Søren Kierkegaard's Journals and Papers

SØREN KIERKEGAARD'S JOURNALS AND PAPERS   Volume 2, F-K

EDITED AND TRANSLATED BY

Howard V. Hong and Edna H. Hong

ASSISTED BY GREGOR MALANTSCHUK

INDIANA UNIVERSITY PRESS

BLOOMINGTON AND LONDON

Library of Congress catalog card number: 67-13025
SBN: 253-18241-7

Manufactured in the United States of America

2 3 4 5 6 7 8 83 82 81 80 79

Contents

Chronology

1837

Between May 8 and May 12. On a visit to the Rørdams in Frederiksberg, meets Regine Olsen for the first time (See II A 67, 68).

Autumn Begins teaching Latin for a term in Borgerdydskolen.

1838

May 19, about 10:30 A.M., S. K.'s entry concerning "an indescribable joy" (see II A 228).

Aug. 8/9 Father dies, 2:00 A.M.

Aug. 14 Father buried in family plot in Assistents Cemetery.

Sept. 7 Publication of *From the Papers of One Still Living*. Published against his will by S. Kierkegaard. (About H. C. Andersen as a novelist, with special reference to his latest work, *Only a Fiddler*.)

1840

June 2 Presents his request for examination to theological faculty.

July 3 Completes examination for degree (*magna cum laude*).

July 19–Aug. 6 Journey to ancestral home in Jutland.

Sept. 8 Proposes to Regine Olsen.

Sept. 10 Becomes engaged to Regine.

Oct. 18 First number of *The Corsair* published by M. Goldschmidt.

Nov. 17 Enters the Pastoral Seminary.

1841

Jan. 12 Preaches sermon in Holmens Kirke (see III C 1).

July 16 Dissertation for the Master of Arts degree, *The Concept of Irony, with constant reference to Socrates,* accepted.

Aug. 11 Returns Regine Olsen's engagement ring.

Sept. 16 Dissertation printed.

Sept. 29 10 A.M.–2:00 P.M., 4:00 P.M.–7:30 P.M. Defends his dissertation. [Around mid-century Magister degrees came to be regarded and named officially as doctoral degrees such as they are now.]

Oct. 11 Engagement with Regine Olsen broken.

Oct. 25 Leaves Copenhagen for Berlin, where he attends Schelling's lectures.

1842

March 6 Returns to Copenhagen.

Nov. 11 S. K.'s brother Peter Christian Kierkegaard ordained.

Johannes Climacus or De omnibus dubitandum est begun but not completed or published.

1843

Feb. 20 *Either/Or*, edited by Victor Eremita, published.

May 8 Leaves for short visit to Berlin.

May 16 *Two Edifying Discourses*, by S. Kierkegaard, published.

July Learns of Regine's engagement to Fridrich Schlegel.

Oct. 16 *Repetition*, by Constantine Constantius; *Fear and Trembling*, by Johannes de Silentio; and *Three Edifying Discourses*, by S. Kierkegaard, published.

Dec. 6 *Four Edifying Discourses*, by S. Kierkegaard, published.

1844

Feb. 24 Preaches terminal sermon in Trinitatis Church.

March 5 *Two Edifying Discourses*, by S. Kierkegaard, published.

June 8 *Three Edifying Discourses*, by S. Kierkegaard, published.

June 13 *Philosophical Fragments*, by Johannes Climacus, published.

June 17 *The Concept of Dread*, by Vigilius Haufniensis; and *Prefaces*, by Nicolaus Notabene, published.

Aug. 31 *Four Edifying Discourses*, by S. Kierkegaard, published.

Oct. 16 Moves from Nørregade 230 (now 38) to house at Nytorv 2, Copenhagen.

1845

Apr. 29 *Three Discourses on Imagined Occasions*, by S. Kierkegaard, published.

Apr. 30 *Stages on Life's Way*, edited by Hilarius Bogbinder, published.

May 13–24 Journey to Berlin.

May 29 *Eighteen Edifying Discourses*, by S. Kierkegaard, published.

1846

Jan. 2 First attack on S. K. in *The Corsair*.

Jan. 10 S. K.'s reply by Frater Taciturnus in *The Fatherland*.

Feb. 7   Considers qualifying himself for ordination (VII¹ A 98).
Feb. 27   *Concluding Unscientific Postscript*, by Johannes Climacus, published.
Mar. 9   "Report" (*Corsair*) begun in first NB Journal (VII¹ A 98).
Mar. 30   *A Literary Review* [*The Present Age* is part of this work.], by S. Kierkegaard, published.
May 2–16 Visit to Berlin.
June 12   Acquires Magister A. P. Adler's books: *Studier og Exempler*, *Forsøg til en kort systematisk Fremstilling af Christendommen i dens Logik*, and *Theologiske Studier*.
Oct. 2   Goldschmidt resigns as editor of *The Corsair*.
Oct. 7   Goldschmidt travels to Germany and Italy.

1847

Jan. 24   S. K. writes: "God be praised that I was subjected to the attack of the rabble. I have now had time to arrive at the conviction that it was a melancholy thought to want to live in a vicarage, doing penance in an out-of-the-way place, forgotten. I now have made up my mind quite otherwise" (VII¹ A 29).

          Date of Foreword to "Bogen om Adler" ("Authority and Revelation"). Not published; MS in *Papirer*.

          Drafts of lectures on communication (VIII² B 79–89). Not published or delivered.

Mar. 13   *Edifying Discourses in Various Spirits*, by S. Kierkegaard, published.
Sept. 29 *Works of Love*, by S. Kierkegaard, published.
Nov. 3   Regine Olsen marries Fridrich Schlegel.
Dec. 24   Sells house on Nytorv.

1848

Jan. 28   Leases apartment at Tornebuskgade and Rosenborggade 156A (now 7) for April occupancy.
Apr. 19   S. K. notes: "My whole nature is changed. My concealment and reserve are broken—I am free to speak" (VIII¹ A 640).
Apr. 24   "No, no, my reserve still cannot be broken, at least not now" (VIII¹ A 645).

Apr. 26   *Christian Discourses*, by S. Kierkegaard, published.

July 24–27 *The Crisis and a Crisis in a Life of an Actress*, by Inter et Inter, published.

Aug.   Notes that his health is poor and is convinced that he will die (IX A 216).

Reflections on direct and indirect communication (IX A 218, 221–24, 233–35).

Sept. 1   Preaches in Vor Frue Church (IX A 266–69, 272).

Nov.   *The Point of View for my Work as an Author* "as good as finished" (IX A 293). (Published posthumously in 1859 by S. K.'s brother Peter Christian Kierkegaard).

"Armed Neutrality," by S. Kierkegaard, "written toward the end of 1848 and the beginning of 1849" (X⁵ B 105–10) but not published.

1849

May 14   Second Edition of *Either/Or* and *The Lilies of the Field and the Birds of the Air*, by S. Kierkegaard, published.

May 19   *Two Minor Ethical-Religious Treatises*, by H. H., published.

June 25–26 Councillor Olsen (Regine's father) dies.

July 30   *The Sickness unto Death*, by Anti-Climacus, published.

Nov. 13   *Three Discourses at the Communion on Fridays*, by S. Kierke-gaard, published.

1850

April 18   Moves to Nørregade 43, Copenhagen.

Sept. 27   *Training in Christianity*, by Anti-Climacus, published.

Dec. 20   *An Edifying Discourse*, by S. Kierkegaard, published.

1851

Jan. 31   "An Open Letter . . . Dr. Rudelbach," by S. Kierkegaard, published.

Aug. 7   *On My Work as an Author* and *Two Discourses at the Communion on Fridays*, by S. Kierkegaard, published.

Sept. 10   *For Self-Examination*, by S. Kierkegaard, published.

1851–52

> *Judge for Yourselves!* by S. Kierkegaard, written. Published posthumously, 1876.

1854

Jan. 30   Bishop Mynster dies.
Apr. 15   H. Martensen named Bishop.
Dec. 18   S. K. begins polemic against Bishop Martensen in *The Fatherland*.

1855

Jan.–May Polemic continues.
May 24   *This Must Be Said; So Let It Now Be Said,* by S. Kierkegaard, advertised as published.

First number of *The Moment.*

June 16   *Christ's Judgment on Official Christianity,* by S. Kierkegaard, published.
Sept. 3   *The Unchangeableness of God,* by S. Kierkegaard, published.
Sept. 25   Ninth and last number of *The Moment* published; number 10 published posthumously. S. K. writes his last entry (XI^2 A 439).
Oct. 2   Enters Frederiks Hospital.
Nov. 11   Dies.
Nov. 18   Is buried.

Translators' Preface

Part of the period devoted to the preparation of Volume II of *Journals and Papers* was spent in the new Søren Kierkegaard Bibliotek of the University of Copenhagen. There we were able to use not only the numerous special reference works but also the growing collection of works which eventually and hopefully will be a reconstitution of Kierkegaard's library (the same editions). We are indebted to the University of Copenhagen and Søren Kierkegaard Selskabet for extensive use of the quarters and the materials, and also to Professor Niels Thulstrup for facilitating these arrangements and for valuable assistance on many things ranging from interpretations of a word to access to unpublished manuscripts.

Dr. Gregor Malantschuk of the University of Copenhagen has continued to share in this volume his extensive and penetrating knowledge of Kierkegaard's works and other writings. He has written the discussions (our translation) of the central concepts found under the topical headings in the notes. For support of this work especially we acknowledge the assistance of the Rask-Ørsted Fond and the Carlsberg Fond.

Undivided concentration on part of the present volume was made possible in the best of settings by a sabbatical leave granted by St. Olaf College and by a genuinely enabling grant from the Louis and Maud Hill Family Foundation in 1965–66. Without this encouragement and substantial provisioning, the whole extensive undertaking and even each part would seem almost interminable.

Permission granted by Gyldendal Forlag of Copenhagen to use the text and absorb the notes of the *Papirer* is again acknowledged.

In the preparation of the manuscript valuable help has been given by Gertrude Hilleboe in the translation of the Latin quotations and by Oliver K. Olson in the translation of the German, Greek, and Hebrew passages. Mary Petersen has graciously undertaken part of the task of typing and retyping. Richard Anderson carefully checked the entire manuscript. Per Lønning and Valter Lindstrom have advised on some vexatious translation problems. Grethe Kjær has contributed variously in various spheres. J. M. Matthew and many others at Indiana University Press

xiii

have helped the manuscript become print. The fine jacket is based on the original design for Volume I prepared by Karen Elnes Foget. To all these colleagues and friends we are gratefully beholden.

St. Olaf College   H.V.H.
Northfield, Minnesota   E.H.H.

A history of Kierkegaard's journals and papers and a full account of the principles of this selection from them are given in the translator's preface to Volume I. Briefly, the entries in the first four volumes of this edition, including the present one, are arranged topically, and chronologically within each topic. Volume V will contain the autobiographical selections. There will be a complete index. Those who wish to follow the serial order of the entries in the present volume, insofar as that can be done on the basis of the *Papirer*, will find appended a table which collates the entries of this volume with the *Papirer* (see pp. 545 ff.)

Within the entries, a series of five periods indicates omissions or breaks in the Danish text as it stands. A series of three periods is used in the few instances of the translators' omissions.

Brackets are used in the text to enclose certain crucial Danish terms just translated or to enclose references supplied by the translators.

Footnote numbers in the text refer to the editors' footnotes, which appear in serial order at the end of the volume. Kierkegaard's notes and marginal comments appear at the bottom of the particular page, at the end of the entry, or in a few special cases as a bracketed insertion within an entry.

Kierkegaard's consciously developed punctuation (VIII^1 A 33–38) has been retained to a large extent. This is evident in the use of the colon and the dash and a minimal use of question marks. Pedagogical-stylistic characteristics (change of pace, variation of sentence-length, and the architecture of sentences and paragraphs) have also been carried over in the main. They are intended as an invitation to reflection and rereading—ideally, aloud.

Søren Kierkegaard's Journals and Papers

FAITH

« 1094

Faith certainly requires an expression of will, and yet in another sense than when, for example, I must say that all cognition requires an expression of will; how else can I explain the passage in the New Testament which says that he who does not have faith shall be punished.

I A 36   November 25, 1834

« 1095

As a contribution to the characterization of the concept "faith," it may be observed that we say a sick person who is apprehensive about dying believes he will die particularly when an expression of will is lacking, and likewise with reference to one who is afraid of ghosts—but on the other hand we may say: I would like to believe but I cannot, for precisely here an expression of will seems to be present.

I A 44   December 31, 1834

« 1096

What Schleiermacher[1] calls "religion" and the Hegelian dogmaticians[2] "faith" is, after all, nothing else than the first immediacy, the prerequisite for everything—the vital fluid—in an emotional-intellectual sense the atmosphere we breathe—and which therefore cannot properly be characterized with these words [*faith* and *religion*].

I A 273   *n.d.*, 1836

« 1097

The *a priori* in faith which hovers over all the *a posteriori* of works is beautifully expressed in the words: I know that nothing in the world, powers etc., will be able to separate me from Christ Jesus, our Lord.[3] His faith sets him upon a rock elevated above all empiricism, although, on the other hand, he could not possibly have gone through all the experiences mentioned here.

II A 190   November 6, 1837

« 1098

The historical anticipation of and also the position in human knowledge corresponding to the Christian "*Credo ut intelligam*"[4] is the ancient "*Nihil est in intellectu quod non antea fuerit in sensu.*"[5]

II A 194   November 15, 1837

« 1099

The *a priori* character of faith can be interpreted in part from the *side of knowledge*, since that which has heaven has overcome every doubt, for doubt is the demonic which lies between heaven and earth, and partly *from the side of action*, since it is the assurance *of victory* (Romans 8).

III A 36   *n.d.*, 1840

« 1100

One can discern that faith is a more concrete qualification than immediacy, because from a purely human point of view the secret of all knowledge is to concentrate upon what is given in immediacy; in faith we assume something which is not given and can never be deduced from the preceding consciousness—that is, the consciousness of sin and the assurance of the forgiveness of sins.[6] Yet this assurance does not come about in the same way as knowledge arises out of doubt by way of an internal consequence, and everyone would certainly sense the frivolity of conceiving of it in this way, or, to put it better, one who conceives of it in this way does not have the above-mentioned position (consciousness of sin); it is rather a free act. Consciousness of sin, however, is not at all an arbitrary human act, which doubt is. It is an objective act, simply because the consciousness of God is immanent within the consciousness of sin. It is for this reason that the consciousness of the forgiveness of sins is linked to an external event, the appearance of Christ in his fullness, which is, indeed, not external in the sense of being foreign to us, of no concern to us, but external as being *historical.*—[7]

III A 39   *n.d.*, 1840

« 1101

The whole Christian life is a complete life and as such has its

1) Immediacy or spontaneity—that is, faith (distinguished from that which in the merely human development is called the immediate because there is an intervening historical issue [*Mellemværende*][8]— sin etc.), and yet immediate faith is simultaneously itself and the con-

dition for itself, the most subjective and the most objective (faith therefore can never emancipate itself from this *I believe*, even though this "I" is an ideal "I." (The aim in knowledge is to let the "I" disappear in its object; the aim of faith is to preserve it in and with the object.

2) Mediacy—that is, the Church (corresponds to what the state is according to the purely human position).

3) Identity, by which every external phenomenon of the Church is surmounted, yet not in such a way that the Church is thereby abolished, but in such a way that the individual is now not merely a factor in the order of things, just as the Church is not, but struggles through the visible to the invisible and through the power of the invisible (which is in the individual not merely as a factor for the whole but continues in the individual) penetrates the visible and consummates itself in the visible.—

III A 216   *n.d.*, 1840

« 1102

Therefore it reads: Cast *all* your cares upon God. This is not so easy—inspecting everything, for one thing, and embracing everything at one time, for another. To believe that God concerns himself with the most insignificant events—not to be too proud to pray to him about them, whereas others are so vain that they egotistically believe God concerns himself with every little trifle which touches them.[9]

III A 127   *n.d.*, 1841

« 1103

In margin of 1102 (III A 127):
Therefore Scripture uses the word *to cast* in order to express the energy involved in the power of resolution—for cares are agile, and even though you make the most ingenious movements, they wrap themselves around you more and more tightly, as did the serpents around Laocoön; they are the cleverest Sophists, against whom all your lessons avail nothing.—[10]

III A 128 *n.d.*

« 1104

And you who say: "Yes, fortunate is he to whom it was given to be faithful over a little, but I was given nothing at all to work with, because the pound which was entrusted to me was not a motivating power but a weight, a burden laid upon my shoulders." It is indeed rare for a human being to be able in truth to talk this way. But if you bore this with humility, if you lost all the world without damaging your soul, if you loved God, if at times even your troubled life was transfigured by gratitude, if you believed God, the depth of his richness, both in wisdom and knowledge—and if you did not dare lift up unblemished hands to God, if that burden deservedly lay still more heavily upon you, if you nevertheless humbled yourself beneath God's mighty hand, did not complain, did not follow the sophisticated advice of the world to forget, did not presume to say: Will these troubles never let up?—if you loved God in the midst of your cares—would you not then be "faithful over a little?"

III A 182   n.d., 1841

« 1105

If faith is regarded merely as knowledge of historical matters, one quite consistently and simply falls into such ridiculousness as thinking that the question whether the earth is flat or round is a matter of faith. Quite properly, therefore Hieronymus says in *Erasmus Montanus*[11] that Erasmus holds deluded ideas in faith, and cites the fact that he believes the earth is round.

IV A 24   n.d., 1842-43

« 1106

The basis of man's being saved by faith and not by works, or more accurately, in faith, lies deeper than one thinks. All the explanation derived from sin is by no means exhaustive. The basis is that even if man himself accomplished the good he could not know it, for then he would have to be omniscient. Therefore no man can argue with our Lord. I dare not call even the most exalted deed, humanly speaking, the most noble deed, a good deed.[12] I must always say: God alone knows if it really is that; therefore it is impossible for me to build my salvation upon it.

IV C 82   n.d., 1842-43

« 1107

Therefore faith is what the Greeks called the divine madness.[13] This is not merely an ingenious observation but something which actually can be sustained.

IV A 109   n.d., 1843

« 1108

It is precisely a matter of being able to believe in God in small things; otherwise one still does not have a right relationship to him. If one were to say of a human being: He is my friend, that I know, and whatever happens, he still remains my friend; but it so happens, strangely, that our views on particular things are always exactly the opposite; nevertheless, in spite of that, I steadfastly maintain that he is my friend—there would be something preposterous in this and it would really be a kind of fanaticism. Likewise it is a matter of drawing God into the actualities of this world, where he certainly is, after all. When Paul was on board the ship which was about to founder, he did not pray only for his eternal salvation but also for his temporal salvation.[14] Perhaps he should have immediately thought: It is all over now, etc. I will think only of my soul's salvation. And yet he was our Lord's apostle.

IV A 117 *n.d.*, 1843

« 1109

When the price of cloves* became erratic in Holland, several shiploads were burned[15]—it was a pious fraud; is a pious fraud really needed in our time?†

Let us check the market in order to make sure that faith is something other than a bit of worldly-wisdom, that it is a power of which few, perhaps, have any idea. Let us run through its dialectic and not talk loosely, as if sacrificing Isaac were merely a poetic expression for sacrificing the best. How many are there who have really tried themselves in such a struggle, and yet people in our day want to go further, as if it were an easy matter to bring about a more unbelieving, more correctly, a less believing, age than our own, whose insipid rationality has pumped all passion out of life.

It is the same for the great ones as for the little people—first one creeps, then one walks in a walker, then one walks holding on to a person's hand, then one walks alone.

The two examples from ancient times of going further are Apollonius and the disciple of Heraclitus.[16]

IV B 76 *n.d.*, 1843

* *Written above:* spices
† Or rather a frank truthfulness which could discipline a no less than pious fraud which has preceded.

« 1110

It is and continues to be a consideration one cannot dismiss out of hand—namely, to what extent should reason be regarded as temptation in matters of faith, to what extent is reason sinful, to what extent again is this—that truth and reason agree—an object of faith?

IV A 191   n.d., 1844

« 1111

There are only 3 positions on the relation between faith and knowledge.
  (1) Paul: I know what I have believed[17]
  (2) *Credo ut intelligam*[18]
  (3) Faith is spontaneity.[19]
In all of them knowledge comes after faith.[20]

V A 1   n.d., March, 1844

« 1112

When one says that faith depends upon authority and, so saying, thinks he has excluded the dialectical, this is simply not so; for the dialectical begins with asking how it happens that one submits to this authority, whether he himself understands why he has chosen it, whether it is a contingency, for in that case, the authority is not authority, not even for the believer, if he himself is not conscious that it is a contingency.

V A 32   n.d., 1844

« 1113

What Jacobi deprecatingly (specifically, that it is not so) says about the good, the beautiful, the true, that they are ideas elicited by need, the category *der Verzweiflung*, really applies to faith (fear and trembling) and is the meaning of faith. It is an idea to be found only in need, and is a category of despair.

Jacobi, S. W. III, p. 435.[21]

V A 40   n.d., 1844

« 1114

In margin of Friedrich H. Jacobi, Werke, IV, 1, p. xliv:
And so faith again becomes only a matter of genius[22] which is reserved for the individual, just like Schelling's genius for action. It happens so

often when one is in the process of shaping a totality-view that he lets such expressions slip in.

v c 13:4   *n.d.,* 1844

« 1115

It certainly is not inconceivable that a man could live his whole life constantly troubled about not having faith and of whom it must be said and to whom it would be said: My friend, you did have faith and your concern was simply the pain of inwardness.

vi a 107   *n.d.,* 1845

« 1116 *Example of Contradiction in Rhetorical Address*

Your sorrow shall be changed into joy, and no one shall take it from you—the apostle did not say this in the beginning of his life—then he would merely have believed it—but at the conclusion; consequently he had experienced it. —As if believing were less and not more than experiencing; as if the certainty of faith were not infinitely greater than the ambiguity of experience; as if it would end with the transposition of faith's infinitely concerned (with passion) certainty into the secure *summa summarum* of worldly wisdom.

vi a 148   *n.d.,* 1845

« 1117

The best proof that there is a just providence is to say: "I *will* believe it whatever happens." All proof is foolishness, a kind of double-mindedness which by two paths (the objective and the subjective) wants to arrive simultaneously at the same point. The believer says to himself: "The most detestable of all would be for you to allow yourself, in any ever so hidden thought, to insult God by thinking of him as having done wrong. There-fore, if someone wishes to write a big book to justify or to indict God— as far as I am concerned, I will believe. Where it seems that I might be able to understand, I will still prefer to believe, for it is more blessed to believe—as long as we human beings live in this world, understanding easily becomes something imagined, a chummy importunity—and where I cannot understand, yes, there it is blessed to believe."

vii[1] *a* 61   *n.d.,* 1846

« 1118

To have faith is simply to achieve buoyancy by taking upon oneself a considerable gravity; to become objective is achieving buoyancy by tossing cargo overboard. To believe is like flying, but one flies with the aid of a counteracting gravity. Considerable gravity is necessary for one to become so buoyant that he can fly. If I want to elevate something, I do it with the aid of a weight; consequently I am lifting it with gravity. Celestial bodies float because they have an enormous gravity; they float with the aid of gravity. It is just like elasticity—height is achieved by compression. And so one may say that the buoyancy of faith is an infinite gravity, and its height is brought about by an infinite compression.[23]

VII[1] A 177   *n.d.*, 1846

« 1119

Faith is always related to that which is not seen—in the context of nature (physically contrasted) to the invisible [*Usynlige*], in the spiritual context (spiritually) to the improbable [*Usandsynlige*].

VII[1] A 203   *n.d.*, 1846

« 1120

The word to the captain from Capernaum:[24] To you it shall be as you have believed—is a consoling, a gladdening word, but it also contains the judgment: Do you really have faith? This could very well be developed further:

> the judgment and the joy that what is done for a man is always according to his faith.[25]

VII[1] A 228   *n.d.*, 1847

« 1121 *Concerning the Relationship between Good Works and Faith*

Good works in the sense of meritoriousness are naturally an abomination to God. Yet good works are required of a human being. But they shall be and yet shall not be; they shall be and yet one ought humbly to be ignorant of their being significant or that they are supposed to be of any significance. Good works are something like a dish which is that particular dish because of the way in which it is served—good works therefore should be done in humility, in faith. Or it is like a child's giving his parents a present, purchased, however, with what the child has received from his parents; all the pretentiousness which otherwise is associated with giving a present disappears when the child received from the parents the gift which he gives to the parents.

VIII[1] A 19   *n.d.*, 1847

« 1122

"If they do not believe Moses and the prophets, neither will they believe if someone should rise from the dead."[26] This is certainly true. Because to believe is not to be fantastically terrified, etc., as one is by a dead
person who reappears. Such a one is perhaps more terrifying than Moses
and the prophets, but he has no earnestness—does not have the earnestness of: You *shall* believe. Such a scare is not fear and trembling; neither is
it the submissiveness of faith.

VIII[1] A 619   n.d., 1848

« 1123 **N.B.**   **N.B.**

May 11, 1848

Most men (if at an early age it is indicated that they must bear some
suffering or other, some cross or other, one of those mournful curtailments
of the soul) begin to hope and, as it is called, to have faith that everything
will improve, that God will surely make everything all right etc., and then
after a while, when still no change has taken place, they will learn little
by little to depend on the help of the eternal—that is, resign themselves
and be strengthened in being satisfied with the eternal. —The person of
deeper nature or one whom God has structured [*anlagt*] more eternally
begins at once to understand that he must bear this as long as he lives, that
he dare not ask God for such extraordinary, paradoxical aid. But God is
still perfect love, and nothing is more certain to him than that. Consequently he resigns himself, and since the eternal is close to him, he finds
rest, continually and happily assured that God is love. But he must accept
suffering. Then after a while when he becomes more and more concrete in the actuality [*Virkelighed*] of life, comes more and more to
himself *qua* finite being, when time and the movement of time exercise
their power over him, when in spite of all effort it still remains so difficult
to live year after year with the aid only of the eternal, when in a more
humble sense he becomes human or learns what it means to be a human
being (for in his resignation he is still too ideal, too abstract, for which
reason there is some despair in all resignation)[27]—then for him faith's
possibility means: will he believe or not that by virtue of the absurd God
will help him temporally.* (Here lie all the paradoxes. Thus the forgive-

---

* Note. This is the inverse movement, which after all is "spirit." Spirit is the
second movement. Humor is not mood but is found, with dialectical propriety, in a
person who unhappily has been cheated of his childhood and then later becomes
spirit and simultaneously aware of childhood.

ness of sins means to be helped temporally;[28] otherwise it is resignation, which can endure the punishment, still assured that God is love. But belief in the forgiveness of sins means to believe that in time God has forgotten the sin, that it is really true that God forgets.)

This is to say that most men never reach faith at all. They live a long time in immediacy or spontaneity, finally they advance to some reflection, and then they die. The exceptions begin the other way around; dialectical from childhood, that is, without immediacy, they begin with the dialectical, with reflection, and they go on living this way year after year (about as long as the others live in sheer immediacy) and then, at a more mature age, faith's possibility presents itself to them. For faith is immediacy or spontaneity after reflection.[29]

Naturally the exceptions have a very unhappy childhood and youth, for to be essentially reflective at that age, which by nature is spontaneous or immediate, is the most profound melancholy. But there is a return. Most people drift on in such a way they never become spirit; all their many happy years of immediacy tend toward spiritual retardation and therefore they never become spirit. But the unhappy childhood and youth of the exceptions are transfigured into spirit.

VIII[1] A 649   May 11, 1848

« 1124

This is the ascent of faith or of coming to faith. Here also is the absurd. Luther[30] speaks (in the sermon on the captain from Capernaum) of how his faith increased: first he believed that Christ could help if he would only come, but when Christ would not do this, he believed nevertheless that Christ could help without coming.

VIII[1] A 661   n.d., 1848

« 1125 *Unless You See Signs and Miracles, You Will Not Believe*[31]

Here we see the justification for placing faith in its own sphere. For if what is commonly called faith—believing that there is a God, a providence, etc. (which is nothing other than knowing, or a spontaneity which can indeed be clarified by thought but is not tested by spiritual trials, does not anguish to the point of the absurd)—if this is what it is to believe, then Christ's words become an anticlimax and Christ comes to say the opposite. For this quasi-faith thinks it believes—but it cannot swallow miracles and the like; it believes, as it is said, in God and Christ but questions miracles. But Christ reverses the relationship: first comes the faith which believes miracles, believes because it sees miracles, and then next, the faith which believes although no miracles happen. These two qualifications are the qualifications of faith, and the marks of offense and the absurd are there. First of all to believe that God will permit something to happen which completely cuts across the grain of our reason and understanding—this is absurd. And when one has believed this, that it will occur, then to believe even though it does not occur. But if one takes away the first qualification of faith—believing because one sees signs and wonders—the spheres are confused, for then knowledge and the highest form of faith come to resemble one another. For knowledge, when it gains permission to call itself faith, requires no miracle; it would rather be free from miracles, simply because miracles are an offense. But the highest form of faith is indeed to believe without seeing signs and miracles.

Here we see an example of how everything is confused if we do not take care to make faith a sphere by itself.

VIII[1] A 672 *n.d.*, 1848

« 1126

Faith is essentially this—to hold fast to possibility. This was what pleased Christ so much in the sufferer, that after suffering for many, many years, he persistently believed with the same originality and youthfulness that in God help was possible. The demoralizing aspect of suffering is the paralysis of foundering in hopelessness: It is too late now; it is all over, etc.

IX A 311 *n.d.*, 1848

« 1127

Luke 24:31. "And their eyes were opened, and they recognized him, and he vanished out of their sight."

This is the relation between the sense perception of Christ and faith: they recognized him—and then he became invisible to them; the one is like an interpretation of the other.

IX A 319 *n.d.*, 1848

« 1128

Christ says: "Why are you afraid, O men of little faith?" He uses two words—no wonder a person is afraid when he has little faith!

X[1] A 62 *n.d.*, 1849

« 1129

Faith's conflict with the world is not a battle of thought with doubt, thought with thought. This was the confusion which finally ended in the madness of the system.

Faith, the man of faith's conflict with the world, is a battle of character. Human vanity resides in wanting to comprehend, the vanity of not willing to obey as a child but of wanting to be an adult who can comprehend and who then will not obey what he cannot comprehend, that is, who essentially will not obey.

The man of faith is a person of character who, unconditionally obedient to God, grasps it as a character-task that one is not to insist upon comprehending.

Now comes the conflict. To insist upon believing what one cannot comprehend, such blind obedience is indeed obscurantism, stupidity, etc. That is, the world wants to alarm the believer through fear of men into the vanity of thinking that he also can comprehend. Here is the conflict. It is a task for the person of character. Or in another way—such a man of faith is perhaps also a superiorly gifted mind. The world becomes aware of him and in general understands well enough that if anyone should be able to comprehend, he must be the one. So the world construes his simplicity of faith as irony, rages at him to make him anxious and afraid, so that he finally must say: Yes, of course I can comprehend—that is, I fear men more than God.

This and all similiar conflicts are the conflicts of faith.

This is my conception.

x^1 A 367   n.d., 1849

« 1130

[*In margin: A definition of faith*, that is, of the Christian conception of faith.]

What is it to believe [*at troe*]? It is to will (what one *ought* and because one *ought*), God-fearingly and unconditionally obediently, to defend oneself against the vain thought of wanting to comprehend and against the vain imagination of being able to comprehend.

x^1 A 368   n.d., 1849

« 1131

When the number of enemies is many, many times larger and almost every day becomes greater, when the defenders have long since recognized this and naturally are firmly and fully convinced that the only rescue is a new defense, and then a person appears who says: You are making a mistake, you are losing everything by defending—attack, and if you were the only one left, one attacker is sufficient; whereas the defenders, whether or not they are superior to the enemies in number, corrupt and lose the cause. If this does not provide a new point of departure, then I do not know at all what this means.

This is the way I relate to the complex of current Christian tactics.

Just as my discourse is continually about faith, so also my entire position is one of reduplicated faith. For essentially it takes faith to assume that a cause which is almost lost by its defenders, that this same cause is triumphant if only it attacks rather than defends itself.

x^1 A 395   n.d., 1849

« 1132

As I have said so often, speculation can comprehend everything—except how I arrived at faith or how faith has come into the world. But philosophy continually takes faith to mean a sum of doctrinal propositions.

It seems to me that I once read this in the third part of the younger Fichte's Grundzüge zum Systeme der Philosophie, die speculative Theologie, Heidelberg, 1846. I have looked for it since but have not been able to find it. However, I perhaps did make a note in one or another journal at the time.

But this is unimportant. However, it is certainly ridiculous to note the cocksureness with which a dogmatician sits and arranges a system—and God knows whether faith is found in the world.

x^1 A 554   n.d., 1849

« 1133

In margin of 1132 (x^1 A 554):

* In my copy I have marked a passage on page 178, but it does not not seem to be the passage I had in mind.

Now, however, I see that this was the passage I was thinking of, for I find it accurately cited in journal NB, p. 125 [VII^1 A 187].

x^1 A 555   n.d.

« 1134

Zacharias Werner in his sermon on White Sunday (the Sunday after Easter) says that Gregory the Great has said "The faith of Mary Magdalene and of Peter is not as instructive as Thomas's lack of faith."

x^2 A 54   n.d., 1849

« 1135 *Luther's Teaching about Faith**

really corresponds to the transformation which occurs when one becomes a man and is no longer a stripling; his teaching about faith is adult religion.

When one is young, it still seems possible to achieve the ideal if one will only honestly, with all his abilities, strive; there is a childlike, if I dare say so—a peer-relationship—between myself and the prototype [*Forbille-det*], if only I will it to the uttermost. Here lies the truth of the *Middle Ages*. It believed so piously that it would achieve the ideal by actually giving everything to the poor, by entering a monastery, etc.

But the religion of manhood is a power higher and can be identified by the very fact that it feels itself a stage removed from the ideal.

As the individual develops, God becomes for him more and more infinite, and he feels himself farther and farther from God.

The teaching about the prototype, then, can no longer plainly and simply occupy the first place. Faith comes first, Christ as the gift. The ideal becomes so infinitely elevated that all my striving transforms itself before my eyes into distracted nothingness, if it is directed at resembling the ideal, or into a kind of devout jest, even though I am honestly striving.

This is expressed in saying: I rest in faith alone. The youth does not notice how enormous the task is; he starts out briskly and in the pious illusion that he will succeed. The adult comprehends with infinite depth the distance between himself and the ideal—and now "faith" must first of all intervene as that in which he actually rests, the faith that fulfillment has been made, the faith that I am saved by faith alone.

So far Luther is perfectly right and is a turning point in the development of religion.

But the deviation in the religion of our day is that we make faith into such an inwardness that it actually disappears altogether, that life is permitted to shape itself purely secularly, *mir nichts* and *Dir nichts*, and that instead of faith we substitute an assurance about faith.

This is the way I partly understood my position earlier through an understanding of Luther, but now for the first time I understand it better. I also have been a youth, and to me it was as if the ideal was much closer, until in the deepest sense I became humbled under the ideal—and then the teaching about "grace" could become properly manifest to me. On the other hand, I have been right and am right in all my polemic against all this modern shadow-boxing.

* *In margin:* Luther's teaching about the faith, or Luther as *point de vüe,* and my understanding of myself.

Just as with the individual man, the race also needs recapitulating lectures or tutors in order to preserve continuity. Geniuses are really such tutors. They are developed far more slowly than other men; they actually run through the basic forms of existence that have been travelled in past world-history. Precisely there lies their significance as correctives. Although the geniuses do prophetically point to the future, they do it precisely by way of a deeper remembering of the past. All development is certainly not a backing up but a going back, and this is primitivity.

The earnestness of youth is *flux, bona fide* to begin with, wanting to resemble the ideal. The earnestness of the adult is first of all to set faith in the middle as the expression of respect for the qualitative difference between all his striving and the ideal. The modern [earnestness] is the shadowboxing of transforming faith into a feigned inwardness.

x^2 A 207   *n.d.*, 1849

« 1136

The condition for a person's salvation is the faith that everywhere and at every moment there is an absolute *beginning*. When someone who has egotistically served himself in the service of illusions is to begin a purer striving, the crucial point is that he believes absolutely in the new beginning, because otherwise he messes up the *transition* with the past. —So it is also with conversion in the stricter sense: faith in the possibility of the new, absolute beginning, for otherwise it remains essentially the past. It is this infinite intensiveness in faith's anticipation, which has the confident courage to believe it, to transform the past into the completely forgotten— and now to believe absolutely in the beginning.

Yet in other respects the criterion of the truth of this faith will be the confidence which in the opposite direction has the courage to comprehend profoundly one's earlier wretchedness. Thus the one corresponds to the other. A person who does not sense this profoundly and have courage for it cannot rightly make the new beginning, and the reason for his not sensing it profoundly is precisely that he secretly nourishes the notion that if he considered it properly it would be so bad that there would be no new beginning for him. Therefore he mitigates it a bit, and in order to be more sure of achieving a new beginning he does not look very closely—and for this very reason he does not make it.

A beginning always has a double impetus toward the past and toward the new; to the same degree that it pushes off in the direction of the past it begins the new.

x^2 A 371   *n.d.*, 1850

« 1137 *The Difficulty of Christianity*

Actually, the difficulty is not, when feeling absolutely one's wretchedness, to grasp the consolation of Christianity, to grasp, if I dare say it this way, this matchless exaggeration that God let himself be crucified for my sake in order to save me and to show how he loves me.

No, the difficulty is to become wretched in this way, to want to risk discovering one's wretchedness.

To be made well with the aid of Christianity is not the difficulty; the difficulty is in becoming sick to some purpose.

If you are sick in this way, Christianity comes with matchless ease, just as it is incomparably easy for the starving person to be interested in food. Especially the food for the preparation of which heaven and earth were set in motion so that it might be delicious and tasty—if one is famished to that degree. Even if the whole world were to laugh him to scorn— what does the starving person care about that compared with getting something to eat. So also with the essentially Christian. If the world disturbs you, then you are not absolutely sick. Imagine that there actually was a hungry person whom everyone would laugh to scorn if he ate the food before him. A few hours very likely would pass by during which he would prefer to be hungry rather than to be laughed to scorn. But if it eventually became a question of death, then he certainly would choose to eat.

x^3 A 184   *n.d.,* 1850

« 1138 *"The Monastery"*

was, nevertheless, a *point de vüe* by which one could determine where he was, whether he had climbed higher toward perfection than the monastery —or had sunk altogether into worldliness.

Then "the monastery" was allowed to drop out, and now for a long time we have gone about foolishly in complete darkness as to where we are, and everything profane has never had it so good.

"Faith" has now become hidden inwardness (not even remotely discernible in men's lives, while they still go on protesting that deep within, etc.) to the degree that eventually a new kind of faith in relation to "faith" becomes necessary, the faith that I believe that I have faith. That which once upon a time inspired not only to witness in word but also in deed has now become imperceptibly concealed to such a degree that not only a third person but also the party concerned himself needs faith to believe that he has faith—yes, ironically, often it takes an extraordinary faith to believe that the man has faith, or he himself needs an extraordinary faith to believe that he has faith.

x³ A 298   *n.d.*, 1850

« 1139 *Faith—a Striving*

Luther is completely right in saying that if a man had to acquire his salvation by his own striving, it would end either in presumption or in despair, and therefore it is faith that saves.

But yet not in such a way that striving vanishes completely. Faith should make striving possible, because the very fact that I am saved by faith and that nothing at all is demanded from me should in itself make it possible that I begin to strive, that I do not collapse under impossibility but am encouraged and refreshed, because it has been decided I am saved, I am God's child by virtue of faith.

This is how faith must relate itself to striving, both in its beginning and during its progress, but it cannot mean that striving is to vanish entirely.

x³ A 322   *n.d.*, 1850

« 1140

Addition to 1139 (x³ A 322), *in margin:*

Luther[32] therefore even urges (for example, in the sermon on the Epistle for the First Sunday in Lent and many other places) that there should be fasting, etc., only that salvation should not be regarded as dependent upon it.

Here comes the dialectical—salvation is not dependent upon it— *ergo*, we think, we can let striving drop out completely. But this was never Luther's meaning; if so, he would have become a champion of dead faith. His meaning is: if salvation is regarded as dependent on this, then it is law, and evil drives a person to strive. When it is faith which saves, then a striving follows which is nurtured by the help of the good. But if no striving at all follows faith but, indeed, even the opposite, then such a one is lost, and why? Is it because the striving did not come? If this is the case, then salvation is still dependent on striving. No, it is because the absence of striving makes it obvious that he does not have faith, and therefore he is lost because he does not have faith.

x³ A 323   *n.d.*

« 1141 *Faith*

If you do not have faith, then at least believe that you will indeed come to have faith—and then you do have faith.

x^3 A 536   *n.d.,* 1850

« 1142 *Faith—Existence*

Usually it is presented this way: first one must have faith and then existing [*Existeren*] follows.

This has contributed greatly to the confusion, as if it were possible to have faith without the existing. We have taken this very much to heart and have abolished [authentic] existence—since faith is much more important, to be sure.

The matter is quite simple. In order to have faith, there must first be existence, an existential qualification.

This is what I am never sufficiently able to emphasize—that to have faith, before there can even be any question about having faith, there must be the *situation*. And this situation must be brought about by an existential step on the part of the individual.

We have completely done away with this propædeutic element. We let the individual go on in his customary mediocre rut—and so he gets faith by and by, just about the way one can learn lessons word-perfect without needing the situation.

Take an example, the rich young ruler. What did Christ require as the preliminary act? He required action that would shoot the rich young ruler out into the infinite.

The requirement is that you must venture out, out into water 70,000 fathoms deep.[33] This is the situation. Now there can be a question of having faith, or of despairing. But there will be nothing meritorious about it, for you will be so thoroughly shaken that you will learn to let meritoriousness go.

Then there is another existing which follows faith. But the first must never be forgotten—otherwise Christianity is completely displaced.

x^4 A 114   *n.d.,* 1851

« 1143 *Christianity's*

and also Luther's intention obviously is not that I identify myself as a Christian by making repeated assurances that I do believe.

No, one's existence [*Existents*] shall be marked by the quality of existence which belongs to Christianity, and then the faith is there, the faith that it is nevertheless by grace that I am saved. Consequently faith is not a substitute for [authentic] existing [*Existeren*], but faith makes sure that the individual does not interpret the qualitative Christian existing (renunciation, self-denial, etc.) as something meritorius. Give up everything—that is the time to make assurances that you believe, that you believe you are saved by grace, that faith saves. When you actually have given up everything, this expresses in another way that you do believe; then the only remaining danger is that you might think that your self-denial is something meritorious.

X^4 A 123   *n.d.*, 1851

« 1144 *The Illumination of All Christianity*

The greatest emphasis a man can put upon himself, upon his *I*, upon the fact that *I* am the one with whom you are dealing—is to require faith. And a man who has understood this would constantly arrange his whole life or put his life in order in such a way that it could only become an object for faith. It is not that he needs to be believed by others; no, it is the affirmation of his sovereignty, which wills to be only an object of faith.

Whether a man has the right to relate to others in this way I do not decide, nor do I deny it.

But *God* is the *I*, the subject who in relation to men must emphasize his *I* in such a way that it is only the object of faith.

With respect to this, God also handles everything in such a way that he can become only the object of faith, always making the relationship one that contends against reason. It is not pride on God's part—he cannot do otherwise.

Take all the difficulties in Christianity which free-thinkers seize hold of and apologists want to defend, and see, the whole thing is a false alarm. The difficulties are simply introduced by God in order to make sure that he can become only the object of faith (although it is also necessarily implicit in his essence and in the disproportion between the two qualities: God and man). This is why Christianity is a paradox; this explains the contradictions in Holy Scripture, etc.

But the intellectual approach wants to put everything into a direct relation—that is, wants to abolish faith. It wants to have direct recognizability, wants to have the most absolute harmony throughout Scripture, and then it will believe Christianity, believe that the Bible is the Word of God —that is, it will not believe It has no inkling of God's sovereignty and what the requirement of faith means.

The apologists are just as stupid as the free-thinkers and are always shifting the viewpoint of Christianity.

To understand or become aware of Christianity, of God's relation to men, one could study the most exhaustive human pride. For it will be recognized precisely by its requirement of faith. Here one would become aware of a good many things. One should not forget, of course, that such human pride is blasphemous and ungodly and that on the contrary with respect to God it cannot be otherwise—he must demand faith, for otherwise he is not God.

But what notion do all these speculative theologians have about what it means to require faith!

x^4 A 422   *n.d.*, 1851

« 1145 *Knock, and It Shall Be Opened unto you*[34]

It is eternally true that if one knocks, the door will be opened. But suppose that the difficulty for us human beings is simply that we are afraid to go—and knock.

Have faith—and if you command it, this mountain will lift itself and throw itself into the sea.[35] It is eternally certain that this is so. But suppose that the difficulty for us human beings is rooted simply in our being anxious and fearful [*angst og bange*] about having such enormous power, so that to us it seems as if the mountain might lift itself up—and then fall upon me.

x^4 A 455   *n.d.*, 1852

« 1146 *To Have Faith*

is really to advance along the way where all human road signs point: back, back, back.

This is because the way is narrow[36] (yet precisely this means something to faith) and dark—yes, it is not only dark, pitch dark, but it is like a dark road where a confusing gleam of light makes the darkness even greater—the confusing gleam of light is the fact that the human road signs point the opposite way.

x^4 A 489   *n.d.*, 1852

« 1147 *All Are Afraid of Decision*

Perhaps someone in our age is a skeptic; he aloofly assesses the clergy as being either stupid men or deceivers. If he were told: Well, let us come to a decision on the matter and take away the illusions—he would perhaps not like it. For he would rather be an aloof skeptic in all indolence and at a bargain price. But if the either/or in Christianity really came to be a matter of earnestness—well, he would choose not to become a Christian, but he nevertheless would understand that he has to buy his skepticism at a considerably higher price than is required now in relation to the triviality by which essential Christianity is now represented.

x^4 A 634   n.d., 1852

« 1148   πίστις—επιστημη

See, here it is. πίστις as it is used in good Greek (Plato, Aristotle, et al.) is regarded as signifying something far lower than ἐπιστήμη. πίστις is related to probability. Therefore πίστις, to produce faith, according to the classics, is the task of orators.

Now comes Christianity and uses the concept of faith in an entirely different sense as related to the paradox (consequently improbability), but also as signifying the highest certainty (see the definition in Hebrews 11:1), the consciousness of the eternal, the most passionate certainty which causes a person to sacrifice everything and life itself for this faith.

But what happens? In the course of time the pace of Christianity is moderated, and then the same old paganism returns, and now we prattle Christianity into the idea that knowledge (ἐπιστήμη) is higher than faith (πίστις), although the conception of Christian faith is in a class by itself, a quality higher than the classical duality: πίστις–ἐπιστήμη.

No, from a Christian point of view, faith is the highest. The paradoxical character of Christianity very consistently is identified by the fact that it turns the purely human topsy-turvy. For, humanly speaking, ἐπιστήμη is higher than πίστις, as paganism assumed it to be,[37] but it pleased God to make foolishness of human wisdom, to turn the relationship around (here, also the possibility of offense is the sign) and to place faith highest of all.

It can all be explained in a very simple way, something I have had to resort to for a long time: Christianity does not exist at all [*er slet ikke til*]; the whole thing is rubbish, not even paganism, because it decks itself out as Christianity.

x^4 A 635   n.d., 1852

« 1149   *The Second Time is a Minus (Subtracts from), the Third Time Still More, etc.*

Every police officer, policeman, every night watchman's report is under oath—but sometimes the party concerned is permitted to take an oath once again; consequently he affirms under oath that which he had affirmed under oath. Glory be to humanity, justice, the police lieutenant, and all of them together.

[*In margin:* With this kind of oath-taking one really dissolves the concept of an oath.]

Yet it is really not this which concerns me. But in Christendom it has gone just about the same way with believing. A Christian is a believer. Christendom, however, for a long time has been a society of people who believe (yes, even to the nth power through that one and that one and that one, etc.) that there have lived men who believed. [*In margin:* By this kind of faith one really dissolves the concept "faith."]

But this is preached so that sweat streams down the preacher's face—to this degree it affects him to believe that there have lived people who believed.

XI[1] A 192   n.d., 1854

« 1150 *A Qualitative Originality*

which relates itself to faith is obliged to put up with the revolting situation of being like unfamiliar merchandise which merchants are not sure has any worth, whether it has great value or little value, or perhaps immense value—therefore they look at it both shrewdly and suspiciously. The price of quantitative originality is given at once.

XI[2] A 18   n.d., 1854

« 1151 *"Teach Them To Observe All That I Have Commanded You."*[38]

With these words Christ leaves the earth. Now if this were in Protestantism, especially in Denmark, it would be extraordinary for Christ to speak of observing everything that he has commanded—it does not sound quite the way we talk about faith alone.

From this it is seen that Christ must associate believing with an idea completely different from that which Christendom has hit upon.

XI[2] A 84   n.d., 1854

« 1152 *Life's Value*

Only when a person has become so unhappy or has penetrated the wretchedness of this existence so deeply that he must truly say: For me life has no value—only then can he make a bid for Christianity.

And then life can get its highest value.

XI[2] A 115   n.d., 1854

« 1153

The New Testament must really have a completely different concept (and also with sheer pathos) of faith than is current today; for Christ explicitly says[39] that the signs which should accompany those who believe are—and now comes the miracle. And in this passage it is not a question particularly of the disciples.

xi^2 A 336   *n.d.*, 1854

« 1154 *Faith*

In the New Testament faith is presented as having not an intellectual but an ethical character; it signifies the relationship of personality between God and man. Therefore faith is demanded (as an expression of devotedness), believing against reason, believing although one cannot see (wholly a qualification of personality, and ethical). The apostle speaks of the *obedience* of faith. Faith is set to a test, is tested, etc.

The confusion of the concept of faith comes most directly from the Alexandrians. Augustine has also confused it by drawing the qualification of his concept "faith" directly from Plato (in the *Republic*).

xi^2 A 380   *n.d.*, 1854-55

FAMILY

« 1155 *God's Tests* {Prøvelser}

 . . . . . Did you never see him, my listener, the loving father who sent his son far away out into the world to become mature and be tested for the work of life; did you not see how tenderly his eyes rested upon him as far as they could follow him, how concerned he was back there at home and how longingly he awaited news from the dear child. And yet it was he himself who placed the test upon him. He was quite free to call him back, to let him grow up and grow old under his own eyes, to keep the poisonous air of every temptation as far as possible from him. But he realized that this would be not father-love but misplaced weakness, and therefore he sent him away; yet the basis of the test was love. . . . . . Or did you never see him who tested the one he loved most in all the world, did you not see how resourceful he was, by heavier and heavier tests, in assuring and reassuring himself more and more deeply of that love which for him constituted his happiness. Did you not see how apprehensive he was, how uneasy, how much more often he wept than the one he tested; and yet it was his own invention; he could be satisfied with this love which he knew he had, but this he would not do, and therefore the basis of the test was love. Is it not true, after all, that we desire to possess through tests only that which we love.

God's tests are rooted in love.

Even if you think the picture of that loving father back home so concerned about his child's welfare is very beautiful and that something would be missing if the illustration is extended to the Almighty Father in Heaven, the incongruity itself is nevertheless elevating; he does not wait for news from us, because he is always with us, and he is not apprehensive about us because he is God Almighty.

Therefore God's tests are, as suggested already in the two chosen sketches:

1. educational [*opdragende*]
2. aimed at the establishment of a deeper relationship with God.

We know very well that in this earthly life we must be educated [*opdrages*] continually in many ways, and we do not want to imagine that we have outgrown this up-bringing—at some time, indeed, this must come to an end, and an intimation of this should be felt already here in this life.

III c 7   *n.d.*, 1840-41

« 1156 *Good Works*

Certainly all of us remember a time when we wanted to delight and, if possible, to surprise father or mother or someone else dear to us with a gift, and when we brought it, somewhat unhappy over its cheapness, face averted (this is how good works should be, bashful), we did not stand with open account book and say: I am giving this to you and now I demand something from you. . . . . . The left hand, free of all self-consciousness, should not know what the right hand is doing.[40] As children we often brought our parents gifts which they themselves had given us; this is the way it always is with God.

III C 17   *n.d.*, 1840-41

« 1157

This is clear in Holy Scripture, and therefore it was much more important to emphasize the latter; but there is also a presentation of the woman as the one who forms the home[41] precisely through her passive sustaining character. The man shall forsake father and mother (this is his first home) and keep to his wife (this is the second home which she develops).[42] This is also beautifully expressed in the word "wife" [*Hustrue*], i.e., faithfulness in the house, a house where faithfulness dwells, or a faithfulness in which love finds its home. Such an expression, so simple and plain and yet so rich in blessing, has nothing at all of romantic love in it.

III B 41:20   *n.d.*, 1841

« 1158

The fulfillment of the duties of motherhood appear to best advantage in collision with conventional forms. This I saw today.[43] I saw a woman of gentility walking along with a little child in her arms. Apparently the child had become tired or weary of walking. In any case, it was not according to plan and arrangement, for otherwise a nurse would presumably have accompanied them. She walked along Østergade and was not at all put out, embarrassed, or ill-tempered, but gazed happily upon her child. It was really a *beautiful* sight.

V A 4   *n.d.*, 1844

« 1159

The young mother (beautiful, erect, a velvet shawl, brisk walker) with her little son.[44] She did not let herself be disturbed at all by the boy's little pranks but said her prayers, followed the service in the hymnbook. She had hit upon the precautionary measure of assigning the child a little space in the pew where he took care of himself while she was wholly absorbed in worship. Generally parents are very busy getting the children to sit still, as if this were their occupation in church. How beautiful to see her choose the one thing needful, and how beautifully she solved the problem. I gave thanks, purely esthetically, to all good guardian spirits, that everything went off quietly, and I shall not readily forget this beautiful picture.

v a 66   *n.d.*, 1844

« 1160

Rachel says:[45] If this is what it is to be a mother—all right. Of how many things in life is this not true: if this is how it is——.

v a 83   *n.d.*, 1844

« 1161

It is certainly true that one learns more from children than from anybody else, but it is also certain that a father can easily be damaged just by this: to have such a creature around whom one may subject to everything and yet demand not only obedience but love, to have someone around toward whom one is constantly in the right—this is a dangerous business.

vi a 24   *n.d.*, 1845

« 1162

"Children shall judge you," says one of the old prophets[46] in proclaiming the most severe punishment upon disobedient Israel. This fits our time —children write in the newspapers, etc. What Socrates speaks of in Plato's *Republic* is relevant here—that ultimately parents are afraid of the children and out of fear of them have to amuse and entertain them exactly the way they want to have it.

vii¹ a 58   *n.d.*, 1846

« 1163 *About God's Love*

"But," says the troubled person, "I do not see God and therefore I cannot know that he is love; nor do I hear him say to me that he is love. In the meantime things happen to me which can least of all be interpreted as being good for me and beneficial to me—how, then, am I to believe that he is love?"

Here it becomes apparent that everything really depends upon a religious upbringing, on the *apriority* which is thereby won, so that it is absolutely settled from the very beginning for a person that God is love. This, the proof that God is love on the basis of an inexplicable impression, an impression which from the beginning is fused with one's whole being, this is really the most important.[47]

VIII[1] A 25   n.d., 1847

« 1164

In earlier times it was a pious custom for families to say grace before meals. Now this is changed. Nowadays people know how to talk almost as connoisseurs about taste and external culture, which is required if eating is to be a human repast and not animalistic bolting of food. But is all this refinement an advance over that pious practice? Is it progress to establish the animal as the standard and to want to distinguish oneself in this respect? Is it an advance over relating oneself to God? Whereas in those times people gathered together at mealtime with the words: Remember God, now they gather together with the words: Remember that you are not animals, or at best remember to be human beings.

VIII[1] A 41   n.d., 1847

« 1165

King Lear's fate can be accounted for as Nemesis. His fault is the madness with which the play begins, of summarily requiring his children to declare the depth of their love for him. Children's love for their parents is a bottomless mystery, rooted as well in a natural relationship. An event can therefore be the occasion which reveals its depth, but it is unseemly, impious, and culpable to wish curiously and selfishly to dissect it, as it were, for the sake of one's own satisfaction. Such a thing is tolerable in an erotic relationship (when the lover asks the beloved how much she loves him), although even here it is pandering.

VIII[1] A 58   n.d., 1847

« 1166 *The Most Rigorous Judgment upon the World*

No one has committed so great a wrong against a human being as the one who has brought up a child in the most ideal view of life and in the strictest discipline and then has sent the child out into the world with this eternally unforgettable impression. Not even the person who seduces a child to gambling and carousing does so great a wrong, humanly speaking, because for this one is not persecuted. But now consider a person strictly brought up, brought up as if related to the gods and who now is sent out into the animal-breed of men—this one will have to suffer. Merely to endure every day this terrible double-vision—whenever he turns inward and scrutinizes his life by the demand of the ideal, he sees how infinitely far he is from being that in the least; anxious and concerned for the salvation of his soul, he understands that this means he must strive even more and still more humbly pray for grace and forgiveness; and then when he turns his gaze outward, he sees that in a certain human sense he is ahead of the others, with the result that for this very reason he is scoffed at and persecuted. If along with other men of the animal-race he would simply ignore God and would be satisfied with the estimation of the metropolis, he would be respected, loved, esteemed.

VIII¹ A 499   n.d., 1847-48

« 1167

How in all the world is it possible for the person who has been brought up in Christianity from childhood[48] and imagines that he is a Christian— how is he ever supposed to get the impression that without Christ he would be lost? Can it ever be anything other than a verbal assurance, some preacher-talk to which neither the pastor nor the deacon nor the congregation gives a second thought? The person continually surfeited with food and drink before he gets hungry—how is he supposed to get the impression that without food and drink he must die of hunger? He can very well say something to this effect, but it remains a simulated something.

It is tragic that a person is brought up from childhood in a security about the highest, a security which ultimately becomes identical with indifference. A pagan was not truly secure but anxious [*angst*]—and then there could be meaning in grasping that without Christ or becoming a Christian he would be lost.

VIII¹ A 537   n.d., 1848

« 1168

To him who knocks, it is opened. And even if God does not open right away—take comfort. Think of a parent who sits in his room making ready something to give joy to his child, who is supposed to come at a certain time. But the child arrives too soon. He knocks on the door, but it is not opened. And the child can see by the light that someone is in the room. Therefore his knocking is heard—and yet the door is not opened.

Then the child becomes despondent. And why is the door not opened? Because the preparations for the child's joy are not entirely completed.

VIII[1] A 586   *n.d., 1848*

« 1169

No—it is upbringing, upbringing, which the world needs. This is what I have always spoken about. This is what I said to King Christian VIII—and this is what everybody regards as absolutely superfluous.

VIII[1] A 616   *n.d., 1848*

« 1170

Actually, the best proof for the immortality of the soul, that there is a God, and the like, is the impression one has of this from his childhood, and therefore this proof, unlike those numerous scholarly and high-sounding proofs, could be stated thus: It is absolutely certain, for my father told me.

IX A 118   *n.d., 1848*

« 1171

It is dreadful to see the carelessness, indifference, and unconcern with which children are brought up—and yet by the age of ten every person is essentially what he will become. Yet almost all bear some damage from youth which they do not heal by the seventieth year; furthermore, all unhappy individualities usually have a background of a faulty childhood.

O, wretched satire upon the human race, that providence has so richly equipped almost every child, because it knew in advance what it means to have to be brought up by "parents," i.e., to be messed up as much as it is humanly possible to be.

X[1] A 468   *n.d., 1849*

« 1172

In margin: On marriage

The danger in getting married is chiefly all the hypocrisy which accompanies it, the fact that a person does what he does for the sake of his wife and children. A person sinks into a secular mentality and cowardliness —and at the same time gives an appearance of holiness to what he does. How lovely of him—he is doing it for his wife and children!

X[2] A 14   *n.d.*

« 1173 *The Greatest Danger for a Child with Respect to the Religious*

The greatest danger is not that the father or tutor is a free-thinker, not even that he is a hypocrite. No, the danger is that he is a pious and God-fearing man, that the child is inwardly and deeply convinced of it, and that the child notices, nevertheless, that an unrest hides deep in his father's soul, to which not even his fear of God and his piety succeed in giving peace. The danger in this situation lies in the child's being prompted to draw a conclusion about God verging almost on the belief that God is not infinite love.

X^2 A 454   *n.d.*, 1850

« 1174 *Infant Baptism, the Bringing Up of Children, Christianity, etc.*

Johannes Climacus[49] correctly points out that in respect to being or to becoming and being a Christian, the accent falls absolutely upon *self-concern*, that the individual is absolutely concerned for himself, to the point—if it is required—of breaking all relationships, all bonds.

But in Christendom the relation has been reversed: we concern ourselves for the children, for the children most of all.

O, we no longer have any conception of Christianity; it is an unchristian lack of resignation for parents to place becoming a Christian within the category of the generation as a matter of course; it is an unchristian kind of love (it is, in fact, only race-love) for parents to be unwilling to understand that to become a Christian is a decision which defines the single individual as spirit, that in this respect one person can do nothing for another, that their baptizing and instructing neither can nor do guarantee that the children are Christian.

O, but the decision to be Christian, what it means, has been completely forgotten, has reverted to paganism's or Judaism's qualities of intimacy in family love, and this about hating father and mother and so on has become a fable, yes, not only that, it is as if Christendom would say: God help Christianity if it thinks again of speaking out and making life strenuous this way. No, we have arranged ourselves very cozily these days here in Christianity with families and all earthly comforts——and this is Christianity!

X^3 A 506   *n.d.*, 1850

« 1175 *God as Father—a Human Father*

God is not Father in wholly the same sense as an earthly father. The earthly father is bound in the natural relationship; he is father whether he wishes to be or not; by making himself a father he has made himself something which imprisons him.

With God it is different, for he is spirit only. If you do not will to be such that God can be your Father, God is then not your Father; he cannot be your Father, nor does he want to be.

But there is still another difference. It sometimes happens that an earthly father, to whom the prodigal son returns in repentance, becomes hard and will not forgive or be a father. But this never happens with God; as soon as you will it sincerely, then God is also your Father.

x³ A 792 *n.d.*, 1851

« 1176 *Christianity—Man*

Does it ever occur to a child that he needs upbringing? Or if you took several children and let them live together, grow up together, would it occur to them that they needed upbringing? Would they think anything else but that they were very fine and splendid children?

But the parents' higher conception sees that they need bringing up and therefore lays down the standard for the child.

It is the same with man. Naturally it does not occur to any man and to any society of men that they are deeply corrupted. It is, quite simply, an impossibility; for men cannot be deeply corrupted if they simultaneously all by themselves, without outside help, can see that they are deeply corrupted.

But a higher conception (Christianity) takes upon itself to proclaim to man that he is deeply corrupted and lays down the standard for him.

But Christianity is not proclaimed in this manner these days. One assumes the natural man's natural conceptions about life; his hankering to enjoy life is regarded as the truth. Thus some of the promises are deleted from Christianity, and it is adulterated so that it fits in with this view of enjoying life.

XI¹ A 522 *n.d.*, 1854

FAUST

« 1177

As far as the criticism of the various versions of Faust is concerned, one can find a basis for classifying them and facilitate a survey of them by paying attention to how such an idea must be reflected in various ages, or how every age must look upon this idea through the prescription glasses of its individuality. For example, the moralizers may use Faust as a wrapper in which they may see the chaff in life; the criticizers may confine themselves to seeing his excessiveness and explain it as a monkish fabrication, etc. A later age must see more deeply.

I A 88   October 7, 1835

« 1178

I would have been happy if Goethe had never continued *Faust;* I would then have called it a miracle; but here human frailty has overcome him. There is a certain strength in seeing the hero of a piece get the worst of it in his struggle, in this case despairing over his doubt; it is precisely this which gives Faust greatness, that is, it is his reformation which draws him down into the common everyday life. His death is the ultimate reconciliation in the work, and we could very well sit and weep over his grave but never think of lifting the curtain which at death made him invisible to our eyes.

I A 104   November 1, 1835

« 1179

It is interesting that Faust (whom I perhaps more properly place in the third stage as the more mediate) embodies both Don Juan and the Wandering Jew (despair). —

It must not be forgotten, either, that Don Juan must be interpreted lyrically (therefore with music); the Wandering Jew epically, and Faust dramatically.

I C 58   December, 1835

« 1180

Does not Goethe's treatment of Faust really lack the enthusiasm for knowledge which nevertheless must be regarded as characteristic of Faust? —Something I have expressed on another occasion is no doubt true—that Faust embodies Don Juan; yet his love life and his sensuality can never be like Don Juan's. With Faust the latter has already become indirect, something into which he plunges himself, driven by despair.

I A 227   August 25, 1836

« 1181

What does it mean and to what extent is it true that every age has its Faust etc.? —No, in the development of the world there is only *one* Faust, only *one* Don Juan, but for the single individual just as for the individual nation in the development of the world there naturally is one for each. Precisely for that reason Faust, for example, can in a certain sense reform, in which case this is the new period's interpretation—which, please note, is not a conception of Faust but is the idea of this age.

I A 292   *n.d.*, 1836

« 1182

That the Faust who is now supposed to represent the age is essentially different from the earlier Faust and from the Faust of every other age is so evident that one needs only to be reminded of it. But how? If we look at the age, we find a host of men who in the elemental Greek sense are πρακτιχοι,[50] whom Aristotle has already assigned to the lowest level of development—preoccupied by their chores of cultivating their land and, as it is called, bringing up their children—that is, as "confirmed consumers" they go on living carefree lives and even in death do something practical for the world—by decaying and enriching the earth. From them something Faustian will hardly develop. On the other hand, there is a great number of men who have either turned their heads to investigate a vanished past or immerse themselves in investigating nature. Because of their busy-ness the Faustian does not appear among them either, inasmuch as the appearance of the Faustian requires first of all that this energetic life be paralyzed in some way or other. —But now there finally appears the type of men we need to observe, namely, those who seek by intuition to comprehend the infinite multiplicity of nature, of life, and of history in a totality-view. But here, too, there is something tragic, for much is already unrolled before their vision and more appears every day, and under all this knowledge of many things dozes the feeling of how infinitely small this knowledge is, and it is this feeling which paralyzes their activity, and now the Faustian appears as despair over not being able to comprehend the whole development in an all-embracing totality-view in which every single nuance is also recognized for its full value, that is, its absolute worth. —But wherein lies the difference? The original Faust's despair was more practical. He had studied, but his studies had not yielded him any return (what he saw next did yield something, even though infinitely little compared with what he wished; Faust's profit from knowledge was a nothing, because in the last resort it was not this question he wanted answered, but rather the question: *what he himself* should do).[51] On the basis of the far more elementary state of the sciences at that time, by means of a survey he could more easily have been convinced of their emptiness, and on account of the special character of the age—enthusiastic action in order to realize its ideal—the question had to be moved over into this area; he had to reconcile life with [that] knowledge. For our time this question has to go back much further since, naturally, as the world becomes older, the intuitive tendency must take precedence, and the question consequently becomes: how can true intuition enter in despite man's limited position. But that which drives men on to this demand for a perfect and true intuition is a despair over the relativity of everything. While he himself uses a rather high criterion (his conviction about this corroborated by having to listen daily to complaints over how fantastical it is), by associating with people who use all the infinite gradations of a criterion all the way from decimals to the diameter of the heavenly orbit, all the way from those who are inspired by the greatest world-historical personages to those for whom the pastor and the deacon are hitherto unsurpassed and unrivalled ideals, all the way from those who have intensely felt and have intensely experienced all the tempestuous emotions of the heart to those who, because once upon a time they were impressed by a juggler, now let us know with a self-assured smile that "they have outgrown those childish tricks" etc.—by associating with such people he gets the idea that he himself is using a much too relative criterion and begins to fear that he is sinking down and losing himself in a bourgeois, philistine mentality. He hears of a discovery which opens vistas over a vast unknown world, which will probably force him to graduate his criterion in quite another way and make vanishing magnitudes of his heroes and his sufferings. He discerns how the most gifted of his contemporaries squeeze out a little yield (speculative abstracting or historical sketching), and he has a secret fear that this possibly may not be what they assume it to be—the most important—but merely what *they* succeed in comprehending and fathoming. He longs for a view which abolishes all relativities and shows him the absolute worth of even the most insignificant thing, because for the true (i.e., divine) view everything has the same magnitude. That such a Faust does not presently lack Wagners is certainly obvious. Herein now lies the despair. The way all of life alters for him now also shows him to be quite different from the first Faust, for while that one with his activist tendency sank into sensuality, this one will back out of everything, forget, if possible, that he ever knew anything, and watch the cows—or perhaps, out of curiosity, transport himself into another world.

II A 29   March 19, 1837

« 1183

In connection with a little essay[52] by Johannes M. . . . . (Martensen) on Lenau's *Faust*, in which it is told that the piece ends with Faust's killing himself and Mephistopheles' giving an epilog, I began to ponder to what extent, after all, it is appropriate to let a work of this kind end in such a way. And here I believe that Goethe was right in ending Part One with Mephistopheles': Heinrich! Heinrich! A suicide would make too much of a character out of the idea; it should be the counter-weight of the whole world which crushes him, as with D. Juan. —Or end in despair (the Wandering Jew). Despair is romantic—not punishment, as it was in the case of Prometheus.

II A 50   *n.d.*, 1837

« 1184

Faust cannot commit suicide. As the idea hovering over all its actual forms, he must complete himself in a new idea (the Wandering Jew).

II A 56   *n.d.*, 1837

« 1185

Faust did not want to learn to know evil in order that he might rejoice over not being so bad (only the philistines do this); on the contrary, he wanted to feel all the sluice gates of sin open within his own breast, the whole kingdom of incalculable possibilities. Everything, however, will not be sufficient. His expectations will be disappointed.

II A 605   *n.d.*, 1837

FICHTE

« 1186

On the whole it is remarkable how much this book[53] has in common with Fichte's *Die Bestimmung des Menschen*.[54] That which in Fichte is more intellectually developed is here more sensuously developed; Fichte's moral world-order and new heaven become here a tent where good works are hung up on the wall (see p. 39), but both are nevertheless unanimous in this—that man simply ought to perform the good without regard to the consequences.

I C 50   March 16, 1835

« 1187

To a high degree Fichte had this spider-moistness, so that as soon as he got the slightest hold he promptly plunged down with the complete security of the form of the conclusion.[55]

I A 231   August, 1836

« 1188

Just like Simeon Stylites,[56] Fichte stands on an enormously high pinnacle performing the most supple (dialectical) movements, and the crowd stands and marvels at him and does not follow him, and the few who try to climb up there parody him (Fichtean School).

I A 252   October 1, 1836

« 1189

The whole idealistic development in Fichte certainly did find, for example, a self, an immortality, but without fullness, like the husband of Aurora,[57] who was immortal, to be sure, but, lacking eternal youth, ended by becoming a grasshopper. —

In despair Fichte threw the empirical ballast overboard and foundered. —

I A 302   *n.d.*, 1836

« 1190

This which I transcribe here[58] was on a scrap of paper and antedates my acquaintance with the younger Fichte,[59] of whose works I have hastily read only *Idee der Personlichkeit*;[60] no doubt it was written in February.

March 19, 1837

Neither Schleiermacher nor Schelling nor now the younger Fichte goes beyond interaction (and speculatively hardly anyone can do this). The one single object of intuition and as such the one truth is the infinite unity moving through infinite multiplicity—the simultaneous infinite becoming and infinite completeness. Infinite multiplicity as such would be a pure abstraction, and likewise infinite completeness. They are discernible only in and with one another by a kind of infinite-space-and-time-filling in the now of beginning; in the same way one may consistently explain individuality as an infinite completeness in infinite becoming,* and therefore the system must be Calvinistic or at least with Schleiermacher regard it [individuality] as the modification of infinite sin and infinite atonement, and just as any individual is predestined, the system is in a way also—omniscience and omnipotence become, therefore, the same, but are seen from two differing angles, and God's consciousness of things is their genesis.†

This system does not really acquire in time (Fichte correctly speaks in one place of *"besondere Zeit"* whereby he is supposed to transcend Schelling, but it stops there) the Christian doctrine of time and of Satan's fall from the eternal and thereby man's into time,‡ or atonement in time, or faith (only the immediate consciousness). Fichte has made an advance insofar as he has gone beyond Hegel's abstraction to intuition.

The first creation gives the immediate consciousness (this is the impression, but as with the wind, one knows neither from whence it comes nor whither it blows); beyond this we cannot go. Christianity is the second creation (therefore Christ is born of a pure virgin, which again is a creation out of nothing; therefore the spirit of God overshadowed Mary

---

* If the infinite multiplicity were simply a given, it would be entirely atomistic.
† God is the actuality of the possible.
‡ Something comparable may be found in F. Baader,[61] where, for example, on man's behalf he declines the honor of being the first inventor of sin[62] and warmly contests Kant's radical evil. —Also belonging here is Günther's theory of original sin conditioned by the development of the race; Adam and Eve were not conscious of sex-differences before the fall.

just as previously it brooded over the waters), a new element, the hearing of the Word—faith, which is the second stage of the immediate consciousness—all this talk about tradition in philosophy is a fraudulent acquisition, an illegitimate child of Christianity. What most likely has given rise to this talk about tradition is that since philosophy has been made the theoretical fulfillment of consciousness, in order to avoid the objection that there is no guarantee of having arrived at normal consciousness, tradition has now been added.

And thus the question of why God created the world can arise, which the old dogmaticians did consider, since there is a revelation; but Fichte *et al.* naturally can never get beyond the universally human immediacy: consciousness.

> I do not transcribe the foregoing because I believe that what is said is something great but because it pleases me to see that some of the observations agree essentially with what bothers me in a later reading of the younger Fichte. The same holds true of the following entry.[63]

II A 31   March 19, 1837

« 1191

How can it be that Fichte places Jacobi, Fries, and Eschenmayer among the reflective philosophers?[64] In their writings have they first developed an epistemology?[65] Or do they appeal to Kantian philosophy? After all, it seems to me that not enough emphasis is placed upon their connection [with Kant], which is the main thing, since otherwise they are to be placed among the constructive thinkers.[66]

II A 592   *n.d.,* 1837

« 1192

It is simple enough to explain everything—by running away from everything, as, for example, the younger Fichte does. He explains all Christianity but admits himself that he cannot explain how it entered into the world. See his just published *Speculative Theologie,*[67] p. 178, lines 14 ff.

If it were generally known that a heavenly communication had fallen down from heaven accompanied by angels, and if someone exegetically explained the contents of the heavenly communication, would he then have explained the heavenly communication? Indeed, the most difficult part would have been omitted.

VII[1] A 187   *n.d.,* 1846

FORCE

« 1193

Augustine[68] draws attention to the fact that not even Christ himself fulfilled the command[69] "When someone strikes you on the right cheek turn the left one to him"; for when one of the high priests' servants struck him on the cheek he said:[70] "If I have spoken wrongly, bear witness to the wrong; but if I have spoken rightly, why do you strike me?" Augustine explains that by this behavior he prevented a new injustice from happening.

Here is the point I have often considered with respect to *meekness*—by its very lightness, which makes even the guilt less (see my discourses, *The Gospel of Suffering*),[71] meekness carried to its ultimate has the double danger of almost strengthening the guilty person in thinking that his guilt is nothing and, in the next place, of being too severe because of the mildness itself. If a man is made aware of his guilt, he might stop doing wrong. In a way the mildness of the unconditional meekness could be almost cruelty, an almost ironical dupery. So wonderfully dialectical are all spiritual relations that, whatever point of departure one takes, by carrying it all the way through one comes to the exact opposite. As with this: meekness undeviatingly carried out can to an eminent degree be the most frightful severity.

x^2 A 564   *n.d.*, 1850

« 1194

On the matter of whether the Christian dares be a soldier, Augustine, believing there was nothing to hinder this, says felicitously: *Non benefacere prohibet militia, sed malitia.*[72] Otherwise he appeals to the fact that John the Baptist[73] did not say to the soldiers: "Throw your weapons away" but "Do no violence or injustice and be satisfied with your wage." But that, after all, preceded Christianity.

x^2 A 565   *n.d.*, 1850

« 1195 *The Suffering Battle*

Force ought never be used; this is the mind of Christianity. Instead

41

one ought to endure injustice in suffering,[74] witnessing also to the truth until the other party cannot hold out in doing wrong and voluntarily gives up doing it.

This suffering battle also has a paralyzing effect. Just as a hypnotist puts his subject to sleep, and one limb after another loses its vitality, so suffering endurance paralyzes injustice; no evil can hold out against it.

But the fact is that this method is so slow; there is an apparently great short-cut which completely satisfies the impatient secular mind, which only all too often is itself in league with injustice: the use of force. Perpetuating injustice and in hasty impatience to want to protect oneself through force against injustice—these are both essentially the same secular-mindedness and essentially the same injustice; at best there is an entirely accidental difference, that the suffering party actually lacks an opportunity to commit injustice.

x^4 A 127   *n.d.*, 1851

« 1196 *Tertullian,*

I believe it is, declares that the Christian must not go to war: one cannot go to war without drawing the sword, the sword which was ordered to be put back into its sheath.

I read this someplace in Böhringer,[75] I, pt. 1, and it seems to be Tertullian.

x^4 A 145   *n.d.*, 1851

« 1197 *Augustine*

says that not to use force to compel one to the truth is "a false and cruel tolerance."

See Böhringer,[75] I, pt. 3, p. 366.
x^4 A 170   *n.d.*, 1851

« 1198 *The Donatists*

said, in opposition to the use of secular force against them: "Christ has given Christians the prototype not of killing but of dying."

See Böhringer,[75] I, pt. 3, p. 384.
x^4 A 171   *n.d.*, 1851

« 1199 *Augustine*

says somewhere, in defense of authoritative faith, that even if someone comes to believe something wrong by way of authority, it would be better than not believing in authority at all. "Even more distressing than to be

deceived by an authority is not to let oneself be guided by any authority."
(See Böhringer,[75] I, pt. 3, p. 253.)

He generally affirms the ethical aspect of authority: obedience and subordination as intrinsically valuable. Also claims that asceticism belongs to being a thinker.

The whole section on this in Böhringer is worth reading again.

In contention with the Donatists, he stresses that his view is not that force is to be used to constrain unto faith (because this cannot be evoked by force), but that force should be used to eliminate hindrances in an individual (passions, etc.), so that faith may appear. (See Böhringer,[75] I, pt. 3. The whole section on Augustine's relationship to the Donatists, especially pages 357 ff. and 367, note, and 368, is what I have in mind particularly.)

x⁴ A 172   *n.d.*, 1851

FORGIVENESS

« 1200 *Christian Confidence*

My son, be of good courage, your sins are forgiven—this is not the freedom which has no experience of the law—confidence is the present tense of hope[76]—hope is like an old woman who stares wistfully—confidence is power and action.* —(a) Confidence before men. (b) Confidence before God. It sometimes happens that our eyes turn toward heaven, and we are astonished at the infinite distance, and the eye cannot find a resting place between heaven and earth—but when the eye of the soul seeks God and we feel the infinite distance, then it is a matter of confidence—but here we have a mediator.

* *In margin:* Hebrews 3:6. τὴν παρρησίαν καὶ τὸ καύχημα τῆς ἐλπίδος[77] (this latter expression is rather a description of the first).

II A 326   January 11, 1839

« 1201

In what sense does an actual *redintegratio in statum pristinum*[78] take place through the forgiveness of sins, also where there is some question of the forgiveness of actual sins? This is of the utmost importance with respect to Christianity's conception of actuality [*Virkeligheden*]. In what relationship does the penitent who has received forgiveness stand to the punishment which actuality itself can provide? Shall he continue to regard it as punishment, or has a transformation taken place whereby it can be regarded as a vicissitude of life?

III A 215 *n.d.*, 1840

« 1202 *On the Forgiveness of Sins*

Christianity has often been spoken of with a certain contempt when compared to the great tasks humanity has otherwise undertaken; the charge has been made that it minimizes what is great in man; or it has been mocked because it is so easy, because it does not require the self-activity of men but rather an inactive receptivity—and this is what faith has been understood to be. But just as Christianity is the easiest of all, so is it also the hardest of all, precisely because it is most difficult for men to control themselves . . . . . therefore the forgiveness of sins. You are not ordered to do this or that; no way is shown for working off your guilt; but you shall believe that there is forgiveness of sins.

It is impossible, you say, you who in your wisdom are already through with Christianity; it is impossible because it is incomprehensible. . . . . . It is impossible, you say, you who would dearly wish that it were true, you who still look continually toward Christianity, because you feel that this must be the source, if it is to come at all. . . . . . It is impossible, you say, you who nevertheless realize that it is real, you, whose repentance became transfigured into a quiet sorrow; it is impossible, you say, and thereby you express your inexpressible thanks to God, who out of his incomprehensible grace and mercy has in Christ reconciled himself with the world.[79]

III C 16   *n.d.*, 1840-41

« 1203

There is no victory more beautiful than that won by forgiving, for here even the vanquished can rejoice in extolling it.

III A 109   *n.d.*, 1841

« 1204

It is better to give than to receive, but it can sometimes be more humble to be willing to receive than to be willing to give. Perhaps there has been someone who in love was prepared to give away everything but was not willing to receive anything.[80]

IV A 66   *n.d.*, 1843

« 1205

Forgiveness of sins cannot be such that God by a single stroke, as it were, erases all guilt, abrogates all its consequences. Such a craving is only a worldly desire which does not really know what guilt is. It is only the guilt which is *forgiven*; more than this the forgiveness of sins is not. It does not mean to become another person in more fortunate circumstances, but it does mean to become a new person in the reassuring consciousness that the guilt is forgiven even if the consequences of guilt remain. The forgiveness of sins must not be the promotional scheme of a wishful thinker who, after having tried many things, ends up wishing to be a completely different person and for this purpose wants to take a chance on the forgiveness of sins. No, only the person who grasps the fact that guilt is something completely different from and more terrible than the consequences of guilt (regarded as misfortune, suffering), only he repents, but he certainly will not fictionalize in this way.

VII¹ A 141   *n.d.*, 1846

« 1206

Heterodoxly one may say that conversion precedes and conditions the forgiveness of sins; orthodoxly one may say: the forgiveness of sins precedes conversion and strengthens men truly to be converted.

VII¹ A 167   *n.d.*, 1846

« 1207 *The Christian Like for Like*[81]

Discourses

Christianity has abandoned "an eye for an eye, a tooth for a tooth," has turned the relationship around, and has thereby introduced a *like for like*: as you relate yourself to men, so God relates himself to you.

Forgiveness is forgiveness

> (forgive and you shall be forgiven;
> forgive us our trespasses as we forgive.)[82]

To judge another is to judge yourself.[83]
When *in life* you are reconciled with your enemy—
then *you* place *on the altar* your gift* to God.[84]

> In the N.T. it is presented as if one offered a second gift: first go and become reconciled with your enemy and then come to offer your gift.[85]

VIII¹ A 114   *n.d.*, 1847

« 1208

In margin of 1207 (VIII¹ A 114):
* For where reconciliation takes place, there the altar is, and reconciliation itself is the only gift which can be offered upon the altar of God.

VIII¹ A 115   *n.d.*, 1847

« 1209

A man rests in the forgiveness of sins when the thought of God does not remind him of the sin but that it is forgiven, when the past is not a memory of how much he trespassed but of how much he has been forgiven.

VIII¹ A 230   *n.d.*, 1847

« 1210

Augustine has said it so well: Certainly God has promised you for-giveness—but he has not promised you tomorrow.[86]

VIII[1] A 459 *n.d.*, 1847

« 1211

..... When he (Stephen) had said this, he fell asleep.[87] —Should one not be able to fall gently asleep when he has prayed for his enemies?

VIII[1] A 475 *n.d.*, 1847

« 1212

*In margin of 1211 (*VIII[1] A 475*):*
One tells a child that he should say something (the Lord's Prayer, for example), and then he goes right to sleep—ah, but for the person who, though innocent, was persecuted, mistreated, and finally condemned to death, there was only one thing to say in the last moment, "Father, forgive them," and then he fell into the sleep of death.

VIII[1] A 476 *n.d.*, 1847

« 1213

It was a miracle when Christ said to the paralytic:[88] Your sins are for-given, arise and walk. But if that miracle does not happen to me now— what miraculous cheerfulness one's faith must have to believe that sin is entirely forgotten, so that memory of it brings no anguish, truly to be-lieve this and to become a new man so that one hardly recognizes himself again!

VIII[1] A 646 *n.d.*, 1848

« 1214

In margin: N.B.
I must continually come closer and closer to the doctrine of the for-giveness of sins.

VIII[1] A 647 *n.d.*, 1848

« 1215 *Something About the Forgiveness of Sins*

The difficulty in personal terms here is at a point quite different from what is generally supposed.

The difficulty is: to what spontaneity does one who believes this re-turn, or what is the spontaneity which follows upon this belief, and how does this belief relate to what is otherwise called spontaneity.

To believe the forgiveness of sins is a paradox, the absurd, etc. —I am not speaking of this but of something else.

I assume, then, that someone has had the prodigious courage of faith truly to believe that God has literally forgotten his sin—a courage which is perhaps not found in ten persons in each generation, this crazy courage —after coming to a mature conception of God and then to believe this, that God absolutely literally can forget.

But I assume this. What then? So now everything is forgotten: he is like a new man. But if no trace at all is left, does this mean that it should be possible for a person to live with the care-lessness of youth? Impossible!

And in this connection, I would point out that to bring up a child rigorously in Christianity is an indescribably dubious matter, because his life is thereby horribly confused until sometime in his thirties.

But would it be possible now for someone who has believed the forgiveness of his sins to become young enough erotically to fall in love.

Here is the difficulty in my own life. I am an old man brought up with extraordinary rigor in Christianity; therefore my life is for me horribly confused; therefore I have been brought into collisions which no one imagines and still less speaks about. And only now, now in my thirty-fifth year, with the help of heavy sufferings and the bitterness of repentance, have I perhaps learned enough about dying away from the world so that I can rightly speak of finding my whole life and my salvation through faith in forgiveness of sins. But really, even though I am spiritually as strong as I have ever been, I am much too old for various things such as falling in love with a woman.

A certain outliving is necessary in order really to feel the need for Christianity. If it is forced on a person before that time, it makes him quite mad. There is something in a child and a youth which belongs to them so naturally that one must say that God himself has willed them to be that way. Essentially regarded, the child and the youth are only psychically qualified, neither more nor less. Christianity is spirit. To construe a child strictly under the qualification "spirit" is an act of cruelty, in a way is like killing him, and has never been Christianity's intention.

And the reason all Christianity in Christendom has for the most part become jabbering is that it is taught to children in this way. For rarely, very rarely is a child brought up very rigorously in Christianity, which nevertheless, however fanatic it may be, is far better even though it slays his childhood and youth. Christian upbringing is very often gibberish and amounts to nothing at all. After all, it is better to have suffered through all these agonies in childhood and youth by being stretched (as in torture) within the qualification of spirit, which one is not as yet, to have suffered through these agonies so that one's childhood became sheer wretchedness —and then finally sometime in complete rapture to understand: See, now I am able to use it; now Christianity exists for me and is everything to me. This is far better than foolishly never to have been one thing or the other.

VIII¹ A 663   *n.d.*, 1848

« 1216 *Something on the Forgiveness of Sins*

Just as the first impression of a true and deep love is the feeling of one's own unworthiness, in the same way the need for forgiveness of sins betokens that one loves God. But all by himself no man can ever come to think that God loves him. This must be proclaimed to men. This is the gospel, this is revelation. But precisely because no human being can by himself come to the idea that God loves him, in like manner no human being can come to know how great a sinner he is. Consequently, the Augsburg Confession[89] teaches that it must be revealed to a man how great a sinner he is. For without the divine yard-stick, no human being is the great sinner (this he is—only before God).

But both parts correspond to one another—when a person does not comprehend what a great sinner he is, he cannot love God; and when he does not love God (through the proclamation to him of how much God loves him), he cannot comprehend how great a sinner he is. The inwardness of the consciousness of sin is the very passion of love. Truly the law makes one a sinner—but love makes one a far greater sinner. It is true that the person who fears God and trembles feels himself to be a sinner, but the person who in truth loves feels himself to be an even greater sinner.

VIII¹ A 675   *n.d.*, 1848

« 1217

The eternal consolation in the doctrine of the forgiveness of sins is this: You shall believe it. For when the anxious conscience begins with heavy thoughts, and it is as if they could never in all eternity be forgotten, then comes this: You shall forget. You *shall* stop thinking of your sin. Not only are you permitted to let it alone, not only do you dare pray God for permission to dare forget—no, you shall forget, for you shall believe that your sins are forgiven.

O, the most appalling arrest of all—when a person's memory is as if eternally arrested at his sin— But you shall forget—this can help.

This discourse is divine discourse, the direct opposite of human discourse, which is merely anxious and desperate about not being permitted

to forget, yes, about being unable to forget even if permission is given—
You *shall*.

IX A 177   *n.d.*, 1848

« 1218

Luther's sermon[90] for the Nineteenth Sunday after Trinity is excellent. He shows here that a Christian's piety is the forgiveness of sins,
that sins' forgiveness belongs to the pure God-relationship, far beyond sin
—and virtue. The forgiveness of sin is a totality-qualification based on
my being in relationship to God.

IX A 482   *n.d.*, 1848

« 1219

A sophistical observation could be made with reference to the Gospel
about the unmerciful fellow-servant:[91] the master cancelled his debt of
10,000 talents and he would not cancel a fellow-servant's debt of 100
denarii; but is not the cancellation proportionate to the wealth of the one
who cancels—then the 100 denarii were perhaps more for the servant than
the 10,000 talents for the master—the poorer one is, the more damaging,
perhaps, a small injustice is.

But to this one has to answer that the 10,000 talents are not only in
themselves a greater sum, but every single one is a greater guilt, since (in
the parable) it is sin against God, and that which provides the criterion for
guilt is the one who is sinned against. I must view guilt toward me as insignificant simply because I must judge poorly about myself.

IX A 491   *n.d.*, 1848

« 1220

If it seems to you that God can no longer forgive you because you have
sinned once again, that Christ can no longer pray for you—O, think again!
He allowed himself to be born, He endured thirty-four years of poverty and
wretchedness, was persecuted, mocked, and finally crucified—in order to
save you, too—and then He would not want to forgive you if you turn
repentantly to Him!

X¹ A 12   *n.d.*, 1849

« 1221 *A Dramatic Motif*

I am thinking of such a person as a Giordano Bruno or someone like
him, in short, someone who became a martyr for an idea. In a weak
moment he has yielded, has hid himself in order to avoid danger. He is be-

trayed and his hiding place discovered; he is seized—and now he is happy to be forced to remain in danger.

Then I imagine him before the judge (and I will now fashion a few Socratic lines). He demands to know who has given away his hiding place and betrayed him. It proves to be his servant. He is confronted by the servant, who is extremely dejected since he himself now clearly feels his guilt. Then he says to the servant: Don't be distressed; I completely forgive you; certainly not many servants would have acted differently than you did, for I know very well that you were bribed—incidentally, how much did I cost? Servant: I got 250 dollars. Master: Well, now, that is a pretty good payment. You understand, however, that you are rather lucky that I am not angry with you, for in my will 500 dollars is designated for you payable upon my death. If I had become angry, you would have been fooled: you have gotten 250 dollars for betraying me, a 250 dollar bribe—a crime; otherwise you would have gotten 500 dollars without any misconduct, and if I were angry you would have lost more than half. Now, on the contrary, because of the will you get 500 after my death, 250 extra as something you have earned on the side. My friend, those who paid you 250 dollars probably did not admonish you to use the money well; take my advice, then, and use the money well. Do not despair because you were weak enough to betray me, be strong enough to believe both that God will forgive you entirely and that I have entirely forgiven you.

This collision could also be developed on the basis of an earlier crime which had no connection to this man's later life, a crime which his servant knew about—and he had now informed on him.

What I would like to portray is the kind of magnanimity which ordinarily is almost taken for mental illness by the human crowd.

x^2 A 516   *n.d.,* 1850

« 1222   *Forgiveness of Sins*

Hamann quotes a passage (Volume I of his collected works, letter No. 40): "*Wie es von drey Männern Gotters in der Schrift heisst: dass Gott ihnen vergab und ihr Thun strafte ψ 99.*"[92]

These are, as Hamann adds in a parenthesis, "two opposing concepts which seem to rescind each other." But it is nevertheless a significant expression of the Christian concept of the forgiveness of sin.

Already in one of my earlier journals [II A 63] (before I began to be an author) I noted that the forgiveness of sin does not consist so much in the removal of the punishment as in the changed view of it, that it is not punishment, that God is merciful to me. The painful suffering of punishment is perhaps not removed, requires its time, but my idea of it is changed. I no longer bear this suffering burdened with the thought that it is the expression of God's wrath, but I bear it with God as I bear any other suffering.

By definition this is also quite properly forgiveness of sin and also, if you will, remission of punishment. For what is punishment? Punishment is not pain in and for itself; the same pain or suffering can happen to another merely as a vicissitude of life. Punishment is the conception that this particular suffering is punishment. When this conception is taken away, the punishment is really taken away as well.

x³ A 319   n.d., 1850

« 1223 *Atonement*

Christ's death is the atonement for our sins principally by its having made satisfaction for sin. But then one could ask: How could Christ forgive sins while he was alive? This must be explained as an anticipation.

There are some differences, however, if Christ forgives sins during his lifetime and if his death is the atonement. In the latter case God the Father is regarded as the one who forgives and Christ as the one who makes satisfaction and thus influences God's willingness to forgive.

Incidentally, at this moment I do not remember any place where Christ uses the form: I forgive you your sins. In the story of the paralytic he says that he will show that the Son of Man has been granted the power to forgive sins; therefore he says: Stand up, take your bed and walk—both, then, are qualifications of the divine, but he does not then say: I forgive you. To the sinner he says: Her sins, which are many, are forgiven—but not: I forgive you your many sins, and he even gives a reason for their being forgiven, *because* she loved much. To the woman seized in open adultery he says: Go and sin no more.[93]

x³ A 573   n.d., 1850

« 1224 *To Forgive Sins*

is divine not only in the sense that no one is able to do it except God, but it is also divine in another sense so that we must say that no one can do it without God. If men really were able to forgive sins, they still are not adequate for it. Indeed, how poor, pinched, and reluctant, how very conditional is their forgiveness; so the sinner may say: No, thank you, may I rather ask to be punished and suffer my punishment and be spared your miserable, wretched forgiveness, which, even if I were properly saved and become somewhat meritorious, would probably turn up again and in the form of envy the forgiveness would be charged to my account.

How different is the divine from the human! Actually it is man's disposition to detect sin, to find out something evil about a man—then we know that he is no different from the rest of us. The only kind of forgiveness which can be sustained at all is a mutual repaying. It is the Deity's joy to forgive sins; just as God is almighty in creating out of nothing, so he is almighty in—uncreating something, for to forget, almightily to forget, is indeed to uncreate something.

XI² A 3   n.d., 1854

FRANKLIN

« 1225

Franklin's work of 1759, *The History of Pennsylvania*, has the motto: "He who gives up essential freedom to gain a little security deserves neither freedom nor security."

Franklins Liv og Skrifter, ed. Binzer, pt. I, p. 154.[94]

x⁴ A 67   n.d., 1851

« 1226

Franklin (in his *Leben und Schriften* by Binzer, pt. II) discusses the Dunker religious sect, which in order not to hinder free development does not want to draft a written confession of faith. Franklin thinks this is excellent, since generally sectarians are characterized by the very opposite. Well, the latter may be true all right, but those sectarians were nevertheless all too expeditious. What is really inexplicable is how they managed to form a sect on that basis!

x⁴ A 73   n.d., 1851

« 1227 *Franklin*

(*Leben und Schr., v.* Binzer, IV, p. 4, *Der Rummeltopf* No. 1.)
..... *und obgleich Reformation eigentlich jedes Menschen Sache ist (ich meine, dass jeder Andern bessern sollte) so ist es doch in diesem Falle nur zu wahr, dass, was Jedermanns Sache ist, im Grunde keines Menschen Sache ist—und dem gemäss wird auch die Sache betrieben. Nach reiflicher Überlegung halte ich's daher für gut die "keines Menschen Sache" ganz zu der meinigen zu machen etc.:*[95]

This is good. Yet I understand it a bit differently, since at the moment everyone is dabbling at being a reformer; therefore the task must be (the task no one wants to assume): to reform the reformers.

x⁴ A 77   n.d., 1851

« 1228 *The Sense of Justice*

Columbus requested to be buried with the chains so unjustly laid upon him in life.

54

Franklin lived in London as an agent for Pennsylvania and several other colonies. A piece of intelligence came to England from Governor Hutchinson and the Vice-Governor in Boston, picturing the public affairs of the colony in an unfavorable light. This letter came into Franklin's possession, and he sent it to Boston. Franklin was taken to court for illegal possession of the letter; the prosecutor called him a thief, etc. During the trial Franklin maintained silence on the whole matter.

But his biographer (a note in Binzer's *Leben und Schriften*, I, p. 179) states that this treatment made a deep impression on Franklin, as was seen later at the formal signing of the pact between America and France, when he wore the same suit of velveteen he wore on that day and which he otherwise never used.

x^4 A 81 *n.d.*, 1851

« 1229 *Franklin*

An article by Franklin (*der arme Richard oder der weg zum Wohlstand*; Binzer's *Leben und Schriften*, IV, p. 95) contains many good practical ideas, and ends thus: "In this manner the old gentleman concluded his talk. Those who were present listened to him and praised his good precepts and thereupon went and did just the opposite—quite as if it had been an ordinary sermon."

x^4 A 82 *n.d.*, 1851

FREEDOM

« 1230

The concept "predestination" must be regarded as a thoroughgoing abortion. Doubtlessly having originated in order to relate freedom and God's omnipotence, it solves the riddle by denying one of the concepts and consequently explains nothing.

See below [I A 7].

I A 5   August 19, 1834

« 1231

See above [I A 5].

If we consider how the doctrine of predestination has arisen, it is clear that as long as there is no consideration of any freedom which plays a role in the world, it is impossible for the question of a predestination to arise. Only when the conception of human freedom had developed and in reflection was coupled with the conception of God's governance of the world, only then could it arise, and it had to make its appearance as an attempt to solve the problem. But in this connection it is nevertheless curious that the intended solution of the problem now constitutes for us the problem, namely, how these two concepts are to be united.

I A 7   November 23, 1834

« 1232

To what extent is illusion necessary for men's lives—this is a question relative to romanticism. —What about the theory that the course of world events is an inevitable development, and how does this theory work in life? Must it not paralyze all activity, inasmuch as it abolishes not only the obviously egotistical but also the natural and enthusiastic assurance, at least in the moment of battle, that what one is working for is the one right thing? Or is this philosophy practicable only for the past, so that it teaches me to solve its riddle and then lets present life stand again as a riddle which the following generation has to solve. But of what use is this philosophy to me? And are those who like this philosophy in a position to resign and let the world go its crooked way, and what is one to think about them? Is it their fault or the system's? —[96]

I A 205   July 11, 1836

« 1233

There is a very speculative and, in connection with Daub's philosophical view, extremely interesting observation in Volume III of Bauer's journal,[97] p. 127. Prior to this he had discussed the relationship between the natural and the historical sense and had shown the former as a condition for the latter; but now he develops how the individual can freely subordinate the latter to the former (thereby history or freedom under nature, completely) or the former to the latter (and thereby freedom over nature, partially), and draws out the more precise consequences of subordinating the historical to the natural, saying that the subject thereby comes upon the idea: *"an dem Vergangenen sei das anschaulich-Gewesene das Unvergängliche, am Gewesenen das Naturliche das Unverwesliche (das also nicht wie doch der Apostel lehrt 'verweslich gesäet wird, und unverweslich auferstehe' sondern, indem es selbst das an sich Unverwesliche sei, nur bis zu seiner Wiederveranschaulichung den Schein des Verweslichen habe)."*[98]

II A 74   May 29, 1837

« 1234

With a curiously ironical consistency fanatics reveal a strong tendency to exhibit themselves publicly in the same negligee in which their train of thought emerges: the Adamites (among the Hussites) thought that in order to be perfectly free one had to go about stark naked and presumably regarded this as the specific difference between man's later condition and his condition in paradise. The Sanscullottes are just as well known—and now the attempt of the barenecked to reestablish the Nordic spirit is in full swing.[99]

II A 280   October 29, 1838

« 1235

In margin of 1234 (II A 280):
Even though, in view of the importance of his discovery, we forgive Archimedes for running split-naked through the streets of Syracuse, it by no means follows as a matter of course that we are obliged to tolerate these modern versions of return-to-nature.

II A 281   November 2, 1838

« 1236

People almost never make use of the freedoms they have, for example, freedom of thought;[100] by way of compensation they demand freedom of expression instead.

II A 746   n.d., 1838

« 1237

That God could create beings free over against himself is the cross which philosophy could not bear but upon which it has remained hanging.

II A 752   n.d., 1838

« 1238

What observer of the vibrations of the soul, of the current changeable weather,* psychically understood, does not think of those enchantments of which almost every fairy story has a trace, and how shocking is the similarity when one discovers that there is also a law in the world of freedom, certainly not a law of nature as for those who are enchanted (that the enchantment lasts seven days, seven weeks, seven months, etc.), but a law of sin, shocking because we first discover the law afterward; we believe ourselves free to move about in a mood, and then little by little we are led to discern the opposition of the present mood to the one previous, then the thought strikes the soul like lightning that according to an inner necessity these moods succeed each other according to a law which we are unable to decipher: ταλαίπωρος ἐγὼ ἄνθρωπος! τίς με ῥύσεται ἐκ τοῦ σώματος τοῦ θανάτου τούτου[101] (Romans 7:24). Or when as in certain fairy stories the thought expands so that it is no longer a particular individual but a whole process which lies under this enchantment. And how few there are who themselves are not enslaved by this law, are not moved by this impression; how few dare to work for their rescue; how long it takes before the fairy story finds the instrumental person who is capable of bearing these difficulties and has the courage to risk everything. Or in quite different situations, how inquisitive people are when the unhappy one desires to be alone with his sorrow; then even all of beautiful Melusina's love, her deeply moving sorrow over his misfortune, could not halt her husband's inquisitiveness.[102]

II A 456   June 17, 1839

« 1239

In margin of 1238 (II A 456):
*Should not the divine saying also have validity in the world of the

psyche: "As long as the world lasts, seed time and harvest, summer and winter, day and night shall not cease?"

II A 457   *n.d.*, 1839

« 1240

That philosophy must begin with a presupposition ought not to be regarded as a *defect* but as a *blessing*; therefore this *an sich* becomes a curse from which it can never be free. The conflict between consciousness or mind as empty form and as the fixed image of a moving object corresponds to the same problem in freedom: how the contentless *arbitrium*, which like the scale has nothing to do with the content but as infinitely abstract elasticity maintains itself victorious and indifferent for all eternity—how this comes to be positive freedom. Here, too, we find a presupposition, because this *liberum arbitrium*[103] is really never found, but world-existence [*Verdenexistentsen*] itself has already provided it.

III A 48   *n.d.*, 1840

« 1241

A perfectly disinterested will (equilibrium) is a nothing, a chimera; Leibniz[104] demonstrates this superbly in many places; Bayle also acknowledges this (in opposition to Epicurus).

In what relationship does the will stand to the last act of understanding; does the will follow necessarily the final cognition of understanding? See para. 311.

IV C 39   *n.d.*, 1842-43

« 1242

It is really extraordinary that Chrysippus uses the statement, "Every statement is either true or false," to prove that everything happens according to fate. Here the idea of mediation seems to be necessary in order to find a providence.

(See Tennemann,[105] IV, p. 272.)

IV C 55   *n.d.*, 1842-43

« 1243

It is most remarkable that almost all the skeptics have always left the reality [*Realitæt*] of the will uncontested. Thereby they would actually arrive at the point they should reach, for recovery takes place through the will. The manner in which the skeptics usually expressed themselves is very striking. They thought that as far as action is concerned one might as well be content with probability, just as if it were less important to act rightly than to know rightly.

IV C 56   *n.d.*, 1842-43

« 1244

Doubt is certainly not halted by the necessity of knowledge (that there is something one must acknowledge) but by the categorical imperative of the will, that there is something one cannot will.[106] This is the will's concretion in itself, by which it shows itself to be something other than an ethereal phantom.

IV C 60   *n.d.*, 1842-43

« 1245 *Problemata*

Is the past more necessary than the future?[107]

This can be significant with respect to the solution of the problem of possibility[108]—how does Hegel answer it? In logic, in the doctrine of essence. Here we get the explanation that the possible is the actual [*det Virkelige*], the actual is the possible. It is simple enough in a science, at the conclusion of which one has arrived at possibility. It is then a tautology.

This is important in connection with the doctrine of the relation between the future and God's foreknowledge.

The old thesis that knowledge neither takes away anything nor adds. See Boethius,[109] pp. 126-27, later used by Leibniz.[110]

IV C 62   *n.d.*, 1842-43

« 1246

If freedom [in repetition as a religious movement] now discovers an obstacle, then it must lie in freedom itself. Freedom now shows itself not to be in its perfection in man but to be disturbed. This disturbance, however, must be supplied by freedom itself, for otherwise there would be no freedom at all or the disturbance would be a matter of chance which freedom could remove. The disturbance which is supplied by freedom itself is sin. If it gets the right to rule, then freedom disperses itself and is never in a position to realize repetition. Then freedom despairs of itself but still never forgets repetition. But in the moment of despair a change takes place with regard to repetition, and freedom takes on a religious expression, by which repetition appears as atonement, which is repetition *sensu eminentiori* and something different from mediation, which always merely describes the nodal points of oscillation in the progress of immanence.

IV B 118:1   *n.d.*, 1843-44

« 1247 **N.B.**

All talk about a higher unity which is supposed to unite absolute dis-
parities is simply a metaphysical attack upon ethics.[111] And also all this
stupid talk about the positive and the positive,[112] that someone else is a
negative spirit but the person speaking is a positive spirit—humbug! A
person has just as much negativity as he has positivity. Freedom never forgets this dialectical origin of freedom. This can happen only when one
dabbles in his categories—one speaks of the good and praises it, one cites
an example, and see, it is a pure, immediate qualification as, for example,
a good heart, what is called a good man. They say that a person should
doubt everything, and when they write about Hamlet[113] they are scandalized that Hamlet had the disease of reflection but still had not
even reached the point of doubting everything———Alas! Alas! Alas!
Siebenbürgen.[114]

V A 90   n.d., 1844

« 1248

In freedom's possibility it holds true, however, that the more profoundly this [actual sin] is grasped, the more profoundly and definitely the
possibility of guilt appears within it, just as it holds true of spontaneous
genius that the greater the genius the more profound the relationship to
fate.

In freedom's possibility, freedom droops. This is, as mentioned, the
closest psychical approximation to the qualitative leap which posits sin.
To say that the Church teaches original sin, that the Catholic Church
teaches it thus and the Protestant Church thus, to erect a speculative concept which explains original sin and sin *at all*—this is indeed the task of
the learned and the wise in our time. The more concrete understanding
of it in the specific individual, that is to say, the way I have to understand
it, is a simpler, less complicated task, which I have chosen.

——

What is developed in these two paragraphs had no place in the previous chapter[115] because the position here described is not a state of innocence and yet does not come after the qualitative leap.

V B 55:26   n.d., 1844

« 1249

Liberum arbitrium,[116] which can equally well choose the good or the
evil, is basically an abrogation of the concept of freedom and a despair of

any explanation of it. Freedom means to be capable. Good and evil exist nowhere outside freedom, since this very distinction comes into existence through freedom.[117]

V B 56:2   n.d., 1844

« 1250

No compulsory school system qualifies a pupil for admission to eternity.

VII¹ A 71   n.d., 1846

« 1251

The whole question of the relation of God's omnipotence and goodness to evil (instead of the differentiation that God accomplishes the good and merely permits the evil) is resolved quite simply in the following way. The greatest good, after all, which can be done for a being, greater than anything else that one can do for it, is to make it free. In order to do just that, omnipotence is required. This seems strange, since it is precisely omnipotence that supposedly would make [a being] dependent. But if one will reflect on omnipotence, he will see that it also must contain the unique qualification of being able to withdraw itself again in a manifestation of omnipotence in such a way that precisely for this reason that which has been originated through omnipotence can be independent. This is why one human being cannot make another person wholly free, because the one who has power is himself captive in having it and therefore continually has a wrong relationship to the one whom he wants to make free. Moreover, there is a finite self-love in all finite power (talent, etc.). Only omnipotence can withdraw itself at the same time it gives itself away, and this relationship is the very independence of the receiver. God's omnipotence is therefore his goodness. For goodness is to give oneself away completely, but in such a way that by omnipotently taking oneself back one makes the recipient independent. All finite power makes [a being] dependent; only omnipotence can make [a being] independent, can form from nothing something which has its continuity in itself through the continual withdrawing of omnipotence. Omnipotence is not ensconced in a relationship to an other, for there is no other to which it is comparable —no, it can give without giving up the least of its power, i.e., it can make [a being] independent. It is incomprehensible that omnipotence is not only able to create the most impressive of all things—the whole visible world—but is able to create the most fragile of all things—a being independent of that very omnipotence. Omnipotence, which can handle the world so toughly and with such a heavy hand, can also make itself so light that what it has brought into existence receives independence. Only a wretched and mundane conception of the dialectic of power holds that it is greater and greater in proportion to its ability to compel and to make dependent. No, Socrates had a sounder understanding; he knew that the art of power lies precisely in making another free. But in the relationship between man and man this can never be done, even though it needs to be emphasized again and again that this is the highest; only omnipotence can truly succeed in this. Therefore if man had the slightest independent existence over against God (with regard to *materia*),[118] then God could not make him free. Creation out of nothing is once again the Almighty's expression for being able to make [a being] independent. He to whom I owe absolutely everything, although he still absolutely controls everything, has in fact made me independent. If in creating man God himself lost a little of his power, then precisely what he could not do would be to make man independent.

VII[1] A 181   *n.d.*, 1846

« 1252

An unwillingness to give in and to change in little things is hardly a token of independence; it rather shows a dependence. If the object is a matter of indifference, the change is consequently also a matter of indifference; therefore the basis of one's unwillingness to change must be the great importance of showing someone else or the others that one will not change. But this, that it is very important to *show* one's independence is precisely dependence.

VII[1] A 210   *n.d.*, 1846

« 1253

That which has made my life so strenuous but also full of discoveries is that I have never been forced finitely into anything but have had to choose decision infinitely. But out of this a difficulty has arisen. In the decisions of the spirit a person can make up his mind in freedom, but in relation to finitude (for example, physical well-being) he actually must be compelled. Finite decisions are in a certain sense too small for him to approach from the infinite—therefore he must be compelled. To "be compelled" is the only help in finite affairs—freedom's choice is the only salvation in the infinite.

VIII[1] A 178   *n.d.*, 1847

« 1254

If all the wonders of the world could be placed in your hands, everything, everything, and then add to that the willingness of the fates to humor your every whim—you might want to accept it, but on the condition that you and you alone would rule over your life, that there would be no God. Consider what you would lose, among other things, in having nothing, absolutely nothing, as the object of wonder, absolutely nothing impinging upon the shape of your life—absolutely nothing to wonder about, how wisely, how indescribably lovingly God has shaped your life. For every person's life, the very poorest, is such that if he would be content to be himself and then rejoice and wonder over God, he would discover the infinite wisdom of the divine in his life also, just as the smallest flower gives witness to God.

VIII^1 A 522   *n.d.,* 1848

« 1255

Every human being who has even once understood himself penetratingly understands further that he could never possibly be satisfied with being the master of his fate, that for a human being there is satisfaction and joy and blessedness only in obeying.

VIII^1 A 525   *n.d.,* 1848

« 1256 *Mynster's Sermon about Joseph, the Stepfather of Jesus*

It is deceitful to talk like this (p. 114):[119] "Whatever happens to me that I cannot prevent, wherever I am led and I cannot go another way—this is God's will." Well, thanks for that! It certainly leaves out the difficulty, the difficulty that a man shall himself *choose*. It appears to be so *geschwindt* and easy, this statement which sounds so Lutheran, and yet when it is supposed to be true in the highest sense it is rarely seen: I cannot do otherwise; God help me, Amen. In this we hear immediately that the person who is speaking is someone who knows what it is to choose.

But the fact of the matter is that Mynster has managed his way gradually through life with probabilities; he has almost never acted authentically; otherwise it would be impossible to talk in this way.

IX A 109   *n.d.,* 1848

« 1257

To have to live quite independently is undeniably the most strenuous life. What goes without saying when a person has the bonds and curbs of relationships—that he cannot do this or this may not be done, etc., so that no time is wasted in deliberation, inasmuch as it simply is an impossibility —this often takes much time and emotional energy if one is quite independent. Yet on the other hand one certainly learns to know himself and life in quite another way.

x^1 A 26   *n.d.*, 1849

« 1258 *Concerning the "Voluntary"*

I now well understand why Christianity adheres to the voluntary.[120] The existential authority to teach corresponds to the voluntary. Who is to teach poverty? He who is fighting to acquire a fortune or has one can certainly talk about poverty, but without authority. Only the voluntary, the person who voluntarily gave up wealth and is poor, only he has authority. Who is to teach disdain for honor and esteem? He who is himself decorated with honor and stars and ribbons bound in gilt-edged velvet [*in margin*: bound in silk with back or front of velvet] can certainly "lecture," "declaim," and also teach it, but without authority, and it can easily become a subtle nicety, also, to have all these things and yet elevate himself beyond them. The actually despised person cannot do it either—here the voluntary has its place, the person who voluntarily gave up honor and esteem (or waived claim to it). —Meanwhile there is a particular dialectical difficulty here. If an esteemed person teaches that people should disdain honor and esteem, men say: Thanks for that. If it is a person who actually has no honor or esteem, people say: Well, never mind what he says. No one has any regard for him.

This "voluntariness," meanwhile, is a strange thing. It is extraordinarily lofty and extremely dangerous; in countless ways it can be perverted into pride, vanity, etc. But certain it is that Christianity has demanded voluntariness, and certain it is that the "voluntary" has absolutely, literally disappeared; and certain it is that Christianity, when the voluntary has completely disappeared, has essentially been abolished.

Voluntariness is the precise form for qualitatively being spirit.

But there is a lower form of religiosity which thinks more childishly about God, which childishly believes that God has nothing against, is almost pleased with, a child's rejoicing and the object of his rejoicing. Thus one remains essentially in the physical-mental categories except that everything is referred to God.

Voluntariness is the highest form of religiousness and is therefore to be recognized by the fact that here God is most rigorous. Religiousness is classified according to ascending rigor. It is as with a child in relation to his parents. If the child wants to be a child, then the parents are gentle. But suppose a child some Saturday says to his parents: Instead of going out to play I would rather stay home and do some work. The parents have nothing against it, but nevertheless they automatically become rigorous about it, for they now insist that the child must finish it freely and gladly. If at midday the child begins to complain about the job, the parents disapprove and say: You should have remained a child and made use of your freedom. It is the same with God in respect to the voluntary. By the voluntary, however, one must not think of the dangers to which a man exposes himself for the sake of the truth by witnessing to the truth and against evil but, as the Middle Ages understood, of the voluntary relinquishing of the temporal, except that this had some [direct] relationship to serving truth and itself wanted to be an expression for the religious.

Voluntariness has disappeared. Christianity has become too mild. If I were to describe it exactly, I do not know anything better than what occurred to me just today. Upbringing in Christianity from childhood makes it too mild; it is somewhat like a child's being brought up by his grandparents rather than by his parents. God is not so much our father as our grandfather.

Yet it must be remembered that God is by no means an enemy of the voluntary; that would be a self-contradiction, since he demands it in his Word.

But precisely because God has become a grandfather, it is so difficult to enter properly into the fear and trembling which is a part of the voluntary, or which truly actualizes the voluntary.

If ultimately God to me is as mild as a grandfather, then the voluntary is false and frivolous.

This matter has occupied me very much. I myself recognize that I have a too mild conception of God. This is the reason I have not ventured the voluntary and why I have never used authority. Even exposing myself to the *Corsair's* attack is not being the voluntary. In part it is quite simply acting in the direction of witnessing for the truth, and in part it could just as well have led to the opposite result, that I had won—yes, there was even a human possibility of that; and this would also have happened if the shabby envy of the distinguished people had not supplied a counter-artillery, which interfered. But the fact that this happened was accidental.

And yet the tiny bit of the voluntary, if I may say so, which my life evidences is still too high for most people. So far has Christianity retrogressed!

If I should now think of beginning the voluntary, it would have to be in such a way, without my daring to say it, that I would carry it through. I would say to God: I understand very well that in your Word you require the voluntary, but I cannot hide from you that in my soul there is the thought and assurance—wherever it came from—that you will think just as much of me if I leave it alone and childishly remain man, and this appeals to me more—whereas the other makes me apprehensive. Just the same I am ever mindful that so it is in your Word. Could you not help me ever so little to begin gradually, please, since I seem to understand that this in a certain higher sense pleases you, even though I understand that in respect to the voluntary you become more strict and must continue to be that; please, please! —See, there we have it. One never comes to the voluntary this way; God remains too mild. It is always the grandfather, who the child suspects is not very rigorous. To repeat, if rigorousness disappears, then the "voluntary" also disappears.

x^2 A 159   *n.d.*, 1849

« 1259

In margin of 1258 (x^2 A 159):
Christianity has become too mild. Only when it is prodigiously rigorous can one venture the voluntary without thinking of it as being meritorious. If Christianity is mild, it is almost unavoidable that the notion of meritorious works slips in, since there is fundamentally no basis for the venturing.

x^2 A 160   *n.d.*, 1849

« 1260

That a bare and naked *liberum arbitrium* is a chimera is best seen by the difficulty, the long, long continuous effort, which is necessary merely to get rid of a habit, even if one ever so earnestly has made a resolution. Or it is seen when one considers the spiritual trials in which a man is fighting against things beyond his control, fighting against them in the anxiety of death, and at first, because of the anxiety [*Angsten*], for a time elicits rather than removes them, until finally he gradually becomes victorious in a long, long drawn-out battle.

x^2 A 243   *n.d.*, 1849

« 1261

Is it not a peculiar yet profound use of language that someone may say: There is absolutely no question here of any *choice*—I *choose* this and that. (A similar observation is found J. Müller,[121] but not so precisely formulated.) Furthermore, Christianity can say to a man: You shall choose the one thing needful, but in such a way that there must be no question of any choice—that is, if you fool around a long time, then you are not really choosing the one thing needful; like the kingdom of God, it must be chosen *first*. Consequently there is something in relation to which there must not be, and by definition there can be, a choice, and yet there is a choice. Consequently, the very fact that there is no *choice* expresses the tremendous passion or intensity with which one *chooses*. Can there be a more accurate expression for the fact that freedom of choice is only a formal condition of freedom and that emphasizing freedom of choice as such means the sure loss of freedom? The content of freedom is decisive for freedom to such an extent that the very truth of freedom of choice is: there must be no *choice*, even though there is a choice.

This is "spirit." But precisely because men are a long way from being spirit, precisely therefore does freedom make so much trouble for them, since they continually remain suspended in freedom of choice. The reflection which is associated with the indolent and base stares fixedly at freedom of choice instead of remembering that there must be no choice—and then chooses. However surprising it may seem, one may say therefore that only fear and trembling and only constraint can help a man to freedom. For fear and trembling and constraint can master him in such a way that it is not a question of any choice—and then one very likely chooses the right thing. In the moment of death, most people choose the right thing.

But of what use is science and scholarship? None, none at all! It relaxes everything in calm, objective observation—and thus freedom becomes an unaccountable something. From a scientific-scholarly point of view Spinoza is and remains the only consistent one.

Here it is the same as with believing and speculating, and, as Joh. Climacus has said, it is like sawing:[122] It is one thing to make oneself objectively light and another to make oneself subjectively heavy—but we want to do both at the same time.

Freedom really *is* freedom only when, in the same moment, the same second, it is (freedom of choice), it rushes with infinite speed to bind itself unconditionally by the choice of attachment, the choice whose truth is that there can be no question of any choice.

It is the indescribable wonder of almighty love that God can really concede to man so much that he, in regard to himself, can want to speak almost like a suitor (here is a beautiful play on words: to make free, to propose [*at gjøre fri, at frie*]): Will you have me, or will you not—and then wait one single second for the answer.

Alas, but man is not sufficiently spirit. He thinks: Since the choice is left to me, I will take my own time and *first of all* think it over very *earnestly*. Tragic anti-climax! "Earnestness" is precisely to choose God immediately and "first of all." And so man lies there and conjures with a phantom: freedom of choice, whether he has it or whether he does not, etc.—and even does it in a scientific-scholarly way. He does not notice that he has missed freedom. And so he diverts himself, perhaps, for a while with the idea of freedom of choice until it changes again, and he begins to doubt whether he has freedom of choice. And now he has also lost freedom of choice. It is because of an utterly wrong maneuver (speaking militarily) that he confuses everything. By staring fixedly at "freedom of choice" instead of choosing, he loses both freedom and freedom of choice. Nor can it be attained again by reflection; if it is to be gained again, it must be by intensified fear and trembling, called forth by the thought of having wasted it.

The most tremendous thing conceded to man is—choice, freedom. If you want to rescue and keep it, there is only one way—in the very same second unconditionally in full attachment give it back to God and yourself along with it. If the sight of what is conceded to you tempts you, if you surrender to the temptation and look with selfish craving at freedom of choice, then you lose your freedom. And your punishment then is to go around in a kind of confusion and brag about having—freedom of choice. Woe to you, this is the judgment upon you—you have freedom of choice, you say, and yet you have not chosen God. Then you become ill; freedom of choice becomes your fixed idea; finally you become like the rich man morbidly imagining that he has become impoverished and will die of want. You sigh that you have lost the freedom of choice—and the mistake is merely that you do not sorrow deeply enough so that you get it back again.

x^2 A 428   *n.d.*, 1850

« 1262

It is quite right, as J. Müller[123] pointed out earlier, that freedom cannot be regarded indiscriminately as a capacity for good and for evil, for then evil is really also a good. Nor can one say that the basis of evil is the misuse of the will, for the very misuse of the will is precisely the evil.

x^2 A 438   *n.d.*, 1850

« 1263

The Greeks say that a man himself shapes his situation and circumstances.[124] The proverb says: Everyone is the blacksmith of his own fate.

Julius Müller[125] expresses the same thing beautifully when he says that a man's choice becomes his fate. At first glance this does not seem even well-phrased, for if he himself chooses it, then there can be no talk about its becoming his fate, then it is his choice; but perhaps what he chose turns out to have much more in it than he thought and involves completely different consequences—thus it becomes his fate.

x^2 A 518   *n.d.*, 1850

« 1264 *Freedom of Conscience, Freedom of Belief, etc.*

Ideally, it must be acknowledged, every human being has freedom of conscience, freedom of belief, etc.

But what then? Where are the men so spiritually strong that they can use it, genuinely able to stand absolutely alone, alone with God.

Here is the untruth, the demagogical flattery in talking as if every human being were such a great fellow—if only there were no constraint, no law. O, my God! No, the truth is that everyone who is subjectively a person to the degree that he consults only with God and his conscience and is able to endure it—such a person does not give the time of day as to whether there are laws or regulations against it; for him such things are nothing but flimsy thread. Yes, if he is in truth great, he desires all possible opposition lest he run wild or go wrong, but that human regulations would be able to compel him—no, that he does not fear; before God and in his conscience he knows that he need not.

But people want to eliminate injunctions and constraints etc. in order to play the game of being such real men that we can stand alone under such conditions—but, instead, it is precisely the opposition given us, if we win over it, which alone is able to prove that we are real men.

Take away all constraint, which is just what men need and especially in the highest concerns [*in margin:* and logically all the more, the higher the concern]—and the mass of men will either cease to be anything at all or will fall into the hands of parties, etc.

But it is so vain and so flattering to our vanity to think: We want to be almost like apostles or at least like Luther—take away all constraint and that's just what we will be. O, you fools or sophists, the apostles, Luther, etc. were just what they were because there was all possible constraint and opposition against them—but they overcame it. Had there been no constraint, we should never have come to see that they were what they were.

Nowadays people want to have all constraint removed and then play the apostle—which is about the same as if someone wanted to eliminate cannons, gun-powder, and bayonets and then play the brave soldier. Precisely in order that it shall become clear whether it really is "conscience" alone which decides (not a belch, a lazy notion, caprice, confused thoughts, foolish aping [Efterabelse], etc.), precisely for this reason there must be opposition and constraint. The qualification "conscience" is so inward that it takes all the filtering possible to find it; but if it is found, if it really is that and only that which determines me—then all regulations be hanged —I laugh at them. It is precisely because "the conscience" is infinitely sacred to the man who is at all conscientious that he wants opposition, constraint. He would rather discover in time with the aid of constraint that it perhaps was not his conscience at all which determined him to will to risk this or that step rather than to discover too late that he was under an illusion concerning the most sacred of all, concerning his conscience.

The person who in truth can stand alone in the world this way, consulting only with his conscience—he is a hero. And he might well say: Do not be embarrassed on my account; you may want to tighten the constraint still more; I would even be glad for that.

But take away all constraint and let us flatter each other that we all, each one of us, are such heroes.

There is a clamoring for freedom of conscience, freedom of belief, etc. in these times when someone who really has a thought is already a great rarity. What does this clamoring mean; does it signify strength, heroism? Not quite. It signifies softness; it signifies that we are weaklings, coddled, who are eager to play the hero at bargain price.

It was not like this with our forefathers; when the berserker felt power in his bones he shouted for others to come with shields and if possible to force him down—for he knew well enough that he had power. Nor was it like this with the heroes of faith, who did not demand that all constraint be removed. O, no, on the contrary, they yearned for it, and a quite different kind of constraint than is even remotely conceivable among us; they yearned for imprisonment, chains, the stake, in order to prove that they had freedom of conscience, freedom of belief, etc. Now men want the state to loosen every bond, to give or perhaps make a present of freedom of conscience, freedom of belief. In the old days men believed that it was the conscience which gave freedom of conscience, that if one had conscience, freedom was sure to come along, but that, on the other hand, to eliminate every constraint, to loosen every bond, meant at best to make it as free and as convenient as possible for everyone to have no conscience and to imagine that he had one.

*   *

It is above all an entirely mistaken dialectic to conclude that the greater, the more serious the good, the more intolerable all constraint. No, no. In relation to insignificant things, even the slightest constraint is intolerable, as, for example, if the wearing of hats were prohibited by law, and every one, all men and every man, was ordered to wear a cap. On the other hand, the greater and the more serious the good, the better I am able to bear some constraint, in order that I can have an opportunity to test myself and to get to know myself, in order that the decisive steps are not made too easy for me—because in the last resort there is really no constraint which can compel the spiritual; at most it can make him buy freedom dearly.*

Therefore all this talk about eliminating constraint comes either from coddled men or from those who perhaps once felt the power to fight but are now exhausted and find it nicer to have all constraints taken away.

x³ A 618   n.d., 1850

« 1265

In margin of 1264 (x³ A 618):

* Consequently what men want is this: they do not want to be forced out into such decisions where it becomes decisive and obvious that one has conscience and acts only by virtue of conscience. They should then say: We are weak and fearful; we do not have such courage or such powers— therefore we want constraint eliminated. There is at least some meaning in this. But in the lying thieves' slang of the day it is phrased: We battle for freedom of conscience.

x³ A 619   n.d., 1850

« 1266 *Freedom*

The true Christian is not much concerned with forms, for he is conscious in himself and in God that if it should become necessary: I shall break them and no earthly power at all will be able to bind me. He is like someone who carries a loaded pistol (although in an infinitely purer sense) —he knows the way out. He is like the Stoic who went about with the thought of suicide (although in an infinitely purer sense)—he knows the way out. Therefore he does not get into a big ferment, and for this very reason can endure a great deal, simply because he is conscious within himself and in God that if a certain point is reached, the martyr's way out beckons to him.

But the more effeminate people are, the less they have of this cheerful confidence or the more they have of a well-grounded fear that when the showdown comes, the whole thing will misfire, and with all the greater zeal they fortify themselves with external forms.

It is basically the same anxiety, the same secular-mindedness, which becomes apparent in zealousness for free forms, as if this were everything, the same secular-mindedness which expresses itself in amassing money because one believes neither in providence nor in himself. The greater the faith in God, the less one feels the desire to hoard; the greater the faith in God, the greater the indifference toward all this contention about more forms.

x^4 A 13   *n.d.*, 1851

« 1267 *Epigram*

In our age everything must be free—yes, one must be free, even if he does not care about it at all; one must be free, otherwise they will kill him —to this extent everything must be free.

x^4 A 99   *n.d.*, 1851

« 1268 *Freedom*

That abstract freedom of choice (*liberum arbitrium*) is a phantasy, as if a human being at every moment of his life stood continually in this abstract possibility, so that consequently he never moves from the spot, as if freedom were not also an historical condition—this has been pointed out by Augustine and many moderns.

It seems to me that the matter can be illuminated simply in the following way. Take a weight, even the most accurate gold weight—when it has been used only a week it already has a history. The owner knows this history, for example, that it leans towards off-balance one way or the other, etc. This history continues with use.

So it is with the will. It has a history, a continually progressive history. A person can go so far that he finally loses even the capacity of being able to choose. With this, however, the history is not concluded, for, as Augustine rightly says, this condition is the punishment of sin—and is again sin. The concept "sin" captures in every way. It is not something external so that the punishment is something else; no, the punishment, although punishment, is yet again sin.

x^4 A 175   *n.d.*, 1851

« 1269 *Freedom of Choice*

Usually the freedom of being able to choose is presented as an extraordinary good. This it is, but it nevertheless depends also upon how long it is going to last. Usually one makes the mistake of thinking that this itself is the good and that this freedom of choice lasts one's entire life.

What Augustine says of true freedom (distinguished from freedom of choice) is very true and very much a part of experience—namely, that a person has the most lively sense of freedom when with completely decisive determination he impresses upon his action the inner necessity which excludes the thought of another possibility. Then freedom of choice or the "agony" of choice comes to an end.

See Böhringer,[126] I, pt. 3, p. 550.

x^4 A 177   *n.d.*, 1851

« 1270 *Necessity Changed to Freedom*

In the hymn "When I think of the hour" etc. there is the expression:
"Close the door";[127]
yet the deceased one does not need to do it himself; the survivors take care of that in order that it be completely closed. But there is the convivial, poetic view, as if the deceased one himself transformed this into his own free act and closed the door in order to have it good there within his sleeping chamber.

In margin: One could be humorous and say that it expresses how slaphappy [*kisteglad*, literally chest-happy] the deceased is in his coffin [*Kiste*], how happy he is that they properly shut the lid of his coffin, that is, over being able to close his own door.

x^4 A 245   *n.d.*, 1851

« 1271 *Independence*

How is it that in our time only a wealthy person is regarded as an independent man? I wonder if it is not because we have completely forgotten or transformed into a fable the fact that being able to live on roots, water, and bread is a more secure independence.

x^4 A 257   *n.d.*, 1852

« 1272 *I Will Not—I Cannot*

With respect to something which one knows to be God's will—how could a man dare to say: I will not!

So we men have discovered how to say: I cannot. Is this any less rebellious? If it is God's will that you do it, how is it possible that you cannot. Thus it amounts to: I will not.

x^4 A 656   *n.d.*, 1852

« 1273   *The Swindle*

When a child gets his will, he is jubilant, jumps up and down and dances, claps his hands, thanks his father again and again, and shouts: What a nice father!—and does it all the more the more he believes that there is something wrong here, that it is not his father's will at all which is being done.

But I still would not regard this situation as dangerous, for the father is still in the external, palpable sense a power who can end the whole game by saying: Nonsense!

It is different when the other party is not a palpable power in the external sense.

As I have often said to and of myself: I do not fear the living as much as I fear the dead, and why? Because face to face with a living person I dare use a portion of my ingenuity to get him to come over to my side— and he can, indeed, assert his own position. But a dead person! A dead person does not talk directly to me; only through myself do I get to know what may be the dead person's will. In one sense it is made very easy for me to use sophistry here so that little by little I craftily, sneakily get the dead person's will to be what I want. And thus when I get my own will I overflow with self-satisfaction, the sense of life stirs powerfully within me, I feel so happy, and imagine, too, that this is my reward because I am doing the dead one's will. Appalling!

And now the relationship to God. God is not in the external, palpable sense a power who, face to face with me, asserts his rights. His will is proclaimed to me, yet not in such a way that I can go and ask him at any moment—no, I have his will in his Word. But the more specific understanding—and what is thus broadly articulated in his Word is realized first of all in action on the part of the individual through a more particular understanding of his whole concretion—the more particular understanding I have in and through myself.

How natural and easy it is to get God's will altered little by little, to get it to be something other than what it is, to get it to be what I wish, what would make me happy.

And then when I do it—no wonder I am happy, for I did what would make me happy.

So I overflow with happiness—and I perhaps say to myself: After all, you can see it was God's will, for God wants to make his creatures happy, wants us to rejoice in life—yes, except the ones he loves, for "they shall weep and lament; I will show him what he must come to suffer for my name's sake!" But I conclude that it is God's will since I am happy—and I give thanks again and again: God is love, after all, I say—and in this manner I go to meet eternity.

Humanness consists in this, that the whole human race shouts as if with one voice, in unison: It is God's will which helps me to be happy in this life—for God is love. And Christianity shouts: "You shall weep and lament; the world will rejoice." But how in the world can anything which makes me weep and lament be God's will? Yes, this is Christianity.

But, to repeat, God is not an external, palpable power who bangs the table in front of me when I want to alter his will and says: No, stop! No, in this sense it is almost as if he did not exist. It is left up to me.

Further, my flesh and blood are diametrically opposed to his will! If with an anxiety like the mortal anxiety of the anguished conscience I do not guard against altering God's will—yes, it is then so infinitely easy to fool myself—and God does not let himself be heard directly.

How stringent this is, and the stringency is precisely that God behaves as if nothing has happened.

x^5 A 13   n.d., 1852

« 1274 *The Way Is Narrow.*[128]

In just these few words lies a stipulation of the voluntary. If Christ did not have voluntariness (which is related to "imitating" [*Efterfølgelse*] him) in mind, he might well have said: The way is sometimes narrow and sometimes easy, narrow for some and easy for others, etc. But he says: The way is narrow. If we do not admit that this contains a reference to the voluntary, it still, in any case, is something different from what we usually talk about when we say that earthly life can have its tribulations. Particular emphasis is placed upon the way being narrow; therefore it must come either from the voluntary or from God, who sends suffering to the Christian in particular—consequently by willing to be a Christian one does not become free from suffering but the very opposite.

XI^1 A 23   n.d., 1854

« 1275

In margin of 1274 (XI^1 A 23):
In any case freedom, the voluntary, self-determination, etc. are implied by the words—enter by the narrow gate[129]—for here it is left to the

individual himself whether he will or will not, whether he will or will not expose himself to sufferings and troubles and tribulations.

XI[1] A 24   *n.d.*, 1854

« 1276 *The Freethinker (an About-face)*

It may almost be said that the freethinker in our time suffers persecution from the government—because he proclaims Christianity.

How does this about-face happen, how did everything get turned around this way? The orthodox Church does not proclaim Christianity but lets itself get mixed up with Epicureanism. So the freethinker takes it upon himself, out of chicanery, to be sure, to proclaim Christianity or what Christianity is—and for this he is punished by the state.

XI[2] A 119   *n.d.*, 1854

« 1277 *The Truth, Christianity, Will Make You Free!*[130]

The fact of the matter is that man prefers to be free from the kind of liberation which God and Christianity have in mind, yes, defends himself against it at any price. It is just as if one were to say to a molar: I will liberate you, loosen the gum, cut the nerve, etc. To that the molar might say: No, thanks, I have it good just as I am. So it is with the sensate man in respect to the liberation which Christianity talks about—God and man do not understand each other or talk the same language.

XI[2] A 261   *n.d.*, 1854

« 1278 *It Hurts to Be Saved*

July 5, '55

In margin: The demons in the gospels—to pray to be free from being saved.

XI[2] A 424   July 5, 1855

FRIENDSHIP

« 1279

What is friendship without intellectual interaction, a refuge for weak souls who are not able to breathe in the atmosphere of intelligence but only in the atmosphere of animal exhalations? How wretchedly it drags itself along in spite of all the external means with which one tries to patch it up (by drinking *Du's*,[131] etc.). What a caricature it is, except for those who straightforwardly admit that friendship is nothing else than mutual insurance.[132] How disgusting to hear those insipid stereotyped screeds about mutual understanding, about friendship. Certainly understanding is part of friendship, but not the kind which makes the one continually aware of what the other is going to say. No, it is essential to friendship that the one never knows what the other is going to say; when that point is reached friendship is past. But that kind of understanding leads such persons to believe that they understand everyone else, too. Out of this comes the self-satisfaction with which they say that they expected one to answer precisely as he did answer, etc., which frequently is not true and has its basis in their presuming that everyone's conversation is just like their own, insipid, trivial, and pointless, and they have no intimation of the whole host of individualizing traits etc. which make every observation interesting. It is always well to avoid such people, since in spite of their understanding, they always misunderstand. How distressing for someone who is having doubts to hear from such a "sweet person" that "he has experienced the same thing." If the conversation is about a great man, he promptly has a little man whom he thinks to be just as great; naturally all phenomena are fetched out of his duodecimo horizons* (a good example: *Raketten med Stjerner* complained that Sibbern was now beginning to write and found this doubly regrettable because it was at the very same time that Messrs. Blok Tøxen and Lange laid down their pens).[133] If the conversation is about a great thinker, he promptly has an opinion because he perhaps has heard the man's name at some time. As the years pass, as far as their conversation is concerned, people generally tend to become more and more like hand-organs, mobile automatons (with built-in muscle flexing), something like ship captains, who, even with the opportunity to walk the longest and most beautiful avenue, nevertheless prefer their standard skipper walk.[134]

II A 22   n.d., 1837

« 1280

In margin of 1279 (II A 22):
* The basis is that they, too, naturally are moved by the train of events and by the mightier spirits, and they reproduce them by way of parody, just as tame geese and ducks beat their wings, cry out, and quiver for a moment when a wild goose or duck flies over them.

II A 23   n.d., 1837

« 1281

What deep feeling there is in the story that if one wants to give a brownie something beyond its frugal requirements (something to eat or a piece of old clothing), the brownie has to leave the place where he has been the good fairy.[135] So also friendship and all feeling vanish when payment is offered.

II A 175   October 8, 1837

« 1282

. . . . . A friend is not what we philosophers call the necessary other, but the superfluous other.[136]

III A 119   n.d., 1841

« 1283

People sometimes complain that they find no friends.[137] But this is very often untrue and one's own fault. It all depends on what a man wants in the world. If he has merely finite aims, no matter what they are he will always find a few who must agree with him. But if a person wants the highest, with every sacrifice he still finds no friend, for there is no common interest here which can unite them, since there are no interests but rather the very opposite, sheer sacrifice. In this regard a friend usually would only hold one back, and therefore one ought to be careful.

VIII[1] A 80   n.d., 1847

« 1284

Job[138] endured everything—not until his friends came—to comfort him—did he become impatient.

X[1] A 194   n.d., 1849

« 1285 *The category—Christ a Friend We Have in Heaven—Is Sentimental*

For his peace, quiet, and felicity a man needs a God in heaven whom he—O unspeakable bliss!—dares call his father, regarding himself as the child. —Then he needs a savior and redeemer so that despite his sin he dares to believe that God will be his father. —Then he needs a holy spirit who strengthens him in the struggle and witnesses with his spirit.

But a friend! Just like that, purely and simply a friend! Has the Christian become so old that he is no more a child and God is presumably no more his father? Well, then it is high time for him to look around for a friend. But if he is a child—a child usually does not have what one calls friends in the proper sense.

This business of a friend in heaven is a sentimentality which has made a thorough mess of Christianity. Yes, one may call Christ the Friend of sinners, for this is the same as Savior and Redeemer. But simply to call Christ a friend in heaven, this does away with God the Father and makes Christ into something altogether wrong.

When we have become so old that we delude ourselves even into having to be our own providence, we ought to look around for a friend, a friend who cannot actually help us but sympathizes with us. This is what we have finally made Christ into, a friend "on whose breast I can lean my tired head" (as it says in one of Mynster's sermons).

X^3 A 200   *n.d.,* 1850

« 1286 *The Rigorous Christian*

ought to be sufficiently fair and human to resign himself to the fact—yes, he should almost apologize to his most intimate friends and others—that he is what he is, that he does not take part in what largely dominates their lives, and which, humanly speaking, can nevertheless be very lovely and lovable, that in a sense they can derive no pleasure from him.

X^3 A 263   *n.d.,* 1850

GENIUS

« 1287

There no doubt are men in whom genius manifests itself just as inconveniently as genius in stampeding cows.

I A 83   *n.d.*, 1835

« 1288

A thesis: great geniuses are essentially unable to read a book. While they are reading, their own development will always be greater than their understanding of the author.

II A 26   *n.d.*, 1837

« 1289

The difficulty in judging great men (namely, that of securing a criterion) is removed by the criterion which they usually carry in their pockets, by the throng of personalities, in themselves important, who gather around them and thereby provide an intermediate instance, a vantage point from which one can observe the genuinely great man, a relativity by which to evaluate him.

II A 278   October 20, 1838

« 1290

Genius, like a thunder storm, goes against the wind.[139]

II A 535   August 8, 1839

« 1291

A genius who is misunderstood by his age takes comfort in the thought of a better future.[140] People think this is noble talk; whereas it is insipid. The world always remains about the same; or is the generation which embraces what he has said better because he has said it? The generation which admires him at the same time crucifies a contemporary whom the next generation, again, admires; for the world remains the same and what it cannot tolerate is contemporaneity with greatness. —I cannot understand how such things can occupy a genius so much. For example, to hope to meet Socrates sometime in order to confer with him in a beautiful dialogue—and then not care a fig for the present and the future.

VI A 21   n.d., 1845

« 1292

When a skipper sails out in his coastal fruit boat, he usually knows the whole course in advance; but a man-of-war puts out to sea and the orders are received only after it is out on the deep. So it is with the genius. He lies out on the deep and gets his orders. The rest of us know something or other about this and that which we undertake.

VI A 93   n.d., 1845

« 1293

A *genius* and an *apostle* are qualitatively different,[141] are qualifications which belong each to its own qualitative sphere. The genius is the primitive, the original, the seminal point of departure within the sphere of immanence; the genius's point of departure is his personal identity with himself. The genius's originality is the genius himself. A person called by a revelation and to whom a teaching is entrusted has his point of departure within the sphere of transcendence; the revelation as the paradoxical point of departure is beyond the called person's [*den Kaldedes*] personal identity with himself; the point of departure is by virtue of the paradox. A genius is born and develops; but a person called by a revelation and to whom a teaching is entrusted is indeed a specific person beforehand and he cannot regard the revelation as a factor in his life-development; he is and remains *qua* person identical with himself, but the revelation and the revealed teaching cannot be assimilated to the qualifications of his personality. The genius develops and becomes what he is κατὰ δύναμιν, but a person called by a revelation and to whom a teaching is entrusted is entrusted with the teaching by virtue of a paradox, and he is held fast in this relationship. The so-called paradoxes of a genius are merely symptomatic, an excessiveness occurring in the process of development; an apostle is made what he is *qua* apostle by a paradox, and his is the qualitative paradox. Therefore entirely different categories must be used for evaluating a genius than for evaluating an apostle.

In margin:
The difference between a genius and an apostle is also the qualitative difference that the new which a genius may have to give still remains within the sphere of immanence, in which every relationship between man

and man *qua* man must find its explanation. The genius is not paradoxically different from other men. The new which he may bring must be such that, regarded essentially, it belongs to the race; then immanence can absorb the difference between the genius and other men. But an apostle is a paradox.

This is to be developed first.

In the capacity of a genius an apostle could very well have something new to bring, and everything would be in order if he had not begun with a revelation or if he solemnly revoked it.

On an accompanying scrap:

The difference is suggested by the words. *Genius*, as the word (*ingenium*) says, means the innate or congenital. *Apostle* accentuates the fact that this man has been sent on an errand by God. That a man is sent on an errand by God entails no change in the man at all—he does not become more intelligent, more learned, or more eloquent, etc.—no, he is simply on an errand.

VII² B 261:8   n.d., 1846-47

« 1294

The true genius, from whom the genuinely pure impact of the idea comes, is always weakly related at first (this is possibility—anxiety—he himself stands in the way). The same thing happens to him as to the fireman. At the very beginning the force of the water in the hose is so powerful that it almost knocks the fireman over and he reels almost like a drunken man, but the next moment he is in control again and produces an extraordinary effect.

VIII¹ A 395   n.d., 1847

« 1295

In *A Thousand and One Nights* there often appears the theme of a human being marrying a genie,[142] but in order for this relationship to be happy, the human being must make a pledge of silence and never ask why, no matter what the genie does. This is the relationship to superiority.

An example of this is found in the story of night No. 871.

IX A 3   n.d., 1848

« 1296

When a country allows a boy to perpetrate boyish pranks and insists that its distinguished citizens put up with them and pretend that everything is just fine—then the country also ought to make it perfectly plain that he is a boy and the pranks are boyish pranks—that he is not to be regarded as a genius because of his boyish pranks.

IX A 157   n.d., 1848

« 1297

People take pleasure in admiring a genius who has no awareness of himself, who at one time produces perhaps a masterpiece and at another a piece of trash and does not himself really know which is which. Precisely because he is without awareness, it flatters them to give an opinion. But a genius who is great precisely because of his awareness arouses opposition and obstinancy. It annoys people that he himself knows how well it has been done; furthermore, they are a little worried about expressing admiration since it is almost like taking an examination—since he himself knows which is which.

IX A 275   n.d., 1848

« 1298

Geniuses are like thunder storms—they go against the wind, terrify men, cleanse the air.[143]

The established order has invented various storm-diverters against or for geniuses—if it succeeds, so much the worse for the established order, for if it succeeds once, twice, three times, the next thunder storm will be all the more terrible.

There are two kinds of geniuses. The characteristic of the one is roaring, but the lightning is meager and rarely strikes; the other kind is characterized by reflection by which it constrains itself or restrains the roaring. But the lightning is all the more intense; with the speed and sureness of lightning it hits the selected particular points—and is fatal.

X^1 A 590   n.d., 1849

« 1299

God creates out of nothing. If we use a customary expression and say that a genius creates, we would have to say that in order to create he must see to it that there is nothing. Everyone who begins with something never manages to create. Let us take an example. The genius of being able, in the Socratic sense, to deceive.[144] If a person about to begin thinks that there are 6 or 100 definite ways to do it, he is not a genius. The genius has nothing prepared, nothing at all; he has absolutely nothing—merely the power, and that which it produces is a production or creation of genius, if this expression is to be used for a human production.

x^2 A 563   *n.d.*, 1850

« 1300 *Nullum unquam exstitit magnum ingenium sine aliqua dementia*[145]

The explanation is very simple. In order truly to be the great genius, a man must be the exception. But in order that there shall be earnestness in being the exception, he must himself be unfree, forced into it. Herein lies the significance of his *dementia*. There is a fixed point at which he suffers; he cannot ever run with the crowd. This is his anguish. His *dementia* perhaps has nothing at all to do with his real genius, but it is the pain by which he is tormented into isolation—and he must be in isolation if he is to be great, and no man is able freely to hold himself in isolation; he must be constrained if it is to be in earnest.

x^3 A 499   *n.d.*, 1850

« 1301 *Genius—Talent*

Talent ranks according to the sensation it awakens; genius according to the opposition it awakens (religious character according to the offense it causes). Talent conforms immediately and directly; genius does not conform to the given. Talent warms up the given (as they say in cookery) and makes it apparent; genius brings something new.

But just as our time in all respects has invented shabby substitutes, so also here—it lets men of talent pass for geniuses, so that the men of talent, freed from the sufferings of genius, enjoy the direct relationship which men of talent have with their contemporaries—and they are also honored as geniuses.

This all hangs together with the self-deification of the human race and the enormous power of contemporaneousness, for people no longer wish to identify themselves with the definition—one who brings something new. Therefore they really want to abolish the genius, deify the genus, and let men of talent forge ahead.

XI[1] A 120   *n.d.*, 1854

GOD

« 1302

A strict doctrine of predestination traces the origin of evil back to God and thereby does not remain even as consistent as Manichæism, for the latter system posits two beings; the former unites these two contradictories in one being.

I A 2   May 30, 1834

« 1303

It seems to me that the same discovery which Copernicus made in astronomy was made in dogmatics when it was discovered that God is not the one who changes (God could neither become gentle nor angry), but that man changes his position in relationship to God—in other words: the sun does not go around the earth, but the earth goes around the sun.

I A 21   September 29, 1834

« 1304

In the rationalistic dogmaticians[146] it is usually stated as a central thesis: God is unchangeable[147] (in love), and Christ's appearance was really only a declaration of this. Consequently, a sharp philosophical mind can be introduced into the Christian position without naming Christ—if, that is, this man can grasp the idea of God's unchangeableness, for it is still, after all, characteristically Christian. But now in order to justify the significance of Christ, they say that one cannot convince men of this (God's unchangeableness), or that they are unable to grasp this without an extraordinary medium, and this then becomes Christ's appearance; but they still cannot deny that it is nevertheless a peculiar way for God to show his unchangeableness—to let him who is sent merely to inform mankind about this suffer and die, while sinful man receives no punishment.

I A 29   November 8, 1834

« 1305

In the development of the doctrine of atonement, as maintained by Clausen,[148] the incentive to which Scripture[149] gives great prominence, love to God, disappears. By maintaining in this way that absolutely no change has taken place in God with regard to us, we are led back to a completely Kantian standpoint; then we ought to improve ourselves because our reason tells us to, and thus God comes to play a very subordinate role.

I A 30   n.d., 1834

« 1306

Monotheism always lies concealed in polytheism, without therefore hovering everywhere as an abstract* possibility, as with the Greeks ("the unknown god").

May 29, 1837

* On the other hand, abstract polytheism is found in the Jew's *plural* expression "Elohim," without either a collective or distributive predicate.

Genesis 3:22, מִמֶּנּוּ אַחַד, the plural coupled with the singular here alludes to the absolute unity of plurality (see Göschel).[150]

II A 73   n.d., 1837

« 1307

So impossible is it for the world to continue without God that if God were able to *forget the world* it would instantly disappear.

II A 622   n.d., 1837

« 1308

God's providence is great precisely in small things; whereas for men there is something lacking here—just as lace seen through a microscope is irregular and unlovely, but the texture of nature under the same scrutiny proves to be more and more ingenious.—

II A 657   n.d., 1837

« 1309

The relation between Christianity and Gnosticism[151] is significantly indicated by the relation between the two definitions at which they arrive: Christianity at the λόγος, Gnosticism at the "Name" (Christ was the name of the invisible God); the latter is abstract to a high degree, just as all Gnosticism was an abstraction, for which reason the Gnostics could not really arrive at a time-and-space-filling creation but actually had to assume creation as identical with the fall.

II A 237   July 26, 1838

« 1310

God creates out of *nothing*—marvelous, you say. Yes, of course, but he does something more marvelous—he creates saints (the communion of saints) out of sinners.

II A 758   n.d., 1838

« 1311

Who are you who dissects hearts, even you who want to do it for the Lord who ransacks hearts and emotions, for him, the heart-inspector, who knows what lives in your heart better than you do yourself, where so many a secret thought has gotten a free hand in the secret parts, in the secret place where he but seldom has looked with pleasure when you have, according to Christ's command, done well in the secret parts. Whoever is not with me is against me. Or who are you who wants to make your Lord and God as finite as you yourself are, he for whom 1,000 years is as a day. Remember that you are created in his image and according to his likeness, and this is the highest, the most glorious thing that can be said—and you wilfully and arbitrarily want to create him in your image and form him according to your own likeness.

II A 330   January 18, 1839

« 1312

. . . . . Would you want the Kingdom of God to be no more superabundant than your earthly reason could calculate it to be? Would you want the depth of God's wisdom to be no more unsearchable than your own cleverness could search out? Would you want God's decrees to be no more intricately tied than could be untied by your keenness? It may seem that what I am saying is crazy, utter foolishness. But I would like to ask if you have ever felt yourself to be so unfortunate in the world that you perceived, even though you had all the wisdom your most glowing imagination could depict, that you nevertheless could not rescue yourself from life's predicament? Have you ever felt yourself to be so poor that you had to say: Even if I had all the treasures and glories of the world, even if I were placed on the pinnacle of the temple and everything I surveyed was mine, I would still not be any richer? And yet, did you not become joyous again, did you not become rich again? And where did this joy come from, this richness, if not from God? And was the joy not more blessed and the richness more overwhelming than anything you had dreamed of; was it not so great and glorious that perhaps a secret fear sneaked in, a secret concern that it might be taken away from you because you had not given it to yourself? But also at the same moment you were consoled by the thought that you were in the hands of him from whom this blessing came; you felt that there is a love which transcends all sense and understanding, and that this love is not the love with which you love God but the love with which God loves you.

II A 391   April 7, 1839

« 1313

In margin of 1312 (II A 391):

O, the depth of the riches![152]—thus speaks the Apostle Paul after having finished one of the most profound expositions the world has ever heard; in these words he reposes, as it were, not exhausted from the work but blissful in the contemplation. He reposes, I say, for I know of no better expression, I know of nothing comparable to his reflective activity other than the creating activity of God. As God's spirit brooded over the deeps, so broods his thought over all of world history. I know of nothing comparable to his profound feeling of the marvelous ordering of the world except these words: And, behold, it was very good[153]—nothing comparable to the peace of his contemplation except God's blessed resting from his work.[154] And now, when Paul, in this connection bursts forth: "O, the depth of the riches!" etc., who can but feel that here is where the exclamation belongs, that there is a point, as it were, where the world lies behind us like a quiet evening, clear and transfigured, reflection's ascension where this exclamation in its deepest and widest sense is at home, that there is only one moment in which such a hymn of reverie belongs, a moment which gives us face to face a foretaste of heaven.[155] Yet it is precisely this interruption in our text which I find so superb. It is an exclamation* which can be ascribed to every Christian's life, to every hour lived in God, for God is in truth no less in the unique life of the individual than he is in the noise of the complications of the world, and he is no less in his governance of the individual human being than he is in the bending of mighty nations under his powerful hand, if only we will turn to him in true devotion, if only we might be able to say with true enthusiasm: O, the depth of the riches!

* This is a gift which no true Christian can deny.

II A 392   May 3, 1839

« 1314

God can no more prove his existence [*Tilværelse*] by way of something else than he can swear; he has nothing higher than himself to swear by.

II A 394   April 23, 1839

« 1315

. . . . . And even though we feel that we have frivolously wasted our birthright, God will hear us even then if with tears we like Esau say: Father, if you have one more blessing, bless me also. And if Isaac found a blessing for his thoughtless son, why should not our heavenly Father, who is rich in blessings, find one for us, too.

II A 402   April 28, 1839

« 1316

"Even now in this hour the Lord speaks," for the Lord's compassion is like the books which are "printed in this year"—eternally young.

II A 407   May 4, 1839

« 1317

In margin of 1316 (II A 407):

It is the same with his grief: Would that even in this hour you knew the things that make for peace. Luke 19:41.[156]

II A 408   *n.d.*

« 1318

. . . . . and especially in our time, when ideas are so confused, when the developments in the world are so fast and so loud, when the inherent selfish drives of men have burst their bonds in so many ways, especially in our time we can so very easily place ourselves in a wrong relationship to Christianity; it can so easily—more or less clearly according to the soul's clarity of self-consciousness, more or less vehemently according to the heart's possessing more or less truth—become an offense, so that God has to stop us on our way as he stopped Paul: Saul, Saul, why do you persecute me, or if the movements of offense have not been very strong: Man, why do you not understand me, why will you not be kindled by the love with which I have loved you before the foundations of the world, why do you plug your ears against my father-voice? Like a father who in anguish watches his son wander off on his own path, I have left nothing untried to call you to myself; how often I have wanted to gather you as a hen gathers its chicks under its wings.

II A 410   May 5, 1839

« 1319

It is really remarkable that whereas all the other qualifications pronounced about God are adjectives, "love"[157] is the only substantive, and one would scarcely think of saying "God is lovely." Thus language itself has expressed the substantive character of love implied by this qualification. —

II A 418   May 12, 1839

« 1320

The fear with which the insane feel the mysterious intellectual superiority of the skilled physician must approximate somewhat the first, almost hostile, stage of the *fear of God*.[158]

II A 472   July 7, 1839

« 1321

God's fatherly love—

III A 29   *n.d.*, 1840

« 1322

Addition to 1321 (III A 29):
Or did you never see him as the loving Father.
   1) bringing up
   2) effecting a deeper fellowship of love.

III A 30   *n.d.*, 1840

« 1323

Nihil extra deum
Nihil præter deum[159]

III A 45   *n.d.*, 1840

« 1324

It takes more courage to suffer than to act, more courage to forget than to remember;[160] and perhaps the most wonderful thing about God is that he is able to forget men's sins.

III A 101   *n.d.*, 1841

« 1325

The pagans believed that the gods reserved revenge for themselves because it was sweet; the Jews think that revenge belongs to God because he is just; the Christians, because he is compassionate. No wonder the pagans were greedy for revenge since they wished to taste the sweets which the gods had reserved for themselves.[161]

III A 102   *n.d.*, 1841

« 1326

And it is not only in the external world that God lets his light fall upon the good and the evil, his sun shine upon the just and the unjust— no, every Sabbath in his Church he lets his benediction shine upon the good and the evil. —

III A 104   *n.d.,* 1841

« 1327

I know that neither angel nor devil, neither the present not the future, etc.—yes, when you are able to say this, you have conquered the world, for we indeed mentioned everything which might have the power to separate us from God[162]—the terrors of the present, the anxieties of the future, the terrible haunting images from the past—

III A 131   *n.d.,* 1841

« 1328

The thought that God is love in the sense that he is always the same is so abstract that it is fundamentally a skeptical thought.[163]

IV A 102   *n.d.,* 1843

« 1329

Certainly God is love, but not love to sinners. This he is first in Christ: i.e., the Atonement.

IV A 104   *n.d.,* 1843

« 1330

Another consequence of the trend of understanding and wisdom in our time is that nothing has come to be farther from a man than God, although nothing is nearer to him; for this reason religion assumes a certain silly solemnity in which there is no meaning and the name of God is named with the same empty veneration elicited by the ink-stand which in the supreme court represents the king. In our age, therefore, a simple and natural effusion of the religious becomes almost blasphemy, and the manner in which one in the Old Testament permitted himself to address God would scandalize, as something unseemly and in conflict with ritual, and yet those men certainly maintained a completely different, deep respect for God.

IV A 106   *n.d.,* 1843

« 1331

There is something strangely tragic and comic in the fact that God in heaven is the only potentate who is permitted to preserve his incognito; usually men are busy enough discovering such things.

IV A 125   *n.d.*, 1843

« 1332

Insofar as all philosophy is able to conceive of the relationship of the divine to the human, Aristotle[164] has already expressed it felicitously when he says that God moves all things but himself is ἀκίνητος.[165] (So far as I can remember, Schelling[166] pointed this out in Berlin.) It is really the abstract concept of unchangeableness, and his influence is therefore a magnetic charm something like the sirens' song. Thus all rationalism ends in superstition.

IV A 157   *n.d.*, 1843

« 1333

Strange that Spinoza[167] continually objects to miracles and revelation on the ground that it was a Jewish trait to lead something directly back to God and leap over the intermediate causes, just as if this were a peculiarity only of the Jews and not of all religiousness, so that Spinoza himself would have done so if he had been basically religious, and as if the difficulty did not lie right here: whether, to what extent, how—in short, inquiries which could give the keenest thinking enough to do.

IV A 190   *n.d.*, 1844

« 1334

The idea of proving the existence [*Tilværelse*] of God is of all things the most ridiculous. Either he exists [*er til*], and then one cannot prove it (no more than I can prove that a certain human being exists [*er til*]); the most I can do is to let something testify to it, but then I presuppose existence)—or he does not exist, and then it cannot be proved at all.[168]

V A 7   *n.d.*, 1844

« 1335

What the contemplation of nature is for the first (human) God-consciousness, the contemplation of revelation is to the second immediate God-consciousness (consciousness of sin). This is where the battle should take place—not to saddle people with the probability of revelation but to silence them and lay their God-consciousness under a consciousness of sin.[169]

v A 8   n.d., 1844

« 1336

God is really the *terminus medius*[170] in everything a man undertakes. The difference between the religious and the merely human person is that the latter is not aware of this—therefore Christianity is the highest connection between God and man, because it specifically has brought this into consciousness.

v A 42   n.d., 1844

« 1337

Is it not a *coup de mains*[171] that God's mighty hand, laid upon a human being in order to humble him, is in the same moment the hand of blessing.

v A 50   n.d., 1844

« 1338

We busy ourselves with the holy, go diligently to church, pray, read devotional literature—alas, as far as it goes we do more than many others. But suppose God did not care at all for this, suppose that with the superiority of infinity he said: Of what concern are you to me. Is there anyone who could bear up against this thought?—although to refrain from thinking it does not involve the same difficulties.

v A 65   n.d., 1844

« 1339

Shelley observes (in the introduction to the poem *Prometheus*) that the idea of Prometheus appears far more beautiful to him than the idea of the devil, for Prometheus is pure, noble, not corrupt and corrupting as is Satan.[172] This is true, but the trouble is something quite different: in the very presence of God to think such a justified idea as Prometheus. Presumably Satan is great, but his very corruption makes it possible to think of him together with God.

v A 89   n.d., 1844

« 1340

Yes, neither do I know the difference[173] [the difference between the

God (*Guden*) and man] as long as I do not stay by the single difference, nor, if I do not know the difference, can I know whether it is present. Thus this individual human being has become the God,[174] for if the understanding holds fast to some distinguishing mark, then it is not because this is the distinguishing mark but because the understanding is arbitrary enough to want it to be the distinguishing mark. In this way the understanding has brought the God as close to itself as possible and yet as far away as possible, and this is the most ironical thing imaginable—the God himself has become pure negativity. Historically one can perhaps show this to be the most fantastic thing conceivable; whether this assumption has ever been historical or not makes no difference in the case, but in this way the understanding itself has made the Incarnation a paradox, which only [the Incarnation] itself can produce.

VB 5:8   *n.d.*, 1844

« 1341

. . . . . But this is what is lacking—No one *wonders* any more. They journey to far countries and tell us about it, and we make comparisons, and marvel over the differences. Is this to wonder over *God*? When a man lived in some isolated place and saw only one single tree, one little shrub, perhaps, a running brook, how he marvelled—at God. The less one has in which to marvel over God, the more one marvels over God.

When that favorite of fortune, who rose from poverty and insignificance in a little island to become emperor of the mightiest countries, led the troops and wanted to inspire them, he said: Four hundred generations are looking down upon you—ah, just to repeat it makes one shiver—how it must have inflamed the fighting! But when we say to a man: God in heaven looks down and sees what you are doing—no one marvels, no one is moved, it is as if it meant nothing—and yet does not the eternal mean more than 4,000 years?

The forgiveness of sins is proclaimed, but who marvels at it? No one. No one says: Is it possible—oh, is it possible? No one believes it and says: It is possible, it is possible!

No one wonders; no one is scandalized.

VI B 163   *n.d.*, 1844-45

« 1342

If the subjects of a country where a king is on the throne were to set about investigating whether or not it is right to have a king, he would become enraged.[175] This is the way man acts toward God—he forgets that God exists [*er til*] and ponders whether it is proper, acceptable, to have a God.

VI A 121   *n.d.*, 1845

« 1343

. . . . . But there is no one who *fears* God: we do not hear him in the thunder—we are too intellectual for that; we do not see him in the fates—and inwardness we do not have at all.[176] But just as everything is adjusted for the convenience of finitude, so God himself has been domesticated. The pastors have him on a leash, conditioned to the way they pull on the rope.

VI A 127   *n.d.*, 1845

« 1344

In this case the Incarnation would have direct analogies in the incarnations of paganism; whereas the distinction is: incarnation as man's invention and incarnation as coming from God.[177]

VI B 98:81   *n.d.*, 1845

« 1345

Alas, when a government has to justify itself in print first of all, it looks ridiculous. But God's relationship to the world is not like that of an earthly government; after all, he has the creator's right to require faith and obedience from the created, and also that every created being in his heart shall dare think only what is agreeable to him. God is certainly not like an elected king who can be deposed by the next assembly if he cannot justify himself adequately. The matter is very simple. Punishment has been devised by the loving Father for the guilt of transgression. But just as in a large family with many children the innocent get nipped a little, so it is in the great family teeming with millions—no, not so—the reason it goes this way in a large family with many children is that the father and the teacher are still only human beings, but God is well able to take everything in at a glance, and he who counts the hairs[178] does not get flustered. The innocent therefore do not share the punishment, but they must bear some of the suffering. As soon as the innocent sufferer turns to God and asks if it is a punishment, he straightway receives the answer: "No, my dear child, it is not punishment; this you know well enough."

VII¹ A 62   *n.d.*, 1846

« 1346

In Chapter 46 of Isaiah there is a very profound expression of the difference between an idol and the true God. Jehovah tells Israel that *he carries his people*; whereas the worshippers of idols *have to carry their idols*.

VII¹ A 81   n.d., 1846

« 1347   †

Immanently (in the imaginative medium of abstraction) God does not exist[179] or is not *present* [*er ikke "til"*]; he *is* [*er*]—only for the existing person[180] [*Existerende*] is God present, i.e., he can be *present* [*være "til"*] in faith. A providence, an atonement, etc. *exist* or *are present* only for an existing person. When everything is completed, providence is in reposeful plenitude; when everything is completed, atonement is in reconciled equilibrium—but they are not *present*. Faith, therefore, is the anticipation of the eternal[181] which holds the elements together, the discontinuities of existence [*Existentsens*]. If an existing person does not have faith, then [for him] God neither *is* nor *is* God *present*, although understood eternally God nevertheless eternally is.[182]

VII¹ A 139   n.d., 1846

« 1348

10) . . . . . They say that God is unchangeable;[183] the Atonement teaches that God has become changed—but the whole thing is an anthropopathetic conception which cannot stand up under reflection.

In other words, by thinking abstractly about God's abstract unchangeableness a person wants to transform himself. But suppose that this is precisely what a human being cannot do. The trick is that by thinking abstractly a person wants to make himself just as *unchanged* as God is unchangeable. What the Atonement expresses is therefore directly opposed to the objection; it teaches that God has remained unchanged while men changed, or it *proclaims* to men-altered-in-sin that God has remained unchanged. Every objection attacks essentially the last clause (that men are changed by sin), but slyly assumes the appearance of profundity by speaking about the first clause, that God must have been changed. We transform the whole thing into a phantom-battle about the predicates of God, instead of simply asking the objector whether or not he has become changed from what he eternally must be assumed to be. If he actually has been changed, then *eo ipso* the proclamation of God's unchangeableness is his most urgent need. For a reconciliation it is by no means necessary that both parties be changed, for if the one party is in the right, it would be madness for him to be changed. But if his unchangeableness (as proclaimed in the Atonement) is an abstract something, then there is another reason for its not being a reconciliation, for then the one party is not a party to it at all but is an abstract something and there is only an impersonal relationship between them. In such a case, the Atonement is an absurdity like praying to the sun. If the sun—let us say, in a pagan land where the sun is worshipped—suddenly became dark and they thereupon tried to appease it and it shone again, and they believed it was reconciled, this would be an absurdity because the unchangeableness of a natural phenomenon is incommensurable with a personal approach. In relation to a natural phenomenon a human being therefore cannot be changed in such a way that this change has some relationship to it. A person's being a sinner is not a change which is commensurable with a relationship to the sun or the moon. This relationship must be between the two reconciled parties, so that the change of one party (the man in sin) has a relationship to the unchangeableness of the other party (God). Here it is again evident that it is especially the significance of the change of sin and the reality of this change which must be maintained if everything is not to be confused.

Conscience is in [the sphere of] immediacy, and it accentuates infinitely the distinction between good and evil. One must then assume (if the objection* is to mean anything) that by thinking abstractly a person is capable of becoming so abstract that he no longer has any conscience or that the ethical has completely evaporated and he has become metaphysically volatized. But this is impossible. As God has limited a human being physically, so he has also set bounds to him in a spiritual sense, if in no other way, simply by his being a creature, one who has not created himself. With his imagination a human being is able to see for millions of miles, but with his physical eyes he cannot see so far; and no matter how long he continues to indulge in this fantasy, his eyes still never see any farther. Thus it is also with immediacy. By means of abstract imaginative thinking a person wishes to transform himself (although if this self-creation were to succeed, it would simply mean his annihilation); yet at the same time he does continue to exist [existere], to be present [at være til], and therefore

* The objection, therefore, usually comes from those who have to be called unhinged individuals, who have grown dizzy out in the infinite (Adler,[184] for example, who thought that one could not distinguish between the voice of God and the voice of the devil).

it can never succeed. Even the most persistent abstractedness in a human being still cannot wholly renounce immediacy; on the contrary, he becomes continually more conscious of it in trying to escape it, if for no other reason. The immediate is his foothold, and no matter how he may soar, no matter how extravagant he becomes in imagination, he can nevertheless never completely abandon his foothold. This description, to be sure, applies only to the outer reaches of the erroneous path, and to prevent its going so far the ethical appears as soon as possible and invites one to follow the moral immediacy of conscience—and then begins the religious. It would be ridiculous if someone, in view of the fact that he is able to see infinitely far in imagination, were to put out his eyes, "because it is not worth the effort to look at crumbs." But if someone, in view of the fact that God must be unchangeable, were to abandon his moral immediacy (i.e., to try to abandon it), this the ethical condemns as sin. And he shall not succeed in this, although one might very well succeed in putting out his eyes, for the eyes are only a particular, but the moral immediacy is the human being himself in the sense of limits, but also in the sense of root and ground.

VII[1] A 143   n.d., 1846

« 1349

Precisely because God cannot be an object for man, since God is subject,[185] for this very reason the reverse shows itself to be absolute: when one denies God, he does God no harm but destroys himself; when one mocks God, he mocks himself.

The more pure a person is, the more he approaches inability to be an object to other persons. Nevertheless there of course always remains an infinite qualitative difference here.[186]

VII[1] A 201   n.d., 1846

« 1350

What I find hard to understand according to the orthodox Christian view is that in the single individual's God-relationship there comes to be any comparison with others,[187] so that in being related to God a person becomes aware of how others are related to God, whether or not they are made happy in the relationship, whether or not they do what God requires of them, etc.

This is the way I think of it. When a man (the single individual) is related to God, he must readily grasp that God has the absolute right, the unlimited absolute right, to require everything of him, and yet on the other hand, that the God-relationship itself is absolute blessedness, is the absolutely unlimited depth of happiness. But if this is the relationship, then consideration of and comparison with any other man are forgotten. This is obviously the meaning of the parable about the workers in the vineyard.[188] But if this is the meaning, then it is sinful to compare oneself with others. If someone says, "I gladly endure all evil, all of your persecution, for the sake of God" and then adds, "but you, my persecutors, you will suffer in the next world"—then the second part is secular mindedness. The relationship to God is clearly such a good, such an extraordinary freight of blessedness, that if I have only this, my happiness is absolute in the most absolute sense, but it diminishes through the secularized comparison that my enemies will be excluded.

VIII[1] A 24   *n.d.*, 1847

« 1351

In paganism God was regarded as the unknown.[189] More recently it has been assumed presumptuously that to know God is a trifle. Nevertheless, although God has revealed himself, he has taken some precautions, for one can know God only in proportion to one's being known, i.e., in proportion to one's acknowledging that he is known. This is enough to ward off all impertinence.

VIII[1] A 30   *n.d.*, 1847

« 1352

Imagine a girl unhappy in love talking to a rock about her grief—just as immovably does God listen to your complaining if you imagine yourself to be the object of his *preferential* love.

VIII[1] A 57   *n.d.*, 1847

« 1353

To love God is the only happy love, but on the other hand it is also something terrible. Face to face with God man is without standards and without comparisons; he cannot compare himself with God, for here he becomes nothing, and directly before God, in the presence of God, he dare not compare himself with others, for this is a distraction. Therefore in every man there is no doubt a prudent fear of really having anything to do with God, because by becoming involved with God he becomes nothing. And even though a person, humanly speaking, honestly tries to do the will of God, directly before God it still seems as if he had never moved from the spot and his slight advance vanishes as a nothing before the holiness of God. Therefore in every human being there is no doubt a prudent fear of really becoming involved with God. They desire this relationship at a distance and spend their lives in temporal distractions, for all this busyness in life is still really a distraction.[190]

VIII[1] A 63   n.d., 1847

« 1354

Instead of all this preaching about lofty virtues, faith, hope, and love, about loving God, etc. (for how many really bother about this since, after all, it is regarded as something important if a man goes to church one day a week), someone ought rather say something like this once: Never get involved with God, and above all never in any really intimate way. Get involved with men and imagine that together with them you are involving yourselves with God, because you name the name of God just as meaninglessly as the physicians scribble embellishments on prescriptions. Never let yourself be alone with God lest you venture too far out, but see to it that your God-relationship is like everybody else's so that you can get someone to assist you right away if God should leave you in the lurch. This way you will be able to live pleasantly and comfortably, believe in God and the lofty virtues, and now and then in passing toy with the whimsical thought whether God really exists—your God-relationship is no more inconveniencing than this. Never involve yourself with God so long that any spiritual trial [*Anfægtelse*] has a chance to begin; if you think about God once a week and bow before him the way the others do, I guarantee that you will never be subjected to spiritual trials. But—for God in heaven's sake never get involved with God in such a way that he becomes your only confidant, the only one you seek night and day to involve yourself with, the only one you are really prepared to make yourself understood to, whereas you perhaps forget to chatter about understanding with men—just suppose then that he left you in the lurch when you had come to understand that he truly is the one and only help and therefore you had not bothered about other helpers—just suppose that he left you in the lurch—just suppose that he did not exist! No, stick to the world of actuality; don't go to church too often; never go alone to God, for that is dangerous, he could make too strong an impression upon you, and it is not legally correct either, for in the relation to God you must always make sure of having something to hold on to so that he does not absolutely reduce you to nothing. Never pray to God in solitude, never so that your heart would prompt you to boundless confidence—no, learn certain formulas which you know for sure others have used to good advantage.

If one were to talk this way, he would talk far more accurately both with respect to the situation of most of the listeners and their wants than if he used all those high-flying phrases.

..... And then shut your eyes to everything else and do not let yourself be disturbed by men.

VIII¹ A 77   *n.d.*, 1847

« 1355

Everything goes its busy way, everyone takes care of his own affairs, the wind blows, the river runs—it is as if God were infinitely far away—alas, and it is 1,800 years since Christ lived!

VIII¹ A 94   *n.d.*, 1847

« 1356 *"Mary has chosen the better part."*[191]

Which is the better part? It is God—consequently everything. The better part is everything, but it is called the better part because it must be chosen. One does not get everything as everything, for one does not begin in this way; one begins by choosing the better part, which, however, is everything.

VIII¹ A 111   *n.d.*, 1847

« 1357

Giordano Bruno[192] expressed it superbly: God is not like a man who can play a zither but does not have a zither. This describes altogether splendidly the relation between God's capability and God's performance.

VIII¹ A 148   *n.d.*, 1847

« 1358

People say that one ought not waste the gifts of God, but the best of all God's gifts, his love, that gift of being permitted to call him Father, permitted to love him—how we waste this! How many even think about this! It is terrible. God in heaven offers his love to every man, but no one cares about it at all. At most, the pastor proves with three reasons that God is love.[193] —After all, the pastors' "reasons" are one of the most effective reasons for Christianity's having become as tame as it is. There is an unholy inversion in all this business of having to prove everything first. I wonder if it would ever occur to anyone really in love to prove the blessedness of love with three basic reasons? But the fact is that men no longer

believe—alas, and so they want to help themselves with the artificial legs
of a little scientific scholarliness.

VIII¹ A 327   n.d., 1847

« 1359

. . . . . Man proposes and God disposes. The fact that the high priests
sealed Christ's grave was indeed a notarized signature—documentary
proof that he had arisen from the dead and had not been stolen.

VIII¹ A 356   n.d., 1847

« 1360

As a rule most men have two counsellors—one in the moment of
danger when they are afraid—and then when things are going well they
would rather have nothing to do with him, for the sight of him reminds
them of how weak they were, and now they are pleased to make believe
that they have conquered with their own strength—not with God's.

VIII¹ A 379   n.d., 1847

« 1361

In Gerhardt's *Meditationes sacræ*[194] there is a rather remarkable
treatment of "God is love." What a person loves most is his God; *ergo*
God is love. What a person loves most is indeed his love; but what he
loves most is his God; *ergo* God is love.

VIII¹ A 516   n.d., 1848

« 1362

Why is there a kind of pretentiousness about being recognized by
a king? Precisely because the king is only a human being and consequently
cannot possibly know everyone but only a select few. Of God, you are
simply to believe that he does know you—here there is no pretentiousness at all.

VIII¹ A 524   n.d., 1848

« 1363

God is the one who lifts up, who presses down. If the world would
idolize you, God is the one who presses down; if the world collapses over
you, God is the one who lifts up.

VIII¹ A 569   n.d., 1848

« 1364

I am certainly able to comprehend that a bird can live; it does not know at all that it exists [*er til*] before God—and I am certainly able to comprehend that a person can endure existing before God when he himself is unconscious of doing that. But to be conscious of the fact that one exists before God—and then be able to live![195]

VIII¹ A 573   *n.d.*, 1848

« 1365

Only the God-relationship gives significance. This is eminently evident in the life of Christ. There was a day, a day which presumably had its events which everyone spoke of as being very important—on that day a woman anointed Christ's head.[196] How insignificant—and yet all the rest has been forgotten and only she is remembered. But it seems to me that divine worth, the consciousness of being God, never came forth more markedly in Christ's life—not even when he performed a miracle—than when he showed what infinite reality [*Realitet*] his life had, so that such an insignificant event deserves to be remembered eternally, that an unknown woman, a vanishing nobody, becomes immortal merely because one day she anointed his head!

VIII¹ A 670   *n.d.*, 1848

« 1366

In the last analysis, the only thought in which a man can rest is that when he does something according to the best planning, and it nevertheless goes badly—God is the one who can still bring some good out of it, that the best a man really does is not much else than to do badly, and God on the other hand does nothing else than to make it good. O, behind all of self-concern's anxiety over responsibility, whether one has properly considered everything, behind all despondency over the thought about consequences, whether or not he has made a mistake—there still dawns or shines this assumption or this assurance that one is not therefore without God in the world, that God is present [*er med*], not as a distinguished indifference but as love which takes part with us in everything. Just as the child, behind all his concern, has the consolation that his father is present —and whatever happens, even if in doing what he thought was the best the child makes a mistake, the father is truly there and can surely bring some good out of it all anyway.

IX A 34   *n.d.*, 1848

« 1367

That a human being has been able to live on for 10, 20, 30 years without having noticed that God exists [er til]—O, it is frightful to deserve God's being so angry with him. For God is the one who loves, and the first form of love is this that in love he makes one aware that he exists so that one does not fool around without becoming aware of God. But it is the wrath of God to permit a human being to walk as an animal whom he does not call.

IX A 75   n.d., 1848

« 1368

There can really be something very humble in a person's saying that he is the object of God's love; by this he can mean that he has no merit at all, that it is a kind of arbitrariness for God simply to throw his love upon him. This is the way to understand "chosen by grace," "humility."

When, for example, someone declares that God loves all men equally and the other people do not feel the same way as the speaker does, and he then says: Yes, but you do not abide in God—then it almost looks as if God loved this man *because* he abides in him. But this is not so. It is true that God loves all equally, and it becomes clear only to the individual that God loves him; but God loves the others just as much.

Yet it is also very true that, humanly speaking, there is a difference between men in regard to how they relate to God. Nevertheless in the relationship to God the impiety and presumption of imagining that God loves him because he abides in God could hardly ever occur to a man.

IX A 77   n.d., 1848

« 1369

In margin of 1368 (IX A 77):

This is similar to praising luck for the great things one accomplishes, so that one does not wound men by presenting oneself as having accomplished them.

See Plutarch, Chapter XI: How One Can Praise Himself without Offending.

IX A 78   n.d., 1848

« 1370

The greatest possible misunderstanding between man and man about the religious life occurs between a man and a woman when the man wants to impart religion to her, all the blessedness implicit in being before God, and then he becomes the object of her romantic love.

IX A 113   n.d., 1848

« 1371

Why do men usually have such a fantastic conception of God? Because they do not live alone. The one makes the other anxious and afraid that God is something far too great etc.

O, one who suffers in the world in such a way that he has become solitary—to him it will become quite natural to think of God's infinite sublimity—and yet relate himself to him as a child to his father. Such a person will surely become resourceful in the holy occupation of reflecting that the greatness of God increases in proportion to his concern (not like human greatness, alas, in proportion to unconcern) for the most insignificant things. Consequently, if I were the most insignificant of all men, then to be completely persuaded and convinced that he is thoroughly concerned about me would be the very way to honor God's goodness. He is not like a physician running around in a hospital, able to spend only five minutes at each bed.

IX A 116   n.d., 1848

« 1372

The relationship between God and a man is quite simply this. The man does not dare demand that God give him revelations, signs, and the like. No, the man must have the bold confidence to be himself, and if he cannot, then he must begin praying for this confidence, which is not a commentary on his own importance but on God's love being so infinite; if he can count the hairs on my head (and to say this of him is indeed honoring his love), it is also sure that he cares about me.

Then the man behaves as follows. When it becomes clear to him how he would do this or that if he were in charge—naturally, it must not be anything sinful or ungodly—he does it—he does not wait for God to intervene with revelations and prevent him from doing it if it is foolish. No, the man goes ahead and does it; but while he is doing it he calls upon God and says: This is how I am taking care of the matter; it is very possible that I am doing it completely wrong and will have many unpleasant consequences for myself, but at present I do not know anything better, and I also know that I dare not shirk any longer what must be done. Consequently I am doing it; but I tell you and call upon you, because you are indeed my father and a love which I cannot comprehend. As I let my

action slip from my hand, I surrender it and myself to you in unconditional obedience; do with it what you will; in this way I am positive that
even the most foolish action will eventually become good.

O, that a man has this assistance, and that this assistance is sheer love!

IX A 182   *n.d.*, 1848

« 1373

Ah, now I understand it! Socrates' dæmon was always merely dissuad-
ing because Socrates' God-relationship was dialectical. The immediate
God-relationship is positive, but the dialectical God-relationship begins in
a certain sense with nothing, and God first comes in the next round. If I
have no immediacy, then I must always make the first step myself. God
does not immediately or directly tell me what I am supposed to do. I do it;
according to my best deliberation I regard it as the best, and I present it
now to God, humbling myself and my resolution, my plan, my action
under God.

IX A 242   *n.d.*, 1848

« 1374

There is, however, a whole area of life which one calls the daily trifles
—whether I should go here or there, whether I should wear a heavy coat or
a light coat, etc.—which are very difficult to make commensurable with
the God-relationship. God would really rather not have it. For this reason
he created man and woman—and says: Get married; such matters most appropriately fall into the sphere of assistance one to another. It is like a
father's relationship to his child. He says: I really cannot play with you all
day long; find yourself a playmate. It is a very dangerous relationship if
the father must also be the child's playmate, if the child has no other association than with his father. It is the same with the God-relationship.
However, a father does do this for a sick child. And if there is a man who
was so unfortunate that he had to renounce the joy of marriage—without
even remotely considering this as a token of his being somebody great,
quite the contrary, probably overestimating marriage and suffering his
unhappiness more deeply—then God undertakes to help him in life's trifles
as well, and for such a man many unimportant things can become commensurable with the God-relationship in a moving way.

IX A 247   *n.d.*, 1848

« 1375

As in all other respects, so also in this man has abolished the God-relationship. Where today does one meet an existence which expresses that a God exists [*er til*], a providence which has a bearing on the most insignificant matters? No, we say this kind of thing but existentially express that it is still most prudent and proper to help oneself, to seek the assistance of men for one's cause, etc.—in short, the merely human criterion is and remains the criterion.

This is why men cannot at all grasp what to me is fear and trembling —whether I have the right, after all, to be active in this respect. Equipped with an inborn talent for tactics, able to win everyone to myself with my knowledge of men, etc., I dare not utilize the least of these for my cause, for then it would be as if God said to me: I see! You want to steer yourself —well, then, I do not need you.

In my mind it is absolutely just as important to express this truth that God is along [*er med*] as it is for the truth to be presented. This truth ought not become a figure of speech or something which the physician writes above his prescription.

I follow in the wake of all this Hegelian-Goethean human self-complacency in satisfying one's contemporaries—i.e., abolishing God and making the age into God—and therefore I have to beware lest I jargonize the truth into this disfigured form rather than God-fearingly to express that *God is the man of the house*. Coddled and confused as the generation is by these antecedents, it must naturally regard my behavior as pride and arrogance—it is also the fear of God, and these two qualifications the secular mentality can never distinguish from one other.

O, in this confusing human-swarm, it is even a great thing that there is among them a human being who has one hour a week to think (for to read newspapers and to run to meetings is really not thinking)—and it is this confused mob which is supposed to judge the truth.

IX A 254   *n.d.*, 1848

« 1376

That no reflection exhausts the God-relationship or the relationship to God can be seen also in this way: no man can relate himself to God absolutely at every moment and at ever moment absolutely; to do this he would have to be more than man. Consequently there also have to be remoteness, rest, recreation. Let it now take place in reflection. The pious man consequently perceives that he must have rest, must give up thinking uninterruptedly about God or about his God-relationship. What does he do, then? He asks God's permission, as it were, to do so. But note that here reflection takes over again, for he is still in reflection. If at every moment of the "rest" there is the thought whether right now he also has permission for it, whether he is not taking too long a vacation, etc., then the rest-period is just as strenuous as what he wanted to rest from, for the rest is again the God-relationship.

IX A 305   *n.d.*, 1848

« 1377

This, too, is a form of worship: to say directly to God, "I am a poor insignificant man, I cannot keep on every moment, literally every moment, thinking of you. Permit me, then, to rest a little, to divert myself a little, so that I do not make you petty, you who are eternal love—alas, the way I myself am not far from becoming gloomily petty toward myself." And then, period, for otherwise reflection intrudes that very moment with the thought that God certainly must know best whether a man needs diversion (as if he should spontaneously, perhaps with a revelation, say to a person: Now you need diversion) and otherwise can give a person the strength to hold out. That is—there must be unconditional surrender, and then immediate action.

Right at this point the real meaning of religious sociality is to be found—that is, when the ideality of the God-relationship has become too strong for an individual (since he cannot, after all, demand direct revelation from God, and his reflection traps him), he must now have another person to discuss it with. From this we see that sociality is not the highest but is really a concession to human weakness. Here, also, is the significance of the idea that God relates himself to the whole race. The idea of the race, of sociality, is then a middle term between God and the single individual.

This is the inverse movement. But wherever there is to be preaching for spiritual awakening, wherever the price has to be jacked up, there individuality must be made relevant. Ordinarily this is most necessary, for men as a rule live enough of a relaxed and indolent life as it is.

There is alleviation, on the other hand, in making use of sociality. It is not good for man to be alone, it is said, and therefore woman was given to him for community. But it is true that being alone, literally alone with God, is almost unendurable for a man, is too frightfully strenuous—therefore man needs community. God and man are separated by an infinite qualitative difference; when the relationship becomes too strenuous, the category of community must come between as a middle term—also with regard to the many little worries which certainly can torment a man but which I dare say would almost be the height of foolishness to take to God in prayer. It is as if God points away from himself, as if he says, love that he is: Yes, my child, it is all right to stop; remember, after all, that I am God; however humble, however faith-full, however ardent your prayer and your devotion, you cannot and must not think of me at every moment.

Here is a danger point, for the highest culmination of true religiousness may only narrowly escape taking on the appearance of presumption. For even the most humble consciousness of being less than a sparrow before God, a nothing—yes, it is fine, but there still may be presumption in this consciousness of wanting to think about him at every moment and being conscious of existing before him. It is right to be conscious of one's nothingness before God, but it is demanding too much to want to have this consciousness every moment or, if I dare say so (in order to indicate the fallacy of thinking that it is like a love affair), to want to see the beloved every moment even if one understands ever so deeply that before him one is nothing.

IX A 315   n.d., 1848

« 1378

Christ himself says:[197] The person who wants to erect a tower first sits down and makes a rough estimate of how high he is able to build it. Fine. But now comes the real problem (and this next matter, the problem, the preachers always leave out)—what does it mean to make a rough estimate? Does it mean a merely human estimate of one's particular capacities, of the situation and circumstances? If so, then what is religion? But if in his estimate he is to determine the size according to what he wants to attain, relying upon God, then the estimate is indeed incalculable. Here again we have the confusion arising when a person expresses one idea at one moment and another the next but does not relate the two. What does it mean—relying upon God, we attain everything? Does it mean that relying upon God I attain everything I attain?—which, it must be admitted, is as good as nothing. In that case the whole thing is humbug. Or does it actually mean: Relying upon God, we attain everything?

Or let us assume that a man attains the ability to apprehend the truth —ought he not promptly begin to do it? Or, if he makes an estimate and finds that he does not, humanly speaking, have the capacities for it, should he give it up—and is he then guiltless?

Suppose a person understands that the truth means to be put to death for Christianity or for the sake of truth (indeed, from a Christian point of view the only truth). But while making his rough estimate he decides that he does not have the capacity for it—what then? Is he guilt-less, then, if he says: I am not going to do it. What becomes of the idea: relying upon God, we attain everything—when we never once, relying upon God, resolve to do the truth we understand.

O, woe, woe to these 100,000 career preachers who do nothing but preachify men into nonsense.

*   *

But the matter is not so difficult. God has a certain craftiness (in the good, maieutic sense of the word); he will have no nonsense afterwards, and he will have it clear whether it is in reliance upon him that a man ventures or not. This is why the intermediary consideration is slipped in: make an estimate. That is, if in making an estimate you are convinced that you do not have the capacities, humanly speaking—and yet begin, conse-quently in reliance upon God—and you fail, then it must be because you did not have true reliance. This means that God does not desire a contrac-tual relationship with a man but desires unconditional obedience, so that a man takes the guilt upon himself if he fails, and he does not blame God. If it succeeds, then it must be by the help of God; if it fails, it is my fault. God is crafty in this way because he *unconditionally* wants to be loved or wants to be loved unconditionally. And if you love God unconditionally, then this love will be everything to you, everything else, the outcome, is a matter of indifference.

IX A 347   *n.d.,* 1848

« 1379

What comfort and blessedness there is in the truth that God who is love is the unchanged (which again, in another sense, one could regard as love or as a characteristic of his love, for a love which changes certainly is not love!).[198] Suppose that you enter into relationship with a loving per-son—at first he was, if you please, love itself, but now so many years have gone by and so much has happened during that time that your relationship has gradually changed him. But God is unchanged love—a spring, cool every morning, is not more unchanged; the sun, warm every dawning day, is not more unchanged; the sea, every morning refreshing, is not more un-changed than God unchanged is love.

IX A 374   *n.d.,* 1848

« 1380

In his sermon on the Gospel for the Third Sunday after Trinity (the good Samaritan), Luther[199] observes that the scribe only asks: Who then is my neighbor, not, Who, then, is my God, for he fancied that in the relationship to God he had fulfilled the law.

IX A 441   n.d., 1848

« 1381

What is wrong about the Pharisee (the Pharisee and the tax-collector) is not that he feels superior; humanly speaking, it is true that he is superior to the tax-collector. What is wrong is that he does this in God's house, face to face with God. In association with men it may very well be inordinate and pusillanimous fear and trembling for me to employ God's standard; there I speak as a man; and when others obviously seek merely earthly advantage and do it brazenly with the show of goodness, then I say: No, this I will not do, and in this respect, at least, I am superior. But I do not have the cheek to come to God with such rubbish.

IX A 476   n.d., 1848

« 1382

In the God-relationship there are the orders given to a man (and consequently to every man): "Do not be concerned about the others, not at all; you have only to do my will scrupulously or as fully as you are able." Fine—but this person is living in the realm of actuality [*Virkelighed*], and God is not an actual something in the external sense and does not walk about. When a person obeys God in this way, cares solely and exclusively about his will and has no interest, as the saying goes, in howling with the wolves he is together with, that is, when he thinks only about understanding and doing God's will and not about being understood by men—then he is *eo ipso* sacrificed. It seems almost as if the God-relationship were a seduction. God is cunning, so to speak; he is the invisible one who quite secretly is really responsible for the development of a persons' life in this way, but God gives no sign, and thus the faithful person becomes a sacrifice. To an extent it would have been appropriate for God to intervene in an extraordinary way to aid the faithful, as was the case in former times.

Doubt of this sort must be answered with: Hold your tongue; believe. No miracles are needed; God who holds everything in his hand at every moment has possibilities to burn. And in any case the absolute relationship to God means that humanly and externally it is as if one were abandoned by God, for the true relationship is that the relationship in itself is the highest.

One can also understand being abandoned by God thus: it is God, if I may say it in this fashion, who sits and whispers in a person's conscience:

Be concerned only about me—and it is I who, by being a palpable entity, am externally in the power of contemporaries. And note, the more a person follows God's will, alone and solitary (without the falsifying middle-term of due regard for contemporaries in order to be understood by contemporaries as one follows God's will), the more complicated and suffering his life will become.

But only believe—and the relationship will become all the more inward.

X[1] A 20 *n.d.*, 1849

« 1383

This is the law of the relations between God and man in the God-relationship.

DIVISIO

There is an infinite, radical, qualitative difference between God and man.[200]

This means, or the expression for this is: the human person achieves absolutely nothing; it is God who gives everything; it is he who brings forth a person's faith, etc.

This is grace, and this is Christianity's major premise.

SUBDIVISIO

Although, of course, there can be nothing meritorious, unconditionally nothing, in any action whatsoever, any more than faith could be meritorious (for then the *Divisio* or major premise is dissolved and we are in the minor premise), this nevertheless does mean daring in all childlikeness to be involved with God.

If the *Divisio* is everything, then God is so infinitely sublime that there is no intrinsic or actual relationship between God and the individual human being.

Therefore attention must be paid scrupulously to the *Subdivisio*, without which the life of the single individual never gets off the ground.

Generally one must pay careful attention to who is speaking. The *Divisio* or its content can be said in such a way that it is the expression of the most profound godly fear, but also in such a way that fundamentally it is a fraud to elevate God up so high. This can be done in order either to be free to live just as one wishes within a secular view of life or to lead a religious still-life without venturing out into the dangers.[201]

X[1] A 59 *n.d.*, 1849

« 1384

In our time the question is especially one of recovering childlikeness so that it is possible for a person, an individual human being, to be truly related to God in the small things of his life. Surely it is generally assumed that God is so infinitely sublime that no one could imagine wanting to play buddy-buddy with God. But the tragedy is that the elevation which is predicated of God has become a triviality and essentially an indulgent discharge from the God-relationship. And, as stated, here the most rigorous orthodoxy can very easily become a self-deception with its doctrine that it is God who works everything in us and that we accomplish nothing at all, for incommensurability can also be indulgence.

X^1 A 60   *n.d., 1849*

« 1385

The tragedy in Christendom (and it is also tragic for the few genuine Christians there are) is that the conception of God's sublimity, of Christ's sublimity, has become so infinite that it has really become fantastic and that there remains no actual Christian life to speak of, at best a little Jewish piety.

Scriptures repeat again and again that we should suffer in common with Christ or in community with Christ. To understand this as being ordinary human sufferings (to lose one's wife, to lose one's property, to become sick, etc.), which were just as fully present in paganism, is, however, obvious perversion.

Monastic asceticism etc. was youthful immaturity. But every person is required to witness to the truth with his life, and please note, not in an illusory way, such as by becoming a pastor (office, paid occupation) but by supporting the truth. If one does this, then genuine Christian suffering will also come.

But to Christians both God and Christ have become all too infinitely distant majesties for the single individual to associate thought of them with life's minor details so that he becomes in truth the single individual [*den Enkelte*]. Escapism and excuses, cowardice and timorousness continually say: Are you supposed to be a single individual like that among all these countless millions? This is nonsense, for the answer must be: No, every individual should be this.

The difficulty, especially for the intellectual, is first of all to have in truth the infinite conception of God's sublimity and the sublimity of Christ and then the childlike openness to become involved with them in the concerns of one's own personal life in a wholly childlike way.

The difficulty arises from this sort of introspection: Who in all the world can or dares risk involvement with God when he considers that his serial number in the race is, for example, No. 27,000,000,000 etc.? But one ought not think this way; he should simply shut his eyes, think only of God, become a poor single human being to whom God's infinite love gives childlike openness, and above all rejoice in the thought that every human being has permission to do this—yes, he shall do this.

But the conception of God exercises no power over the lives of men simply because it has become so fantastically elevated. A person says: Of what use is the little bit I am able to do, and what need does God have of it, he, the infinitely sublime; with my human prudence I am doing the best I can to look out for myself and my life, and I humbly bear in mind that God does everything. To this I would reply: Humbug, and I would add: Tragic duplicity, for here the expression of fear of God can be a cosmeticizing of the indolence, cowardice, and practicality of the secular mentality.

The matter is simple. One must be quite a blockhead to imagine that God has need of him. No, one loves God with his whole heart, and then in childlikeness rests assured that he who resides in heaven and thinks of every sparrow in its particularity allows a person to act according to his highest capacity, yes, that his doing this—if he first prays for God's permission—that this, understood in childlike simplicity—is pleasing to God.

O, that men would learn to think humanly of God! There is nothing said here about childishly and foolishly becoming buddy-buddy with God. No, first of all, first the infinite conception of God's infinite sublimity, and then, then the next, the childlike openness to become involved with him earnestly and in truth. But Christendom has made God so sublime that in the long run we really have spirited him away or smuggled him out of life. And at times even among the few more religious persons it is apparent that with all their talk about God's sublimity they have spirited God away.

In the conversation of the apostles one continually gets the impression that they had been personally in the company of Christ, had lived with him as with a human being. Therefore their speech is very human, although they never do forget the infinite qualitative difference between the God-man and other human beings.

But now finally in Christendom the full circle has been made so that everyone says: Among all this countless multitude of human beings should I be such a single individual—and *summa summarum* (if every individual says it or every individual has the right to say it), it turns out that God does not get a single one. And yet God has to have human beings; he has use for them. Therefore the relationship is really the very opposite: every single individual should really be such a single individual—this is God's requirement. And this will happen with every single individual who, in fear of God, begins not with the *mass* but with himself.

x¹ A 64   *n.d.*, 1849

« 1386

Job is correct in saying (9:20) that even if he were blameless, before God he could not be blameless, because he would become anxious [*angst*] before the judge. This is what I have developed in *The Gospel of Suffering*[202]—the misrelationship between or the qualitative difference between God and man.

x¹ A 196   *n.d.*, 1849

« 1387

There is a beautiful word to express that the whole creation serves only one lord, points to only one: *uni-versum* (the universe).

x¹ A 203   *n.d.*, 1849

« 1388

That true humility and pride are one can also be seen in this that there is something very proud in saying: I fear only God—otherwise nothing. And yet only this is fear of God, for to fear God and then also something else is not genuine fear of God.

x¹ A 332   *n.d.*, 1849

« 1389

In a sense Christ did not need to prescribe it as a duty for the greatest to be like a servant—this lies in the very nature of true superiority. If a man is a little superior to another, he is the master and rules. If he is absolutely superior, he is like a servant, for then in his relation to another his (the absolutely superior one's) center of gravity will be his God-relationship, and thus he becomes like a servant. The less significant the other person is, the more the superior one becomes like a servant. This is how a humble woman (by her very humility) can make her far superior husband the serving one; whereas in his relation to another, a stronger man, he is the master, for here the God-relationship does not directly emerge. Had Christ not been God, he would not have become absolutely like a servant, either.

x¹ A 408   *n.d.*, 1849

« 1390

We certainly do speak in Christendom about a revealed God, but for how many is he not still a hidden and concealed God?

In Tersteegen[203] I have read a similar observation, although not developed in this way, but that prior to a certain time God had been hidden for him, and he gathered from this that hitherto he had loved God too little—this or something like it in Tersteegen.

x¹ A 479   *n.d.*, 1849

« 1391

Here one rightly sees the subjectivity in Christianity. Generally the poet, the artist, etc. is criticized for introducing himself into his work. But this is precisely what God does; this he does in Christ. And precisely this is Christianity. Creation is really fulfilled only when God has included himself in it. Before Christ God was included, of course, in the creation but as an invisible mark, something like the water-mark in paper. But in the Incarnation creation is fulfilled by God's including himself in it.

x¹ A 605   *n.d.*, 1849

« 1392 *The Religious Person Who in Truth
Believes That God Is His Father*

Let me imagine such a person. Let it be a man who owns nothing and has no worldly advantages. Let us suppose that he visits a baron on his estate. The baron has the kindness to show him around the estate. Among other things he climbs a hill from which he can look about, and when the baron, pointing to the whole domain, says: All this is my father's, these woods which you see, in which there is much wild game, etc.—the religious man says: Yes, but please look up, Herr Baron. Everything which you see, every bird that flies in infinite space, this is my father's. After all, your father's barony, too, is my father's.

How many are there in every generation who have the courage to believe in this simple way that it is literally true that God is their father. In the clear, starry night, [how many] in humble faith dare to say to themselves: "This is my father's," just as fully and completely convinced as the baron that this is his father's.

x¹ A 629   *n.d.*, 1849

« 1393

What is true of one's relationship to God is not true of one's relationship to another human being—namely, that the longer they live together and the more they get to know each other, the more intimate they become. It is the reverse in the relationship to God—the longer one lives with him the more infinite he becomes—and the less one himself becomes. Alas, as a child one still thought that God and man could play happily together. As a youth one dreamed that if he really and truly made an effort, like someone passionately in love, even though beseeching—that then the relationship might still be achieved. Alas, when one has matured he discovers how infinite God is, discovers the infinite distance. This is the upbringing, and it has something in common with Socratic ignorance—with which the beginning was not made but the ending—it ended with ignorance!

x^2 A 72   *n.d.*, 1849

« 1394

This is how one rises in the world: when a person has reached one rung of the ladder, he hankers and tries to go higher. But when a person has become involved with God so that God truly has hold of him and uses him, this is how he rises: at every higher rung he is supposed to climb, he begs like a child to be exempted, for he well understands that, from a human point of view, suffering and wretchedness and spiritual trial [*Anfægtelse*] mount on the same scale. How often an apostle has pleaded for himself in this way.

x^2 A 125   *n.d.*, 1849

« 1395

If a desert Arab suddenly discovered a spring in his tent, so that he would always have spring water in abundance—how fortunate he would consider himself! It is the same with a man who as physical being is always turned outward, thinking that his happiness lies outside himself. Finally he is turned inward and discovers that the springs lie within him, to say nothing of discovering the spring which is the God-relationship.

x^2 A 169   *n.d.*, 1849

« 1396

All of us think of God essentially as being mild, an old man whom one can make listen to reason. Really, now, come on out farther, there where the blessedness is indeed infinitely greater—but where the rigorousness is also something different. Imagine one of those powerful monarchs of the Orient—and watch one of the servants, the first in rank, approach him—

what an expression of submission! And yet this is only a metaphor. But, to repeat, there farther out, where in consternation, perhaps only in retrospect, a person believes that he has incurred God's disfavor in some way (alas, even if it were only the misunderstanding of anxiety and one had not actually made a mistake)—then it seems to him that God would not look at him for 70,000 years. 70,000 years![204] O, for him it is still only seven days —but for the miserable, unhappy man who languishes in fear and trembling! And yet, yet, that this frightening ruler is nevertheless my father, yes, my father, that I, when in wonder I go into the light night and behold the stars, that I then dare to say: All this is my father's!

x^2 A 186   *n.d.*, 1849

« 1397

"If God is for us, who can be against us."[205] On the face of it this seems very clear. But if one is to speak in a genuinely Lutheran way,[206] he has to say: Precisely when God is for us, the whole world is likely to be against us. But—and here comes the consolation—what this means is that if God is for us, then the opposition of the whole world can accomplish nothing against us. The apostle's interpretation of the words (who then can be against us) is clear—who could possibly be against us in such a way that he becomes the stronger one. Scripture[207] answers these words thus: He who is within us is stronger than the one who is in the world.

x^2 A 226   *n.d.*, 1849

« 1398

Really and truly to become involved with God and to have anything to do with him is almost beyond human strength and endurance. —Then all the blessedness of his love is perceived, all one's past sins and mistakes are forgotten—and strengthened by this indescribable bliss, one is supposed to begin. And then, in the very next hour, one's striving is so deficient that God is completely justified in saying: Once again you are personally guilty of wasting everything. —O, in one sense, a frightful exertion; but how infinitely different and greater the task of patience—to be God!

x^2 A 232   *n.d.*, 1849

« 1399

Since God himself has *created* and *sustains* this world, one ought to guard himself against the ascetic fanaticism which as a matter of course hates it and annihilates it.

No, putting it Christianly but gently, I would present the relationship in the following manner. This world is like play and playthings to the child. The father can even find playing beautiful and can enter into it like a child; yet he requires that the child shall be weaned gradually from it.

It is the same with upbringing in God's kingdom or in Christianity. God is not an impatient or cruel man who tries to take a person by surprise and harm him. God is the God of patience.

Yet God wants men to understand that they must once and for all make such a clean break with this world that the spirit really comes into existence [bliver til]. And he wants us, even now, gradually to wean ourselves away.

But no carnal fanaticism, for there is, alas, a fanaticism which is essentially carnal.[208]

You are to believe that God is fatherly enough to rejoice in a child-like way with you whenever you according to your human conception are happy. But you are to remember that there must be a striving, that there shall be striving in order that the mind can be transformed away from the earthly.

This is the way I understand it, but I also understand that it is need-ful, it is still needful for Christendom and for myself, that He stepped forward, He, who by being most effectively rigorous with himself ventured to be rigorous with us, in order that we could be prompted both to strive and to appreciate leniency.

But God is gentle. This I have always understood. My own life shows me this. For whenever I wish to enjoy myself, it never occurs to me promptly to *pray* God to cooperate with me and grant that I may really enjoy myself—which would be nonsense, as if God were a fantastic bogey-man; nevertheless, I do have a rather uncommon sense of the hold God has on me every second. Most people would perhaps completely lose their zest for life if they should ever understand to the degree I do how God at any second is able to transpose a person into a more rigorous spot, and it would probably go the same with me as with them if I were to understand it in an even greater measure and in an even greater measure were always to have it immediately present.

x^2 A 241   *n.d.*, 1849

« 1400

Yes, it is true, how satirical—imagine all of a sudden the application of the Old Testament command, "You shall not form for yourself any image of your God," to our time, when God has become abstract. How turned about the world is—is it progress or retrogression?

In his *Vorschule der Theologie*,[209] para. 108, the younger Fichte has drawn attention to this.

X^2 A 443   *n.d.*, 1850

« 1401

The thought that God tests [*prøver*], yes, tempts [*frister*] a man ("lead us not into temptation") must not horrify us. The way one looks upon it makes the crucial difference. Disbelief, melancholy, etc. immediately become anxious [*angst*] and afraid and really impute to God the intention of doing it *in order that* man shall fail. However remote it may be that the melancholy anxiety in a man would think of having such thoughts about God, yet in the profoundest sense he really does think in this way, but without knowing it or becoming aware of it, just like the hot-headed person who is said not to know what he is doing. The believer, however, immediately interprets the matter inversely; he believes that God does it *in order that* he shall meet the test [*Prøven*]. Alas, in a certain sense this is why disbelief, melancholy, anxiety, etc. so often fail in the test, because they enervate themselves in advance—it is punishment for thinking ill of God; whereas faith usually conquers.

But this is rigorous upbringing—this going from inborn anxiety to faith. Anxiety is the most terrible kind of spiritual trial [*Anfægtelse*]—before the point is reached where the same man is disciplined in faith, that is, to regard everything inversely, to remain full of hope and confidence when something happens which previously almost made him faint and expire with anxiety, to plunge fearlessly into something against which he previously knew only one means of safety, to flee, and so on.

The person with inborn anxiety can very often have even a visionary idea of God's love. But he cannot concretize his relationship to God. If his idea of God's love has a deeper ground in him and he is devoutly concerned, above all else, to nourish and preserve it, then in many ways and for a long, long time his life can go on in the agonizing suffering of getting no impression *in concreto* that God is love (for anxiety continues to be too overpowering for him and prevents him from seeing the danger, the test, the temptation, etc. in the right way, that they are for him to meet), while he still all the more firmly attaches himself to and clings to the thought: Yes, but God is love just the same.

This is a sign that he is being educated or brought up to faith. To hold fast this way to the thought that God is love just the same is the abstract form of faith, faith *in abstracto*. Then the time will come when he will succeed in concretizing his God-relationship.

x^2 A 493   *n.d.*, 1850

« 1402

How many men have any idea at all of how strenuous life becomes in an actual relationship to God. This alone—to be completely deprived of the habitual security which most people have when they have reached a certain age, believing that their period of development has now essentially rounded off and has now become merely repetitious, almost routinely repetitious—just this alone, to have this security completely withdrawn! And, on the other hand, this daily fear and trembling, every day, every moment of the day, the possibility of being thrown into decisions of prime importance—or, more correctly, that one is in this position because every spiritual existence is out in the depths of "70,000 fathoms."[210]

x^2 A 494   *n.d.*, 1850

« 1403

There is a kind of religiousness, yes, the most common kind, which still continues to appear in analagous forms. Earlier, in the first centuries, many thought that a person related himself to God only with respect to his eternal salvation; as far as earthly and temporal affairs were concerned, one had to stick with the old gods.

[*In margin:* This is related to Neander's *Denkwürdigkeiten*,[211] II, somewhere in the notes.]

It is the form: existentially to live in completely different categories, but to have made sure of one's eternal salvation by a kind of insurance.

x^2 A 569   *n.d.*, 1850

« 1404

In II Samuel 23:15 we have an example of sacrificing the will (Arndt[212] also refers to this in the preface to Book III, p. 667): when David had a powerful longing to drink the water of the well at Bethlehem and the three heroes broke through the enemy lines and brought the water to the king, he poured it out for the Lord.

Incidentally, this is a religious counterpart of the story about Alexander, who did not do it for God but out of human magnanimity and heroism.

x^2 A 591   *n.d.*, 1850

« 1405

To be involved with God, actually to be religious, without bearing the marks of being wounded—well, I do not understand how such a thing could be possible. In the relationship to God to be able to say: To a certain extent I will get involved with you, I will concede you a place in my feelings, but no more; I will not be a spectacle in the world as the religious man must be because by his relationship to you he has become heterogeneous with this life; I will live healthy and strong in this earthly life, become a complete man in the worldly sense—and then have a feeling in my innermost being. One who in truth has become involved with God is instantaneously recognizable by his limp, as they say, or he knows suffering heterogenity in this life.

But to become involved with God in any way other than being wounded is impossible, for God himself is this: *how* one involves himself with Him. As far as physical and external objects are concerned, the object is something else than the mode; there are many modes; someone perhaps stumbles upon a lucky way, etc. In respect to God, the *how* is *what*. He who does not involve himself with God in the mode of absolute devotion does not become involved with God. In relationship to God one can not involve himself to a certain degree, for God is precisely the contradiction to all that which is to a certain degree.

$$x^2 \text{ A } 644 \quad n.d., 1850$$

« 1406 *If——What If*

If someone were to say to the believer: But suppose it ends with God's having duped you—he would answer with Luther:[213] Be quiet, man, God does not do that. And if the person were dissatisfied with this answer, he would say: Well, all right, if that's the way you want it; but I still would not lose anything by concentrating everything on the one thing which occupies me. For even if I renounced much in this life because I believed it to be God's will and it still, as you say, ended with God's deceiving me, I still would not have occupied myself with getting these things, since either I would be aware that God could deceive a man, thus that God is a deceiver—that is, that everything is nothing—or I would have desisted because of concentrating everything on becoming involved with God.

$$x^3 \text{ A } 75 \quad n.d., 1850$$

« 1407 *In the Presence of God*

Well, yes, there are two ways, but the latter of the two really ought to be the more blessed: either everything is more and more propped up externally by good fortune, and you thank God, or you learn to be able to endure more and more, to do without more and more, learn it by fellowship with God.

x³ A 247   n.d., 1850

« 1408 *The Highest Form of Godliness*
—and the Highest Egotism.

The terrible thing is that the highest form of godliness, complete abandonment of everything earthly, can be the highest egotism. This happens when one's way of life expresses that the others are not really religious in the deepest sense of the word.

And yet this absolute form of surrender is precisely what Scripture requires.

x³ A 264   n.d., 1850

« 1409 *Absolute Devotion to God*

The God-relation is like the relation to superiority, particularly to absolute superiority: there comes a moment when it almost seems as if God's love were a deception whereby he deceives the pious.

This is the moment when it really comes home that the God-fearing person must be torn out of his conceptual setting and his world of ideas and be transposed into the world of God, to learn from him what love is.

At the beginning a person lives in relation to God in such a way that with the facility of a child and according to the religious impression of the period he thinks he loves God, understands that God is love, is grateful for all the many good gifts, etc.

But look, now God continually sends opposition; the Christianity which is proclaimed as consolation changes to a prodigious burden which is laid upon the believer, so that instead of being consoled he must suffer for Christianity etc.; then it seems to him as if God were in a certain sense a deceiver who draws a person farther and farther out and instead of accommodating himself to man designs everything to capture man in the service of his own interests. It begins with God's being the love which loves men, and then it appears that God is the one who wants to be loved; he has not the slightest intention of altering his conception of what love is, and his conception of what love is makes you, humanly speaking, unhappy in this life.

This is spiritual trial [*Anfægtning*], but it is entirely in order that it goes this way; even the apostles experienced this in relation to Christ.

And yet God is infinite love, but he has only the spirit's conception of what constitutes your happiness and blessedness—alas, and you are flesh and blood. If you are to become blessed in your relationship to him, your conception must be transformed, and this transformation, this rebirth, is a very painful operation, and in the process there comes the moment when it seems to you as if God were like a superior sort of seducer.

Certainly God is no egotist, but he is the infinite *I* who cannot possibly be altered to please you, but you must be altered to please him.

Completely forget everything, including yourself, in thinking about God, that he is love—yes, then you are blessed in your relationship to him —but then you have also become spirit.

x^3 A 359   *n.d.*, 1850

« 1410 *The Situation of the Apostles*

How horrible it must have been for the apostles when for a time it seemed as if Christ had deceived them—luring them with attractive prospects—and then reversing the whole thing so dreadfully.

But it cannot be otherwise for a man in his relationship to God. There has to come a moment (specifically, when all his purely human world of concepts has to be toppled and he has to be shifted over into God's concepts), when God seems to him to be a deceiver. He will have many weak moments when he will pine for the old days, and it will seem to him that he could love God better if the relationship were as it once was, when God coaxed him by adapting to his own ideas.*

This is the truth. But the difference between my way of talking about it and the usual way up until now is that the latter (probably because the persons concerned do not involve themselves either with God or Christ) sling some fat phrases about love and God is love and Christ likewise— whereas I picture how it is when the whole thing is taken in earnest. Really and truly, anyone who has the remotest idea of what it actually is to die to the world also knows that this does not take place without frightful agonies. No wonder, then, that he cries out, sometimes also rebels against God, because it seems to him as if God deceived him, he who from the beginning became involved with God on the understanding that God would love him according to man's idea of love and now sees that it is God who wants to be loved and according to God's idea of what love is.

But, of course, it still holds true that God is nevertheless infinite, infinite love. The error, of course, is in man—that in moments of weakness he does not have the courage, confidence, and faith to rejoice that God deigns to involve himself with a man.

Just hold fast to this—that it is out of infinite love that God has to perform this excruciatingly painful operation—this will surely help.

But painful it certainly will be. And then comes spiritual trial [Anfægtelse]. One is anguished by the thought that God is angry and this is why he gives a person all this pain—instead of its being out of his infinite love.

x³ A 373   n.d., 1850

« 1411

Addition to 1410 (x³ A 373), in margin:

* But we human beings seldom come any farther in the relationship to God than to fall in love, and few come even that far. But falling in love is self-love; erotic love is self-love. In erotic love I keep my own idea of what is lovable and find that the object completely suits my head and my heart; this is why I love the beloved so ardently—that is, I ardently love myself. So also with the God-relationship. One man can endure much longer than another with respect to what love can do unto the beloved and still be love; but when his whole concept must be totally overthrown, then inevitably the moment comes when God seems to be a deceiver; this is the crisis, until faith more than conquers.

x³ A 374   n.d., 1850

« 1412

You who have loved us *first*, O God—alas, we speak about it as if it were something historical, that you had loved us first only that one time, and yet you do it constantly; many times every single day throughout life you always love us first. When we awake in the morning and turn our thoughts to you—you are the first, you have loved us first. Even if I arise at daybreak and instantly turn my thoughts to you in prayer, you are too quick for me; you have loved me first. When I collect my thoughts from all my distractions and meditate on you, you are the first. And so it is always—and then we talk ungratefully as if it were but once that you loved us first.

x³ A 421   n.d., 1850

« 1413 *God as Father—and the "Neighbor"*

Number 339 of the hymn book begins:

> O, God, to call you Father
> Is sweet to every man,
> But one who hates his neighbor
> Of child's rights has none.

Yes, he not only does not have the rights of a child but he has no "Father." God is not my Father or any man's Father in a special way (frightful presumptuousness and madness!); no, he is Father only in the sense of being the Father of all. When I hate someone or deny that God is his Father, it is not he who loses but I—then I have no Father.

In these areas there is always the reversed echo.

x³ A 581   *n.d.*, 1850

« 1414 *The Relation to God*

When everything smiles upon you and you overflow with joy or feel completely happy over existence [*Tilværelse*]—and then you think of God, then perhaps your expression flowers more vigorously and richly.

When you are dispirited, depressed, then your expression is perhaps meager—but, but in the final analysis it is without a doubt more obvious that it is you who are in need of God, and to God this is the one thing pleasing, that you in truth need him. When you rejoice, you can be truly grateful to God, but it is still possible that what moves you is not this genuine need of God, however beautiful and well-intentioned your gratitude may be.

Therefore the second is more pleasing to God. For God is spirit; he does not find additional pleasure in men's hymn singing any more than in the smell of incense. What is most pleasing to him is that a human being genuinely needs him, essentially feels that he needs him.

If you have rich gifts to bring to God (the happy richness of songs of praise, the plenitude of eloquence, and everything of this poetic nature, and in all sincerity, for otherwise it is all empty), then it is perhaps more pleasing to you to approach God; but when you are wretched, disheartened—then it is more pleasing to God that you approach him, for he has only one joy: to communicate, and therefore the one most welcome is the one most in need.

x³ A 585   *n.d.*, 1850

« 1415 *Christianity in God's Interest— and Christianity in Man's Interest*

Man's interest is in having an established order of things religious, the more complicated and grand the better, since in this there is all the more security and a distance from decisions, something we humans prize so highly.

God's interest is that there be no established religious order at all, for the more immediately all are responsible to him, the better hold he has on the ears of everything.

But to represent Christianity in God's interest in the strictest sense is beyond a man's power; that requires an apostle, at least.

How can the two be joined: an established order—there is no established order? In this way—that we human beings confess [*tilstaae*] that an established order is for the sake of our human frailty, consequently is a concession, which has come about because every one individually at one point or another must have reduced what it is in the most rigorous sense to be a Christian, thus helping to bring about an established order, which again helps us to reduce Christianity.

But the fact is that as a rule the highest thoughts are never included. So we devised an established order. In contrast to that we think of the lower qualification of immaturity and party spirit, etc. Well, in that case, an established order is of course the highest. But then it ends with our idolizing "the established order." We forget that on the other side of "the established order" lies, as an ideal, the thought: no established order.

The order is as follows: I. There is no established order. But this is so infinitely too high for us men that we must pray for ourselves and "by grace" get an established order. II. An established order. III. Immaturity and party spirit spoiling it all by wanting to be higher than the established order.

x^3 A 658   *n.d.*, 1850

« 1416 *A Difficulty from Another Quarter*

Suppose there were a person who had sufficient heroism or acquired sufficient heroism actually to come to hate father and mother etc. for the sake of Christianity. My God, it must be frightful to be able to do this, frightful to live so alone. Take the opposite—think of the most eminent human talent—and then to have fellowship only with a sparrow—yet this is not so frightful as a person's (a poor human being's) having to live all day long and day in and day out solely in fellowship with God. Is this because I trivialize God? No, it is because I think that there is an infinite qualitative difference between God and man. Therefore in that sense we cannot speak of fellowship with God, and man cannot endure the fellowship, cannot endure continually having only the impression of God's presence.

x^3 A 694   *n.d.*, 1850

« 1417 *The Fear of God Is Profitable for Everything*

Yes, it is as one takes it. The way the world is at present, the fear of God is about as impractical as anything could possibly be—all practical folk will no doubt agree to that.

As it is everywhere with the New Testament, this is the greatest satire on Christendom.

x^3 A 743   *n.d.,* 1851

« 1418 *God's Upbringing*

The following collision could very well be imagined.

A religious individual [*Individualitet*] prays to God: Will you take over my upbringing yourself, O God. This prayer is heard. What does God do? He takes a stick, as it were, and begins to beat up the fellow. Alas, the poor wretch, he is completely bewildered by this. He had really believed himself to be the object of God's love—and now this dreadful beating. He becomes completely despondent, believes he has completely forfeited God's grace. Meanwhile God says: Yes, *if* one has said A he also ought to say B; if he himself asked to be brought up—it pleases me that he has confidence in me—then it also ought to be to his benefit. And God continues to beat him.

Finally the fellow is completely fagged out and collapses—and look, suddenly there is a transformation, and he exclaims: O my God, thank you, thank you. I forgot that I asked you to bring me up yourself. During the worst of it I was unable to make up my mind or maintain how it was to be understood, but now I remember it again.

After all, is it not the same with anyone who actually involves himself with God? In a magnanimous moment he is greater than himself and ventures to involve himself with God. God keeps his word and involves himself with him. But then it is too much for him: it seems to him that he has completely lost God—until the understanding is there again —and in heightened blessedness.

x^3 A 747   *n.d.,* 1851

« 1419 *In Relation to God*

the most difficult situation is one in which a person in a certain human sense is right or is not entirely wrong. Face to face with God it is just about easiest of all when one can say: I was a scoundrel, I behaved liked a scoundrel; forgive me.[214] Repentance is, after all, the easiest and most natural relation to God.

This is why in situations in which, humanly speaking, I still think I am right, over against God I personally prefer simply to gain genuine peace and rest—to assume that I nevertheless am really a scoundrel but that God will surely forgive me.

x^3 A 772   n.d., 1851

« 1420 *"The Highly-Trusted"*

That a human being in the presence of other human beings has dared refer to a special relation to God—this I do not understand, and furthermore, I do not understand it in this way.

Suppose that a person dared to be convinced of his having a special relation to God—it seems to me he would have to say to God: In infinite, ineffable gratitude for this grace, I am willing to suffer everything; O, but is it not true that you do not want me to speak about this to anyone; is it not true that if I presumed to speak to anyone about my relation to you, you would be angry about it as being the greatest presumption and ingratitude. And on the other hand, I also pray that above all you will not require anything like this of me; I would almost die of shame, and it would grieve my spirit to death.

I shall now pursue this further, thinking and speaking in a purely human way.

To this God might answer: What you say may be, humanly speaking, true and beautiful; but in part I have chosen you precisely in order that it should be declared in the world or because I want to have it declared, and what you say is really human egotism: you want to enjoy the relationship to me. No, to the contrary, what I require—and for this very reason I have entered into relationship with you—is that you shall declare it in the world. Do you fear that it will be taken in vain, that you will be honored and respected of men, something you think would grieve your spirit? Rest at ease; it is eternally impossible. Such things can happen only to those whom it does not grieve at all, those who in truth have no relation to me. No, by saying it, you will have pronounced, humanly speaking, your destruction. Men will hate, abominate, curse you. You may also find that, humanly speaking, it always looks as if I, too, had left you in the lurch, because, since I am spirit, you can have only a spirit-relationship to me, only the spirit-witness in faith, as long as you live in this world. Yet also in this there will be blessedness sufficient for you, and then you have eternity before you.

x^3 A 781   n.d., 1851

« 1421 *A Radical Consolation for One*
      in Extreme Spiritual Trial {Anfægtede}

Does only the person who has a gracious God and Father have a God
and Father? I wonder if the person who has, alas, an angry God and
Father does not also have a God and Father? O, my friend, if this is your
predicament, or if you are being spiritually tried [*i Anfægtelse*] in this
way, continue to cling to this radical consolation; only do not let go of
God, and you will find that there is help in this. The one danger is to let
go of God. Even if his wrath were to hang over you all your life, this still
is not nearly so dangerous.

But no doubt a man is seldom spiritually tried as hard as this.

x^3 A 790   *n.d.*, 1851

« 1422 *Misunderstanding*

When someone sees what he calls God's cause in difficulty, it is very
natural to want to rush to its assistance and then also hope that somehow
God will make it a little easier for him in other respects.

Alas, no! Who really comprehends the eminence and the elevation
of the divine? Suppose that God's cause were almost lost, humanly speaking. Now someone comes along and humanly, yet honestly, wants to help.
And God, who has been waiting calmly in heaven, answers: Well, now,
so you want to be examined? —For it does become a comprehensive
examination.

Imagine—it is humanly unimaginable!—a human being as sure of
his cause as that! Humanly speaking it looks as if all is lost. Then someone comes, in all honesty, and wants to help him—and he answers: Yes,
but it will be an examination and it will be hardest for you. And remember
that he is someone who, humanly speaking, in all honesty wants to help,
for if he is a deceiver it is another matter, and then this kind of eminence
is not needed for putting one at a distance.

But this divine eminence! O, a poor human being can so easily make
the mistake, as if God or God's cause stood in need of anyone. The relationship is *always* this, even in the most desperate moment, humanly
speaking, for God's cause, [the relationship] is *always* the same: the closer
you come to God the more rigorous he becomes. He does not make the
mistake of rejoicing over this help—no, it becomes your examination. But
no clubbing with God, no fraternizing.

x^4 A 132   *n.d.*, 1851

« 1423 *Anselm*

He shows the necessity of satisfaction not only from God's side, in order to satisfy God's honor, but also from man's side.

Assuming that man could become saved by a compassionate act on God's part, but without satisfaction, man would still not be able to be saved. The fact that satisfaction was not made would continually torment him and disturb his bliss; or one would have to think that he did not even care if satisfaction were made or not, and that would indeed be wickedness. See Böhringer,[215] II, pt. 1, p. 406

x^4 A 211   *n.d.*, 1851

« 1424 *A Mediator*

is necessary for me, among other reasons, simply to make me aware that it is God with whom, as we say, I have the honor of speaking; otherwise a man can easily live on in the indolent conceit that he is talking with God, whereas he is only talking with himself.

x^4 A 252   *n.d.*, 1851

« 1425

Addition to 1424 (x^4 A 252), *in margin:*

Seen from this aspect, the Mediator in a certain sense means the buffer; he is like the courtier who informs us that we cannot get to talk directly to the king lest we stupidly and thoughtlessly go in and talk to the king as if we were peers.

What consistency there always is in the divine! Always a redoubling [*Fordoblelse*]—when he subtracts he also adds. He subtracts, involves himself with us human beings, sends a mediator—yes, but in another sense the Mediator expresses aloofness, that God does not naïvely become involved with a man as friend with friend—no, now there is a mediator.

Yet we have come closer to God; but just as in relation to the ideal every step forward is a step backward, so it is in relation to God: approach, withdrawal, and yet, *actual* approach.

x^4A 253   *n.d.*

« 1426 *The Most Blessed Comfort, the Eternally
Certain Proof That I Am Loved by God*

Here is the syllogism—love (that is, true love, not the self-love which loves only the distinguished, the excellent, etc., and consequently actually loves itself) relates itself inversely to the greatness and excellence of the object. If I am infinitely, infinitely a nobody, if in my wretchedness I feel more miserable than the most miserable person of all—then it is eternally, eternally certain that God loves me.

Christ says: Not a sparrow falls to the earth without his will.[216] Ah, I offer a lower bid, before God I am less than a sparrow—the more certain it is that God loves me, the more quickly the syllogism is completed.

Yes, one could suppose that God could overlook the Emperor of Russia—God has so much to look after, and the Emperor of Russia is so great. But a sparrow—no, no!—for God is love, and love relates itself inversely to the greatness and the excellence of the object.

You feel yourself abandoned in the world, you suffering one, no one cares for you, and so you decide: God does not care for me, either. You fool! Shame on you, you slanderer, to talk this way about God. No, if there were a person of whom it literally could be said that he is of all people the most abandoned—he is the one, the very one, whom God loves. Or if he were not absolutely the most neglected, if he still had a little bit of human comfort—and if this also were taken from him—in that very moment it would become even more certain that God loves him.

x^4 A 254   n.d., 1851

« 1427 *The More One Gets Involved with God,*
the Greater the Difficulties

It is, however, completely in order that this is so; otherwise the God-relationship surely would be taken in vain, and it would be particularly the earthly mentality which would be involved with God.

x^4 A 304   n.d., 1851

« 1428 *God's Unchangeableness*

It is unbelievable how recklessly we men speak of the consolation in the thought that God is unchangeable. Yes, of course God is unchangeable, but what good is it to me, am I really capable of having anything to do with an unchangeable being? For a poor, unsteady human being this is the greatest possible strain; the pain I have to go through is far greater than everything I can suffer because of another man's changeableness.

This is how serious the matter is. But then it must be said that despite all this we *must* go through with it, and that then the blessedness is there as well. But this sentimental flirtation, this brashness with which we generally speak of the consolation in the thought of God's unchangeableness, is an illusion.

x^4 A 311   n.d., 1851

« 1429 *David's Psalm: "This is too high for me."*

In the psalm[217] where David praises God's omnipresence so gloriously and says: If I take the wings of the morning and fly to the most distant sea, thou art there, etc., David says: This is too high for me.

Yes, quite right, that is the way it is. All this unspeakable bliss—when it is heard in a quiet hour (consequently at the distance of imagination): O, how soothing, how soothing that God is so near to me, at every moment—how blissful for a man just to think it.

But now if it is to be actuality and not just a presentation of it—how dreadfully strenuous to have God so near to me. In fact, I scarcely dare cross my floor, scarcely dare stir, scarcely dare say a word—lest it displease God—and before God (if he is present, I am indeed before God) the least trifle is equivalent to the greatest decision—exactly as a sparrow is an object to him, yes, as he counts the hairs on my head.

This explains the truth in David's declaration: This is too high for me. For David was an experienced man. But on the other hand, again, we see here the total confusion prevailing in Christendom—for everything is confined merely to presentation, and where the religious life begins is not to be seen at all—yes, from the character of the preaching I will be able to prove indirectly that the average pastor does not live in the religious at all!

x^4 A 485   *n.d.,* 1852

« 1430 *The Unknowability of God*

In contrast to the Church Fathers' firm conviction of the unknowability of God, Aëtius maintained "that he knew God just as well if not better than he knew himself." (See Tennemann, *Geschichte der Philosophie,* VIII, p. 176). It would have sounded still more ridiculous if he had replied: God? Sure, I know him very well. In any case Socrates[218] would certainly have found it quite ironical that Aëtius thought he knew God even better than he knew himself. Alas! I wonder if he really knew himself!

x^4 A 567   *n.d.,* 1852

« 1431 *The God-relationship*

The thought: to do this or that, to offer this or that, to venture this or that—in order to serve the cause of God—this thought has never moved me, for I have always found it somewhat nonsensical that an Almighty One, for whom millions of worlds are nothing at all, should have a cause for which it is important that Peter or Paul does this or that.

No, I cannot go along with this. For me it is better if I think of God as an examiner who says: I would like this and that from you. I do not mean thereby that this should now become useless activity—no, it is supposed to be of benefit—but the idea that God could have a cause in the sense that a man could automatically be a colleague seems to me to have been justifiable childishness once upon a time but now is sheer nonsense, for it is predicated on God's having a cause in the sense that he is one of the adherents, he who really is all.

No, it is not God who has a cause, but every individual human being has a cause, and it is God who from his infinite sublimity looks on with his blessing and now, in relation to the infinite totality of the whole, may allow a man to suffer, still encompassing him just as fully in infinite love and expecting, as it were, a man to do this and that, to endure this and that, because it fits into the whole. But it is never God who has a cause. At best this could be said as an accommodation, in the same sense as parents play along in order to make the child happy. But God does not have a cause in the sense that there is something which has not been fought out, something of concern to him but of doubtful outcome in the cause of the Almighty One, who infinitely and eternally has been victorious from eternity and without battle.

It cannot be denied that the idea that God very clearly has a cause, that it is important to God that you and I fight for his cause—it is undeniable that this idea has in its time inspired many people and made it easy for them to sacrifice everything. But it is no good; it is still a flight of fancy and would have been a frightful conceit if men at that time had had such a developed idea of God's infinite sublimity which must now be held. On the other hand, it is certain that this infinitely blissful peace with which we think of God as infinitely elevated above the world can easily have an intellectually stupifying effect on us human beings, so that we become spectators instead of men of action. But it is no good; we are obliged to follow through again to action, to the same boundless enthusiasm which men at earlier times had in the illusion that they were somehow helping God by fighting for his cause.

Here again there is a redoubling [Fordoblelse] which makes it so difficult to break through, a redoubling which is ever present where there is to be enthusiasm on the other side of or after illusion. With one eye, as it were, to see all of man's effort as the greatest childishness, yes, as the most indifferent thing in the world (for he, the Almighty One, has millions of resources and has always been infinitely victorious) and then, nevertheless, to be able to strain himself to the utmost fully as much as someone inspired in sober earnestness by the thought that his persistence, his daring, were crucial to the point of determining no more nor no less than that God would be victorious or would lose.

I am tempted in a sense to say: O, you fortunate ones! What would not a man be able to endure if he could first of all get the firm idea that his striving is so infinitely important that God depends on it. In another sense I consider myself fortunate, for how fortunate it is to have an infinitely more elevated conception.

He must increase, but I must decrease.[219] These words could be applied to the relation of the human race to God. With every forward step man makes, God becomes infinitely more sublime—and thereby man decreases, even if this happens through a step forward.

Then comes the danger—that this infinite elevation of God has a stupifying, paralyzing effect so that man loses desire and courage and confidence and joy in venturing and suffering—because it does not make the least difference either way (although, if I am right, precisely this is infinitely inspiring!)

And as God has become for us men so infinitely sublime that there can no longer be a matter of what a more childlike age believed in a straightforward way—that God has a cause which we fight for—then even the highest good, eternal salvation, has similarly become too elevated, incommensurable with our efforts. Therefore there is only "grace." There were times when man with childlike earnestness soberly believed he could fulfill the requirement and earn eternal salvation. And in truth, what could a man not succeed in accomplishing if he once could get the firm idea that he really has it in his power to earn eternal salvation, that this task is commensurable with his powers. I could be tempted to say: O, you fortunate ones! And yet, how fortunate to have an infinitely more elevated concept about the highest good.

No, no striving can earn eternal salvation. Therefore there is "grace." But here the danger appears again, the danger that grace may have a stupifying, paralyzing, soporific effect—because it nevertheless is fruitless to strive, and because it nevertheless is grace.

Once more the redoubling! That the most strenuous human effort is still fool's play, a wasted inconvenience, a ridiculous gesture, if it should be an attempt to earn salvation—and still (if I am right, this is still the infinitely inspiring) to push on just like one who soberly and seriously believed that by his efforts he could earn salvation.

x^4 A 640   *n.d.,* 1852

« 1432 *The God-relationship*
Father—Son—Holy Spirit

As a rule the relationship is present thus: it is Christ who leads us to God; man needs a mediator in order to come to God.

But this is not the way it is presented in the New Testament (note especially the Gospel of John, particularly John 6:45: No one can come to me unless the Father who sent me draws him), nor can it be this way if it is true that the heightening of the God-relationship is characterized by the lowering of oneself.

It begins with the Father, or the relationship to God as Father, without a mediator. This is simply the child-relationship. Nothing is too exalted for the child; he says *Du* to the emperor in the same way he says *Du* to the nursemaid. To the child it is perfectly clear and completely as it should be that God is his Father.

But when a man has reached a certain point of maturity God has become too infinitely exalted for him to dare call him Father as a matter of course—that is, if the words are not to become an empty phrase. In a certain sense God sees it the same way.

Then it is that God directs one to the Son, to the Mediator (John 6:45: No one can come to me unless the Father who sent me draws him). The man will himself feel it to be presumptuous unceremoniously to call God Father, and in a certain sense God sees it the same way. Therefore it is as if he said: In the Mediator I can be a father to you.

So the Mediator comes. The Mediator is also the prototype [*Forbilledet*]. Now there is a lovable youthfulness in the relationship whose very mark is a lovable simplicity which finds nothing too exalted. One finds it quite as it should be to have so infinitely exalted a prototype and in his lovable illusion is piously convinced that it can be done; in the good sense of the word the two of them, the prototype and he, the striver, are peers.

But when a man has reached a certain point of maturity, the prototype becomes so infinitely exalted to him that he does not dare begin trying to be like him in an informal and, in the good sense of the word, comradely sort of a way. In a certain sense the prototype himself also believes that this really would be presumptuous.

Meanwhile the prototype has to be seen from another side; he is also the "Atoner." It is this side which that lovable youthfulness actually is unaware of, for in his lovable eagerness the person is promptly on his way trying to be like the prototype, for he sees no problems whatsoever in respect to the prototype's infinite sublimity. Consequently this youthfulness lacks, for one thing, the category of the prototype's infinite sublimity (that he is, after all, qualitatively different from the merely human) and, for another, has an unrealistic idea about his own powers.

Yet the "Atoner" must not supplant the "prototype"; the prototype remains with his demand that there be a striving to be like him.

Consequently the prototype directs away from himself (just as the Father directed one to the Mediator), to the "Spirit," as if he said: You cannot begin this striving naïvely; that would even be—as you yourself feel—presumptuous (something that lovable youthfulness was too naïve to see, and therefore it does not feel guilty of presumption in what it does). No, you must have a Spirit to help you.

Thus it is not the Spirit who leads to the Son and the Son who leads to the Father; no, it is the Father who directs to the Son, the Son who directs to the Spirit, and not until then is it the Spirit who leads to the Son and the Son who leads to the Father.

This—if I dare put it this way—is God's tenacious grip on his majesty, which is anything but domineering or aristocratic—no, it is inseparable from his being. The more he gives himself, the more he involves himself with man, the closer he comes, or precisely inasmuch as he wills to do that, man is—even though elevated—lowered. To tell the truth, he is elevated, but he is elevated by getting an infinitely higher concept of God, and in this way he is lowered.

How elevating! No human sovereign is able to protect himself against indiscreet forwardness in this way. But God is protected, for the closer you come to him the lower you become—that is, the nearer you come to him the more infinite a concept you get of his infinite sublimity, but thereby you are lowered. "He must increase, but I must decrease" is the law for all drawing near to God. Even if he were a million steps removed, he would not thereby be protected against indiscreet forwardness, for it just might be achieved sometime. But to be protected by the law of inversion—that to come closer is to get farther away: infinite majesty!

"But then in a way I lose God." How? Indeed, he increases! No, if I lose anything, I lose only my selfishness, myself, until I find complete blessedness in this adoration: He must increase, but I must decrease.

But this, after all, is the law for all true love. Indeed, it would surely be self-love if I wanted to increase along with God as he increases.

No, he must increase and I must decrease; only in this way does he become my Father in spite of everything; he becomes my Father in the Mediator by means of the Spirit.

x^5 A 23   *n.d.*, 1852

« 1433 *Gradations in the God-Relationship*
—God's Majesty

1) In paganism and anything pagan the distinguishing mark of the God-relationship is: happiness, prosperity; being loved by God is marked by being successful in everything.

2) In Judaism the shift begins: to be God's friend etc. is expressed by suffering. Yet this suffering is essentially only for a time, is a test [*Prøvelse*]—then comes happiness and prosperity even in this life. But it is essentially distinguishable from all paganism in that being loved of God is still not as completely direct as being a Pamphilius of fortune.

3) In Christianity being loved of God is suffering, continual suffering, the closer to God the more suffering, yet with the consolation of eternity and with the Spirit's testimony that this is God's love, this is what it is to dare to love God.

The gradation in God's majesty corresponds to these three stages.

In paganism God's majesty is merely a superlative of a human majesty—and therefore the distinguishing mark is something direct.

Only in Christianity is God's majesty pure majesty, qualitatively different from what it is to be man, paradoxical majesty, and therefore distinguishable by suffering.

———

Take the same idea in other ways. Think of God's confidence or understanding with God. If the sum and substance of the understanding is that all an individual's happiness and prosperity are from God, then this is not a relationship of the spirit and in the highest sense is not confiding in God, for God is spirit.

No, when that which comes from God is suffering—but the understanding with God is that this suffering indicates God's love—this is the confiding of the spirit. God is indeed spirit. And as such he must redouble [*fordoble sig*]. But the redoubling consists precisely in this—that it is suffering which comes from him and that nevertheless this is to be the expression for love.

———

All that which an older piety (Luther, for example) explained by the devil, that it was the devil who sent sufferings, I explain with the help of God's majesty.

It cannot be otherwise if you actually want God to be God and you have anything to do with him. That is, if the most blessed thing of all is granted to you—to love God. God can, of course, love the sparrow without the relationship becoming one of suffering, but here there can be no question of a spiritual relationship or of loving God in return.

When God involves himself with a man, he says something like this: I love you, be eternally convinced of it, I, who am eternally love. This does not mean unqualified suffering, although it may begin. O, but if this love of mine stirs you, and you wish—and this is indeed my will—gratefully to love your God in return, then it must become suffering. Just do not become impatient, and you will find that you will do well. But I cannot alter my majesty in such a way that when the most blessed of all is granted you or permitted you—to love your God—that things become easier—no, they will get harder, there is more suffering—yet behind all this is my confiding that this is love. To want to have permission to love me and then also to want everything made easier is wanting to have your cake and eat it, too.

This is how I see it. But as I always say to myself and to everyone: Go slowly; if the going gets rough, then try a lower relationship to God, but in such a way that you nevertheless begin again where you eased up; you are not under the law but under love.

x^5 A 39   *n.d.*, 1852

« 1434 *Sadness*

It is altogether certain that the more an individual is involved with God, the more difficulties enter his life. It sometimes seems as if God allowed everything to go wrong for him—and yet he can have the blessing of being able to affirm that God does it out of love alone. Now his sadness lies in the fact that others cannot understand it this way. And therefore he could perhaps desire the relief merely of having the others remain ignorant of all these misfortunes and sufferings, because they do not participate in his understanding of them; he does not, however, ask to be freed from the sufferings. Yet it is very seldom that a man is truly so spiritually advanced that he rightly lives in such an understanding with God that the suffering, the misfortune, etc. actually signify to him God's love.

x^5 A 55   *n.d.*, 1852

« 1435

The New Testament teaches how we human beings should serve God; the human invention which we call Christianity is—how we let God serve us.

x^5 A 116   *n.d.*, 1853

« 1436 *The Majesty of God—the Only Thing That Interests Him Is Obedience*

It is easy enough to see that only one thing remains which can interest him for whom everything is equally significant and equally insignificant—obedience. This is the absolute Majesty.

This is not the case with a relative Majesty; there is always one or another "what" that interests him. These are the differences—for him one thing is more important than others; for him something is significant and another thing is insignificant, etc., but precisely thereby he is excluded from infinite sublimity, real Majesty—which is interested only in obedience.

But this conception of the majesty of God and of obedience does not really please us human beings. Therefore we have managed to get it abolished and have permitted ourselves to pretend that we are able to trick God into distinctions, as if there were something important to him, an important "what." We have invented this for the benefit of those better favored, who by living their lives on the basis of the differences between man and man consider themselves to be closer to God. We have invented it also because we ourselves would rather deal with differences. Thus a man will gladly govern and rule perhaps a whole country and then in addition would like to have this be something important to God, who, after all, is not very particular about trifling things. See, there is the rub! To repeat, it is so terribly hard for a man to realize that the only thing which interests God is obedience, that the most insignificant thing of all can be transformed into what is more important than all world history—as soon, that is, as it pleases God to accent it as a task of obedience.

It is so easy to deal with God in this way—that it is only the all-all-most-important things that occupy him; and it is so frightfully rigorous to have to deal with God in this way—that only obedience interests him, and therefore the all-all-all-most-insignificant things can interest him. However, the first way is a belittling of God's majesty, and only the latter is the expression for God's majesty.

XI^1 A 5   *n.d.*, 1854

« 1437 *A Personal God*

The abundance of talk about how blessed it is to have a personal God is like all the other hypocrisy one hears.

In one sense, yes, but in another it is really far easier to have a blind fate to deal with, for in blind "fate" there is nothing inciting; one has to be as insane as Xerxes to be incited by the sea and natural forces.

But a personal power—when it begins to "tempt"—and a personal power such that the most insignificant thing can correspond to the most frightful decision: O, in one sense this is agonizing, agonizing.

But this we omit; we take only the other side—that is, we lie, pretend, and chatter here as in everything else.

I doubt very much that there could be found among us one single person who in the old Christian or Jewish sense is able to have anything to do personally with a personal God. In relation to those heroes, we are a bunch of old rags, duplicates, a heap of bricks, mass-men, a school of herring, etc.

XI^1 A 35   *n.d.*, 1854

« 1438 *That Christianity Has Been Cunningly
Abolished in Christendom,*

that this has not been done openly, that people have not revolted against Christianity in order to discard it but have cunningly made it seem as if they were Christian, yes, as if everything were zealousness and support for Christianity, that they have done this as cunningly and perfidiously as possible by teaching in the name of humility something Christianity does not want and forbidding as presumption and a tempting of God something Christianity particularly wants—the fact that this has taken place cunningly is also the reason why it is so dangerous, for thereby the whole crowd of what could be called nice people, humanly speaking, are *bona fide* along in the conspiracy without ever suspecting that they are criminal conspirators. No one can so easily be a *bona fide* part of a revolt which is in character, but with cunning it happens far too easily.

Incidentally, one has to hand it to these swindlers who are masters in this cunning (for that matter, in a certain sense I am willing to admit that the master κατ' ἐξοχήν really is human nature itself) for craftily knowing how to take advantage of human frailty and to get Christianity so twisted around that it is precisely the nice, good-natured folk who are obliged to presume this to be Christianity.

Christianity in the New Testament leans toward foolhardiness, the rashly risked venture: Dare to believe, become involved with God, you can do everything if you only believe, etc. Nothing is more difficult to get into an ordinary human being—and nothing is more difficult to get out of a human being than this tedious modesty which thinks that it is worshipping God to be so unpretentious, so modest.

The fact of the matter is that the ordinary man has no idea of Majesty, that the law for the Majestic is wholly different—yet, exactly the opposite —from the law for ordinary civil affairs. Let an ordinary citizen get the whim (yet such whims are really not for ordinary citizens) to say to someone, "Ask of me what you will"—what then? —The ordinary citizen becomes angry if the other then asks too much. A king, on the other hand, not only becomes angry, he gets into almost a raging fury if someone to whom he said, "Ask what you will," asks for a trifle. His Majesty will say: Either the man wants to insult me and make a fool of my royal capacities or he is as good as dead, a blockhead, an idiot, an ass whom I would rather not have in my sight.

And now this divine Majesty! He offers everything—and nothing insults him, nothing revolts him, except this puny human wretchedness which does not dare ask, does not dare aspire, does not dare believe, this puny human wretchedness which, after all, in a way makes a fool out of him for having been loving enough to want to become involved with men.

But we preachify and preachify and swill it into the children: Modesty and unpretentiousness, do not demand too much, and be humbly satisfied with mediocrity—this is true worship, well-pleasing to God.

XI¹ A 188   *n.d.*, 1854

« 1439 *The Examination*

God's judgment of this temporal existence [*Tilværelse*] and this world is: it is a sinful, evil world; it is a vale of tears. This he says in his Word.

But precisely because existence is supposed to be an examination, this world is as fascinating and lovely as it is in many ways.

God has a very good understanding of what examining means. He does not place man in a world which forces him in every way to recognize that it is a vale of tears—and then declare in his Word that it is a vale of tears in order to see whether man will believe him. No, this would be a stupid examination, and it would never be believed. No, the world seems a lovely, nice world, unequalled—and now God says in his Word: The whole thing is a lie and sin and a vale of tears; now let us see if you will believe me.

XI¹ A 359   *n.d.*, 1854

« 1440 *God and the Human Race*

Having introduced Christianity into the world, God can involve himself with the human race on one of two conditions, *either* in such a way that individuals are found who are willing to venture out so far in hating themselves that there can be any possibility of God's using them as apostles, *or* in such a way that the true situation is honestly and unconditionally admitted. The latter is my primitivity [*Primitivitet*], never thought of before in Christendom, and I have cast it in such a way that it becomes an appeal to God to accept it.

As far as the former is concerned, this is certainly the instruction of the New Testament.

But with respect to venturing so far out that there can be any possibility of becoming an apostle, the following must be noted. This is something so dreadful for a human being that it is permissible to say: I dare not.

But, to repeat, God will involve himself with the human race on only one of these two conditions.

But when it pleases the human race to place dishonesty between itself and God with regard to Christianity, then he cannot and cannot want to involve himself.

And this is what we have done. Christendom is the dishonesty which has introduced the variation: We are too humble to want to be apostles. This is dishonesty, and it makes a fool of God with respect to what he has had proclaimed in Christianity. In Christianity he offers the condition that any and every man can become an apostle—on God's side there is nothing to hinder. But to become an apostle is, of course, so dreadfully agonizing that a man is allowed to say: I dare not, I am incapable of it, etc. But one thing is not allowed, he has no right to say: I am too humble to aspire to anything like that. It is this dishonesty (which is Christendom) which has made it impossible for God to involve himself with the race.

And when the race places dishonesty between itself and God with regard to Christianity, then God is not a petty tyrant who flares up and beats men. O, no, he is too aristocratic for that, his righteousness too severe. He has eternity—here we meet again. In time he uses the punishment which he personally understands to be sufficiently terrifying: to ignore. And in this respect he is sufficiently majestic; he ignores the centuries, the million times trillions of specimen-men or copies.[220] It is only we men who are fooled, as if these enormous masses were something in and for themselves.

God ignores the race. Christendom has been God-forsaken for a long time. And this will continue until once again honesty about Christianity is placed between us and God—then we shall either get apostles or the turning which I propose will be made, and this turning will find grace before God.

XI¹ A 381   *n.d.*, 1854

« 1441 *A Second-hand Relationship to God*

is just as impossible and just as nonsensical as falling in love at second-hand.

The ridiculousness of a second-hand relationship to God is evident in another way. Since God is the closest one of all to a person, at every moment the closest one of all, it is clear how ridiculous it would be to want to have a relationship to him at second hand, that is, to put distance between oneself and the one who is closest of all and who intends to come even closer. It is as ridiculous as Sexton Link's leaving the student "to go to a grocery store and borrow a directory in order to find the address of the man he wanted to talk to" and then coming back, saying, "How strange—this is the place."[221] The only difference is that Sexton Link arrived at the right place; whereas one who wants a second-hand relationship to God does not arrive at the right place in this way.

XI¹ A 464   *n.d.*, 1854

« 1442 *An Actual God-Relationship*

As stated elsewhere, an actual relationship to God is of such infinite worth that even if it were only for a moment and in the next moment one were kicked, struck, tossed, hurled far away, and forgotten (which, as a matter of fact, is impossible both because God is love and because that relationship can be remembered eternally, so that the end still has to be that one lays hold of God again)—it is still worth infinitely more than everything the world and man have to offer.

But an actual relationship to God is also entirely different from becoming a professor of it, getting married on it, making a living from it, consequently, with family, making a living (of, on, from, with) off the fact that someone else has had an actual relationship to God and in the only way possible, in frightful anguish and suffering.

XI¹ A 553   *n.d.*, 1854

« 1443 *Backward Progress*

In a piece[222] by Prof. Jacobi (about the Irvingites, 1854) I see that the Mormons assume that God is not everywhere present but moves with great speed from one star to another. Splendid! Generally progress means, compared with a more childlike age, that more spiritual conceptions are achieved, as if a more childlike age had fancied that God moves with great speed from one place to another—and now the modern age understands that God is everywhere present. But here the movement is in reverse! It is very characteristic, and presumably I am not wrong in assuming this to be the influence of trains and the invention of the telegraph. In all probability there is in store for theology a completely new development, in which all these modern inventions will be employed to decide the conception of God.

XI^1 A 591   n.d., 1854

« 1444 *God—Appearance*

To assume that God is related directly to the world of appearance (if this is not at variance with God as spirit and in general with the entire outlook of Christianity) would also involve us in the difficulty of having to assume that this world is a splendid world. The sensate man who thinks that this world is a splendid world thinks therefore that the nearness of God is related directly to appearance: the more phenomena, the nearer God is. But Christianity[223] teaches that this world lies in sin, which implies that God is related paradoxically to appearance, only tangentially, just as one may be able only to touch something but nevertheless can gear into it decisively, yet without being in continuity with it.

XI^2 A 53   n.d., 1854

« 1445 *A Point of View for the History of the Human Race*

If I were to express myself on this—although generally I am not concerned with such things and assume that it is unethical to be occupied with the history of the race instead of with my own existence—I should state this point of view.

God has only one passion: to love and to be loved. It has pleased him, therefore, to go through existentially with men the various ways of being loved and of loving.

He himself, of course, takes roles and disposes everything in relation to them. At one time he wants to be loved as a father by his child, then as friend by friend, then loved as one who gives only good gifts, then as one who tempts and tests the beloved. The idea in Christianity, if I dare say so, is to want to be loved as a bridegroom by his bride in such a way that it becomes sheer testing. Now he changes almost into equality with man, accommodatingly, in order to be loved in this fashion; then again the idea is to be loved as spirit by a human being—the most strenuous task. And so on.

My thought is that God is like a poet. This is why he puts up with evil and all the nonsense and wretchedness and mediocrity of triviality, etc. The poet is related in the same way to his poetic productions (also called his creations). But just as it is a mistake to think that what a particular character in a poem says or does represents the poet's personal opinion, so it is a mistake to assume that God consents to all that happens and how. O, no. He has his own view of things. But poetically he permits everything possible to come forth; he himself is present everywhere, observing, still a poet, in a sense poetically impersonal, equally attentive to everything, and in another sense personal, establishing the most terrible distinctions—such as between good and evil, between willing according to his will and not willing according to his will, and so on.

The Hegelian rubbish that the actual is the true [the identity of being and thought] is just like the confusion of thrusting the words and actions of the dramatic characters upon the poet as his own words and actions.

But it must be kept clear, if I may put it this way, that God's wanting to work as a poet in this fashion is not a diversion, as the pagans thought —no, no, the earnestness lies in God's passion to love and to be loved, yes, almost as if he were himself found in this passion, O, infinite love, so that in the power of this passion he cannot stop loving, almost as if it were a weakness, although it is rather his strength, his omnipotent love. This is the measure of his unswerving love.

$$\text{XI}^2 \text{ A } 98 \quad n.d., 1854$$

« 1446 *God Is Love*

This is the thesis of Christianity.

There is a twofoldness in it: God loves—and God wants to be loved.

These two in equilibrium make true Christianity: exactly as much promise as obligation, always equally as much promise as obligation.

If someone were able to adhere on the greatest possible scale to the fact that God is love in the sense that God loves him and then suddenly came to see the other side, that God wants to be loved—he would certainly become anxious [angst] and afraid. Just as it can be grand and glorious for a poor girl to become the object of a very powerful man's love, who loves her with all his soul—but in another sense there is an enormous difference when she perceives the earnestness of his passionate desire to be loved— just so it is for the Christian. In one sense nothing is more blessed than this certainty that God loves him, and also the degree to which God is love, the fact that it is his essence—in another sense nothing is more dreadful than to be pulled up to this highest level of existence [*Tilværelsens*], where in one sense God's wanting to be loved is so frightfully earnest.

Christendom naturally has agreeably wanted to play the game of taking God by the nose: God is love, meaning that he loves me—Amen!

XI² A 99   *n.d.*, 1854

« 1447 *The Majesty of God*
           One Aspect of Lutheran Doctrine

Luther declares that all sufferings and spiritual trials [*Anfægtelser*], all troubles and persecutions, and so on come from the devil; if there were no devil, being a Christian would be a life of milk and honey.

This conception is not truly Christian* and in part is related to Luther's assumption that Christianity is an optimism, that opposition and sufferings are only accidentally related to being a Christian and therefore originate from an external power; therefore if there were no such power, being a Christian would be sheer fun and games, since being a Christian in and by itself does not intrinsically involve suffering.

In part this view is related to Luther's not elevating divine Majesty high enough in essential majesticness. If the situation is such that over against God there is a Majesty like Satan, so powerful in relation to God that God with his best will still cannot avert suffering from his faithful, the *summa summarum* is that humanly speaking God has a cause, and thereby God is degraded.

But men like very much to think that God has a cause, for then human busy-ness begins right away—and they calculate that the price of being a Christian has been significantly reduced. If, humanly speaking, someone —say he is a somewhat elevated Majesty—has a cause,[224] what then? Then *he must use* men. He must make use of men. Take a few analogies. If someone *must buy* on the stock exchange, the broker understands at once that here is a business opportunity, for the customer *must* buy. If someone *must sell* to a dealer in used books, the dealer understands immediately that here is a business opportunity, for the customer *must* sell. And so it is when one must make use of men.

This, however, is the idea which Christianity, especially Protestantism, has pursued, and thereby God has fallen from being the infinite Majesty, who humanly speaking has no cause, to the level of a Majesty who must make use of men. Finally, in procuring men for him, they have practically followed Vespasian's principle about money: One must not smell the money.[225] Christianity came into the world as something wonderful to raise men to the highest ideality, but mankind turned the whole thing around—the requirement for being a Christian was reduced to almost zero, for God has to make use of men.

Compare Christ's answer to those who would be disciples. You see, this expresses that God has no cause, humanly speaking. Clad in the form of a poor servant, without a place to lay his head, knowing what enormous machinery had been set in motion against him—we should think that such a man would have use for men, especially when they bid as high as you about whom this discourse centers. But no, Christ maintains unchanged the price of the unconditioned. As he says to Pilate and the mob of people: I am nevertheless a king[226]—so his reply here has majesty, as if he were saying: My friend, I am a Majesty who does not have to make use of men. Oh, a miracle is not nearly as majestic as such a reply given in character.

*   *

Later Protestantism has completely abandoned the devil in the sense of a participating power. Along with it went the shot of pessimism which still remained in Luther's Christianity, and Christianity became purely and simply sweet sugar candy, an idyllic life of begetting children and all that.

The depravity of later Protestantism lies in letting this whole aspect, for Luther such a decisive aspect, disappear, without intending to replace it with another interpretation, an interpretation which Luther still maintained rightly according to Scriptures—that to be a Christian involves suffering. The depravity is letting this whole aspect disappear, pretending as if this were nothing, and continuing, as they claim, Luther's interpretation.

Yet a Protestant pastor in our age, especially in Denmark, is practically a private citizen who is paid for Sunday orations on just about anything that occurs to him.

*   *

That Christians must suffer does not come from the devil.

The suffering comes from God—and right at this point begins the most extreme spiritual strenuousness in the Christian life. If a person thinks of a being who is pure love, it is then the most excruciating effort for his heart and mind to grasp that this love in a certain sense may be like cruelty. Man is not able to bear this redoubling [Fordoblelse]; so we have made the following division: God is love and from him comes everything good and only the good; everything evil, all troubles, and so on come from the devil. Otherwise we could not maintain that God is love; the most we can maintain is that punishment for our sins still comes from him.

But this contradiction, that humanly speaking love makes the beloved unhappy, yet out of love, but nevertheless, humanly speaking, unhappy —this thought is fatal to a human orientation. So we have made use of the devil to help ourselves, just as we help a child by talking about a bogeyman who does what we are unwilling to tell the child that God does, because we wish to promote in the child the idea of associating only goodness and gladness with God.

But the suffering comes from God. And it never has an accidental relationship to being a Christian, either. No, it is inseparable from it.

The suffering and the inevitability of it are connected with the majesty of God. His majesty is so infinite that only the paradox can designate it or be the expression for it, and the paradox is this—to be so majestic as to have to make the beloved unhappy. [*In margin:* Lesser majesties are known by the fact that they make the beloved happy—the direct relationship.] Infinite majesty! Yet it must never be forgotten that this majesty is love.

The suffering is related to the qualitative difference between man and God and to the collision of the temporal and the eternal in time, which must involve suffering.

The suffering is related to God's being the examiner. But if the examination is to be in earnest, the examiner must carry it to its ultimate. God, who gives an examination in faith and in whether a person loves him, must also carry it to the ultimate (himself suffering more than the one examined). What a human being would like to have is that it be plainly recognizable that he is loved by God. Only rarely, very rarely, is there someone with enough inwardness not to desire this. But in truth the relationship cannot and must not be thus, if God is spirit. The examining must go to the opposite extreme, where the beloved seems to have been abandoned by God. This is the examination in which there can be different grades but essentially all get the same grade.

God is the examiner. This is a very suggestive term. An examiner really has not the slightest thing in common with one who, humanly speaking, has a cause. But of course in our nonsensical age all concepts are reversed and finally we have no word to signify the relationship of sublimity. A schoolmaster in our age means someone who needs the children; a physician means someone who needs the sick; an author one who needs readers; a teacher one who needs the learners—and so an examiner is one who needs you who are subjecting yourself to the examination.

XI² A 130   *n.d.,* 1854

« 1448

*In margin of 1447 (XI² A 130):

It is particularly this kind of Christianity (refined Judaism) which makes a hit as "childlike Christianity,"²²⁷ and since, of course, a child cannot assimilate pessimism, we can just as well pour optimism into it and also lick along ourselves—and thereby be the occasion for the child's behaving like a fool later on in the fancy that he is a Christian or despairing when he gets to understand properly what Christianity is, despairing simply because this Christianity has been poured into him as a child.

XI² A 131 *n.d.*, 1854

« 1449 *God—and the Devil*

When I raise objection in several places²²⁸ to the conception which everywhere introduces the devil as the source of suffering for the Christian, it is not my intention to explain away this power. Indeed, the New Testament itself also presents Christ as having been tempted [*fristet*] by the devil.

No, my aim is to block the idea which is so easily smuggled in, the idea that God has a cause in the human sense—and simultaneously the criterion for being a Christian is readily reduced.

If the situation in any way whatsoever is such that God wants to have Christians because he has some use or other for Christians, has something he wants to use them for, the ideality of being a Christian will immediately be threatened, disturbed, just as God's majesty is also degraded. If the situation is such that God is a Majesty who is embattled with the devil, another Majesty, and wants to have Christians for this battle in order to make use of them in this battle, it is then impossible to maintain the ideal qualifications for being a Christian.

The ideality for being a Christian is established so high in the New Testament that even if God got only one single Christian, not one jot must be removed from the requirement. This is the ideal, and this is infinite majesty.

The mutiny from below, however, is always spying to find, if possible, that the Majesty in some way is in the situation of having use for Christians, perhaps must make use of Christians. And the very second this is discovered, that very second finitude has really taken power away from the infinite Majesty—and now the bargaining begins.

Take a figure which illustrates what it is meant to illustrate if you do not forget that there is no arbitrariness in God (the ideality he has established for being a Christian is not something arbitrary, a caprice). Imagine that a king got the idea that he wanted soldiers only of a certain height, a certain build, and with a certain color of eyes and hair. Now then, if His Majesty is in the situation of having to wage war with another king and needs soldiers—what then? Then finitude, that little humpbacked rag picker, says: "Your Majesty is in a tight spot and ought not be so almighty stubborn about this specific requirement, for it is impossible to get even an approximate number of soldiers according to the specifications—and Your Majesty does need soldiers."

This, you see, is why finitude wants very much to impute a cause, humanly speaking, to God, to make him busy, indeed, just like someone in hot water—for then God must make a deal, knock off something from the requirement for being a Christian—"He must indeed make use of Christians."

The unconditioned, being-in-and-for-itself, is so frightfully strenuous for a human being, and therefore we would like to get rid of it, force a purpose upon God—and in that very second he becomes dependent upon finitude. Whoever has a purpose must also want the means, and if he must have the means, then he must adapt himself—here it is again: God cannot maintain the ideality of what it is to be a Christian, and he must give in a little—for "otherwise he gets no one at all"—and, of course, he does have a definite purpose and therefore he wants to have Christians: *ergo*, the requirement is lowered.

This is why I repeatedly say[229] that God is pure subjectivity, has nothing of objective being in himself which could occasion that he has or must have intentions. Whatever is not purely transparent subjectivity has at some point or other in its objective being a relationship to an environment, a relationship to an other and therefore has, must have, intentions. Only that which infinitely subjectively has its subjectivity infinitely in its power as subject, only that has no intentions.

But the unconditioned, the being in-and-for-itself, is fatal to a human being. Assume the unconditioned requirement, and then suppose that a man is nevertheless allowed to raise the question: Why, why must I unconditionally give up everything—and then suppose the answer: Because God wants to use you as an instrument to influence other men. This would be an alleviation; the unconditioned would be somewhat mitigated, be somewhat less fatal because this "why" and along with it an intention have been shoved between this man and the unconditioned. But look closely and you will see that the unconditioned is no longer the unconditioned, being-in-and-for-itself. And when you know that, you will see that some-thing lurks here which gradually turns the relationship around and, *summa summarum*, God becomes a majesty with a cause, humanly speaking, and consequently cannot hold unconditionally to the unconditioned.

This is why I have a suspicion about the way men use the expression "to serve God," because one cannot serve God as one serves another Majesty who, humanly speaking, has a cause, has intentions. No, the only appropriate expression for God's majesty is: worshipping him. The distinction is commonly made between worshipping God, thinking more particularly of feelings, moods, and their expression in words—and serv-ing God by one's actions. No, your action is indeed true worship, and it is true worship when it is freed from all busy-ness, as if God had an in-tention. Worshipfully to give up everything—but not because God must make use of you as an instrument, no, by no means—to give up every-thing as being unconditionally in the category of luxury and superfluity: this is what it means to worship.

When this is the case, it is certain that you "worship," and it is also certain that God's majesty is not degraded.

Such is this infinite Majesty, which nevertheless is love, is love itself, suffering, as I have often said,[230] suffering in love for the beloved, but still without altering his majesty.

But we must not do what Christendom has done—reduce the majesty of God in order to maintain the conception of God as love.

XI² 133   *n.d.*, 1854

« 1450 *Divine Providence*

Providence is indeed everywhere present and thus in one sense is the closest of all. But in another sense he is infinitely far away. That is —he refuses to intervene forcibly, he omnipotently constrains his own omnipotence because it has pleased him to want to see what will become of this whole existence.

In a sense he is like a natural scientist conducting an experiment: no doubt he is easily capable of getting at something in another way, but he wants to see whether or not it can be produced by the particular procedure of the experiment, and he constrains himself in order to watch the experiment; he waits patiently—yet with infinite interest. —Or God is like a maieutic in relation to the learner. He certainly has the ability to tell the pupil the right answer immediately, but instead he constrains himself, patiently endures perhaps several years while the learner ex-hausts himself inventing new nonsense.

But just as the experimenter and the maieutic are anything but indifferent men, so God also is infinitely interested.

Yet, seen from this point of view, what makes life so frightfully overwhelming for a poor human being is that God has and employs such enormous proportions, which again indicates majesty (just as, although a poor analogy, the experimenter and the maieutic rank according to how long each can hold out and according to the range of the scale on which he can lay out the experiment). God uses centuries or lets centuries be tossed away in gibberish and mistakes: this proportion is just too enormous for a poor human being.

In a certain sense it can be said that there is no providence at all, just as if there were no experimenter or the experimenter were no one, since, after all, he does not intervene but merely lets the concatenated forces develop. And yet the experimenter is sheer awareness and attention and is constantly present—all of which is but a poor picture of God's being present, although in yet another sense he refrains completely from intervening.

Only once has providence omnipotently intervened—in Christ.

XI^2 A 170   *n.d.*, 1854

« 1451 *To Be in Relation To God*

God is at one and the same time infinitely close to man and infinitely far away.

To come into relation to God is a voyage of discovery somewhat comparable to an expedition to the North Pole, so rarely does a man ever actually press forward on this way, to the discovery. But to fancy having done it—that almost everyone and every century have done this.

But if this journey of discovery of God is an *inland journey*, the main point of it is specifically to preserve one's individuality and then inwardly simply to remove the obstructions, push them aside.

Here is the limit to human busy-ness and conceitedness. If an emperor were to open his purse-strings and give two million dollars a year to pay 10,000 well-fed pastors—to discover God—this naturally would be ridiculous; it is even more foolish than to chuck the money away. If all Christendom started a drive for donations of four farthings in order to pay 10,000 pastors for the purpose of getting hold of God—this would be nonsense. Yes, God be praised, money is not able to do everything; neither can associations.

XI^2 A 171   *n.d.*, 1854

« 1452 *A Personal God*

This is what the professors and preachers prattle about; they try to prove that God is personal, and this is what makes the congregation happy.

I am not going to speak here about how ridiculous it is to want to prove it, for it cannot be "proved"—it must be believed. What I really want to discuss is that here as everywhere men waste their time and their lives solving problems they themselves create. Yes, God always makes fools of the wise.

Assume that someone, a professor, devoted his whole life to a scientific and scholarly attempt to prove the personality of God—suppose that he finally succeeded—what then? Then he will have succeeded at the end of his life in standing at the beginning, or in standing at the end of the introduction to the beginning. And this whole introduction to the beginning is something man himself has foolishly created, problems man himself has concocted. But as has been said previously, this is the way it is in everything religious, everything essentially Christian—men invent a species of antecedent difficulties, the introduction to the matter itself, and thereupon waste their time and powers and lives and then die, never making a beginning in the thing itself.

No, God is personal; that matter is certain enough.

But, by this, unless something else happens, you have not advanced. Here, again, is a human illusion. We fancy that as soon as the professor finally proves that God is personal, then he straightway is personal for all of us. Perhaps this is also the reason we so eagerly transfer the matter into another sphere, the sphere of proofs rather than the sphere of faith —in order that we may quickly and positively, once and for all, be done with this, or have certainty.

No, God is indeed personal, but it still does not follow that he is straightway personal for you. Take a human relationship: a superior personality is certainly personal, but does he not have it in his power to be personal in relation to the inferior one or to relate objectively to him, although it still is true that the superior one is and remains personal.

So also with God. Assuredly he is personal, but whether he will be that toward the individual depends on whether it so pleases God. It is the grace of God if he will be personal in his relation to you; and if you throw away his grace, he punishes you by relating to you objectively. And in this sense it can be said that the world (despite all proofs!) does not have a personal God; for the world does not please God, and his punishment is to relate objectively to it, although he nevertheless remains just as fully personal.

But while the preachers and professors prattle to the millions about proofs of the personality of God, the truth is that long ago there ceased to be men capable of bearing the pressure and the weight of having a personal God. There is something jolting and soul-stirring in the truthfulness with which a patriarch or an apostle talks about dying weary of life, for truly having to do with a personal God can certainly make a man weary. Figuratively speaking, a workhorse, even if it has worked hard at the plow, has no inkling of what it means to be as tired as is a trained performing horse when it has been ridden. —Alas, even if my life did not otherwise have enough torments and sufferings, this alone would be sufficient, this loathing which comes over me every time I think of the nonsense on which men waste their time and their lives. It would certainly be loathsome to think of men living on filth instead of food, eating vermin, etc.—but it is just as loathsome to think that men buy and pay an exorbitant price (to the preachers and professors) for nonsense—and live happily on it.

XI² A 175   n.d., 1854

« 1453 *The Common Man—the Cultured Man*

Just as the common man puts God at a distance, or himself creates the scruples and problems which put God at a distance, specifically because the common man does not want to be uplifted but would rather cling to his notion that God is so infinitely exalted that it just cannot make sense that anyone could address him quite simply and directly— so also does the cultured man invent similar difficulties which likewise put God at a distance. The cultured man says (and this is actually more stupid than what the common man says): It is not possible to approach God directly—no, one must push through to God along the way of science and scholarship.

Alas, and all the time the God of love sits in heaven and waits for someone to become involved with him—while men are busily engaged in removing themselves from God in various ways—maintaining all the time, please note, that what they are doing is done in order to approach God.

Thus, insisting that we are coming closer to God, we put him at a distance. But is not this really what we instinctively and cunningly want?* Is not the truth of the matter really this—that man is just like a child who would rather be free from being under his parents' eyes; is not this what men want—to be free from being under the eyes of God? To this end their instinctive cunning has discovered that this can best be done in the guise of making great efforts to approach God, while these very efforts place God at a distance. This is especially true of the cultured man.

XI^2 A 179   *n.d., 1854*

« 1454

Addition to 1453 (XI^2 A 179), *in margin:*
* Is not the whole of human life like the princess in A *Thousand and One Nights*, who sustains life by the telling of stories—is not this the reason for all these efforts to put God at a distance, under the pretext of approaching him, because, as children know that their pranks and hubbub will have an end when the parents come home, men secretly know that the impression of God's actual closeness would stop this whole hubbub, occasioned simply by our surreptitious support of each other in the notion that God is far away, putting him at a distance under the guise of working to approach him.

XI^2 A 180   *n.d.*

GOETHE

« 1455

If I were to state briefly what I really regard as masterly in Goethe's *Wilhelm Meister*, I should say that it is the capacious governance which pervades the whole work, the entire Fichtean moral world-order,[231] even more doctrinairely developed in the novel, which is inherent in the whole book and gradually leads Wilhelm to the point theoretically postulated, if I may put it that way, so that by the end of the novel the view of the world the poet has advanced, but which previously existed [*existerede*] outside of Wilhelm, now is embodied and living within him, and this explains the consummate impression of wholeness that this novel conveys perhaps more than any other. Actually, it is the whole world apprehended in a mirror, in a true microcosm.

I C 73   March, 1836

« 1456

Goethe indeed has irony and humor but hovers above both—to that extent different from Greek tragedy.

I A 224   August 19, 1836

« 1457

Is it the customary Goethean experience of the world which led Goethe (in his *Faust*) *to have Mephistopheles lead the new student astray particularly with regard to the faculty's curriculum*, which he does by ridiculing the arduous pursuit through directing him to a course of study and at the same time leading him astray about it, scaring him away from it, thwarting and destroying the great plans of one who could have gone forth strengthened by such a pressure. This easily leads one to think of Hamann, who also in this respect is πρότυπος,[232] his biography in *Schriften*,[233] I, p. 172.

I A 233   September 9, 1836

« 1458

In his *Aus meinem Leben*,[234] what is Goethe but a talented defender of insipidities? At no point has he realized the idea, but he talks

158

himself out of everything (girls, the idea of love, Christianity, etc.) he can.

In margin: And all this is rather cheap, if you will, and Goethe is only a shade different from a criminal who also poetizes guilt away, "puts it at a distance by poetizing."[235]

V A 57   n.d., 1844

« 1459

It is Goethe, I believe, who says somewhere:
> *Ach, da ich irrte, hatt' ich viel Gespielen,*
> *Seit ich die Wahrheit kenne, bin ich fast allein.*[236]

VII¹ A 8   n.d., 1846

« 1460

Every Sunday every pastor preaches about a purely personal relationship between God and man. But the great minds—Goethe (in *Aus meinem Leben*,[237] S.W., XXIV, p. 65) cites as an illustration that as a child he wanted to build an altar to God and sacrifice to him, but it caught on fire, and then adds: This holds for any personal and immediate approach to God.

This shows that no one pays any attention to the pastors; and it is wisdom, the profoundest wisdom granted a person, privately to believe the exact opposite.

IX A 89   n.d., 1848

« 1461

Goethe always presents his feminine characters solely in the light of masculine egotism. Take Clärchen! A man like Egmont who stands on the stage the way he does, even in peril of his life—that he can be so completely sure that Clärchen would not betray by a single word or look anything of what she knows and is infinitely interested in, that she can love mere man to this degree—yes, this insignificant little maiden is simply femininely great, an unusual girl—in quite another sense than the silly way in which we usually speak of an unusual girl (a little refined, etc.), a character which, in complete agreement with Goethe, I rate very low. Take Margaret! To maintain this feminine insignificance in the presence of such a pronounced personality as Faust—yes, this is feminine greatness. But Goethe was such an egotist that he really never once had sufficient integrity to value sympathetically all that was squandered on him. Even the diminutive "Clärchen" is in a sense an injustice if nothing more is said, for her insignificance is simply greatness, even if it is quite correct that Egmont calls her "Clärchen," but perhaps it could be stressed that it was only Egmont who called her this.

x² A 465   n.d., 1850

« 1462 *Goethe as Representative of the Modern Lack of Character—the Sins of Understanding, More Frightful than Other Sins*

Apparently Christianity is letting its cause come up for trial; in any case it will be necessary to go back to Luther; the question of the public worship service especially must come up, the objective preaching, the fact that it has no character. It may be advantageous, perhaps, to show the modern lack of character in another area, in its representative Goethe, where the matter is probably not as serious since Goethe did not pass himself off as being a teacher of Christianity and had not dedicated himself by a sacred vow and was not consecrated by ordination and the communication of the Holy Spirit to teach Christianity.

There is imaginatively within a man a relationship of possibility to the good, the noble, the altruistic, etc. (and this every man has more or less).

It is providence's purpose (and thus also the intention of Christianity) that this relationship of possibility should draw the man out so that he walks in character according to the good, the noble, the altruistic, sets them into actuality [*Virkelighed*] where he then experiences the truth of the infinite difference between possibility and actuality, that what in possibility is so beckoning is so difficult in actuality.

Children and youth and women sometimes for their whole lives relate themselves essentially to imagination; the mature man, then, should walk in character according to that which stirred the child, the youth, the woman.

But this very seldom happens. And as in the individual, so in the whole race—this development comes to a standstill with reason.

Take an egotistical, richly endowed nature with a strong desire to enjoy life. He is both too richly endowed and too intellectually developed not to see that life is all too meaningless without ideas, ideality, and a relationship to them.

But he is also a pure egotist with an egotistical sensibleness. What does he do, then? He splits. Aided by imagination, he relates himself to the noble, the good, the altruistic, the high-minded—and it is glorious enjoyment, that he knows well. He throws himself into it, surrenders to it, so to speak—but see, the very instant the good by means of imagination would draw him out in such a way that he walks in character, sets these ideals into the midst of actuality—something which, because of his greater understanding and intelligence, he has a rather good idea would become suffering—at that very instant he breaks off and is the egotist. Poetically he possesses ethical ideality, he exhausts himself poetically—but for himself he is a shrewd one about his earthly advantages and is not foolish enough to walk in character according to the good. Charming! He has double profit—first the direct worldly profit which one acquires by being an egotist, and then the appearance of high-mindedness which the poetic production casts over him.

One "poetizes" noble, unselfish sacrifice—and one *is* a crafty peddler: and so one has even more profit than the peddler, for one also has the appearance, the look of being an altruistic person etc., since men in their simplicity confuse a person with the poetic production.

Now think of a teacher of Christianity à la Goethe, one who with the assistance of observations and descriptions (this corresponds to "exhausting oneself poetically") acquires the appearance of saintliness and who *is* a cold egotistical rationalist who knows to the minutest detail how to watch out for his advantage, and also the profit from these observations and descriptions.

There is enough talk—and severely judgmental talk—about all the frightful immorality which in the ages of "passion" frightfully confused the highest things with the most tragic debauchery. I wonder if it is as abominable as this forfeiting of one's heart, this damaging of one's soul—to be able to make the highest and most holy things into a poetic game and calmly, sensibly calculate to get profit out of it. Take someone who, under the influence of religious inspiration, as he thought, talked in heavenly tones about Christian love—and on whom passion then played a trick so it turned out that he seduced some girls who were enchanted by his imagination (for this must be maintained—it was not his intention, it was not a coldly calculated plan)—consider this and then its counterpart, someone who with the hard heart of reason knows exactly how to change his relation to the good into a poetic relationship and now enchants everyone by this presentation. Almost worshipfully they look upon him as a saint, this person who always shrewdly knows how to turn around in such a way that he never enters into the character of the good but merely takes all the profit, also the profit of an almost worshipful admiration—which is worse!

x⁴ A 582   *n.d.*, 1852

GRACE

« 1463

It seems to me that the Catholic-Protestant issue could be brought to a head by asking whether the choice whereby man receives divine grace is prepared by the activity of the Holy Spirit or whether it has its foundation solely in man. The Protestants have certainly declared themselves for the former position in assuming that all human nature is incompetent and must first be transformed, so to speak. According to Dr. Möhler[238] (to whom I especially refer) the issue for the Catholics is not so clearly defined. He says (Clausen's and Hohlenberg's *Tidsskrift*, II, 1, p. 137): "The divine call which is issued to men for the sake of Christ expresses itself not only in the external invitation through proclamation of the gospel but also in the internal activity of the Holy Spirit, which awakens the latent powers in man." Shall we conclude from this that man, according to Catholic doctrine, cannot himself receive the grace (which is offered–?–to him) but must first be inwardly prepared to receive it through the awakening of his powers—and thus they presumably cannot be charged with Pelagianism? But in other places Möhler does not seem to want to admit this. On the whole, I think that the resolution of this question by both sides would lead to a better understanding each of the other.

I A 37   November 26, 1834

« 1464

Striking, pertinent, and very pregnant is the whole position on law in the O.T. in contrast to the N.T. as found in Hebrews 12:24: "*αἵματι ραντισμοῦ κρεῖττον λαλοῦντι παρὰ τὸν "Αρελ.*"[239] (Revenge. Punishment—love. Grace.)

I A 82   August 10, 1835

« 1465

It is not Christian righteousness one sees portrayed at Vesterport as blindfolded and holding scales; it is Jewish justice. Christian righteousness is *single-eyed* grace, which does not weigh with complicated calculations. Christian righteousness is not blind or blindfolded, nor is it deaf, and therefore it does not need scales.[240]

II A 656   n.d., 1837

« 1466

As long as we live in this time of grace, even though our condition is deeply tragic and our despondency borders on hell's despair, our prayer nevertheless is granted once in a while, and Lazarus gets permission to dip his finger to quench our tongue.[241]

CLAUDATUR PARENTHESIS[242]
II A 507   n.d., 1839

« 1467 *Something about Devotional Discourse*

Soon an orthodoxy will be emphasizing the power of the sacraments, what the sacraments confer, the enormous grace and new life (the miraculous); soon it will censure and ridicule a free-thinker who is offended by the Lord's scanty means. But if faith itself sees the greatness, no wonder then that it does not regard them as too scanty, but then faith ought to say this and not change the weapons.

VI A 154   n.d., 1845

« 1468

When Paul[243] insisted that he was capable of anything only through grace, this kind of talk evoked the effect it should, because to the pagans this was not a platitude. But in Christendom it has long since become a platitude, and reflection slyly plays underneath. Just as when one is obviously in style although he is casually dressed, if casual dress is the style, so also to protest that all one is capable of is by grace is a sly trick, because it is established custom to honor this as an expression of humility.

X[1] A 214   n.d., 1849

« 1469

Yes, I certainly do realize very well that to want to build one's salvation on any works, to dare come before God with anything like this, is the most abominable sin, for this means a scorning of Christ's Atonement.

Christ's Atonement is everything, unconditionally, because it makes no difference, after all, what a man does. However, it still holds true that the boundlessness of this Atonement neither makes a man completely indolent nor stifles the childlike which simply and in a childlike way wants to do what it can as well as possible, always with God's permission, please note, not arbitrarily, always thanking, always regarding it as a nothing in relation to the boundlessness of Atonement.

x^1 A 507   n.d., 1849

« 1470

With regard to the claim of ideality, it may be right to present the ideal higher than one himself is existentially if he then, note well, makes an admission concerning himself. In this area it may be right, for indeed one ought to express striving. But with regard to grace it would be nonsense if one proclaimed grace for others and denied that it is for himself. Grace pertains to a receiving, not to my worthiness but rather to my unworthiness. Without any embarrassment at all I can speak of grace because I thereby also speak indirectly of my own unworthiness.

x^2 A 188   n.d., 1849

« 1471

The fact that Jesus died for my sins certainly expresses the magnitude of grace, but that he will involve himself with me only on this condition also expresses the magnitude of my sins, the infinite distance between myself and God. Therefore we may say: This is the majestical or respectful expression for God's majesty—namely, that such a sacrifice, such a middle term, is required in order for me to dare approach him so that he will involve himself with me. In the most profound sense, then, the Atonement could not have been invented by "man," for no human being all by himself could imagine anything as exalted as God's elevation. Only God himself knows how infinitely exalted he is. The remarkable thing about it is that just when God expresses his condescension he also expresses indirectly his infinite elevation. I am willing to become reconciled with men, he says (what condenscension!) on the condition that my son be allowed to be sacrificed for you—what an infinite distance of elevation, if this is the sole condition!

x^2 A 189   n.d., 1849

« 1472 *Grace*

Grace is not something settled and completed once and for all— one needs grace again in relation to grace. Think of a man—grace is declared to him, the gracious forgiveness of all his sins, God's mercy. Good —but tomorrow is another day and the day after tomorrow, and perhaps he will live fifty years. Now comes the difficulty—does he lay hold of grace worthily at every moment from this moment on. Alas, no, therefore grace is needed again in relation to grace.

The easiest thing of all is to die; the difficult thing is to live. In grace everything is intensively compressed—the situation of death is still a factor. But when I have to keep on living, the infinite decision continues to be dialectical, as in this relationship: that grace is needed in relation to grace.

This means that life is a striving.

x^2 A 198   *n.d.*, 1849

« 1473

In his sermon about the son of the widow of Nain Luther[244] makes an important distinction: the gospel does not tell us what we ought to do but where we are to receive power to do what we ought to do.

At the same time, however, the teaching about the prototype [*Forbilledet*] comes once again. For example, self-denial is not diminished, but from the gospel I learn to believe that God and Christ help me toward self-denial.

"Grace" is really related to the composite of the temporal and the eternal which man is. When a solid is spun about too rapidly, there may be spontaneous combustion. So also when the requirement of the eternal and of ideality precipitously breaks in upon a man and makes its demand upon him—then in despair he may lose his mind. At such a time he might cry out to God: Give me time, give me time.

And this is grace—and this is why temporality is called the time of grace.

In eternity there really can be no question of grace. Temporality, to be sure, in one sense is anguish—and yet in the divine sense it is the time of grace.

Faith, which relates itself to and grasps grace, intervenes redemptively. In faith there is rest.

Faith relates itself to grace, and see, now the very opposite enters in: now in one sense there is absolutely nothing to be in a hurry about, for, to be sure, everything is done. Here is the Atonement, justification.

Only in this way can a poor human being be kept in the struggle. In order to gain courage to strive, he must rest in the blessed assurance that everything is already decided, that he has conquered—in faith and by faith.

So he begins his striving, but faith, relating itself to grace, is always at hand to strengthen him to strive patiently, always giving time, the time of grace.

A human father or mother has enough trouble accommodating to a child—what a miracle of patience for God in heaven, or when one is God in heaven, to have patience with a human being's striving.

x^2 A 219   *n.d.*, 1849

« 1474

"Grace" is usually taken to be a dead, once-and-for-all decision instead of being related to striving, since it is—to recall one of Baader's expressions—an advance payment. But this matter of striving is always so difficult, and in a certain sense the easiest situation for the Christian is death, simply because then there is no more talk about striving. For the thief on the cross it was also in a certain sense comforting that it was not a matter of any striving.

x^2 A 223   *n.d.*, 1849

« 1475   *"Grace" and "Law"*

"Grace" has been pushed into an entirely wrong position; we use grace to slough off the requirement of the law. This is meaningless and unchristian!

No, the requirement is and remains the same, unaltered, perhaps even sharpened under grace. The difference is just this: under the law my salvation is linked to the condition of fulfilling the requirement of the law. Under grace I am freed from this concern, which at its maximum must bring me to despair and make me utterly incapable of fulfilling even the least of the law's requirements—but the requirement is the same.

The law's requirement is a tightening. To be sure, tightening such as the tightening of a bowstring creates motion, but one can tighten a bowstring to the breaking point. This is precisely what the law as such does. Yet it is not the requirement of the law which breaks, but that which is added—the fact that your eternal salvation depends upon your fulfillment of the requirement. No human being can endure this. Indeed, the more earnest he is, the more certain is his simultaneous despair, and it becomes completely impossible for him even to begin to fulfill the law.

Then comes "grace." Naturally, it knows very well what the trouble is, where the shoe pinches. It takes away this concern, the appendage of the fulfilling of the law, which is precisely what made the fulfilling of

the law impossible. "Grace" takes away this concern and says: Only believe—then eternal salvation is assured to you. But no more, not the
slightest abatement of the law's demand; now you are to begin to realize
precisely this. But there will be rest and peace in your soul, for your
eternal salvation is assured to you if only you believe.

Just as we have botched all of Christianity by messing it up with
human sympathy, we have also botched up "grace." We have this silly,
imbecilic notion of "grace," that our Lord has now become a doddering
old man who does not know what is going on. No, if our Lord was ever
comparable to an old man, it was rather in Judaism, for he himself understood full well the impossibility of getting the law fulfilled. But in
Christianity he became like the young teacher who keeps a sharp eye on
things: Now I want genuine earnestness, now that I have paid the
earnest money of grace. In Judaism God sat, as it were, up in heaven, saw
that the law was not fulfilled, scolded and punished, but nevertheless let
matters slide. Then came Christianity, and God became young, as it were.
He stepped down to earth, himself became man, went among men, and
said: I want the law fulfilled—here is grace, but now there must also be
earnestness. If I dared to put it this way, I would be tempted to say: It is
as when a new teacher comes to a school, a new teacher who in one
respect is infinitely more gentle and yet in another respect more inflexible
with regard to getting the work done. The old teacher scolded and punished, was perhaps too rigorous also, but be that as it may, the work was
not done. Then comes the new teacher. At the outset he makes the concession of infinite gentleness, and the whole school is reborn and rejuvenated—and then, then he says, "Now we shall begin"—and the requirement, the work—yes, it is the same as before.

I could be tempted to present this in a figure which naturally does
not illuminate but yet perhaps can awaken. Take a group of adult disciples. The old teacher has treated them in the old-fashioned way—like
boys. He scolds and punishes, but there is no progress in the instruction.
Then a new teacher comes. He makes them free, saying: Gentlemen, my
friends, etc.—but the requirements for the instruction, no, he does not
reduce them, and they must pull in the harness in quite another way
than before under the old teacher.

$$x^2 \text{ A } 239 \quad n.d., 1849$$

« 1476 The Requirement—Indulgence

The requirement is the universal, that which holds good for all, the
criterion by which everyone must be measured. Therefore the require-

ment is what must be proclaimed. The teacher has to declare the requirement and in this way incite unrest. He dare not scale down the requirement.

Indulgence must not be proclaimed. Indeed, it cannot be proclaimed, since it is completely different for different people in their innermost private understanding with God.

The proclamation of the requirement is to drive men to God and
Christ in order to find what indulgence they need, what indulgence they
dare ask for before God, and the proclamation of the requirement constantly holds them to God.

But we have turned the relationship around. The teacher (pastor
and priest) does not proclaim the requirement but indulgence. Instead
of acknowledging that the indulgence is the deepest secret of the individual conscience with God, face to face with the requirement, we have
turned the relationship around and for mutual contentment and edification declare indulgence pure and simple. The requirement is omitted
completely or we say it pertained only to the apostles and then each one
enthusiastically declares indulgence to the others—indulgence, which is
still one of the prerogatives of God's majesty and thus can be bestowed
only by him to the single individual, that is, to every individual but to
each one separately.

Do I have the right to say to another person (except in the very
special situation of anxiety and illness etc., although I still would have
to say to him that he must turn to God and there he will find peace):
God does not require this of you (even though it is the New Testament
requirement), not to mention whether I have the right to take it upon
myself to be a teacher, to be paid for it, and then to proclaim to an entire congregation: God does not require this (even though it is the New
Testament requirement), God is gracious etc.? —No, this I have no
right to do. I must proclaim the requirement, and then I must add: If
it is too burdensome for you, turn to God (as I myself, who also need
indulgence, have done); then you will surely come to an understanding
with him, but also before him, about what can be conceded to you.

But we have taken indulgence in vain. It has become a kind of fable
which we tell to one another (this is something like "preaching"), that
God is not very strict etc. And yet the intention is quite different.

God is the sole bestower of grace. He wants every person (educated
up to it through proclamation of the requirement) to turn, each one
separately, to him and to receive, each one separately, the indulgence
which can be granted to him. But we men have turned the relationship

around, robbed or tricked God out of the royal prerogative of grace and then put out a counterfeit grace.

x³ A 72   *n.d.*, 1850

« 1477 *The God-relationship*

If it were possible to deny yourself more inwardly and more truly, for 70 years more inwardly and more truly than 1,000 Christians, if it were possible to work harder than 1,000 martyrs—it is still grace that you are saved, just as the worst sinner is saved by grace.

In a way it might seem as if what one does is a matter of indifference —O, yes, if you are inhuman.

But if God were not infinitely elevated in this way, he would not be God; then he would be more or less the needful one instead of being what he is, grace.

The confusion lies in the fact that you compare yourself with others —alone before God the matter is utterly simple.

x³ A 106   *n.d.*, 1850

« 1478 *"Grace"*

To be permitted to live on sparing oneself in this way, coddling oneself, and thus to have an easy life—and then to believe that one is saved by grace, this is human wisdom. But it is not Christianity.

It is Christianity when one has to experience that it is precisely Christianity which, humanly speaking, makes a person unhappy, when consequently one is tempted to claim merit for sticking it out—and then in his sin to humble himself infinitely before God and to understand that he is saved by grace, simply and solely—this is Christianity.

x³ A 269   *n.d.*, 1850

« 1479 *Grace—Christendom*

Just like those countries in which a rich and prolific nature produces everything and men do not need to work, so Christendom, by means of "grace" which has been taken in vain, is more demoralized than even paganism was.

x³ A 270   *n.d.*, 1850

« 1480

Christianity requires everything, and when you have done this, it requires that you shall understand that you are nevertheless saved simply and solely by grace. This is divine grace, different from the human conception of grace.

x^3 A 353   *n.d.*, 1850

« 1481 *Groan*

Alas, sometimes it can be like this: which then is worse, the anxiety when the law is preached—or the anxiety that I still might take "grace" in vain. Yet this is precisely why there is grace—to root out this anxiety, too.

x^3 A 410   *n.d.*, 1850

« 1482 *Grace More Rigorous than Law*

It can also be looked at this way—just because grace is shown to me and I am reprieved, precisely in this lies the requirement to exert myself all the more. This is the way Luther[245] presents it, too, in his sermon on the Epistle for the Seventh Sunday after Trinity.

But here it holds true, lest I drive a poor man mad, that this must yet again be taken as an inward deepening in grace, more inwardly and more deeply to understand how deeply I need grace.

In addition, it is easy to see, as I have so often said, that the moment of death is the easiest situation in which to become a Christian or to accept grace, for here the difficulty of new striving drops away.

If I am going to live, then there has to be new striving. This should be all the more pure, considering that I received grace for the past. But soon or immediately this striving, too, comes to need grace—and again grace—because after having received grace it is so imperfect. And thus it multiplies.

What does this mean? —It means that there are two ways. Either one believes he is achieving perfection by his striving, or one understands even more deeply how he stands in need of grace.

If I were to define Christian perfection, I should not say that it is a perfection of striving but specifically that it is the deep recognition of the imperfection of one's striving, and precisely because of this a deeper and deeper consciousness of the need for grace, not grace for this or that, but the infinite need infinitely for grace.

Yet how easily this again can be taken in vain! Yes, it is entirely true, but I could almost be tempted to say that just by this it is recognizable as being truly Christian. Judaism is not nearly so easy to take in vain; the God of the Old Testament cannot so easily be taken in. But when he revealed himself in Christ—yes, that was the ultimate that he could do, and for that very reason it became in a sense so easy to take in vain; however, behind it all, again, waits the terrifying earnestness of the eternal.

The genuinely Christian thesis: A man is capable of nothing at all —does not this seem to have become Christendom's password for the discontinuance of all striving? It is the same with everything essentially Christian! Christianity actually begins there where the most enthusiastic person, almost in despair over his sin, with the most intensified zeal stands prepared to sacrifice everything—and lest this zeal become either presumption or actual despair (presumption, as if a man had achieved something himself; despair, that he still is achieving nothing), Christianity wants to humble this zeal and also to bring peace, and now it says: A man is capable of nothing at all—it is grace alone.

It is precisely this thesis that all secular mindedness has appropriated to itself, saying: A man is capable of nothing at all; he is saved by sheer grace—so let's not waste a second being concerned about the salvation of our souls; it can do no good anyway, since a man is not capable of anything at all, and moreover, it is not necessary, since we are saved by grace. And so they rewrote that gospel. For in the gospel story[246] they were actually excluded, those who excused themselves from coming because one had gotten married, another had bought a pair of oxen (note in passing: it hardly corresponds to our grandiloquent phrases about marriage when the gospel offhandedly parallels getting married with buying a pair of oxen; it is something like Diogenes Laertius's use of parallel construction with Greek naiveté when he says of Pythagoras, in order to indicate his purity, that no one saw him in love-making or in the toilet).[247] They rewrote the gospel, and the new ending became: All the invited guests who were absent came along just the same.

In my opinion the very thing which is most terrifying about Christianity is that in a certain sense it can be tricked so easily. It has no external marks as does the law; it almost takes the wheedling words of comfort right out of the secular world's mouth in speaking continually about a man's being unable to achieve anything at all, that it is grace alone; in a sense it makes it so infinitely easy to deceive God, oneself, others—terrifying earnestness!

Precisely when God became in Christ the God of mercy, he also became—if I dare say so—more gentlemanly than ever before. In the Old Testament it is more as if he looked after his affairs—yes, if I dare say so, he contended with men about his affairs, stood on his rights, etc. Then he decided to do everything—and now he becomes infinitely more gentlemanly; it is almost as if he invites men to deceive themselves—

terrifying earnestness. It is the same with God as with a father in relation to a prodigal son. For a long time he does something for him. In all that time he is not so very dignified and remote—he gets angry, he asserts his rights, etc. Then he decides to do everything, and now he becomes infinitely gentlemanly. By doing everything, he makes it possible for the son to fool him completely in a certain sense—frightful earnestness! The father no longer wrangles with his son, does not scold —no, he has done everything, and from that moment it is as if an infinite silence had come to pass. Earlier when the father would at least do something, it was not nearly so easy to take this something in vain, for the father was watching. Now he has done everything, has made it so infinitely easy for the son to take everything in vain—terrifying earnestness!

To do everything is therefore the most decisive *discrimen*, a terrifying either/or. When God sent Christ into the world, he did infinitely everything, he saved the race, every single one—yes, or he abandoned it forever, every single one.

In Christ God is brought to the ultimate—infinite, infinite love and compassion—or in the same degree to severity, so terrifyingly rigorous that for the time being he will not even let you notice it, as when wrath becomes silent and precisely then is at its peak.

The utmost is always the most terrifying. Even the utmost gentleness always has this terrifying quality: there is nothing more extreme.

x³ A 784   *n.d.*, 1851

« 1483 *Irenæus*

The reciprocal relationship between law and gospel.

They are alike:
> 1. in respect to their authorship—they both originate in God
> 2. in respect to their aim—the upbringing of men
> 3. in respect to their essential content—to obey God, to follow his word, to love him above all and one's neighbor as oneself, to abstain from all evil.

They are different:
> 1. in respect to the range of content—the law gave ceremonial laws; the gospel abrogated them but thereby extended the law
> 2. in respect to the proclaimer—the prophets, Christ
> 3. in respect to their different positions—who should have upbringing—the law is for slaves in order to crack their stubbornness; the gospel is for free men

4. in respect to methods of upbringing—the law from the outside in; the gospel from inside out

5. in respect to the ethical requirement—obedience required by both, but a greater obedience in the gospel

6. in respect to inclusiveness—the law was specified for a single people; the gospel for all.

See Böhringer, *Die Kirche und ihre Zeugen*,[248] I, pt. 1, pp. 239-240.

x⁴ A 134   *n.d.*, 1851

« 1484 *Law—Gospel*

Christianity is gospel——but, but, nevertheless Christ declares that he has not come to abolish the law but to fulfill it, make the law more rigorous, as in the Sermon on the Mount. When this is disregarded, then the gospel and grace are taken in vain.

Then came the Reformation. It is said that the Reformation affirmed "grace" in contrast to law. (As in Ullmann, *Reformation v. der Reformation*, I, xiii: "*die Reformation ist . . . . . Reaction des Christenthums als Evangelium gegen das Christenthum als Gesetz!*"[249] Quoted in Petersen: *Die Idee der Kirche*[250] III, p. 345 n.) Good. But here Luther probably did not take enough care. The norm is: for every higher degree of grace, law must also be made more rigorous in inwardness—otherwise the whole secular mentality rushes forward and takes "grace" in vain. And this is precisely what happened in the Reformation.

x⁴ A 230   *n.d.*, 1851

« 1485 *The Most Dreadful Error in Judgment—*

if someone had chastised himself in all the ascetic practices over a long period of time and had finally reached the point of what might be called a genuinely good deed—and then erroneously judged it, thought it should have merit before God. Alas, the greatest of all transgressors is far closer with his simple "God be merciful to me, a sinner."

What Luther[251] emphasizes is very true, that the more one does his best to do good works with the idea of becoming saved, all the more anxious does he become, and his life becomes sheer self-torment. Far happier is the sinner who sighs briefly and to the point, "God be merciful to me, a sinner."

Yet it must also be remembered that this can easily lead to wanting to live out one's life in worldliness out of fear of being ensnared in the traps of meritoriousness and self-tormenting if one undertook something which would not be to one's worldly advantage, etc.

x^4 A 419   n.d., 1851

« 1486 "Imitation"—Mildness

Because as children we have become pampered and spoiled in Christianity—it is almost impossible to bring up a child in Christianity, for neither the conception of sin nor imitation [Efterfølgelse] can be properly introduced to a child—the slightest rigor seems to be almost presumptuous.

O, how men have been weakened by this doctrine of grace!

Luther says that this whole doctrine is to lead to the battle of the anguished conscience. Have you seen anyone among us whom you could imagine to have the Christian presuppositions? I have not seen one. But everything is done by "grace"; the preachers speculate in grace. Actually they regard grace as an enormous endowment which they possess and let us men pay for at high prices.

Of course, if Christianity is to be presented according to the New Testament, it will be very difficult to introduce money as a middle term for the preaching. But "grace" in the sense of indulgence (and as soon as "imitation" is taken away "grace" is essentially indulgence) lends itself perfectly to money transactions.

x^4 A 618   n.d., 1852

« 1487 "If You Would Be Perfect, Go, Sell What You Possess"

In the first place, Christ does not speak as a pastor preaches nowadays. He does not say: You presumptuous one, what detestable presumption for you to consider wanting to be perfect, etc.! No, Christ speaks very directly, as if he thought wanting to be perfect was something good about the young man. Yes, in the New Testament it says that Christ thought well of him, because there really was in him a stirring in the direction of wanting to be perfect.

How frightfully demoralized we have become through the way in which we apply "grace." This is how the preaching really sounds: To want to strive after perfection is presumption, detestable presumption. Nothing shocks God as this does. There is nothing he so assuredly consigns to hell. No, stay in your filth and effeminacy—and then "grace."

Frightful! No, the relationship should be like this: Your striving is to be as rigorous as possible, and then it is nevertheless by "grace" that you are saved. Notice that it is not those of us in filth who are to say this about the one striving in this way (something we are mighty quick to do in order to reassure ourselves that it is nevertheless really grace, so that we can just as well stay in filth): no, but the one who is striving is to say this himself. It is also true that the longer one strives the higher he will discover the task to be—so it is "grace" after all.

What frightful demoralization "grace" has helped bring about! How in the world shall a human being get courage and desire to strive when from childhood on he is brought up in and preached full of this—that to want to be perfect is presumption, something which God and Christ would never lend a hand to, since in their eyes just this is detestable presumption, and you can be sure that every suffering along this path is punishment from God.

A righteous God: and in the New Testament the matter is turned in such a way that imitation [Efterfølgelse] is precisely what is required, and God is so far from being opposed to it that, on the contrary, a Spirit (who also can very well become necessary) is promised who helps one along on this path.

But when one from childhood up is demoralized by the mildness which the whole environment preaches, what is to come of it! How is a Chinese woman whose feet are unnaturally stunted from infancy ever going to walk if she is incessantly confronted by the idea that to want proper feet and to want to walk is presumption.

What demoralization! Just as the physician bungles a case to make himself indispensable, so the pastors demoralize men—to make themselves indispensable.

x^4 A 619   *n.d., 1852*

« 1488 *"Grace"—"To Reveal the Thoughts*
       of Many Hearts"

It was said of Christ that he would reveal the thoughts of many hearts,[252] and this he did.

But, actually, this is the point in all Christianity, the point Christianity continually makes manifest.

How? Simply by proclaiming "grace," that it is grace. He who proclaims the law forces men into something; at least they try to hide themselves when faced with the law. But "grace," the fact that it is grace, makes them completely unconstrained. Face to face with "grace" a person really learns to know what lies deepest in a man.

Tell a child to do something—this does not mean the child does it;

but you do not really get to know the child's nature. No, but say: "You are free, you may do what you want to"—then you find out what lies deepest in the child.

You can say: "It is grace"—and then by glad and grateful striving (because it was grace) endure more than someone who shivers and shakes before the law, while you still continually say: It is grace. If this is true, then gratitude is harbored deep in the ground of your soul. You can also shirk everything, constantly referring to the fact that it is all grace—yet, even if you shirked everything, one thing you cannot get away from— that it becomes manifest that you harbor this within you.

A rigorous proclamation of the law can result in demoralization, but the most dangerous demoralization is and continues to be the demoralization brought about by the use of grace.

x⁵ A 7   n.d., 1852

« 1489 *Proclamation—Proclamation*

To proclaim Christianity in such a way that the proclaimer himself does not need Christianity—yes, only once has Christianity truly been preached thus, by Christ himself, who was Christianity, who won grace.

Every other proclamation must be by someone who personally needs Christianity, and consequently this will also sound through his proclamation.

Does this then mean that he is to coddle himself, since in his proclamation, "I rely on grace," he also says: By the help of grace I enjoy life and exempt myself from suffering because (in order to protect himself properly, he perhaps would say) it certainly is not I who should save the world or win grace—I grasp it, make use of it.

Perhaps he does make very good use of grace and presents the matter all wrong.

Is it Christianity's intention to eliminate striving by means of grace? No, Christianity simply wants to have the law fulfilled, if possible, by means of grace.

To that end Christianity acts like this. When this and this are required of a man, but in such a way that whether or not he does it decides his eternal salvation, he must sink down in despair at once, suffocate in despair, just as if he had lost his breath. That this is decisive for his soul's salvation puts too dreadfully great a pressure on him—this is why he cannot. Christianity thinks somewhat along these lines: It is anxiety which makes him unable to do it; it is anxiety which makes him totally incapable of doing it—take the anxiety away, and then you will see that he can do it all right. The situation is like that of a child who has been made so anxious he cannot do anything—the wiser teacher will perhaps say: It is anxiety which makes him incapable, take that away and you will see that he can do it, all right, at least a good share of it.

It is the same with Christianity and grace. Take away this anxiety for the salvation of his soul—this is what makes him incapable. This is removed by grace—you are saved by grace, by grace through faith. Take this anxiety away, and you will see that he can do it, all right.

Christianity's intention is: now as never before under the law we shall see what a man can achieve.

But instead of this we have used "grace" to prevent acting. Instead of "grace" as the basis of courage and mobility for action it is applied in such a way that it even causes an unnatural obstruction; it is applied in such a way that by means of grace one sinks deeper and deeper into softness and effeminacy in order to require continually more and more grace. We continually run across this kind of thing: Since we are all saved by grace anyway, why should I exert myself; anything could happen if I were promptly to begin making an effort, and I would be responsible for this myself—for I can keep clear of any kind of effort and say it is grace.

Christianity's intention is that precisely this should give a man the courage and the desire to exert himself, that whatever happens to him at least this ought not happen to him—that, however badly things turn out, he loses his eternal salvation—because for this there is grace. He can then venture all the more intrepidly. We men, however, do it thus: Even the least little venture is foolish—since there is grace anyway.

$x^5 \, A \, 8$ *n.d.*, 1852

« 1490 *It Is All Grace*

But this does not mean that one is to sneak out of self-denial, no, no. But only that it is not under penalty, which is what makes self-denial so hard and agitates the mind. On the other hand, it is moving, as if Christ said to a person: Everything is given you by grace—now look at me, at my sufferings—should that not move you and stir you to want to deny yourself?

I remember from my childhood and youth something apropos of this which often comes to mind as having been helpful to me. I got so very tired of copying father's letters, and he merely said to me: Well, well, I shall do it myself then. At once I was willing. Ah, if he had scolded, alas, then there would have been a quarrel, but this was moving. In the same way much self-denial may fall heavily on a man and embitter him if it is under penalty, but the look of the suffering Savior and his words: Everything is given to you; it is pure grace; now look at me and my suffering which acquired this grace—yes, this is moving!

x⁵ A 54   *n.d.*, 1852

« 1491 *My Grace Is Sufficient for You*[253]

In one way or another these words are usually understood as follows: the apostle has begged to be exempted from a suffering, a torment, but the answer comes: My grace is sufficient for you, for my power is made perfect in weakness.

In this case I do not quite understand how the reply "My grace is sufficient for you," is suitable. In this case the reply should rather be: Be assured of my grace; do not let this suffering disturb you as if it were a disgrace.

I have wondered if the apostle's words are not to be understood differently, namely: when a person strives to the uttermost to be only an instrument for God and to the point where in self-denial he has no will of his own and is wholly in God's hand and at his disposition, to the point where he actually is only an instrument, the individual perhaps runs up against a stone wall, something he cannot succeed in conquering unconditionally—and so it was even with the great apostle. This has grieved him inexpressibly; to him it was like infidelity toward God, lack of love. He had prayed to God that he might succeed in conquering this also, perhaps a triviality in itself, but something which had become very important to him just because of this struggle—and then the answer came: My grace is sufficient for you; my power is made perfect in weakness—that is, it would even be dangerous for you if you completely and unconditionally succeeded in being an unconditioned instrument, for it might tempt you to arrogance—your limitation is simply an aid to humility, but do not be disheartened—"My grace is sufficient for you." Your limitation is to keep you from being tempted to claim merit before me; my grace is sufficient for you and my power is made perfect in weakness; your weakness will help make it clear to you that it is my power and not yours.

x⁵ A 56   *n.d.*, 1852

« 1492 *"Grace"*

The Christian requirement is infinite. It must be proclaimed. With respect to grace—which also must be proclaimed—each person must personally turn to God and in his conscience come to an understanding with him as to how and why he relies on grace.

But I do not have the right to say to another person whose life does not express the requirement: Set your mind at rest with grace. No, no, grace is God's majestic right; only God has the right to say to the individual—"There is grace." I have to proclaim that there is grace, infinite grace, but I dare not decide for another man where he dares to apply grace in such a way that it diminishes the striving or sets his mind at ease in this respect. As far as someone who is dying is concerned, it is something else; for him there is essentially no question of any striving.

But this is the frightful deception which permeates all Christendom —that human authority has appropriated "grace" and now makes a business of it, at times sells it for money, then again wins the amiability and esteem of men by confirming them in cheerful enjoyment of life—for, after all, there is grace.

No, no! This is the Christian rigorousness which must not be altered —where grace is concerned, each man must address himself to God, be alone with him, and no man should have the audacity to want to be an intermediate authority between God and another man.

This is why the infinite requirement must be proclaimed—to thrust men, each one individually, to God—for there (indeed, this is how the proclamation reads), there is grace, but no man has the right to say to another: Be lenient with yourself, for after all there is grace.

To repeat, grace has been regarded in Christendom as an enormous deposit, a kind of hereditary trust we men can dispose of together. We forget that God is not dead—he lives, and he reserves the right to be the only one who has grace at his disposal. Therefore each individual has to turn to him alone. And every Christian proclamation has to direct the individual to him, "for there is grace, infinite grace."

x^5 A 64   n.d., 1853

« 1493 *An Immediate God-Relationship; Grace in First Place or Beforehand; the Objective*

We ordinary human beings do not have a direct or spontaneous God-relationship; therefore are not able unconditionally to express the unconditional, and we always need grace beforehand, because even the most sincere beginning is always imperfect compared to the demand of the ideal—consequently it is like a new sin.

Thus grace in first place.

But then once more the need for the objective is felt still more deeply. And this is offered in the sacraments, in the word, yet not magically.

In margin: See next page [i.e., x⁵ A 103]: grace in first place.

x⁵ A 101   *n.d.*, 1853

« 1494 *Grace in First Place*

This is true even of the objective, the sacraments and the Word.

Consider the Lord's Supper. When I think of going to Communion, I confess that up to now I have not succeeded in going worthily to Communion. This I repent, grace is offered to me, this is grace in second place, grace afterwards, related to the past.

But now I am going to Communion again—am I worthy now? Do I dare say now that I am worthy? This might very well be required of me in gratitude for the grace related to the past.

You see, there it is! The sacrament promises me grace and strengthens me in grace, but I must have grace in order to dare use the sacrament. It cannot be otherwise, unless I have a direct or immediate relationship to God so that in immediacy he says to me: Today at four o'clock you shall go to Communion—for then I have no responsibility.

As it is with the Lord's Supper, so it is with Baptism, assuming we have not been baptized as children—when do I dare say that now I am worthy to accept Baptism, which will assure me of grace in relation to the past. You see, this is why in earlier times they postponed Baptism as long as possible. Tertullian[254] advises against hastening Baptism. But as early as Basil, for example, early Baptism is encouraged, the sooner the better.

Generally in earliest times all interpretation of Christianity was marked by imitation [*Efterfølgelsen*], but it also rested in the naïveté that an ordinary man as such and as a matter of course can have the God-man as prototype [*Forbillede*]. They postponed Baptism as long as possible. They supposed that Baptism atoned only for the past, that later sins had to be atoned by good deeds, that martyrdom insured the forgiveness of sins even better than Baptism.

x⁵ A 103   *n.d.*, 1853

« 1495

It is one thing that all who are saved are saved by grace, but does it follow from this that all are saved?

x⁵ A 108   *n.d.*, 1853

« 1496 *Elemental Balderdash*

With the help of "grace" the point has now been reached, especially within Protestantism, of smuggling Christianity completely out of everything. We are all saved by grace—the matter is decided once for all—and thereupon we arrange our lives according to the best paganism.

The intention of Christianity was to introduce "grace" into life in order to transform all life.

x⁵ A 109   *n.d.*, 1853

« 1497 *"Grace"*

We are all saved by grace. Fine! But even though God is so infinitely gracious, O, as infinitely gracious as only divine grace can be—I wonder if there still is not one thing he wants, yes, because of the nature of the case, must require: that a person who shares in grace at least should have some true conception of how great the requirement is?

But it will be easy to show that the official proclamation of Christianity conceals *the part* about how infinitely great the requirement is for being a Christian (the requirement to imitate [*følge efter*] Christ, to forsake the world, to die to the world, and, which follows, to have to suffer for this teaching—the official preaching, however, at best brings in "grace" on a basis of public morality, as if this were approximately the requirement).

But if someone does not have a true conception of the magnitude of the requirement, he cannot have a true conception of the magnitude of grace—he really takes grace in vain. Is he, then, saved by grace? Or must there not always remain one exception, although the sentence reads "All are saved by faith"—the exception of the person who takes grace in vain. If we say that a rich man fed all his people, did he also feed the man who left the food untouched and did not eat?

xI² A 284   *n.d.*, 1853-54

« 1498 *"Grace"*

It is said that a government can hang on for twenty to thirty years by gradually letting up—imagine, then, if the requirement for being a Christian found in the New Testament were put into action, that infinite requirement which infinitely demands everything—one would think that God had thereby made sure there was enough there to ease up on as long as the world should last.

Yet, how long did it take before the requirement was significantly, substantially reduced?

And now we are all Christians in such a way that the only thing we hear anything about is grace, but we hear nothing about what is required, how infinitely much, never once in such a way that we become aware of how infinitely much has been given to us.

Soon the very opposite will be reached, that we regard "grace" as our right, that we turn the entire relationship around, perhaps even pursue our rights right up to God and initiate a lawsuit against him concerning grace.

XI^2 A 285   *n.d.*, 1853-54

« 1499 *"Grace"*

There was once a noble family who possessed great areas of land.

The renters were impoverished—and one of the forefathers of this noble family had not only released them from all past debts but also from payments in the future; yes, he had even sent servants to them to set them at ease by assuring them that the debts and payments had been cancelled.

At the beginning the renters knew very well how much had been cancelled. Later on the servants of the nobleman reminded them of it.

Finally it came to be understood very sketchily—in their lethargy people knew that it had been cancelled, but how much nobody knew and nobody cared about it.

So it had gone from generation to generation. Then a member of that noble family declared: No, this should not be tolerated. Just like my father I will gladly release them from all debts and payments, but this impudence of exploiting one's goodness almost as a right [should not be tolerated].

XI^2 A 286   *n.d.*, 1853-54

« 1500 *Christendom*

Christendom is so far from being a community of Christians that it is actually, as I have shown elsewhere,[255] a falling away from Christianity.

If one looks more closely, Christendom will betray such demoralization that all the other religions will show up better.

Yet this is not altogether inexplicable, for Christendom is demoralized with the help of mildness, grace, promise, God is love, etc. The other religions do not have this intrinsic leniency; they have more of the rigor of the law, and therefore the demoralization is never so deep.

No, demoralization encouraged by mildness is the deepest of all. Let me make a comparison. If a man gets fat and heavy from eating too much—well, this is basically unhealthful obesity. But if he gets fat, pallid fat, on cakes, confections—this is horrible. So it is with the demoralization of Christendom.

Even in hypocrisy there is a difference. To pose and pretend in the face of the law's rigorous demand—this is hypocrisy, but to pose and pretend in the face of grace—this is infinitely more loathsome.

To be insubordinate toward what is hard on me surely is sin; but to make a fool of love is loathsome.

XI^2 A 100   *n.d.*, 1854

« 1501 *Grace* (*Paradox*)

In order to forestall, if possible, the nonsense about grace which has falsified Christianity in "Christendom" and demoralized men, permit me in a few words to show the relationship.

The matter is very simple if one only remembers that "grace," like everything else Christian, is in the sphere of paradox. The falsification of grace, like the falsification of everything else Christian, occurs by dragging grace down into the sphere of the direct or the immediate.

What is meant by the paradox of grace? It means grace with a negative sign, suffering. Grace is negatively recognized by the fact that it brings suffering. The Christian concept of grace is so very elevated because the divine majesty reflects not upon this life but only upon the eternal; therefore when the eternal is introduced into this life, everything gets reversed.

Consequently grace, too. Grace means to be saved from eternal perdition—in God's view, infinite grace.

But in weak moments the relationship appears quite different to a man. What is a weak moment? It is a moment when the eternal is not present to him. And when the eternal is not present to him, the temporal becomes important to him—and when it becomes apparent in time that being a Christian brings, as the New Testament teaches, suffering, which one could avoid if he were not a Christian, the entire relationship is reversed, and grace becomes that which brings suffering, anguish—so far is it from being "grace" directly.

Hold God's conception of eternity, of man's guilt, and of an eternal lostness—then Christianity is pure grace, and this suffering for a few years in this life is infinite, infinite grace. Hold your conception of this life—and grace is anything but grace; it is an affliction, the greatest affliction, since to be a Christian is the most intensive suffering in this life.

Blessed is he who is not offended! See, this is the way it all hangs together: just because everything Christian is in the realm of paradox, the possibility of offense is always infinitely near. This majesty of grace is, in a lower sense, nothing but suffering, affliction—then how infinitely near lies the possibility of offense if one does not prefer Christendom's way out, the way out by changing Christianity into outright nonsense, whereby in a certain sense offense can be avoided, even though it must come, I think, in another sense, if one considers that such nonsense is supposed to be—the divine. This means that in a deeper sense the sign of the "possibility of offense" is missing, so that it must be said of this non-sense-Christianity that it cannot possibly be the divine since there is nothing to be offended by.

XI² A 182   *n.d.*, 1854

« 1502 *The Blessedness of Heaven*

Once it was understood to be a task, an effort scarcely possible for us to form an idea of nowadays.

Then the matter was turned in this way: No, it is sheer grace, no effort can seize hold of it, it is sheer grace—but then one's life is also sheer gratitude on a scale scarcely possible for us to form an idea of nowadays.

Now we have achieved the truly *profound* expression for grace: grace to such a degree—to such a degree that it is not worth thinking about.

At one time a man sold everything in order to buy the blessedness of heaven from heaven's majesty: nowadays we get it gratis the way we get a pretty box or a decorated sack when we make a purchase. And not only that, it has been made a crime of high treason to want to do the least thing, even merely to think about salvation—it is indeed an insult to the majesty since he himself desires to give it gratis to such a degree, just as it would be an insult to the merchant to want to pay for what he gives gratis. God wants grace to be gratis to such a degree that he does not even want to be thanked for it. No, to repeat, the blessedness of heaven is obtained not so much as a gift—but as the sack the sugar or coffee come in.

XI² A 226   *n.d.*, 1854

« 1503

A human being is saved by grace alone—are all of us therefore saved? Are these one and the same?

XI² A 342   *n.d.*, 1854

« 1504 *Is It the Law That I Proclaim?*
Do I, Myself in Anxiety, Perhaps Want
To Bring Anxiety upon Others?

In truth, no. See for yourself!

Imagine a government which from generation to generation cancelled a debt of 100,000 dollars which each individual inhabitant of the state owed, each individual—well, we can imagine it!

It went on like this from generation to generation—unchanged. But although this was unchanged, a change nevertheless took place. From generation to generation people grew more and more accustomed to this unchanged arrangement, so that finally—well, they did not deny that a debt had been cancelled—it made no greater impression upon them than if it had been four shillings which had been cancelled. What, then, if someone said: No, it should not be like this. In fairness to our benefactor it ought to become clear how great the debt is—how great his benefaction. And it is to the recipient's interest to become properly aware of the greatness of the debt—and of the benefaction. It is in the recipient's interest, so that his gratitude might really be proportionate to the gift.

If someone did that, would this be an attempt to make himself and others anxious about how they could ever possibly repay this debt? No, this would not be what he is doing.

From a Christian point of view, it is the same with "grace." In fairness to God it ought to become clear how great the guilt is—but then it must first be made clear how great the requirement is. And it is to man's interest that this happen, so that his gratitude in no way has to be proportionate to the infinite greatness of merciful love [but to the greatness of the guilt forgiven by that infinite merciful love].

Tell me, is this severe, anxiety-creating? Would it not rather have been a sin against you not to make you aware, so that you seemed to be a much more ungrateful person than you are? In resentment you might sometime cry woe unto me and every one who could have and should have made you aware but instead contributed to your remaining what in your innermost heart you are not—an ingrate—for this you are not.

XI² A 367   *n.d.*, 1854-55

GRATITUDE

« 1505

Often I have wondered when I felt inclined to thank God by suggesting that however wretched and miserable things are, there is still something good (for example, that I can really sleep at night, etc.)—is this true gratitude, or is it cowardice, fear that it will be taken away in the next moment and that I shall despair?

II A 667   n.d., 1837

« 1506 *Give God the Glory*

This sounds humiliating to you to whom it has been granted to do great things, you who are tempted to take the glory for yourself (Christ did not take it—did not look upon it as plunder).[256]

To you of humble fate it sounds consoling, uplifting. Let not your soul be bowed down; do not damage your soul; give God the glory. And if it is really a good which you have received, you surely know that it comes from God: all good gifts, all perfect gifts are from above.

III A 140   n.d., 1841

« 1507

And when everything seems to storm in upon us, when everything totters, when all depends on bending without breaking, he who from a full heart can say: All God's gifts are good when they are received with gratitude[257]—in this gratitude and by this gratitude he has overcome the world.

III A 143   n.d., 1841

« 1508

. . . . . and discover that it is a mystery deeper than any thought which has ever arisen within a man's heart,[258] that God is one who hates all ceremonies, that one dares without further ado (*ex tempore*) to speak with him without an appointment etc. in the joy of life, during sorrow-filled nights; that one always has occasion to thank him, and that when one forgets this, he is loving enough to remind one of it. I meditate upon

how proportionately God shares with man, for it must be far more difficult for him to love a human being in such a way that he is not crushed
by God's love, far more difficult for him to make himself so small that a
human being really can love him.[259]

And when one does not have a single human being who understands
him, then he is willing to listen and he can remember far better than any
man, even better than one can himself. And when one's thoughts are so
confused that one does not know whether he is coming or going, God
has not forgotten even the slightest thing one has prayed him to remember; and if it were not so, everything would be a matter of indifference,
whether one himself could remember it or not.[260]

III A 240   n.d., 1842

« 1509

If one is to have an actual relationship to God—that is, have something to do with him every day (not just on New Year's Day or on one's
wedding day or baptism day)—he quickly learns that he must see his
way to understanding everything God does as good or learn always to give
thanks. Otherwise there appears all this childish drivel about thanking
God because this is good or this and that were so wonderful and the next
moment about sighing and praying for patience because this or that is
so bad. It is impossible to have an actual relationship to God and still
remain in one's merely human and earthly conception of good and evil,
pleasant and unpleasant.

VIII¹ A 253   n.d., 1847

« 1510

There is something odd about the idea that thanking God for benefits (i.e., earthly and temporal advantages and good luck, etc.) adequately constitutes Christianity. In this way, Christianity is easily transformed into heightened life-enjoyment (*eudæmonism*). The pagan
became anxious [*angst*] when especially good luck came his way, for he
had a certain distrust of the gods.[261] But there is also something else
involved, because his anxiety, truly understood, expressed what follows
from attaching oneself closely to worldly things. But in Christianity!
We hanker after and chase after earthly goods and then—in order to rid
ourselves of anxiety—thank God. Aha! This is precisely the way in which
such a Christendom becomes even more secular-minded than paganism.
Thanking God for good days should first and foremost mean undertaking to examine oneself, how one clings to such things; it should

mean that one learns to think lightly of all such things. But, instead, we clutch even more tightly and then thank God—in order to keep on possessing these things with complete complacency and security. Alas, how we cheat ourselves out of Christianity!

VIII¹ A 333   n.d., 1847

« 1511

Let us talk something like this. Imagine that you possess the goods of every possible good fortune and along with them the taste and genius to utilize them, an inventiveness in enjoyment—yes, as if your whole life were arranged in poetic enchantment; and everyone who came from distant lands* to visit you—all, all unanimously admired your mind and spirit and were speechless with wonder over your success. What would you lack? Perhaps you are thinking I will say: You lack someone with whom to share your happiness. By no means, this is granted to you as well, for the wish is in my hands, indulgent in everything. Consequently you have a beloved, the epitome of charm, lovely as that rose of Sharon in the Song of Solomon, even more lovely, more blushing than eastern voluptuousness, more coy than northern femininity; she is more diverting than Scheherazade (in A Thousand and One Nights) and for more than a thousand and one nights. What do you lack now? You are perhaps thinking that I will say that everything is still so insecure, that luck often changes, that you lack the assurance of its continuation. By no means; this is granted to you too. What then do you lack? Perhaps you are thinking I will say: Death is so uncertain—no, always so certain; this is disturbing. By no means; this is granted to you, too. Seventy years are absolutely assured to you—what now do you lack?

You lack having God and his governance to wonder over, because, after all, you are the architect of your own fortune, you are your own providence.

Look, there was one window lacking in that covetous young man's palace.²⁶² The view from all the others was enchanting—but he correctly understood that he could not complete this window (let us imagine it thus)—and the view from this window was to God, to God's providence. O, is it not true that if we turn the whole thing around, you are still better off: instead of that enormous palace with the twenty-three win-

In margin:
* Travelling even from the lands closest to the borders of the realms of phantasy.

dows you nevertheless have nothing less than a palace; you have a small room with only one window and even that is not altogether completed —but it is though this window that you see out to God.

VIII[1] A 678   n.d., 1848

« 1512

After all, the pagans were far more sensitive to what is religiously appropriate in everyday life than we Protestants, especially. Consider merely how at their meals, festivities, and almost everywhere they thought of the gods *first of all*.

X[1] A 504   n.d., 1849

« 1513

That the positive is higher than the superlative, unity higher than number, and simplicity higher than multiplicity is seen in this illustration. Anyone would feel it unseemly to say in expressing gratitude to God: A thousand thanks, many, many thanks. One simply says (and this is precisely the pathos): Thank you, God.

X[1] A 639   n.d., 1849

« 1514 *The Ten Lepers*

This Gospel,[263] or, more correctly, the manner in which this text is usually preached, shows again how little we actually conceive of Christianity as something present, how little we are aware of the situation.

Much is said in a general way about ingratitude; what is forgotten is the particular point that by thanking Christ the lepers would lay themselves open to suffering insult for his sake; we forget that the priests (to whom, according to Christ's word, the lepers addressed themselves) naturally would have done everything in order in God's name to prevent them from being grateful to Christ.

On the whole I could almost be tempted to regard it as a test Christ sets before them, for in saying: Go to the priests and show yourselves to them, he certainly knew that the priests would say everything to prevent them from thanking Christ, make it into a crime against God, a blasphemy.

X[2] A 206   n.d., 1849

« 1515 *Human Ingratitude*

Look just once at the sea and the clouds and the sea gull—strain every nerve to hold this picture, for perhaps it is the first and last time you might have anything to remember.

But who sees in this way. Yet suppose it became the first and last time —and suppose you forgot it and became blind—well, the God who has created all this, him you can abundantly see.

Ah, how ungrateful we men are!

x^3 A 627   *n.d.*, 1850

« 1516 *Savonarola*

says someplace that he must remind them about what he had said so often: A great benevolence can be repaid only by great ingratitude. (*In margin:* see Rudelbach, *Savonarola,*[264] p. 208).

Excellent! For a benevolence which obtains for me another kind of benevolence, a direct payment, is certainly *eo ipso* not such a great benevolence. Suppose it to be a great benevolence—but it is rewarded with much gratitude—it becomes somewhat less. No, when it is rewarded with ingratitude, then only is it altogether a benevolence; if it is rewarded with much ingratitude, then it is quite truly a great benevolence. Payment I have, then, at any rate. For from the recipient's great ingratitude I have the payment that my great benevolence becomes in truth a great benevolence.

x^4 A 269   *n.d.*, 1851

« 1517 *Savonarola*

Bernard says: Ingratitude dries up the springs of compassion, but Savonarola adds: Gratitude opens them.

See Rudelbach, *Savonarola,*[265] p. 372 and p. 373.

x^4 A 278   *n.d.*, 1851

« 1518 *Christian Gratitude toward Christ*

Christ has desired only one kind of gratitude: from the individual, and as practically as possible in the form of imitation [*Efterfølgelse*].

Instead of this, humanity has arranged the matter in quite another way: a people, a state, a country, the race, in short, a chorus among whom there is not one single person in the character of imitation—but then, to make up for it, there are so many more: a chorus which thanks Christ for its salvation.

Here it is again, always the substitute: statistics, the generation, an abstraction.

This shows again that Christianity does not exist [*er ikke til*], for this kind of gratitude is either pagan or Jewish—not Christian. Christ came into the world specifically to save—out of statistics, out of the generation, out of abstractions.

xi¹ A 176   n.d., 1854

« 1519 *Thanking God for the Good Days*

In Christendom this is what we call Christianity, this is what we are instructed in from childhood and are prompted and coddled to call Christianity: thanking God for the good days, for joy and the enjoyment of life.

But right here and now let us measure the distance from what is true Christianity.

Whether this thanking God for the good days is true Christianity depends specifically on the extent to which the good days and the enjoyment of life for which thanks are given have a genuinely Christian context. But now if Christianity's thought is that this existence [*Tilværelse*] is an institution for punishment, if it is God's thought that this life is the suffering of punishment, something he has had proclaimed—and then we human beings, because God does not constrain us (on the contrary, he wants to see whether of our own free will we shall draw near to his thought), make use of this to set everything in motion to get joy and pleasure out of this life—then to thank God for this is so far removed from being piety that it really is making a fool of him.

Think of a penal institution where to a certain degree prisoners have the power to plan their lives the way they want to—but they recognize that the authority's idea is that their life should be the suffering of punishment: if then they do everything to make life for themselves very enjoyable, cozy, and pleasant—and then are ready to thank the authority for the good days they have—this would be making a fool of the authority, for it would be just the opposite of his intention.

xi² A 224   n.d., 1854

« 1520 *The Witness to the Truth*

And so when a witness to the truth dies, he says to God: Thank you, thank you, O infinite love, for all the sufferings. And God says in return: Thank you, my friend, thank you for the use I have had of you.

xi² A 245   n.d., 1854

GREEKS

« 1521

The Greeks knew how to fit even Echo (who, seen from a romantic viewpoint, is highly parodical, and therefore to be taken humorously) into their harmonious view of life, and it was a friendly nymph.

II A 134   July 20, 1837

« 1522

The Greeks lacked a sense of miracle, just as in their art they did not portray their ideals in *preternatural magnitude.*

II A 298   November 22, 1838

« 1523

The Greeks had far purer intervals in their music, and therefore their tones were more full and exuberant—but they were unable to die and in their dying to lose themselves in heaven.

II A 716   *n.d.* 1838

« 1524

It is very significant that the Greeks called a lunatic θεοβλαβής,[266] for insanity surely has its root in the wrath of the gods, who deprive one of the opportunity to improve himself and utilize his time.

II A 744   *n.d.,* 1838

« 1525

There has been much talk about the sadness implicit in the Greek's conception of the powerless, bloodless bodies of the dead in the underworld—but how much happier are the prospects in our age; the two are scarcely to be compared when one considers that a man's whole spiritual movement in death is contracted in a reduction to one single immortal paragraph.

II A 555   September 6, 1839

GUILT

« 1526

An example of dialectic in regard to guilt and innocence.

An old sensualist, yet still witty and ironical (a diplomat), guides some young girls into an exhibition of Greek sculpture. There are some young men in the company. One of the young girls, the most innocent of them all, blushes, not because she is disturbed, but because there is something in the old scoundrel's countenance which wounds her modesty. But this blush does not escape his notice; in his face she reads his thoughts —she is mortified; she cannot speak to anyone about it, and she becomes melancholy.[268]

IV A 121   *n.d.*, 1843

« 1527

. . . . . In paganism one saw the furies[269] pursue the guilty, saw their hideous forms—but the gnawing of remorse cannot be seen; it is hidden, a hidden pregnancy fathered by a bad conscience.

VI A 49   *n.d.*, 1845

« 1528

When someone is eager to enter a complaint against another man before God, to initiate a case in God's court, things go with him as with a Copenhagen pickpocket. In collusion with another, he had carried out a big robbery and in the distribution had received among other things three one-hundred-dollar bills. He took one of them to a receiver of stolen goods to get it changed. The receiver took the bill, went into another room—as if to change it. Thereupon he came out again, said "Goodbye," and acted as if nothing else were involved. The event took place, with all judicial caution, just between the two, and therefore the receiver was quite safe. Presumably the pickpocket himself perceived this. In the meantime, however, he became so angry over the affair, over this deceitfulness, that he left and took the case to the police. Of course the diligent, energetic police did everything possible to help the innocent man get his rights, or the one hundred dollars, but they did not regard the case one-sidedly but from a higher point of view, and therefore they quite rightly asked the victim where he himself had obtained the hundred dollars. Alas, the wretched dupe, because of the same one-hundred-dollar bill, it all ended by his being arrested to boot.[270]

VII^1 A 87   *n.d.*, 1846

« 1529

How far we human beings still are from the spirituality which really and truly grieves alone over its sin and alone in the relationship to God. How rare is even a person who has the courage to be completely open to another human being with respect to every secret guilt.

x^2 A 140   *n.d.*, 1849

« 1530 *That "Original Sin" is "Guilt"*

is the real paradox.[271] How paradoxical is best seen as follows. The paradox is formed by a composite of qualitatively heterogeneous categories. To "inherit" is a category of nature. "Guilt" is an ethical category of spirit. How can it ever occur to anyone to put these two together, the understanding says—to say that something is inherited which by its very concept cannot be inherited.

It must be believed. The paradox in Christian truth always involves the truth as before God. A superhuman goal and standard are used— and with regard to them there is only one relationship possible—that of faith.

x^2 A 481   *n.d.*, 1850

« 1531

In margin: Julius Müller. Richard Rothe. Dorner. Part II of J. Müller's *Lære om Synden*, pp. 557 ff.[272]

Here we see the confusion expressed in the usual way. R. Rothe in his *Ethics* attacks Julius Müller and shows the error to be J. M.'s too strong an emphasis on the consciousness of guilt; and then he says: "The proper loathing of evil depends on the objective quality of the same [evil], not on man's subjective relationship to it. The only proper hatred of evil is that which hates and denounces it *because it is evil*, that is, because it is contrary to God and our essence, and only *therefore*—not because it deserves [to be hated] from our side." Can a more immoral pronouncement be imagined! And this is scholarship! Here we see the result of all this objectivity with respect to the doctrine of sin as well, where "earnestness" is precisely the subjective, that I am a sinner. J. M. correctly repudiates it, shows that sin thereby actually becomes *Uebel*, suffering, and the like. But J. Müller does not make it qualitatively ethical enough.

The second customary example of confusion is Dorner. He upbraids J. M. for stressing too much the individual personality and overlooking the concept of race. Well, thanks—precisely that is the demoralization of the age.

J. Müller is an able man, but he is no great ethicist; he lacks Socratic powers and that kind of training. He is essentially an antiquary; he has not accomplished the $\mu\epsilon\tau\acute{\alpha}\beta\alpha\sigma\iota\varsigma$ $\epsilon\grave{\iota}\varsigma$ $\mathring{\alpha}\lambda\lambda o$ $\gamma\acute{\epsilon}\nu o\varsigma$[273] to an existential thinker.

Yet in the same portion I see a satisfactory observation by Dorner: "It is first of all in the presence of Christ that a man actually confronts the most profound decision; all earlier sins are provisional and in the deepest sense do not decide a man's total worth." Here we have the truth that properly the option-situation in the presence of Christ is qualitatively calculated to make a man an individual. It is the genuine conversion of the mass into individuals; it is the decision of eternity, and eternity will come to the aid of memory in this respect. (Incidentally, Anti-Climacus in *Sickness unto Death* sheds some light on this.) But Dorner is wrong in not regarding man as originally structured or intended to be the single individual, so that he has become mass-man through a qualitative decision.

The relationships are: first, the foundation for being the single individual—and through guilt becoming spirit-less—that is, mass, along in the mass. But then comes "salvation," that is, the second time, the choice of Christ.

But Dorner sees the atonement and salvation as actually the first beginning instead of—as is implicit in the concept of Salvation—the second time. Strictly speaking, can I be "saved" by an "atoner" out of a situation, no matter how disastrous, into which I have not by my own guilt plunged myself? According to Dorner Christ does not become "the second time" but "the first time"; thus the whole past falls away as if it were something like a dust-cover which is not bound to the book, or a careless draft on inferior paper compared to the document on bond paper.

This makes the matter far too easy. The sharpening of the choice-decision with respect to Christ comes precisely from its being "the second time." If one takes Dorner's position, he could be tempted to assume that Christ came once again into this life—as Savior in a stricter sense.

The untenability of Dorner's thinking shows itself in still another way. For if it is true that all prior sins are merely something provisional in the sense of being insignificant, something which cannot as such be an object of God's wrath, that prior to Christ the individual is actually hidden in the mass and merely participates in this universal guilt, which is not properly guilt anyway since the individual is not really guilty (consequently we arrive at a negative result rather than the positive one that every individual in the race is guilty as well)—if this is so, why in the world did Christ come into the world? If guilt was no greater than that, he was not necessary. In such a case Christ comes to the world as proclaimer of the law and as demand.

This no doubt is inconsistent with something else in Dorner, that he most likely assumes that Christ really came into the world to save the race, to make satisfaction for the race. But this again is something extremely unclear: a race which has guilt—a race in which each individual has no guilt.

The truth, as I pointed out earlier, is that man was structured and intended to be the single individual; through guilt he became the mass. Now comes Salvation; but Salvation—that is, the fact that it is "the second time" also sharpens the relationship, and therefore the choice-decision in the presence of Christ is even more qualitatively intensified, and if the decision is to reject Christ, the sin and guilt are even more qualitatively intensified.

X^2 A 500   *n.d.*, 1850

« 1532 *Unhappiness—Guilt*

Human sympathy defends itself against the unhappy man by explaining his unhappiness as guilt: thus one is rid of him.

And all the time we are all of us Christians.

X^3 A 284   *n.d.*, 1850

« 1533 *The Impossibility of Meritoriousness*

Suppose that someone in the consciousness of his guilt genuinely desired to make something right again.

Imagine now that he succeeds to an amazing degree—what then? Then he is in the situation of having to thank God again and again for being successful, in the situation perhaps of having assumed new guilt for not being genuinely grateful to God, by imagining sometimes, perhaps, that what he has done could merit a little consideration in return.

But what is the basis of this meritoriousness? No, it is an impossibility. If meritoriousness appears, then it is by way of a guilt, that in relationship to God the man forgets, as they say, to whom he is talking, has the audacity to talk with God as we human beings might stand and talk with one another; for in our relationship meritoriousness is not excluded.

x^3 A 638   *n.d.*, 1850

« 1534 *Repentance*

Dismay over guilt and sin is probably not very strong at first. On the contrary, only after a long time has passed and there has been progress in the good—when such a person perhaps accidentally comes to hear or read how another man guilty of the same thing has been lost—then dismay awakens. In the very first moments of guilt, sin has the power of self-preservation in a man, and in a certain sense this gives palpable powers, the powers of despair—for not wanting to dwell on the guilt.

x^3 A 719   *n.d.*, 1851

« 1535 *Forgetfulness*

When, for example, a hired girl has broken something, the first thing she does is to see to it that the master does not find out about it right away. After a time—perhaps even a long time—she says: Well, that was a long time ago—and it seems to her as if it were nothing at all.

So it is with most men, great and small. This is light-mindedness.

Melancholy is just the opposite—the longer the elapsed time, the more dreadful the guilt seems.

x^3 A 775   *n.d.*, 1851

« 1536 *The Book of Job*

The significance of this book is really to show the cruelty which we men commit by interpreting being unhappy as guilt, as crime. This is essentially human selfishness, which desires to avoid the earnest and disturbing impression of suffering, of what can happen to a man in this life —therefore in order to protect ourselves against this we explain suffering as guilt: It is his own fault. O, human cruelty!

Job is concerned with proving himself right, in a certain sense also in relation to God, but above all in relation to his friends, who instead of consoling him torment him with the thesis that he suffers because of guilt.

x^4 A 396   *n.d.*, 1851

« 1537 *Human Righteousness*

The most profound satire on the human race is its notion of what is right and of its righteousness. Practically to assume that stealing is the one and only crime—O, how you deceive yourselves; O world, how avaricious you are, etc.

XI^2 A 4   *n.d.*, 1854

« 1538

Addition to 1537 (XI^2 A 4), in margin:

Abraham à St. Clara declares somewhere that he has often pondered who is more guilty—the one who gossips or the one who listens to it. One could similarly be tempted to ask: Who is a greater sinner—a thief or the person who literally looks upon stealing as the only kind of sin.

XI^2 A 5   *n.d.*

HAMANN

« 1539

With respect to a Christian's views of paganism see Hamann,[274] I, pp. 406, 418 and 419, especially p. 419: "*Nein—wenn Gott selbst mit ihm redete, so ist er genöthigt das Machtwort zum voraus zu senden und es in Erfüllung gehen zu lassen—: Wache auf, der Du schläfst.*"[275] On page 406 one sees the complete misunderstanding of a Christian and non-Christian in Hamann's answer to an objection by Hume: Well, that's just the way it is.

I A 100　September 10, 1836

« 1540

Hamann[276] *draws a most interesting parallel between the law (Mosaic law) and reason.* He goes after Hume's statement: "*die letzte Frucht Weltweisheit ist die Bemerkung der menschlichen Unwissenheit und Schwacheit*"...... "*Unser Vernunft,*" Hamann goes on to say, "*ist also eben das, was Paulus das gesetz nennt—und das Gebot der Vernunft ist heilig, gerecht und gut; aber ist sie uns gegeben uns weise zu machen? Eben so wenig als das Gesetz der Juden, sie gerecht zu machen, sondern uns zu überführen von dem Gegentheil, wie unvernünftig unsere Vernunft ist, und dass unsere Irrthümer durch sie zunehmen sollen, wie die Sünde durch das Gesetz zunahm.*"[277]

September 12, 1836

See Hamann, *Schriften* I, p. 405.

Another passage, p. 425. "*Ist es nicht ein alter Einfall, den du oft von mir gehört: incredible sed verum? Lügen und Romane müssen wahrscheinlich sein, Hypothesen und Fabeln; aber nict die Wahrheiten und Grundlehren unseres Glauben.*"[278]

I A 237　n.d.

« 1541 *Something about Hamann*

It is most interesting right now in our time when the recognized achievement of thought holds that the important thing is to live for one's age, and that the abstract immortality which men previously rejoiced in is an illusion—it is most interesting right now to see that there nevertheless is something to living for a posterity[279] and being misunderstood by contemporaries. People move continually between these two extremes. Whereas a few stand isolated in the world, balancing with the agility of a Simeon Stylites,[280] or at most beating their wings like tame geese, admired, or more correctly, stared at by the gaping crowd, despised by the philistines, served by angels; there are on the other hand, enormous numbers who, strictly speaking, are living in the present age, who are to the body politic much like the brass hammers of a clavichord which swing at the slightest touch and cannot possibly maintain a definite impression; they are like certain patients who always get a little attack of every epidemic, a class of people so numerous that they have brought a kind of spiritual ventriloquism into the whole society. One hears a confused sound and scarcely knows whether he himself is speaking or someone else, and is easily tempted to say with Soldin: Rebecca, is it I who am speaking? To live in the age and die in the age in this fashion is not particularly inspiring, and yet there is not much left for the majority of men who have, for better or for worse, pawned their reason for the motto: Conform to the age. Certainly this has not been the idea of the few great men who first expressed this view of life, but the tragedy is that whenever a rational man opens his mouth there immediately are millions ready posthaste—to misunderstand him. Well, God help them. If in military fashion he should hear the password from the last generation (there is a password which God whispered in Adam's ear, which one generation is supposed to deliver to the next and which shall be demanded of them on judgment day)—God help him, it must be frightful!

So much for that misunderstanding, and I also hope that it will advertise that every man who in the proper sense is to fill out a period in history must always begin polemically, precisely because the subsequent stage is not purely and simply the result of the previous one. Was this not the case with Holberg, was it not the case with Goethe, and so on? And must it not be this way? Must it not be, as in a royal procession (the new which is to come), that the bodyguards go first to clear the way? Here, again, so much depends upon how quickly the new follows on the heels of the polemic, and whether it is the truth which must be fought for day after day for years or is merely one insignificant modification or another.

I A 340   *n.d.,* 1836-37

« 1542

Isn't Hamann[281] being extremely ironical when he says somewhere that he would rather hear the truth from the mouth of a Pharisee against his will than from an apostle or an angel?

II A 2   n.d., 1837

« 1543

Hamann and personal life on the whole in its immediate origin from the depths of character are the *hyperbole* of all life.

II A 623   n.d., 1837

« 1544

To what extent is there an element of correspondence between Hamann's deep *personal protest** against the reality-significance [*Realitets-Betydning*] of existence [*Tilværelsens*] and the genuinely serious *doubt* in modern philosophy. —

II A 214   n.d., 1838

« 1545

*In margin of 1544 (*II A 214*):*
* Precisely because there is such a thing, one must say that the God-man idea is not merely an object of cognition but is also an edifying or up-building thought which disperses all dissatisfaction with the world, rectifies every mistake, a thought which steps forth consolingly when even the great in the world seem so petty, when the mind is alarmed over how the insignificant in the world can still get their rights, too.

II A 215   May 20, 1839

« 1546

The inscription on a tile stove in Kold's Tavern in Fredensborg[282] applies to Hamann: *allicit atque terret.*—[283]

II A 442   May 22, 1839

« 1547

Hamann's relationship to his contemporaries—Socrates' to the Sophists (who could say something about *everything*).

III B 17   n.d., 1840-41

« 1548

The dogmatic thesis around which everything centers in Hamann πάντα θεῖα καὶ πάντα ἀνθρώπινα—[284]yet it does not remain the center, but the thoughts spill out chaotically.

Irony remains aristocratic. (The philosophers.) Humor reconciles with all existence (πάντα θεῖα πάντα ἀνθρώπινα).

III B 20   n.d., 1840-41

« 1549

Hamann,[285] VIII, p. 307

It is a most interesting story* which Lucian tells about Demonax. Not only the person who revealed the Eleusinian mysteries but also the one who would not let himself be involved in them was punished. The latter was the case with Demonax. The Athenians, who even before they heard his defence were prepared to stone him, were nevertheless moved when they heard his explanation that he could not permit himself to become involved in the mysteries, because he could not fulfill the condition to [keep silent about them].

* In margin: This is found in Lucian II.[286]

IV A 39   n.d., 1843

« 1550

"Write"—"For whom?"—"Write for the dead, for those in the past whom do you love."—"Will they read me?"—"Yes, for they come back as posterity."[287]

On old saying.

"Write."—"For whom?"—"Write for the dead, for those in the past whom you love."—"Will they read me?"—"No!"

An old saying slightly altered.

Rebus und Grundsätze durcheinander.[288]
Hamann, I.[289]

IV B 96: 1a, 1b, 1c   n.d., 1843

« 1551

Ein Laye und Unglaübiger kann meine Schreibart nicht anders als für Unsinn erklären, weil ich mit mancherley Zungen mich audsdrücke, und die Sprache der Sophisten, der Wortspiele, der Creter und Araber, Weissen und Mohren und Creolen rede, Critik, Mythologie, rebus und Grundsätze durch einander schwatze, und bald κατ' ἄνθρωπον bald κατ' ἐξοχήν argumentire.[290]

Hamann.

IV B 96:4 *n.d.*, 1843

« 1552

Speaking of abstract definitions, Hamann puts it excellently: *"die Jungfraukinder der Speculation."*[291]

V A 29   *n.d.*, 1844

« 1553

Addition to V B 42 [title page of *The Concept of Anxiety*]:

Socrates ————— Hamann

†   †

400 b. Chr.   1758 after Chr.

Socrates mein Herren war kein etc. (in *Sokratiske Denkwürdigkeiten*).[292]

V B 43   *n.d.*, 1844

« 1554

Addition to V B 42:

Motto

Is it not remarkable that the greatest master of irony and the greatest humorist, separated by 2,000 years, may join together in doing and admiring what we should suppose everyone had done, if this fact did not testify to the contrary. Hamann[293] says of Socrates: "He was great because he distinguished between what he understood and what he did not understand." If only Socrates could have had an epitaph! Many an innocent person has drained the poisoned cup, many a one has sacrificed his life for the idea, but this epitaph belongs to Socrates alone: Here rests Socrates; he distinguished between what he understood and what he did not understand.

Or perhaps better simply to quote Hamann's words.

V B 44   *n.d.*, 1844

« 1555

Addition to V B 42:

The age of distinction is long past, because the system abrogates it.

He who loves it must be regarded as an oddity, a lover of something that vanished long ago. This may well be; yet my soul clings to Socrates, its first love, and rejoices in the one who understood him, Hamann; for he has said the best that has been said about Socrates, something far more remarkable and rare than that he taught young people and made fun of the Sophists and drained the poisoned cup: Socrates was great because he distinguished between what he understood and what he did not understand.

V B 45   n.d., 1844

« 1556

Hamann's so-called marriage of conscience, which was not a civil marriage—how does all this hang together? Roth in the preface to Volume III[294] merely mentions it and says that there are documents, but that he dare not publish them. In addition, he quotes Reichardt's *Urania* for 1812.

Must be investigated.

VI A 5   n.d., 1844-45

« 1557

There is something rather curious about this: Hamann says that God forgets nothing but that there are ideas and flashes which men get no more than once in a lifetime—and this statement appears twice in the third[295] and in the fifth[296] volumes. I have marked them in my copy.

VI A 6   n.d., 1844-45

« 1558

Amazing! Yesterday I spoke with Jørgen Jørgensen, who has now become an avid reader of Hamann. In Hamann's writings he has found evidence that Hamann was not married to his wife but lived with her out of wedlock, consequently as a concubine. And I, who have looked for this most eagerly, have not found it. At one time this would have been of the greatest importance to me. And yet it would not really have helped me, but it would have given the matter a little different twist if I had known that Hamann had dared to do such a thing. Of course I have thought of the possibility, but I did not know that Hamann had carried it through. But at the time I was sure that it could not be done that way.

In margin: see Journal JJ, p. 160 [i.e., VI A 5].

VIII[1] A 251   n.d., 1847

« 1559

Hamann rightly declares: Just as "law" abrogates "grace," so "to comprehend" abrogates "to have faith."[297]

It is, in fact, my thesis. But in Hamann it is merely an aphorism; whereas I have fought it through or have fought it out of a whole given philosophy and culture and into the thesis: to comprehend that faith cannot be comprehended or (the more ethical and God-fearing side) to comprehend that faith must not be comprehended.

x^2 A 225   *n.d.*, 1849

« 1560

. . . . . With Argus-eyes I am watched by all those who are nothing, by all those who achieve nothing, who will nothing. What Hamann says is excellent (III, letter no. 67):[298] "Argus was a human being who had nothing to do, which is indicated by his name."

x^3 A 51   *n.d.*, 1850

HAMLET

« 1561 *Rötscher*[299]

Börne[300] who *en passant* calls *Hamlet*[301] a "Christian tragedy." The mistake in Shakespeare is precisely that Hamlet does not have religious doubts. If he does not have them, then it is sheer nonsense and indecision if he does not settle the matter straight away.

V B 148:16   n.d., 1844

« 1562 *Two Esthetic Observations*
Which I Still Want to Record

I. *Hamlet and Ophelia.* Hamlet cannot be regarded as really being in love with Ophelia. It must not be interpreted in this way, even though psychologically it is quite true that a person who is going about hatching a great plan is the very one who needs momentary relaxation and therefore can well use a love affair. Yet I do not believe that Hamlet is to be interpreted this way. No, what is indefensible in Hamlet is that, intriguing in grand style as he is, he uses a relationship to Ophelia to take the attention away from what he actually is keeping hidden. He misuses Ophelia. This is how it should be interpreted, and one can also add that precisely because he is so overstrained he almost goes so far that momentarily he actually is in love.

II. *Don Quixote.* It is a mistake that Don Quixote ends by dying and dies as a rational man. Don Quixote ought to have no ending. On the contrary, Don Quixote ought to end with the momentum of a new fixed idea, in which he would now appear, as he himself says, as a shepherd. Don Quixote is endless fantasy. Therefore it is prosaic to let the story end with his dying after he has become sensible. It is an attempt to transform Don Quixote into a kind of moral tale instead of keeping it properly in the realm of romantic comedy.

XI[1] A 501   n.d., 1854

HEGEL

« 1563

It is obvious that in time the romantic gradually declines more and more, precisely to the same degree as necessity is advanced (Hegel), in such a way that Christianity does not remain romantic at all (for example, Schleiermacher, a necessary development). To what extent does the antique, which thus enters in, resemble so-called actual antiquity. (The present tense of beauty.)

I A 170   June 12, 1836

« 1564

When the Indian teachers interpret the doctrine of evil in such a way that it turns out (see Schlegel, *Werke*,[302] Vol. I, p. 213) that God is just as much the source of evil as he is of good and *in a way* place the devil in the Trinity (Schlegel, ibid.); is this not Hegelianism? And to what extent is this consistent with the idea of the romantic which one usually associates with Indian thought?

I A 211   August 1, 1836

« 1565

It is quite curious that, after being occupied so long with the concept of the romantic, I now see for the first time that the romantic becomes what Hegel calls the dialectical, the other position where

Stoicism—fatalism
Pelagianism—Augustianism
humor—irony
etc.

are at home, positions which do not have any continuance by themselves, but life is a constant pendulum-movement between them.

I now perceive also that when Heiberg[303] transferred Hegelianism to esthetics and believed that he had found the triad: lyric–epic–lyric-epic (dramatic), he was right; but [it is doubtful] that this can be carried through on a far greater scale: classical–romantic–absolute beauty, and in such a way that precisely the Heiberg-triad becomes meaningful, since the classical, as well as the romantic and absolute beauty, has its lyrical—its epic—its dramatic.

To what extent, for that matter, is it right to begin with the lyrical; the history of poetry seems to indicate a beginning with the epic.

I A 225   August 19, 1836

« 1566

The Hegelian cud-chewing involving three stomachs—first, immediacy—then it is regurgitated—than down once more; perhaps a successor master-mind could continue this with four stomachs etc., down again and then up again. I do not know whether the master-mind understands what I mean.

I A 229   August 25, 1836

« 1567

Of course, Hegel's logical trinity can be treated the way everything can—it can be carried to the extreme by applying it to the simplest of all objects where it no doubt is true, but unfortunately ridiculous. Thus someone might make use of it on boots and show the immediate position, then the dialectical position (that they begin to squeak), and the third position of synthesis.

I A 317   January 5, 1837

« 1568

Insofar as Hegel was fructified by Christianity, he sought to eliminate the humorous element which is in Christianity (something about this is found elsewhere in my papers [I A 207]), and consequently reconciled himself completely with the world, with quietism as a result. The same thing happened with Goethe in his *Faust,* and it is curious that the second volume came so late. He could easily produce the first volume, but the problem was how to calm the storm once it was aroused. The second volume, therefore, has a far more subjective character (indeed, on the whole Goethe has sufficiently expressed how his experience occasioned one or another work of art); it seems as if he makes this confession of faith in order to calm himself down.

II A 48   *n.d.,* 1837

« 1569

Hegel's subsequent position swallows up the previous one, not as one stage of life swallows another, with each still retaining its validity, but as a higher title or rank swallows up a lower title.—

II A 49   *n.d.*, 1837

« 1570

Just as in domestic life there is a type of person who, as it is excellently phrased, peddles gossip among families, so there is a goodly number of men who with regard to the question of the union of Christianity with philosophy really gossip, since, without knowing either party very well, they have gotten to know in a second- or third-hand way someone with a master's degree who during his foreign travels has drunk tea with this or that great scholar, etc.[304]

II A 52   *n.d.*, 1837

« 1571

Hegel really began where Charles V ended—in a monastery setting clocks.

II A 678   *n.d.*, 1837

« 1572

Those who have gone beyond Hegel are like country people who must always give their address as *via* a larger city; thus the addresses in this case read—John Doe *via* Hegel.

II A 697   January 17, 1838

« 1573

When certain people[305] maintain that they have gone beyond[306] Hegel, it must be regarded at best as a bold *metaphor*, by which they are trying to express and illustrate the thoroughness with which they have studied him, to describe the terrific running start they have made to get into his thought—and with their momentum they have not been able to stop but have gone beyond him.

II A 260   September 12, 1838

« 1574

The Hegelians devise many abrogations [*Ophævelser*][307] of the concept which are not worth bothering about [*gjøre Ophævelser over*].

II A 766   *n.d.*, 1838

« 1575

Hegel is a Johannes *Climacus*[308] who does not storm the heavens as do the giants, by setting mountain upon mountain—but enters them by means of his syllogisms.

II A 335   January 20, 1839

« 1576

When one sees the abuses to which orthodox Hegelians have pressed their master's categories, as if they contained a kind of salvation, who does not come to think of the γενεαλογίαι ἀπέραντοι,[309] against which Paul warns in I Timothy 1:4.

II A 371   February 19, 1939

« 1577

It is now clear that the category of bad infinity,[310] which the Hegelians are always gunning for, has actually been partially eradicated by these attacks, but it seems to me that the Hegelians themselves propound it again only in another form. Just as plants with one shoot of the stalk pushing itself out from the other without any marking other than the exposed joint would be a picture of the attacked bad infinity, just so a flower which in its developing continually bisects and thereupon unites again in order to bisect again would be a picture of the victorious bad infinity. In relation to the other this view is merely *a new pattern*; the essential nature is the same and also the treatment.

II A 381   March 12, 1839

« 1578

All relative contrasts can be mediated [*medieres*]; we do not really need Hegel for this, inasmuch as the ancients point out that they can be distinguished. Personality will for all eternity protest against the idea that absolute contrasts can be mediated (and this protest is incommensurable with the assertion of mediation); for all eternity it will repeat its *immortal* dilemma: to be or not to be—that is the question (Hamlet).[311]

II A 454   June 14, 1839

« 1579

Just as there are times when the optical nerves of a neurasthenic become so microscopically sensitive that he can *see the air*, so that for him* it is no longer a medium, so too in a spiritual sense there come ecstatic moments[312] when all of existence seems so poetic, so dilated and transparent to contemplation, that even the most insignificant insignificance of the most ordinary productions and rush jobs of the bad infinity[313] seem, at least allegorically, to intimate the deepest truths, yes, seem to have their reality [*Realitæt*] only insofar as they are such allegories, to have their existence thereby and therein.

II A 487   July 20, 1839

« 1580

* *In margin of* 1579 (II A 487):
It is generally characteristic of the whole more recent development always to be conscious of the medium, and it must end almost in madness, just as if someone, every time he saw the sun and stars, became conscious of the revolving of the earth.

II A 488   *n.d.*

« 1581

DISCURSIVE RAISONEMENTS AND INCONCEIVABLE PERTINENT PROPOSALS CONCERNING THE CATEGORY OF THE HIGHER LUNACY

Preface

I believe that I would do philosophers a great service if they were to adopt a category which I myself have discovered and utilized with great profit and success to exhaust and dry up a multitude of relations and qualifications which have so far been unwilling to resolve themselves—it is the category of the higher lunacy. I ask only that it not be named after me, but that goes without saying, and besides, in analogous situations we are not accustomed to name something after the active party but after the passive one; the switch is not named after the one who switches but after the one who first gets it.

It is the most concrete of all categories, the fullest, since it is closest to life and does not have its truth in a beyond, the supraterrestrial, but in a subterranean below, and thus, if it were a hypothesis, the most grandiose empirical proof of its truth could be made.

It is this category by which the transition is formed from abstract lunacy to concrete lunacy. The formula for it from one side is given by Baggesen,[314] VII, p. 195:

The Unity of Lunacy [Galskabs] in the Duality of all
Creation [Alskabs],

but expressed speculatively it is

The Unity of all Creation in the Duality of Lunacy.

All creation implies multiplicity, that is, *Quodlibet* or the loonier the better.

The duality of lunacy. We no longer can be content with discrete and partial insanities, but the concepts genus and species must have their validity here, too.

II A 808   n.d., 1839

« 1582

*In margin of 1581 (*II A 808*):*
This work is dedicated to each and all of the cottagers in Bistrup[315] and above all to all the esteemed contemporaries who are looney enough to understand what I mean.

II A 809   n.d.

« 1583

*Addition to 1581 (*II A 808*):*
(Within this category I would treat the ridiculous combinations of two contending parties' several [*besondre*] follies in higher unity. The orthodox and the politicians,* for example, in the cause of parish freedom.[316] Philosophers and theologians, etc.)

II A 810   n.d., 1839

« 1584

*In margin of 1583 (*II A 810*):*
* Indeed, it seems as if the politicians and the orthodox are really on intimate terms with each other; apropos of this, I have never become really intimate with anyone with the exception of my brown-striped trousers.

II A 811   n.d.

« 1585

*Addition to 1583 (*II A 810*):*
First there should be developed under the title "*summistisk summa summarum*"[317] a compendium of the meager *quantum satis*[318] of each part, and thereafter would come unity or the discursive *raisonement*, which is continually interrupted by an *apropos* of a polemical and sarcastic nature.

II A 812   n.d., 1839

« 1586

In margin of 1585 (II A 812):
Concerning matters of conscience—I wish I could see through the crowns of hats when people hold their hats in front of their eyes to pray; I dare say faces would be caught there which physiognomists have not yet described.

II A 813   *n.d.*

« 1587

It does seem that there ought to be a continued and intensified fore-shortening and abbreviating of the abstract, the metaphysical (both in the sense in which painters foreshorten the perspective and in the stricter sense of foreshortening, since the doubt, through which the system works itself forward more and more, must be overcome and thereby become less and less talkative), but if in so doing metaphysical thought[319] also declares that it thinks historical reality, it is on the wrong path. After the system is complete and has reached the category of reality, the new doubt appears, the new contradiction, the last and the most profound: by what means does the metaphysical reality bind itself to historical reality (The Hegelians distinguish between existence [*Tilværelse*] and reality: the external phenomenon exists, but insofar as it is taken up into the idea it is real. This is quite correct, but the Hegelians do not define the boundary, to what extent each phenomenon can become real in this way, and the reason for this is that they see the phenomenon from the bird's eye perspective of the metaphysical and do not likewise see the metaphysical in the phenomenon from the perspective of the phenomenon.)—namely, the historical as the unity of the metaphysical and the accidental.[320] It is the metaphysical, insofar as this is the eternal bond of existence, without which the phenomenological would disintegrate; it is the accidental, insofar as there is the possibility that every event could take place in infinitely many other ways; the unity of these (divinely regarded) is providence, and (humanly regarded), *the historical.* The meaning of the historical is not that it is to be annulled but that the individual is to be free within it and also happy in it. This unity of the metaphysical and the accidental is already resident in self-consciousness, which is the point of departure for personality. I become conscious simultaneously in my eternal validity, in, so to speak, my divine necessity, and in my accidental finitude (that I am this particular being, born in this country at this time, throughout all the various influences of changing conditions). This latter aspect must not be overlooked or rejected; on the contrary, the true life of the individual is its apotheosis, which does not mean that this empty, contentless *I* steals, as it were, out of this finitude, in order to become volatilized and diffused in its heavenward emigration, but rather that the divine inhabits and finds its task in the finite.

III A 1   July 4, 1840

« 1588

It is strange what hate, conspicuous everywhere, Hegel has for the up-building or the edifying,[321] but that which builds up is not an opiate which lulls to sleep; it is the Amen of the finite spirit and is an aspect of knowledge which ought not to be ignored.

III A 6   July 10, 1840

« 1589

The view that Hegel is a parenthesis in Schelling seems to be more and more manifest; we are only waiting for the parenthesis to be closed.

III A 34   *n.d.,* 1840

« 1590

Whereas the philosophy of the recent past had almost exemplified the idea that language exists [*var til*] to conceal thought (since thought simply cannot express *das Ding an sich* at all), Hegel in any case deserves credit for showing that language has thought immanent in itself and that thought is developed in language. The other thinking was a constant fumbling with the matter.

III A 37   *n.d.,* 1840

« 1591

How beautifully Hegel says it in his *Æsthetics,* III, p. 362:[322] "*Denn das Hauptrecht dieser grossen Charakteren besteht in ihrer Energie, sich durchzusetzen, da sie in ihrer Besonderheit zugleich das Allgemeine tragen; während umgekehrt die gewöhnliche Moralitæt in der Nichtachtung der eignen Personlichkeit und in dem Hineinlegen der ganzen Energie in diese Nichtachtung besteht.*"[323]

III A 186   *n.d.,* 1841

« 1592

Dec. 6

An observation which contributes to the question of the relationship of philosophy to actuality [*Virkeligheden*] according to Hegel's thought, which one frequently grasps best in his occasional utterances, is found in his *Æsthetik*, III, p. 243.

III C 31   December 6, 1841

« 1593

A passage where Hegel himself seems to suggest the deficiency of pure thought, that not even philosophy is alone the adequate expression for human life, or that consequently personal life does not find its fulfillment in thought alone but in a totality of kinds of existence [*Existents-Arter*] and modes of expression. Cf. *Æsthetik*, III, p. 440, bottom of page.

III C 33   *n.d.*, 1841-42

« 1594

The secret of the whole of existence [*Tilværelsen*], movement, Hegel explains easily enough, for he says somewhere in *Phenomenology*[324] that something goes on behind the back of consciousness (see Introduction, p. 71). Plotinus manipulates in a similar manner in order to make one into two. "*Diese (die Vernunft) als Eins anfangend, beharrt nicht als Eins, sondern wird sich selbst* unbemerkt *ein Vieles, gleichsam unter ihrer eignen Last erliegend.*"[325] (See Marbach, *Geschichte der Philosophie,*[326] II, p. 82.)

IV C 59   *n.d.*, 1842-43

« 1595

What is a category?

As far as is known, modern philosophy has not supplied any definition, at least not Hegel. With the help of his inverse process he always leaves it to the reader's virtuosity to do what is most difficult, to gather multiplicity into the energy of one thought.

IV C 63   *n.d.*, 1842-43

« 1596

Addition to 1595 (IV C 63):

The only place in Hegel I have found anything is in the little encyclopedia[327] published by Rosenkrantz, p. 93; he is completely arbitrary in his terminology, which is quite obvious in the classification he makes. Category has thus obtained a place it should not have, and the next question to be asked is: What is it, now, which encompasses this tripartition?

IV C 64   *n.d.*, 1842-43

« 1597

Addition to 1595 (IV C 63):

Strangely enough, Aristotle gives no definition either (must be examined more closely). κατηγορία.[328] (Cicero, *prædicamentum*; scholastics likewise.)[329]

IV C 65   *n.d.*, 1842-43

« 1598

Addition to 1595 (IV C 63):

* Is being, then, a category? It is by no means what quality is, namely, determinate being, determinate in itself; the accent lies on determinate, not on being. Being is neither presupposed nor predicated. In this sense Hegel is right—being is nothing; if, on the other hand, it were a quality, then one could wish enlightenment on how it becomes identical with nothing. The whole doctrine about being is a fatuous prelude to the doctrine of quality.

* *In margin:* See Hegel's *Propädeutik*, pp. 96-97

IV C 66   *n.d.*, 1842-43

« 1599

In margin of 1598 (IV C 66):

If being[330] [*Væren*] were really a quality, then I must also be able to determine it quantitatively, for quantity in contrast to quality is an indifferent determination. I can determine a field quantitatively; it still continues to be a field. But to determine being quantitatively is meaningless; for either it is or it is not, a more or less here is nonsense which would abrogate quality itself.

IV C 67   *n.d.*

« 1600

Addition to 1595 (IV C 63):

Why did Kant[331] begin with quantity, Hegel with quality?

IV C 68   *n.d.*, 1842-43

« 1601

Despite all the assurances about the positivity which lies in Hegel's system, he still has arrived only at the point where in olden days they began[332] (for example, Leibniz).

IV C 73   *n.d.*, 1842-43

« 1602

In the doctrine of being everything *is*[333] which does not change. (This is something which even Werder[334] admitted. See the small books [i.e., III C 29-30].)

In the doctrine of essence there is *Beziehung*. —The irregularities in Hegel's logic. Essentially this segment is only dichotomies—cause–effect —occasion–result—reciprocal effect is a problem, perhaps belongs somewhere else.

The concept is a trichotomy.[335]
Being does not belong to logic at all.[336]
It ought to begin with dichotomy.[337]

IV C 79   *n.d.*, 1842-43

« 1603

Addition to 1602 (IV C 79):
Is mediation[338] the zero point, or is it a third? —Does the third itself emerge through the immanental motion of the two, or how does it emerge? —The difficulty appears especially when one seeks to transfer it to the world of actuality [*Virkelighedens*].

IV C 81   *n.d.*, 1842-43

« 1604

In the Hegelian school, the system is a fiction similar to the one Schelling[339] brought to the world in "the infinite epic," which in its time was quite successful.

IV A 185   *n.d.*, 1844

« 1605

If Hegel had written his whole logic and had written in the preface that it was only a thought-experiment, in which at many points he still steered clear of some things, he undoubtedly would have been the greatest thinker who has ever lived. As it is he is comic.[340]

V A 73   *n.d.*, 1844

« 1606

There is a phrase which, simply uttered, pierces the soul with awesome solemnity; there is a name which, simply uttered together with the phrase from which it is inseparable, makes the child of the age take off his hat and bow down, even someone who does not know the man: *the absolute method* and *Hegel*.[341] The absolute method—this phrase is *einhaltschwer* and yet it passes, as the poet says, from *Munde zu Munde*, but in every mouth it is equally weighty in substance. Nowadays the absolute method is at home not only in logic but also in the historical sciences. O worldly eminence, what a fraud you are—exclaimed the beggar who had envied that rich lord, until he discovered that His Lordship walked on crutches—just as the absolute method does. O worldly eminence, how worthy you are to aspire to be the absolute method, and then to have such a home as Hegel has prepared in logic, not to mention in the historical sciences! To have to take recourse in word-play and witticisms and evasions, to have to help oneself along by half untruths, to have to beg all through life merely to become the absolute, which does not begin *bittweise*, to have to be silent about its not hanging together properly—O, this is a high price! Cromwell the Protector in all his glory could not have been more unfortunate, more fugitive, when he vainly sought a resting place for the night. And yet Hegel was a great, an outstanding logician; this in truth no one can deny him. And yet what he had understood was more than adequate to assure his significance and to make the young student understand in joyful and trusting devotion that Hegel was genuinely a teacher—if only his explanation had been limited to this; but the absolute method is a bad conscience in scarlet. And the absolute method was the superscription—*ergo*, Hegel had also accomplished this. And the logical gimcrackery whereby it is supposed to be the object of pious fetish-worship—to speak ill of it was the prime philosophical high-treason against Hegel. In the same way Nero was incensed at the guard, not because he incited rebellion, not because he said he was a bad emperor, but because he said Nero was a bad zither player.[342]

And, now, in the historical sciences! Too bad that Hegel lacked time; but if one is to dispose of all of world-history, how does one get time for the little experiment as to whether the absolute method, which explains everything, is also able to explain the life of a single human being. In ancient days one would have smiled at a method which can explain all of world-history absolutely but cannot explain a single person even mediocrely; for in ancient days the wise man did not begin this way and did not go beyond in this way so that he never came to understand or he ceased to understand what the simple man understands. In ancient times existence [*Tilværelsen*] was thought to be epitomized in such a way that anyone who understood a single human being would be in position to explain history, if he had the requisite knowledge, because the task of reckoning remained essentially the same. Of course, in ancient days there

was no wise man who had invented the absolute method. The malprac-
tice in Hegel is easily pointed out. The absolute method explains all
world-history; the science which is to explain the single human being is
ethics. On the one hand, this is quite neglected in Hegel, and insofar as
he explains anything, it is usually in such a way that no living being can
exist [*existere*] accordingly, and if he were to exist according to the few
better things to be found there, then he would instantly explode the absolute method. Hegel can manage much better with the dead, for they
are silent. Nevertheless he has adequately guarded himself against them;
but my wish, although I do not know whether or not it can be fulfilled, is
that Socrates, who, according to his own statement wanted to ask the
wise in the underworld whether they know something or not, may get hold
of Hegel in order to question him about the absolute method. Perhaps it
will then become evident that Hegel, who became so extraordinarily absolute in this earthly life, which ordinarily is the life of relativity, would
become rather relative in the absoluteness of eternal life.

The question is simplified as much as possible, and in the treatment of
it we shall again strive to simplify everything as much as possible, for we
do not have such munificence to offer that we dare count on it to make
recompense for neglecting the simple duty of answering what has been
asked. Yet even if the other, which one gets instead of an answer, were
marvelously munificent, it would still be essentially a diversion to which
one devotes himself and a loss in that one gets to know this instead of
receiving an answer to the perhaps insignificant question which nevertheless had the peculiar characteristic of being what one had asked about. It
is a dangerous pet-idea to want to be concrete immediately in answering
an abstract question, whether the concretion consists of a resumé of some
earlier philosopher's thought or the particularity of the historical. The
concretion often has the effect of seductively depriving thought of the
serenity and simplicity which are satisfied with thought itself. The mathematician is content with his numerical calculations and does not wish to
use dollars, marks, or shillings in order to engage the participation of the
materialist. But even though the concrete is more necessary than it is for
the mathematician, one does not begin immediately by making the
thought concrete but *in abstracto* clarifies the thought he wishes later to
point out in the concrete. Thus if a musician wishes to explain to someone that a lead instrument penetrates the rest of the music with its tones
[theme, idea, the abstract] and is the basic constituent of the whole,[343] he
would first play certain passages on that instrument until the learner is

familiar with it and can recognize it among a hundred others playing at the same time; only then would he have the entire orchestra play, and he would ask him to be attentive to the way the tone of that instrument is present throughout. If, on the other hand, he were to begin immediately with the music of the full orchestra [*the manifold*], he would confuse everything for the listener. The concrete is the manifold and as such exercises a charming power over the soul. Suppose it happened that the thought which is to be pointed out in the concrete did not become clear but that the concrete were itself so rich, so variegated, that it captivated the soul and at times became so difficult that in itself it was work enough, so that the learner or the reader, rejoicing in the delight, weary of labor, finally forgot the thought and with unfeigned gratitude felt how much he owed to this teacher. In the beginning the teacher had not made the thought clear in the passionless brevity of abstraction; perhaps he minimized such a method as being deficient; the thought is supposed to become clear only at the conclusion of the whole, at the conclusion, that is, after the learner had seen and heard various things, had been in various mental states, had again and again admired the teacher's prodigious knowledge, both the profound and the foolish thoughts of the earlier philosophers. —You see, this is why we speak very abstractly. We do not have magical charms; if we do not win the reader simply by speaking about the given question, we shall hardly win him by polished dishonesty which knows how to amaze at the outset.

V B 41   *n.d.*, 1844

« 1607

If I attempted to point out how the Hegelian ordering of the world-historical process perpetrates caprices and leaps, how it almost involuntarily becomes comical when applied to more concrete details, I would perhaps get the attention of a few readers. Essentially the interest would be in arranging world history, and perhaps I am the one who should do it. If I were merely to state this, I would probably cause quite a stir. But to regard all this interest as curiosity is, of course, ethical narrow-mindedness; yes, even to regard interest in astronomy as curiosity and silly dilettantism, which in order to advance further disappoints by moving into another discipline, would also be regarded as ethical narrow mindedness. Yet I am happy at this point to remember Socrates "who gave up astronomy and the study of heavenly things as something which did not concern man."[344]

VI B 40:3   *n.d.*, 1845

« 1608

I here request the reader's attention for an observation I have often wished to make. Do not misunderstand me, as if I fancied myself to be a devil of a thinker who would remodel everything etc. Such thoughts are as far from my mind as possible. I feel what for me at times is an enigmatical respect for Hegel; I have learned much from him, and I know very well that I can still learn much more from him when I return to him again. The only thing I give myself credit for is sound natural capacities and a certain honesty which is armed with a sharp eye for the comical. I have lived and perhaps am uncommonly tried in the *casibus* of life; in the confidence that an open road for thought might be found there, I have resorted to philosophical books and among them Hegel's. But right here he leaves me in the lurch. His philosophical knowledge, his amazing learning, the insight of his genius, and everything else good that can be said of a philosopher I am willing to acknowledge as any disciple. —Yet, no, not *acknowledge*—that is too distinguished an expression—willing to admire, willing to learn from him. But, nevertheless, it is no less true that someone who is really tested in life, who in his need resorts to thought, will find Hegel comical despite all his greatness.

VI B 54:12   *n.d.*, 1845

« 1609

All that was lacking was for Hegelian philosophy to have also a visible custom such as baptism, an act which could be performed with small children; thus one could bring it to the point where babies fourteen days old would be everything—Hegelians as well. And if a person baptized at fourteen days as a Hegelian were to announce himself as a Hegelian, if a watchman, for example, had his child baptized as a Hegelian and then brought the child up to the best of his humble abilities and the child had no special aptitudes and grew up to become a watchman, too—but also a Hegelian—would this not be ridiculous. Let it be true ten times over that, unlike Hegelian philosophy, Christianity is not based on differences, that it is Christianity's holy humanity that it can be appropriated by all—but is this then to be understood to mean that everyone is a Christian automatically?

VI B 54:30   *n.d.*, 1845

« 1610

A person can be a great logician and become immortal through his services and yet prostitute himself by assuming that the logical is the existential and that the principle of contradiction is abrogated in existence because it is indisputably abrogated in logic; whereas existence is the very separation which prevents the purely logical flow.[345] Hegel may very well be world-historical as a thinker, but one thing he has certainly lacked: he was not brought up in the Christian religion, or he was mediocrely brought up. For just as the person brought up to believe in God learns that even if every misfortune falls to his lot in life and he never sees a happy day, he must simply hold out, so also the person brought up in Christianity learns to regard this as eternal truth and to regard every difficulty simply as a spiritual trial [Anfægtelse]. But Hegel's concept of Christianity is so far from bearing the imprint of this primitivity of childlike inwardness that his treatment of faith—for example, of what it is to believe—is nothing but pure foolishness [corrected from stupidity]. I am not afraid to say this. If I had the cheek to say of the most simple man alive that he is too stupid to become a Christian, this would be a matter between God and myself, and woe unto me! But to say this of Hegel remains a matter only between Hegel and myself, and at most a few Hegelians, for the stupidity is of another kind, and to say this is no blasphemy against the God who created man in his image, consequently every man, and against the God who took human form in order to save all, the most simple of men as well.[346]

VI B 98:45   n.d., 1845

« 1611 *From the Book on Adler*[347]

On the whole, it is incredible what confusion Hegelian philosophy has brought into personal life—the tragic result of a philosopher's being publicly a hero and privately a philistine and a pedant. One thing continually escapes Hegel—what it is to live; he knows only how to make a *facsimile* of life, and if he is a master in that, he is also probably the most glaring contrast to a maieutic.

We find some astonishing examples among the philosophers following Hegel who have appropriated the Hegelian method. One such philosopher writes a new book, and he becomes aware of it as an element within the effort which began with his first book; but this is not enough, for he becomes aware of his whole effort (which does not yet exist) as an element in the whole philosophical effort after Hegel, and that again as element in Hegel, and Hegel as element in the world-historical process from antiquity through China, Persia, Greece, the Hebrews, Christianity, the Middle Ages. Could it be possible? Would it not be all right for such an assistant professor, upon seeing that we are all too astonished, to say like the preacher who saw his audience becoming much too moved: Don't cry, children; it may all be a lie.

But this unholy desire to construe as an element has become a fixed idea. The ethical view: to strive, and the metaphysical view: to construe as an element, are in a life-and-death struggle with each other. Every living person who is not completely unthinking and absentminded has to choose, but if he chooses the metaphysical, he really commits, spiritually, suicide.

VII^1 A 153   *n.d.*, 1846

« 1612

The relation between Schelling[348] and Hegel is really this: Schelling got rid of the *Ding an sich* with the aid of the Absolute, inasmuch as the *Schattenspiel* was abolished on the far side and everything appears on this side. But Schelling *stopped* with the Absolute, with indifference, with the zero point, from which he really did not proceed, which simply signified that beyond the Absolute is nothing. Hegel, however, intended to get back to the Absolute on the far side so that he could get *momentum*. Schelling's philosophy is at rest; Hegelian philosophy is presumably in *motion*, in the motion of the method.

VIII^1 A 14   *n.d.*, 1847

« 1613

The world regards the God-relationship of the single individual [*den Enkeltes*] as really being selfishness, self-love. Since the world does not really believe in God, in the long run the God-fearing person must really love himself. The God-fearing person does not love what the world loves, but then what is left—God and himself. The world takes God away, and therefore the God-fearing person loves himself. The world regards the fear of God as self-love. It is also self-love to be unwilling to deify the world and contemporary opinion, to want to maintain (as every human being ought to) that one's ultimate judgment and ultimate responsibility are to God. This impiety (the abolition of the relationship of conscience) is the fundamental damage done by Hegelian philosophy. And Hegelian philosophy has now become so popular that finally the street-corner loiterers become the objective spirit. Heiberg, for example, does not think about it this way, yet not because he perceives the sophistry, but because he and his want to be the objective spirit.

VIII^1 A 283   *n.d.*, 1847

« 1614

In margin: Julius Müller[349] on "Sin," part I, pp. 350 etc.

No, no, Hegel is not so wrong in this way. Since Hegel also defines evil as abstract subjectivity, arbitrariness, the single individual's [*den Enkeltes*] encroachment upon the universal, therefore also as egotism, J. Müller would have to be in agreement with him and would be, if it were not clear that Hegel traces the presence of evil back to a higher *necessity*.

No, the error lies mainly in this, that the universal, which Hegelianism considers the truth (and the single individual to be the truth by being swallowed up in it) is an abstraction—the state, etc. He does not come to God, the subjective in the absolute sense, or to the truth—that ultimately the single individual is really higher than the universal, namely, the single individual in his God-relationship.

How frequently have I sworn that Hegel basically regards men, paganly, as an animal-race endowed with reason. In an animal-race "the single individual" is always lower than "race." The human race always has the remarkable character that, just because every individual is created in the image of God, the "single individual" is higher than the "race."

That this can be taken in vain and horribly misused, I concede. But *this* is Christianity. And *here* is where the battle must really be fought.

x^2 A 426   *n.d.,* 1850

« 1615

For a long, long time the race wearied itself with the question of the personhood of God. If only it could be conceptualized, they thought, then the question of the Trinity could be put aside.

What happened? Along came Hegel and Hegelianism. They understood the matter better: they proved that God is personal simply because he is triune. Well, thanks, that is a lift. All this about the trinity was shadow-boxing; it was the old logical trilogy (thesis–antithesis–synthesis), and the "personhood" which resulted from it was something like the X with which they began in those days, since they thought that if they could only get the personhood of God conceptualized, the matter of the trinity could be put aside.

On the whole, the most profound Hegelian confusion with regard to Christianity is that it has no time or understanding for posing the Christian problem *first of all* before one comprehends. Hegel's results (which are proclaimed with drums and trumpets as the explanation of everything) are more or less a form of the problem as one of comprehending or having to comprehend that one cannot comprehend.

Christianity begins about where Hegel ends; the misunderstanding is only that Hegel thought that he was through with Christianity *at that point*—had even gone beyond it.

It is just impossible to keep from laughing when I think of Hegel's conception of Christianity—it is utterly unconceivable. True it is and true it remains, something I have always said: Hegel was a professor of philosophy, not a thinker, and he must also have been a rather nondescript person, without a life-impression—yet a very unusual professor, this I do not deny.

The time will surely come when the idea of "professor" will be equated with a comical person. One thinks of Christianity! Alas, how changed since the time when it had unwavering confessors and now when it has professors who accommodate in all *casibus*.

x^2 A 431   *n.d.*, 1850

« 1616 *The System*

"goes forward by necessity," so it is said. And look, it never for a moment is able to advance as much as half an inch ahead of existence, which goes forward in freedom.

This was the fraud. It was just as if an actor would say: It is I who speak, these are my words—and then has not a single word to say the second the prompter is silent.

x^3 A 786   *n.d.*, 1851

«1617 *Essential Christianity Is Always This* quid nimis[350]

The apostles are scourged, thrown into prison—and then a great earthquake occurs in order to rescue them. From the merely human point of view one might say: This is both too much and too little; I really do not demand that miracles take place for my sake, but then, too, I would just as soon avoid the lashing. Cannot the proclamation of Christianity be mediated so as to become an inoffensive, good, safe position for a man and his family.

O how the extraordinary one must still suffer! It always seems to be verging on madness. The apostle hardly has his daily bread—and in the next moment performs miracles, but without mediation. Mediation, mediation, it is the merely human factor, without which a man never becomes happy.

And thus we have wanted to mediate Christianity! This really means to abolish it. Yet, again, I do not contend against this, that there is mediation, but rather against the shamelessness of wanting to make it something superior. Let us humbly confess that mediation is a grace we must pray about.

But mediation is mob rebellion against the sovereignty of Christianity. We boast that mediation is the only thing that unites men; we also boast that mediation has "the crowd" on its side—and thus we dethrone Christianity.

x⁴ A 385   *n.d.,* 1851

« 1618 *Hegel*

The greater honesty in even the most bitter attacks of an earlier age upon Christianity was that the essentially Christian was fairly well allowed to remain intact.

The danger in Hegel was that he altered Christianity—and thereby achieved agreement with his philosophy.

In general it is characteristic of an age of reason not to let the task remain intact and say: No—but to alter the task and then say: Yes, of course, we are agreed.

The hypocrisy of reason is infinitely treacherous. This is why it is so difficult to take aim.

x⁴ A 429   *n.d.,* 1851

« 1619 *The Wretched Religiousness in Our Time*

Nowadays we do not even have as much as a heresy; there is not even enough character for that—for a heresy presupposes (a) honesty enough to let Christianity pass for what it is and (b) passion to think differently.

No, now we have forgers, this miserable forgery of playing at Christianity, of pretending that it is Christianity we have and are teaching; whereas it is something watered down, effeminate sentimentality, a refined Epicureanism.

O, they were better, much better times when men let Christianity be what it is and either received it in earnest or broke with it in earnest.

But now the forgery is the only Christianity we have—and this is precisely the most dangerous of all. Thus there is no philosophy which has been so harmful to Christianity as Hegel's. For the earlier philosophies were still honest enough to let Christianity be what it is—but Hegel was stupidly impudent enough to solve the problem of speculation and Christianity in such a way that he altered Christianity—and then everything went beautifully.

XI¹ A 14   n.d., 1854

« 1620 *Greek*

There certainly were philosophers before Hegel who had assumed the task of explaining existence [*Tilværelsen*], history. As far as all such attempts are concerned, providence presumably must really smile at them. But it perhaps did not exactly laugh at them, for there was, after all, an honest, human earnestness about them.

But Hegel—O, let me think as a Greek! —How the gods must have grinned! Such a repulsive professor who had completely seen through the necessity of everything and got the whole thing down by rote—ye gods!

It has amused me unspeakably to read Schopenhauer.[351] What he says is altogether true and as coarse as only a German can be—something I marvel at in the Germans.

XI¹ A 180   n.d., 1854

« 1621 *"Windbag"*

It is an extraordinary word; I envy the Germans for having it [*Windbeutel*]; it is also wonderful that it can be used as an adjective and as a verb. A. Schopenhauer[352] makes excellent use of it—yes, I must say Schopenhauer would be in a dilemma if he did not have the word, he who has to discuss Hegelian philosophy and all the professor-philosophy.

The Germans have the word because there is such continual use for it in Germany.

We Danes do not have the word, but that which the word designates is not characteristic of us Danes either. Being a windbag really does not belong to the Danish national character.

However, we Danes do have another fault, a *corresponding* fault, and the Danish language also has a word for it, a word which the German language perhaps does not have: windsucker [*Vindsluger*]. It is used about horses, but it can be taken up into general use.

This is just about the way it is—a German makes wind—and a Dane swallows it—Danes and Germans have been related to each other in this way for a long time.

It amuses me no end, this business of Schopenhauer and Hegel, also what is in store for Germany now, the culmination of Hegelian philosophy, that Hegel was—probably by necessity—a windbag, apparently a product—by necessity—of 1,000 years of world history or at least of the portion which S. correctly designates as the age of philosophical lies.[353]

But if Schopenhauer had to deal with windbags, I have to deal with windsuckers.

XI[1] A 183   n.d., 1854

HEINE

« 1622

Heine is undeniably a humorist (*like all humor, developed from Christianity itself, because, itself humorous, it moved and moves in contrast to the ironically developed world and by its teaching elicited humorous sparks from irony, because it (Christianity) became an offense,* and then irony would not allow itself to be regenerated by humor and subsequently be redeemed, but developed as diabolical humor*), but he could not hold out alone and constituted a contrast to the Church, which develops humorously against the world, because the world now sought to constitute itself as a perennial humorous polemic against the Church.

II A 142   August 26, 1837

« 1623

In margin of 1622 (II A 142):
* Just as Christianity offended Paul.

II A 143   n.d.

« 1624

For Heine Christianity appeared in such a baroque form that he became frightened. During these sufferings the poetic in his soul relaxed in lovely, lyrical productions (*Buch der Lieder*),[354] but then reflection entered in. This should really have made Christianity its object in order, if possible, to find out whether it actually is as it seemed, but instead in Heine it made his own mournful features its object (in a profound sense he is our age's knight of the mournful visage); he became enamored of it, and the phenomenon proceeded to entrench itself so that what arouses our melancholy in his *Buch der Lieder* arouses our disapproval in his prose, and he becomes rigid in it [his mournful visage].

II A 729   April 16, 1838

HISTORY

« 1625

It would be interesting to see by means of systematic historical research the various metrical forms as a necessary outgrowth of the whole age to which they are indigenous.

Our age has the romance and the novel.

I A 148   March, 1836

« 1626

Everything becomes still more tragic, if I may say so, when it is made historical, is made into something which happens not only to me but to the whole world, but of course only in case one has first of all grasped his own need and then gives it this historical background. Thus Heine: *es ist eine alte Geschichte, wird immer aber neu, und wem sie jetzt passiret, ihm springt das Herz entzwei*[355]—yet there is here already more reflection upon it; but in its naïve form it appears chiefly in, for example, many of the poems in *Knaben Wunderhorn*.[356] There is an example in the novels[357] by the brothers Bernhard: in *Børneballet*,[358] at the end of which one sees the same lieutenant who has poisoned the heroine's life, yes, as good as murdered her, try to get an adolescent girl, whereby the story, so to speak, begins all over again. In a certain sense getting the story to begin all over again can be comical, because one makes life into a hurdy-gurdy piece which, when played, begins all over again.

I A 208   July 20, 1836

« 1627

Will not light opera as developed here destroy itself in a way, simply because the musical element has been made so important and the point is constantly one of finding the connection between the musical number and the opera from which it is taken; but its stock will soon be exhausted, at least as far as it is adaptable to light opera (as commonly known—popular), and therefore the new light opera will finally reach the point of using the same musical number in another production (which has already happened, if I am not mistaken, in *Nei!*)[359]—and so on, until it destroys itself. *Is this not a proof of the transitory significance of light opera—significance as a stage of development.*

I A 242   September 14, 1836

« 1628

As far as a comprehension of the relation of contemporary history to the past is concerned, many people are like the person who along the way hears the church clock strike, but since he is on the move, he cannot know if the clock began striking with the first stroke he happened to hear. He continues walking in this illusion (that it was the first stroke), with the result that he counts two although it is seven o'clock, etc.

I A 247   September 20, 1836

« 1629

What I call the mythological-poetic in history is the nimbus which hovers over every genuine striving in history, not an abstraction but a *transfiguration*, not the prosaic actuality, and every genuine historical trend will also give rise to such an ideomythology.

I A 264   October 17, 1836

« 1630

In reflecting upon history great care must be taken lest the genuinely historical disappear through one's fingers, and in this connection I cannot forebear copying a remark by G. Phizer in his *M. Luthers Leben* (reviewed in Rheinwald's *Reportorium*,[360] XV, p. 129, from which the quotation is taken): "*Bei einer solchen angeblich erhabenen, grossartigen und tiefsinnigen, in der That aber frivole Behandlungsweise der Geschichte gelten die Personen nur noch als Träger oder Symbole gewisser, willkührlich in sie gelegter Ansichten, verlieren ihre Eigentümlichkeit und allen Charakter, so wie der auf solche verwöhnte und gekitzelte Geschmack die derbere aber nahrhafte Kost der wirklichen, markigen nicht nach Belieben ausgedeuteten und abgezogenen Geschichte nach und nach verschmäht.*"[361]

II A 14   *n.d.*, 1837

« 1631

The development of world history is something like arguments—the discussion gets so involved with parenthetical matters that finally it is almost impossible to recollect the original issue.

II A 183   October 24, 1837

« 1632

There are few words by which men unknowingly say so much as by the word *orientate*; it is a world-historical memento—all history proceeds from the east, the starting point of the human race.

II A 650   *n.d.*, 1837

« 1633

It requires a trained eye to see what is round, because it cannot be seen all at once and the inner sense must exercise diligent control over the external eye's hasty, inquisitive, and desultory observations lest one mistake a sphere for a polygon. The same is true when considering the cycle of history—lest the observation of multiplicity weaken the impression of continuity. That everything is new is the angle of refraction;* that nothing is new is the bond of unity; but these must be in and with each other—only in this does the truth lie. Yet this likeness among the different is not to be conceived abstractly, not as the Sophist Protagoras did.† A comparable sophism is the idea of mediation.

* *In margin:* the infinite tangential possibilities of the periphery.

† Heise,[362] II, p. 152: that all things are like each other.

III B 14   *n.d.*, 1840-41

« 1634

When I speak[363] of the stillness and silence of contemplation, I do not mean, for example, that one should use just as much time (or even longer) to comprehend history as history itself covers.

III B 15   *n.d.*, 1840-41

« 1635

Concerning the relation between what is right for all ages and what is right for particular ages—the thesis that Christian doctrine maintains that something is right before God decides it[364]—see Plato's *Euthyphro*, para. 182.

There is a scepticism here, however, if the boundary is not exactly defined. Leibniz's analogy that the laws of harmony exist [*er til*] before any one plays (see para. 181)[365] proves nothing. Only abstract truth can be proved in that way. But Christianity is an historical truth; it appears at a certain time and a certain place and consequently it is relevant to a certain time and place. If one says that it had existed [*har været til*] before it came into existence [*blev til*], just like harmony, then one says no more about it than about any other idea, for it, too, is ἀπάτωρ, ἀμέτωρ, ἀγενεαλόγητος.[366] If one maintains this rigorously, then the essence of Christianity is enervated, because in Christianity it is precisely the historical which is the essential; whereas with the other ideas this is accidental.

IV C 35 *n.d.*, 1842-43

« 1636

In the old days people became consequential by being noble, wealthy, etc.; now that we have become more liberal and more world-historical, we all become consequential by being born in the Nineteenth Century. —O, you amazing Nineteenth Century! O enviable fate!

V A 38 *n.d.*, 1844

« 1637 *Relationship to the Historical*

Something demonic[367] in wanting to attack the historical in the New Testament, as if this were the main thing.—

Yet no one has freely and openly posed the problem of doubt in relation to Christianity—Lessing[368] might be the only one.

V B 64 *n.d.*, 1844

« 1638

Rare thinking! If a historical point of departure can decide an eternal happiness, then it can also *eo ipso* determine eternal perdition. We easily understand the one, and we cannot understand the other—that is, we do not think either of the parts but talk our way glibly into the first and are a little shocked by the second. If anyone can think the one (the deciding in time of eternal happiness through a relationship to a historical phenomenon), then he has *eo ipso* thought the other. If time and the relationship in time to a historical phenomenon can be an adequate medium for determining eternal happiness, then it is *eo ipso* adequate for deciding an eternal perdition. To that extent, then, all the extremely curious proofs with which a pious orthodoxy has fenced in this dogma are a misunderstanding, just as the proofs are also quite curious and completely devoid of the specific concept and its consequences.

VI B 35:25 *n.d.*, 1845

« 1639

This is the turning point in world history. Christianity is the religion of the *future*; paganism was the religion of the present or the past (preëxistence). Even Judaism, in spite of its prophetic nature, was too much in the present; it was a future in the present tense. Christianity is a present tense *in futuro*.

VIII[1] A 305   *n.d.*, 1847

«1640

With the help of history we want to understand everything—and with the help of history we still only understand everything inversely or backwards, or we understand nothing. We constantly come to a wrong conclusion. We know that this man and that man were great: *ergo*, his actions were good—that is, we do not understand his actions and therefore do not recognize them again when done by a contemporary. On the strength of the results we conclude that the actions were right, but if as yet there is no result to what a contemporary does, we do not dare believe in it.

Christ prays for his enemies.[369] How many thousand times has a preacher, moved to tears, moved others to tears. But let us look at the situation of contemporaneity. For a person who is regarded by everyone to be an upstart, a crackpot, or a hypocrite—for him to dare to pray for his enemies—that is, those who are around him—well, now, this is regarded as lunatic obstinacy and pride.

IX A 112   *n.d.*, 1848

« 1641

Things have been turned around in Christendom and thus that mythical Christ is supposed to have come from the time of childhood—the age of childhood composes myths. Charming! It is just the opposite. First comes the historical Christ. Then, after a long time, the mythical —an invention by the intellect, which then imputes it to that time of childhood, making it look as if the intellect now had the task of explaining this myth—this myth which it had itself composed.

IX A 160   *n.d.*, 1848

« 1642

It is amusing to read an orthodox writer who is preoccupied with proving a particular item in Christ's life so that, being historical, we can accept it. —O, he who in faith has accepted the most absurd, humanly speaking, of all absurdities—that a simple human being is God—finds it impossible to be baffled by some detail. The fact is that we perceive from this, indirectly, that this orthodoxist is not quite clear about his own relationship to Christ; therefore he admits that it is difficult to believe, for example, Christ's Ascension—if it is not historically certain. For such an orthodoxist it is and has at all times been impossible for Christ to be the paradox.

IX A 196   *n.d.*, 1848

« 1643

History ventilates. When all these *real* people who, exploiting their advantage (especially their coolness about what history will judge of them), have perhaps been altogether brazen and cheeky in the contemporary situation—when all these real people have gotten their due and are no longer impudent but dead and buried and forgotten as if they had never lived—then he still stands there, he whom history designated, he who humbly had to endure the tortures of contemporaneity.[370]

IX B 45:4   *n.d.*, 1848

« 1644

Happy the man who is able to hold the opinion and then is inspired by the opinion that Christianity has been progressively triumphant from century to century. Happy the man who is able to be so carried away, without once being disturbed by the objection that present-day Christendom is therefore an expression of the much greater triumph of Christianity now than in the beginning. Alas, I am able to understand only that Christianity was most true in the first generation, in contemporaneity, and became less true with each generation. On the whole I am unable to understand nothing else than that every thought (when truth is defined as inwardness) is most true in the person in whom it first arose, and by continued communication it steadily becomes less and less true.

X[1] A 415   *n.d.*, 1849

« 1645 *Christ's Passion-story*

It can be said that this is the most moving (considered from Christ's side) and the most shocking (from the environment's side) event which has occurred and which is conceivable, because Christ's story always *is* ideality and not like history, which usually is not pure ideality, and therefore the poet can add ideality to it. But here the ideality is the historical, the greatest contradiction possible, again an expression of the fact that Christianity in its pure ideality explodes all existence [*Tilværelsen*], just as the graves burst, and the veil.

X[4] A 208   *n.d.*, 1851

« 1646 *Generation-Christianity—the Historical*

Christianity relates to the single individual [*den Enkelte*] and exists only where it is primitive. Nowadays we have gotten the whole thing turned around: Christianity is supposed to be related to the race. From generation to generation this falsification is perpetuated—believe because or by virtue of the fact that the others have believed.

The first generation was right. It handed over to the next: We have believed. But from then on we come to the generation which delivers to the next generation—not the testimony that we have believed, but that the preceding generation had believed, that we believe that the preceding generation had believed! Imagine this continued from generation to generation—O, abysmal confusion! A sure way to abolish Christianity!

From this one can also see to what extent the Grundtvigian position misses the point of Christianity.

x⁴ A 505   n.d., 1852

« 1647 *Christendom*

In Christ God volunteered his willingness to become involved with the human race.

But what has the human race done? Instead of becoming involved with God it has changed this into *history* about: how God in Christ has involved himself with the apostles, or history about how God in Christ has involved himself with man. In short, instead of becoming involved with God, they have made this into something historical which they repeat in progressively diluted form from generation to generation.

And how has the race done it, has it behaved with honor and decency toward God? No, no! The truth is that to become involved with God is, from the merely human point of view, the most dreadful of all agonies for a human being.

Thus "man" could have said to God: We dare not; the grace you show us is so great that it makes us unhappy.

But the race has not done this. No, it has hypocritically said: We are too humble to want to be apostles. But this is making a fool of God. This is why Christendom is as God-forsaken as it is idea-forsaken, a mass, a dark body. For the law of the mass is that the individual is just like the others. Thus the singling out of individuality, which produces transparency, drops off, and all become copies, a dark lump.

xi¹ A 388   n.d., 1854

« 1648 *"History"*

And this also belongs to the human confusion, this belief that a young man is supposed to be educated by history. Good lord, what is history! Let us be honest and not succumb to the human conceit that the human race is something so important and significant that its history is very educative.

History is a process. Rarely, rarely is a little drop of idea introduced. The process consists of forming this into nonsense—employing centuries and millions and trillions of people and proceeding on the claim that it is for the purpose of perfecting the investment of idea.

It is this which is so important that the young are to be educated by it, presumably to be perfected in nonsense in good season.

With every decade new and ever new discoveries are made in order to succeed, if possible, in getting everything made over into history, so that every bacon peddler can find a place in history, just as the camera takes pictures of everybody.

No, Omar[371] was right: burn the whole works, for either it is in the Koran or it is a lie.

That which is divinely and infinitely important is to save the primitivity, if possible to preserve the youth in the impression of being the only person in the whole world. What historical education tends to do is to engulf the youth with the nonsense of the sea of millions. Divinely, salvation is in "the individual" [*den Enkelte*]; the race naturally believes that it is in "the race."

XI[1] A 446   *n.d.*, 1854

« 1649 *Christianity—Christendom*

Christianity is: the contact between the divine and the human.

And it is this which has become history, and, note well, in such a manner that each subsequent generation, continually increasing the distance, has become the history about the previous generation's having been the history about the previous, etc., backwards. . . . .

And this is the perfectibility of Christianity!

Christianity has been made into—the history of Christianity, without noting that this simply means to remain outside Christianity, and of course more and more so with each generation.

When we receive a package, we undo the wrappings to get at the contents. Christianity was a gift from God, but instead of receiving the gift,

Christendom has undertaken to wrap it up, and each generation has furnished or produced a new wrapping around the others—and in this way they thought they were getting closer and closer to Christianity.

Christianity has become history. Yes, if there were not the difficulty that the first generations observed the single state, then I am sure that in Christendom, whose religion is intended to be a religion of the spirit, it long ago would have become orthodox that it depends not only upon apostolic succession but upon—the veterinary consideration—true lineage through procreation.

The greatest difference among men is this: to feel God so near that he stands, so to speak, right beside one, near at every moment—or to live on blissfully in the idea that God is removed from one by the distance of 1,800 years of history, and that God's nearness is a historical question.

XI² A 234   *n.d.*, 1854

« 1650 *Christendom—Absence of Spirit*

Christianity is, or becoming a Christian is: to submit oneself to the God-ordained examination by existence [*Tilværelsens*].

Christendom is a society of men who call themselves Christians because they occupy themselves with obtaining information about others who a long time ago submitted themselves to this examination, together with what happened to them in this time of examination—spiritlessly forgetting that they themselves are up for examination.

XI² A 235   *n.d.*, 1854

HOLY SPIRIT

« 1651

The Holy Spirit is the divine "We"[372] which embraces an *I* and a third person (an objective world, a realm of existence); the presence of two subjects makes a plural, and the presence of a first person gives this preference [over an objective third or object].

II A 731   April 23, 1838

« 1652

John 16:10. The Holy Spirit will convince the world of righteousness, because I go to my Father and you will see me no more.

What is understood here by righteousness? It could be related to Paul's teaching[373] that Christ is raised for our justification.

Perhaps it is more correctly understood in this way—the Holy Spirit will convince the world of righteousness—that is, of my righteousness, that I am who I said I am. Then the ending, because I go to my Father and you will see me no more, fits. Christ's returning again to the Father is the justification of Christ's truly having come from the Father. The next verse, concerning judgment, that the ruler of this world is judged, also confirms this interpretation.

IX A 337   n.d., 1848

« 1653 *Hugo St. Victor*

His little essay "The Seven Gifts of the Holy Spirit" (See Helfferich,[374] II, pp. 332 etc.) is also excellent. There is real value in the man. His individual sentences are so pithy that they are practically themes—for example: If you pray for your spirit, you pray for Spirit (the Holy Spirit).

His description of how the Holy Spirit as remedy saves from illness is superb. "Do not be afraid to use the remedy against illness. The illness does not spoil the remedy, but the remedy breaks the illness." If you use the remedy, the suffering arises from your unwillingness to use the remedy properly and thoroughly. "Two opposites struggle with each other: the remedy and the illness, the remedy for you and the illness against you. There is no healing without resistance to the illness: one does not have a hard time of it unless there is resistance to the remedy. The hard time you are going through is the struggle between the opposing factors"—but why do you also want to resist the remedy. "But just the same do not complain of the remedy but of the illness. The remedy will benefit you, the illness will harm. This is why the sickness all by itself probably has peace but not well-being. The remedy all by itself has well-being and creates no hardships. But when the two come together, the battle of the opposites constitutes the hardship by which the one seeks to enter in order to help and the other seeks not to leave in order to harm. But this hard time is the fault of the illness, not of the remedy."

"By the coming of the Holy Spirit you are enlightened and quickened, you who were blind and dead, quickened that you may perceive. One thing you see, another you see ahead; one thing you perceive, another you perceive ahead. You see the evil and see it ahead. You see the present, and what is coming you see ahead. You perceive the guilt, and ahead you perceive the punishment. Before the coming of the Spirit, you were as if blind and did not see, and you were as if dead and did not perceive; you did not see because you did not look backward, and you did not perceive because you did not pay attention. —The healing struggle comes when you, sensitized to the evil, feel pain in order to amend it. If you felt no pain, you would not reform it: if you felt no fear, you would not be attentive. First of all you are enlightened concerning the guilt, so that you may see it; next, concerning the punishment, so that you may fear it; and finally you are sensitized because of the guilt so that you may perceive the pain and reform yourself. If we did not see the punishment which we fear, no one would feel pain over the guilt in which he finds pleasure. Therefore the punishment which follows the guilt is shown to you so that the guilt in which you actually take delight will pinch you and disconcert you and you will finally wake up to the fact that this which seems so delightful is an evil, because the bitterness which is tasted on account of it or after it is such a great evil. Thus you become enlightened and concerned, because you see what terrifies, what possesses, what pains." "Every punishment is indeed an evil, but not every punishment is evil, for what is an aid and benefit unto something else is a good. By punishment we are freed from punishment, that is, eternal punishment."

x^2 A 353   *n.d.*, 1850

« 1654 *The Holy Spirit*

The Holy Spirit is called "the Comforter." This name might lead one to think that the Holy Spirit should comfort the disciples and then also the Christians because Christ went away and was no longer visible among them.

But this is not the way it is. Christ as the prototype [*Forbilledet*] is still a form of the law, yes, the law raised to a higher level, and therefore Christ's suffering is the most rigorous judgment upon the world and the race in that there was not a single one who would persevere with him. (We see here how immensely confused that preacher-prattle is which, carried away in a soulful moment, without thinking, or with as much thought as flesh and blood can be said to have, wishes to be contemporary with Christ.) To be contemporary with Christ is the most rigorous examination ever possible. If this were to be perpetual, then the Jews were under milder judgment under the law.

But then Christ dies—and his death is the Atonement: here is grace.

The Holy Spirit whom Christ will send is really the dispensator of grace, the grace which Christ won.

From this comes the name "the Comforter." A man does not need grace only in relation to the past. This is how men usually think: All your sins are forgiven you: satisfaction has been made. Fine; but if I do not die tomorrow, then it is soon apparent that although "grace" has been allotted to me, since that time I have been far from pure and perfect. To that extent the situation has become still worse, because before I received grace I always had the consolation that grace was still to come, but now I have misused even the grace. Therefore I need "grace" again in regard to the bad use I made of grace,* and so on and on——. Grace is the everlasting fountain—and the Holy Spirit the dispensator, the Comforter. The Holy Spirit is the Comforter also in the sense that Christ as the prototype is a requirement which no human being meets. As long as Christ is visibly present as the prototype, he cannot prevent its becoming judgment. Therefore his life has two aspects: he is the prototype—then he dies, and now he is transformed: he becomes for all eternity the "grace" for our imperfect striving to be like "the prototype."

x^2 A 451   *n.d.,* 1850

« 1655

* *In margin of* 1654 (x^2 A 451):

Note. Therefore there was something profound in the early view that Baptism should be on the deathbed. They understood that Christianity, humanly speaking, is the conception of life for which only one situation is favorable: the situation of death. The difficulty appears when there is to be striving. Acceptance of grace is deferred until it [striving] is past —then one receives grace. But this is either melancholy or even secular-minded shrewdness, which takes Christianity in vain.

x^2 A 452   *n.d.*

« 1656 *The Sigh of a Contender*

Even though everyone opposed me, even though misfortune followed on the heels of misfortune (something which often pains more than the opposition of men, which one understands must come), one thing still remains, O God, the witness of the Spirit. When you who have everything at your disposal, who at all times have millions of possibilities, when you, infinite love, let all this go against me, or insofar as I bring some of it upon myself by a mistake, when you, infinite love, let me make the mistake, when it then seems as if you had backed out—there is one association still remaining between us, the witness of the Spirit.

If there were no witness of the Spirit, if through the Spirit you did not essentially hold on to the very one you test most stringently, I would not know whether I am coming or going, it would be impossible for me to know where I am, whether opposition and misfortune are your fatherly discipline in order to frighten me back, or whether opposition and misfortune simply mean that I am on the right way, the narrow way, where the witness of the Spirit is the only sign.

x^3 A 297   *n.d.*, 1850

« 1657 *The Testimony of the Spirit,*

strictly understood, is present only when the immediate testimony witnesses to the contrary. When everything is going the way you want it to, even if you relate everything to God, you can still not be sure that the joy you feel is the testimony of the Spirit, for it can also be simply the particular heightening of your own life by means of your good fortune and prosperity. But when everything goes against you and you nevertheless perceive deep within you a testimony that you are on the right path and ought to continue further along this path where everything will probably go against you increasingly: this, you see, is the testimony of the Spirit.

x^3 A 360   *n.d.*, 1850

« 1658 *Nonsense*

They pray God to give them the testimony of the Spirit—and forget that "the testimony of the Spirit" is really present and is decisively present only when all the spontaneous, immediate testimonies have been nullified. How many really have the strength to bear the testimony of the Spirit? They do not know what they are saying with respect to religion; far too many (pastors and lay people) are like the Jew who signed a petition insisting on the Norwegian constitution without knowing that it expelled Jews from the country. This is the way they consort with Christianity, and if they knew themselves at all they would have to thank God for not granting their prayer at present, for a person has to be very far out [beyond the immediate] before he is actually helped by the testimony of the Spirit, he has to be essentially on the way to becoming spirit—and how many are that far out?

x^3 A 365   *n.d.*, 1850

« 1659

Eve was created as company for the man; the Holy Spirit is called the Comforter.

x^3 A 787   *n.d.*, 1851

« 1660 *The Holy Spirit*

. . . . . In the lives [*Existentser*] we actually live—insignificant, finite, and secularized—we make each other believe that we pray to a Holy Spirit to stay by us, that it is the Holy Spirit who guides us. No, let us at least be honest and hold the Holy Spirit in honor and say: We are afraid to pray to a Holy Spirit for aid. The matter could become too serious for us if the Holy Spirit actually did come—and help us.

This is 50% more earnest than preacher-chatter.

x^4 A 329   *n.d.*, 1851

« 1661 *The Holy Spirit[375] is "the Comforter"— To Die to the World—To Be Born Again*

Why is the Holy Spirit called the Comforter?

Very simple. If the sign of being in relation to God and the sign of God's loving me is supposed to be that I succeed in everything, then I need no Spirit to comfort me; the whole relationship is not a relationship of spirit at all.

No, but when the sign of the relation to God is suffering, when God's loving me has its very expression in my having to suffer (and God as "Spirit" cannot express his love otherwise; this is the way it is taught in the New Testament, where, for example, Christ expressly says to Paul that he will see what he will have to suffer for his name's sake—consequently suffering is the expression of love, the expression for being the beloved), then there must be a "Spirit" in order to comfort.

[*In margin:* "The Spirit" is also called "the Comforter" with respect to "imitation" [*Efterfølgelsen*], yet a person can never attain to the point that he in any sense dares to put his confidence in it.]

What is it to die to the world [*afdøe*]? It is to suffer the pain of God's really becoming Spirit for a person, and through this the mark of the God-relationship becomes suffering.

What is it to be born again? It is through the pain of dying to the world to be transformed into being spirit and enduring suffering as the mark of the God-relationship.

The most intensified egotism is to love oneself and then, to boot, to make oneself believe that succeeding in everything is proof of God's love. Dreadful egotism. The greatest distance from this is to endure, in blessed joy and in victorious joy, suffering as the mark of the God-relationship.

$$x^4 \text{ A } 588 \quad n.d., 1852$$

« 1662 *The Spirit is the Comforter, the Intercessor*

I am sure that in an earlier journal [i.e., x^4 A 588] I have already noted what I wish to emphasize once again.

When the mark of the God-relationship is success, prosperity, earthly blessings, with a sprinkling of adversities at most, which no one avoids anyway—then there is no need for a Spirit who is the Comforter.

But if a man has to live in the situation where in inwardness with God he dares think that he is God's instrument, is loved by God, serves God's cause (and this is how it is presented in the New Testament)—and yet empirically it looks as if God is on the side of the opposition, whom he lets have the power, the power to mistreat this man in every manner —when a man in his inner being dares think that he is beloved of God, and empirically it continually looks as if the opponents were beloved of God, the ones with whom God sides, since this man comes to suffer worse than any criminal at the hands of the powerful and favored ones— when a man in his inner being dares think that he is beloved by God and yet understands that empirically this will be expressed by his coming to suffer more and more, yes, the more he clings to God (just as if God progressively left him more and more in the lurch)—well, then there is truly need for a Spirit who is the Comforter, the Intercessor, who can speak to him, "remind him" that this is exactly what Christ foretold and his life expressed, so that above all the person suffering in this way does not become weary and in human impatience quite naturally and humanly change the relationship so that the suffering and adversity are regarded as a sign of God's disfavor, a sign that I should not continue on the way I am going, that I have gone astray, or probably am even arrogant and puffed-up and ought to turn back penitently.

Take "Christendom" as it is now: the way people live nowadays, there can be no question of needing any Spirit (for people are living in the category of extroversion, not conversion)—and yet they talk endlessly about the Spirit and about community.

X⁵ A 49   *n.d.*, 1852

HOPE

« 1663

Hope is the foster-mother of the Christian life.

II A 566   n.d., 1839

« 1664

There is all the difference of heaven and hell between the proud courage which dares presume to dread [*frygte*] everything and the humble courage which dares to hope everything.

III A 217   November 15, 1840

« 1665

You complain that many of your expectations[376] become disappointments, that none of your most eager desires is fulfilled; you are so wretched that you have even lost the desire and the courage to hope—this we will not deny, partly because we all have many fatuous expectations and partly because our Lord teaches us not to expect everything to be fulfilled. Yet there is still an expectation which cannot possibly be disappointed, for you do expect the resurrection of the dead, which is a blessed longing [*Længsel*], for you do expect to be gathered together with those who were dear to you, a prolonging [*Forlængsel*], for you do hope finally to see your life transfigured in God—an expectation that God will work out everything for the best, inasmuch as your life is not yet past and you do not know the time or the hour.

III A 129   n.d., 1841

« 1666

In margin of 1665 (III A 129):
We know, of course, that there have been those who have not been disappointed in their expectations, who learned early to harden their hearts, who now with a certain proud self-satisfaction look out over those whose heads are bowed down in affliction—they certainly are not disappointed. Yet there was a time in their lives, too, when their hearts were stirred by great ideas, when hope shone round about them—at

246

that time they certainly did not expect to experience seeing themselves like this—withered, barren, and unfruitful.

III A 130   n.d.

« 1667

Everyone hopes at least for something when he goes out into the world—and then wants to be faithful over that little.[377] But the one who goes out into the world possessing nothing but a precious memory, expecting nothing, but is faithful to the memory, is also faithful over little, and he shall be set over more, for such a memory shall become for him the eternal.

V A 55   n.d., 1844

« 1668

That Christianity is like this, that it is preceded by humor,[378] shows how much living out of life it presupposes in order rightly to be accepted. Christianity was certainly not proclaimed to children but to the world of superannuated philosophy, science, and art. For this reason the paradox is something else than, say, the marvelous, just as the hope Christianity proclaims is opposed to understanding. But the dialectic of hope goes this way: first the fresh incentive of youth, then the supportive calculation of understanding, and then—then everything comes to a standstill—and now for the first time Christian hope is there as possibility. The fact that ecclesiastical chatterboxes have confused this as well as all Christian speech is none of my business.

VI B 53:13   n.d., 1845

HUMOR, IRONY, THE COMIC

« 1669

The irony of life must of necessity be most intrinsic to childhood, to the age of imagination; this is why it is so striking in the Middle Ages; this is why it is present in the romantic school. Adulthood, the more it becomes engrossed in the world, does not have so much of it.

I A 125   February, 1836

« 1670

It is very interesting to see the singular comedy played with the world—for example, in the Scandinavian hero stories—when the person from whom one would expect the least suddenly rises up with a power and might which is not particularly pleasing to those who have taken advantage of his apparent stupidity to make fun of him. (All of the Hamlet type; I may cite as examples *Ketil Hæng's Saga*,[379] III, 2, p. 3 *passim* and *Buesvingers Saga*, III, 2, p. 211.) This, however, is not so remarkable, since it is nature which, so to speak, has for a long time allowed the fire to glow under the ashes, which later flames up all the more powerfully, and this is precisely the situation here in that a sudden disappearance constitutes the transition to the later brilliant period. —But still more remarkable is the example of the curious kind of ironizing over the world which occurs when the world with all its cleverness stands in the presence of an individual who plays the mad man and yet triumphs over all of them—such as I find in Schwab, *Buch der schönsten Geschichten und Sagen*,[380] in the character of Robert der Teufel (p. 357), where he is advised by a hermit he consults to behave like a fool and a deaf-mute and to take food only with the dogs and to sleep with them. Meanwhile he does great things for the king he is with, yet without anyone's suspecting it except the king's daughter—but again he plays the role of the fool. —From this we could make a transition to a study of the significance of *fools* in the Middle Ages: how to a large degree fools were, if you please, the chorus in the world's tragedies which were performed in the Middle Ages, how the fool's relation to his master was a fruit of the cleavage which had become established between the nobility and the

248

poorer classes, how this constituted a transition to the relation of a Wagner, a Leporello, and a Sancho Panza to their respective masters—in order thereby to arrive from another side at the same idea we discussed on another occasion.

March, 1836

It almost seems as if it takes two individuals to form one whole man; this explains the enthusiasm for the prince or lord which the fool often displayed. When I say that it takes two to make one individual, I of course do not mean the knight's relation to his squires, for *they* did not play any independent role, but to the fool, who represented intelligence.

I A 145   *n.d.*, 1836

« 1671

Humor in contrast to irony—and yet as a rule they can be united in one individual, since both components are contingent on one's not having compromised with the world. This non-compromise with the world is modified in humor by one's not giving two hoots for it, and in the other [irony], however, by one's trying to influence the world and for precisely this reason being ridiculed by the world. They are the two opposite ends of a teeter-totter (wave motions). The humorist, when the world makes fun of him, feels like the duck which must often go under in its battle with life and then again often rises above it and laughs at it. (When, for example, Faust does not understand the world and yet laughs at the world, which does not understand him.)

I A 154   April, 1836

« 1672

One who walked along contemplating suicide—at that very moment a stone fell down and killed him,[381] and he ended with the words: Praise the Lord!

I A 158   *n.d.*, 1836

« 1673

Irony, the ignorance Socrates began with, the world created from nothing, the pure virgin who gave birth to Christ——

I A 190   *n.d.*, 1836

« 1674

Does not the irony in Christianity lie in this that it made an attempt to encompass the entire world, but the seeds of the impossibility of doing this lay within itself, and this is connected with the other, the humorous, its view of what it actually calls the world (this concept properly belongs to the humorous and therefore in a sense the humorous occupies a middle ground), because everything which hitherto had asserted itself in the world and continued to do so was placed in relation to the presumably single truth of the Christians, and therefore to the Christians the kings and the princes, enemies and persecutors, etc., etc., appeared to be nothing and to be laughable because of their opinions of their own greatness.

I A 207   July 19, 1836

« 1675

Precisely because it actually is mood which dominates in Holberg, at many points his dramas (*Erasmus Montanus, Jeppe*, etc.) slip over into tragedy, skip over the ironical point of view which moderates it, just as tragedy based on immediacy easily takes on a tinge of comedy (through accidentals which as such become ridiculous) or irony lies dormant from the outset, as in the hero stories, for example.

I A 238   *n.d.*, 1836

« 1676

Irony is native only to the immediate (where, however, the individual does not become conscious of it as such) and to the dialectical position; whereas in the third position (that of character) the reaction to the world does not appear as irony, since resignation has now developed in the individual, which is precisely the consciousness of the limitation every effort must have, insofar as it is to continue in a structure of world-order, because as striving it is infinite and unlimited. Irony and resignation are two opposite poles, the two opposite directions of motion.[382]

I A 239   September 13, 1836

« 1677 *August, 1836*

For the ancients the divine was continually merged with the world; therefore no irony.

I A 256   August, 1836

« 1678

Does not some of what I have called irony approach what the Greeks called Nemesis—for example, the overrating of an individual the very moment he feels most distressed about some guilt—for example, the scene in *Faust*[383] where the jubilant peasants receive him and thank him for his and his father's skill during the epidemic, likewise often the Wagner-type admiration.

I A 265   October 27, 1836

« 1679

The quiet and the security one has in reading a classic or in associating with a fully matured person is not found in the romantic;[384] there it is something like watching a man write with hands which tremble so much that one fears the pen will run away from him any moment into some grotesque stroke. (This is dormant irony.)

II A 37   *n.d.*, 1837

« 1680

In margin of 1679 (II A 37):
The development of the concept of irony has to begin here where the fantastic, grandiose ideas are gratified and reflection has not yet disturbed the ingenuousness of this position. But now one observes that it does not go this way in the world, and since he is unable to surrender his lofty ideals, he likewise has to feel in some manner the world's ridicule (irony—romantic, the previous was not romantic but a gratification in the form of achievement) (this irony is the world's irony over the individual and is different from what the Greeks called irony, which was the ironical gratification in which the single individual hovered above the world and which began to develop as the idea of the state disappeared more and more—therefore in Socrates; but in the romantic position, where everything is struggle, irony cannot gain entrance in the individual but lies outside of it; I believe this distinction has been too much overlooked), and finally the third position, where irony is outlived.

II A 38   *n.d.*

« 1681

Hamann could become a good representative of the humor in Christianity[385] (more about this another time), but in him the trend toward humor necessarily developed one-sidedly (a) because of the humor intrinsic to Christianity, (b) because of the isolation of the individual conditioned by the Reformation, an isolation which did not arise in Catholicism, which since it had a Church could oppose "the world," although in its pure concept as Church it probably was less able to be predisposed to do this, and in any case it nevertheless could not develop humor to an apex opposing everything and thereby rather barren, at least devoid of prolific vegetation and bearing only dwarfed, scrawny birch (the reason this was not the case with Hamann is to be found in his profound sensibility and enormous genius, which had depth corresponding to the degree of its narrowness in width—and Hamann found a real delight in inviting his knowledge-greedy contemporaries, platter-lickers, to his long-necked stork flask—but just the same he can be a very good representative for the true center of this position), and (c) because of his own naturally humorous disposition. Thus one can truthfully say that Hamann is the greatest humorist in Christianity (meaning the greatest humorist in the view of life which itself is the most humorous view of life in world-history—therefore the greatest humorist in the world).

II A 75   *n.d.*, 1837

« 1682

The humorous, present throughout Christianity,* is expressed in a fundamental principle which declares that the truth is hidden in the mystery (ἐν μυστηρίῳ ἀποκρύφη),[386] which teaches not only that the truth is found in a mystery (an assertion which the world generally has been more inclined to hear, since mysteries have arisen often enough, although the ones initiated into these mysteries promptly apprehended the rest of the world in a humorous vein), but that it is in fact *hidden*† in the mystery. This is a view of life which regards worldly wisdom humorously to the nth degree; otherwise the truth is usually *revealed* in the mystery.

Insofar as Christianity does not divorce itself from romanticism, no matter how much Christian knowledge increases, it will still always remember its origin and therefore *know* everything ἐν μυστηρίῳ.[387]

The humorous in Christianity appears also in the statement: My yoke is easy and my burden is not heavy,[388] for it certainly is extremely heavy for the world, the heaviest that can be imagined—self-denial.

The ignorance of the Christian (this purely Socratic view,‡ as in a Hamann, for example) is, of course, also humorous, for what is its basis but a forcing of oneself down in this way to the lowest position and looking up (that is, down) at the ordinary view, yet in such a way that behind this self-degrading there lies a high degree of self-elevating (the humility of the Christian which in its polemical form against the world increases his own wretchedness, while on the other hand in its normative form it involves a noble pride (the least in the kingdom of heaven[389] is greater than John the Baptist) or in its abnormality a haughty isolation from the course of ordinary events (the historical nexus).

Thus miracle plays an important, primary role in this view of life, not because of the power gained in this way for Christianity but because all the most profound ideas of the sages become (in this view) as nothing, along with Balaam's prophesying ass.[390] The more insignificant the miracle is, if I may say so, or the less it enters into relationship with the historical development, yes, even to the point that this view, so to speak, tempts God—that is, wanting a miracle performed only to disconcert the professors of physics—the more pleased it is; indeed, this view would rejoice most of all over the changing of wine into water at Cana.[391] Yes, when it rejoices over the miracle of Christ's rising from the dead, then this is not the true Easter joy but rather the amusement over the Pharisees and the soldiers and their great big stone in front of the tomb. Therefore this view usually dwells upon the crib, upon the rags in which the child was wrapped, upon the crucifixion between *two thieves*.[392]

II A 78   June 3, 1837

« 1683

In margin of 1682 (II A 78):

* I see that Daub[393] in his lectures on anthropology, recently published, makes a very brief similar observation about why the ancients did not have humor. See p. 482.

II A 79   April 17, 1838

« 1684

In margin of 1682 (II A 78):

† And the concept of revelation can in itself very well include the concept of the hidden, just as the word "door" is used to designate that one does not come back, שעדי-נוות,[394] death's door. —

II A 80   May 14, 1839

« 1685

In margin of 1682 (II A 78):

‡ The Socratic principle expressed in the realm of action is: God be merciful to me a sinner[395] (this appears precisely in contrast to the Pharisee and the other one is praised for it).

II A 81   *n.d.*

« 1686

In margin of 1682 (II A 78):

The extent to which humor appears in Christ's own utterances—see, for example: Consider the lilies of the field, yet I tell you even Solomon in all his glory was not arrayed as one of these;[396] you have revealed these things to the blind, the poor in spirit;[397] Martha, Martha.[398] These are all utterances which with the addition of a polemical cast would all be humorous but in Christ's mouth are redeeming. Also the utterances: There is more joy in heaven over one sinner who repents than over 100 who do *not* need repentance[399] (how the irony emerges here!)*. It is easier for a camel to go through the eye of a needle than for a rich man to enter the kindgdom of heaven.[400]

* Since the meaning can never be that there was a single righteous person who did not need repentance. The same meaning is seriously expressed in the words: Let him who is without sin among you be the first to throw a stone.[401]

II A 84   *n.d.*

« 1687

In margin of 1682 (II A 78):

Another feature with regard to humor in Christianity is that in the Middle Ages parody developed within Christianity itself (see how excellently it is sketched in Walter Scott's *der Abbt*; Stuttgart: 1828; part II, p. 40 etc.: *der Narrenpapst, der Kinderbischof, der Abt, der Unvernuft*, where it is also poetically conceived, since, to be sure, it takes place here as a well-merited nemesis of ridicule upon Catholicism). This is an unconsidered observation and should be digested in an essay.

II A 85   *n.d.*

« 1688

If I have conceived (see another sheet [i.e., I A 154]) of the romantic position as a see-saw, the ends of which are characterized by irony and humor, then it follows naturally that the path of its oscillation is extremely varied, all the way from the most heaven-storming humor to the most desperate bowing down in irony, as if there were a certain rest and equilibrium in this position (Wieland's "Irony"), for irony is first surmounted when the individual, elevated above everything and looking down from this position, is finally elevated beyond himself and from this dizzy height sees himself in his nothingness, and thereby he finds his true elevation. —See *Prindsessinn Brambilla*.[402]

June 2, 1837

This self-overcoming of irony is the crisis of the higher spiritual life; the individual is now acclimatized—the bourgeois mentality, which essentially only hides in the other position, is conquered, and the individual is reconciled.

The ironical position is essentially: *nil admirari*; but irony, when it slays itself, has *disdained* everything with humor, itself included. —

II A 627   *n.d.*, 1837

« 1689

How close the immediate, spontaneous expression often lies to irony, and yet how far away. For example, Oehlenschlaeger:

> O flower, as it goes with you
> so it goes with me.
> Like a cornflower the wretched poet
> stands and grieves.
> He only stands in the way of the *nourishing grain*—
> What does he achieve.[403]

Is it the same immediacy, although far more profound, which keeps Christ's discourses and for the most part the whole New Testament from having an ironical and humorous imprint, although one single stroke would immediately give the expression the strongest possible coloring of irony and humor?

II A 101   June 30, 1837

« 1690

Irony presumably can also produce a certain tranquillity (which then may correspond to the space following a humorous development) which, however, is a long way from being Christian redemption* (brothers in Christ—every other distinction completely disappears, becomes nothing in proportion to being brothers in Christ—but did not Christ make distinctions, did he not love John more than the others—Poul Møller in a most interesting conversation on the evening of June 30). It can produce a certain love,† the kind with which Socrates, for example, encompassed his disciples (spiritual pederasty, as Hamann[404] says), but it is still egotistical, because he stood as their deliverer, expanded their narrow expressions and views in his higher consciousness, in his perspective; the diameter of the movement is not as great as in the case of the humorist‡ (heaven—hell—the Christian has to despise all things—the ironical man's highest movement is *nil admirari*). Irony is egotistical (it contends with the bourgeois, philistine mentality and yet retains it even though in the individual it mounts in the air like a songbird,§ little by little throwing out its cargo, until it runs the risk of ending with an egotistical "Go to the devil," for irony has not yet slain itself by looking at itself, in the sense that the individual sees himself in the light of the irony. Humor is *lyrical* (it is the most profound earnestness about life—profound poetry, which cannot form itself as such and therefore crystalizes in baroque forms—it is hemorrhoidal *non fluens*—the *molimina* of the higher life).

The whole attitude of the Greek nature (harmony—beauty) was such that even if the individual disengaged himself and the battle began, there was still the imprint of having arisen from this harmonious view of life, and therefore it soon came to an end without having described a full circle (Socrates). But now there appeared a view of life which taught that all nature is corrupt (the deepest polemic, the widest wing-stretching), but nature took revenge—and now I get *humor* in the individual and *irony*‖ in nature, and they meet in that humor wants to be a fool in the world and the irony in the world accepts them [men of humor] as actually being that.

Some say that irony and humor are basically the same with only a degree of difference. I will answer with Paul,[405] where he talks about the relationship of Christianity to Judaism: *everything is new in Christ.*

The Christian humorist is like a plant of which only the roots are visible, whose flower unfolds for a loftier sun.

II A 102   July 6, 1837

« 1691

In margin of 1690 (II A 102):

* Therefore Socrates' influence was simply to awaken—midwife that he was—not redeeming except in an inauthentic sense.

II A 103   October 30, 1837

« 1692

In margin of 1690 (II A 102):

† And therefore so enormously different from the more recent idealistic-philosophical go-to-the-devil.

II A 104   *n.d.*

« 1693

In margin of 1690 (II A 102):

‡ Humor can therefore approach blasphemy; Hamann would rather hear wisdom from Balaam's ass or from a philosopher against his will than from an angel or an apostle.[406]

II A 105 n.d.

« 1694

In margin of 1690 (II A 102):

§ It is no heavenly ladder on which angels *descend* from the *opened* heaven,[407] but it is an assault-ladder, gigantic, which Christianly means to take God's kingdom by force.[408]

II A 106 n.d.

« 1695

In margin of 1690 (II A 102):

‖ Irony in nature must be worked out, such as the ironical juxtapositions (man and monkey) etc. found in various forms in Schubert's *Symbolik*;[409] this was something the Greeks knew nothing about, as far as I know.

The medieval fairy story *Lune*,[410] for example, has a man who, standing two miles away from a windmill, makes it go by *laying his finger on one nostril* and blowing through the other.

II A 107 n.d.

« 1696

In margin of 1690 (II A 102):

Jean Paul[411] is the greatest humorist *capitalist*.

II A 108 n.d.

« 1697

Irony no longer stands out the way it used to. I have often thought[412] it was a kind of irony of the world when, for example, a horsefly sat on a man's nose the very moment he made his last running leap to throw himself into the Thames, when in the story of Loki and the dwarf,[413] after Eitri has gone away and Brock stands by the bellows, a fly settles on his nose three times—here the ironical appears as one of Loki's intrigues to prevent him from winning the wager, and in the other case it is a grandiose human plan which is horridly ridiculed by a horsefly.

II A 112 July 8, 1837

« 1698

There certainly was humor in the Middle Ages, too, but it was within a totality, within the Church, and was partly about the world, partly about itself. Therefore it does not have much of the sickliness which I believe belongs to this concept. This was also why some of the modern humorists became Catholics, desired a community again, a backbone which they did not have within themselves.

II A 114   July 11, 1837

« 1699

See this book pp. 10 and 11 [i.e., II A 101-108].

Humor is irony carried through to its maximum oscillations. Even though the essentially Christian is the real *primus motor*, nevertheless there are those in Christian Europe who have not achieved more than irony and for that reason have also not been able to accomplish the absolutely isolated, independently personal humor. Therefore they either seek rest in the Church, where in united humor over the *world* the solidarity of individuals develops a *Christian irony*, as was the case with Tieck and others, or, if the religious is not in motion, form a club (*The Brothers of Serapion*[414]—which in Hoffmann's case was nevertheless not something palpable, actual, but ideal). No, Hamann is still the greatest and most authentic humorist, the genuinely humorous Robinson Crusoe, not on a desert island but in the noise of life; his humor is not an esthetic concept but life, not a hero in a controlled drama.

II A 136   August 4, 1837

« 1700

See pages 10 and 11 and 19 [i.e., II A 101-108, 136].

Now I perceive why genuine humor cannot be caught, as irony can, in a novel and why it thereby ceases to be a life-concept, simply because not-to-write is part of the nature of the concept, since this would betray an all too conciliatory position toward the world (which is why Hamann[415] remarks somewhere that fundamentally there is nothing more ludicrous than to write for the people). Just as Socrates left no books, Hamann left only as much as the modern period's rage for writing made relatively necessary, and furthermore only occasional pieces.

II A 138   n.d., 1837

« 1701

In margin of 1700 (II A 138):
"For how could Hamann ever think of publishing the whole body of his works"[416]—he who, completely in agreement with Pilate, whom he declares to be the greatest philosopher, said: What I have written I have written.

II A 139   *n.d.*

« 1702

In margin of 1700 (II A 138):
Therefore the humorist can never actually become a systematizer, either, for he regards every system as a renewed attempt to blow up the world with a single syllogism in the familiar Blicherian manner;[417] whereas the humorist himself has come alive to the incommensurable which the philosopher can never figure out and therefore must despise. He lives in the abundance and is therefore sensitive to how much is always left over, even if he has expressed himself with all felicity (therefore the disinclination to write). The systematizer believes that he can say everything, and that whatever cannot be said is erroneous and secondary.

II A 140   *n.d.*

« 1703

The ancients' use of irony is completely different from that of the moderns. First of all there is its relation to a harmonic language, the compact Greek in contrast to modern reflective prolixity, but the irony of the Greeks is also *plastic*, for example, Diogenes, who does not merely make the observation that when a poor marksman shoots, the best thing is for him to stand close to the target, but he walks ahead and stands close to the target. O, I would like to have heard Socrates ironize!

II A 141   *n.d.*, 1837

« 1704

See page II [i.e., II A 102].
The humorous expression for the Christian is "weakness:" they are weak in *Christ* (for then God is strong in them; therefore Paul says that he will *boast of his weakness*, find pleasure in his weakness, II Corinthians 12:10 etc.) See Calvin[418] on II Corinthians 13:4: *nos infirmi sumus in*

illo. Infirmum esse in Chr., hic significat socium esse infirmitatis Chr. Ita suam infirmitatem gloriosam facit, quod in ea sit Christo conformis: neque jam amplius horreat probrum, quod sibi commune est cum filio dei, sed interea dicit, se victurum erga eos Chr. exemplo.[419]

As is usually the case with regard to the humorous interpretation of Christianity, the much-worked dogmatic question concerning Christ's life becomes important—whether Christ bore the divine life in his state of debasement[420] κατὰ κενῶσιν or κατὰ κρύψιν[421]—the latter is genuinely humorous.

II A 146   August 27, 1837

« 1705

In margin of 1704 (II A 146):
There also seems to be something humorous in II Corinthians 13:7, where Paul hopes that the congregation may do no wrong, "not that we may appear to have met the test, but that you may do what is right ἡμεῖς δὲ ὡς ἀδόκιμοι ὦμεν,"[422] since, indeed, to the very same degree that they grew in goodness, his honor increased in a sense, unless the meaning is that he wishes them progress in the good to such a degree that compared to it he himself may become ἀδόκιμος.[423]

II A 147   August 27, 1837

« 1706

When an ironist laughs at the whimsicalities and witticisms of a humorist, he is like the vulture tearing away at Prometheus's liver, for the humorist's whimsicalities are not *capricious little darlings* but the *sons of pain,* and with every one of them goes a little piece of his innermost entrails, and it is the emaciated ironist who needs the humorist's desperate depth. His laughter is often the grin of death. Just as a shriek wrung from pain could very well appear to be laughable to someone at great distance who had no intimation of the situation of the person from whom it came, just as the twitch of a muscle on the face of a deaf-mute or a taciturn person could appear to someone to be laughable, that is, caused by laughter in the individual (like the dead man's grin which is explained as the muscle twitch of rigor mortis, the eternally humorous smile over human wretchedness)—so it goes with the laughter of the humorist, and it probably betrays a greater psychological insight to cry over such a thing (note —not a jeremiad, for one of the sad things about man is that he troubles himself about so many irrelevancies)—than to laugh over it.[424]

II A 179   October 11, 1837

« 1707

Therefore [because of the attainment of tranquility] only then is humor maturely reflective—in the face of all empiricism it is an unshakeable, authentic frame of mind related to genius; whereas irony at every moment exempts itself from a new dependence—which from another angle means that it is dependent at every moment.

II A 192   November 9, 1837

« 1708

When irony (humor) in its polemic has put the whole world, heaven and earth, under water and in compensation has enclosed a little world in itself—it lets a raven fly out when it is ready to be reconciled with the world again—and then a dove, which returns with an olive leaf.

II A 195   November 15, 1837

« 1709

Humorists develop God's side
> (Mohammed etc.
> Pythagoras)

"Realists"—the human side
You poor wretches, you poor man, the poor men[425]

II A 591   n.d., 1837

« 1710

When a person first begins to reflect upon Christianity, it undoubtedly is at first a cause of offense before he enters into it; yes, he may have wished that it had never come into the world, or at least that the question about it had never arisen in his consciousness. Therefore it is nauseating to hear all this talk by meddlesome, intervening intermediaries about Christ as the greatest of heroes. Therefore a humorous view is far preferable.

II A 596   n.d., 1837

« 1711

The whole attitude of the Greek nature (harmony) had the effect that even though battle divided them, the struggle never became acute—then there was harmony in nature—irony in the individual—now comes the revenge—irony in nature and humor in the individual. If someone says that irony and humor are identical, only different in degrees, I will say what

Paul says of the relationship of Christianity to Judaism: "All is new."

II A 608   *n.d.*, 1837

« 1712

The sympathetic egoity. Irony.
The hypochrondriacal egoity. Humor.
    One is closest to himself.

II A 626   *n.d.*, 1837

« 1713

Now I perceive why genuine humor cannot be caught, as irony can, in a novel and why it thereby ceases to be a life-concept, simply because not-to-write is part of the nature of the concept—just as Socrates left no books, neither did Hamann, only as many as the modern rage for writing made relatively necessary—occasional pieces.—[426]

II A 658   *n.d.*, 1837

« 1714

Irony in relation to ancient linguistic structure—before the modern reflected prolixity.

II A 659   *n.d.*, 1837

« 1715

To what extent may there be humor in prayer, in which there is a disregard for all secular relatively, an informal *du*-relationship[427] to God.

II A 660   *n.d.*, 1837

« 1716

But humor is also the joy which has overcome the world.

II A 672   *n.d.*, 1837

« 1717

Irony is an abnormal development which, like the abnormality of the livers of Strasburger geese, ends by killing the individual.

II A 682   January 1, 1838

« 1718

A man who lets himself be skinned alive in order to show how the humorous smile is produced by the contraction of a particular muscle—and thereupon follows this with a lecture on humor.

II A 689   January 6, 1838

« 1719

The humorist, like the beast of prey, always walks alone.

II A 694   January 13, 1838

« 1720

Wit always depends upon an association of ideas, but the difference lies in whether it ricochets upon the player (the periphery) or upon the red ball[428] (the center).

II A 562   September 11, 1839

« 1721

Humor can be either religious or demonic (in relation to the two mysteries).

III A 46   n.d., 1840

« 1722

Precisely because humor wants to have the absolute without the relative, it fumbles about in the most desperate leaping, always within the most appalling relativity—

The same glass magnifies[429] (a blade of grass is worth more than all ingenuity) and diminishes (rather hear wisdom from the mouth of a Pharisee against his will than from an apostle)—[430]

III A 49   n.d., 1840

« 1723

When Socrates says at the end of the *Apology* that it is impossible to call death the greatest evil since we do not know really what it is, this is still spoken with irony[431]—but with a little modification the same thing could be said humorously.

III B 4   n.d., 1840-41

« 1724 *Introduction*

That it [irony] is not an esthetic concept—but the *molimina* for a life-view—the relation of paradox* to thought—personality—the style is the man—Socrates had to stand still to come to himself—the Middle Ages was occupied with encircling the world—there is humor in Clement of Alexandria's praise of writing allegories so that the heathens could not understand.

III B 5   n.d., 1840-1841

« 1725 *Immediacy—Whimsy*

To what extent there is immediacy in the comic—after all, there is really nothing immediate—to what extent it points back to something of the sort—

III B 6   *n.d.*, 1840-1841

« 1726

* *Addition to* 1724 (III B 5):
The significance of the polemical—the comic has the polemical as a necessary element.

III B 7   *n.d.*, 1840-1841

« 1727

In the case of Swift, it was an irony of fate that in his old age he entered the insane asylum he himself had erected in his early years.[432]

III B 9   *n.d.*, 1840-41

« 1728

Irony conceived according to its definition becomes a factor understood by the Greeks as σωφροσύνη[433]—which shears away the salacious as insipid.[434]

III B 10   *n.d.*, 1840-41

« 1729

Humor by definition becomes a polemical factor in the Christian view of life.[435]

III B 11   *n.d.*, 1840-41

« 1730

The demonic humor which attempts to draw even the divine along into the humoristic "Go to the devil" (thus Heine: the heavenly family etc.).[436]

III B 16   *n.d.*, 1840-41

« 1731

Irony is the birth-pangs of the objective mind (based upon the misrelationship, discovered by the *I*, between existence [*Existentsen*] and the idea of existence).

Humor is the birth-pangs of the absolute mind (based upon the mis-relationship, discovered by the *I* [*self*], between the *I* and the idea of the *I*).[437]

III B 19   *n.d.*, 1840-41

« 1732

There is irony in the identity of asking and answering only insofar as people are permitted to remain in their ignorance (such as when someone said to me that it must be hard to take a shower bath in the winter when the water is many degrees colder, and I answered—as if conceding the worth of the remark—that as yet it had not happened to me).

III B 21   *n.d.*, 1840-41

« 1733

Irony as *negative* creation. —blowing soap bubbles—.

III B 22   *n.d.*, 1840-41

« 1734

The concept of divine irony. Attempts were made to emancipate the divine, but this was possible only by means of the idea that it floats freely above all finite qualifications, denying them all, but the concept of positive *freedom* was not achieved, that divine irony moves freely within all these finite qualifications. Because the divine and the human were confused, a similar attempt arose from the human side.

When trust and faith in the gods were lost, it became no longer possible to maintain the divine except in its purely negative form—the reflex of this in the realm of consciousness is *ignorance*, and the corresponding factor in the realm of action is irony.

Earlier the divine was maintained as the individually human; now this has been annihilated and has been replaced by the abstractly human —the pure "I."

III B 23   *n.d.*, 1840-41

« 1735

We recognize humor immediately only in such a reply as *credo quia absurdum*.[438] Ignorance, however, is something quite different.

III B 24   *n.d.*, 1840-41

« 1736

A traveling humorist who is making preliminary studies, preparatory work for a theodicy—he travels about seeking as far as possible to experience everything in order to prove that everything is a disappointment.

III A 98   n.d., 1841

« 1737

The category of the comic is essentially contradiction.[439]

III A 205   n.d., 1842

« 1738

The comic is really a metaphysical concept. It brings about a metaphysical reconciliation. —Hegel's development of the comic[440]—Martensen's parroting.[441]

IV C 108   n.d., 1842-43

« 1739

Jesus Sirach does not seem to be fond of irony. See 41:19: Better a man who hides his foolishness than a man who hides his wisdom.

IV A 115   n.d., 1843

« 1740

One of the gospels tells the parable of two sons,[442] one of whom always promised to do his father's will but did not do it, and the other always said "No" but did it. The latter is also a form of irony, and yet the gospel commends this son. The gospel does not let repentance enter in,[443] either, that he repented of having said "No." By no means. This suggests that it is a kind of modesty which keeps the son from saying that he will do it. A man of any depth cannot be unacquainted with this modesty. It has its basis partly in a noble distrust of oneself, for as long as a person has not done what is demanded, it is still possible for him to be weak enough not to do it, and for that reason he will not promise anything.

IV B 96:13   n.d., 1843

« 1741

The comic is always based upon contradiction.[444] If a man tries to establish himself as a tavern keeper and fails, this is not comic. However, if a girl tries to get permission to establish herself as a prostitute— and fails, which sometimes happens, this is comic—very comic, inasmuch as it contains many contradictions.

V A 85   n.d., 1844

« 1742

Addition to 1741 (v a 85):
If the tavern keeper was debarred because there were so many of them, it would not be comical, but if he was debarred because there were so few, it would be a laughing matter, just as when a baker upon being asked for something by a poor person answered: No, Mother, you cannot get anything; we cannot give to everybody; there was another one here recently, and he didn't get anything either.[445]

v a 86   *n.d.,* 1844

« 1743

There are many loud-talking, flippant people who are stupid enough to assume that their stupidity is earnestness and are earnestly stupid enough to want to get others to believe it. This kind of so-called earnestness is the easiest of all attitudes; whereas earnestness is the finest fruit of exhaustive reflection. If one does not have a sense of humor to control his earnestness, he becomes earnest just as Holberg's Jeronimus did. This accounts for the hypocritical shriek, "He is not serious!" against everyone who is not sufficiently stupid but is witty and jesting and then serious at the right time. But just the opposite is the case: he who does not constantly dare to submit his earnestness to the test of jest is stupid and comical.

VI A 3   *n.d.,* 1844-45

« 1744

If a king disguised himself as a butcher and a butcher happened to resemble the king in a striking way, people would laugh at both of them, but for opposite reasons—at the butcher because he was not the king, and at the king because he was not the butcher.

VI A 22   *n.d.,* 1845

« 1745 *Definition of Irony*

Irony is the unity of ethical passion, which in inwardness infinitely accentuates the private self, and of development, which in outwardness (in association with people) infinitely abstracts from the private self. The effect of the second is that no one notices the first; therein lies the art, and the true infinitizing of the first is conditioned thereby.[446]

VI A 34   *n.d.,* 1845

« 1746[447]

13) The immorality does not lie in the laughing but rather in the ambiguity and the titillation in the laughing, when one does not really know whether to laugh or not and one is thereby prevented from repenting for having laughed in the wrong place.

14) Thus there may be someone who is able to be comically productive only in flippancy and hilarity. If one were to say to him: Remember, you are ethically responsible for your use of the comic, and he took time to understand this, his *vis comica*[448] perhaps would cease—that is, it would be unauthorized, without the direct implication that he actually did harm with it while he used it.

15) In contrast to the flippancy and wantonness (as productive) and ambiguity and sense-titillation (as receptive) of ringing laughter [stands] the quiet transparency of the comic. A person ought to practice laughing not in connection with the objects of his antipathetic passions but in connection with the objects of his gentleness and consideration, that which he knows he cannot totally lose, the area where he is protected by the opposition of all his emotions against the ambiguous, the selfish, the titillating.

VI B 70:13, 14, 15   *n.d.*, 1845

« 1747

People think it comical for someone to have a false conception, and they laugh when it is expressed. Even Holberg[449] uses such comic effects, although this really is not genuine but only situational—for example, people on a mountain assuming that the earth is flat. But, after all, this is not so terrible—there is more of the comic in the opposite situation, that someone can be so smug about knowing the earth is round. If having an untrue conception of something is comical, then we are all more or less comical, and some disclosure or other awaits us to render us ridiculous. But the comic of this kind, as was said previously, is of a subordinate order, and yet the sense for and the understanding of the comic is so undeveloped that this kind is almost always used and very seldom the purely comic.

The purely comic arises when a man knows the right thing and yet shows that he does not know it. Here is the essential contradiction. A man knows that God exists [*er til*]—and he says: I know it, damn it all! He knows everything is uncertain, and yet "Experience has taught him" to cling to the "certainty," namely, to the certainty which is in fact uncertainty.

VII^1 A 19   *n.d.*, 1846

« 1748

An ironist who is in the majority is *eo ipso* a mediocre ironist. To be in the majority is what the man of immediacy wants. Irony is suspect both to the right and to the left. Therefore a true ironist has never been in the majority. The comedian or entertainer is.

VII^1 A 64   *n.d.*, 1846

« 1749

If you want to be and want to continue to be enthusiastic, then promptly pull the silk curtain (irony's) of quips and bantering and be enthusiastic in secret. Or put mirror glass in the windows so that your enthusiasm is hidden, because curiosity and envy and partisan-sympathy see only their own mugs. Generally speaking, there is no safer hiding place for inwardness than behind mirror glass. And this can be done if in your association with anyone you deftly and agilely practice reflecting correctly, just as a mirror does, and changing your phenomenal deportment in relation to his, so that no one manages to converse with you but only to converse with himself—although he thinks that he is talking with you.

VIII^1 A 169   *n.d.*, 1847

« 1750

A good example of the contradiction which belongs to the comic. A pastor who uses a manuscript in the pulpit and steals a look at it. Just at the moment when, with a bold, sweeping, upward motion, he says the words, "The soul rises upward," he discovers he has not looked at the manuscript long enough to make such an expansive gesture—and he must now look at the paper.

VIII^1 A 478   *n.d.*, 1847

« 1751

A desiring, hoping, craving individuality can never be ironical. Irony (as constituting an entire existence) consists of the very opposite—to have one's grief just where others have their desire. Not to be able to have the beloved is never irony. But to be able to have her all too easily, so that she herself coaxes and begs to become yours—and still not be able to have her—this is irony. Not to be able to gain privileges in the world is never irony, but to be able to have them beyond all measure so that a whole age almost pleadingly thrusts power and office upon you—and still not be able to receive them—this is irony. These forms of irony require a person to have a secret, a melancholy secret or a secret of melancholy wisdom. This is why an ironist can never be understood by a person dominated by desire, for he thinks: O, to have my desire fulfilled!

Irony is a kind of hypersthenia, which, as is well-known, may be fatal.

VIII¹ A 517   *n.d.*, 1848

« 1752

Lines of a humorist. "I am so positive that I honestly wanted what was right in the matter that I, who otherwise would be likely to scurry to the ends of the earth in fear and trembling before our Lord, I am sure that I dare to say it directly to his face."

IX A 107   *n.d.*, 1848

« 1753

The reason most people cannot maintain a sustained impression of Christ in abasement is that they have not even the slightest idea of what it means to pass oneself off for someone else and the determination required to prevent anyone from peering through. Basically they all imagine that if they had lived contemporaneously with Christ, they would have glimpsed something. On the other hand, they have no idea at all of the self-renunciation required to carry through an incognito. They really do not credit Christ with being able to keep quiet. They have no awareness, therefore, that it honors Christ to believe that he succeeded in being neither more nor less than a despised man, an incognito which not even Satan himself saw through, an incognito which was open only to faith. They are stupid and undialectical enough to believe with human foolishness that they flatter him by protesting that they would have suspected something—this, I should think, is a way of flattering oneself and not the masquerader.

On this matter I have made studies which in a human sense will always be useful.

Most people have no idea of what it means to enter into a character-role* (for how many, indeed, live so audaciously and ideally), have no idea of the difference between saying to another person: I shall assume this or that guise, and then standing directly opposite him and carefully doing everything to carry through the character-role. I have attempted this with irony. I told a man that I am always somewhat ironical. What happened? We understood each other—I had revealed myself. But the very moment I stepped into character, he was bewildered. At that moment all direct communication was cut off; my whole appearance, visage, and speech were nothing but question marks. Aha, you are being ironical, he said. He of course expected me to answer *yes* or *no*—that is, to communicate directly. But the moment I stepped into character I tried to be completely true to it. Now, however, it was impossible for him to be sure whether or not it was irony—precisely this was the irony of it!

But men live so senselessly, so effeminately. This is why they have no idea of what it means when it pleases God to want to be incognito.

Let us take a minor character—Socrates. How many have the slightest idea of what it means to say that for him irony was an impersonation, that it was by no means a matter of trying to become understood but simply of remaining true to character, consequently of becoming misunderstood. He wanted to be misunderstood, because he wanted to be incognito. It was no holiday charade to entertain the cousins and nephews—and thus he lived day in and day out for many, many years.

* *In margin:* Or the difference between instructing and the existential art of being this or that. When I am giving instruction it is actually through my assistance that the others understand; in the second case I have removed myself completely from relationship to them, keeping myself solely to myself in order to carry through my character-role. Consequently their understanding will depend upon what powers they have in themselves—that is, I examine them.

IX A 151   n.d., 1848

« 1754

Where is the comic in making a poster for a play and writing: Among other characters, the widow Johansen, *née* Petersen?

In margin: Or if one added: engaged to student Marcussen.

IX A 279   n.d., 1848

«1755

In margin of 1754 (IX A 279):

The comic element is, of course, in the discrepancy between such determinants of actuality and merely being a character in a play.

IX A 280   n.d.

« 1756 *Lines for a Poetic Individual*

Granted that eternity is too earnest a place for laughter (something I have always been convinced of), it seems that there must be an intermediary state where a person is permitted to laugh outright. The person who with extreme effort and much self-sacrifice discovers the comic really has no opportunity to laugh himself out; he is too tense and concerned for that. Thus it seems an intermediary state ought to be assumed. And no doubt the pious pagans, for example, Socrates, would be found in this intermediary state.

IX A 398   *n.d.*, 1848

« 1757

There is something noteworthy in the thought that weeping is a divine invention, laughter, the devil's. Of course, if I were or imagined pure earnestness, absolutely ideally, there would be nothing laughable, for this earnestness always points ethically at a man and therefore finds nothing to laugh at but finds the same thing to be something to weep over instead.

It is also noteworthy that the world manifestly tends toward the comic, to the greater and greater development of laughter, all of which hangs together with the world's retrogression. Nowhere do we pause with pathos; we shudder at nothing—but say: Knock it off and see the comical side; human corruption is comical, and we try to express it comically. The demoralization of nations, all the insidious disease in public life, all this wretchedness and fraud and deceit which merely surpasses itself in ever new resourcefulness—is presented comically (for example, Scribe). This signifies that the view of life behind it is despair: All is phoney—so let us laugh. It is reminiscent in a certain sense of the chorus of a drinking song: Everything is lousy—so let us clink the glasses. But laughing is a refinement. It is tragic and indeed immoral for a woman to be of easy virtue, but the woman who is capable of being delighted by loose-living, comically conceived, has sunk far more deeply.

IX A 399   *n.d.*, 1848

« 1758

There is, of course, an essential difference between this worldly hankering for laughter and the urge to laugh which has a purely esthetic basis. Sometimes we laugh at men simply because we do not presume to judge them ethically—for example, as hypocrites—and therefore rather give an esthetic explanation of the phenomenon as stupidity.

IX A 400   *n.d.*, 1848

« 1759

Alas, in the theater we laugh at *Kammeraterne*,[450] but in actuality we laugh at the single individual [*den Enkelte*] who refuses at every point to join a clique. The person who will not do this loses all earthly and worldly advantages (money, honor, esteem, etc.); and if he is one who could easily attain these things if he would only pick up a few comrades to help him—well, isn't that peculiar and laughable!

God help us, for the moral the drama is supposed to convey to people demoralizes them even more, this witty familiarity with wretchedness.

IX A 420   *n.d.*, 1848

« 1760 *Humorous Lines*

"Did you hear N. N. preach today?"

"Yes, I did."

"What do you think of the sermon?"

"Well, there were some really good things in it—for example, the Lord's Prayer."

IX A 437   *n.d.*, 1848

« 1761

The best proof of the depth to which the fundamental demoralization of the age has sunk is the fact that what once was the judge's call to repentance (consequently ethical in terms of ethical character) has now become an assignment for subtle ingenuity which wittily and interestingly entertains the age—with the sins of the age. And we all laugh, and the author is not a bit better than what he presents as bad. Dreadful!

Who has more talent for depicting the vileness of the age, the power of lying and of self-love and of sordidness over the world, than Scribe! And those comedies (nauseating, that it is comedy [*Lystspil*, literally, delight-play]!) are admired and relished by the age—and Scribe himself is absolutely just as sordid as the world he depicts.

What an abyss of perdition! At the bottom of it all lies despair. To want to do even the least bit to halt this demoralization, to want at least to save oneself—this would be regarded as ridiculous madness. No, let it go, one hears, let it hit bottom—and although we sink in it, we entertain ourselves with witty comedies which expose the perdition. Done for, they say, we are all done for; nobody should complain about anybody—let's all laugh! The crazier the better, they say. Let's not only be miserable scoundrels but refine it with witty and clever knowledge and virtuosity in depicting it dramatically.

This is how judgment is delivered in the world. Even though the age is as bad as it is, the latter makes it 100% worse. I dare say that ultimately they will want the judgment in the next world to be witty!

x^1 A 148   *n.d.*, 1849

« 1762

Christianity does not really exist. Christendom is waiting for a comic poet *a la* Cervantes,[451] who will create a counterpart to Don Quixote out of the essentially Christian.

The only difference will be that no poetic exaggerations will be required at all, as in Don Quixote—no, all he needs to do is to take any essentially true Christian life, not to mention simply taking Christ or an apostle. The comic element arises because the age has changed so enormously that it regards this as comic.

That a person actually is earnest about renouncing this life, literally, that he *voluntarily* gives up the happiness of erotic love offered to him, that he endures all kinds of earthly privation, although the opposite is offered to him, that he thus exposes himself to all the anguish of spiritual trial [Anfægtelse], for spiritual trial comes only to the voluntary—and then that he, suffering all this, submits to being mistreated for it, hated, persecuted, scorned (the unavoidable consequence of essential Christianity in this world)—to our entire age such a life will appear to be comic. It is a Don Quixote life. —All this about the eternal can be very fine and acceptable—if a person also gets the earthly, or at least gets permission to aspire for it even if he does not get it—now this is something. But to renounce voluntarily—this is too high. There was a time when this was too high and a person admiringly said: I cannot do it; for our age is too high and it is regarded as ridiculous. Just take some lesser examples. The pathos of the age has already abandoned the idea that a girl whose love affair turned out badly would remain faithful to "the deceiver." To get married is the pathos of the age, if such a thing is pathos at all. And since all that is beyond this is regarded fundamentally as the uncertain, the problematical, the extremely dubious, it is comical (it is inherent in the category) for a person to concentrate absolutely everything on this. We would say to such a girl: How can you be so foolish as to want to believe such a man; get hold of yourself, life still is beckoning to you. Alas, when it comes down to it, God in heaven is regarded as the most cunning of all deceivers and betrayers, one who catches a man's imagination, lures him out to concentrate everything on this uncertainty—and then—no wonder this is found to be comical! In a less rational age to be deceived is regarded as a something unfortunate, tragic, disturbing—in a rational age where reason in everything, it is found to be comic: it is inherent in the category.

The frightful aspect is that men still want to keep the name of Christian, the idea that all are Christians. And if someone tells Christendom quite frankly how things stand, he is persecuted as one who is not a Christian, persecuted by Christians.

x^2 A 32   n.d., 1849

« 1763

There is really something low, something coarse in most of Holberg's comedies, and this explains why they are so popular, for they are bound up with an altogether common, human, teasing, and grinning malice.

To present as comic, or in an actual situation to laugh at that under which a man suffers—no, I could not bring myself to do that. When such is the case, I do not feel at all inclined to laugh; I would either try to help the man straighten out his affairs or I would try to avoid him. An old man who, having acted rashly and married a young wife, fears being made a cuckold and now really suffers under this imagined notion. But I do not consider this comic; as I said, I would either try to convince him that it was a mistaken notion or I would let him pass for what he once was—but not a Troels'[452] sort of comedy or witticism.

The more I think about this, the more I see how demoralizing this kind of comedy is; and the more I come to think of you, you noble one [Socrates], you were the only one who nobly and profoundly understood what comedy is and when it is appropriate to a high-minded spirit. It is absolutely necessary that the person concerned be himself happy in his ridiculous delusion; as soon as he is himself unhappy in his ludicrous delusion, he is not to be laughed at. In the next place, this noble irony is not to be represented before grinning crowds and not as sensate strength, but as you [represented it], you noble simple soul, by far the weakest at the moment, while the Sophists had both power and honor and esteem and were themselves extremely happy in the delusion which a whole contemporary age shared with them, so that they were far from suffering under it, and only you, you noble wise man, saw the ridiculousness of the delusion.

x^2 A 304   *n.d.*, 1849

« 1764 *Humor*

If in another sense it were not madness, it would be an example of humor if a person were to say to God: Although brought up rigorously in Christianity, I am, as you know, born in the Nineteenth Century and therefore have my share of the universal superstitious belief in reason, etc. —the humor would lie in the words "as you know."

x^3 A 228   *n.d.*, 1850

« 1765 *Wittiness of the Occasion*

I have always believed and said that the occasion, actuality, is wittier than all the witty authors.

Disinclined as I am to write about such things, I will nevertheless give this as an example.

The man who has best understood the present situation in Denmark, all the political yowling of half-men devoid of character, the man who has written and writes the wittiest satire on it is a merchant (on Farve Street, I believe) who advertises a long list of things for rent in the Shoppers' Guide, a list which ends with: Bingo and Bedpans. The ass— I could be jealous of him; he is wittier than the wittiest author in Denmark. Bingo—yes, that is the whole thing. But it is not played at such high stakes that it is a matter of life and death—no, for that the other is needed: bedpans. The time of heroes is past: here bingo and bedpans are for rent.

XI^1 A 343   *n.d.*, 1854

« 1766 *Christianity (Irony)*

If someone were to say, "Christianity is God's irony over us men," I would reply: No, my good man, but we men have the power to transform Christianity into irony, into biting irony.

The matter is very simple. In his majesty God sets the pitch so high that if a person is unwilling to let go of his finite common sense, will not abandon flat, self-indulgent mediocrity—then what God calls help, salvation, grace, etc. is the most biting irony. Finite understanding is scarcely to be blamed for saying: No, thanks, I would rather not have that help, salvation, and grace.

As soon, however, as a person wills as God wills, is willing to be instructed by God concerning the relation of the temporal and the eternal, is willing to see and to appropriate God's conception of the eternal, is willing to believe God—then of course God is sheer, pure love and mercy.

But Christendom's escape by making God somebody who babbles through his nose some drivel about salvation, grace, etc. in such a way that the secular mentality finds this kind of talk to be very sensible—this escape is high treason.

As I have noted somewhere else [i.e., XI² A 8], no pagan people worshiped such a ridiculous and repulsive deity as does "Christendom," which worships and adores a drooling driveller. Even the crudest pagan took better care that his god rose somewhat above and stood a little higher than the human, whereas Christendom has excelled in making God entirely human.

Perhaps this will be called an exaggeration. But this is not the case; on the contrary, the matter can be explained in this way: Christianity in its truth has the highest conception of God—God is spirit, love's majesty —but the demoralization of this highest concept yields the very lowest conception of God.

To charge "Christendom" with lies, hypocrisy, and so on is therefore really too lofty, makes it into more than it is. No, the most appropriate charge is: the whole thing is unbecoming. It is unbecoming for a grown-man to ride a hobby-horse and thus it is also unbecoming to call something Christianity—as they intone in the name of Christianity— from which all the divine marks have been rubbed away long ago and all concepts long ago restamped with human nonsense.

XI² A 183   *n.d.*, 1854

« 1767 *Irony*

My entire existence is really the deepest irony.

To travel to South America, to descend into subterranean caves to excavate the remains of extinct animal types and antedeluvian fossils—in this there is nothing ironic, for the animals extant there now do not pretend to be the same animals.

But to excavate in the middle of "Christendom" the types of being a Christian, which in relation to present Christians are somewhat like the bones of extinct animals to animals living now—this is the most intensive irony—the irony of assuming that Christianity exists [*at være til*] at the same time that there are one thousand preachers robed in velvet and silk and millions of Christians who beget Christians, and so on.

In what did Socrates' irony really lie? In expressions and turns of speech, etc.? No, such trivialities, even his virtuosity in talking ironically, such things do not make a Socrates. No, his whole existence is and was irony; whereas the entire contemporary population of farm hands and business men and so on, all those thousands, were perfectly sure of being human and of knowing what it means to be a human being, Socrates was beneath them (ironically) and occupied himself with the problem—what does it mean to be a human being? He thereby expressed that actually the *Treiben* of those thousands was a hallucination, tomfoolery, a ruckus, a hubbub, busyness, etc., worth a zero in the eyes of the ideal, or less than zero, inasmuch as these men could have used their lives to concentrate upon the ideality.

The irony with respect to Christianity has one element more than Socratic irony has, inasmuch as men in Christendom not only imagine themselves to be human beings (here, of course, Socrates stops) but also imagine themselves to be something historically concrete, which being a Christian is. Socrates doubted that one is a human being by birth; to become human or to learn what it means to be human does not come that easily—what occupied Socrates, what he sought, was the ideality of being human. What would Socrates think now if he were told that men have long since become so perfectible that they have made great progress in nonsense to the extent that there now is sense in saying that a child is just about born a Christian, yes, "even of a particular denomination."

xi² A 189   December 3, 1854

« 1768 *Philanthropy (Christianity)*

Paul says: Even if I gave away all I have to the poor but have not love, what would it profit *me?*

This "me" is very characteristic of Christianity. We turn the whole thing around in such a way that the others are supposed to have the benefit of one's philanthropy—therefore what counts is the philanthropy itself.

Alas, no, the essentially Christian is not activism. Unlike the world, Christianity is not hard pressed for money so that the question is simply one of getting hold of some money and thus philanthropy is made into a virtue in and by itself. No, Christianity has no such use for money at all. Therefore the apostle says: What does it profit *me?*

Here we see, incidentally, how close irony always is to Christianity, so that it is really only our emotions which make us deaf to irony. The apostle speaks with concern for the eternal: What would it profit *me?* Socrates would have been able to say the same thing, teasingly: What would it profit me, would I become better, wiser, if without love I gave everything to the poor?

XI² A 190   n.d., 1854

« 1769 *Jesuitism*

No eminently primitive person has ever lived without being accused of being a Jesuit by his contemporaries.

The matter is easily explained. The fact that he has the future within him gives him that simplicity in action which his contemporaries call Jesuitism. He acts by virtue of the future; whereas his contemporaries always carry on their business in the time-honored fashion.

His God-relationship lies in this tension.

Such a heterogeneous person has also, from one point of view, something comic about him, or his tremendous pathos is mantled in something comic. There is nothing comic about someone with the rank of cabinet minister who acts like a cabinet minister, but that someone by virtue of bearing the future within himself acts more energetically than any cabinet minister is in a sense comic. That someone who is acclaimed by millions acts by virtue of that acclaim is not comic, but that someone acts by virtue of bearing within himself the future's millions has something comic about it. When the millions are visible there is nothing comic, but to have the millions within oneself is comical.

XI² A 255   n.d., 1854

IDEA, IDEALS, IDEALITY

« 1770

It is strange that people are so enraged by the Jesuits; in a certain sense to the degree that a person is inspired by an idea and concentrates on its realization, he is a —Jesuit.

I A 196   June 17, 1836

« 1771

There are certain people who live in an imaginary grandiose world (or a marvellous historical world) and then carry this yardstick directly over to the most insignificant events, which produces something just as ridiculous as measuring a small box with a fathom line.

II A 148   August 27, 1837

« 1772

There are people who treat the ideas they pick up from others so frivolously and disgracefully that they ought to be prosecuted for illegal traffic in lost and found property.

II A 695   January 17, 1838

« 1773

Just to have been the object of more severe judgment even once is something which cannot be forgotten, even though one has improved.

III A 242   n.d., 1842

« 1774

If a person has one idea, but an infinite one, he can be carried through his entire life by it, easily and swiftly, just like the Hyperborean,[453] Abaris, who, carried by an arrow, circumnavigated the entire earth.

Herodotus,[454] IV, 36

IV A 21   n.d., 1842-43

« 1775

Every time world history is to take an essential step forward and

280

along a difficult path, there immediately appears a formation of authentic lead horses: the unmarried, solitary men who live only for an idea. Johannes von Müller[455] says there really are only two forces which steer the world: *die Ideen und die Frauen*—but if things are to go right, ideas alone must steer.

VIII[1] A 54   *n.d.*, 1847

« 1776

. . . . . Show me one single person who was nothing and yet worked with all his power for an idea; show me one single person like that for whom things have not gone wrong. To be nothing is precisely the burr under the saddle of earnestness; to be nothing is precisely what makes delusions impossible; only when a person is nothing can he in truth serve an idea, but it does not follow that everyone who is nothing does it. —But the point is, when a man is also something—in short, when infinite advantages go along with it, then men look at them, and thus they understand the man. He proclaims the truth; it is his occupation and his bread and butter—aha!

This is why the more shrewd contemporaries who are aware of the burr want such a person along with themselves in a bread-and-butter job— for then he is no longer a burr under their saddles.

IX A 202   *n.d.*, 1848

« 1777

In his sermon on the Gospel for the Tenth Sunday after Trinity, Luther[456] relates that according to Josephus 90,000 Jews were taken prisoner and carried away from Jerusalem, and the price on them was so cheap that 30 of them sold for a penny. Here is an instance where the gospel's declaration that we are worth more than sparrows does not hold true, for they were sold at 2 or 3 for a penny. But the punishment of God was also involved here.

In margin: At times like this, one feels so horribly the pressure in being this contradiction, man—the ideal which is required of every single individual human being, and then, suddenly, seeing that man is nevertheless only like an animal.

IX A 423   *n.d.*, 1848

« 1778

The case with most men is that they go out into life with one or another accidental characteristic of which they say: Well, this is the way

I am; I cannot do otherwise. To this providence replies: So you cannot do otherwise; I shall teach you, and then begins to work them over—and thus the majority of men are ground down into conformity. These are the mass of men in each generation. Then in each generation there is a small part who cling so tightly to their "I cannot do otherwise" that they lose their minds. Finally, there are a very few in each generation who in spite of all life's terrors cling with more and more inwardness to this "I cannot do otherwise." They are the geniuses. Their "I cannot do otherwise" is an infinite thought, for if one were to cling firmly to a finite thought, he would lose his mind. And if he does not have character enough to persevere in this way, then he is ground down into conformity.

IX A 459   *n.d.,* 1848

« 1779

With regard to ideality, the ages we can learn from are: the child, the youth, the young girl, the old man. From the active man and the busy housewife one does not learn anything about ideality. Why not? Because they are essentially occupied with finite ends. This proves that ideality is a more abstract relationship to actuality, is tangential.

X¹ A 434   *n.d.,* 1849

« 1780

In margin of 1779 (X¹ A 434):
There is in one of my earliest journals (during my student days) this: Christ is a tangent. This is not an inappropriate observation. What is a tangent? It is a straight line which touches the circle at only one point. But the absolute is indeed this very point.

X¹ A 435   *n.d.*

« 1781

As soon as the category "the single individual" goes out, Christianity is abolished. Then the individual will relate to God through the race, through an abstraction, through a third party—and then Christianity is *eo ipso* abolished. If this happens, then the God-man is a phantom instead of an actual prototype.

Alas, when I look at my own life! How infrequent the man who is so endowed for the life of the spirit and above all so rigorously schooled with the help of spiritual suffering—yet in the eyes of all my contemporaries I am fighting almost like a Don Quixote—it never occurs to them that it is Christianity; indeed, they are convinced of just the opposite.

Christendom as it is now makes Christ into a complete phantom as far as existence is concerned—although men do profess that Christ was a particular human being. They have no courage to believe existentially in the ideal.

Yes, it is true, the human race has grown away from Christianity! Alas, yes, in quite the same sense as a man grows away from ideals. For the young person the ideal is the ideal, but he relates to it with pathos. For the older person, who has grown away from the ideal, the ideal has become something quixotic and visionary, something which does not belong in the world of actuality.

In the hour of my death I shall repeat again and again, if possible, what every word in my writings testifies to: Never, never, with a single word have I given occasion for the mistaken notion that I personally mistook myself for the ideal—but I have been convinced that my striving has served to illuminate what Christianity is.

Reason and reflection have taken the ideal away from men, from Christendom, and have made it into something quixotic and visionary—consequently, being a Christian must be set a whole reflection farther back, being a Christian now comes to mean loving or desiring deeply to be a Christian, striving to be one: so enormous has the ideal now become.

In reference to this see the essay, *Armed Neutrality*, where I have parelleled this with the transition from being called σοφοι[457] to being called φιλοσοφοι.[458]

x¹ A 646   *n.d.*, 1849

« 1782

Everything that *neither* occupies within the state a certain assigned sphere for its activity and therefore is subordinate to it *nor* directly acknowledges working for finite ends makes a claim to be in the service of ideas and as such ought to be kept chaste and pure, unaffected by attachments to finite advantage.

Activity for an idea is also recognizable by the fact that it addresses itself κατὰ δύναμιν to all, to the people. An official and the like have their assigned spheres of activity, but an author or an artist relates to the whole people. A businessman, for example, can also in a sense be said to address himself to all, insofar as they want to do business with him, but he also acknowledges forthrightly that he works for a finite end.

How mad and immoral, then, that something which by its form of existence [*Existents*] makes a claim to serve the infinite and to be higher than a particular, defined, limited activity within the state, that this, take journalism for example, is in fact in the hands of tradesmen!

The significance which lies in being higher than relativities at least ought to be bought at a financial sacrifice.

x² A 474   *n.d.*, 1850

« 1783

The dreadful dilemma in which we are living has been occasioned by the desire of people, from generation to generation, to unite to work for an infinite and finite goal. All this can do is engender confusion. Let it merely become clear which is which.

Work for a finite goal is indeed an honest thing to do. The dishonesty appears as soon as someone wishes to adorn such work with the appearance of also being for an infinite goal.

No, no! All work for an infinite goal must be regarded as a luxury in the noble sense. Test yourself and see how far, how much, how long you can work in this manner, without compromise in any way; just keep it unadulterated, and then you will be of use. If you do not find the time or opportunity at all to work in this way—well, you do no harm whatsoever if you honestly acknowledge that you are working solely for a finite goal. Not only do you do no harm—no, you do good, for when the person comes who can and will work for an infinite goal, he is more readily understood, instead of always being exposed to becoming a martyr because of the dishonest and abject jumbling on the part of those who actually are working for finite goals and have perpetrated the sham of also working for the infinite goal.

x² A 510   *n.d.*, 1850

« 1784 *Seeking the Kingdom of God First of All*

It can truly be said that everyone whose striving at the very outset and later at all times is commensurate with one or another finite τέλος is not seeking the kingdom of God first. Yet it does not follow that everyone whose striving has the heterogeneity of infinitude can be said to be seeking the kingdom of God first. But ideality he does have, nevertheless.

An example of making one's striving commensurate with a finite τέλος at the very outset. When someone wants to be active in preaching Christianity and this effort at the very outset becomes for him commensurate with finitude—for example, which pastoral appointment shall I try to get, preferably in a city or out in the country, in case of the latter, shall it be Jutland, or Zealand—so that, when he has first of all obtained such a position, he may preach undauntedly that a man should seek the kingdom of God first of all. If the urge to be active in this manner is defined by the infinite, he probes to see if he has the enabling qualifications for this kind of activity, and if he does not, he promptly begins to acquire them, and if he has them, he begins right away, does not waste a second; if it can be done in no other way, he goes right out on the street and begins. Very likely he comes into conflict with the existing order of things, is arrested, etc., etc., never gets an office and a job. This, you see, is the result of seeking the kingdom of God first of all. Homogeneity with the world, on the contrary, means to seek worldly advantage first of all—in this case one does not collide, either.

x^3 A 238   *n.d.*, 1850

« 1785 *The Middle Term between the Requirement of Ideality and Where We Are*

It is easy to see that the New Testament (especially the gospels) contains only the requirement of ideality, and absolutely.

Nowadays we are accustomed summarily to say that this was meant only for the apostles and does not apply to us.

You, my God, what a curious God you are, to give a holy book which applies only to a few men, who, indeed, received it orally—and does not apply to the whole human race.

No, everyone has to relate himself to the requirement of ideality, and, as stated elsewhere [i.e., x^3 A 233], the apostolic way is not to relate to the demand of ideality but to divine authority.

Everyone has to measure himself before God by the requirement of ideality, and then before God—but responsibly—flee to grace.

x^3 A 268   *n.d.*, 1850

« 1786

That Christ's life expresses the idea is self-evident.

And this constitutes the dialectical movements of the idea.

When the absolutely extraordinary steps out on his own, his contemporaries are amazed that he is capable of absolutely everything. They follow him rejoicing, worried and curious about one thing only, what finite aims he has, does he want to be king or merely prime minister, etc.

Now he stands at his highest pinnacle. Now his contemporaries and he have to come to an understanding. Now they will get to see what his earthly aims are.

What do they see? He remains standing on this peak and rejects every finite *telos*, wants nothing earthly at all, not even assurance regarding the most insignificant things.

Now comes the transformation. As far as his contemporaries are concerned, he cannot be categorized; his extraordinariness changes into nothingness; he has become nothing, the shabbiest of all. And the charge against him is: It is his own fault that he did not take the opportunity.

And yet ideally he is standing at the same point, at the same high point, and the eulogy over him is: He did not take the opportunity.

x³ A 312   *n.d.*, 1850

« 1787 *The Christian Order of Precedence*

(1) If you have money and want to be perfect, then give everything to the poor. (2) If you have money and want to use it for some beneficial enterprise or other, that also is fine. (3) If you have money and want to use it to enjoy life but, please note, in a permissible manner, it is true that Christianity tolerates this. (4) If you must earn, then Christianity prefers that you limit your necessities in order to have more time for the religious rather than that you spend a lot of time earning money in order to have all the more to use. Christianity is suspicious of earning money. At the same time Christianity is lenient if you will regard the right to use so much time to earn money as an indulgence. But if you make earning money into the earnestness of life, then you have fallen from Christianity.

x³ A 347   *n.d.*, 1850

« 1788 *Attaching Oneself to the Established Order*

Automatically to praise attaching oneself to the established order and to pretend that this is "earnestness," also modesty and humility, can be a great big lie. Attaching oneself to the established order in this unqualified way can signify the desire to evade all work for or even inquiry into the idea as such. We say: I take the world as it is; I waste no time but begin immediately to arrange things so as to get as much enjoyment out of life as possible.

But earnestness simply means devotion to the idea: the ideality with which a man searches for the idea first of all and for the present does not give a hang about the others and is indifferent to their possibly completely erroneous interpretation.

The genius produces an essentially lasting existential revision. That which others do not find time to think about—because they must immediately go right into the relativities—is the very thing that occupies him. He thinks about the reality [*Realiteten*] of this matter of getting married

—the others start at once with the assumption that a man should get married since the others are doing it and merely ask which girl they should take, etc. So it is in all areas. And this is the reason that geniuses usually amount to nothing.

x^3 A 395   *n.d.*, 1850

« 1789 *The Ideal*

Every step forward toward the ideal is a backward step, for the progress consists precisely in my discovering increasingly the perfection of the ideal—and consequently my greater distance from it.

One cannot love the ideal selfishly; for then progress would make me happy only if I were to come closer to the ideal in a *direct* way—yes, in a certain sense I might then wish the ideal not to be all too perfect or that I might not learn too much about its perfection—so that I could better attain it.

To love the ideal in truth (so that as a consequence progress is retro-gression, or my making progress means that I step back out of respect because I see its sublimity even more perfectly) is therefore like hating oneself.

x^3 A 509   *n.d.*, 1850

« 1790 *Dialectic*

We think of "motion" as being unrest, uproar, etc., but "motion" carried to its logical conclusion is like a magic spell which in the external sense sets everything at rest.

In the highest sense "motion" is the movement of the ideal—and this separates men absolutely, makes them single individuals and makes every single individual introspective, so that he has enough to do with himself—but then not the slightest uproar arises.

x^3 A 524   *n.d.*, 1850

« 1791 *The Ideal*

. . . . . It is not being true when someone, after having become aware of the ideal, dares be neither one thing nor the other and finally scarcely dares to exist. After all, is it not a kind of vanity to fancy oneself, insignificant as he is, capable of approximating the ideal?

No, full of cheerful courage and confidence, and like a child, one works to the best of his ability, sometimes takes humorous delight and sometimes in fear and trembling feels grief in thinking what a worthless fellow he is—but then is cheerful again, and above all indescribably happy that he at least understands the ideal, happy to let the ideal be beyond him this way, to his own destruction.

Or is it not true love really to feel that one is a worthless fellow, and if someone says: No, then I dare not fall in love—then he is sick and about to become, in a pitiful sense, a worthless fellow. No, this is precisely why I feel desire to be in love, really to feel what a worthless fellow I am and really to feel what a pure love is.

Giødvad told me yesterday that I most likely had discouraged one or two theological candidates from becoming ministers by making the conception so ideal. I answered that as far as such a person is concerned, it would be the same with everything; by presenting ideally what it is to be a man I could ultimately discourage him from being a man and thus it could end in suicide. Then I showed him that such sickness was a matter of egotistically loving oneself instead of loving the ideal and hating oneself, loving the ideal which makes one a worthless fellow—and then always cheerful and happy over existing [være til].

x^3 A 525   n.d., 1850

« 1792 *World-shift*

That a world-shift has taken place can be seen from the fact that it is necessary to redefine man's relationship to the ideal [*in margin:* Of course, not a new ideal, but a new definition of the relationship to the old ideal, a new understanding of the old ideal]; the present generation has no norm.

Luther's definition is taken in vain; reason has blockaded communication with the ideal; but if it is to come again, Luther's definition must be modified.

Now all progress toward the ideal is retrogressive (which I have pointed out elsewhere [i.e., x^2 A 125, 189, 194; x^3 A 509]). Therefore I believe that we shall come to characterize ourselves as Christ-lovers, because to be Christian has become too great a task. Childlike simplicity did not observe what an infinite requirement is involved in being a Christian; therefore it could believe that this is possible; nowadays it is apparent that the requirement for being Christian is so enormous that humanness becomes satisfied with a relationship to it, a striving toward it.

The sequence was actually this: first, the universally human; then the poet with ideals; then the religious which required that the ideal ought to be realized in actuality. But now there will be need for the presentation of the religious in poetic form. This is a step forward compared to what prevails now when meaninglessness and mediocrity actually have taken the place of the religious, so that the poet in the ordinary sense is even higher than the religious.

In any case, there no doubt must be something poetic in the religious domain, mainly just to get hold of existential ideals again and to encounter the existential ideals.

This will be the break. Then it will become apparent whether a new generation will get the power to make an attempt again to actualize the ideals existentially.

x³ A 576   n.d., 1850

« 1793 *Contemporaneity with Christ or an Apostle*

Undoubtedly this contemporaneity makes the relationship most strenuous, for such an *existing person* jacks up the price of the idea.

But then again it helps to have someone who is so far along and who commands with authority.

As we are now living, we men have at best an understanding of the ideal (something poetic),[459] but to get it going existentially at all in the everyday there also has to be such an objective rigorousness, a rigorousness and authority like that of an apostle, for I would rather keep Christ out of it entirely in order not to carry the matter too far. A person can still be conscious of having a willingness—but what is lacking, if it is to amount to anything, is an objective rigorousness. It is impossible to supply this rigorousness oneself, for every self-redoubling [*Selv-fordoblelse*] still does not contain any more than this self contains.

x³ A 670   n.d., 1850

« 1794 *Inversion*

How difficult it is for a man just in this respect to resist and be true! For the lower one's striving, the more effective he is at the moment. How easy it is for this extensiveness to seem to him to express that what he is doing is higher than a purer service of the idea, which, the purer it is, appears at the moment to be all the more superfluous, a ridiculous exaggeration.

x³ A 689   n.d., 1850

« 1795

Just as one speaks of being shot by elf-arrows, I would say: wounded by ideas.

x⁴ A 39   n.d., 1851

« 1796 *The Impression Which Must Be Made*

The impression must be made by the ideals. For example, in ideality a witness to truth is essentially higher than any actual witness to truth. Therefore from the elevation of the ideal the impression is even stronger.

The mitigation, again, lies in the fact that the whole thing happens through the poet, who says: This I am not.

x^4 A 80   *n.d.*, 1851

« 1797 *The Book of Job*

When the three friends (who are older men) have become weary, so to speak, of answering Job or have lost their composure in relation to him and are not far from conceding that he is right, the young man, Elihu, begins.

This can be understood as follows. In one sense the ideality of faith is most authentically—that is, most ideally—represented by the young man, because he as yet has no experience. The older, the experienced— alas, with such a man it happens only too easily that faith has suffered a little damage; therefore he is more inclined to accommodate, to ease up a bit, etc. But youth still has only the pure ideality.

x^4 A 146   *n.d.*, 1851

« 1798 *What It Means To Be a Christian*

The ideality involved has been lost completely. As a result being a Christian is construed to be something everyone can be very easily. And then it becomes a matter of distinction to go further, to become a philosopher, a poet, and God knows what.

To bring this to a halt I have affirmed ideality. At least one ought to acquire respect for what it means to be a Christian; then everyone can test or choose whether or not he wants to be a Christian.

They scoff at prayer (as in the little piece, "The Conflict between Ørsted and Mynster," by H—t).[460] If I were to enter in here, what would I do? I would idealize prayer in all its infinitude so that it would turn out that there is perhaps not a single person who is fit to pray.

This is the way it must be done. One must have sufficient resignation to keep himself in the background in order to introduce ideality, infinitely exalted. Then the matter will surely take a different turn.

x^4 A 282   *n.d.*, 1851

« 1799 *Why Are the Ideals So Rarely Presented?*

Very simply, this has its roots in human egotism.

If someone were to present them, he would at least want to profit by it—to be himself the ideal, to be admired as such, etc. On the one hand, this would turn out to be a mediocre presentation of the ideal (and is romanticism), and on the other hand, such an aspiration is rather alien to our age of good sense.

Consequently if someone were to present the ideals he would not personally claim to exemplify them. Good common sense says: "I am not crazy enough to let people see that I know how great the demands are (something most contemporaries do not know)—it would rob my life of all the advantages of my efforts. I am not crazy enough to let people see that I know how great the demands are—if I am not able to fulfill them, it would only result in my own humiliation. And, besides, 'the others,' as soon as I came with such a presentation, might get it in their heads to force me to put the ideal in practise, badger me with it. No thanks, I am not crazy; neither do I hate myself. I want to have advantage from achieving a little more than the others. Therefore I live by the old rules and do not traffic in this about the ideal."

This, you see, is why the ideals are not presented.

X^4 A 344   *n.d.,* 1851

« 1800 *What Characteristics Must One Have Who Is to Effect a "Stop" in the Realm of the Spirit?*

To stimulate with the help of ideals he must have *sadness*—the thousands and thousands busily active in the service of mediocrity can only be stopped by ideals—sadness in order to captivate and stimulate those who still have receptivity and are willing to yield—when brought to a stop.

He must have satire, again with the help of ideals. Satire to enable him to crack fatally the incessant busyness of mediocrity—and bring it to a stop.

This is the power he must have, a two-fold power, yet viewed basically one and the same.

But he himself must not be any kind of a power, because then, instead of merely effecting a stop, he could very likely begin something new or separate the two parts.

No, just as sadness and satire, this one-and-the-same twofold power, is the stopping power, so he in whom this stopping power resides must not be a power but an impotence, a weakness—a poet, and of course without attachments, neither to any party nor to any particular human being.

And when, divinely understood, such a poet is weakness, he is compelled whether or not he is so inclined, and when, divinely understood, he is also a weakness in unconditioned obedience to the power who compels him, then he is the "stopper."

*   *

The "stopper" will be the first one to understand Christendom. Just as all the spooks and trolls and that whole phantom bunch disappear in the morning with the breaking forth of the sun, so ideals will throw light upon that not less phantom nonsense about millions and millions of Christians who beget Christians, those swarms of Christians who gad around with each other where we all are Christians—ideals will throw light upon them, and—look—they have vanished, there was not even one Christian!

God is interested in ideals. Man supposes—this is precisely the most convenient for man—that he is able to please him with a substitute, the numerical, by procuring for him more and more millions of—non-Christians. Instead of striving to the uttermost ourselves in the direction of the ideal, we prefer, each according to his situation, to procure for God 10 or 100 or 100,000 or a million non-Christians who have become non-Christians through the influence—how meritorious!—of a man who for his part freed himself from striving to the uttermost.

XI² A 294   *n.d.*, 1853-54

« 1801

Christ—and Pilate
or
God—and man
or
the ideal—and the practical man

XI¹ A 43   *n.d.*, 1854

« 1802 *The Criterion for Being Human*

A falsification has taken place: from generation to generation, ever more insanely, the criterion for being human has been altered, has been diminished.

Although in a certain objective sense Christianity is proclaimed as an objective doctrine—because of the altered criterion there is no one who is fit to be Christian; *ergo* Christianity is poetry, mythology, and this is what is called orthodoxy.

In the New Testament the criterion for being human is this: the New Testament contains the requirement, the God-man as the prototype—and every man, unconditionally every man of these countless millions, falls quite simply under this requirement without any nonsense or middle terms.

We live in such a way that we have brought the ethical into direct line with differentiations such as genius and talent. Just as a person tranquilly says: I am no genius (because it quite rightly neither can nor should occur to him that he ought to be that), we say in the same relaxed way: Well, I am unable to practice self-denial. Charming! And not only that, but just as one wants to be praised for his humility when he is not a genius and does not aspire to be one either, so we want to be praised also for humility because we are humble enough to be satisfied with ethical shabbiness.

Excellent! Imagine a school where the pupils speak of being diligent in the same sense that they speak of being intelligent, in the same relaxed way! Furthermore, where the pupil even wants to be praised for humility for being deficient in diligence and says: I am humble enough to be satisfied with being lazy.

*   *

In the New Testament the criterion for being human is: the eternal —not a people, a century, a country, the remarkable aspect of a contemporary age, the present age just as it is, a miserable present age, etc. And now think of those dreadful falsifications, tending toward what I would designate in a few words as the Goethean, the Hegelian, to satisfy the age.

Moreover, the New Testament criterion for being human is to be a single individual—nowadays everything is association.

XI^1 A 130   *n.d.,* 1854

« 1803 *Hypocritical Falsification.*

The law of existence is: the more insignificant, the easier (the life of plants is easier than that of animals, the animals' than man's, the child's than the adult's, the simple man's than the wise man's, etc.)

Therefore worldly shrewdness continually tends to make life insignificant (abolishing the ideals, higher striving, etc.), since in this way life becomes easy.

Christianity has made being a human being as significant as possible —that is, being in kinship with God and striving to be like God, imitation [*Efterfølgelse*]. Of course, Christianity has also made it as laborious and anguished as possible (just as it has made being a human being as significant as possible).

This is what men cannot stand. But we are not honest enough to admit the true motives. Therefore we hypocritically abolish Christianity by saying we are much too humble to aspire to anything so lofty.

"Significant" and "laborious," "insignificant" and "easy" are correlatives; take one away and you take the other away also. So we hypocritically say: I do not aspire to the "significant," because I am too humble for that—this means: I want to get rid of the "difficult." And this is the case as soon as I get rid of the significant.

XI^1 A 194   *n.d.*, 1854

« 1804 *Pearls—and their Use*

The diver who fetches up pearls from the ocean floor leads a poor life—and the pearls are perhaps sparkling on some trashy woman's breast as a reward for her degradation. So it is in the world, with both pearls and the truth, with ideas and discoveries—the diver has only the labor, and it would not be surprising if he gets only ingratitude and persecution as his reward.

It has always been this way—until the most wretched of all generations—when Goethe tampered with the laws of existence and became a genius on the basis of talent.

Among us it was Mynster who fashioned himself on the model of Goethe—tampering by way of adulterating the criterion.

XI^1 A 197   *n.d.*, 1854

« 1805 *The Law of Subordination*[461]

Since no man is the ideal, it is readily seen that everyone knocks off a little—the apostle, also.

But subordination and the significance of subordination imply that the person whose life is less strenuous does not have the right to say to the person whose life is more strenuous: You knock off, too.

This is what has been done, and as a result of this sophistry every effort ceases and we get this utter nonsense about grace.

XI^1 A 336   *n.d.*, 1854

« 1806 *Strength—Weakness*

When a girl's beloved dies or is unfaithful to her and she says it will be the death of her—and then a year later is married, people say: Who would have believed that she was so strong.

The truth is—she was weak.

But idea-strength is regarded as weakness, and palpable strength is regarded as strength. A person who has the strength to live devoid of ideas is called strong; a person who has the strength to reap profit on all sides is called strong, etc.

XI[1] A 337   *n.d.,* 1854

« 1807 *Duty toward God*

This then is the rascally shift, as noted elsewhere, by which we have abolished Christianity: there are no duties toward God—whereas the New Testament is totally the duty to love God. But we teach (and call it Christianity) that there are no duties toward God. If someone were a little farther along than the others so that there could be any question of an ideality which could be related to God, then this means (this we teach and call it Christianity) that he should turn to the others and help them along, for God points away from himself and there is no duty toward God.

Splendid! The matter is very simple—mankind's interest quite naturally lies in fitting everything into mediocrity, for mediocrity is the *conditio sine qua non*[462] for an easy life. Therefore it is important for mankind to draw every ideality down to the mass, down to mediocrity. And to make sure of getting there, we enlist God's help, that it is he who points away from himself.

What rascality, and how tricky to call this Christianity. In the New Testament it is precisely ideality, the intensive, one who is driven to the highest, which interests God—the masses do not interest God at all. "Let the dead bury the dead" is the cry; just press on. Yes, God in his majesty is so aristocratic that he spends millions on a single one (yet it must always be remembered that every single one of these millions could, according to Christianity, be the single one. According to the New Testament, God is so keen on the intensive that he squanders the extensive on the most frightful scale.

Yet for this very reason it is very strenuous to have anything to do with God—and it is natural that under the name of Christianity men have gotten Christianity made over into its very opposite: amiable mediocrity, instead of the most excruciating strenuousness toward ideality.

Make it very simple in order to see how infinitely elevated Christianity is.

If there were someone who could truly be said to be significantly more developed than his contemporaries in Christian understanding, insight, and striving, what is more natural than for him to think that now his task is to try to help others and that God will aid him in this, and the result would be that he might become honored, respected, and esteemed by his contemporaries as their teacher.

But this is not the tack New Testament Christianity takes. When such a person as the one just depicted turns to God, God would say to him: "No, no, my friend, not that way. You are now out so far that there is hope for you; therefore I shall cudgel you some more and help you along so that your contemporaries, instead of hoisting you on their shoulders, which would spoil the whole thing—you and them—will beat you to drive you farther out." Because ideality, the intensive, is God's interest, he squanders millions, millions—which, please note, nevertheless consists of single ones, every one of whom could be the single one.

It is a terrible thing to be involved with God. The more you are involved with him, the wilder it gets and the more he cudgels you.* He is just as infinitely concerned with one person of intensity, yes, one, as he is infinitely indifferent to millions and trillions. God is always the inverse of man. Man believes numbers mean something; for God it is precisely numbers which mean nothing, nothing at all.

If one may put it like this, it is true that God still knows how to speak very well for himself. He says to such a single individual: My little friend, I understand all too well what you are humanly suffering, that you are suffering by being heterogeneous to persons dearest to you, from having to give them up or find them turned against you as enemies, instead of relaxing and having a good life with them. But, my little friend, believe me, I intend that all will be infinitely well with you, as only infinite love can intend it.

Alas, yes, as a girl must have said many times of her seducer: It is useless to resist him, useless, *vergebliche Mühe*, he is able to speak for himself—it is even more true of God. He is able to speak for himself, and therefore, therefore—therefore he cudgels again: O infinite love!

XI¹ A 402   *n.d.,* 1854

« 1808

In margin of 1807 (xi¹ A 402):

* Therefore mankind felt an unspeakable relief when it got Chris-

tianity turned around in such a way that it got rid of God and Christianity came to mean there is no duty toward God. Man thinks he will have the easiest time of all when there is no God at all—then man can play the lord. After that God becomes at most a handsome ornament, a luxury item—for there is no duty toward God.

XI¹ A 403   n.d.

« 1809 *The Ideal—the Carrier*

There are two levels of advancing ideals before men.

The first is the level of those who advance the ideals before men in such a way that they themselves are honored, praised, and rewarded with all kinds of earthly goods. In the same degree as the reward increases, becomes greater, the ideal becomes less recognizable, less clear. The carrier actually stands in its way and draws attention away from it, until finally, when he approaches the maximum of earthly reward, he destroys the ideal by concealing it.

The other level of carriers, the true carriers, are those who, themselves suffering, advance the ideals before men. In the same degree as such a carrier suffers more and more and his life becomes unhappier and more wretched, also through the persecution and opposition of men, in the same degree the ideal is seen more and more clearly. Therefore the carrier does not stand in the way of the ideal at all, does not cloak it in any way with his carnality or finitude.

XI¹ A 429   n.d., 1854

« 1810 *Substitute*

To compensate for the hollowness of nuts,[463] we get all the more of them.

This is ridiculous compensation and also a curse. If the nuts are hollow, it still would be better if there were just three or four of them—what agony to have to crack a million hollow nuts in order to be convinced that they are hollow nuts.

So it is with human beings: compensating for specimens or copies devoid of ideas—we get all the more of them. Although no one wants to strive toward the idea, everyone is in the service of the substitute, serving by multiplying and begetting children.

The numerical is the most ridiculous parody of the idea—by addition we are supposed to achieve that for which addition is really subtraction. But, of course, in the brute sense, numbers have power.

XI¹ A 432   n.d., 1854

« 1811 *Maturity—Immaturity*

There are certain thoughts, the loftiest of which every human being has an impression or memory of in his youth—but then he gets sensible and these thoughts are forgotten.

As exceptions there are some single individuals [*Enkelte*] who do not have a period of youthfulness. Their youth runs on in dark melancholy —and only when they have reached adulthood, when they also are fully educated and matured—only then do these thoughts awaken, and with the enthusiasm of youth.

XI¹ A 447   *n.d.*, 1854

« 1812 *The Honesty of Ideality*
or
Either/Or

An orientation toward quality, always an eye to quality, is required for the honesty of ideality (which is spirit or a purity of spirit)—therefore either/or.

Mediocrity, on the other hand, sordidness, niggardliness, shabbiness, etc., are immersed in: "also," that is, wanting to be along quantitatively, approximately, etc., instead of honestly manifesting quality and giving it its due.

Example. If there is someone who really handles an instrument with some competence and if he has the honesty of ideality referred to, then in the presence of an expert he will immediately manifest that quality: He is an expert and I, no, I am not an expert. He will abhor misusing the competence he has by claiming to be a virtuoso, too, or by claiming equality with the virtuoso, or by diminishing him in any way. On the contrary, he will use his comparatively greater insight based on his competence in order to make others aware of the expert and of his expertness. This is the honesty of ideality; yet the common thing—niggardliness, sordidness, shabbiness—is to say "also," if not quite as good, still "also"— "we lords."

If this honesty of ideality were more common in the world, how different everything would appear! Excellence needs a middle instance with enough insight to point out excellence. The tragedy in the world is precisely that the middle instance is generally dishonesty, which, instead of decently letting either/or, that master of ceremonies of ideality, show it to its place and gladly accepting it, wants to pretend to be excellence also, if not quite as excellent, nevertheless "also."

So it goes in all relationships. Take the most important one—the relationship to Christianity. If pastors had this kind of honesty of ideality, things would be entirely different with Christianity. But they do not have this kind of honesty at all. It is disgusting how they have spoiled everything just because they "also" claim to have experienced, to have suffered—well, not quite as God's great instruments have, but nevertheless "also." They themselves have suffered the ordinary sufferings just as everyone may have, and now they take the apostle and talk as if they had suffered not quite as the apostle had, perhaps, but nevertheless "also."

I am most deeply opposed to this kind of behavior. No, even though compared with men generally I can be said to have suffered unusually, I am far from making the most of this in order to fraternize with the apostle or weaken his impression with my wretched "also." On the contrary, I have immediately pointed out the quality and used my acquaintance with suffering to point him out—"for I am only a poet."

With the aid of mediocrity's cheap dishonesty, Christendom has managed to lose the prototypes [Forbillederne] completely. We need to reintroduce the prototypes, make them recognizable, something which can be done only by: either/or. Either you have quality in common, or you are on another qualitative level—but not this "also—well, not quite, but nevertheless—also."

But with respect to what is a qualitative level different from oneself, even though one is the very next lower approximation, if one has the honesty of ideality not to be concerned about approximations but only elevates these qualities, then he finds his sole joy in pointing out what is a quality higher.

This is the theme in *Fear and Trembling*,[464] in the presentation of the relation between the poet and the hero.

$$XI^1 \text{ A } 476 \quad n.d., 1854$$

« 1813 *How Deceitfully Disguised!*

As the situation now stands, wanting to be a Christian in a way different from the customary meaningless counterfeit is regarded as something so insignificant and cheap that it is hard to see why anyone should want to be that.

Then if anyone makes known again what Christianity understands by being a Christian, the world will rage against such a person and accuse him of being dreadfully conceited. For Christianity actually presents the relationship as follows: the difference between being a Christian and being a man is just as great as between being a man and being an animal.

But then, again, being a Christian is such a horror and agony that gradually and in a very subtle way men managed to become free from this kind of being-a-Christian. Thus ideality has been abolished and this is how what we now have was contrived—namely, that being a Christian is something so insignificant and cheap, something everyone so plainly is, that it does not deserve mention. It is silly to say that one is a Christian or that *cum emphasi* he wants to be one, since, after all, he is that naturally, just as we do not find it silly for a person to want to be a councillor of state *cum emphasi* but certainly find it silly for him to want to be a man *cum emphasi*, for—good lord—we are all that, after all. And just as it is not regarded as silly for someone to make a pregnant observation *cum emphasi*, but for someone on a fine summer day to say *cum emphasi* that the weather is fine today is certainly regarded as ridiculous, for the emphasis has no relationship to the nothingness in the meaninglessness he is saying. Emphasis very likely has the same relationship to the nothingness of being a Christian, something we all are, of course, etc.

XI[1] A 515   *n.d.*, 1854

« 1814 *Our Age*

No individuals, no persons, are born any more whose lives respond to the idea. No, men are no longer men; women are no longer women. In place of ideality we have managed to make prudence into a kind of ideality.

XI[1] A 539   *n.d.*, 1854

« 1815

*In margin of 1814 (*XI[1] A 539*):*
Just as a ship capsizes when it does not respond to the rudder, so the race degenerates if it does not respond to the idea—alas, and this is what is called man's perfectibility, as if we were to call a child's naughtiness its perfectibility and strive to develop it.

XI[1] A 540   *n.d.*

« 1816 *Hypocrisy—Hearty Nonsense*

Formerly, when Christianity was shocking to men, forgeries tended toward hypocrisy. The appearance of accepting the Christian requirement was produced—but it was hypocrisy.

Nowadays, when Christianity is anything but shocking to the minds of men, now when it has become such a familiar, good-natured, decent chap—now the forgeries tend to be hearty nonsense and the Christian requirement is treated as something quite cozy; it is mucked up to such an extent that it almost amounts to the life of a bourgeois.

This forgery, of course, is the most dangerous of all—I wonder if any of the Church fathers who fought for the faith against heresy, I wonder if any heresy-judges ever really had the slightest intimation that anything like this could get to be orthodoxy.

$$\text{XI}^2 \text{ A } 77 \quad n.d., 1854$$

« 1817 *Abnormality*

True religious ideality, simply because it is always before God, may seem to be what men call a triviality, somewhat as they tend to regard the greatest crime as an abnormality. Splendid—yes, it is an abnormality. In the very same way a darning needle will consider it an abnormality if the finest English needle cannot take what the darning needle takes before it betrays any stress, or the table knife will consider it an abnormality if the finest, sharpest honed surgical scalpel "can't take the least thing" without being affected.

No, this abnormality is health, a higher health. It is an abnormality or sickness only when it becomes nothing but nonsense. It surely is not an abnormality that the microscope, let us say, is able to see the most insignificant triviality. No, seeing the trivial is an abnormality only when it means seeing imprecisely, but if the vision is precise, then it is health and advantage to be able to see even the very insignificant. It surely is not an abnormality on the part of a watch to be able to indicate both the minutes and the seconds, something a clock might call a kind of pusillanimity, an abnormal restlessness. No, if the watch very accurately indicates the minute and second, this surely is a superiority.

$$\text{XI}^2 \text{ A } 195 \quad n.d., 1854$$

« 1818 *The Human Race*

The whole thing works out this way; this is the way I explain all that nonsense which is Christendom, plus the fact that Christianity has become the very opposite of what it originally was.

Christianity is God's thoughts. To God the meaning of being human was an ideality of which we have scarcely an intimation. The fall was such a guilt and brought such a degradation that a person cannot adequately feel the pain of it without having an impression of the prior ideality.

All this has been progressively lost in successive generations. Step by step we have become habituated to the idea that the wretched state in which we are living is the natural condition; every generation has begun with the wretchedness of the generation just past and has proceeded to increase the wretchedness with which the next generation begins.

Christianity must therefore become meaningless, and to salvage a kind of meaning there is in a certain sense nothing to be done but to change it into the opposite of what it presently is.

The ideality which is lost and by which the degradation to animal creatures becomes all the more perceptible—yes, it is as if it had never been. For a long, long time, for generations immemorial and in continued decline, the race has been very well satisfied with being animal creatures, finds the pleasure, the earnestness, and the meaning of life in it, and must ultimately find it screamingly funny if anyone were to think of returning to Christian conceptions and their necessary presuppositions.

Imagine a family of noble blood demoted to slavery as punishment for a crime—imagine someone of the tenth generation with a background of eight or nine generations who have lived as slaves, the son like his father —the result will presumably be that the tenth-generation man is well satisfied with the conditions of life, feels at home in his station by birth, which was his father's before him, and grandfather's before him, etc. And if someone were to come to this tenth-generation man and explain to him that he is of noble lineage, he would be laughed to scorn and would discover that the persons involved care least of all, yes, even become embittered because someone seeks to disturb their routine, the routine in which they had contentedly lived for a long time, the son like the father and the father like the grandfather, etc.

So it is with Christianity. With the imperturbability of the eternal, unmoved as the North Star, Christianity points to the fall as its presupposition. But in the meanwhile, through the consequences of repetition, the fall has burgeoned into such a frightful prolixity that it is like an enormous parenthesis, so colossal that no one has sufficient range of vision to see that it is a parenthesis. And within this parenthesis life goes on lustily, the degradation continues, and in constantly increasing proportion from generation to generation the next generation becomes less significant than its predecessor with whose insignificance it began, and also more numerous—and now the two greater powers, insignificance and numbers, join to reduce man to such a triviality that the Christianity of the New Testament, if brought into touch with it, must be looked upon as nonsense.

And then they hit upon the idea—what an enormous discount!—that Christianity is not related to the man, to the individual, but to the race. "Never mind us human beings," they thought. "We don't mind saying that it is nonsense to bring Christianity into relation with a single one of us, but perhaps 100,000 millions taken all together might suitably be related to Christianity."

But this is no help. Even if this change of substituting the race for the individual did not radically confuse Christianity, it still would not help, for the race is so degenerated that it is not suitable for the Christianity of the New Testament, does not have the conceptions which are the presuppositions of Christianity.

But God's memory stretches far enough to encompass all parentheses.

Men, however, have long, long, long ago totally forgotten that it is a parenthesis into which we have entered, that Christianity was introduced precisely as the divine *claudatur*.[465] No, we live pleasantly within the parenthesis, propagate the race, and organize world history—and it is all a parenthesis.

Question: is a parenthesis-man immortal?

XI^2 201   *n.d.*, 1854

« 1819 *Ideals—Social Morality*

What social morality is for the criminal world ideals are for the world which observes social morality.

What the criminal world wants is to get rid of social morality, whether by rebelling against it or by devious means; in quite the same way the world, which still observes social morality, is occupied with getting rid of ideals by outright rebellion against them or by devious means, or by the hypocritical appearance of going along with them etc.

The eternal binds to ideals in the very same way that this world binds to the observance of social morality. From a Christian point of view, therefore, someone who by preaching Christ manages to make 20,000 a year and to go around decorated and dressed in velvet is just as much a thief as anyone who steals in this world, for all these thousands, velvet and all, achieved by preaching Christianity is thievery and can only be achieved by proclaiming under the name of Christianity something which is not Christianity.

But the situation is such that in this sinful world it is regarded as a great accomplishment if one can push through this egotism—complying all the while with social morality. And then the observance of social morality is regarded as Christian virtue—and thus we are all Christians!

XI² A 264   *n.d.*, 1854

« 1820 *To Hate Oneself*

Simply wanting to have the ideals out in the open is already on the way to hating oneself. One who loves himself does not want to have the ideal out where it will disturb his self-satisfied enjoyment of life.

*   *

If you have a habit which you yourself frown on but which you still cannot manage to resolve to give up—well, then do this. If up to now you have concealed it from others, then make a change and force yourself to let others know about it—this is on the way to hating yourself. For a bad habit is happy to identify itself with the person to the extent that he wants to hide it. Therefore, when the person concerned says to the bad habit, if I cannot withstand you, if I am too weak even for that, I can do one thing, I can torment you, tease you, by disclosing you to others. The bad habit also knows very well that only when the person involved loves it so much that he hides it, only then does it really have power over him.

XI² A 313   *n.d.*, 1854

« 1821

No, God in heaven is the only power who does not hold sales or reduce the prices; his prices remain eternally unchanged, more firmly fixed than the North Star.

And every generation and every individual in the generation, right where he is, must come to self-understanding in relation to these eternally unchanged prices (which are found in the New Testament); this is the primary condition for all reformation and all progress.

If anyone assumes that this ideality (to be a Christian) is just like every other ideality, so that when things naturally start slipping for a man (at times it cannot be helped) the price must be reduced—well, the price still must not be changed; we must rather take stock of ourselves and see how much we are drawing on "grace." God cannot change the price, for then *eo ipso* he would not be God, but he can help us poor human beings with grace; he cannot, however, serve a most honored public (even though that public were all mankind) by changing the price.

XI² A 344   *n.d.*, 1854

« 1822   *Whether the Race Is Not So Degenerate*
That Individuals Able To Bear Christianity
Are No Longer Born

That the "free thinker" in a certain sense is a great boon to Christianity cannot be denied. He stresses that aspect of Christianity by which it is an offense.

Here we are faced by what I mean by the degeneration of the race.

Everything Christian presupposes a dialectic or is so constituted [*lagt an*] that the individual must be able to undergo a redoubling [*Fordoblelse*] within himself. To be able to see sharply and clearly that Christianity involves the thrust of offense, to be able to see that Christianity makes one, humanly speaking, unhappy, and then despite all this to enter into Christianity—I doubt that men so structured will appear any more.

Nowadays everything must be done quite automatically. If people are going to enter into something, they have to see very clearly that it is to their advantage, have to have finite reasons etc.—in short, men have sunk down into sheer meaninglessness which has no relationship at all to the ideality which is Christianity.

And corresponding to this meaninglessness of individuals, Christianity has been remodelled into some kind of soothing syrup which, like other sweets, is offered for sale by pastry women (clergy in silk and velvet) and which further corrupts people.

XI^2 A 267   *n.d.*, 1855

« 1823   *The Ideal*

The ideal is enmity toward the human. —Man naturally loves finitude. The introduction of the ideal is to him the greatest agony; of course, if it is introduced very poetically as fascinating make-believe, well, this he accepts with pleasure.

But when the idea is introduced as the requirement, an ethical religious demand—it is the most terrifying agony for man. In the most agonizing way it slays for him everything in which he actually has his life. In the most agonizing way it shows him his own wretchedness. In the most painful way it keeps him in sleepless unrest; whereas finitude quiets him down in a life given over to enjoyment.

This is why Christianity has been called and is enmity toward the human.

*   *

This is how humans respond to the ideal. Young girls become rosy with excitement when they hear of it; the young man's heart beats violently; the unmarried man respects it; the married man does not turn entirely away from it—but the farthest away from the ideal is mother, Mrs. Ordinary Woman. The real fury against the ideal proceeds from family life, from the lioness, or, to say it another way—and it is sometimes true —from the sow with her young.*

*   *

Anyone who thinks he has brought ideals to bear—and has not been hated and cursed by men—has brought the ideals to bear in a deceitful way, in such a way that they were a delight to the imagination, something like Heiberg's battling "the public"[466] and at the same time organizing "a cultured public,"[467] which is shadow boxing.

XI[2] A 271   *n.d.*, 1855

« 1824

In margin of 1821 (XI[2] A 271):
* All who have learned this about ideals have therefore also commended the single state. To marry means making the relation to the ideal so difficult for oneself that ordinarily it is synonymous with giving up the ideal.

(To be married the way Socrates was is something quite different from what is generally understood by marriage. Socrates saw in marriage a hindrance and for that reason—married, and for that reason was *happy* with Xanthippe, or counted himself fortunate—namely, because of the difficulty.)

XI[2] A 272   *n.d.*

« 1825 *The Idea—Number*

These are the poles. And the infinite difference between man and man is this: to feel impelled to the idea and to be capable of being tranquilized by human numbers.

Only one who has felt the need for the idea and has pressed through to the idea and has endured the suffering of bearing the idea, only such a person has need for immortality and has pressed through to it.

But such individuals long since ceased to appear and have been a rarity in all periods with generations as the criterion, a rare instance in a single generation. The millions need nothing more than numbers; they are specimen-men or copies [*Exemplar-Mennesker*].

There are, of course, levels. The utterly insignificant specimen-men are able to be tranquilized by the human numbers in the city where they live; the somewhat more significant ones need something larger, a large city, a country, contemporaries, history, but they are all specimen-men, tranquilized by human numbers. Regarded in the light of the idea, 17,000 centuries of millions *qua* number are no more than half a dozen, which, again, $= 0$.

The specimen-man tranquilizes himself with human numbers. If something is true, he needs no higher proof than that such and such a number (according to his level as specimen-man) have regarded it as true. On the other hand, if the ideals are presented to specimen-men, they immediately identify themselves by their objection: This is going too far; you won't get anyone to accept this. Consequently human numbers decide what is truth. Looked at in terms of the idea, of course, it is completely irrelevant whether many or few or no one will accept it. The idea-man is recognizable simply by not being at all occupied by such things. For the idea-man the human number $= 0$; for the specimen-man, it is everything. He is so much in the power of this thought that he is very concerned about being comfortably buried in a place where many others are buried; he would perhaps doubt his immortality if when he died he were thrown out in some out-of-the-way place where no others are buried. In short, the specimen-man imagines (and this is as upside-down as possible) that immortality is connected with being a crowd, that his life depends upon numbers, that is, he has no need of immortality, at most a need for an illusion which for an appropriate consideration is satisfied by the social class of job-holders called "the clergy," "ever striving by oath upon the New Testament and by prompt service and honest dealing to guarantee their honored customers" and so on.

Although the specimen-man has nothing to do with the idea, he has the obvious advantage of a life which is infinitely easier than the life of the idea-man. Yes, five minutes of the sufferings in which the idea-man breathes every day would be enough to annihilate every specimen-man; for him it would resemble being transported into a foreign atmosphere. To be accurate, it must be said that the specimen-man cannot suffer, for the idea specifically belongs to authentic, agonizing suffering. We human beings are of the opinion that plants cannot really suffer because consciousness is required for suffering. Likewise, for genuine intensive suffering the idea is required.

That very suffering which belongs to the qualitatively intensive daily life of the idea-man, the suffering of being set apart from being ordinarily human, set completely outside the crowd, this suffering the specimen-man, who is of course at home in the crowd, does not have and cannot imagine. Yet this suffering, and in its most agonizing form, decidedly accompanies being an idea-man. Only the human bite, if I dare say so, isolates an individual in such a way that he can become an idea-bearer. The human bite, to be bitten by men! The isolation which arrogance or peculiarity or misanthropy originally gives is by no means sufficiently iso-lating. No, loving men—something the idea-man always does—he must collide with them in such a way that as thanks for the most disinterested, well-intended action, he is rewarded with bestiality; he has experienced, daily, that beyond a certain point men are animals in clothes. The idea-man must be rejected, cast off by men. This is required if he really is to become an idea-man. Specimen-men or copy-men must be regarded as not knowing what they are doing when they treat him this way, for this very isolation is the condition for his being brought to the last extremity of human existence so that he relates himself to the idea, or, to speak re-ligously, so that God can get hold of him and he really comes to be in-volved with God, something not one individual in a generation does, although in every generation there are thousands of job-holders with fam-ilies who make a living prating to the millions about the fact that men have lived who have done this, and thereby they strengthen themselves and the millions in thinking that this nonsense about others is the same as really getting involved with God themselves.

Yes, to touched by an idea (shot by the elves), to be an idea-man, an idea-bearer, or to use a religious expression, which I prefer, to be chosen by God, is agony to such a degree that, speaking merely humanly, it is unconditionally, unconditionally the most terrible of all the terrible misfortunes which can happen to a man. And in every weak moment the chosen one himself thinks so, too. Yet, be still, be still, do not despair, do not in one single moment of impatience squander what in eternity is unbounded happiness!

But, speaking merely humanly, to be a chosen one is the most terrible of all terrible misfortunes.

The very moment God chooses an individual, he blocks him off, sets madness between him and the others in order to prevent an under-standing between them. For God is no friend of that hearty nonsense or of those battalions arm in arm. He wants men as single individuals. And in order to guarantee that the chosen one does not in an unguarded mo-ment prattle himself into the hearty crowd, a kind of madness is set between him and the others. To be bearers of the idea, to be a century, perhaps two or three, before one's time is about the same as to be excluded from relationship by madness. On the whole, what was said in the childhood of the human race about having seen God is, rightly understood, entirely true. The consequence of having seen God is death, but not in a physical sense, no, but death to everything natural and human, to live as one dead. The consequence of having seen God is—madness, but not understood in the sense that the chosen one becomes mentally ill, no, but that a kind of madness is set between him and others: they cannot understand him.

Thus he lives in the most agonizing isolation. He endures bestial treatment from men, for when the idea is to be introduced, men become so outraged that the animal side comes to the fore.

Literally, there is not a single one who can understand him. Nor is he able to help anyone, because he could never want to encourage anyone to mimic him, and he knows full well he could never get anyone to relate himself to the idea as he has. No one can rejoice with him. When a man's work involves temporal and earthly wages, when he serves thousands and is distinguished by titles and rank, amounts to something, something big in this world, he can invite family and friends to rejoice with him; but what is infinitely more joyful, in a Christian sense, for the sake of eternity, to be rewarded with being laughed at, insulted, and persecuted—this joy he himself perhaps finds difficult enough to regard as joy, infinitely joyous, but under no circumstance can this kind of joy be the occasion for parties, neither large banquets nor small family gatherings. No one can sorrow with him; no one understands why and how he suffers. Detested, despised, and excluded as if he hated men (which, however, he does not do at all simply because loving God he destroys, as it were, everything in which the mass of men have their lives and for which they live), he can expect the participation of people generally only in the form of malice. He is incessantly martyred in the agony of being related to the generation but living among specimen-men who, physically, are just like him. And no *direct* alleviation can be expected from God. God is rather the very one who, with the most calculated cruelty, martyrs him when men are unable to do it—yet in love drilling it into him that he has to do this out of love, that otherwise he could not be used, and that in eternity he will thank him for it as one gives thanks for the most ineffable benefaction.

So he lives. As long as he lives, intensively concentrated, he is much too strong for his contemporaries, like a fatal poison, and therefore he is hated, excluded, detested, and finally put to death. To his contemporaries he is like an essence. A glass of it—heaven help us, the kitchen maid will say—that's enough to kill the whole town; one drop of it in 30 jars of water gives the most refreshing, delicious taste, enough to raise the dead. So it is also with him. During his life, all those who are called preachers, professors, all those oathbound animal-creatures, are the most zealous to put him to death and, as with the Savior of the world (to take the highest example) in his time, to save the world from this poison. When he is dead, when assistant professors, preachers, and professors have first thinned him out in their own water and then in the water of the thousands whom they teach—this is magnificent!

You lowest dregs of humanity, you oathbound liars—yet I feel it useless, yes, even presumptuous to imagine myself able to prevent the future from being like the present. It would even be presumptuous if, having surveyed "Christendom," I consider what you, the Savior of the world, have achieved, the numerous generations of well-fed, larded, prolific teachers of Christianity you have procured, you who have spoken, both gently and severely, with words which must have been able to move stones and crush rocks, against taking that to be Christianity.

XI³ B 199   n.d.

IMAGINATION

« 1826

Most super-clever people, when they come in touch with the higher levels of the poetic, the more visionary and imaginative, have somewhat the same experience as did Colonel von Plessen who, when his horse became uneasy about some *unheimliche* phenomena during the night, sat up straight on his otherwise *well-trained* horse because he was *a good horseman* and was going to force it on, but it was impossible; yes, he could not even dismount but had to sit for a whole hour through its most horrible capers.

See J. Kerner, *Eine Erscheinung aus dem Nachtgebiete der Natur* (1836), p. 299.

II A 621   *n.d.*, 1837

« 1827 *Situation:*

A man standing on a pontoon bridge detects through his field glasses that something is moving in the water; subsequently he sees that it is the shadow cast on the bottom by a little animal lying on the surface and about to drown. He first tries to save it by throwing himself down full length and using a pole, but the current makes this impossible. He then takes off his clothes, wades out with the field glasses in one hand to keep the creature in sight, since the movement of the water disturbs a steady view—and finally rescues it. Meanwhile a number of people have gathered to see what he is doing. A policeman comes along and arrests him because he went in the water at a place where it is not allowed. He then takes out his little animal, which is no bigger than a ladybug, shows it, and explains that he ventured out in order to save it—and the whole crowd laughs at him, and the policeman fines him!

The error does not lie in their not being able to understand his compassion (there is no question of this at all) but in their inability to perceive that a trifling little thing, through the power of a man's imagination etc., can come to occupy him *absolutely*.

V A 24   *n.d.*, 1844

« 1828 *The Medium of Imagination—Actuality*

Take a stick. You hold it in your hand, and it is straight. Thrust it into the water and it looks broken. You pick it up again and say, "Yes, but good lord, it is still straight"—but please thrust it into the water again, and it will appear broken.

This is the way rhetoricians and their ilk present Christianity. They take it out of the medium of actuality (they do not express it existentially), and therefore Christianity looks completely different than it truly is—please venture it existentially in the realm of actuality, and you will see that it looks completely different, that exaltation becomes abasement, etc.

x^3 A 616   *n.d.*, 1850

« 1829 *But from Him Who Has Not, Even What He Has Will Be Taken Away*[468]

This seems to be a contradiction, the very opposite of the proverb: One who has nothing has nothing to lose. How can something be taken from one who has nothing.

It is very simple. Not to have means "not actually to have," to imagine that one has it. From him, then, is taken—that is, the fragmentary intimation of having which he has is taken away in such a fashion that he becomes more and more stupid in his imagining that he has something. The delusion is not taken from him—this would be his good fortune—no, only that fragment by which it might still become clear to him that he was deluded.

Thus it is in all Christendom and established Christianity: to have Christianity in imagination means that they do not have it. And from them is taken—i.e., they sink deeper and deeper in the delusion.

x^4 A 478   *n.d.*, 1852

« 1830 *Sophistry*

In Wieland's *Agathon*[469] it is superbly stated that Hippias does not, to be sure, deny that the good is beautiful and virtue magnificent, etc., but he says (and here is the sophistry) that it is something which delights the imagination through depiction and consideration—but it is not something by which one orders his life, nothing normative or regulative.

What, then, of "quiet hours" and this kind of Christian proclamation! If the above description does not fit this kind of thing I know of nothing which fits.

What enormously dangerous sophistry! All the artistry of "quiet hours," all the mastery in depicting, considering, describing—and then the secret, that of course it is not like this in practical life; one does not order his life according to such things.

The secret—yes, for care is taken not to mention this in the quiet hours so that the true situation becomes evident.

The greater the artistry employed in depicting and considering—the less this listening leads to acting accordingly—in fact, the listeners are all the more charmed and bewitched into mere imaginative infatuation.

x^4 A 479   *n.d.*, 1852

« 1831 *Optical Illusion*

Councilor of State David told me about a North American prison warden who provided his penitentiary with painted iron bars etc. but made sure that the prisoners never came close enough to see that the whole thing was an optical illusion; he insisted that the painted iron bars were just as effective as real ones.

It is the same with the proclamation of Christianity! During "quiet hours" a person emotionally surrenders himself in imaginative emotions to spiritual dissipation and imagines himself willing, if demanded, to sacrifice everything, portrays the exalted, noble life with the passion of an actor (and who but an actor ordinarily has such inflamed passionateness)—and for daily use he sees to it with all possible cowardly shrewdness that his life never eventuates in any decision whereby it could become evident what kind of a fellow he is.—What more does the congregation want? This, after all, is just as useful as any actual witness to the truth. Maybe even better, they perhaps think. For this purely abstract possibility —no, it was never that perfect, even when the most honest witness to the truth became a martyr. The abstract possibility is the essence of all perfections, but the most excellent work of the greatest author would still not be as perfect as the work John Doe could produce, if he wanted to. And this abstract possibility is offered to the congregation every Sunday by these noble "good shepherds," who with the help of abstract possibility reap the profit of esteem and rank as instruments of earnestness, of the truth—and also get all the earthly profit as well.

x^4 A 533   *n.d.*, 1852

« 1832 *Imagination*

is what providence uses to take men captive in actuality [*Virkeligheden*], in existence [*Tilværelsen*], in order to get them far enough out, or within, or down into actuality. And when imagination has helped them get as far out as they should be—then actuality genuinely begins.

Johannes V. Müller[470] says that there are two great powers around which all revolves: ideas and women. This is entirely correct and is consistent with what I say here about the significance of imagination. Women or ideas are what beckon men out into existence. Naturally there is the great difference that for the thousands who run after a skirt there is not always one who is moved by ideas.

As far as I am concerned, it was so difficult to get me out and into an interest in ideas that a girl was used as a middle term against me in a very unusual way.

XI[1] A 288   *n.d.*, 1854

IMITATION

« 1833

And if Christ will not even permit us to follow [følge] him, in the same way as he denied the prayer of the demon-possessed man, εἶναι σὺν αὐτῷ (Luke 8:38), nevertheless, like him, we shall go home to our family and our home and proclaim the goodness of God and what has happened to us. Luke 8:39.

II A 324   January 9, 1839

« 1834

If to grieve and lament were right, then it would be futile to name our Lord and Master as our prototype [Forbillede]; for he surely did not sit down and weep over the world's sins, and yet he bore the sin of the whole world,[471] which we do not have to do.

III A 132   n.d., 1841

« 1835 *An Ascension Discourse*

Just as in teaching a child to walk one gets in front of the child and turns toward it—consequently does not walk alongside the child but is oneself the goal (how delicious if it is the mother!) toward which the child is to walk alone—so also Christ in his Ascension gets in front, does not walk beside the disciples; he is himself the goal toward which the believer strives while he is learning to walk alone. There he stands at the goal, turns toward the believers, and stretches out his arms just as the mother does. Even though she stands so far away that she cannot reach the child, she stretches out her arms and motions with them as if she already embraced the child, although there is still some distance between them. That much solicitude she has, but more solicitous she cannot be, for then the child does not learn to walk.[472]

V B 237   n.d., 1844

« 1836

In the world of nature the imitation [Eftergjørte] is the most insignificant of all. Imitation diamonds are worthless. In the world of the spirit it is the reverse. There is an original hope, youthful hope, but it is not the highest; faith's hope is the highest. And the whole intrinsic world of spirit is precisely the world of imitation, and yet far more glorious.

VII¹ A 208   n.d., 1846

« 1837

Contemporary Christendom really lives as if the situation were like this: Christ is the great hero and do-gooder who once and for all has guaranteed us salvation, and now all we have to do is be happy and satisfied with the innocent goods of earthly life and leave the rest to him. But Christ is essentially the prototype [*Forbilledet*]; therefore we should *be like* [*ligne*] him and not merely reap benefits from him.

VIII¹ A 303   n.d., 1847

« 1838

The religious prototypes [*Forbilleder*] are frequently very abstract. We do not see them tested and tried in ordinary human sufferings, in sickness, in physical weakness and all that goes with it.

VIII¹ A 335   n.d., 1847

« 1839

. . . . . The conformity [*Conformitet*] with Christ prized so highly by the superstition of the Middle Ages in the form of having the stigmata, the wounds of Christ, upon one's body (Francis) was simply an exaggeration—but the conformity of being derided etc. is the true conformity.[473]

VIII¹ A 349   n.d., 1847

« 1840

In margin of 1839 (VIII¹ A 349):
For the task is, as Gerhard says somewhere (in *Meditationes sacræ*),[474] not only *frui Christo*, but above all *imitari Christum*.[475]

VIII¹ A 350   n.d.

« 1841

. . . . . You talk about wanting to find consolation in Christ. All right, but you had better watch out lest there be something egotistical here. You are supposed to be like [*ligne*] Christ. All right, then try this— at the very moment you yourself are suffering most of all, simply think about consoling others, for this is what he did. The task is not to seek consolation—but to be consolation. To seek the company of the cripples, the despised, the sinners, and the publicans.

VIII¹ A 432   n.d., 1847

« 1842

If Christ had said, "Thus have I lived and suffered; you are not to concern yourselves with all this; you are only to look to me and let all be well." —And if someone would say: No, I'm not satisfied with that; I want to strive to be like [*ligne*] Christ—then this would be arrogance; and this approximates Mynster's theology.[476] But, merciful God, the very essence of Christianity has been left out of this, because it is Christ himself who exhorts and encourages, yes, commands and orders us to be like him. What is Christianity? It is the doctrine of and the instructions for being like Christ. Usually there is something fraudulent in all this about looking to Christ and then being happy, i.e., happy in totally different categories. O sheer deceit, wherever one turns!

VIII¹ A 449   n.d., 1847

« 1843

The fundamental defect in Christendom is that the essentially Christian has been given an absolutely wrong position. The essentially Christian, so it is said, should be consolation—consolation, tranquillity, alleviation, etc. But, after all, Christianity itself says that it is Christianity for which men will have to suffer (all Christians will be persecuted, says Paul;[477] suffer on account of the Word, according to the parable of the sower).[478] What a contradiction in terms—what they, seduced by all this chatter about consolation, have jumped at is what they are supposed to suffer for. But such is the result of all this priestly altering and modifying. Christianity must be embraced—then everything follows naturally. But Christianity has become sheer milksop. This is the reason contemporary Christians achieve nothing, are incapable of enduring anything, and are just like children who have never had any requirement placed upon them but have been pleasantly and sweetly coddled.

But the entire age does not want to hear anything about the absolute; everything must be defined according to a finite teleology. Christianity has also gone in this direction. What is Christianity really good for? The very question is a basic lie. Just as the Royal Danish Council could not make up its mind about what pastors are really good for and therefore has gotten them busy counting sheep and ducks, so also Christianity has become a kind of consolation insofar as one is pinched financially. And this is Christianity!

VIII¹ A 536   n.d., 1848

« 1844

In Tauler's *Nachfolgung des armen Lebens Jesu Christi*,[479] which I am presently reading for my edification, I find (pt. 2, para. 33, p. 137) a striking similarity to what I have developed in *Christian Discourses* (third section, second discourse). The following is especially excellent: that love prefers to obey counsel rather than commands. Consequently, as I have presented it, renunciation of all things is Christian counsel; Christ desires that you do it but does not command it. Nor does he judge every person who does not do it to be no Christian.

VIII¹ A 587   n.d., 1848

« 1845

Luther is entirely right in naming these among the marks of the Christian (no. 7): they (Christians) inwardly sorrow and are grieved, are agonized, and yet do not give up, but outwardly they are poor, despised, sick, frail, so that in all things they may become like their master, Christ, and receive the blessing he promises all who suffer persecution for his name's sake.

See Rudelbach, *Biographier*,[480] the article on Jesper Swedberg, p. 553.

IX A 7   n.d., 1848

« 1846

I understand very well how I ought to conduct myself in order to be understood—honored and esteemed—how I could gain these benefits even by preaching Christianity. But this is simply unchristian—that the one who preaches Christianity is not himself what he says is Christianity. Christ has not inaugurated assistant-professors—but imitators [*Efterfølgere*]: Follow me. It is not *cogito ergo sum*—but the opposite, *sum ergo cogito*.[481] It is not: I think self-renunciation, therefore I am self-renouncing, but if I truly am self-renouncing, then I must certainly have also thought self-renunciation.

The one who preaches Christianity shall therefore (he *shall*, it is something he has to take care of himself) himself be just as polemical as that which he preaches.

IX A 49   n.d., 1848

« 1847

Everything Christ expresses belongs essentially to a Christian's life. He whose life does not express this *ecce homo* is really not a true Christian. But it is a matter of integrity that one does not express an *ecce homo* which, because of the particular contemporary point of view, is the object of admiration—such as voluntary poverty and celibacy in the Middle Ages.

IX A 82   *n.d.*, 1848

« 1848

Because Christ simply expresses that he was a human being like everybody else, he is truly the prototype [*Forbilledet*], but he also constitutes the eternal strenuousness in what it means to be a human being. He makes the divine commensurable with being a completely ordinary human being. He gives no one a discount; he does not stand outside as an object for lazy and sterile gawking and admiration, but behind, in order to force men out.

IX A 101   *n.d.*, 1848

« 1849

Wherever human compassion either from within or without cries out to you: Spare yourself, Christianity answers: The prototype [*Forbilledet*] did not spare himself. Which means that he submitted everything to God. So also when stress and strain, humanly speaking, go beyond your powers, you shall not spare yourself but submit everything to God; let him decide to spare or not to spare. In any case you must in no way spare yourself but pray God for permission to spare yourself, and this confession of weakness will still keep you in the God-relationship, to begin again where you left off.

IX A 323   *n.d.*, 1848

« 1850

In the course of many centuries there came a time when people paid an enormous amount of money to get a fragment of the cross to which he was nailed. And if it had been possible—this impossibility—that somewhere in Judea, perhaps on a less frequented footpath, a genuine print of his foot was found, what would one have given to own this little piece of land, in order literally to set one's foot in his actual footprint!

IX A 396   *n.d.*, 1848

« 1851

How tremendously taxing contemporaneity with the ideal is becomes apparent if one merely speaks of what kind of clothes Christ went around in, whether he wore a hat or a cap—it becomes almost irresistibly comical. But in contemporaneity earnestness is this tremendous intensification, the mark of which is precisely the comical, i.e., that there is no escape whatsoever through a delusion, by shaping a more ideal form, etc. It is the same with the question of his diet, because in retrospect he is so ideal that the question simply cannot arise, or it becomes almost comical. Dreadful earnestness!—that in contemporaneity the ideal has all of these accidental and finite human characteristics—"as we are," "like one of us"—and nevertheless is God.

x¹ A 179   n.d., 1849

« 1852

I must now take care, or rather God will take care of me, so that I do not go astray by all too one-sidedly staring at Christ as the prototype [*Forbilledet*]. It is the dialectical element connected with Christ as the gift, as that which is given to us (to call to mind Luther's standard classification). But dialectical as my nature is, in the passion of the dialectical it always seems as if the contrasting thought were not present at all—and so the one side comes first of all and most strongly.

x¹ A 246   n.d., 1849

« 1853

If the terror of eternity (either eternal salvation or eternal lostness) is removed, then wanting to imitate [*følge efter*] Jesus becomes, after all, fantastic. For only this earnestness about eternity can oblige and also motivate a human being to venture in such a decisive way and justify his action.

But since all of us now live in the relaxed notion that we will all be saved just as we are, the rascal and the just man, the one who was righteous to the utmost of his power and the one who chiselled a little, all, all of us, just as we are, become equally justified—well, then people are right to regard it as basically fantastic and ridiculous for someone to want to sacrifice everything to imitate Jesus.

Earnestness lies specifically in the ethical, and if the ethical is taken away and, for example, Christ is made the ideal, and if anyone wants to be like [*efterligne*] him in this way—this is taking him in vain. The issue is heaven or hell—and this is the reason for wanting to imitate him, i.e., to be saved—this is earnestness.

O, what sufferings are approaching! It is quite certain that in the near future there will be for the second time on earth suffering as terrible as during the introduction of Christianity, for this is what is at stake. Once it was introduced into the world and it conquered the raw passions; now prudence and everything related to it have abolished Christianity in Christendom itself so that it must once again be introduced into Christendom, but the battle becomes a battle with prudence and shrewdness.

x^1 A 455   *n.d.*, 1849

«1854

An adherent [*Tilhænger*][482] is not an α *intensivum*[483] but an α *privativum*.[484]

x^1 A 631   *n.d.*, 1849

« 1855

What we men might call intellectuality is not at all prominent in Christ as the prototype [*Forbilledet*]. This is why it would offend us to think of Christ as laughing, an idea expressed in the words of the hymn: How he weeps who never laughs.

It is a misconception, however, for a Christian person to want to be so ideal that he cannot laugh. Furthermore, in the edifying discourse there is even an essentially appropriate comic element which is just as true and just as pedagogically right as tears and severity.

x^1 A 673   *n.d.*, 1849

« 1856

The prototypes [*Forbillederne*] are anonymous, or eternal images: "the publican," "the sinner"[485]—a name distracts so easily, merely sets tongues wagging, so that one comes to forget himself. The anonymous prototype constrains a person to think of himself insofar as this can be done.

x^2 A 36   *n.d.*, 1849

« 1857

In his sermon on the Gospel for the Fourth Sunday in Advent, Luther[486] himself says that every sermon begins with preaching the law (and this is indeed forever unchangeable).

I find that what he says about preaching the law corresponds to what I am accustomed to say concerning the use of the prototype [*Forbilledet*] in order to preach men to bits so that they turn to grace. The basic error in the Middle Ages was that men childishly (and to that extent forgivable) persisted in the naïve thought that they could succeed in approaching, in resembling, the prototype. Yet it is true that the prototype must be the prototype, that is, there ought to be striving toward likeness, and yet at the same time the prototype is that which by its infinite distance crushes the imitator [*Efterligneren*], as it were, or thrusts him back into an engulfing distance—and yet again the prototype is himself the compassionate one who helps the person to become like him. The doctrine of the prototype, rightly understood, encompasses everything.

But back to Luther. Luther says that when the law is thus rightly proclaimed to a man, he becomes aware of his wretchedness—and then he becomes embittered about the law—and this is precisely the judgment upon him. This is absolutely correct. The law captures totally, not by thundering about this one or that one of a man's actual sins, but by making him in total desperation a rebel against the law, from which he nevertheless cannot tear himself—and thus he is captured.

x^2 A 47   n.d., 1849

« 1858 *The Epistle for the First Sunday in Advent*[487]

The whole thing is really a metaphor: to rise and dress (put on Christ).

Life is compared to a day. One awakens (night is past—day has come). So one gets up, dresses (puts on Christ).

With regard to the Atonement, to put on Christ means, *for one thing*, to appropriate his merit (in the parable of the king who prepared his son's wedding feast there was one without a wedding garment),[488] and *for another*, to seek to be like [*ligne*] him, because he is the prototype [*Forbilledet*] and example [*Exemplet*]. This is essentially an expression directed toward inwardness. Just as the expression he uses of his teaching, that it is food, is the strongest expression for appropriation, so the expression of putting on Christ is the strongest expression that the resembling [*Efterligningen*] must be according to the highest possible criterion. It does not say of Christ that you shall try to resemble Christ (to say this implies indirectly that the two still remain essentially unlike); no, you are to put on Christ, put him on yourself—as when someone goes around in borrowed clothes (this is *satisfactio vicaria*)—put him on, as when someone who looks strikingly like another not only tries to resemble him but *re-presents* [*gjengiver*] him. Christ *gives* you his clothing (*satis-faction*) and asks you to *re-present* him.

x^2 A 255   *n.d.*, 1849

« 1859

As the prototype [*Forbilledet*] Christ gives absolute expression to that which naturally no human being achieves: absolutely holding to God in all things. Consequently his life must with unqualified necessity collide absolutely with the world, with men, and he became the most forsaken and hated and wretched of all. Then the voice of mockery sounds: "He sticks to God—now let's see whether God wants him!"[489] The malice in this mockery is not anything peculiar to those Jews; it is in every man. For there is strife between man and God, and one must choose sides.

A man can experience something similar in a lesser degree. Even to be moderately earnest about holding to God is a sure way to make a failure of everything temporal and earthly, for the more one holds to God the more he endeavors to make his cause pure and unselfish and his striving sacrificial—all of which becomes his misfortune; but the person who stakes his lot with men knows that the trick is to secure for himself earthly advantages which he can share with others.

Nevertheless men do notice that in spite of everything such a man's life is still a power, and they do not like him but almost hate him. And when finally there comes a sort of analogy to the suffering of Christ—being forsaken by God—the mockery rejoices and adores Nemesis for what happens to him. It sounds something like this: He should have stuck with us. Earlier it went like this: Join up with us, for to love us is to love God; to stick together with us is making the most of life.

Everyone who is just moderately earnest about holding to God is in a certain sense *eo ipso* squandered, even though for faith this is the most blessed of all. He misses everything in this life and is hated for it; if the latter happens, besides being squandered he is also sacrificed.

So it is; yet this must never be heard; if someone merely says this, his fate will be like that of one so squandered and sacrificed. It must not be heard, for it disturbs men's selfish doctrine that to stick together is to love God.

x^2 A 317   *n.d.*, 1849

« 1860 *The Asceticism of Christianity*

We congratulate ourselves on having explained away all asceticism from Christianity, showing how far Christianity is from the foolishness of such things as monastic flagellation.

But wait a little! Something is always left out, and that is the paradigm: the Lord of Lords in the form of a poor servant without a place to lay his head, the self-denial exemplified by this prototype [*Forbillede*] which Christianity requires—but this, in fact, is asceticism and quite different from remaining in the world (in contrast to monastic flight from the world) in order to be honored and esteemed and to enjoy life. In short, where have they found the text which is now orthodox Christianity —that Christianity is the enjoyment of life (which both Mynster and Grundtvig have, each in his own way)? As I have pointed out in another journal [IX A 362], the one who remains in the world to suffer for the truth is in the right over against the hermit's flight from the world, yes, but the convivial, beribboned person who remains in the world to enjoy himself in the completely ordinary human sense hardly has the right to castigate the monastic. Let us not deceive each other. Everyone knows full well what is meant by enjoying life. That such a one can nevertheless be exposed to ordinary human suffering, sickness, etc. (just like every pagan) is part of being human, and yet it is a new lie, again, the audacity with which one classifies such sufferings in the category of Christian suffering.

X^2 A 326   *n.d.*, 1849

« 1861

Luke 24:28: "He appeared to be going further, but they constrained him, saying, 'Stay with us, for it is toward evening and the day is now far spent.' So he went in to stay with them."

This is a figurative characterization of Christ's relationship as prototype [*Forbilledet*] to the believer. In one single step the prototype is so far in advance that the believer is demolished. But the believer still must strive. Therefore the prototype may patiently yield a little; thus in spite of the infinite imperfection there is nevertheless a slight advance. But then it frequently happens that for a moment it seems as if the prototype would "go further," and now more than ever the imitator is defeated—then he prays for himself: Stay with me. This is the lingering which a man needs, even though for the prototype it is the suffering of patience.

X^2 A 347   *n.d.*, 1849

« 1862

It is entirely clear that it is Christ as the prototype [*Forbilledet*] which must now be stressed dialectically, for the very reason that the dialectical (Christ as gift), which Luther stressed, has been taken completely in vain, so that the "imitator" [*Efterfølgeren*] in no way resembles the prototype but is absolutely undifferentiated, and then grace is merely slipped in.[490]

With regard to contemporaneity with Christ as the criterion, which has been treated also in other journals [i.e., IX A 95, 153; X¹ A 132; X² A 253], it must be remembered that Christ's death is indeed the Atonement and in one sense grace really begins here. As long as Christ lived, grace in this sense was not present; his own life was for him a testing in which he himself was tried. —In another sense his entire life was grace; as Scripture says, grace and truth became revealed in Christ.

X² A 361   n.d., 1849

« 1863

Christ is the prototype [*Forbilledet*], but as the prototype he jacks up the requirement even higher than the law. He says to men: If you are like this, if you are love in this way etc.—you are like [*ligner*] me; and if amid good and happy days you perhaps have little love etc.—this is not being like me. No, when everybody is hostile to you and hates and persecutes you etc., if you then are love like me, then you are like me. Then man despairs. But instantly the prototype changes and is also "the Savior," who holds out a rescuing hand to help him be like the prototype. He casts himself into the arms of the prototype. But then he shrinks back again because of being a sinner. But the prototype changes again and is the Redeemer. This is the love of Jesus Christ. Inasmuch as there is to be striving, he is the prototype whom one ought to resemble, but the prototype is also the Savior and Redeemer who helps the Christian to be like the prototype.

X⁶ B 241   n.d., 1849-51

« 1864 *Contemporaneity with Christ—Dying to the World*

Let us imagine someone saying: That which impels me to Christ and binds me to him is not so much the consciousness of sin as it is what Peter says: To whom shall we go.[491] I assume that the relationship to God, salvation hereafter, is contingent upon Christ, and therefore I adhere to him.

Fine. But think now of contemporaneity. What does Christ express? Being dead to the world, living in poverty, in contempt, in persecution. If you are going to adhere to him now in the situation of contemporaneity, then you must conform to his life. For Christ has not recited a doctrine about dying-to-the-world; he is himself existentially what it means to die to the world.

Is eternal salvation really so great a good to you that you value it as an absolute good at this price? As a matter of fact, at this price a good can be only the absolute good.

How pedagogically cautious Christianity is! It does not come out immediately with the whole difficulty, something Christ does not do either. It says: Do you want eternal salvation? If you answer "Yes," Christianity then says: Well, attach yourself to Christ, attach yourself most intimately to him—but he expresses what is meant by being dead to the world.

x³ A 171   n.d., 1850

« 1865   *A Less Rigorous Way To Enter into Christianity*

The assurance of an eternal life is bound up with Christ.

Thus if the matter of eternal life becomes absolutely important to a person, he adopts Christianity.

Yet no essential change has taken place in the man. He goes on living in his own particular categories, except that by his relationship to the eternal he is attached to Christ.

But then if he himself becomes aware that to be involved with Christ in this way means to be wholly involved, he will constantly be driven by life's dilemmas into actual imitation [*Efterfølgelse*].

Then, too, little by little, the divine elevation of suffering will stir and move and beckon him.

Meanwhile there will always be the question whether such a relation to Christianity can stand the test in the real crisis, when it is manifest that religion is not primarily consolation but that primarily it plunges me into suffering and adversity.

x³ A 207   n.d., 1850

« 1866

It is easy to see that a person has to be utterly broken before he takes refuge with one crucified. Nowadays we say: He suffered and died simply to save me. Fine, but it is equally true that the fact that his whole life was suffering was to leave me footprints[492] in which to walk.

It really does not do to wheel away from a crucified one into a dance hall, to let him be crucified in order that I shall live to the tune of: Enjoy life—and even more—enjoy life unabashedly, for there is One who has let himself be crucified for you. Even if it were possible that the Crucified One could have had something like this in mind, it would still be offensive to every better person.

The error of the Middle Ages was all that monastic asceticism. What Christianity demands of the Christian, on the contrary, is to witness for truth—and then the suffering will come, to be sure.

x³ A 272   n.d., 1850

« 1867 *The Mixing of Judaism and Christianity*

The little fragment of religiousness we see in Christendom (and it is little enough) is actually, as I have noted elsewhere [i.e., x² A 80], Judaism, with a little admixture of some Christianity.

This is how we live—we believe (only God knows, by the way, how many do, but *eh bien*, I assume it) that there is a God, a Father in heaven. This God guides everything; whether it is going to go well or ill with me in this world, whether I am to have prosperity or adversity, etc., lies in his hands. This means that nothing is decided here, what the fate of the devout will be in this world; at times a devout man has it good and prosperity smiles on him, while another devout man has daily adversity, and yet both are devout; their lot in life does not indicate whether or not they are devout. —This God has written his law in the hearts of men and also let it be revealed in another manner. But this God has never presented himself as the pattern or prototype [*Forbillede*].

This is the kind of religiousness we have now, and then we bring Christ in merely as the tranquilizer, as grace.

But Christ is also the prototype. In relating to Christ and at every moment I do relate myself to Christ, I pledge myself to discipleship, to imitation [*Efterfølgelse*]. This has been completely abolished. Or is this what it is to follow Christ—to let him, so to speak, go his way in suffering —and thereby acquire grace—and then I take it and go my way.

As soon as there is a prototype, there is the obligation to imitation. What does imitation mean? It means striving to conform my life to the prototype.*

But the fact that there is a prototype establishes a necessary relationship between being a devout man and what happens to a devout man. The devout man who is not marked in a very specific way is *eo ipso* not a devout man.

Now try this. I can pray to God to have an easy life, for God has not established a necessary connection between piety and suffering in this world. The prototype, however, expresses that piety means to suffer in this world. Can I now pray to Christ for an easy life? Impossible, for in praying to Christ about this I am indirectly asking him to help me to escape from imitation, which is precisely what he demands. And yet in Christendom we invoke the very name of Christ to make quite sure of having an easy life—with the help of grace.

The terrifying aspect of Christianity is still not the suffering which comes but the fact that I must understand that involvement with Christ means that suffering must come. Therefore I can very well beseech him to help me persevere—but not to be exempted, since this is mocking him.

Christianity could not even appear as terrifying as this to the contemporary disciples, for they saw no necessary connection between suffering and Christianity; on the contrary they hoped for the very opposite, until the suffering came. But the contemporaries did not have the prototype in quite the same sense (for contemporaneity with him was in the period when the prototype unfolded, which did not end until his death); neither did they have "grace," which was won by the prototype's suffering and death. But grace should not be understood to mean that I get permission to get out of suffering; it means rather that I shall be dealt with gently and that I shall be freed from the anxiety of meritoriousness, as if I myself had to earn salvation by suffering.

x^3 A 276   n.d., 1850

« 1868

In margin of 1867 (x^3 A 276):

* And suffering will surely come. For the moment an imitator [*Efterfølger*] introduces into the world an action properly characterized qualitatively as being essentially Christian, he will of course collide with the world, with Christendom. Any essentially Christian action is characterized by the *quid nimis* which creates an offense. If you are a millionaire and give 100,000 dollars to the poor, you make people happy; if you give it all, you will collide. Accept a big salary and a distinguished office in order to proclaim Christianity, and you will perhaps make people happy; renounce everything, every personal advantage, in order to proclaim Christianity, and you will collide.

x^3 A 277   n.d.

« 1869 *Christianity—Suffering*

In respect to everything else in the world, it holds that if I begin something, it is possible that I may succeed, but it is also possible that I may fail—but not in respect to Christianity. Here if suffering does not come, then my life has not expressed true Christianity at all.

If this is not true, then the prototype [Forbilledet] is in some way an untruth. Either the prototype expressed something merely accidental (that by living at a certain time he met with opposition etc.) and therefore is not essentially the prototype, or there ought to be more prototypes (one expressing that the truth is to suffer, another that it is to float, etc.) and in that case "the prototype" is indeed untrue, for there is only one.

But you say: "If a man is a professing Christian and then otherwise lives as the others, he must leave his fate in the world to God."

I am not going to speak now about the potential precariousness of professing Christ if nothing more is meant by it than is now understood in Christendom—being baptized as a child, etc., or as a theological candidate seeking a position—for if this is professing Christ, then the chances are that there will be no collision with the world; whereas from a Christian viewpoint one certainly takes upon himself great responsibility by participating in such deceptions. But I will not speak of this. But in addition to professing Christ (saying I am a Christian and believing what a Christian shall believe), acting in an essentially Christian manner is also required (which corresponds in particular to the presence of a "prototype" and to true Christianity as imitation [Efterfølgelse]).

Try it, then; enact in your life an action marked by Christian quality, and you will see collision for sure. This world lies in sheer relativity—and the Christian quality is absolute—such action must in life and in death collide with actuality [Virkeligheden]. Certainly no human being, not even an apostle, can bear the absolute when he enacts it, so that to bear it is to be it—which also accounts for everything breaking, the veil of the temple, the graves,[493] all existence [Tilværelsen], all this relativity—but in addition the collision will endanger his life.

But the situation is that action characterized essentially by Christian quality is perhaps not seen once in each generation; it reaches only a certain degree, and thereafter comes the collision.

X³ A 283   n.d., 1850

« 1870 Christianity—Dying to the World

That this is the way it is may be seen by this alone—it says: You shall love Christ.

But to love is to be transformed into likeness [i Lighed] to the beloved; otherwise it is merely wanting to profit by the beloved.

Yet when someone wants to do it, wants to love Christ—then all of Christendom screams: This is presumptuous!* But on Sunday the preacher prates that this is what we must do.

The distinction is this—the preacher-prating on Sunday is a diversion; the other is to be earnest about it, and this we do not want to do. We sit and conjure up the highest for men and say that this is what each must do—and then if he wants to take it in earnest, we say: This is presumptuous![494]

x³ A 294   n.d., 1850

« 1871

In margin of 1870 (x³ A 294):

* But if it is presumptuous to want to do it, then it is also presumptuous of the preacher to encourage it.

And so "it is presumptuous." If simply wanting to love Christ to the extent that one strives to be like [*at ligne*] him, if this were quite obviously something just plain great (for example, like wanting to love a princess, etc.), then it is quite legitimate that one abandons the whole thing in order not to be presumptuous. But to love Christ is just what flesh and blood in its innermost being shrinks from most of all; therefore it is a dubious matter that everyone who avoids it is supposed to have the right to say it is in order not to be presumptuous. But here again we have all the official hypocrisy which is preserved in Protestantism: possibly it is piety which out of godliness does not dare risk it (although it nevertheless is always a dubious matter), and it may be an utterly profane shabbiness which makes use of the opportunity to get free of it and then, to boot, collects the bonus that this is in order not to be presumptuous.

x³ A 295   n.d.

« 1872 *To Be Saved from One Evil or Another by a Miracle of Christ—and Dying to the World*

The fact that Christ performed miracles, healed the sick, etc. is customarily used to show how obvious it is that everyone simply must desire to be his contemporary in order to seek his help.

Let us look at this matter more closely. The question will always be— to what kind of an existence [*Existents*] does the one who has been helped return after being helped.

Christ's meaning is clear—the one who has been helped should now unite with him, become his imitator [*Efterfølger*], forsake this world, and how this is to be understood he can see by observing Christ, and he will also easily discover what the result of uniting with him will be.

But, if this is so, then most human woes are easier to endure than this operation so painful for flesh and blood—actually to die to the world.

Let me illustrate. There is living at the same time as Christ a man on whom fortune has smiled in every respect—except for one aching torment which disturbs this life of his. O, this life, he says, this life, which otherwise is happier by far than most men's lives. If this cross could be taken away, how he would enjoy life, how grateful he would be to the one who helped him!

Imagine that he lived at the same time as Christ lived. I will not dwell on the point that it would scarcely occur to such a man to turn to Christ, that he probably would be afraid beforehand that the affair could become too serious for him. Yet let us make this assumption.

So he turns to him. Let us assume that Christ will help him—but Christ adds this: Then you must become my disciple [*Discipel*] by imitation. What happens? I think the man will say: This is an awkward situation. I wanted to get rid of this cross so that I could properly enjoy life, and you are willing to help me on the condition that I then completely die to this world. But if that is the case, then I am better off staying as I am, enjoying life the best I can despite this torment—than to be helped in this way. On the other hand, if I were actually to die to the world as you require, then this torment is not so dangerous that it makes any sizable particular difference.

Take a cripple. Yes, one who wishes to enjoy life on a grand scale (a Lord Byron, for example) could certainly wish to be healed—but not on the condition that he has to die to the world once and for all. On the other hand, if one is going to die to the world once and for all, it makes no great difference one way or the other whether or not one is a cripple.

But here, again, this is flirting with Christ. This makes him into a miracle-doctor who miraculously helps one—and we forget that he is a teacher.

And even if Christ did not obligate to imitation the person he helps —every better person would still feel obligated to do it—if he has been helped by a miracle. And thus the matter is still the same. If there were someone who wishes to enjoy life and Christ helps him without saying a word about imitation—ah, simply to be guilty of such ingratitude would be enough to disturb his enjoyment of life, even if he could not decide to become an imitator. Of the ten lepers only one turned back—

but I wonder if the nine really had great joy in having been healed; I wonder if they were not constantly reminded of having taken Christ in vain.

In order to perform miracles Christ presupposes: faith. Essentially this means that the one who wants to be helped must be prepared to will to die to the world. Then he is helped, but then he is pledged in imitation to die completely to the world.

This is the relationship—and then all this about miracle loses its fascination.

X^3 A 314   *n.d.*, 1850

« 1873 *The Religious Need of Our Times*

is not a new masterwork in eloquence and profundity, not a hitherto matchless acumen in concepts of faith, etc.—no, the sickness of the age can consume all this in a half year, and there is no advance. No, one who for Christ's sake gives up something, however insignificant, denies himself, does more good.

Action is what our age needs.

No doubt it was sometimes presumptuous when in an earlier age men almost chummily attempted to be like the prototype [*Forbilledet*]. No doubt it was a misconception all too childishly to fraternize with God and think that he sat and looked at me denying myself and giving up this or that trifling thing. Ah, but those times had one great good— a childlikeness which made it possible to get hold of the tasks.

Nowadays, on the contrary, the ideal is so terribly far removed from the single individual that it has become merely an idea of the race; the ideal is so terribly far removed from the single individual that it never occurs to him in the remotest way to want to strive toward likeness [*Lighed*], as if this were just as unprofitable and foolish as to bark at the moon. The ideal is so distant from the individual that between him and the ideal there lies a whole world of prosaic prudence which would find it ridiculous if he undertook such things; yes, he, too, he would consider himself ridiculous.

You see, this also is presumption.

X^3 A 331   *n.d.*, 1850

« 1874 *The United Brethren*

do not accentuate imitation [*Efterfølgelsen*]—in place of a blood-theory lyric there is all this staring at Christ's suffering.

X^3 A 338   *n.d.*, 1850

« 1875 *God—Christ*

When a person is related only to God, then the relationship is like that of a child to a father.

When Christ enters into the relationship, then man is treated like an adult. Imitation [*Efterfølgelsen*] and voluntariness show that the requirement here is higher than for a child.

Yet it must also be remembered that Christ is also grace, and the very one who will help a person to strive.

x^3 A 378   *n.d.*, 1850

« 1876 *Concerning Imitation* {Efterfølgelse}

Do you perhaps not know that there is something called "imitation"? Does it perhaps consist of repeating the same words Christ has said, or does it not rather concern existence [*Existentsen*]?

Or is it perhaps a doctrine, so we again play "pass-me-by."[495] We present the doctrine, but of course we have nothing more to do, somewhat like that dock clerk who wrote in such a way that no one could read it and then replied to his co-worker's complaint that his job was to write and the co-worker's business was to read.[496]

x^3 A 400   *n.d.*, 1850

« 1877 *The Prototype* {Forbilledet}

When Jesus Christ lived, he was indeed the prototype. The task of faith is not to be offended by this particular man who is God, but to believe—and then to imitate [*følge efter*] Christ, become a disciple.

Then Christ dies. Now, through the apostle Paul, comes a basic alteration. He puts infinite stress on the death of Christ as the Atonement; the object of faith becomes the atoning death of Christ.

In this way the prototype *qua* prototype is shifted further away. As long as Christ was living and the prototype walked and stood here on earth, existence [*Tilværelsen*] was as if shattered—the absolute always shatters existence.

Now comes the alteration: the prototype is turned in such a way that his very death, his death of Atonement, becomes particularly emphasized.

While the apostle is enunciating this doctrine, his life meanwhile expresses imitation. But in order that no blasphemy may appear, as if the apostle thought he could attain to Christ by imitating him, he draws attention away from imitation and fixes it decisively upon the death of Christ the Atoner.

This is Christianity for us men. Christ's life on earth is Christianity, which no man can endure.

Then in the course of time imitation or discipleship, again misconceived, is emphasized.

Then Luther puts the relationship straight again.

But then Luther is misused.[497] Imitation is excluded completely and "grace" is taken in vain.

Imitation there must be, but not in such a way that one becomes self-important by it or seeks thereby to earn salvation. No, grace is the decisive factor.

But if the relationship is to be true, then it is particularly "grace," grace alone, which must be declared by the person whose life nevertheless expresses imitation in the strictest sense. If the person who is preaching grace is someone whose life expresses the opposite of imitation, then it is taking grace in vain. No, but when someone whose life rigorously expresses imitation preaches grace, then the relationship is true—grace, in very truth, is kept at par value. The more it might seem, humanly speaking, as if such a person were almost looking for credit, the more true his proclamation is that it is sheer grace by which a man is saved.

Here we see again that Christianity is related to the person who proclaims it—consequently it is as far as possible from a "doctrine."

x^3 A 409   *n.d.*, 1850

« 1878 *The Judgment of My Contemporaries upon Me*

Now there will again be an uproar claiming that I proclaim only the law, urge imitation too strongly, and the like (although in the preface to the new book, *Training in Christianity*, I presented grace). And they will say: We cannot stop with this; we must go further—to grace, where there is peace and tranquillity.

You babble nonsense. For the average man Christianity has shrivelled to sheer meaninglessness, a burlesque edition of the doctrine of grace, that if one is a Christian he lets things go their way and counts on God's grace.

But because everything which is essentially Christian has shrivelled to meaninglessness this way, they are unable to recognize it again when its pathos-filled aspects are delineated. They have the whole thing in an infinitely empty abstact summary—and thus think they have gone further, beyond the succcessive unfolding of the pathos-filled aspects.

Nothing can be taken in vain as easily as grace; and as soon as imitation is completely omitted, grace is taken in vain. But that is the kind of preaching men like.

x³ A 411   n.d., 1850

« 1879 *Blasphemy*

Although there is Sunday palaver about Christ as the exalted proto-type [*Forbillede*] the Christian strives to resemble, it is always understood that no one is foolish enough to want to do any such thing.

This is what Christendom calls piety, fear of God. If, however, some-one makes an attempt to place "the prototype" into actuality in such a way that discipleship or imitation might get to be in earnest, then they say: "This is blasphemy." —Consequently, the truth is blasphemy.

x³ A 447   n.d., 1850

« 1880 *What Is Christianity?—or, More Correctly, What Christianity Is*

Christianity is not doctrine.

Christianity is a *believing* and a very particular kind of existing [*Existeren*] corresponding to it—*imitation* [*Efterfølgelse*].

Note: Christianity is not to be defined as a faith [*en Tro*], which is somewhat like "doctrine"—but is a believing [*en Troen*].

Consequently Christianity is a believing and an imitating.

We can put faith first and imitation second, inasmuch as it is neces-sary for me to have in faith that which I am to imitate. We can put imi-tation first and faith second, inasmuch as it is necessary that I, by some action which is marked in some measure by conformity to the Christian ethic (the unconditioned), collide with the world in such a way that I am brought into the situation and the situational tension in which there can first be any real question of becoming a believer.

The fact that the situation of act or deed is the presupposition for becoming a believer, consequently that to believe corresponds to situa-tion,[498] proves the reciprocal relationship between faith and imitation.

x³ A 454   n.d., 1850

« 1881

Addition to 1880 (x³ A 454), *in margin:*

Christ, who never gets mixed up with proving the truth of his teach-ing or giving reasons for it, uses only one proof: "If any man's will is to do my father's will, he shall know whether the teaching is from God or whether I am speaking on my own authority."[499] This implies that an action-situation is necessary in order to come into the tension in which the decision of faith can come into existence [*blive til*]; it is a venture. It is not a matter of proof first (as men have twisted it about) and then the venture (which is a self-contradicting piece of nonsense)—no, first the venture, then the proof comes afterward—you will experience that the teaching is truth. But men do not wish to venture anything, and therefore they have made Christianity into doctrine, and then one sits down to prove it without any essential change in his personal existence taking place. People become hollowly inflated by the security of the three grounds of proof, even more inflated than a pasha with a helmet crested with three horse's tails.[500] They turn up their noses at the Socratic approach, "If there is an immortality," and call it mere subjectivity—while Christ recognizes this alone as proof of the teaching: If any man wills . . . . . he shall know.[501]

x^3 A 455   *n.d.*

« 1882 *The Milder Christianity and How the Transition to Christianity in the More Rigorous Sense Is Made*

Let us imagine a very superior person and his relationship to a child or a young girl. He takes it upon himself to do for the child or the young girl what the young person is unable to do yet and requires only one thing: Do not worry about a thing; just be happy and contented in your innocent way. If the child or the young girl were to go and prattle and continually ask for permission to do something to help, the superior person would be displeased and say: Leave it all to me. The only thing I ask is that you simply be happy and satisfied and let me take care of it. If the child or the young girl were to ask at least to be allowed to sit the whole day and do nothing else but thank him, he would again be displeased and would say: That is not what I wish; all I want is to make you happy.

This is just about the way it is in the mild Christianity which comes from being brought up in Christianity from childhood.[502] [*In margin:* Although this kind of Christianity in childhood is also a rarity.] The individual permits Christ to have done everything, which, indeed, is unconditionally true for all Christianity, but the individual lives on childishly occupied with the rest of life, relying on Christ to take care of his salvation and confident that all he had to do himself is to be happy. The individual does not even become so inwardly contemplative that he is disturbed by the thought that this security and unconcern might be an ungodly flippancy. In any case this security and unconcern never become a task for the individual, as if there were something to win, for in that case it becomes an enormous task—out of misplaced self-concern and the like to win this security and unconcern.

But in the whole context of this milder Christianity there is no mention at all about the imitation [*Efterfølgelse*] of Christ.

This is where the more rigorous Christianity begins. Of course, the fact remains that in respect to man's salvation Christ is everything and man himself is not capable of achieving anything, but although this is true, or just because it is true, Christ says, as it were, to the single individual: If you want to thank me, then become my imitator.

Then being born again becomes something in earnest. Then come all the collisions with the environment, all the suffering.

And even if imitation were not required, the Christian who actually becomes inwardly contemplative, and consequently in a more rigorous sense a Christian, would still collide. For at present he is living in this world, and if he does not want to adapt and conform his life to this world —and that he cannot want—then he must *eo ipso* collide.

x^3 A 552   *n.d.*, 1850

« 1883 *Imitation* {Efterfølgelsen}

True imitation does not come about by preaching: You must imitate Christ, but from preaching about what Christ has done for me. If a man really comprehends and feels profoundly and truly how infinitely much it is, then imitation is sure to follow.

x^3 A 602   *n.d.*, 1850

« 1884 *"Imitation"* {Efterfølgelsen}

When Christ at the end sends out his apostles, he says, Go therefore and teach all nations and baptize them[503] . . . . . and he who believes.[504] Consequently Christ does not add here, he who imitates me; here grace is predominantly emphasized.

As the prototype [*Forbillede*] Christ still belongs to the proclamation of the law; Christ's own life as the prototype was the very fulfilling of the law.

And precisely by fulfilling the law he ransomed us from the law to grace.

But then imitation comes again, not as the law but after grace and by grace.

x^3 A 615   *n.d.*, 1850

« 1885 *"Imitation"* {Efterfølgelsen}

"Just as Christ humbled himself and took the form of a poor servant —so also the Christian on whom God has bestowed earthly power and wealth should live humbly in all this glory."[505]

This parallel is still not quite accurate; it leaves out the voluntariness, the authentic discipleship or imitation.

And I do not like it when the omission of something very crucial is made out to be nothing at all. We could at least be truthful before God and admit [*tilstaae*] our weakness instead of reducing the requirement.

x^3 A 666   *n.d.,* 1850

« 1886 *"Imitation"* {Efterølgelsen}

Imitation or discipleship does not come first, but "grace"; then imitation follows as a fruit of gratitude, as well as one is able.

Take the human love-relationship. The lover should not torture himself, wondering whether at every moment he fulfills his beloved's every possible requirement. This is not love but earning love, wanting to earn it, and forgetting that the beloved is not a creditor but a lover. No, it begins with joy over being loved—and then comes a striving to please, which is continually encouraged by the fact that even if he does not, he is still loved.

But in the relationship to Christ the problem is that of simply becoming spiritual enough really to grasp how infinitely much Christ has done for me, what a terrible evil sin is, and what a superlative good eternal salvation is.

x^3 A 667   *n.d.,* 1850

« 1887 *"Imitation"* {Efterølgelsen}

We are not to talk about discipleship or imitation the way Paulli talked the last time I heard him (26 Sunday after Trinity, the Gospel):[506] He said: We have now followed [*fulgt . . . efter*] Christ through the succession of holy days during the past year. This is nonsense, a careless association of ideas with the words "to follow after" [*at følge efter*], an attempt merely to get them said, as if everything were "all right" then, "and we cannot accuse him of leaving out imitation [*Efterølgelse*]."

x^3 A 668   *n.d.,* 1850

« 1888 *Contemporaneity with Christ—Grace*

In contemporaneity not even Christ can reduce the requirement in the slightest, for indeed his own life would thereby be altered, and he must fulfill the law to the uttermost.

Therefore he is not angered, either, that no one can be his disciple.

Then he dies, and the death is the coming into existence [*Tilblivelse*] of grace.

Dying,* he diminished the demand for the thief, for here there could be no question of requiring "imitation" or "discipleship" [*Efterfølgelse*]. Nevertheless, just because there can be no question of imitation in this case, we cannot categorically say either that it is reduced. At the same time it is nevertheless shown here that imitation *qua talis*[507] is not the absolute condition; in that case Christ would have had to perform a miracle and let the thief climb down from the cross, would have given him life—to see what would happen with his life of imitation.

x^3 A 712 *n.d.*, 1851

« 1889

In margin of 1888 (x^3 A 712):

* And in life he also did the same with respect to the many he helped and whom he allowed to go away without demanding imitation [*Efter-følgelse*]; only toward those whom he himself wanted for *disciples* [*Disciple*] or who themselves wanted to be *disciples* was he obliged to be so rigorous.

x^3 A 713 *n.d.*

« 1890 *"Imitation"* {Efterfølgelsen}

Alas, it can be said that imitation usually "follows behind" [*følge efter*] in a very peculiar sense—so far behind that it is almost not following at all.

x^3 A 721 *n.d.*, 1851

« 1891 *Decline in Christendom*

First of all Christ was the prototype [*Forbilledet*]. Then this aspect was abolished and only his death was emphasized.

Then came the derived prototypes. But even this was too strenuous. Instead of remaining as prototypes they were changed into intercessors who pray for us.*

In short, the human technique of getting rid of everything called discipleship or imitation [*Efterfølgelse*] prevails everywhere. Therefore the cunning with which we attempt to get a contemporary smuggled away as an object of admiration. Therefore, too, Socrates' cunning in remaining in the background. Anti-Climacus has also developed this in *Training in Christianity*.[508]

* *In margin:* This observation is found in Neander, *Chrysostomus*,[509] I, p. 51, where he expressively calls this way of thinking a way which *"die Stützen der Unsittlichkeit statt Vorbilder der Sittlichkeit sucht."*

x³ A 750   n.d., 1851

« 1892 *What Does Christ Require?*

First and foremost, faith.

Next, *gratitude*.

In the disciple [*Disciplen*] in the stricter sense this gratitude is "imitation" [*Efterfølgelse*]. But even the weakest Christian has this in common with the strongest disciple: the relationship is one of gratitude.

Imitation is not a requirement of the law, for then we have the system of law again. No, imitation is the stronger expression of gratitude in the stronger.

Imitation is not the law's demand that a poor wretch of a man must torture himself. No, even Christ is against this kind of extorted discipleship. He would no doubt say to such a person if he otherwise found gratitude in him: Don't be carried away, take your time, and it will come all right; in any case, let it come as a glad fruit of gratitude; otherwise it is not "imitation." Yes, one would have to say that such fearfully extorted discipleship is rather a perverted mimicking [*Efterabelse*].

x³ A 767   n.d., 1851

« 1893 *"Christendom"—Christ*

All of Christendom's art is constantly employed in getting rid of "imitation" [*Efterfølgelse*].

"Established Christendom" really dates from the time Christmas was declared the supreme festival (in the Fourth Century). The Savior of the world is now a baby. And why would anyone want to be saved by a baby? Because men thought: Here there can be no question of imitation. To be saved by a baby is something like "learning" from the lily and the bird, which is also preferred to an actual "teacher."

Thus there is an oscillation between two extreme poles—either stressing only Christ's death (for then one also escapes imitation) or the baby Christ.

It is "imitation" which must be emphasized once more. Certainly not in the almost comic variation of the Middle Ages. No, imitation in the sense of witnessing to the truth and suffering for it.

Here, incidentally, the asceticism etc. of the Middle Ages will have its significance. Specifically, to become capable of being a witness of the truth, tutoring is necessary in order to be capable of doing without etc. The mistake of the Middle Ages was to make asceticism and the like the absolute τέλος. Thus the Middle Ages copied [copierede] Christ rather than imitated [efterfulgte] him. Christ did not teach poverty in and for itself; he taught poverty to enable witnessing to the truth.

But the Middle Ages were still far out in front of the modern variation, which completely leaves out imitation and transposes Christianity as mere doctrine into the domain of instruction or esthetically into artistic expression along the lines of eloquence and the like.

x³ A 776   n.d., 1851

« 1894 *Christ in Glory*

. . . . . Then he died—and then he was taken up in glory.

Nowadays it is too easy to cut short all too hastily (as was pointed out in *Training in Christianity*),[510] shout hurrah for him, as it were—and forget about imitation [Efterfølgelsen] on our part.

But it is too easy to cut short all too quickly in another way, too. Origen expresses it well: ". . . . . Even (in glory) he weeps over our sins, cannot rejoice as long as we continue in our wrongdoing. How can he who sacrificed himself on the altar to atone for our sins, how can he be joyful when the lamentation of our sins ascends to him! He does not want to drink the wine of gladness in the kingdom of God alone; he is waiting for us. But when, you ask, will his joy, his work be perfected? When he has made me, the last and most wretched of all sinners, perfect and whole." This last sentence is an excellent turn, especially when regarded as a blank in which each can write his own name. Its excellence, after an enormous supra-historical sweep, consists in bringing the matter back to—me.

(See Böhringer, *Die Kirche und ihre Zeugen*,[511] I, pt. 1, pp. 189-190, Origen.)

It is also possible to interpret Christ as prototype [Forbillede] too much, as being like someone who has finished his own examination and now does not think of the others, rather than that his life, his suffering and death (which certainly were the examination of obedience for him) are still essentially redemption and reconciliation, that is, for others.

x⁴ A 131   n.d., 1851

1895   *Christ as the Prototype* {Forbilledet}

Take a human relativity. Think of an existential ethicist. It is always to the advantage of the contemporary age to push him out front as an object of admiration and thus get rid of him as one whom they should resemble. We make him esthetically into the extraordinary, who is admired and admired[512]—in order to get rid of him ethically.

This is the way the whole human race has continually behaved toward Christ.

It is curious to see how quickly Christianity is slackened with respect to the existential [*det Existentielle*]. Already in the Third Century there is a substantial easing up on the requirement for being a Christian: One can very well be a Christian and yet avoid the danger of confession, yes, be a Christian—and sacrifice [to the public gods to avoid persecution].

As a result Christianity made enormous numerical advance—and lost intensity.

Now comes the elongating train of Christians-as-a-matter-of-course, and now begins the tactic of pushing Christ way outside. In the Fourth Century men lose themselves in reveries of admiration and adoration of the God-man—aha!, but imitation, they are not so scrupulous about including that!

From that time Christianity is disoriented. And in this wrong direction it moves steadily forward—yes, it goes forward! Just ask the Nineteenth Century whether Christianity goes forward! Then Christ becomes a myth, a clever poem—and finally he becomes, so to speak, that snake with eight heads which Linnæus proved never existed.

The more admiration increases, the easier Christ becomes—and at the time when he existentially made the strongest impression there was no time for admiration.

Ethically, admiration must immediately be converted into action in the direction of imitation; to the same degree as admiration is permitted to take time to be admiration, to the same degree one is ethically astray.

x⁴ A 148   n.d., 1851

« 1896 *Essential Christianity*

All prototypes [*Forbilleder*] show that the more a man becomes involved with God the more unhappy and miserable, humanly speaking, he becomes*—and this doctrine we have trivialized into something to preach for a living. All preaching for a living must be on the basis of the proposition: The more you are involved with God, the better things will go for you.

Consider "the prototype." Bear in mind what is already difficult enough to imagine, that he, the Righteous One, must suffer all these many things; but one thing still stands firm, you think—God did not forsake him. But that happened, too. God did forsake him. We see something similar in the derived prototypes, that in the most agonized part of their lives there comes a moment when they, too, feel themselves forsaken by God, when they, too, must drink the bitter cup that the world wins its point against them even in this sense that they themselves lament that God has forsaken them.†

Essential Christianity, therefore, means: The more you truly become involved with God, the greater the intensifying misery, humanly understood, even though it is a blessedness in an infinitely exalted sense —and then to have God forsake you. True, it is only for a moment, but nevertheless it is dreadful, dreadful that God is like this (and yet infinite love)—dreadful that being involved with God is like this.

x^4 A 273   *n.d.*, 1851

« 1897

In margin of 1896 (x^4 A 273):
* This is the most rigorous form of being a Christian. This does not hold true of the milder form, which makes Christianity an inwardness, which lives quietly in a cloister or quietly in the world but does not in the more rigorous sense witness for Christianity—then the increase of inwardness is not linked to such an inversion and in particular not with the double danger of inversion.

x^4 A 274   *n.d.*

« 1898

In margin of 1896 (x^4 A 273):
† Note. So it is, for example, with Savonarola when he is in prison, and on the whole this suffering belongs to the specific suffering of the witnesses to truth.

x^4 A 275   *n.d.*

« 1899 *Christian Piety—Jewish Piety*

Strictly speaking, I have never seen a Christian. Among so-called Christians I have seen some beautiful examples of Jewish piety.

Jewish piety rests in the thought: Adhere to God and everything will go well with you; the more you adhere to God the better, and in any case you always have God to hold onto.

Christianity expresses something entirely different: The more you adhere to and involve yourself with God, the worse it becomes for you. It is almost as if God said to a man: You had better go to Tivoli and enjoy yourself with the others—but above all do not not get involved with me; it gets to be sheer misery, humanly speaking.

Strictly speaking, to be a Christian is: to die (to die to the world)— and then to be sacrificed; a sword pierces his heart first of all (dying to the world), and then he is hated, cursed by men, abandoned by God (that is, sacrificed).

In this way the essentially Christian is superhuman. Yet this is the "imitation" [*Efterfølgelsen*] demanded of the Christian in the New Testament.

I am incapable of this. I am able only to come so far out that I use "the prototype" [*Forbilledet*] as a source of humiliation, not for imitation, and once again to my humiliation, because I cannot use the prototype in any other way.

x⁴ A 293   *n.d.*, 1851

« 1900 *Tone*

And when a man dies, one who throughout his life, in daily suffering and torment of soul, presumably bloodlessly yet with blood has been sacrificed to men, then it seems to me that he should at least have the consolation that his life accomplished something. Alas, anything but. No, when he is dead—then the speakers stand up, the orators, the faithless disciples, and now in loud voices praise his noble unselfishness etc. (perhaps they had everything prepared while he still lived and only awaited his death)—and thereby earn money, fame, and honor for themselves. How abominable!

Consider the ultimate! Was the vileness before Christ even half as great as that after him? No. That his innocent suffering and death, that not even this could affect men—this is a greater vileness. Yes, not only did this not move men to imitation [*Efterfølgelse*], no, they made money out of it, honor and reputation. The profit stood waiting; they found it most profitable to orate about how he suffered. Note that what he accomplished pointed toward imitation. True, there were those whom he moved to suffer as he had suffered, but vileness made capital of each of these, again, making money and the profit of reputation on them.

Alas, if there is someone whom the prototypes [*Forbillederne*] do not move so deeply that he comes in a more rigorous sense to suffer as they suffered but in whom there is nevertheless a little grain of truth so that he at least does not want to make money and profit on the sufferings of the prototypes—this is enough to bring some suffering on him, because just this is too much for the world. And while he suffers, vileness is already standing there waiting—"If only he were dead," and then his life also will be cashed in and made into profit.

And when the dead one is highly praised by this vileness which makes a profit out of his suffering, it appears as if the world were now a better world—but alas, it is worse. This profiteering vileness is even worse than all the opposition to him.

x^4 A 321   *n.d.*, 1851

« 1901 *The Apostle, the Disciple—Christendom*

For at least 1,500 years we have turned things around in this way: "The apostle, the disciple [*Disciplen*], is the extraordinary [*Overordentlige*]. God forbid that I be so immodest as to claim or crave to be such a personage. No, I am modestly and humbly content with something less."

O, the abysmal craftiness of the human race which has completely perverted Christianity by this means.

The fact of the matter is that we would rather be free from the glory of having to die to the world according to the criterion of the disciple— and then, to boot, we want to have the bonus that being free from all these sufferings and anguish is also modesty and humility—God forbid! Good lord, what knaves we humans are! We manage to get the ethically normative and the definition of the relationship to it transformed into the esthetically extraordinary and a relationship to that.

We are now at the time, as the watchman says, for the matter to be turned around completely, and the requirement to be held aloft is this: All of us, each one, should be an apostle or "disciple." This provides another interpretation. This above all is the criterion by which we are to be judged. Everyone who does not become a martyr has in one way or another exempted himself by some knavish trick and is accountable to God for it.

This changes the situation. We can spare ourselves all these antics about being too modest and humble to seek such a thing—and then at least see to it that we are honest enough to admit how it is with us.

Ethically understood there is no extraordinary; ethically the extraordinary is normative for all of us, the requirement with which each of us must come to terms by way of admissions [*Tilstaaelser*].

But we have shifted the spheres. We have transposed the ethical into the esthetic, and the apostle becomes the esthetically extraordinary—and we have built churches for them and made a great fuss over them, for we would rather be free from imitation [*Efterfølgelsen*], thank you.

Ethically the extraordinary is the norm. "The disciple" is the criterion, the requirement. On this basis we are judged, and above all we ought to beware of increasing our guilt by the hypocrisy that out of modesty and humility we do not become disciples. Dreadful! Just imagine that it may at some time become customary to regard an honest man as the extraordinary, and that a thief would then say: I am not so immodest as to claim to be an extraordinary—I prefer (rather than as an honest man to have to give up his illicit gain) to keep the illicit gain and then also be honored and respected as modest and humble.

This is how we have behaved in respect to the Christian ethical norm: the disciple.

The movement has been steadily backward. First the God-man as "prototype" ["*Forbillede*"] was abolished; it was too lofty; but we still kept the apostle, the disciple. Then the apostle and the disciple were abolished; they became the extraordinary, which we smuggled out, but we still kept the witness to the truth. Then we abolished him, too, and trimmed away more and more, until finally the prototype is the shopkeeper.

From all this we see that the fundamental guilt of Christendom is really practising indulgence. We abolish imitation and retail Christianity at various prices. This is the history of the Church, or the history of Christendom. Indulgence was practised long before it reached the height which Luther complained about. And when Luther was scarcely dead, yes, even while he lived, he was used to promote further indulgence.[513]

x^4 A 340   *n.d.*, 1851

« 1902 *Historical View*
"Imitation" {"Efterfølgelsen"}

It is "imitation" (to suffer for the doctrine and what belongs to it) which must be emphasized again; in this way the task relates itself dialectically to the point where Luther eased up.

And just why must "imitation" be emphasized? Could it be in order to lay a yoke upon men's consciences, or could it mean ascetic self-torturing and that we have learned nothing from the past?

No, imitation must be stressed in order, if possible, to maintain a little justice in Christendom, and to bring a little meaning if possible into Christianity, in order to humble men by means of the ideals and teach them to rely on grace, and in order to stop the mouth of doubt.[514]

This point of view of Christianity has been completely displaced. In the New Testament the matter is very simple.

Christ says: Do according to what I say—and you shall know.[515] Consequently, decisive action first of all. By acting your life will come into collision with all existence [*Tilværelsen*], and you will get something to think about besides doubt, and in a double sense you will need Christianity both as the prototype [*Forbilledet*] and as grace.

Nowadays we have swung the whole thing around. Christianity is an objective doctrine—before I get involved, it must first justify itself to me. Good night to all Christianity! Now doubt has conquered.

This doubt can never be halted by reasons, which only nourish doubt. No, but doubt can be halted by "imitation." It is the other way around, my friend. You must be—not objective—but subjective. Do you dare to doubt—does your life express imitation in the remotest way?

See, this is a different kind of talk. We have completely abolished imitation, and at most we hold to the paltriness called social morality. In this way men cannot become properly humbled so that they genuinely feel the need of "grace," because the requirement is no more than "social morality," which they fulfill tolerably well. Furthermore, when imitation is not required—there is a fine opportunity for becoming objective and transforming both Christianity and Christ into their exact opposites— Christ as a kind of teacher who is to be judged by the public and who therefore must see to justifying his doctrine.

Luther's situation was quite different in his time. Then "imitation" was in full motion and off course. Now, however, imitation has been completely abolished. Therefore it must be stressed again, dialectically, well instructed by all the old errors.

x⁴ A 349   *n.d.*, 1851

« 1903 *Christianity*

My most profound doubt, which has now been removed.

How inconceivable it has been to me, the gentleness of Christianity which I have heard these millions and millions talk about.

This is how it has looked to me. I have really believed (however humbled I have been before my Lord and Savior) that I would come off better if I only had to deal solely with my God the Father, that it is "the mediator" himself who makes things difficult. For if I have only God to deal with, no "imitation" [*Efterfølgelse*] is required. And then it looked like this: If I, miserable and suffering like the most wretched of people, turn to Christ—and he helps me: What then? Then he says: But you must imitate me [*følge mig efter*], die to the world, suffer for the teaching, be hated by all men—in short, agonies never suffered before on this scale by any human except by a Christian. But good God, to be helped in this manner!

Now I understand that imitation is not to be applied in this way; I understand that it is intended to keep order, to teach humility and the need for grace, to put an end to doubt.

Then comes the reassurance and the blessedness—and then it would not be impossible for a man to be so moved by all this love and feel so blessed that it becomes love's joy for him to die to the world.

Does there not come a moment when a man says: There really is grace; and imitation, as Luther[516] says so superbly, ought not plunge a man into despair or into blasphemy. If that moment comes, then, in spite of all its pain, imitation is a matter of love and as such is blessed.

x^4 A 352   *n.d.*, 1851

« 1904 *"Imitation"* ["Efterfølgelsen"]

There is more significance in Catholicism simply because "imitation" has not been relinquished completely.

"Imitation" (properly understood, and therefore not leading to self-torturing or to hypocrisy and works-righteousness, etc.) really provides the guarantee that Christianity does not become poetry, mythology, and abstract idea—which it has almost become in Protestantism.

"Imitation" places "the single individual" [*den Enkelte*], every one, in relationship to the ideal. See, this spikes Christianity as mythology and poetry.

But Protestantism (by abolishing imitation and by means of hidden inwardness) has almost reached the point that Christ is not the ideal, the prototype [*Forbilledet*] (to which every single individual must relate himself, honestly confessing how it is with him), but an idea. And the individuals in the race, the separate individuals, are specimens, mere copies; each one enjoys himself in his own way without thought of being involved in the ideal. There is, after all, no ideal; there is an idea: Christ—and the human race. Hurrah for me and you, I say.

The matter is distorted even worse than that. When Christ is the prototype and every single individual is supposed to strive—to have to strive in this way means suffering. Therefore it is necessary to have the command: *you shall*—otherwise it never works. Now we have turned the relationship around—to strive after the ideal is arrogance, shameless pride —this is how we talk (as Professor Heiberg,[517] for example, in the preface to *Clara Raphael*).

Here again we have hypocrisy. We not only exempt ourselves from the rigorousness—no, we interpret rigorousness as pride, and then going scot-free is supposed to be commendable humility.

If someone were to venture out in striving toward the ideal—what would happen? The very thing which would help him when the suffering begins would be precisely this "You shall." There is no nonsense about this "You shall," and it means every one. Now they say instead: Detestable pride, the suffering is well deserved—punishment for pride.

God and Christianity reckon with precision: Every single human being *shall* relate himself to the ideal, no matter how far away he is from it. This is so that Christianity can hold a general inspection of these millions. The Protestant mind is free with men, reckons with very large round numbers, exempts all of us from striving toward the ideal, and makes the race that which relates—not to the ideal, for this the race cannot do (*en masse* there can be no relating to the ideal) but to an idea, an abstract idea—and then how far away is this from making Christianity into mythology and talk about Christianity into poetic effusions and moods?[518]

O Luther, Luther, alas, the Reformation went as easily as it did because the "secular mentality" understood that "this is something for us."[519] O, you honest man, why did you not suspect how sly we human beings are! Why did you not have eyes in the back of your head so you could have prevented what was going on behind your back!

Luther had an easy time of it because the "secular mentality" quickly saw this was a neat way to get rid of the rigorousness of Christianity. And it will be difficult to get this relationship straightened out again (without, of course, missing the essential truth in Luther), because the "secular mentality" understands all too well that the issue centers on making the matter more rigorous.

If "imitation" is not applied at least minimally in order dialectically to maintain justice and to set the relationship in order—namely, that Christianity involves the single individual, every single individual, who must relate himself to the ideal, even though it only means humbly to admit how infinitely far behind it he is—then the "race" has taken over and Christianity is mythology, poetry, and the preaching of Christianity is theatrical, for the guarantee of distinction between theater and Church is "imitation," its earnestness, and the sobriety involved in making men into single individuals, so that every single individual relates himself, is obliged to relate himself, to the ideal.

x⁴ A 354   n.d., 1851

« 1905 *Christ Did Not Come To Abolish the Law—Imitation* {Efterfølgelsen}—*We Human Beings*

In truth Christ did not come to abolish the law—he himself is the fulfillment of the law, and has presented himself as the prototype [*Forbillede*]. That there is a prototype who is the fulfillment of the law and whom we should imitate—this is a thoroughly qualitative intensification. 1,718 law-makers writing laws all day long still cannot exhaust the whole law the way this life does which every second is the fulfillment of the law —and to think that we are supposed to imitate this!

But "imitation"—this is what we human beings must try to get rid of in every possible way. Christianity in man's interest must get rid of "imitation"; in any case, there may be few enough who enter into it. Men have been willing to enter into "imitation" only on one condition, that it be profitable. Otherwise imitation must be eliminated if Christianity is to please men. Thus they make the objective so important, the sacraments, etc., but in a way completely different, please note, from the gospels and what Christ himself did.

Imitation! I do not mean this to be understood as the kind of imitation consisting of fasting and flagellation etc. No, imitation [*Efterfølgelsen*] means following [*følgende*] the prototype in willing to witness for the truth and against untruth, but without seeking any support whatsoever from any external power whatsoever, consequently neither attaching oneself to any power nor forming a party—but if one holds to this he is *eo ipso* sacrificed. No wonder that we men are unable to get involved with this imitation.

Nevertheless imitation must be stressed again, at least dialectically, in order to teach standing in need of grace; it must be emphasized that imitation is demanded of everyone—then let him rely on grace.

x⁴ A 366   n.d., 1851

« 1906 *"Imitation"* {Efterfølgelsen}

The two main devices by which we have gotten rid of imitation, even the very notion of imitation, are:

(a) We center all our attention upon an objectivity, doctrine, for example, or the sacraments, and then in lofty tones speak disparagingly about the subjective—rascals that we are!

(b) We center all our attention upon the race, community, Church, in short, upon a collective—whereupon the category "the single individual" disappears. Christ relates to this collective but not in this way to the separate individuals, and "imitation" disappears along with "the single individual," because imitation is related categorically to the single individual—and then in lofty tones we speak disparagingly about wanting to be the single individual, either that it is foolishness or morbidity or vanity—rascals that we are! What was it the greatest thinker in the Middle Ages, Thomas Aquinas, used to defend "indulgence"? It was the doctrine of the Church as a mystical body in which we all, as in a parlor game, participate in the Church's *fideicommissum*.[520]

Every conception of Christianity which does not use "imitation" at least dialectically to train the need for grace and to prevent Christianity from becoming mythology and to maintain justice ethically—every such conception is on the whole "indulgence."

$$x^4 \text{ A } 369 \quad n.d., 1851$$

« 1907 *No One Can Serve Two Masters*[521]

Introduction

[*In margin:* The theme is to be: Christ as the prototype (*Forbilledet*).]

The gospel says: No one can. The whole world says the very opposite: In fact, it can be done very nicely. And no one has ever lived who did not more or less serve two masters. —Nevertheless, the gospel does not trim off the observation, mediating it or saying that "to a certain degree" is sufficient.

There is only one who has actually succeeded in serving only one master, he who said the words, "No one can serve two masters," Jesus Christ, the prototype.

But then how did he have to live? First in poverty and insignificance, and then as total sacrifice.

And how did it go with him (to what did he have to acquiesce in order not to serve two masters)? He had to suffer for it, because all the others wanted to serve two masters and they wanted to force him to do it, too. He had to suffer this in order not to serve two masters. He was persecuted (by those who wanted to serve two masters), forsaken (by those who wanted to serve two masters), betrayed (by those who wanted to serve two masters), condemned, and crucified. Ah, is this what it is to serve only one master? Yes, this is how it is.

But Christ does not want to trouble us by presenting himself (though it is the truth) as the only one who has served only one master and now with the rigorousness of the law requiring the same of us.

No, he mitigates it all for us. He points to some other teachers, to the lily and the bird (who, however, like him have no arbitrary will of their own—and this is the point, if one is to serve only one master).

"Consider them," he says; yes, consider them. O, do not forget that it is now autumn and soon the lily will be withered. Do not forget to consider it before that happens. Soon the bird will fly away. Do not forget to consider it once more before its departure. Then comes winter, a long, long winter during which you will neither see nor hear these delightful teachers. Consider them! It is autumn—but notice whether or not this disturbs or distresses them. No, as we read in the hymn, "Say to sorrow—yes, tomorrow"—this is the way they act, untroubled about tomorrow.

Yet we are not to interpret this to mean that imitation [Efterfølgelsen] is changed into a poetic jest about the lily and the bird as prototypes. No, it is precisely the prototype, Christ as the prototype, and "imitation" which must be stressed in our time, at least dialectically—in order to introduce meaning and a little discipline into "Christendom," in order to stop the mouth of doubts, in order to teach science and scholarship propriety and respect within the Christian sphere.

x^4 A 410   *n.d.*, 1851

« 1908 *Christianity*

To be sure, when a man has become thoroughly unhappy—Christianity tastes good to him. This is why most men resort to Christianity at the time of death.

But—so the human objection might actually read—if I am one of the happy ones, have I the right voluntarily to make myself unhappy in this way in order that I can get a real taste for Christianity?

This is the question of the voluntary, of the imitation of Christ [Christi Efterfølgelse]—not so much as a consequence of faith as it is a matter of coming into the situation where I can become a Christian. The one who has involuntarily become unhappy, humanly speaking, has less difficulty, because spiritual trial [Anfægtelse] is really associated only with the "voluntary."

Luther rightly orders it this way. Christ is the gift—to which faith corresponds. Then he is the prototype [Forbilledet]—to which imitation corresponds.[522]

Still more accurately one may say: (1) imitation in the direction of decisive action whereby the situation for becoming a Christian comes into existence; (2) Christ as gift—faith; (3) imitation as the fruit of faith.

x⁴ A 459   n.d., 1852

« 1909 *Imitation* [Efterfølgelsen]—*the Atonement*

Although the present situation calls for stressing "imitation"—even though (instructed by the error of the Middle Ages) in another sense— the matter must above all not be turned in such a way that Christ now becomes only prototype [*Forbillede*] and not Redeemer, as if atonement were not needed, at least not for the advanced.

No, no, no—for that matter, the more advanced one is, the more he will discover that he needs atonement and grace.

No, the Atonement and grace are and remain definitive. All striving toward imitation, when the moment of death brings it to an end and one stands before God, will be sheer paltriness—therefore atonement and grace are needed. Furthermore, as long as there is striving, the Atonement will constantly be needed to prevent this striving from being transformed into agonizing anxiety in which a man is burned up, so to speak, and less than ever begins to strive. Finally, while there is striving, every other second a mistake is made, something is neglected, there is sin—therefore the Atonement is unconditionally needed.

Although it is the utmost strenuousness, imitation should be like a jest, a childlike act—if it is to mean something in earnest, that is, be of any value before God—the Atonement is the earnestness. It is detestable, however, for a man to want to use grace, "since all is grace," to avoid all striving.

The situation is like that of a child when he is, as we say, "a little angel," caught up in goodness; the spoiled child is identified by the way he exploits the fact that his parents are very kind and affectionate and is utterly remiss, in short, everything his parents do not want him to be. It would also be distressing if the diligent child desired to be rewarded because he is "caught up in goodness." No, nothing so predictably prevents reward and meritoriousness as being caught up in goodness. For a moment it appears disappointingly to be the very opposite, because if I am only caught up in goodness, then nothing is stringently required, but all is grace—then it seems as if the slightest scrap of striving would be meritorious. O, my friend, precisely this—that nothing is stringently required, that you are caught up in goodness, precisely this makes it impossible for even your greatest striving, even that, to be meritorious. Yes, when something is stringently required, there can be discussion of merit. But where all is grace, there is no meritoriousness possible; it is impossible to transform merit into grace. But, as I said, it is scurvy and mean for someone to want to make use of this to avoid striving.

x⁴ A 491   *n.d.,* 1852

« 1910

Addition to 1909 (x⁴ A 491), *in margin:*

Note. For there can be a question of meritoriousness only in the face of what stands on a level equal to your own, therefore in the face of the "requirement." But "grace" stands infinitely above you and therefore has made meritoriousness impossible. "Grace," therefore, is simultaneously the expression for God's infinite love but also the ultimate expression of majesty, manifesting the infinite elevation of God. At the distance of "grace" you are in one sense infinitely further from God (even though in another sense infinitely closer, that is, by fleeing to his love hidden under "grace") than at the distance of the law and the requirement. For in the face of the law and the requirement it is as if God condescended to haggle with you, and on the other hand as if you still might be able to fulfil the law. But at the distance of "grace" God has set you at an infinite distance once and for all—in order to have mercy. At the same time that God in Christ came infinitely closer in "grace," he also made sure of an infinitely higher majestic expression of distance: "grace."

x⁴ A 492   *n.d.*

« 1911 *Christianity in God's Interest—in Man's Interest*

Christ's life is Christianity in God's interest.

The moment he dies, Christianity is transferred over into man's interest. "The apostle" transforms the prototype [*Forbilledet*] essentially to the Redeemer. A consequence is that "the apostle" also posits hetero-geneity between the God-man and every other human being. The Atone-ment, that Christ's life and death are the Atonement, is the expression for the heterogeneity between him and every human being. "Imitation" [*Efterfølgelsen*] tends toward likeness. "The apostle" imitates him and is crucified—but he affirms the Atonement as essential, since otherwise the apostle becomes a kind of Christ.

To be sure, it is precisely the apostle who had not been a witness to Christ's life, had not lived with him, the later apostle, Paul, who most strongly stresses the Atonement and almost overlooks imitation.

Thus from generation to generation Christianity in the Church has been transformed egotistically into something more and more according to man's interest: the Atonement makes imitation into a nothing, or we completely cheat our way out of imitation. Then Christendom more and more develops a bad conscience, and the thought that to relate oneself to God should mean suffering becomes completely foreign; and the very opposite—success and prosperity—becomes the sign of being related to God—and then Christianity is really abolished.

x^4 A 499   n.d., 1852

« 1912 *"Imitation"* {["Efterfølgelsen"]}

It is clearly recognized that this is not a matter, as in Catholicism, of believing in Christ's Atonement—and then calmly continuing one's activities as a bandit. But the question persists: what ethics shall be adopted so that one dares to call himself a Christian.

In place of this lunatic way of trusting in grace and continuing to be a bandit, Protestantism has established social morality. Social morality approximates the existential [*Existentielle*] which is required of Christians —and then faith in the Atonement.

But take care. Christianity is infinite gentleness, sheer mercy. If someone lies dying—even though he had 70,000 murders on his conscience, etc.,—the Atonement provides satisfaction. But, but, he dies and consequently is not in a position to lead a new life. The question is: on what existential level does Christianity allow a man to live out his life, year after year.

Is social morality this kind of existential level? Well, look around, and what do you see? It is a secular mentality over and over more secularity, in actuality a scurvy betrayal of everything higher.

And then we want to introduce the Atonement into this or add it to this—and this is supposed to be Christianity! Once a week in a quiet hour there is mention of striving—but of course we have made sure that our lives are anchored in illusion and consequently it is pure imagination to suppose such talk means anything. This is Christianity!

x^4 A 500   n.d., 1852

« 1913 *Catholicism—Protestantism*

What we men are trying to do is to get rid of "imitation" [*Efterfølgelse*], to get it set aside.

This is how we go about it. We take Christ purely as "Redeemer" and omit the qualification "prototype" [*Forbilledet*]. But this is not enough. After a while the Virgin Mary becomes a kind of redeemer to whom we pray that she will pray for us to "the Redeemer." And then "the apostle" becomes a kind of redeemer to whom we pray that he will pray for us to "the Redeemer," and then the martyr to the apostle and on up, and the witnesses-to-the-truth to the martyrs and on up, and then the priest to the witnesses-to-the-truth and on up. This gigantic rigmarole is calculated, naturally, to put "imitation" at a distance.

This is a dreadful error. Yet there is something human in all this. If I want to live a life of enjoyment and am conscious of the fact, and yet I want to be related to the prototypes who express the very opposite (suffering), then, humanly speaking, it is rather touching that I want to change the prototypes to a kind of redeemer, that I want to express how heterogeneous my life is in relation to theirs; it is a kind of honesty towards the prototypes.

Protestantism is more astute. We live in sensate and secular enjoyment (and this is called Christianity)—and then get rid of the prototypes, the middle-instances, by the hypocritical "I am too humble and modest to aspire to be the extraordinary." What kind of extraordinary? Living in poverty and wretchedness, being hated, ostracized, and at last slain?

The more I think of this the more it seems to me that Protestantism (however true Luther's concept is), that the hypocrisy of Protestantism is actually heightened and refined hypocrisy.

x^4 A 521   *n.d.*, 1852

« 1914 *When the Middle Ages Came To Regard*
as Extraordinary Christians Those Whose Lives
Expressed "Imitation" {"Efterfølgelsen"} in
Renunciation and Asceticism, the Meaning
of Christianity Was Demolished, the Way
To Striving Was Blocked, and Bargaining
Took Over

From the time the extraordinary [*Overordentlige*] arose (in the sense that one becomes the extraordinary by doing what is required), things got worse and worse in that direction. Then came *meritoriousness*, but how in the world could meritoriousness otherwise have arisen if imitation [*Efterfølgelsen*] had been clearly maintained simply as the requirement. Consequently meritoriousness entered in, and after that all the blasphemous lunacy associated with it.

But the error lay in getting extraordinary Christians. This was a falsification of Christianity. One cannot become the extraordinary by fulfilling the ethical requirement. "The apostle" is not the extraordinary because of his voluntary poverty and the like. No, this is what is required, and in so doing he is a Christian. But he is the extraordinary through his immediate God-relationship. Only in this sense can Christianity admit to extraordinary Christians.

Thus haggling conquered here. Haggling can be done in two ways: either by being freed from the requirement or by being declared the extraordinary. Christendom came to consist of these two kinds: either Christians who were completely exempted from "imitation" (these are actually not Christians, and it should be noted that this is only an approximation of Christianity) or Christians who did strive in the direction of imitation but gained the title of extraordinary Christians—and this untruth had the result that neither was Christian.

It was the secular mentality which conquered here. In general, men wanted to get rid of imitation—and yet be Christians. Thus there was no other way but to let those who expressed "imitation" advance to "the extraordinary" in order to be rid of them and be able to continue to be Christians with a secular peace of mind. And "the extraordinary" found pleasure in this recognition—again the secular mentality.

A swing must be made in the other direction. The so-called "extraordinary Christians," or persons corresponding to what the Middle Ages understood by the "extraordinary Christian," can be called Christians, plain and simple Christians. The rest of us must be demoted to "approximations of Christians," apprentices, and the like.

This is the way "Christendom" as delineated is related to the delineation [of Christianity] as it is in the New Testament. For "the extraordinaries" (once it was conceded to them that there is something extraordinary here) it was impossible to strive without entering into meritoriousness, because the extraordinary or that such [a life] is called the extraordinary signifies that "imitation" is the extraordinary, is not the requirement, for if it is the requirement, it is impossible that doing what is required can become the extraordinary. And the other Christians were entirely exempted from imitation.

x^4 A 556   *n.d.*, 1852

« 1915 *Without "Imitation"* {"Efterfølgelsen"}
Christianity Is Mythology, Poetry

Modern atheists attack Christianity and call it mythology, poetry.

Then come the defenders (we could satirically call them the rescue squad which we call in case of a fire), the official preaching. They assure and swear and fulminate that it is detestable, that for them Christianity is anything but mythology, poetry.

Aber, aber—regarded as a whole their preaching completely leaves out imitation (even their sermons are almost silent on this, and their lives express just about the opposite of the imitation of Christ [*Christi Efterfølgelse*])—*ergo*, Christianity is for them, in spite of all their protests, mythology, poetry.

There is something curious about assurances which may point indirectly to a contrary proof. If a man stands and swings an axe wildly and declares by everything holy that he is a cabinet maker, one replies quite confidently: No, anyone who handles an axe that way is certainly not a cabinet maker despite all his protests and assurances.

x^4 A 626   *n.d.,* 1852

« 1916 *"Imitation"* {"Efterfølgelsen"}

How sly we human beings are! We have turned things around in such a way (in order to get rid of "imitation") that it is supposed to be arrogance and pride to venture out in this way. This slyness has finally completely altered God and Christ for us. Instead of God's simply wanting us to do this and helping us with his Spirit, God has become so elevated that he seems to mock us if we would make a beginning on it, just as if a very strong man were to say mockingly to a child: Lift the weight you see me lifting.

x^4 A 650   *n.d.,* 1852

« 1917 *The Prototype* {Forbilledet}—*Grace*

This is a redoubling [*Fordoblelse*] established at the same time by God; the one seems to contradict the other, but they complement each other.

God's thought, if I may put it this way, was probably something like this: Now the human race must develop all its ability; through grace everything has been done on my part to encourage and quicken the will to be like [*ligne*] the prototype [*Forbilledet*].

But "man" is shrewd; he does not let himself get involved in redoubling. For a time he chose the prototype and cast grace aside, replaced it with meritoriousness, and became, in supposed striving after likeness to the prototype, as impertinent as possible toward God—yes, however ridiculous it is, it was almost a case of going beyond the prototype in perfection—that is how serious this striving after the prototype was!

Then man changed—and now he omitted the prototype but stole "grace." If he previously had been all too impertinent and importunate toward God, now he behaved as one who had stolen something—he ran away with the stolen goods (grace) and hid in a secularized mentality as far from God as possible. This is Protestantism. And surely the demoralization in Protestantism is the deepest the world has ever seen.

x⁵ A 9 *n.d.*, 1852

« 1918 *Grace—Imitation* [Efterfølgelsen]

In relation to your past or to some particular event in your past—yes, even though your life deserved the most severe punishment ever imposed—it still holds true: there is grace; through faith in the Atonement you are forgiven. So infinitely open-handed is grace.

But now let us turn to the other side—and look, grace holds again here where the question becomes specifically: What kind of life shall I lead in the future? Is it possible that, trusting in grace, I calmly construct my whole life in a way which I myself must admit has no relationship whatsoever to the essentially Christian strenuousness, to "imitation"—do I have the right to do that? Or the one who arranges a very secure career for himself through preaching Christianity—is this not the same as admitting that one's life once and for all is kept outside of this essential striving and that it is my intention to keep it this way? Do I have the right to do that in the power of "grace"?

Is this not taking "grace" in vain? As mentioned, in relation to something in my past there is now nothing to do; consequently there I appropriate grace, and this is how faith is to be appropriated. But, now, what about the future?

What daily existence corresponds in any way whatsoever to the Christian requirement? Or is there an element of imitation in living secularly as all the others do and then for a quiet hour once a week listening to a sermon or even preaching oneself? Here again it holds true—if I have lived in this way up until now—well, it is something past, and I am forgiven for it; grace is offered. But the very same moment the question arises: Do I have the right to live the same way tomorrow, do I have the right to think that I am not able to adopt another way of life, pretty much as if I were about 70,000 years old—for if this were so I would only be making a simulated movement during the quiet hour every Sunday and consequently would not move from the spot—do I have the right to do that by virtue of "grace"?

x⁵ A 27   *n.d.*, 1852

« 1919 *The Spirit is the Comforter*

Consider a man who is conscious of his guilt and offense. For a long time he goes about in quiet despair and remosefully broods over it— then he learns to flee to grace, and he is forgiven everything; everything, everything is infinitely forgiven.

Blissful! But now as he walks out, as it were, from the sanctuary where he heard this word of grace, he shuts the door behind him—and now is supposed to begin—what then? Let us visualize it. When this infinite grace was proclaimed to him, he was also told: Now begin a new life—and he found this requirement so reasonable that in speechless gratitude he felt it was unnecessary for him even to be told about it.

Now he is supposed to begin. Introduce now the requirement of the ideal—and remember it was a completely new life he should begin— in that very moment he is unable to lift a finger, for whatever he undertakes means new and even greater guilt, for what he is doing, even the best, is still shabby in relation to the ideal.

Consequently, the moment he shuts the door of grace, as it were, and goes out full of holy resolve to begin a new life, alas, blissfully stirred by the thought that now all is forgiven and he will never get into that situation again—that very same minute, that very same second, he is on the way to new guilt—in the form of "the best he can do."

In that same moment he must return again and knock on the door of grace. He must say: O, infinite grace, have mercy on me for being here again so soon and having to plead for grace, for now I understand that in order to have peace and rest, in order not to perish in hopeless despair, in order to be able to breathe and in order to be able to exist at all, I need grace not only for the past but grace for the future.

See, this is grace in first place, of which I am speaking.

For that purpose there is also "the Spirit." The Spirit is the Comforter. It is not only vitalizing, enabling power for "dying to the world"—but is also the Comforter in relation to "imitation" ["Efterfølgelsen"].

Christ is the Atoner. This is continually in relation to the past. But at the same moment he is the Atoner for the past he is "the prototype" ["Forbilledet"] for the future.

Here, alas, is the difficulty. Measured by the criterion of "imitation," the first step in my future will again make me in need of the Atoner— indeed, I cannot even make a beginning because I am stifled by anxiety [Angst].

Then "the Spirit" is the Atoner.

X^5 A 44   n.d., 1852

« 1920 *Christ as the Prototype* {Forbillede}—
and as the Redeemer

If there is any question of a difference between the "gospels" and the "epistles," it must be that in the "epistles" there is stress on Christ as the Redeemer, on his reconciling death, on grace; in the gospels Christ is more the prototype.

It may also be said that if Christ were only the Redeemer, then his death would be primary and he need not have lived so long on earth, need not have let himself be born as an infant, grow up, and so on.

At the same time, however, it must be noted that in order to become the sacrifice, some time would nevertheleess be needed, for his death must also still be man's guilt; therefore in any case some time is needed to bring about the situation that the *race* put him to death.

Insofar as it can be said that in the gospels the "prototype" is more prominent, this is nevertheless counterbalanced by the fact that nothing is really told of the rest of his life, which would have been of importance if he should be emphasized especially as the prototype. On the other hand, the three years he lives in the public eye, these three years in which he is the prototype or endures being the prototype, these three years are certainly about the shortest time needed within historical dimensions to bring about the catastrophe which became his atoning death. Consequently at no time in these three years does he exist simply and solely as the prototype, but his existence is related to the catastrophe in which he is, for which he was eternally intended, and for which he freely had intended himself—the Redeemer.

$$x^5 \, A \, 45 \quad n.d., 1852$$

« 1921 *That Christ Permitted the Situation to Develop
to the Point of His Being Put to Death Is Not
a Direct Prototype* {Forbillede} *for a Man*

I am thinking of the turn which H. H. (*Two Minor Ethical-Religious Treatises*[523]) gave to the matter. Christ is love—how then could he have the heart to permit men to become guilty of his death; would it not be love to ease up a little? In answer to this, H. H. points particularly to the other side, that Christ is also the truth and therefore could not yield but had to let it reach its climax.

But there is also another vantage point in the matter which, as far as I remember, H. H. does not call attention to, namely, the fact that

Christ let the situation develop to the point of his being put to death is love itself, for his death is indeed the Atonement, the Atonement also for the sin of those who took his life. If he had not been put to death he would not have attained his destiny, for he did in fact come to the world to suffer and die.

But it is not possible for any man to come into this situation. No human being has the right to think that his sufferings will be atoning or beneficial for others in the sense that he and God alone are aware of it. No, this would make him more than human. No, as a human being he is to let God guide and counsel and even use his reason and every permissible means to avoid suffering.

x^5 A 87   n.d., 1853

« 1922 *Christ as Prototype* [Forbillede]—
         the Apostle as Prototype—Grace—
         the Christian Requirement Must Still Be Proclaimed

Christ is the prototype. This is true, and surely this is what must be particularly stressed in our time. But he still is not altogether literally the prototype, because he is, of course, heterogeneous to an ordinary human being by a full quality—and still he is the prototype. What does this mean? It means that in being the prototype he is also intended to teach us how greatly we need *grace*. The change or the successive steps in the change which is the movement in Christian history is basically this. To the degree that a person becomes more and more aware of how infinitely ideal the prototype is, yes, that he is heterogeneous by a full quality, to that degree grace must be more and more affirmed; whereas in the beginning and naïvely in the Middle Ages people went all out for copying [*efterligne*] the prototype—Luther put a stop to it. In my situation I believe that grace must be put in the first place, as I call it. What I do take a little exception to in Luther's position is that he did not more clearly and definitely indicate that thereby the New Testament's, particularly the gospel's, requirement for being a Christian was eased. I am not objecting so much to the relaxation, because this may be the case inasmuch as every advance toward the ideal is a step backward, but then it should be indicated and "grace" all the more emphatically applied—that is, not in empty forms of speech but in an accurate accounting.

Not even "the apostle" is a wholly direct prototype, that is, neither I nor anyone else can undeviatingly and directly copy his life. Generally speaking, no prototype should be that, for then human life would not sufficiently have the rigor of personal responsibility, and then one guilt could never come into existence—that of presumptuously wanting to copy the prototype. No, the very fact that the prototypes are irregular is part and parcel of the paradox—and yet it seems that to be a prototype means that others should decline their lives accordingly. And so it is, and yet, the prototype is also irregular, the prototype does what no human being has the right to do; yes, humanly speaking, it is quite in order if we place "the apostle" in the defense box, for no man has the right to act in that way. The apostle therefore has no other defense than this: I have a direct relationship with God.

So it goes generally. God empowers a single individual man, makes him his instrument. He has, then, a direct relationship with God and, aided by this, turns all human concepts upside down. Now, if a person without this direct relationship with God (and someone who himself has a direct relationship with God is himself an apostle and consequently does not need the other person as prototype) wants to copy him directly, this is an offense. In a certain sense the apostle must humanly shudder at what he is doing as an apostle, but he has nothing more to say than: God drives me to it.

Yet "the apostle" is the prototype. But the fact that the prototype is an irregular has been wisely arranged this way by God, both in order to tighten men properly in the tension of rigorous imitation [*Efterfølgelse*] and humility and also in order to test and to judge the presumptuous ones who want to copy the prototype literally.

No, the prototypes cannot be copied literally. Generally, the older the world and mankind become, the more it develops intellectually. But the more it develops intellectually, the more ideal become the concepts of God and the God-man, but the more ideal these become, the more difficult imitation becomes, and the greater the emphasis which must be placed upon fleeing to grace.

Let each one test himself. I wonder if there is a single person alive in our time who in a beautiful and true way is naïve enough to be able to call God "his friend." To be a friend of God! No! Or to call Christ his brother! No! No, I can call God Father—even a little child does this— but the little child is not a friend of his father. I can call Christ my Savior, my Lord, my Redeemer, my benefactor, perhaps even my friend, but, please note, not in the sense that I dare call myself his friend—but "my brother" is inappropriate for me. Is this because I am such a worm compared to the millions who talk about being friends of God and brothers of Christ? I do not think so; but, no matter, the rising intellectuality has made ideality so high that the prototype does not have the effect of emphasizing imitating as much as it emphasizes relying upon grace.

But one of the components ought to be: either/or. The mistake Mynster[524] and the whole official clan make is that they know neither how to apply the prototype to "imitation" nor how to use this advantageously with regard to relying upon grace.

This last is what I wanted and now want: I want to apply the Christian requirement, imitation, in all its infinitude, in order to place the emphasis in the direction of grace.

x^5 A 88   n.d., 1853

« 1923 *Despairing Presumption—Despairing Humility*

It is quite correct that in Catholicism there have certainly been many examples [*Exempler*] of despairing presumption in the realm of wanting to be like [*ligne*] Christ, to be like the prototype [*Forbilledet*], wanting to be perfect, etc. Nevertheless, there is always present in Catholicism this element of good—namely, that imitation [*Efterfølgelsen*] of Christ is demanded, imitation with all that this means remains firm.

On the other hand, what has Protestantism devised? It has devised despairing humility, an invention of the secular mentality which once and for all declared imitation to be too exalted—and then arranged matters with thoroughgoing secularity and thereby achieved two conveniences: one, freedom from the strenuousness of "imitation" and, two, being honored, regarded, and esteemed for one's humility.

Which is worse? O, Luther, who more than you has been used by adherents [*Tilhængere*] for the very opposite of what he intended?

x^5 A 139   n.d., 1853

« 1924 *Withholding the Communion Wine from the Laity*

Perhaps it was not merely a craving for power which led the clergy to withhold the Communion wine from the laity, but also, if you please, a sense of propriety, because the life the layman generally leads—his entire occupation, striving, and effort—does not seem to have any relationship to this fearful covenant of drinking Christ's blood. We must remember that the situation in the Church at that time was not as it is now, especially in Protestantism, where everything that makes Christianity a covenant has been crossed out and it is taken only as a "gift," in fact, so thoroughly thoughtlessly as a gift that finally we give the whole thing over to our Lord.

Therefore it could be a sense of propriety. But then the question arose whether or not the priests should also be forbidden the cup.

When one thinks back, it is really shocking: this is the Savior of the world; he knows he is the sacrifice; now, for the last time, he is sitting at the table with his disciples—and they, too, are destined to be sacrificed; and then he hands them the cup and says: This is my blood, which is shed for you—then they drink the wine with the understanding: Now it is our turn to shed our blood. How shocking, then, to think of the colossal nonsense of millions and millions of Christians and the prolonged scholarly conflict about the sacrament *sub utraque specie*—and through the centuries the covenant has more and more been forgotten. How simply Cyprian[525] solved the whole difficulty involved in the question as to whether or not the cup should be withheld from the laity by answering: If they are required to shed their blood for Christ's sake, we dare not deny them Christ's blood.

XI¹ A 4   n.d., 1854

« 1925 *Christianity*

This is the true correlation.

The God-man is the prototype [*Forbilledet*], who of course does not live more than once, no more than *qua* Redeemer he dies more than once.

The God-man is the prototype. Christianity, then, is existence's [*Tilværelsens*] examination: Will *you* be a disciple or at least relate yourself truly to this?

It begins from the beginning with every generation—all this about the history of Christianity is rubbish, a trick; likewise, it is rubbish to change the question of unconditionally relating oneself to the unconditioned to an approximating-effort continued from generation to generation, because where the requirement is either/or, a fraction of a generation's effort is nonsense; furthermore, it is nonsense to want to strive jointly (perhaps along with millions), because where the requirement is either/or, numbers mean nothing at all.

Christianity is to be proclaimed to all, all—it does not want anybody to be able to excuse himself on the basis of ignorance, but the outcome of the examination is something else again.

It begins from the beginning with every generation. Right here lies the possibility that frightful, truly Christian collisions can occur also in "Christendom": to hate one's father and mother and so on. Since each new generation must on its own responsibility look to the N. T. to see what Christianity is, the interpretations can very likely be so at variance that a Christian collision becomes possible. In a Christian sense, all this talk about direct continuity with previous generations, about holding fast to the faith of the fathers, etc., is rubbish and trickery. No, we have only the N. T., and every generation has to begin from the beginning, and insofar as it has anything to do with what went before, it has to begin with a revision of the most immediate past.

If, as we humans have made it out to be, Christianity is perfectible, has a history, and so on, then it is downright irresponsible of the God-man to forsake the earth without saying in advance that after a few hundred years everything will be so transformed that his description of what Christianity is simply does not fit anymore.

XI¹ A 22   *n.d.*, 1854

« 1926 *Either/Or*

Either this is Christianity: To be a Christian means to be in kinship with God, but then the prototype [*Forbilledet*] and imitation [*Efterfølgelsen*] are also characteristic and the words "Blessed is he who is not offended"[526] means that to be a Christian is to become, humanly speaking, unhappy in this life and being willing to become that.

Or Christianity expresses: Paganism's dream that humans are in kinship with God is much too elevated—Christ is the Mediator, ... and as far as everything else is concerned, you people can be happy according to your own wisdom of life, but you are reduced to a lower level. In this case "imitation" disappears completely, and the expression "Blessed is he who is not offended" must be understood thus—Do not be offended that it can no longer be granted to you, that you are not in kinship with God but have been reduced to a lower level.

The first conception is clearly that of the New Testament and of the early Church—the other is Protestantism in particular.

XI¹ A 27   *n.d.*, 1854

« 1927 *The Prototypes* {Forbillederne}

It will always be true of the prototypes that in contemporaneity their contemporaries will feel sorry for them as the most unfortunate of all people.

They will be victorious—after their death. Then after some years their contemporaries will be utterly forgotten, and all will consider them blessed—and professors and preachers will make money and more by extolling them. The whole relationship is reversed; it becomes "humility" not to aspire to be anything as extraordinary as this.

xi¹ A 41   n.d., 1854

« 1928

. . . . . In vain Christ (the debased, the poor, the persecuted, the crucified) cries out to men: Imitate me [Følg mig efter]; in vain the apostles give this call, in vain the martyrs—between men and the Savior of the world, between men and the apostles, a class of men interpose themselves who with their families make a living by—presenting the sufferings of Christ and the apostles—thereby preventing imitation. It is of the utmost importance to them that nothing should be heard about imitation.

In truth, even if these villains do not consume widows and orphans, they do, however, do something just as abominable—they eat the martyrs.[527]

xi¹ A 104   n.d., 1854

« 1929 *Imitation* [Efterfølgelse]

Christ comes to the world as the prototype [Forbilledet], constantly enjoining: Imitate me.

The relationship was soon turned around because men preferred *to adore* the prototype, and finally in Protestantism it became presumption to want to resemble the prototype—the prototype is only the Redeemer.

The apostle imitates Christ and enjoins: Imitate me.

The apostle was soon turned around; men adored the apostle.

And this is how it skids downward.

There lived among us the now deceased Bishop Mynster—in a Christian sense simply a criminal.[528] At the same time in another sense he was a more than ordinarily gifted man. I am sure that many who have lived among us regarded Mynster as too lofty to imitate and who therefore were content to adore him.[529]

There is this one thing which is the divine invention—the only kind of adoration God requires is imitation. Man is willing to do only one thing—adore the prototypes.

xi¹ A 158   n.d., 1854

« 1930 *A Question*

When a man like Bernard of Clairvaux or Pascal, both of them significant characters, let such a confusion go undisturbed as the Pope's calling himself Peter's successor [Efterfølger] (and thus nonsensically parodying the imitation [*Efterfølgelse*] of Christ), there is still the question of whether this is connected with their wanting to coddle themselves or their perhaps unconsciously and with instinctive cunning refraining from risking what would of necessity come to be martyrdom, a bloody martyrdom.

xi¹ a 306   *n.d.*, 1854

« 1931 *The Objections to Christianity*

may be dismissed with one single comment: Do these objections come from someone who has carried out the commands and orders of Christ for the existential—if not, all his objections are nonsense; for Christ continually declares that we must do what he says—and then we will see that it is truth.

But the trouble is not with these objections but with those hordes of characterless professors, preachers, etc. who have no intention of acting according to Christ's commands but write folios against nonsensical (from a Christian point of view) objections.

xi¹ a 338   *n.d.*, 1854

« 1932 *Christendom*

Christ makes his appearance in the middle of actuality [*Virkeligheden*], teaches, suffers—and says: Imitate me [*følger mig efter*]; imitation [*Efterfølgelsen*] is Christianity.

Before long the generation finds imitation to be inconvenient and hits upon something new. They say: To imitate in this way is a little too earnest. Let us rather go out to the meadow and play at Christianity but call it Christianity. That is, they introduce another actuality, an artistic actuality, or they introduce Christianity into the arts, removed from actuality by the distance of imagination, and in this medium officials and dignitaries hired for the purpose play Christianity in costume.[530] And this is supposed to be Troy[531]—or what was it I was going to say—this is supposed to be Christianity!

*   *

Christendom is a kind of emanation, a continual diluting (what we in self-congratulation have called spreading Christianity), or it is, as printers say of a line out of place, a transposition, a slanting away, and the law for this obliquity (away from original Christianity) is: to adore and worship rather than to imitate.

Even the apostle altered Christ somewhat, to some extent diverted attention from him as prototype [*Forbillede*] and what this signifies.

But he was, after all, the apostle, true enough. But that did not last long. Men did a repeat performance and substituted adoring and worshipping the apostle for imitating the apostle.

We do the same with the martyr, the witness to truth.

Then Protestantism sees that this is confused—and so Protestantism promptly resolves to discard all that part of Christianity which is inconvenient.

This is Christianity and Christianity continues to be this—paid positions which constitute almost the only (and also the most curious) change Christianity has brought about. A teaching of renunciation of this world enters the world, and after having existed 1,800 years, about the only result achieved is the creation of 1,000 or 100,000 paid positions. Truly Christianity is perfectible!

XI[1] A 391   n.d., 1854

« 1933 *Christendom is a Metaphor*

Think of a very long railway train—but long ago the locomotive ran away from it.

Christendom is like this. The ideal, the prototype [*Forbilledet*] was the locomotive—yes, truly, no locomotive which human ingenuity ever designed or ever will design can be compared with this perpetual motion which is the restlessness of the eternal.

As mentioned, the locomotive has run away from the train.

In the meantime generation after generation has imperturbably continued to link the enormous train of the new generation to the previous one, solemnly saying: We will hold fast to the faith of the fathers.

Thus Christendom has become the very opposite of what Christianity is. Christianity is restlessness, the restlessness of the eternal. Any comparison here is flat and tedious—to such a degree the restlessness of the eternal is restless. Christendom is tranquillity—how charming, the tranquillity of literally not moving from the spot.

Christianity is a locomotive—in Christendom Christianity is a locomotive with the most peculiar characteristic for a locomotive, that it does not move from the spot, that is, it is not a locomotive, or, more correctly, the locomotive has run away from Christendom long ago.

XI[1] A 396   n.d., 1854

« 1934 *The Prototype* [Forbilledet]—*the Redeemer*

"The prototype" slays all, as it were, for no one achieves it. "The Redeemer" wants to save all.

Yet Christ is both, and that swindle which takes redemption and grace in vain is not Christianity.

XI¹ A 492   n.d., 1854

« 1935 *The Prototype* [Forbilledet]

Protestantism has reached the point where wanting to imitate [*efterfølge*] the prototype is bluntly regarded as presumption.

How can this be explained? In this way. When we think of the prototype's life we really think of the outcome of his life—so there is truth in saying: I do not aspire to anything like that.

But actually the prototype's life was not the outcome of his life—no, his life, as it says in scripture, was to be a worm and no man,[532] and he speaks of it himself as sheer wretchedness and suffering. How loathsome, then, to say in the face of this: I am too *humble* to aspire to anything like that.

But this human speech is a fraud from beginning to end. Let God proclaim "joy" and human speech comes along and immediately takes the word "joy" and makes out that Christianity means: Enjoy life. Likewise with the prototype. The prototype manifests the highest. But hold on, what does the highest show itself to be—sheer wretchedness, need, being a worm, behold the man.[533] And now what does man do with the aid of his swindle-language—he takes the words "the highest" and says: I am too humble to aspire to the highest or to will the highest.

And this is Christendom, a society of Christians, whom even Paul's description of paganism (Romans 1-3) does not fit, since a still more loathsome mendacity has replaced the savage, wild excesses. In a certain sense I am tempted to say that one cannot properly get at the corruption of Christendom by means of the New Testament, because the New Testament has to do essentially with the demoralization of Judaism and paganism but, of course, not with what has been produced by the misuse of Christianity. Yet it is easy to see that this must be the most dangerous, for the stronger the medicine the more dangerous the results of misuse.

XI¹ A 550   n.d., 1854

« 1936 *Atonement*

Protestantism, especially here in Denmark, has gotten Christianity turned around in this way: Christ has suffered, is dead, and his life and death make satisfaction for our sins and gain for us an eternal salvation—now we can and should enjoy life properly and at most thank him once in a while, although this is not really necessary.

What men are taught in the name of Christianity is nothing but sheer cannibalism, inhuman cruelty.

In ordinary life if it were a question simply of dying, not of eternal perdition, any man with any good at all in him, if his crime deserved the death penalty and now an innocent person must die for him—any such man would surely have to say: No, this just makes it worse; there would be some mitigation in my suffering the punishment of death as I deserve, instead of an innocent person's having to suffer for it for me, whereby I get a murder on my conscience besides, because it is my guilt which murders him. However willing or not the other person is to suffer death for him makes no difference one way or the other.

The situation is certainly different if it is a matter of an eternal perdition, of being saved from it by another who suffers the punishment of death for me.

But now suppose that Christ had not required imitation [*Efter-følgelse*]—how then could a person with any good in him, aware that another had suffered the most excruciating death to save him, had suffered because of his guilt, how could it then occur to him to want to enjoy this life! Might not one who had experienced something like this say: My life is essentially devoted to sorrow. Has not salvation been bought in such a costly way that it would be a mitigation if one could purchase it by his own suffering.

XI[1] A 573   n.d., 1854

« 1937 *Illusion*

Christ is the prototype [*Forbilledet*]; his life eternity's examination.

Just because it is eighteen hundred years since he lived does not mean that the examination has changed in the least. Just because no one has subjected himself to the examination for a long time does not mean that it has changed.

But we are Christians with literally no conception at all of the examination, of its requirements—this is how far we are from subjecting ourselves to the examination.

What an illusion to think that because "time" is cunning enough to deceive us that it is also able to fool the eternal!

XI[1] A 588   n.d., 1854

« 1938 *Swindles*

That the whole business of Christendom is a swindle is apparent in the relationship the proclamation, the official preaching, has to life. On

Sunday it is taught that Christ is everyone's prototype [*Forbillede*]—and if anyone on Monday were to talk about Christ as his prototype people would call this presumption, terrible arrogance, and so on.

Consequently the preaching of Christianity is Sunday jargon. Likewise the master of the royal household wears all his regalia when he "rides in the opening session of the nobility"—but it would be ridiculous for him to walk around in such regalia every day!

This is supposed to be Troy![534] And this is supposed to be Christianity!

XI[2] A 197   *n.d.*, 1854

« 1939 *The Prototype* {Forbilledet}

Generally what presents itself as the extraordinary does not want to have imitation [*Efterfølgelse*], replication [*Efterligning*]. The extraordinary wants to be admired; he is almost angry if others want to copy [*efterabe*] him; there is something embarrassing about it. Therefore it is modesty to refrain from it.

But Christ demands imitation [*Efterfølgelse*]; his life is related to a judgment hereafter. But he is also the prototype oriented to the universally human, of which everyone is capable.

Now human craftiness comes in again; we invert getting out of imitation, as if this were humility, and invert wanting to imitate Christ, as if this were presumption, as if he (generally like the extraordinary) would be angry about it, offended by it. O, human hypocrisy!

XI[2] A 358   *n.d.*, 1854

« 1940 *That "Christendom" Is Mankind's Centuries-old, Progressively Successful, Prolonged Struggle—To Protect Itself against Christianity*

Sept. 22, 1855

Christ has required "imitators" [*Efterfølgere*].

A true imitator of Christ will soon come to be thrown headfirst out of this world. If another imitator comes along, the same thing will happen, quickly and decisively—all action.

But suppose instead of imitators there come people who go around prattling about the fact that others have risked life and blood—now the expanding begins; all nonsense is sociable, astoundingly fertile, spawning nonsense.

The generation following these drivellers are, according to type, not imitators but likewise drivelling preachers and professors and authorities who regard themselves as the true teachers of Christianity. In addition to the nonsense this generation is able to produce by itself, in the name of historical scholarship it takes over the nonsense produced by the prior generation.

This is the law: instead of action, an increasing, limitless mass of nonsense which is called scholarship and which must be studied, so it is said, before one can understand Christianity.

In fact, what is not wanted is precisely an understanding of Christianity, which is easy to understand. And this insuperable mass of historical and learned nonsense is introduced as an aid to understanding Christianity in order more surely to prevent an understanding of Christianity.

There are insects which protect themselves against attackers by raising a cloud of dust; likewise "man" instinctively protects himself against ideas and spirit by raising a cloud of numbers. Numbers are the opposite of idea and spirit. If you want to be insured against having to deal with idea, with spirit, simply get together battalions, legions, millions who strive, perhaps with united powers—then spirit vanishes and you have achieved what you really wanted, a halting on the animal side of human nature.

Of course there are never very many who understand this, since to be able to understand this the very change at which Christianity aims—to become spirit—must have occurred. The animal-man is related immediately and spontaneously to number; this is what he believes in.

*   *

Is this Christianity's view of the present world: it is an evil, sinful world, but for that very reason Christianity has come into the world to transform the world, and therefore God's purpose and aim is to get a nice, congenial world out of this world and let it stand?

Or is not Christianity based more upon the following view: This present world has come into existence [er blevet til] through a fall away from God, exists [er til] against his will, and every day it exists it is against his will; he wants to have it back again. Omnipotently to destroy the world is not what he wants, because the whole world is not constituted [lagt *an*] in that way. It is a world of freedom which in freedom fell away from him and which he wants back again. For God this present world is lost; it goes without saying that everyone who is born simply augments the mass of the lost.

In order to get the world back and motivated by mercy he has Christianity proclaimed. The prototype [*Forbilledet*] shows what it means to be a Christian, that it is suffering from beginning to end, even abandonment by God. Mercy, grace, infinite grace now consists in enduring hell on earth through becoming a Christian, and then being eternally saved. But to be a Christian means accepting gratefully the infinite grace of having to be an imitator of Jesus Christ in life and in so doing be eternally saved by grace, an imitator of Jesus Christ, cursed by mankind, hated, tormented in every way, and finally abandoned by God. And every imitator of Jesus Christ is oriented in such a way that if he can be said to have any other life aim than working out his salvation in fear and trembling, it must be to get rid of this world.

If it were not so, if God's intention were to get a nice, congenial world out of this one, then the human race would actually be without guidance. For the New Testament, the proclamation of Christ, predicates this world as an evil world, and all the marks of being a Christian are related to this. But if God intended this world to be transformed into a nice, congenial world which then endures, the marks of being a Christian must become the very opposite.

But the "human race" very conveniently forgets that for God there is neither time nor number; a thousand years are like a day and a number so large that it takes a thousands years to say it is nothing at all to him. He continues with his own. Out of grace he will have mercy upon this lost world. He offers the condition—infinite grace—but not like a fussy pedant. Whether there are many or only a few single individuals who want to be saved does not alter him or his condition; it is not he who is to be saved but the others.

On a grand scale the human race has the same bad habit as the individual man—when he is invited he comes rolling up right away with his wife and a half dozen children. Thus when God has grace proclaimed to the race (but, please note, to each single individual), what happens is not what God submitted—the battalions of the race come rolling up and want to be saved by battalions. No, not that way. First the humiliation (which for many will be unto despair) of enduring being only a single individual, drowning in this enormous world, disappearing—and then perhaps becoming saved. The other way, being eternally saved by battalions, is undoubtedly cosier and also has something in common with excursions to the amusement park and other pleasant diversions.

From a Christian point of view, in order to be saved any idea and any consolation based on numbers must be eliminated, that is, life must be taken from the animal-creature. Just as a bird is killed when deprived of its air supply, so the life of animal-man is taken by the removal of numbers.

To be deprived of human numbers, to have to stand alone, abandoned, mocked, ridiculed, etc., is what animal-man fears most, most of all, because *qua* animal-creature he lives in fear of men. Therefore animal-man has courage to do the most frightening things as long as he simply has human numbers with him, knows that others are doing the same thing or that the others think that he displays courage. Therefore this is the very collision Christ points to in particular: to suffer from men means Christianly precisely to fear God in contrast to fearing men, in contrast to what men as animal-creatures fear most of all—human numbers. Incidentally, from this point of view it is easy to understand that in all the centuries of Christendom not one single proclamation like Christ's proclamation is to be found. Very quickly there were human numbers of Christians, and from that moment on it was possible to be a Christian in the fear of men. All the most rigorous asceticism of the Middle Ages was based on the fear of men and did not suffer from men.

I know very well that what I write here will in the course of time be declared to be the loftiest wisdom. I also know that when that happens the shape of the world will not have changed one whit, because those who will be busy showing how profound and true this is will be, of course, assistant professors—those animal-creatures. Yes, those animal-creatures. I know very well that in this sinful world where everything is egotism there is the custom of calling the common man a simple animal-creature.[535] But I protest against this. In one sense we all are animal-creatures. But if any class of men deserves to be called animals in comparison with the rest of us, it is preachers and professors.

We recognize the animal in the child by the way it wants to put everything into its mouth; this is a very characteristic trait of the animal. But to be animal to the extent of wanting to put truth and spirit into one's mouth, to live off truth, to live off others' having suffered for the truth, oneself pledged by an oath to that one thing to which those others have aspired—imitation—this is beastly! Curiously enough, this bestiality is found in conjunction with the finest culture and good breeding, which is so discriminating that it does not even see the garbage collector or, if such a being dared speak, would loftily let him understand that he is only an animal. Strangely enough, the relationship is the reverse, and the garbage collector is a human being, but this elegantly dressed, finely cultured, bemedalled man of distinction is an animal, an animal who animalistically puts truth into his mouth, thinking truth is something to eat, an animal more loathesome than any beast of prey, even living off the sufferings of others, something no beast of prey does, for it lives off its prey and if it causes its prey to suffer in depriving it of life, it still does not live off the sufferings of its prey.[536]

XI² A 434   September 22, 1855

IMMEDIACY

« 1941

The double meaning of "immediacy" in Aristotle. Trendlenburg, *Erlaüterungen*,[537] p. 109, reference to para. 51.

In Hegelian philosophy the immediate is used partly arbitrarily and partly surreptitiously (as the sensuous).[538]

V A 75 n.d., 1844

« 1942 *New Discourses on the Lilies and the Birds*[539]

But perhaps you say: O, to be a bird which lifts itself into the air more easily than anything that has gravity, so easily that it can even build nests at sea. O, to be like a flower in the meadow. —This means that the poet extols as the highest happiness something to which human yearning strives to return—how unreasonable to make this the instructor for the person who is supposed to move forward.

Immediacy or spontaneity is poetically the very thing we desire to return to (we want our childhood again etc.), but from a Christian point of view, immediacy is lost and it ought not be yearned for again but should be attained again.

In these discourses, therefore, there will be a development of the conflict between poetry and Christianity, how in a certain sense Christianity is prose in comparison with poetry (which is desiring, charming, anesthetizing and transforms the actuality of life into an oriental dream, just as a young girl might want to lie on a sofa all day and be entranced)—and yet it is the very poetry of the eternal.

Of course the lilies and the birds, that is, the sketching of nature will this time have an even more poetic tone and richness of color, simply to indicate that the poetic must be put aside, for when poetry in truth shall fall (not because of a preacher's dull and dismal jawing), it ought to wear its party clothes.

VIII[1] A 643 n.d., 1848

« 1943 *Christianity*

Christianity is opposed to spontaneous, immediate human nature (the immediately natural) to such a degree that I have to say (I know this by personal experience): Such a thing would never occur to me (would not originate in my heart). Yes, Christianity is opposed to the natural man to such a degree that if anything but Christianity were to advise me to undertake such a thing (or more accurately, that Christianity not only advises but commands me to it), I would not dare undertake it, because it would not only appear to me to be self-torment but also presumption toward God.

It is natural to desire what is pleasing, to rejoice in life, to enjoy life —and then to bring God in as the one to thank for all this. If I am to make a beginning in essential Christianity and I renounce myself or I venture in such a way that I experience opposition in the world and suffer, then suddenly and swiftly there is a change, as if this suffering were the expression of God's displeasure with me and therefore the sign that I should not take this path—because (this is the natural conclusion) the sign of the God-relationship is that my undertakings succeed so that I can enjoy life, etc.

What is the matter? The trouble is that it naturally never occurs to me at all that I should be in relationship, in kinship (which is Christianity's thought). I desire (as a conformist) to enjoy life—and then to thank God. Think of a sparrow, let it have everything it wants—and then imagine that it gives thanks to God—it still is not in relationship with God for all that. But Christianity wants this very thing, that it be taken seriously that a man is to be in relationship to God.

God is spirit—consequently (for a sensate being) only in dying to the world, in self-denial, in suffering (not in pleasure) is relationship with God possible.

O divine sublimity, which does not, like the gods of the pagans, maliciously lie in wait to persecute or punish his enemies—and does everything good for those who worship him. —No, in divine sublimity you let the punishment for the ungodly be simply this—that without you (ah, there's where the punishment is!) things go all right for them. But your worshippers are identified by the fact that they must suffer. They are involved with you and therefore they must suffer.

As far as we can see, the reason Christ had to suffer was that to be in kinship with God means to suffer. Reconciliation there is, nevertheless, even though not quite the way human cruelty has invented it *à la Phalaris's* ox:[540] that Christ should suffer and be martyred in order that I could enjoy life in luxury, in splendor, and in magnificence. No, no, "imitation" ["*Efterfølgelsen*"] belongs here, too. And only through suffering can a sensuous being be in kinship with God.

X^4 A 471   *n.d.,* 1852

IMMORTALITY

« 1944

The more intense earthly life is, the flatter eternity becomes. By the Greeks, therefore, life after death was regarded as a mere shadow of actual life; whereas for Northmen, Christians, etc., present life is merely an outline of future life, although they have not been successful in depicting their heaven.

Generally speaking, did the idea of a future life evolve from the individuality of the Greeks, or was there some outside assistance?

I A 151 *n.d.*, 1836

« 1945

The baying of dogs in the distance, calling one to far off, friendly, familiar places—conveys the most beautiful proof of the immortality of the soul.

II A 639 *n.d.*, 1837

« 1946

The principal problem with respect to the question of the immortality of the soul will probably center more upon the nature of immortality than upon immortality itself, specifically, whether at death the soul may be considered as tightly embracing the contents of its action or as dissolved in the divine all. This is so remote from signifying that the soul thereby is surrendered that within ourselves we can perceive analogies to this, in which the purely subjective consciousness walks in the shadow ahead of a far more objective consciousness and in which existence [*Tilværelsen*] gains a transparency, and the question is still whether or not these moments are not of a higher kind than the moments of action.

II A 387 March 28, 1839

« 1947

That the letter kills can be seen in the Sadducees, who adhered so strictly to the letter of the law that they denied the immortality of the soul.[541]

II A 424 May 19, 1839

379

« 1948

According to the apostolic injunction a Christian must live in such a way that his life may express that he really would be the most wretched man of all men if there were no immortality. But if we have earned honor and money, participated in great affairs, enjoyed life—well, then we cannot be called the most wretched of all if there were no immortality. But if we have forsaken all this—yes, quite right, then we would certainly be the most wretched of all if that for which we have forsaken all were not forthcoming.

VII^1 A 244   *n.d.*, 1845-47

« 1949

Arndt,[542] II, chapter 8, para. 2: *Denn wie Dich Gott findet* (namely, in death) *so wird er Dich richten*.[543] The orthodox have the idea that a person remains eternally in the condition in which death finds him. This explains their dread of dying and their attempt to make a trial test of dying or to experience in advance the situation of death.

IX A 391   *n.d.*, 1849

« 1950

The final and most impressive thought for holding men in check—when finite considerations and punishment are no longer effective—is immortality[544]—and this we have turned into a problem, something which must be proved.[545] This is like lifting a cane to hit someone and saying: Now you are going to get a good thrashing—that is, if this is a cane I have in my hands—and then, instead of striking, give three reasons to prove that it is a cane, and thereupon say Amen, i.e., completely forget to strike. O, dreadful nonsense—but so it goes with preaching.

X^1 A 372   *n.d.*, 1849

« 1951

The person who really grasps his immortality or that an eternal life awaits him will learn quickly enough to flee to grace.

X^2 A 584   *n.d.*, 1850

« 1952 *Immortality*

Cicero says (in *De natura deorum*, bk. II, near the end) that the gods have no advantage over man, except immortality, *but this is not necessary for living a happy life.*

Surely the way in which immortality is shoved upon people in Christendom is very confusing, making them think that they feel a deep need for immortality.

On the whole, immortality first appeared with Christianity, and why? Because it requires that a person shall die to the world. In order to be able and willing to die to the world—the eternal and immortality must remain fixed. Immortality and dying away correspond to each other. The hope of immortality is nourished by the suffering of dying away. But in Christendom we want to cheat our way into everything, and thus also into immortality.

x^4 A 440   *n.d.*, 1851

« 1953 *Immortality*

One of our poets (Ingemann) is supposed to hold the sentimental view that even every insect is immortal.

He is right, one is tempted to say—for if people born *en masse* as they are nowadays are immortal, it would not be unreasonable that insects, too, are immortal.

It is all this milksop chatter, so hearty and animated, regular preacher nonsense, which always excels, heartily, in watering down all concepts so that they end up as nothing, yes, almost nauseating! Immortality—this was once the high goal to which the heroes of the race looked forward, humbly acknowledging that this reward was so high that it had no relationship to their most strenuous striving—and now every louse is immortal!

Ingemann really should have been a clergyman, wrapped in velvet, front and back, and with gold tassels on his shoulders. Although I generally do not like anyone to ridicule a man's name, there is something to what Heiberg[546] called him: no-man [*Ingenmand*].

It is disgusting, and what is particularly disgusting is that to thousands this kind of stuff seems beautifully touching! If only this swindle-industry would seize hold of the idea and the clerical rascals (*Gaudiebe*)[547] would get a "Christian government" to thinking that Christianly something ought to be done for the insects, these immortal creatures, that some spiritual counsellors ought to be appointed, in any case some ecclesiastical offices established.

xi^1 A 463   *n.d.*, 1854

« 1954 *Immortality*

Immortality was once the high goal of the greatest possible effort, relating to the entire formation of character in this life. Nowadays if a man and woman merely couple—an immortal creature immediately results, and with a sprinkle of water on its head—a Christian, with the expectation of eternal salvation.

Isn't this really too cheap a way to produce immortal works?

In Christendom, Christianity, which is spirit, has changed to a kind of brutality, a kind of bestiality.

So it goes, and no one gets suspicious; all of this is regarded as magnificent.

XVI[1] A 547   *n.d.*, 1854

« 1955 *To Hate Father and Mother*

This collision is obvious when regarded like this: if a man's life is intended for the eternal, this tremendous goal, how alienated he must become from that which binds him in the relationships of finitude.

This alienation is indeed like hating the very relationships which are most important to the man when they completely absorb this life. These relationships are such that if he does not belong to them unconditionally (and this he cannot do if his life is to be exerted for the eternal), it is like hating them.

But men live out their lives in the foolish opinion that the lives we live here on earth will automatically continue in all eternity, that we will take the city we live in, everything, everything, straight into eternity. This is why men who would shudder at the strangeness and the isolation of emigrating to another continent nevertheless think they are going to live for eternity.

XI[1] A 577   *n.d.*, 1854

« 1956 *The Demoralization of the Human Race*

proceeds at an increasing rate.

Individuals (*sit venia verbo*)[548] become less and less significant. On the other hand, they are developing more and more into an external power by forming a mass and in this way brazenly bidding defiance and thereby making their possible deliverance less and less possible.

In the meantime Professor Snuffler and the clergy declaim that man is immortal—and prove it. O, yes—but then also prove that the creatures who are now called men are men.

Immortality! What significance can this really have for men who in respect to everything are accustomed, even in most insignificant matters, to being members of a party, a group, and for whom being members of a party and a group is—everything.

XI[2] A 237   *n.d.*, 1854

INDIRECT COMMUNICATION

« 1957

Yet the communication of the essentially Christian must end finally in "witnessing." The maieutic cannot be the final form, because, Christianly understood, the truth doth not lie in the subject (as Socrates understood it), but in a revelation which must be proclaimed.

It is very proper that the maieutic be used in Christendom, simply because the majority actually live in the fancy that they are Christians. But since Christianity still is Christianity, the one who uses the maieutic must become a witness.

Ultimately the user of the maieutic will be unable to bear the responsibility, for the maieutic approach still remains rooted in human sagacity, however sanctified and dedicated in fear and trembling this may be. God becomes too powerful for the maieutic practitioner and then he is a witness, different from the direct witness only in what he has gone through to become a witness.

IX A 221   *n.d.*, 1848

« 1958

Unqualified indirect communication belongs to being more than human, and no man, therefore, has the right to use it. The God-man cannot do otherwise, because he is qualitatively different from man. In paganism it is demonic, but this has no place in Christendom.

As soon as a person is decisively, personally Christian, he dares not carry the dialectical so high that he posits the possibility of offense. The God-man cannot do otherwise, simply because he is the object of faith.

In paganism, therefore, the abstract indirect method could certainly be used, for the possibility of offense was not present. And also thus in relation to Christendom (which is very far from being purely Christian, but is closer to paganism) [it may be used] by one who has not unconditionally stepped forth as personally being Christian in a decisive sense. For where the proportions are such as these, offense cannot become more than a kind of awakening.

IX A 260   *n.d.*, 1848

« 1959 *Indirect Communication*

It is not true that direct communication is superior to indirect communication. No, no. But the fact is that no man has ever been born who could use the indirect method even fairly well, to say nothing of using it all his life. For we human beings need each other, and in that there is already a directness.

Only the God-man is in every respect indirect communication from first to last. He did not need men, but they infinitely needed him; he loves men, but according to his conception of what love is; therefore he does not change in the slightest toward their conception, does not speak directly in such a way that he also surrenders the possibility of offense—which his existence [*Existents*] in the guise of servant is.

When a person uses the indirect method, there is in one way or another something demonic—but not necessarily in the bad sense—about it, as, for example, with Socrates.

Direct communication indeed makes life far easier. On the other hand, the use of direct communication may be humiliating for a person who has used indirect communication perhaps selfishly (therefore demonically in a bad sense).

I have frequently felt impelled to use direct communication (it must be remembered, of course, that even when I did, it was far from being carried through completely and, indeed, it was only for a short time), but it seemed to me as if I wanted to be lenient with myself and that I could achieve more by holding out. Whether there is pride here as well, God knows best—before God I dare neither affirm nor deny this, for who knows himself well enough for this?

When I look back on my life, I must say that it seems to me not impossible that something higher hid behind me. It was not impossible. I do not say more. What have I done, then? I have said: For the present I use no means which would disturb this possibility, for example, by *premature* direct communication. The situation is like that of a fisherman when he sees the float move—maybe it means a strike, maybe it is due to the motion of the water. But the fisherman says: I will not pull up the line; if I do, I indicate that I have surrendered this possibility; perhaps it will happen again and prove to be a bite.

For me indirect communication has been as if instinctive within me, because in being an author I no doubt have also developed myself, and consequently the whole movement is backwards, which is why from the very first I could not state my plan directly, although I certainly was aware that a lot was fermenting within me. Furthermore, consideration for "her" required me to be careful. I could well have said right away: I am a religious author. But later how would I have dared to create the illusion that I was a scoundrel in order if possible to help her. Actually it was she —that is, my relationship to her—who taught me the indirect method. She could be helped only by an untruth about me; otherwise I believe she would have lost her mind. That the collision was a religious one would have completely deranged her, and therefore I have had to be so infinitely careful. And not until she became engaged again and married did I regard myself as somewhat free in this respect.

Thus through something purely personal I have been assisted to something on a far greater scale, something I have gradually come to understand more and more deeply.

x³ A 413   *n.d., 1850*

« 1960   *Is a Person Free to Speak at All to Any Other Person about the Important Things?*

That he is free to speak with him about the weather and so on, I knew very well.

But the other thought has preoccupied me all my life and to such a degree that I did not know whether I dared say it: Is a person free ....., because the very moment I say it I have actually broken the silence of the relationship to God.

There is [*er til*] a God; his will is made known to me in Holy Scripture and in my conscience. This God wants to enter into the world. But how is he going to be able to do that without the cooperation of—that is, *per* men. We can say, we can all say: Yes, that is what he does, but certainly it is not *per* me. This means that not one of us wants to be the single individual [*den Enkelte*], and if God is going to enter in, it has to be *per* the single individual.

And how does a person become the single individual? Well, if he does not relate himself solely to God regarding the most important things, saying: Now I am going to think about these things and then act to the best of my ability in such a way that you, O God, can get hold of me, and therefore I do not speak to any other man; this I dare not do unless he does it—then he does not remain the single individual. The very moment I talk with anyone else about that which is supreme to me, about what God's will with me is, at that very same moment God's power over me is diminished.

O, but how many are there who are able to comprehend this priority of God in a human being so that being free to speak with another person about matters which are most important to him is a diminution, a concession we must pray for, because no mere man can persevere in being unconditionally the single individual.

x³ A 659   n.d., 1850

« 1961 *Sanctified Ingenuity*

When worldly shrewdness (that is, worldly reflection) is the particular evil, all tactics must become indirect.

In an earlier day the tactic for the purpose of awakening was direct. One who was conscious of having grown more in Christianity stepped forth in the character thereof, directly recognizable as more advanced.

Now the operation becomes indirect. He must guarantee that he is existentially more advanced than the established order. Thereupon he turns aside and makes the admission: I feel that I am not a Christian; Christianity is so infinitely elevated that I am no Christian.

At first the established order will perhaps think this wonderful. But it had better look around. —It has been tricked. With its claim to being Christian the established order is way behind him, and he who insists that he is not a Christian is ahead.

They will perhaps say: He is a fool. The established order had better look around. In the game *Gnavspil*,[549] when the fool goes he takes only one along with him—here he takes everybody along.

x⁴ A 91   n.d., 1851

« 1962 *To Declare Maieutically That One
Himself Is Not a Christian*

Take the Socratic position: error and evil are puffed-up knowledge—therefore Socrates is the ignorant one and remains that until the end. Likewise, to be a Christian has become an illusion, all these millions of Christians—therefore the situation must be reversed and Christianity must be introduced by a person who says that he himself is not a Christian.

This is the way I have understood it. But to what extent ought this tactic be maintained to the end, and to what extent should I stick to it?

For me the entire operation has been a matter of being honest with myself: whether and to what extent I wanted to become a Christian in the strictest sense. Devoutly (for I felt myself to be ordained to this task, my only one) I undertook intellectually the task of making clear what Christianity is, and the pseudonym[550] also declared himself not to be Christian.

But when the one who enters upon this operation is himself in the situation of having to determine whether he actually wants to become a Christian in the strictest sense, this tactic cannot and ought not to be maintained to the end. Otherwise the most appalling thing that could happen—that by jacking up the price of being a Christian he ultimately (let us take the extreme) would get everyone to give up Christianity and he himself would give it up. Furthermore, such a person, himself detached, could take a demonic delight in torturing those who call themselves Christians by attaching to them heavy burdens which he himself has not yet taken up.

So it is with me. But suppose that someone else had undertaken the enterprise of maieutically introducing Christianity, declaring himself not to be a Christian, someone else who from the outset had in deepest inwardness made up his mind about being and wanting to be a Christian in the strictest sense—ought this maieutic position then be maintained to the end or is there not a difficulty here which is not present in the Socratic position? To be specific, Christianity teaches that a danger is involved, persecution goes along with confessing that one is a true Christian —this is no doubt evaded by the person who in introducing Christianity declares himself not to be a Christian. True enough, the evil in "Christendom" is precisely that all are Christians and thus there is no danger connected with calling oneself Christian but rather an advantage, and here again, in reverse, the danger might come through not wanting to declare oneself to be a Christian. Yet to this Christianity might reply: "Because there is no danger connected with being a Christian in the sense that these millions are Christian, I do not for that reason take back my word that suffering, mockery, and persecution are still to be expected if one genuinely wants to be a Christian and confesses to being one—and this you evade by introducing Christianity in such a way that you declare yourself not to be a Christian." And so it is, too. The scruples I have expressed in a little essay (*Armed Neutrality*) (because I do not want the point of contention to be my claim that "I am a Christian" but that "I know what Christianity is") about claiming to be a Christian because of the fear that on judgment day God might say to me: You have dared to call yourself a Christian—these scruples are removed by what I have pointed out here, that on judgment day God could very well say to such a person: By declaring yourself not to be a Christian, you have evaded suffering for confessing that you are a Christian (with respect to Socrates, there is no ignominy etc. connected with calling himself wise, something he evaded by calling himself ignorant).

But let us suppose that the person who introduced Christianity maieutically (in order to get rid of the illusion, the notion of being Christian because one is living in Christendom), declaring himself not to be a Christian, let us suppose that he not only from the beginning made up his mind about wanting to be a Christian in the strictest sense but that he completely ordered his life (although continually declaring himself not to be a Christian) according to the requirements of Christianity concerning renunciation, dying to the world, and lived in voluntary poverty [*in margin:* and everything involved in "imitation" ["*Efterfølgelse*"], dying to the world, being born again, and so on, which I myself was not aware of in 1848] and thereby was definitely exposed to the suffering and persecution which are inseparable and are essential Christianity—can he continue to the end with this formula: I am not a Christian? The answer to this must be: Christianity nevertheless always requires the confession of Christ, and yet the suffering he suffers may not necessarily be for Christ's sake; perhaps he could also be secretly proud of having no fellowship with other Christians.

If the formula "I am not a Christian" is to be maintained to the end, then it must be done by an "apostle" but in an entirely new style. He must have an immediate relation to Christ and then only in death explain how it all hangs together. Whether or not this will ever happen, I cannot say.

x^4 A 553   *n.d.*, 1852

« 1963 *The Criminal Dialectician*

Just as someone who is himself in the profession recognizes a master among the examining judges not by his virtuosity in any particular area but by the way he conducts the inquiry, so that the minute he sees it he promptly exclaims: Look, here is the master——just so the criminal dialectician is identified by how he structures the case, how he poses the problem.

A criminal dialectician is precisely what Christendom needs.

xi^1 A 335   *n.d.*, 1854

INDIVIDUAL

« 1964

It is dangerous to isolate oneself too much, to withdraw from social relationships.

I A 177   n.d., 1836

« 1965

Addition to 1964 (1 A 177):
If you do not need the lead-strings of a social group, you can dispense with the aid of a go-cart, which your contemporaries provide.

I A 178   n.d., 1836

« 1966

In what relationship does the development of each individual stand to the whole—the earth turns on its axis and goes around the sun—the romantic outlived—to what extent does each individual traverse the whole development of the world—go from the beginning up to the present stage of development?[551]

I A 248   September 25, 1836

« 1967

Previously the tendency was to make fractional men out of human beings; today they are changed into an abstraction. Everybody looks exactly alike ("venturesome, sensitive, enthusiastic Danes"), and now it becomes easy for a Wehmaler[552] to come forward and paint Hungarian and Danish national facial types, portraits which are painted before seeing the individual. Everything is directed toward getting everyone a national physiognomy, just as one has a national costume.

I A 337   n.d., 1836-37

« 1968

Faust may be paralleled with Socrates. Just as the latter expresses the individual's emancipation from the state, Faust expresses the individual after the abrogation of the Church, severed from its guidance and abandoned to himself; this is an indication of his relationship to the Reformation and is a parody of the Reformation insofar as it one-sidedly emphasizes the negative aspect.

II A 53   *n.d.*, 1837

« 1969

There are people who in life stand like interjections in speech, without influence on the sentence—it is the hermits in life who in the highest degree govern a case—for example, O! *me miserum!*

II A 168   September 29, 1837

« 1970

How horrible if all history disappears before a sickly brooding over one's own wretched history! Who will point to a middle course between this self-consuming while reflecting as if one were the only human being who has ever lived or ever will—and a foolish confidence in the ordinary human *commune naufragium?* This is what an authentic doctrine of a Church should bring about.

II A 172   October 7, 1837

« 1971

There is nothing more dangerous for a man, nothing more paralyzing, than a certain isolating self-scrutiny, in which world-history, human life, society—in short, everything—disappears, and like the ὀμφαλοψύχιται[553] in an egotistical circle one constantly stares only at his own navel.[554] —This is why it is so profound that Christ alone bore the sin of the world —alone—not merely because no one would or could understand him, but also because he had to take upon himself all the guilt as only man bears it, to an extent and in the degree appropriate to him as a member of the human society.

II A 187   November 3, 1937

« 1972

In my opinion, Erdmann's formulation[555] (p. 104) of the concept *mysticism* is unusually felicitous. "The object shall remain what it was, that is, the same for the *gegenüberstehendes I* and the *I* which it was, that is, the same *I* itself as the single *I* in relationship," for the mystic does indeed forsake society and has even polemically separated his *I* and yet with this isolated *I* wants to come into relationship with the universal.—

KIERKEGAARD

II C 41   November 13, 1837

« 1973

It would be horrible on judgment day, when all souls come to life again, to stand utterly *alone,* alone and *unknown* by all, all.[556]

II A 643   *n.d.,* 1837

« 1974

The hero in a novel is just about to make a remark when the author takes it out of his mouth, whereupon the hero becomes angry and says that it belongs to him and he shows that this remark is appropriate only to his individuality, and "if things are going to be like this, I just won't be hero any more."[557]

II A 652   *n.d.,* 1837

« 1975

There are some people who make the same mistake in their relationship to the development of the period as a person singing in church who forgets the organ and the rest of the congregation and admires his own deep bass, as if it were not the singing of all in unison which so powerfully fills the church but his own voice all by itself.

II A 211   April 1, 1838

« 1976

There are on the whole very few men who are able to bear the *Protestant* view of life. If the Protestant view is really to become strengthening for the *common man,* it must either structure itself in a smaller community (separatism, small congregations, etc.) or approach Catholicism, in order in both cases to develop the mutual bearing of life's burdens in a communal life, which only the most gifted individuals are able to dispense with. Christ indeed has died for all men, also for me, but this "for me" must nevertheless be interpreted in such a way that he has died for me only insofar as I belong to the many.

II A 223   April 6, 1838

« 1977

The more latitude individual differences are given, the greater the loss of continuity—instead of a *continent* one gets a South Sea of islands—perhaps this development is coming, and this is why that part of the world is preserved.

II A 267   October 3, 1838

« 1978

I had a sorrow in my youth
which never leaves me
as long as I live. It is the greatest sorrow
that anyone can have. It is to love
the one he can never have.

The greatest sorrow the earth can bear
is to be deprived of his heart's most
dearly beloved; the greatest sorrow
under the sun is to love the one
he can never reach.

I bought this ballad[558] a few days ago at one of those ordinary book-shops which also do bookbinding and sell the products of the widow Tribler's publishing house. These two stanzas pasted in here are in my opinion excellent and are an example of the objectivity previously mentioned [i.e. II A 383] which always characterizes the genuinely popular. Strangely enough, while it seems to transcend the individual, it commends itself most to the people who have individuality, just as a sermon ought to be neither an address limited to a particular occasion nor an abstraction either—but have the ideal individuality in mind.

II A 385   March 23, 1839

« 1979

There are certain occasions when a person especially feels how hard it is to stand utterly alone* in the world. The other day I saw a poor girl walking utterly alone to church to be confirmed.[559] And I saw an old man whose whole family had died out—he was carrying his little grandson, his last comfort, in a coffin under his arm, and some time later I saw him in the cemetery sitting like a cross on a family grave.—

II A 400   April 28, 1839

« 1980

* *In margin of* 1979 (II A 400):
God knows where the expression *mutters-alene* actually comes from![560]

II A 401   *n.d.*

« 1981

Individuality is the true period in the development of creation. As everyone knows, a period is written when the meaning is completed, which can also be expressed (looking backwards) by saying that the meaning is there. Thus not until individuality is given is the meaning completed or is there meaning in creation, and in this way we see the possibility of reducing all philosophy to one single proposition. The divine and the human are the two dots (:) which end in the period, which is remarkable also in this respect, that (:) is not a greater dividing indicator than (.) but a lesser.

II A 474   July 10, 1839

« 1982

Just as in language one occasionally comes across a word which by its very nature (by derivation, *ex radice*) contains a multiplicity of meanings, a disposition to a life rich in content, but the process of time truncates it more and more and finally specializes it to denote something evil so that only the philologist is ever struck with the thought of its tragic fate and only an occasional uncorseted author dares to use it in its original meaning, whereby to the amazement and later to the offense of the world it looks splendid, and yet this experiment, this *playing* (word-play) with its existence, is soon abandoned and the word is allowed to sink once more under the *dura necessitas*[561] of the development of language—so does it also go with the single individual human being.

II A 516   July 28, 1839

« 1983

The very meaning of omnipresence is not merely that God is everywhere present at all times but also that he is totally present in his presence, present in his absoluteness in every single individual, wholly present in every one and yet in all. He is not, as it were, fragmented and partially present in everyone and totally present by addition—this is pantheism; but he is totally in each and every one and yet in all—this is theism, personality, individuality.[562] But after one has grasped this, organic development will acquire its more profound and full worth, just as assuredly as an army would not be the poorer because every soldier is a general in spirit.

III A 38   n.d., 1840

« 1984

The main thing is to save as many of the universally human qualities in an individual life as possible.[563]

III A 136   n.d., 1841

« 1985

When you were happy, have you ever said to yourself that you could easily go through life alone? When you were heavy-hearted, have you ever said that it seemed as if even God in heaven was not able to help you?

III A 236   *n.d.*, 1842

« 1986

There is really only one single quality—individuality. Everything revolves around this, and this is also why everyone understands qualitatively with regard to himself what he understands quantitatively with regard to others. This constitutes individuality, but not every one wants to have it.[564]

V A 53   *n.d.*, 1844

« 1987

The person who appeals to "They say . . . . . ," to the approval of the age, of the times, to prove the rightness of the truth (not with respect to factual truth, for this, to be sure, is purely historical, but with respect to the eternal, the eternal truth) does nothing with his proof but refute the truth; for the truth is this—namely, that everyone must make a personal accounting to God. This he does not want to understand (that is, the truth), and yet he wants to prove its rightness.

V A 60   *n.d.*, 1844

« 1988 *On Solitariness*

Ecclesiastes 4:10. Woe to him who is solitary; if he falls there is no one to lift him up.[565]

V B 235   *n.d.*, 1844

« 1989

In the old days they believed that whatever one hears concerns the individual himself (*de te fabula*),[566] that everything concerns himself; now everybody believes that he can tell a fable which concerns all mankind but not himself.

VI A 20   *n.d.*, 1845

« 1990

Suppose that you go to church every Sunday, read devotional books often, and everything you hear and read applies to you, but yet the kind of suffering which you experience every day is never mentioned. Suppose that every time *Amen* is pronounced it is your solitary edification to say: Would to God that everything mentioned here might be my task. Suppose that horses could have devotional gatherings and that suffering hunger, being cruelly whipped, being kicked in the stall, being tormented, being hunted out in the open in winter are all discussed—but there is one horse among the listeners who goes home despondent every time because everything that is said, everything the other horses intimate to each other when they put their heads together in the harness or confidentially* share with each other out in the pasture, this he understands well enough, but what he suffers is never talked about.†

In margin: A horse that comes galloping gladly every time they assemble evenings in the pasture, hoping by listening closely to find out something—until, troubled, it turns around again and seeks its own solitary refuge.

* *In margin:* or, by neighing call each other together for collective deliberation.

† *In margin:* or, as they stand and toss their heads on a dewy summer morning and the meadow looks so inviting.

VI A 106   *n.d.,* 1845

« 1991

Of all debaucheries, the brilliance of this putrefaction* is still the most nauseating. Let a man sin personally in his youth, let him seduce girls, let him crave wine—there is still hope that this may some day rest on his conscience as sin. But this refinement, this wretched glitter of perdition —that the individual evaporates into the generation, confuses himself with Rome and Greece and Asia—this mildew of pomposity, with the result that the individual does not belong to those who lustfully in a physical sense are *deliciis diffluentes*[567] but, intellectually understood, are *diffluentes* in the nincompoopery of thoughtlessness.[568]

* *In margin:* pantheistic.

VI A 120   *n.d.,* 1845

« 1992

Simply to take an example near at hand—with respect to what I have here expressed I am convinced that every second student will say to himself: What he says I also know and I can say it just as well as he can. Perhaps so, I relinquish with pleasure any and all prominence. I only wish that what can belong to all and perhaps does belong to all may actually belong to me. I only wish that I may actually know that which all can know and perhaps all do know. But reflection is so athletic that it will assert itself in comparisons even down to the last "clip, clip" [of the levelling],[569] even with regard to expressing the conception of levelling. One person says it and gets a few listeners, one person writes it and gets a few readers, and these now think of themselves as outsiders—in the brief moment of disappointment. It makes no difference whether you pipe or you sing, whether you are busy or lazy, you must launch out into the deep, and in the deadly peril of destruction you must learn to help yourself, whether you are accused of arrogance in not accepting help from others or are accused of egotism in not helping (an impossibility for the person who has understood this) others.[570]

VII^1 B 121:6   *n.d.*, 1845-46

« 1993

. . . . . But I have heard that this is the meaning of life, that the individual weans himself away from the benefits of differentiation, if these tempt him, that he hardens himself against their invasion, if these tempt, in order with equal magnanimity to find equality in the universal, in what is common for every person as a human being. How beautiful to lose himself thus, magnanimously to understand what benefits all, enthusiastically to regard everything else as loss, whatever vainly wants to rest upon differentiation or abandoned wants to remain in the differentiation! I have heard further about life's meaning, that the individual in this magnanimous concern must be concerned about himself as if he were the only person, as if everything pertained to him when this everything is the universal rule, the universal demand, the universal task, the universal reward.[571] How beautiful to win the universal for himself in this way! Equality sanctifies this meaning of life; in the understanding of it there is peace, blessedness in the appropriation of it, love in the struggle for it, unity in victory, the purest human love in self-concern, in the concern over self-concern, because it demands of itself what it loves in all! —This I have heard! A signature is really not needed. Who said it is infinitely unimportant. There is no differentiation; it is not that one is higher for having said it and the other sits lower down because of hearing it, that one is benefited by being able to express it, the other the ill-treated stepchild who was denied this gift; for equality means that all are capable of doing it—alas, if there is no equality, then no one would attain it.

S. KIERKEGAARD
VII¹ B 199   *n.d.*, 1845-46

« 1994

True magnanimity can never be rewarded in the world, quite simply because if the so-called magnanimous step is of such a nature that the contemporaries can immediately understand that it is magnanimous, then it is not in a great sense truly magnanimous and thus it does have its reward. True magnanimity must also include becoming misunderstood and nevertheless doing the right, the noble thing. The honor and admiration of men is just as much a reward as money and an important position.

VII¹ A 149   *n.d.*, 1846

« 1995

A person can very well eat lettuce before it has formed a heart, but yet the tender delicacy of the heart and its lovely coil are something quite different from the leaves. It is the same in the world of spirit.⁵⁷² Busyness makes it almost impossible for an individual to form a heart; on the other hand, the thinker, the poet, the religious person who has actually formed his heart never becomes popular, not because he is difficult, but because a quiet and protracted occupation and intimacy with oneself and a remoteness go along with it. Even if I could raise my voice and say something of which everybody would approve, I would not say it if it was of a religious nature, because there already is a kind of religious indecency if the main point is to cry aloud; for religiousness the main point is rather to speak quite softly with oneself. Ah, it gets so turned around! We think that religiousness, instead of being a matter of every individual's going alone into his private room to talk softly with himself, is a matter of talking very loudly.

VII¹ A 205   *n.d.*, 1846

« 1996

Wanting to hide in the mass or the crowd, to be a little fraction of the crowd,* instead of being an individual, is the most corrupt of all escapes. Even if this makes life easier by making it more thoughtless in the din—this is not the question. The question is that of the responsibility of the single individual [*den Enkelte*]—that every single human being ought to be a single individual, ought not to make a racket along with a few others for a so-called conviction, but by himself before God ought to make up his mind about his conviction, just as in the next world eternity will single out the busy one who thought that he was in a group, single out the poorest wretch who thought he was overlooked, single him out as individually responsible, so distinctly individual that an eternity seems to lie between him and the next man. This is eternity's accounting—for there is a double accounting: that of temporality in which achievements are counted up and all that came of the individual's life by his engaging in life's play of powers, and that of eternity, which is made to see if the accounting tallies. For the first accounting can look very splendid inasmuch as it describes achievements, but nevertheless there can still be a lot of hidden irregularities, yes, the most critical irregularities. This is why it is so good to go to the house of sorrow, to enter into the heavy service of those who suffer in order rightly to see what the highest is; for if one is important in a big enterprise, perhaps is king over a whole nation, then it almost seems as if there would not be time for eternity's accounting. Although there are a great many public functionaries who keep accounts of national administrative affairs and who again are subordinate to the lord and king of the country, none of these public officials makes the accounting of eternity.

* *In margin:* Adam hid among the trees—but still he did not escape God. God in heaven does not talk to men as to an assembly; he talks to each one individually.

VII[1] B 158:3   *n.d.*, 1846

« 1997

The whole development of the world tends toward the absolute significance of the category of the single individual [*den Enkelte*],[573] which is the very principle of Christianity. We acknowledge this principle *in abstracto*, but we still have not come especially far in actualizing it. This explains why people still get an impression of proud, haughty arrogance when someone talks about the single individual, instead of recognizing that precisely this is complete humanity—that everyone is a single individual. Sometimes the misunderstanding is expressed piously. Thus when the deceased Bishop Møller[574] of Lolland says (in the introduction to his *Guide*) that it would be too bad if the truth (Christianity in particular) were accessible only to a few individuals and not to all, he certainly says something true but also something false, for Christianity is accessible to all, to be sure, but—note well—this occurs through and only through each one's becoming an individual, the single individual. But neither this ethical courage nor the religious courage is in good supply. Most men become very much afraid when they must, each one for himself, become the single individual. The whole thing twists and turns like this—one moment it is supposed to be arrogance to present this view of the single individual, and then when the single individual attempts it, he finds out that this thought is too great for him, too overwhelming.

VIII¹ A 9   *n.d.,* 1847

« 1998

Why did I make such a great, great fuss about the category of individuality?[575] Very simply, through this and by this stands the cause of Christianity. Let those who defend the Bible etc. and those who attack see what they accomplish without it and what they accomplish against it. Christianity still has so much power over men that if every man were only placed under the eternal responsibility of individuality he would become a Christian. All the rest are merely remedies which feed the sickness. Doubt has entered in and, just like cholera, hangs on. Every scholarly argument therefore merely feeds doubt; every organization-minded effort feeds doubt. Only God and eternity are powerful enough to cope with doubt (for doubt is precisely man's rebellious force against God), but if God and eternity are to get the better of it, then every human being must enter into the compression chamber[576] of individuality.

Very likely if I were to lecture on this many would go along—but would a person enter into the compression chamber of individuality by *going along?*

VIII¹ A 125   *n.d.,* 1847

« 1999

In the old days being a Christian was expressed by entering a monastery (the category of individuality); now the category of individuality must be used in the opposite way in order to become a Christian. —The homeopathy involved.

In reflection the category of individuality is the monastery—i.e., what the monastery was in immediacy

VIII¹ A 126   *n.d.,* 1847

« 2000

Abraham of St. Clara[577] somewhere makes the very penetrating distinction that when a person has withdrawn from the world (in an external sense) but is not in communion with God and therefore has the world with him in his thoughts, he is not solitary—he is a recluse but not solitary.

VIII¹ A 210   n.d., 1847

« 2001 *Text for a Friday's Sermon*

Mark 9:50—"Have salt in yourselves."
The individual's God-relationship.

VIII¹ A 262   n.d., 1847

« 2002

He who stood and fell at the pass of Thermopylæ did not have a sounder position than I have at the pass and the narrows of the category of the individual—through which the age must go—for precisely when it walks this path over my body I shall have been victorious, which he was not.[578]

VIII¹ A 286   n.d., 1847

« 2003 *The Most Horrible Collision*

imaginable would be a bird, for example, a swallow, in love with a girl. The swallow would be able to know the girl (as distinguished from everyone else), but the girl would not be able to tell the swallow apart from any of the 100,000 other swallows. Imagine the swallow's distress when upon its arrival in the spring it said, "Here I am," and the girl answered, "I do not know you."

As a matter of fact, the swallow has no individuality.[579] We see from this that individuality, this difference of separateness, is the presupposition for loving. Because of this, most men are not truly able to love because the distinctiveness of their individualities is too slight.

The greater the distinctiveness of individuality, the more pronounced the individuality, the more knowers there are, and the more there is to know.

In this far deeper sense one sees the significance of the Hebraic expression—to know one's wife,[580] the significance of what is said about the differences between the genders, but the same thing is far more profoundly true about the psychical (*Sjælelige*), the imprint of individuality.

VIII¹ A 462   n.d., 1847

« 2004 *"The Single Individual"* {"den Enkelte"} *A Hint*

"The single individual" is the category through which, in a religious sense, the age, history, the generation must go.[581] And the one who stood and fell at Thermopylæ was not as secure as I who stand at this narrow pass, "the single individual." His particular task was to keep the hordes from pressing through that narrow pass; if they pressed through, he had lost. My task is easier, at least at first sight, and exposes me far less to the danger of being trampled down, since it is as an insignificant servant to help, if possible, the hordes press through this narrow gate, "the single individual," through which, please note, no one in all eternity gets through without becoming "the single individual." And if I were to request an inscription on my grave, I should request none other than "that single individual"—even if it is not understood now, it surely will be. With the category "the single individual" I took a polemical aim at the system in the day when everything here at home was system and system—now the system is never mentioned any more. My possible historical[582] significance is linked to this category. Perhaps my writings will be quickly forgotten, as many another writer's. But if this was the right category and all was in order with this category, if I perceived correctly here, if I understood properly that this was my task, even though it was by no means a pleasant, comfortable, or appreciated task, if this was granted to me, although involving internal suffering such as is seldom experienced, although involving external sacrifices which not every person is willing to make—then I stand and my writings with me.[583]

"The single individual"—with this category the cause of Christianity stands or falls, now that the world-development has gone as far as it has in reflection. Without this category pantheism would be unconditionally victorious. No doubt there will be those who know how to tighten this category dialectically in a quite different way (without having had the labor of bringing it forth), but the category "the single individual" is and continues to be the anchor which can hold against pantheistic confusion, is and continues to be the medicine which can make people sober, is and continues to be the weight which can be put on, except that those who are to work with this category (at the levers or in applying the weights) must be more and more dialectical as the confusion becomes greater and greater. I promise to make a Christian of every person I can get in under this category, or, since one human being certainly cannot do this for another, I assure him that he will become one. As "the single individual" he is alone, alone in the whole world, alone face to face before God—then he will no doubt manage to obey. All doubt has its ultimate haunt in the illusion of temporality, that as "a few of us" or as the whole human race we can finally intimidate God (as "the people" intimidate the king and "the public" the councilman) and even be Christ. Pantheism[584] is an optical illusion, a vaporous image formed out of the fog of temporality or a mirage formed by its reflection, which claims to be the eternal.

But the fact is that this category cannot be taught directly; to use it is an art, an ethical task and an art, the practice of which is always dangerous and at times may claim the lives of its practitioners. For the self-willed race and the confused crowds regard the highest, divinely understood, as high treason against "the race," "the crowd," "the public," etc.

The single individual—this category has been used only once before (the first time) in a decisively dialectical way, by Socrates in disintegrating paganism. In Christendom it will be used a second time in the very opposite way, to make men (the Christians) Christians. It is not the missionary's category with respect to the pagans to whom he proclaims Christianity, but it is the missionary's category within Christendom itself, for the inward deepening of being and becoming a Christian. When he, the missionary, comes, he will use this category. If the age is waiting for a hero, it waits in vain; instead there will more likely come one who in divine weakness will teach men obedience—by means of their slaying him in impious rebellion, him, the one obedient to God.[585]

VIII[1] A 482   *n.d.*, 1847

« 2005

The touching naïveté of medieval lyric poetry is rooted in the category of individuality. This naïveté corresponds to the time in a child's life when it says "me wants," when it calls itself by name (Carl, etc.) instead of saying "I." The individuality is not separated but is universal. From this comes the curious dreaming quality which makes it almost doubtful who the subject is, whether the speaker speaks about himself or some unspecified other, because it is "man." This enigma, this mystery, that the lyric is in a way impersonal and yet in this very way so very personal. —As if a flower (a lily, for example) were able to speak and spoke in such a way that one could not be sure which lily did the speaking, but it would still speak as a lily. So it is with medieval lyric poetry: it is just as uncertain which "I" is speaking or which human being is speaking, but it is all the more certain that it is a human being. Alas, in our time things are often turned around: it is quite definite that it is *this* human being who speaks, and yet there is no human being who speaks.

VIII¹ A 568   *n.d.*, 1848

« 2006

Every single human being has an infinite reality [*Realitet*], and it is pride and arrogance not to honor one's neighbor in every single human being. O, if only I could speak with every single human being this way, I am convinced that I would move him.⁵⁸⁶ But it is a fallacy to think that 1,000 men are more than 1; this is to make men into animals. The point in being man is that oneness is the highest, 1,000 of them is less.

Alas, alas, alas, until this dialectic is practiced!

IX A 91   *n.d.*, 1848

« 2007

If I were to permit myself a word of objection to Christianity, it would be this: How did it ever hit upon the idea, not only of addressing itself to all (for this is the kind way), but even of envisioning the possibility of all, at least many.

But on the other hand is not the same thing expressed in a way by the phrase "the single individual" ["*den Enkelte*"], for this, indeed, can be everyone. But the objection would arise from Christianity's seemingly having started out with an inexplicable hope that all would want to follow it—and yet the founder himself certainly knew otherwise, he who knew that he was to be sacrificed, he who most certainly is not deceived, either, by this unholy sham of the countless millions and millions in Christendom.

The divine is to know this in advance and then not let it influence his discourse in the least. The human is—knowing this in advance—to say: that single individual [*hiin Enkelte*]. The divine, with the same knowledge, nevertheless says: All.

IX A 286   *n.d.*, 1848

« 2008

The God-relationship of singleness (that *each* single individual relates himself to God) is still sound and true. What is said of the sparrows⁵⁸⁷ is certainly literally true of men: God knows each single one. Indeed, to be human simply means belonging to the race which has the distinctiveness that every single individual is known as a single individual by God and can know him. The task is precisely to work oneself out of sociality more and more, but genuinely and truly, to be able to maintain longer and longer the thought of God-present-with-me. This is also the significance of "judgment."

But when the God-relationship of singleness in the single individual becomes diseased, the middle term of sociality or of "the other person" is temporarily postulated. This disease can indeed be an almost physical kind of melancholy and the like. But for the most part it is the fanaticism which conceitedly misinterprets what it means to be the single individual relating himself to God, imagines that it is wanting to be or being a most uncommon individual and, furthermore, choosing to do nothing but sit, as it were, and flirt with God. As a matter of fact, no such unhealthy inebriacy can remain in the thought of relating oneself to God as a single individual if he is sobered by the thought that everyone is permitted to do this—indeed, everyone is commanded.

Furthermore, this disease in the single individual's God-relationship can sometimes also be a spiritual trial [Anfægtelse], and then it does not at all follow that a person should yield to it and go seeking company but should struggle against it and bring love of God to glow as it should. This kind of spiritual trial arises because the deep underlying feeling of infinite unworthiness basic to every true God-relationship becomes over-powering, is not transfigured into a greater joy in God, but oppresses one, so that a person becomes momentarily anxious and afraid of ideality and himself—and of God, who seems to be so infinitely sublime that one does not dare think of him at all. It seems as if he must become disgusted and tired of listening to one's nonsense and nauseated with one's sins.

But a person is not to give in; he is to fight against it, thank God that God has *commanded* that one *ought* to pray to him, for otherwise it is hardly possible to force one's way through the spiritual trial. He is to remember that God is love, the God of patience and consolation, and that God is not one who adopts vain titles but is completely different from anything I am able to comprehend of what he says himself to be. That he is not just as kind as the kindest man plus a little more, but that even the kindest man (even though he has never lived but is poetically imagined) is only a sort of caricature who still does not resemble God's love any more than a monkey resembles a man. Remember that God at any moment has 100,000 possibilities for helping you, and equally as many explanations which, if he would, could immediately show you that this thing he has allotted to you is still at this very moment the best, and the reason why he does not do it is simply because he has one explanation more, that not doing it is the best for you.

But it must be true for you that you reflect upon God because you need God, because otherwise everything would collapse for you. Therefore you should pray most sincerely for help in always having work to do and then receive everything from his hand—the necessary diversion as well. And always remember—or bid him remind you—that the task is directed toward being able to hold fast to the thought of God more and more for a longer time, not the way a dreamer does, idling and flirting, but to cling fast to it within your work. There shall be no dreaming, for God is pure act [*Actuositet*], and therefore a mere dreamy loitering over the thought of him is not true prayer.

IX A 316   n.d., 1848

« 2009

Only as an individual can a man ever relate himself most truly to God, for he can best have the perception of his own unworthiness alone; it is almost impossible to make this really clear to another person; besides, it could easily become affected.

IX A 318   n.d., 1848

« 2010

In one sense there is something dreadful in the thought of these countless millions and millions of men. For a moment one is reminded almost of other animal species with their teeming duplicated specimens [*Exemplarer*] in the millions, and of nature's almost horrifying wastefulness. And when one then reflects that every single human being is by nature intended [*er lagt an til*][588] for the highest religiously—and the religious is again the highest! But providence is not only blameless but has graciously made it possible for everyone and cannot be responsible for how many thousands throw it away.

But as soon as men become indolent and seek indulgence, they promptly escape into sociality, where the standard is relative, comparison with others, and man is an animal species. It appears so striking and is so enormously tempting—these countless millions—it is the vision of relativity—but it is a lie; for there is only one ideal, and it is intended for the single individual, not for companies and fraternities.

We think that by attaching ourselves to society we develop a higher perfection—that is a nice idea, but no, it is retrogression! This kind of talk is just as fraudulent as that which says it is earnestness to seek a secure place in the established order of things (in contrast to freely—bound only to God—serving an idea). No, thank you. If this is earnestness, then all the religious paradigms are dreamers. But we want to have sensate security and then, in addition, the honor that it is supposed to be earnestness.

IX A 356   *n.d.* 1848

« 2011

The congregation is a composition of eternity within time. This is evident in the medium. The congregation is in the medium of being [*Værens*], which implies growth and composure. The single individual is in the medium of becoming [*Vordens*]—and this earthly existence [*Tilværelse*] is the time of testing—therefore there is no congregation here.

IX A 450   *n.d.*, 1848

« 2012

Alas, in the theater we all laugh at *Boon Companions*,[589] but in actual life we laugh at the single individual who literally does not want to be a part of a clique in any form whatsoever. For if he is someone who could but does not want to, then he loses all earthly advantages; after all, it is ridiculous of him—he who could have them.

IX A 496   *n.d.*, 1848

« 2013

"The single individual" ["*den Enkelte*"] is a category which may be used in two ways.[590] In times when security prevails and existence [*Tilværelsen*] seems to lie under a spell of apathy, "the single individual" is the category of awakening. In agitated times when everything is tottering, "the single individual" is the category of composure. The person who understands how to use this category will appear quite different in times of peace than in times of commotion, and yet he will be using the same weapon. The difference is the same as that between using a sharp and pointed instrument, like a scalpel, to wound, and using the same instrument to clean out a wound. But never will the category "the single individual," rightly applied, cause any damage to the established order of religious truth. In peaceful times its purpose will be to awaken inwardness to a heightened life in the established order, without changing anything externally. In times of commotion its purpose will be a rescue action of drawing attention away from externality, to lead the single individual to an indifference to external change, and to strengthen inwardness. The category of the single individual always relates to inward deepening. Earthly reward, power, honor, etc. are not involved in its proper use, for what is rewarded in the world, of course, is only change or working for external change—inwardness does not interest the world, which, to be sure, is externality.

IX B 63:8   *n.d.*, 1848

« 2014 *Sharpened*

A Double-edged Weapon

In times of peace the category "the single individual" is the category of awakening; when everything is peaceful, secure, and indolent—and the ideal has vanished—then the single individual is awakening. In agitated times, when everything is tottering, . . . [Text essentially the same as IX B 63:8].

IX B 66   *n.d.*, 1848

« 2015

What has confused everything and above all the whole of Christendom and the whole of Christianity is that the contemporaries, the generation, etc. are regarded as the authority in matters of truth. Everything hinges upon the single individual. This category is the point by which and through which God can come to move the generation. If this is taken away, God is dethroned.

Since this is so, it is obvious that to address myself to a single person very directly concerning the religious truth would be an attempt to make him an authority and consequently would be a deception.

X^1 A 218   *n.d.*, 1849

« 2016

Thomas à Kempis,[591] book I, chapter 20:
"Every time I am with men I always come back less a man." According to Seneca, Epistle VII, "I come home again more niggardly, more arrogant, more sensual, more cruel, and more inhuman, because I have been among men."

This thought I myself expressed a short time ago in this way: To what a degree men would become men and lovable characters if they could be brought as single individuals before God.

X^1 A 286   *n.d.* 1849

« 2017

It was "the evil spirit" which led Christ out into solitude in order to tempt him;[592] from this one could be tempted to conclude that it is always the evil spirit which leads a man out into solitude. There is some truth in this, but it is also the way to the true God-relationship, and it must also be said that this very temptation of Christ in solitude was part of his development, if one may speak this way. Furthermore, God also in a certain sense dwells in solitude. But surely solitude is dialectical; therefore a man rarely amounts to anything, either good or evil, who has never been in solitude. In solitude there is the absolute, but also the absolute danger. In sociality there is relativity and relative danger, yet also, please note, the danger which is more than relative, the danger of missing the absolute, of never discovering that it exists [er til], of never relating one's life decisively to it, however far one is from being it. It is arrogance and fanaticism for a human being to want to be the absolute, but it is truth to understand it to be the standard by which one must be measured, both unto humiliation and also unto *stimulation*, for it is humiliating to see how far short one is, but it must also stimulate one and keep one awake in the endeavor.

X^1 A 463   n.d., 1849

« 2018

That a single individual was in the right against "the crowd"—yes, this we see; but that he carried his point, this we do not see.

X^2 A 179   n.d., 1849

« 2019 *The Stages of the World*

Providence is becoming more and more thrifty; less and less is to be squandered. In old times there lived only an individual; the mass, the thousands, were squandered on him. Then came the idea of representation. Those who really lived were again only individuals, but the mass nevertheless saw themselves in them, participated in their life. The last stage is: the single individual, understood in such a way that the single individual is not in contrast to the mass, but each one is equally an individual.

But the task becomes more and more rigorous for the missionaries who should prepare for this. Formerly the teacher was an individual, but then he had disciples. For the humanness in him there was something consoling in this; he had a kind of human probability that all his striving would not be without a trace, for, indeed, he had disciples, and in the way he expanded in finitude. [*In margin:* and the teacher also had this opportunity to make himself comfortable by means of the disciples, had the relief of the relative criterion.]

But when the last stage begins, the teacher will become the single individual who neither wants nor dares to have a disciple. What terrifying rigorousness! How can one possibly avoid dizziness. In the midst of this whirlpool of millions, where everything is either togetherness or parties, such a single individual stands utterly helpless. He makes himself helpless, for he does not want to have disciples. How easy for the wave of time to wash over him and erase all his effort as a nothing! What faith it takes to persevere in this life day after day, what faith it takes to believe that his life is noticed by God and this is enough! And how squandered such a person is in the service of God! But the greater the squandering in regard to the teacher, the greater the thrift in regard to the generation. Formerly the teacher was spared and the many were spent; now the teacher is spent precisely in order that there be upbringing in the category: the single individual.

$$x^2 \text{ A } 265 \quad n.d., 1849$$

« 2020

The dialectical relationship: the universal, the single individual [*den Enkelte*], the exceptional [*særlige*] individual. . . .

$$x^6 \text{ B } 52:1 \quad n.d., 1849$$

« 2021

. . . If the final copy of *The Accounting* is published separately, a note must be added to the portion saying that religiously there is only the single individual, and in that case also be added in the draft.[593]

Note. This must be emphasized ethically and existentially as decisively as possible, especially in our time, whose particular evil and special demoralization is precisely that, metaphysically or ethically dissipated, we want to abolish what is fundamental for all morality, constructive life, religion—the single individual—and establish the generation, one abstraction or another, fantastical social definitions, and the like, instead, as the world revolution of 1848 has only made clearer and more obvious, so that it is already rather easy to see that "the single individual" is the point of view of the future unto salvation, just as "the single individual" is also the passage way through which "Christendom" must go,[594] since the task will continue to be to introduce Christianity into Christendom, which reverses all Christian conceptions, a prodigious illusion, which, if it is to be thoroughly overhauled and raised up must face the task: to introduce Christianity in Christendom.

x^5 B 244   *n.d.*, 1849-50

« 2022

Instead of all that preacher-prattle and those scholarly folios which make the matter so serious, so immensely serious and important by showing how Christianity satisfies the deepest need of the whole race, so that nothing is said (how frivolous or petty!) about my little *I*, but (magnificent and profoundly serious!) everything is about the whole world—instead of all this I could be tempted to reverse the discussion and say: I feel the need for Christianity; I can easily imagine that you others do not feel this need, for you are better and stronger than I am. There is a wretched hypocrisy about seriousness, that it is being serious to hide behind "the others," these millions, instead of being "the single individual" ["*den Enkelte*"].

x^2 A 457   *n.d.*, 1850

« 2023

Julius Müller[595] makes the excellent observation (II, p. 430) that if one says that the doctrine of personality speaks not of the race but of the single person as atomic—then what does the word "individual" mean? Is not the individual an ἄτομον which in no way can be regarded as a mode or affection of another.

x^2 A 480   *n.d.*, 1850

« 2024 *The Single Individual* [den Enkelte]—*Race*

There is something correct in Göschel's observation that in the concept of *race* man is really independent *personality* prior to and independent of temporal realization or unfolding in personal individuals [*Individer*] (cited by Julius Müller in *Læren om Synden*,[596] II, p. 467).

I have frequently pointed out that the human race in contrast to the animal species is characterized by the fact that the single individual [*den Enkelte*] is higher than the race. Whereas the overlapping factor in regard to particular animal copies or specimens [*Exemplarer*] is the race, here the single individual, that is, every individual, when he in truth is the single individual, is the overlapping factor. The race is a binding together on a lower level.

This has been completely forgotten in our age, when we have also forgotten that man is in kinship with God. But God cannot be in kinship with an animal species; God is spirit and it would be bestial for him to be in kinship with a "race." He can be in kinship only with "the single individual," and only "the single individual" can be in kinship with God.

A particular instance or specimen is less than a race or species; the single individual is more than the species or race, for he is the whole race and also the individuation. Therefore in eternal life the race will cease.

This will be of great significance with respect to the entire doctrine of original sin.

Man rejoices like a pagan over being in the race (an animal qualification); it is the greatest unhappiness and deepest pain to be outside "the race." This repeats itself also in the life of youth, before man has become spirit, which most men never do become, although it is the criterion by which eternity will judge them.

In a Christian sense a man sighs under being "race." By the synthesis he is constrained in and with the race, must assume all the concretions given thereby as his task, participate as an accomplice in the guilt of the race, and by his own guilt increase the guilt of the race—but he longs to be in God.

To imagine "species" or "race" as the middle term in the eternal life, as the middle term for being in God—is bestiality.

Here merely a psychical observation. Imagine a lover whose beloved dies. Suppose then that Christianity offers him his immortality if he is somewhat attentive; there may be many who would say: Immortality is not for me; it is too spiritual.

Likewise for many men the eternal life of Christianity is much too spiritual. An eternal life where there are no general assemblies, no running in flocks, no animal odors, etc.—this would be worse than death.

x^2 A 489   *n.d.*, 1850

« 2025

Why is it that people prefer to be addressed in groups rather than individually? Among various reasons is this one—the single individual, who is probably far superior to them, whom they hardly dare look at if they were to speak with him individually—is physically overwhelmed by the impression of "the many." Each one present at the gathering then attributes this tension to himself and thinks that he himself is the one the other is almost afraid of.

x^2 A 629   *n.d.*, 1850

« 2026 *The Human—the Christian*

The human is—that we are the innumerable, the generation, and I am one with the flock—here is the indulgence, the dissipation. The Christian is—that only one is ever needed—there is in this an almost super-human strenuousness for every one who can grasp it. Humanly, we must all together, if possible, stick together in order to drag the load along—there is in this an alleviation and freedom from concern, for the part each one has to carry is so very little. Christianly, one is enough—furthermore, one who is infinitely incapable of achieving anything—but God is along. The frightful weight of it—conscious of infinite incapability in support-ing God, who is capable of everything. Humanly our minds are fully occupied in making, if possible, seventeen plans at one time—in this there is solace and elation. —Christianly there is nothing to do, only to be infinitely still so that God can have a chance—a frightful strain!

x^3 A 116   *n.d.*, 1850

« 2027 *Is There a Private Relationship to Christ?*

It is possible as far as I am concerned personally that I look upon Christ too much as an examiner, as if I were supposed to strive on my own power and he would merely watch and see how far I can go. I realize this, and I also know that many a time in penitence before God I have confessed that these were actually sinful thoughts, because it is impiety to have such thoughts in relation to a Savior, for love like this is not in the least a Savior's love.

But on the other hand there has been a trend too far in the opposite direction. We imagine we have a private relationship to Christ. We attach ourselves to Christ, we want to work for his cause, as we say; but then we also believe that Christ is not scrupulous with the one who joins up with him in this way.

We forget that with Christ no such private relationship is possible; unchanged, he looks upon the one who attaches himself to him to see whether he honestly and earnestly strives.

But we have wanted to form a regular clique with Christ.

A clique sticks together in such a way that the members among themselves are not particularly scrupulous about whether something is done honestly, honorably, uprightly—but they keep a sharp watch on those on the outside, the others.

For the most part we have forgotten in what sense Christ has a cause.

He who has a cause in the temporal, earthly sense must form a clique and become dependent on the co-partners.

Only in the eternal sense does Christ have a cause. Anything else he will not have. This is why he must be just as scrupulous about the one who attaches himself to him as with all the others.

A man who wants some earthly advantage could be served splendidly by an adherent who successfully carries his cause forward among all others while making an exception of himself—Christ cannot in all eternity use such an adherent; it would be blasphemy.

x³ A 324   *n.d.*, 1850

« 2028

Christianly it is not at all right to stress that all mankind needs Christianity and then to prove it and demonstrate it. The Christian stress is: *I* need Christianity.

x³ A 339   *n.d.*, 1850

« 2029 *"That Single Individual"* {"hiin Enkelte"}

The thing that has puzzled me most in my work is how I came to begin with "that single individual," with willing this utterly true principle, the single individual [*den Enkelte*].

Imagine someone who has been inspired to will something; then inspired in this way he went out into the world and gathered followers; the years went by and now he is an old man. He himself is about the only one who has remained true to the ideal and considers the undertaking bungled in other respects—and now he says: No, it depends only on the single individual. Sociality is essentially retrogression.

Thus it is with an old man at the end of his life—but that a man of some twenty years begins this way—how did he find this out or how inverted or upside down he must have been situated to believe that this is the truth—alas, ordinarily for the young there is nothing more natural than to believe in joining together.

x³ A 349   *n.d.*, 1850

« 2030 *The Single Individual* {den Enkelte}—
            the Crowd—before God

Socrates' greatness was that even in the moment he was accused before the assembly of the people, his eyes did not see the crowd but only single individuals.

Spiritual superiority sees only single individuals. Alas, generally we human beings are sense-dominated—therefore, as soon as there is a gathering of people, the impression changes and we see an abstraction, the mass—and we become changed.

But for God, the infinite spirit, all these millions who have lived and are living do not form a mass—he sees only single individuals.

x^3 A 476   *n.d., 1850*

« 2031 *"The Single Individual"* {"den Enkelte"}

This principle can be set forth only in a poetic way, for it would be presumptuous for anyone to pass himself off as being eminently "the single individual." Consequently it is a striving.

x^3 A 660   *n.d. 1850*

« 2032 *"What Good Can It Do?"*

You say, "What good can it do for me to set myself against the crowd as a single individual?" What good can it do? —Well, perhaps it can even help save your soul so that it doesn't go to hell! Or do you think that when God and eternity pronounce judgment this kind of talk can be of any good to you; do you not suspect that merely to risk such a lame excuse is guilt enough?"

x^3 A 687   *n.d., 1850*

« 2033 *A Possible Foreword to the Edifying Discourse, "The Woman That Was a Sinner"*

If neither *The Accounting* nor *Two Discourses at the Communion on Fridays* is published but only the edifying discourse, which is to be dedicated to my father, the following foreword could perhaps be used.[597]

Foreword

What was said in my first book of edifying discourses, in the *Foreword* to *Two Edifying Discourses* in 1843, that this book "seeks that single individual" [*hiin Enkelte*]; what was repeated verbatim in the Foreword to each new collection of edifying discourses; what was pointed out, after I had exposed myself to the laughter and the insults of the crowd and thus, as well as I could, contributed to evoking awareness, by dedicating the next large work, *Edifying Discourses in Various Spirits*, 1847, to "the single individual" [*den Enkelte*]; what world revolution in 1848 certainly did not witness against or render untrue—emphasis upon the single individual—let me repeatedly remind of this. [*In margin:* If for the sake of recollection it is possible for a thinker to manage to concentrate all his thinking into one single idea, this has been granted to me, the edifying author, whose entire thinking is essentially contained in this one thought: the single individual.]

"The single individual"—of course, the single individual religiously understood, consequently understood in such a way that every one, unconditionally every one, yes, unconditionally every one, just as much as every one has or should have a conscience, can be that single individual and should be that, can stake his honor in being willing to be that, but then also can find blessedness in being what is the expression for true fear of God, true love to one's neighbor, true humanity, and true human equality —O, if only some might achieve it, if it is not, although the task for all, nevertheless too high for all of us, yet not too high in such a way that it should be forgotten, forgotten as if it were not the task or as if this task did not face us in November 1850, so that we may at least learn to forsake not only the mediocre but also the indifferent half-measures which reject an established order, yet without driving through to become in an extraordinary [*overordentlig*] sense the single individual, but rather schismatically organize parties and sects, which are neither the one nor the other.

x⁵ B 117   November, 1850

« 2034 *To Become Sober*

in the Christian sense is extremely difficult for everyone, and no doubt very few become Christianly sober. Curiously, becoming sober does not come by itself, naturally, as we are inclined to think—a quiet transition from clarity to greater clarity. On the contrary there comes a crisis in which one is so confused he does not know in from out, and now it seems as if he were really drunk whereas before he was sober—and yet this is the crisis. It is just as with the person who literally has fallen to drink and now wants to stop—there comes a time when he seems much more drunk than when he was drinking, and it is simply because he is withdrawing from drinking.

Spiritually understood, to be sober requires first and foremost the completely and thoroughly reflected withdrawal of oneself as a single individual before God, alone before God; and then the pure expression of the ethical and what is ethically crucial—a clear and thoroughly worked out consciousness of one's own actual situation.

x³ A 763   n.d., 1851

« 2035 *God*

Take a poet, even the very best—and see how almost all his characters resemble each other—at most he creates a few original or primitive [*primitive*] characters.

And then think of God, who creates all these millions and millions —and not a single one is like another.

x³ A 778   *n.d.*, 1851

« 2036 *That Christianity Does Not Exist* [ikke er til]⁵⁹⁸

can be proved by the fact that life as it is lived [*det Existentielle*] shows that no one believes in "the single individual" [*den Enkelte*] and in intensive action; existence [*Existentsen*] everywhere shows the attitude: Let's be part of a group.

But Christianity is diametrically opposed to this.

And the way one lives his life always expresses what he in fact believes.

What good is it, then, that they profess and profess that they believe in Christianity.

x⁴ A 29   *n.d.*, 1851

« 2037 *Fraud*

In all respects the mint-standard of being a human being has been reduced.

In ancient times they regarded egotism and self-love as wanting to be alone.

But now the race has become so paltry that to be alone has gone out completely; the race is too paltry to provide even such egotists.

To be an egotist nowadays one must be part of a group. Egotism is represented by blocks and parties.

Meanwhile we keep on talking the same old way that egotism is wanting to stand alone—but to be part of a group is cordiality and love.

We do not observe that the whole context of existence has shifted around. The world has become so secularized that no single individual can persevere as an egotist; he cannot *qua* egotist elbow his way through. Egotism has understood this and has abated to the extent that egotism has become somewhat social, blocks and parties, profiting by the hypocritical appearance of being love.

Consequently egotism has become social—and to want to stand alone has therefore become the religious; under the circumstances only the religious person can persevere. But the fact that egotism became social certainly does not mean it ceased to be egotism.

x^4 A 89   *n.d.*, 1851

« 2038 *One Man—Many Men*

God is an omnipotent man who can manage even with only one human being.

But then that single human being must unconditionally, unconditionally, sacrifice everything.

We do not want to be that one human being.

Therefore we grab after palpable help—Let's form a group—we coddle ourselves.

We ought to admit that this is the situation, but we lie and want sociality to be the higher earnestness.

This I do not do: I make the admission that I am not such a single human being; I am only a poet.

In general, the law is very simple; the faster a man accommodates to sociality—"Let's form a group"—the more sensate he is and the less he communicates with God. The one who always and everywhere has to be part of a group is actually abandoned by God and by the idea—that is, it is his own fault, for God abandons no one.

x^4 A 104   *n.d.*, 1851

« 2039 *Vinet*

He says it masterfully: Christianity teaches the fall of the race and the resurrection of the individual. [*In margin: denn ein Christ glaubt an den Sündenfall der Gattung und an die Wiederherstellung des Individuums.*][599]

See *Der Sozialismus*[600] (translated by Hofmeister), p. 23.

x^4 A 188   *n.d.*, 1851

« 2040 *The Single Individual* {den Enkelte}—*Conscience*

It could be said that "conscience" is one of life's greatest inconveniences. Therefore "Let's be part of a group," for if we are part of a group it means good-night to conscience. We cannot be two or three, a Miller Brothers and Company around a conscience. Let's make all this coziness secure by abolishing conscience, by saying that wanting to be a single individual is egotism, morbid vanity, etc.

If you have a conscience—then life is just about barred to you, for the law of the world is: consciencelessness, the best rule of thumb, *hanc veniam damus, petimusque vicissim.*[601]

x⁴ A 370   *n.d,* 1851

« 2041 *Wessenberg*[602]

says (p. 46): Here is revealed a striking difference between paganism and Christianity. The former regards the universe as eternal, the individual human beings as transitory. Christianity holds the world to be transitory and the individual human beings to be imperishable.

This is fine. But this is just exactly the modern mind: the universe, the race, etc. are eternal, the individuals vanishing. That is, the modern mind is pagan.

x⁴ A 401   *n.d.,* 1851

« 2042 *Why Does Tragedy No Longer Appeal?*

Quite simply because faith in personality has been lost. The heroic has actually become ridiculous to the mentality of our age—that one individual human being stands there and gesticulates as if he were accomplishing everything—no, this is ridiculous—we must be part of a group, a party, have anonymous patrons, etc. To the mentality of our age Luther is really ridiculous—a solitary man riding in a cart to the parliament at Worms and wanting to demolish the entire power of the Pope. That he appeals to God is, of course, again ridiculous to the mentality of our age, because according to this mentality God cannot be assumed to relate himself to an individual human being but at best to "a group," a party, a people, etc.

With what dreadful haste everyone in our time wants to form a "group" the minute he has the slightest thing to communicate or to propose! What a confounded, ungodly shortcut we think we can take!

And then it is said that we are all Christians. My God! The formula for existence [*Tilværelse*], which is the paradigm of Christianity, has become ridiculous to the whole race—and then we are all supposed to be Christians!

x⁴ A 415   *n.d.,* 1851

« 2043 *The Single Individual* {den Enkelte}

What makes such great confusion is that everyone promptly has to formulate a theory and obligate everyone else to it.

Someone gets an impression of Christianity—presto! there has to be a theory, and everyone must subscribe to his theory. Then he gets busy developing his theory further (this is itself a direction away from the religious). Then his theory is attacked by others, and he defends it etc.— constantly moving away from true religiousness. He does not personally get around to acting according to the theory but manages to introduce a theory about the opposition to the theory.

No, what should be insisted upon is this: there is a book called the New Testament; I feel obligated by it in this way and that—but I do not theorize; I do not obligate others. I simply say—I feel obligated in this way and express it in action. Truth is not trying to get a random bunch of people obligated to me or to my conception. Truth is that it become known that there is a book called the New Testament and that everyone must alone by himself before God become obligated by it.

x⁴ A 427   *n.d.*, 1851

« 2044   *"Only One Wins the Prize"*⁶⁰³

This can be used as the theme of a discourse (for self-examination) which discloses the hypocrisy practised by "the community," "the parish," just as the first discourse disclosed the hypocrisy in "science and scholarship."⁶⁰⁴

Men know very well that to be, that one is obliged to be, the single individual [*den Enkelte*], is very exhausting and means renunciation of the world, but they beat about the bush. "The single individual" is the qualification of the spirit; the collective is the animal qualification which make life easier, provides a comparative criterion, procures earthly benefits, hides one in the crowd, etc.

"But we are clever, we have discovered—just imagine how clever, how inscrutable!—we have discovered that to want to be the single individual (who appeals only to God) is selfishness, detestable and heartless selfishness. Should I then be such an egotist? Pfui!—especially since by wanting to be the single individual I would lose all earthly benefits, too; whereas by being hearty, hearty in the company of others, I gain all the earthly benefits and also am loved as a lovable, hearty person."

. . . . . "But we are clever, we have—just imagine how ingenious, but let's keep it to ourselves that it is ingenuity!—we have discovered that the collective, the association, the community, the parish are "earnestness," that to want to be the single individual is fantasy, immaturity, exaggeration, and therefore not genuine earnestness. Should I be a visionary, then? No, I am an earnest man who sincerely and heartily sticks with the others—and this way I gain all the earthly advantages and also am regarded and honored as an earnest man. Just look into history (of course this is between us; such things I can confide to you in the lounge, but we avoid saying it officially) at those who have really stood alone, how they fared, how they were completely abandoned and then persecuted, had to live in poverty, and finally were not even permitted to live but were doomed to death. —They were visionaries devoid of earnestness, and to that extent punishment was their fate, even though perhaps too severe, and the punishment imposed by our age—being laughed at by us earnest and reasonable people—is more suitable."

x⁴ A 441   n.d., 1851

« 2045 "The Church"

In various ways the heresies in "Christianity" lie in the doctrine of "the Church." By this we have tried to abolish or supplant what is truly Christian—namely, that Christianity is related to the single individual [*den Enkelte*]—and thus we have produced a lower state of religion, "national religion and a national God," corresponding to paganism and Judaism. We have not paid close enough attention to the sense in which the Church is formed of single individuals, but by making human beings into Christians while still infants we fundamentally postulate that the Church is the chosen people just as the Jews were. But this is Judaism, not Christianity, for a Christian cannot be born—no, the individual becomes a Christian; Christianity is related to the single individual understood as spirit.

x⁵ A 97   n.d., 1852

« 2046 "The Individual" ["den Enkelte"]

The implication, although I do not claim to have actualized it.

It is one thing to introduce a new doctrine into the world; it is something else to appropriate a given doctrine personally in inward deepening.

In the first case disciples may be accepted, a party organized, because otherwise it could easily happen that the doctrine, with the teacher gone, would not get out into the world at all.

It is entirely different with personal appropriation of a given doctrine in inward deepening. Here it is essential that disciples not be accepted or a party organized, because doing so inevitably weakens personal appropriation; here what counts is to work as an individual, to stand as a single individual, to be sacrificed as a single individual.

The task of personal appropriation is the only one there can be any question about in "Christendom," for everyone, to be sure, is acquainted with the doctrine.

Christianity is the unconditioned. The unconditioned can be unconditionally expressed in only one way: by being sacrificed.

This is the meaning of "the single individual." It is the sacrifice or the sacrificed which is needed time and again in order to appropriate the given doctrine personally.

As soon as such a single individual works toward organizing a party instead of sticking to being a single individual, he removes himself farther and farther from the very thing he should be used for. He does not come to express unconditionally the relationship to the unconditioned but gains external power by way of numerical extension and his ideas soon become garbled just as do the ideas to which he wants to be related *qua* corrective—for the numerical is the very thing which tramples upon the unconditioned.

But to give up organizing a party—good night!—no one wants to do that. "Would I be so selfish"—to want to be sacrificed? O you liars and hypocrites with all your talk about wanting to organize a party out of love for mankind. No, you want to form a party in order to get overt or external power, and you know very well that you thereby avoid the martyrdom of laughter and all other kinds.

The idea and the role of the single individual is the critical point in the conception of Christianity. "Christendom" is the situation; the doctrine is sufficiently proclaimed; personal appropriation is the task, by way of "the single individual," the sacrificed one—as soon as it all becomes a party it goes automatically by rote again in a very short time.

Understood in this way the single individual is the extraordinary [*Extraordinaire*]. He understands himself and his action in relation to God; this, he says—and happily it is so—every single person can do; but on the other hand I do not admit on any account that it is done, for my particular task is personal appropriation and precisely because most men have their Christianity seventeenth hand, for that very reason it is my task to work toward personal appropriation. But now if I attract followers and encourage mimicking [*Efterabelsen*]—well, then we are back where we started.

O, but it is hard to persevere in standing alone. Yet this is the task. Think of Luther, that magnificent man, and yet what confusion has come about through him because he could not forbear founding a party. He was a single individual, an extraordinary. His task was personal appropriation in inward deepening, for he did not have a new doctrine to bring into the world, since Christianity was already present, but personal appropriation was what was needed—and then instead of becoming a martyr himself he formed a party and in a very short time Lutheranism was externality and rote as much as Catholicism ever was.

But, as mentioned, by forming a party we avoid all kinds of martyrdom. Formerly martydom always meant blood-martyrs; nowadays we perhaps can also think of the martrydom of laughter. In a rational age the martyrdom of laughter is just what can be expected for wanting to be "the single individual." Fear of men dominates men; no one dares to be himself; everyone in every situation is hiding in "togetherness." And is it not true, in order if possible to help put a halt to this, is it not true that a number of us ought to get together?

x^5 A 121   *n.d.*, 1853

« 2047 *The Single Individual* {den Enkelte]—*Numbers*

No one wants to be that strenuous being—the single individual. But men everywhere are in the service of that deceitful substitute—a group. Let's a few of us join together, form a group—then we can surely do something. This is the most profound demoralization of the human race.[605]

XI^1 A 36   *n.d.*, 1854

« 2048 *Idea—Individual—Specimen*
Also a Word about Myself

As nature has formed the more sensitive organs in such a way that they do not come into immediate contact with objects but are shielded, because otherwise the organs would be destroyed, so ordinary men cannot bear to relate themselves directly to the idea. [*In margin:* Yet it must be remembered that according to Christianity everyone can be the single individual.]

Therefore they relate themselves to the idea only indirectly or mediately, through a tradition, through others, whether by twos or tens or millions. Thus their lives do not come into relation to the idea. Imagining themselves related to the idea, they are very brief about it—and now they have all the better opportunity to occupy their time with finite things, but of course the person who relates himself immediately or directly to the idea thereby has enough to do and usually misses out on the finite.

This is what it is to be a specimen or copy [*Exemplar*], and to be a specimen is the easiest kind of life, a life shielded against direct relationship to the idea, which would be as fatal as sunstroke.

The individual [*Individet*] relates himself to the idea.

In the New Testament to be a Christian is presented in such a way that one cannot be a specimen but must be an individual—"Christendom" has only specimens. [*In margin:* But, according to the New Testament, everyone can be the single individual (*den Enkelte*). Therefore Christianity ought to be proclaimed to "all": Come unto me "all," go out and proclaim to "all nations."]

As far as I am concerned, it is my contemporaries who have made me properly aware of this, have educated me. I have not really collided with my generation, for *The Corsair*[606] was not the public opinion throughout the country. Yet the country is so without character that I have been treated as if I had made myself into something superhuman by being "the single individual" in contrast to the generation. This is not my fault. But on the other hand it has been an education for me.

But this is the way every age will educate the very one who wants to deal with the age. It all looks so nice; indeed, they are so many—what can he achieve against them. And yet, here it is again—he provides the counterpressure.

XI¹ A 42   n.d., 1854

« 2049 *The Economy of Existence*

Think of a clever mother. She has a child, and this child of hers, like all other children, likes very much to hear stories. Now the mother can tell stories, but not more than a half dozen or so.

If the child with heroic stubbornness were able to persist one whole day in wanting to hear stories, this would be enough to put the mother in a dilemma, for she would run out of stories.

Therefore the art of the mother consists in distracting the child. For instance, she has just told a story. The child wants "to hear more." But instead the mother says, for example: Look, Louis, look—there's a queer fly buzzing around. This alters the situation. Now Louis has to go. Perhaps he falls down, bumps himself, etc. The mother has a thousand distractions like that, and Louis is positive that mother is inexhaustible when it comes to stories.

So it is with providence or with existence [*Tilværelsen*] in relation to the idea.

All existence is structured [*lagt an*] very economically—and right here is the divine, even though it also indicates how providence regards us as children. It is structured in such a way that there is enough idea to be adequate for an individual's entire life, even if he could maintain an exclusive interest in the idea according to the highest possible standards. But if a new individual in the following generation could begin where the other left off and be quite as completely and exclusively interested in the idea, existence would then go bankrupt.

Therefore the art of existence consists in fooling little Louis. There is a war going on in Europe for a half dozen years, for example; every day the telegraph dispatcher is sending out etc. etc. etc. etc.—but seen from the vantage of the idea this is of no significance whatsoever, and the idea does not enter the world this way at all—but little Louis gets something else to think about. With regard to what touches the idea—God's relationship to man and man's relationship to God—we learn absolutely nothing by way of a European war.

But how rarely is there even one person so developed that the numerical does not exercise its power over him. Thus the millions live and the millions die; they are just statistics and the statistical is their horizon, their everything, which means that they are merely specimens [Exemplarer].

And Christianity, which—in divine love—wants to make every human being into an individual [Individ], this we have messily humanized into the very opposite.

But no wonder, because to become an individual involves such frightful torments that men prefer to decline with thanks. This I know from my own experience.[606] It is in part deep inner torment, but nevertheless the wretchedness and the wretched, bestial behavior of contemporaries toward me have forced me to be aware. It is with my contemporaries as with Joseph's brothers: They meant it for evil, but God has turned it to good.

XI[1] A 60   n.d., 1854

« 2050 *The Single Individual* {den **Enkelte**}
—*the Crowd, Statistics*

"The single individual" is a spiritual definition of being a human being; the crowd, the many, the statistical or numerical is an animal definition of being a human being.

The operation is, of course, very simple. The single individual ranks *qua* spirit according to the extent he can endure, wholly unchanged, having statistics thrown at him (something like being splashed with mud by street urchins).

The distinction of the God-man means absolutely inalterably to be the single individual, without the change of a letter or an expression, unconditionally, absolutely unconditionally in opposition to the countless millions of the whole race. —Even the apostle needs a few who agree with him.

xı¹ A 81   *n.d.*, 1854

« 2051 *The Single Individual* {den Enkelte}
    —Statistics—God's Sovereignty

No one wants to be the single individual; everyone shrinks away from the strenuous effort.

But this is not the only reason no one wants to be the single individual; there is also a fear of the envy and opposition of the environment. It takes only ten people joined together to make an abstraction, and envy is not directed against an abstraction. "Number" makes us all alike. Ten names joined together have a basically anonymous effect, and the anonymous does not excite envy.

But God is also a sovereign, and when he wills to express his sovereignty he humbles human sovereignty—and therefore he uses only a single individual.

To be such a single individual is then in a certain sense inevitably the most eminent distinction for a human being, but since it is "distinction" in the highest sphere, where everything is paradoxical, it is recognizable by the negative—to be the distinguished one in this way means to be sacrificed.

xı¹ A 82   *n.d.*, 1854

« 2052

Christianity does not join men together—no, it separates them—in order to unite every single individual with God. And when a person has become such that he can belong to God, he has died away from that which joins men.

xı¹ A 96   *n.d.*, 1854

« 2053 *Hypocrisy*

is as inseparable from being a man as sliminess from being a fish.

Thus it is disturbing and disgusting to see the hypocritical way in which we continually excuse ourselves from every effort by changing the ideal demand.

"If a person does the good out of fear of eternal punishment," so it goes, "then it is, for all that, not the good"—*ergo, ergo*, he can just as well do the evil. Unconditionally to renounce everything, unconditionally, is humanly impossible, or no human has ever done this perfectly; after all, man is only relative—*ergo, ergo*, he can just as well hanker, if possible, for everything! No one was ever perfect, absolutely perfect—*ergo, ergo*, one might just as well be a scoundrel.

Disgusting! Would it not be disgusting, too, if one were to say to a child: If you are industrious only from fear of punishment, you might just as well be lazy? Or is it not the educator's idea that the punishment is like an aid which is necessary until the child no longer needs punishment.

I shall introduce here a completely different objection which could be made against the Christian infinite demand upon the individual. Does not Christianity make me into an enormous egotist [*Egoist*], or does it not abnormally develop my self-awareness [*Egoitet*] in that by terrifying a man with the most terrible horror it brings him to be concerned solely and only for his own salvation, completely oblivious to the possible fraility and imperfection of everybody else? It is easy to see that if a man is going to strive earnestly for the unconditioned and is at all earnest about it, he will soon be living in a circle of people who, comparatively, are far behind him; but then is it not as if Christianity would make him into an enormous egotist when it forbids him to delay by wanting to help them and, on the contrary, always orders him further and further out, all of which perplexes his contemporaries, perhaps even prompts them to kill him, so that they bring the greatest possible guilt upon themselves?

To this one must answer: "The truth" cannot act in any other way. If anyone out of arrogance or pride presumes to pursue this game with the weaker ones—well, this becomes his responsibility. But if that which determines him is concern for the salvation of his soul, then he bears no responsibility, then the responsibility rests upon Christianity, upon providence, who will also guide everything for the best.

XI[1] A 148   *n.d.,* 1854

« 2054 *"Christendom"—the Savior of the World*

If someone in this country, someone born in this country of Christian parents, baptized as a child, confirmed—if he earnestly got the idea of raising in earnest the question whether or not he is a Christian, the impression this would make on everybody would be such that they *bona fide* would think the man was nearly crazy.

With this alone I prove that Christianity no longer exists, at least not in "Christendom," and all this talk about a Christian nation is an abominable lie—this society of Christians who have no notion of what it means to be Christian.

New Testament Christianity has been completely altered.

In the New Testament Christ appears addressing men, inviting all, and saying to every single individual: Do you want to be saved. Now, however, we have concocted the nonsensical dogma that Christ saves the race. This is balderdash. If I may say so, even if Christ had wanted this he would not have achieved it. "Race" is a category of corruption and to be saved means to be saved out of the race. Through the race I can belong to the corrupted race, but neither can I be saved by virtue of the race nor, if I am saved, can I be saved into the race.

But we have managed to make being a Christian almost synonymous with being a human being. We are not far from assuming that Christians breed Christians. The category of race has been applied so extensively that individuals have been debased to copies or specimens [Exemplarer], and thus the way has been opened for a life of earthly lust and enjoyment, which specimens are capable of having.

Very likely the theory of Christ as Savior of the race is related to the abolition of the pathos of gratitude for one's salvation. Originally the individual [Individet] and the single individual [den Enkelte] understood that his salvation had cost Jesus life and death. What pathos! His gratitude did not rest until in gratitude he had brought his own life as an offering. But when the salvation turnover occurs in such enormous blocks—the whole race, these millions and millions—this page in the book probably drops out, and it counts up to quite a bit if every one of them just says thanks en passant. In place of that Christian pathos there is something analogous to a contribution list for a few shillings or crowns.

This is utter nonsense. And those confounded preachers who exploit this in order to get 1,000 jobs lined up and to be rare, earnest Christians at a bargain price!

O, if only this could be rooted out of men! The security of belonging to a Christian nation where we are all Christians is very seductive to sensate men. Christianly, of course, this security is "like a house built on thin ice,"[607] but men are not awakened by that.

XI[1] A 168   n.d., 1854

« 2055 *The Infinite Abundance of Existence*

Most men would despair if they were told how enormously abundant existence [Tilværelsen] is, that one human being, just one human being, is enough, is the whole; here the greatest events are possible.

Numbers mean—and this is a consequence of numbers—that a European war is an event. 100,000 millions amount to something—but a single individual is nothing.

XI¹ A 175   *n.d.*, 1854

« 2056 *An Alarming Note*

Those three thousand who were added *en masse* to the congregation on Pentecost—is there not something dubious here at the very beginning? Should the apostles not have had misgivings about the appropriateness of Christian conversions by the thousands *auf einmal?* Has not something human happened to the apostles, so that, remembering all too vividly their despair over Christ's death when everything was lost and now overwhelmed with joy over the effect they have brought about, they forgot what Christianity really is, forgot that if true imitation [*Efterfølgelsen*] is Christianity, such an enormous conquest as three thousand at one time will not do?

It is very difficult, because there is a curious meeting of two thoughts, something like the meeting of two persons in a bottleneck where they cannot pass each other. In Christ Christianity has the orientation of intensity, that is, it is the pure intensity. The apostles' task seems to be oriented toward extensity, the more extensity the better. But to the degree that intensity is accentuated, extensity is diminished and—yet it was surely true Christianity the apostles were to spread.

In Christ Christianity is the single individual [*den Enkelte*]; here is the one and only single individual. In the apostle there is at once—community.* But in this way Christianity is transposed into an entirely different conceptual sphere. This concept has been the ruination of Christendom. This concept is responsible for the confusion that whole states, countries, nations, kingdoms are Christian.

XI¹ A 189   *n.d.*, 1854

« 2057

* *In margin of 2056* (XI¹ A 189):
Then there is the question whether the principle of hating oneself, which belongs to Christianity, is not so asocial that it cannot constitute community. In any case we can get some idea from this about what nonsense this is about state churches, folk churches, and Christian countries.

XI¹ A 190   *n.d.*

« 2058 *That Christianity Does Not Exist, since There*
        Are No Christians—Christianity Seems to
        Have Been Abolished[608]

To have to hold fast to this—to be saved as an individual [*Enkelt*] in contrast to a whole world which is eternally lost, in contrast to the nation to which one belongs, in contrast to all—this is such an immense exertion that only the most terrible fear and trembling and the most terrible pressure of passion can hold a person at that point. —Seen from another side it is also extremely aristocratic to be the single individual [*den Enkelt*] to such a degree.

So things soon slacken off in Christendom. The individual [*Individet*] can no longer hold himself at that point; he wishes a certainty apart from this terrible exertion—here is the root of the misconceived faith in an election of grace, that you are saved by the election of grace and there can be no talk about exertion.

Furthermore, the individual cannot maintain an aristocracy face to face with others; it can even be dangerous—from this comes the misconceived use of grace, whereby the charge of aristocracy is avoided, because if everything is grace, I of course can do nothing about it (if one really could do something about it, as if it were a person's own effort, then mediocrity would not tolerate this aristocracy in him).

Finally, the individual also feels a need to be free—to a certain degree, at least—from the tension of being the only one saved, the single one saved. It is far more *gemütlich* and sensately dependable when there are more, many who are saved, far more dependable to see oneself surrounded by the co-saved than this tension of being on the other side, when the others are lost. Thus little by little the contrast disappears—just about all of us are saved.

Finally mediocrity rises up as one man: If it is by grace alone and only by grace, then we are indeed all saved. And now life is *gemütlich* and worth living.

Christianity begins this way: one is saved, perhaps only one among millions, one in the whole world. Nowadays we have: all of us are saved, the cat and dog, too, perhaps—and this is the same teaching which in the New Testament is Christianity!

XI[1] A 260   *n.d.*, 1854

« 2059 *The Human Race*

Just as there are only specimens [*Exemplarer*] and no individuals

[*Individer*] in every other animal species (that is, each particular one is a specimen and the species), there is also another difference between the human race and every animal species—the ultimate relationship between specimens is never such that there are some specimens whose destiny it is to be sacrificed for the others.

This is the case only with the human race.

And these sacrifices who are sacrificed for the others are different from ordinary men by a whole quality (in no animal species is there anything analogous to this, that one specimen is a whole quality different from others)—actually they are men of spirit. Yet these men of spirit do not begin proudly feeling their qualitative difference. No, the race repudiates them in one way or another, and precisely in this way they are helped through suffering to discover their distinctiveness.

xi¹ A 272   *n.d.*, 1854

« 2060 *The Lack of Character in Our Time*

Part of the lack of character is the modern wretched invention of treating difference of opinion as madness.

To be able to conceive of difference of opinion as a crime, as guilt (as in the Middle Ages), there must be character enough to have an opinion. But this we do not have. Therefore we cravenly pounce on the device of getting the other regarded as insane. Then we play the hypocrite and congratulate ourselves for not being cruel, intolerant, tyrannical—We don't have him executed, do we? Of course not, we are human! We expect to get the common man in on this, too, for since he has so few concepts he is more inclined to regard any heterogeneity as madness—the ordinary person, who is just as willing to stick by someone who is persecuted and slain as he is willing to go along and assume that someone is crazy.

The Middle Ages was far ahead; it still treated those who actually were insane, mentally, as criminals.

xi¹ A 310   *n.d.*, 1854

« 2061 *Homogeneity—Heterogeneity*

The tyrannizing, leveling world of time present is always trying to change everything into homogeneity so that all become mere numbers, specimens.

History, on the other hand, is interested only in what has preserved itself in heterogeneity within its own period, without, however, automatically regarding every such heterogeneity as the truth

The world of time present presumably considers a change to homogeneity as ennoblement, cultivation; the truth is that it consumes the individuals, wastes them.

XI¹ A 319   *n.d.*, 1854

« 2062

In margin of 2061 (XI¹ A 319):

When the individual [*Individet*] has become entirely homogeneous with his world of time present, assimilated, as we say of the digestive process, the age has eaten him, he is as though lost, wasted. Time, the world of time present, tends to change everything into waste or waste gas (*ad modum Brindt*).

XI¹ A 320   *n.d.*

« 2063 *Christianly, Association Is a Swindle*

Let's form an association in order to work on behalf of Christianity, we say. And this is supposed to be taken for true Christian zeal!

Christianity is of another mind and knows very well that this is a swindle, since by association Christianity is not advanced (the larger the number, the smaller the advance) but is weakened.

Christianity always needs only one, but that one exerts himself to the uttermost. This, however, is what we men want to get rid of. Dishonestly and trickily we turn the matter so as to make it appear that true Christian zeal means: to form an association, the more the better.

XI¹ A 368   *n.d.*, 1854

« 2064

In margin of 2063 (XI¹ A 368):

A result of forming an association is that the genuinely Christian collisions (which we men fear most to suffer at the hands of men) disappear. That is why we hear: Let us form an association—in Christian zeal and unity!!!—to work for Christianity.

XI¹ A 369   *n.d.*

« 2065 *The Single Individual* {den Enkelte}—*the Crowd*

The category of the spirit is: the single individual. The animal category is: numbers, the crowd.

Christianity is spirit and consequently relates itself to the category of the single individual.

To work for Christianity aided by the crowd and oriented to the crowd means to shift spirit over into the animal category.

Yet this is the gist of all the effort of Christendom. How abominable this lying disposition which makes this out to be Christian zeal, that we are to be praised and extolled for Christian zeal on the basis of the greater numbers we can get to join together to work for Christianity (as it is called)—whereas the effect actually tends toward watering down and abolishing Christianity.

The common man cannot see this, but those vipers, the jobholding clergy, they ought to be able to see this much.

XI[1] A 370   n.d., 1854

« 2066 *Christianity's Law for Existence*

The law (which again is grace) which Christ by having lived has posited as the condition for being human is: Involve yourself as an individual [*Enkelt*] with God; it makes no difference whether you are clever or simple, highly endowed or poorly endowed; involve yourself as a single individual with God (O, divine grace, to want to have anything to do with a single individual human being, with each and every individual), dare as an individual to involve yourself with him, he will take good care of everything as far as your capacities and possibilities are concerned.

Therefore involve yourself with God *first*; not with "the others" first.

But the trouble is that for poor man there is a terrible anxiety in living and existence [*Tilværelsen*]. He becomes afraid—dares not involve himself with God first. The animal in him is victorious; he reflects: The smartest thing to do is to be like the others.

Every life whose first principle is *like the others* is a wasted life, and since, from the Christian point of view, it happens because of guilt, it is a lost life.

These millions whose law of existence is: First of all like the others —this mass of mimickers [*Efterabelser*]—in a sensate way they appear to be something, something big, something enormously powerful. And in a sensate way this is so, but viewed ideally this mass, these millions, are a zero, less than zero, are wasted, lost lives.

A sparrow, a fly, a poisonous insect is an object of God's concern, for it is not a wasted or lost life. But the mass of mimickers are wasted lives. God having been merciful to men, having demonstrated his grace to the point of being willing to involve himself with every individual— and since grace is pertinent to this, he must in fact require this—and if men then prefer to be like the others, this amounts to high treason against God. The mass of mimickers are guilty of high treason. The punishment is to be ignored by God.

From a Christian point of view, all didacticism is a wasted, lost existence. Assistant professors can get smarter and smarter at falsifying, but it is no use; it is still a wasted life.

To be like the others is the law for all worldly temporal shrewdness.

It is this shrewdness which, from a Christian point of view, is so shrewd that it cheats itself out of eternity.

*   *

Alas, I write this in sadness. Myself unhappy, I loved men and the human crowd with melancholy sympathy. Their brutishness to me forced me (that I might endure it) more and more to involve myself with God.

The result is that undoubtedly I have come to know what Christianity is; but it pains me, this truth.

xı¹ A 384   *n.d.*, 1854

2067 *Being Alone*

The criterion of a man is: how long or how far can he endure being alone without the understanding of others.

The person who in the decisions of eternity can endure being alone for a whole lifetime is poles apart from the infant, from the social mixer, which are the animal definition of what it is to be human.

xı¹ A 415   *n.d.*, 1854

« 2068 *"Two Women Will Be Grinding at the Well; One Is Taken and One Is Left," etc.*[609]

What terrible separation and isolation! How different from paganism and Judaism, in which, just the opposite, the family, the city, the province, and the country share (participate) in the individual, so that, for example, when someone distinguishes himself, immediately the family, the city, the province, the country participate in his fame! Christianity means the unconditional separation of the individual; paganism and Judaism are, inversely, domination by the categories of race and generation.

But of course in Christendom everything is according to pagan or Jewish pattern; in Christendom a man is Christian by being in a family, even by being a distant relative of someone who is Christian. Yes, one is a Christian even though a whole generation removed from Christian ancestors—that is, one is a Christian in a way by which it is impossible to be a Christian.

The apostle says that faith comes by hearing, but in this way one is Christian by hearsay!

XI¹ A 421   n.d., 1854

« 2069 *The Proportions of Existence*

are so enormous that they seem calculated to deceive.

The distances in the universe are so enormous that the gigantic heavenly bodies look like dots—the child, nations in their childhood, actually believe that they are.

In relation to the numerical, it is also this way—the centuries and millions and millions of millions appear deceptively as if they were something, and then it all revolves around some very few individuals.

Yet with respect to the numerical, men always remain children, and there are only very few individuals who understand the reverse, just as with respect to the stars (although they do think the dots are the large bodies): these trillions look as if they were something and yet all revolves around a very few intensive points.

XI¹ A 441   n.d., 1854

« 2070 *You Shall Be the First*

Here it remains; God does not change the terms. Viewed from another side, thank him, O thank him because, tired of letting himself be mocked, he says: Does no one of you want to be first—well, then, you shall be the first. Bear in mind that it was worse for those who were permitted to mock him in this way, that they deluded themselves frightfully.

You shall be the first. Along with being the first comes—quite simply —the collisions and spiritual trials which the New Testament predicts (and which are completely removed from Christianity): you will perhaps be ridiculed by the others, persecuted, perhaps also put to death—but then also, too, comes the blessedness which is predicted in the New Testament.

It is a perennial lie that the apostles were sent out to catch herring; they were sent out to catch whales. You know, of course, that in a frightfully tragic manner confusion entered the company of angels; God in heaven desired to complete the number. The terms were offered to man in Christianity, to every man, unconditionally, every, every, every man. Would that I had a thousand voices and could shout this to the whole world—to every man. Do you want to, or do you not? But this much you yourself must be able to see—that millions of herring cannot be used to fill the place of an angel.

How infamously Christianity has been falsified, and how nauseating that men have not merely taken all the earthly profit to be had in order to be teachers of Christianity but have almost allowed themselves to be worshiped—dreadful refinement—as if they were intermediary authorities.

XI¹ A 455   n.d., 1854

« 2071 *Species—Individual* {Individ}

In every animal species, the type is higher, is the ideal; the copy or specimen [*Exemplaret*] is always an appearing and a disappearing. The type is higher; the specimen is lower.

Only in the human species, because of Christianity, is there another order: the individual is higher than the species.

But to be an individual in this way is of course very demanding; therefore everything human tends toward getting this relationship changed so that the species becomes higher than the indivdual, that is, the individual becomes a specimen, which means that we are animals. But of course to be animal is more comfortable; then one is freed entirely from those strenuous efforts which certainly must appear to people nowadays to be fantastic madness—relating oneself personally to God, thinking that one is tested by God.

XI¹ A 485   n.d., 1854

« 2072 *Judaism—Christianity*

In Judaism God is related to the "nation."

The advance is to be related to the individual [*Individ*]. Christ is the prototype [*Forbilledet*]. The Jews take offense at this. It is also evident that Christianity is inversely related to the numerical, and generally advances are made in a direction opposite to the numerical.

XI¹ A 490   n.d., 1854

« 2073 *The Significance of Cholera*[610]

is in its tendency to train men to be single individuals [*Enkelte*], something neither war nor any other calamity does—they herd men together instead. But the plague disperses into single individuals and teaches them, physically, that they are single individuals.

XI¹ A 506   n.d., 1854

« 2074 *Christianity—Christendom*
      God—Man

This is how the matter stands—I may as well repeat it once again. According to Christianity, salvation means to become spirit, to be saved out of the race, but to become spirit means to become the single individual [den Enkelte]; isolation is a conditio sine qua non, an indispensable condition.

This word about a salvation, a salvation for men, is barely heard before the race, if I may put it this way, replies: "Superb! Now let us join together (there it is!) so that united (abracadabra!) we may seek this highest good."

But, as mentioned elsewhere [i.e., XI^1 A 248], simply by joining together we defend ourselves against God, the idea, the unconditioned, the ideal—and thus also against "salvation."

So a countless throng joins together—and thereby we are perfectly protected against Christianity. And this is "Christendom."

Since there is a qualitative difference between God and man, it obviously is difficult for them to come to an understanding with one another, even with the best intentions on man's side. And the tragedy is that man always counters with numbers.

If (to speak almost playfully about what has cost me suffering enough, which I still do not regret), if God in heaven opened his window and said: I need a man, get me a man—the generation would say: We will make the necessary arrangements at once, collect a few hundred thousand men and women so that you can have as many people as you want. —But God asked for one person. And "man" cannot get this into his head, that one human being is more than millions, that getting millions means getting less.

This belief in millions is eradicated from men only with the greatest difficulty since it is connected with our animal qualifications. Everyone in whom the animal nature is dominant believes wholeheartedly that millions are more than one, but spirit is the very opposite, believing that one is more than millions, but that everyone can be the single one.

Everyone in whom the animal nature is dominant has an abiding belief in being more when he has a family, and what a family is on a small scale the millions are on a large scale, a family. But the point is apparent even in a small setting. For example, if the question has to do with working for an idea, the one who says, "Yes, I am willing, but not just I alone but my whole family!" is not saying the most. No, the one who says the most is the one who says: "I am at your service, I am just a single person." For a single person in relation to an idea is more than a man with a family. But the dominance of the category of race is in the very language we use. This is why the one who said less—"Not only I but my family, too!"—says "not only"; consequently we expect something more in what follows, and yet this is less, because the family subtracts. The one who said "only"—"I am only a single person"—says more, and yet it would be less if he included his family.

XI¹ A 518   n.d., 1854

« 2075 *The* "I"

Generally much is said about every man's being an egotist, wanting his own *I*, asserting himself, etc. This no doubt is true, particularly with reference to everything below him, where he thinks he is able to dominate.

But upwards it is not so. There no one wants to be *I*. Face to face with a power, the *I* pulls in its antennae and becomes third person [*in margin*: or the *I* becoming third person is like a sharp instrument whose point or edge is blunted when it strikes something hard]; face to face with contemporaries no one wants to be *I* but pulls in his antennae and becomes third person, "the public," "they."

And now to have to be *I*, face to face with existence [*Tilværelsen*] itself, bearing all its weight—no thanks, no one wants that.

But it is impossible to be involved with God without enduring the weight of this pressure of being *I*, because God has placed himself at a distance from man and yet in another sense he is the closest of all, and to be a Christian without being involved with God is surely quite impossible.

Yet the thousands live on without having become *I* or as truncated *I*'s, truncated to the third person. They fill their lives with all sorts of things, imagine that they are really involved with God, flatter themselves that they have not ventured farther out because they are so humble. What befuddlement! The first condition for getting straightened out is to see that this notion about humility is rubbish, that one is dragging his feet because of weakness, thin skin, and cowardice. It is untrue, and no human being has ever been genuinely too humble to aspire to the highest, especially the highest which God commands under the liability of eternal punishment. No, my friend, it is self-deception. But you want to be free from all dangers and therefore are the very sort of person who drags his feet out of so-called humility; you are very greedy when you are able to get in touch with someone who has ventured way out, so greedy to get ideas, impressions, expressions, etc.—yet without the dangers.

XI¹ A 533   n.d., 1854

« 2076 *Individual Differences*

In order to be assisted toward the decisive victory one person needs to be encouraged by small victories; another is strengthened by defeat.

XI[1] A 576   n.d., 1854

« 2077 *Christendom*

could be regarded as sheer misunderstanding, a wrong turn which has established the historical in place of the primitive [*det Primitive*]. This historical approach has now become an enormous, long rigmarole; just as in certain fairy tales, all that has preceded must be reeled off again with every new part.

As I have often pointed out, we shudder at the strenuousness of having to be the primitive *I*—and so we become third person and become tranquilized in the historical and trace the historical.

But is it possible to become immortal in third person or by virtue of the history about others who have become immortal?

XI[1] 587   n.d., 1854

« 2078 *Divine Police-precaution*

There are people who have the fortunate gift of managing successfully with all men (and to be sure, it usually goes along with their insignificance)—they have no sharp edges, etc.

Such people God never uses. If he is going to use such a person he first of all crosses up his life in such a way that he is thoroughly misunderstood by men. The human bite is of real value to anyone who is going to be involved with God. God is no friend of the cozy human crowd—no, the one he is going to use is promptly blocked off.

What originally has an intrinsic significance God generally does not need to block off later, for the intrinsic significance in its original state is generally so differentiated from what is common that its becoming misunderstood by men seems almost intentional.

This is police-precaution, but it also is love, yes, almost like falling in love. This is what is done in a love affair when a superior man falls in love with a girl who has the happy gift of living on the best of terms with a host of cousins and cousins—he immediately crosses up the relationship for her and deliberately causes a misunderstanding to prevent the beloved from becoming silly.

As far as I am concerned, the act of separating out, whereby a person is singled out, happened to me, I believe, as early as birth. With me isolation seems to be congenital, and I have instinctively tended to act accordingly. Therefore my isolation is not something God may undertake with an older person. No, my isolation came early and in a sense was my own doing.

$$\text{XI}^2 \text{ A } 69 \quad n.d., 1854$$

« 2079 *A Sense for Majesty*

One can literally say that no man will go very far if he does not have an innate, decisive sense for majesty.

But these individualities [*Individualiteter*] so equipped—who can be said to be *erectioris ingenii* (for just as man's erect walk is his advantage over the animal, so such a person's sense for majesty is an erectness which distinguishes him from ordinary men just as much as walking erect distinguishes man from the animal)—can be divided into two classes.

The one class are covetous, want to be majesty themselves. Even if the grandest maximum is reached, this nevertheless can be only a limited majesty, since the individual himself has to supply it. Meanwhile the common man regards this kind of aspiration as utterly impractical (in the opinion of the common man the law for the impractical always is to stake everything on one thing). Only in the rare case that this succeeds is it admired as a kind of higher practicality, one he cannot quite understand.

The other group are suffering; themselves suffering they want only to manifest majesty, admiring or—here it becomes the highest possible —blessedly worshipping, to manifest majesty, divine majesty. Here majesty can remain true majesty, for such an individuality certainly will not obstruct majesty by wanting to be it himself; no, he will suffer simply in order to manifest it or, completely forgetting himself, he wills majesty exclusively. Such an existence [*Existents*] is interpreted unconditionally at all times and by all practical people [*Practici*] to be *impractical*; for no matter how one shifts and turns it, and whether or not the individual succeeds in what he wills, it always turns out to be of no profit, nothing finite comes of it—and being-in-and-for-itself is and remains, according to the unanimous testimony of all practical people, "unconditionally impractical." "So there is still something, after all, which is unconditional. That is good. I was afraid that practicality [*Praktiskheden*] would have completely abolished the unconditional—by also getting involved with it to a certain degree."

The whole practical world along with its millions and its practices is immersed in *interest*; how could it then have any concept of or respect for uninterestedness, disinterestedness, let alone—if we go up the scale—that disinterestedness is even positively expressed (consequently not merely negatively by not wanting to have any profit) by willing to suffer.

XI² A 124   n.d., 1854

« 2080 *The Single Individual* {Den Enkelte} *(To Be a Christian)—the Race*

To be qualitatively different from the species to which one belongs, inasmuch as one does indeed belong to a species, and to have to continue in the species—this is the formula for the most intensive anguish, also the most painful collision both autopathetic and sympathetic—and it is also the formula for being Christian.

Let me illuminate this a bit more exactly and tie some observations to it.

Take animals. For the particular specimen [*Exemplaret*], belonging to the species is a comfort, a relief, a satisfaction. If living as a particular, a particular animal, or *qua* man as an individual, may be at all compared with being under a certain pressure (the way the living are indeed under a certain atmospheric pressure), one could say it is the species which helps bear the pressure, or that one is not literally a particular individual but is categorized under an abstraction which, so to speak, alleviates the pressure.

Let me put it this way. There are, to be sure, animal creatures which are so abominable and loathsome that the sight of them disgusts not only men but almost every living thing. Imagine now that such a creature said to the creator, "Why did I become such a loathsome thing? It is a frightful anguish simply to arouse disgust the way I do." The answer to this must be that it came into existence [*blev til*] because its existence [*Tilværelse*] is also a part of everything. But something else must be said: By belonging to a family of the same species, your condition is alleviated. Yes, no doubt this is the way it is—that everything which belongs to a species, by being homogeneous with it, is content; the contentment resides in being homogeneous with its species. The particular cannot have any idea of anything beyond this or of its not being glorious to be like the species to which one belongs. And so the particular is also content with the sight of the many others who belong to the same species.

Consequently the situation would become different and harder if such an animal were absolutely alone, if it were—supposing that such a thing occurred—both the specimen and the species in one. Still it would always have the composure which one has by being homogeneous with one's species and would not have to suffer anything from others of the same species.

But note that here the collisions begin—when within one and the same species there is exhibited a qualitative difference, yet without becoming a new species but having to continue within the species, which then naturally hates and detests this bastard to the bitter end. A bastard! In the animal world also the species from which the bastard is formed detests the bastard. But then it comes again, the bastard then becomes a species by itself and again has the contentment of being homogeneous with its species.

To be a Christian (as this appears in the New Testament) means a qualitative difference from being man, yet within the category of being man.

And this is the most intensive anguish and the most painful collision. In being a Christian (according to the New Testament) the divine is put together with being human in such a way that this composite is qualitatively different from being man, and yet he is man and is to live among men.

Christendom, as is well-known, has solved the collision in the following utterly simple manner: it makes being a Christian into a qualification of the species so that all collisions fall away.

This, of course, is nonsense or swindling. In the New Testament the mark of being Christian is precisely this: qualitative heterogeneity from being man and yet—a man among men, inasmuch as the Christian belongs to the species.

That this is the most anguished suffering is readily to be seen.

That it is the most painful collision both autopathetically and sympathetically is not difficult to see, and it is only the latter I will dwell on.

In everything I have read about conversions, the transitions of becoming a Christian, in none of them, even in the most famous and historical conversions, have I seen the pain in becoming a Christian described, the hesitation exposed, nor the pain which seems to me to be the most valid of all—the pain of sympathy. Is it not inhuman to break with one's species in this way, to become blessed in such a way that others, all others, perhaps become unblessed! For the mirage which is conjured up by getting Christian empires, countries, and states is of course meaningless. No, to become Christian in the sense of the New Testament is actually to be separated eternally from what, humanly speaking, is called humanity—and thereby from men. In the New Testament Christianity (it is not concealed) is enmity to man—this is the way contemporary paganism and Judaism regarded it. It is a life and death struggle and enmity between being God and being man. And just as when two nations make war on each other, the one nation captures some of the other nation's men in order to use them against it, so also the Christian is adopted by God (as the New Testament puts the matter)—and used against men and humanity. It is true that God does it out of love—but it must be remembered that this interpretation does not help the one who does not understand the matter in this way, who is not a Christian, so other men must, according to their view, see in the Christian their deadly enemy, un-man, someone who is qualitatively different from the species yet wants to be within the species.

In order to be loved by men it is necessary that your life express *to a certain degree,* or that your life express *just like the others.* The human is immersed in relativity. If you want to be more egotistic than the others, you are interpreted as being an egotist. But—please note—if you do not want to be just as egotistic as the others, then this becomes again another kind of egotism, for then you are encroaching upon the whole mode of human existence around you in a disturbing way. This is the way we humans live with one another—we make a mutual confession to each other, a silent agreement which we do not discuss further, but we know very well among ourselves that we are all egotists. But let us be reasonable; let everyone have a certain consideration for others and limit his egotism; then we can all lead a more or less happy life here on earth. But egotists we cannot bear, egotists who want to be more egotistical than the rest of us around here—and [we cannot bear] egotists who want to be less egotistical than we all are.

How, then, could we possibly tolerate a Christian with his ideality (which the New Testament also teaches), which is hatred of the world, hatred of himself, hatred of men, hatred of all that in which men have their lives.

But this is not the point at present; I speak of the hesitation about becoming a Christian, the hesitation arising from sympathy, whether it is not unhuman to break with one's species.

I have sought enlightenment about this in vain, have sought in vain a man who has even been aware of this.

Today, of course, it is fruitless to search. Everywhere there are swarms of millions of Christians, who are Christians of course, just like all the others of course—and are begetting more Christians at top speed. One really cannot find enlightenment among them. Their existence as a reply to what I want to know is just as meaningless as if someone who was trying to determine the solvency of "the currency which the bank owns" received for his enlightenment bank notes shipped *en masse* from every direction. What I am seeking is a primitivity [*Primitivitet*]. I call out, as it were, to the world, from the present back through the centuries: Where is the primitivity which primitively vouches for this whole thing, where is the primitivity which has primitively experienced and lived through becoming a Christian as primitively as I can characterize it. If such a one is found, then I must also find this hesitation, this collision, and consequently the answer to what I am asking about.

But I do not find it! I am fast becoming dejected! Even well-known Church fathers—if one looks very closely it really appears as if they, too, are not completely free from this human grandiloquence, talking in stronger expressions about what they have experienced than what literally was the truth.

It is of the nature of true primitivity (and without this it is impossible to become Christian) literally to be alone, alone with God. Only when this is the case can the collision of sympathy properly appear, for then one really gets the species properly on his conscience. But when you look more closely at even the most celebrated conversions to Christianity, you will see that this being alone before God is not taken very strictly. As we talk in daily life about a girl being very much in love and believe that she at most has a sister and a girl friend with whom she talks about her beloved—but in fact she does not in the deepest sense have inwardness—so also is the transition of becoming a Christian. A pagan is converted to Christianity—but he takes his mother with him, perhaps his wife, his children. A pagan is converted to Christianity, but he has friends with whom he talks about this most inward resolution of his inwardness. In this way the collision cannot really appear. In the first place, if a person has confidants in his inward relation to God, one solitary one—his inwardness is lessened 50%. In the second place, the person who takes his beloved along with him when he goes over to Christianity thereby makes it easier for himself to let go of the other men. But Socrates (oh, Socrates, you one and only!)[611]—is it not true that he who really becomes involved with the idea fears most of all to be in error.[612] He therefore seeks in no way to arrange things to avoid collisions, no, no, he probably uses the utmost zeal in seeing to it that the collisions can come. Whoever becomes involved with ideas lets himself be examined by existence [*Tilværelsen*] at once, but he also examines. His examination consists in not wanting to buy at the cheapest possible price, because he understands that all this talk about a cheaper price, in the light of the idea, is nonsense; in the light of the idea there is only one price—the highest. One gets the idea at this price or it amounts to nothing. At the cheaper price one gets bamboozled. The person who wanted to become a Christian and said to himself: I cannot make this transition if I cannot take my beloved along—and then was lucky enough to get her talked into becoming Christian—avoided the true Christian collision and accordingly became Christian "also."

Because the transition in becoming a Christian is not according to the true Christian dimensions, because of this I do not find manifest the truest hesitation about becoming a Christian: whether or not, humanly speaking, I wrong men, both by allowing them to become guilty in hating me, persecuting me, perhaps putting me to death, which must follow with and from becoming a Christian in the New Testament sense (this point H. H. has especially emphasized in his two ethical-religious treatises;[613] and later I have seen it suggested some place by Clement of Alexandria, I believe, noted in my copy of Böhringer[614]), and by eternally separating myself from them, from their ideas, their whole being, for eternity, so that eternal salvation is waiting for me and eternal judgment for them.

He who conducts himself in such a way that he says: In order that I can make the transition to being a Christian more easily, I must have my beloved with me—is actually an egotist opposed to being a man. He who magnanimously loves humanity says—also for the sake of the idea —No, precisely in order to verify this I will keep the beloved away from me, suspended, so that by letting go of the others I also let her go—so that I shall not buy too cheaply this which ought to be the hardest and heaviest. He who in the transition to becoming a Christian takes along with him his beloved and mother and father and the children and some friends and this and that so very easily makes a mistake and does not notice at all that the transition to being Christian is to let go of the human. He takes along with him what for him amounts to the species. This means that such a person neither poses nor answers the problem— and the latter surely comes if the former just occurs.

XI² A 125   *n.d.*, 1854

« 2081 *Christendom*

As a single individual [*Enkelt*], quite literally as a single individual, to relate oneself to God, to turn personally to God—this is the formula for being a Christian.

Christendom goes on with these millions of people who, as mentioned, say, each one of them and mutually to one another: How marvellous that each one of us, absolutely every one of us, can turn personally at any time to the majesty of heaven. This is how they talk, and this is what is preached. But when it comes to a showdown, each one says: The most prudent thing is not to get involved literally as a single individual with that infinite majesty—and therefore the *summa summarum* is that no one at all does it.

On the surface it seems as if this were something which everyone does; indeed, we are all Christians, all these millions, and everyone can do it, and it is a blessing that everyone can do it and at any time of the day, etc. On the surface it seems, therefore, as if personally turning to God as a single individual were such a perpetual and perpetually occuring event every single day that it is almost as meaningless as stopping at the grocery store next door for a few cents worth.

The truth of the matter is somewhat different. The truth of all that chatter about how blessed it is that everyone and so on is that no one does it. And the truth about the assumption that the perpetual occurrence of personal turning *qua* a single individual to God would make it a meaningless event is that if it happens once, it is an event utterly without parallel, more important than both a European war and a world war, a catastrophe which radically moves existence.

Nothing is more certain. Coming close to God brings catastrophe. Quite literally turning *qua* a single individual to God brings about the most intense catastrophe of existence [*Tilværelsens*]. Even a slight but significant approach (consequently a small number, because number subtracts) brings a relative catastrophe. Nothing is more certain. It is as certain as when a chemist, knowing that a drop of a certain substance in a glass of water produces a fizzing, says with certainty when a drop from a bottle is put into a glass of water and there is no fizzing: "It wasn't that particular substance"—so certain is it that to come close to God brings catastrophe.

Yes, so it is—God be praised. Without being a soul-searcher one can nevertheless check that despicable lie by those detestable, repulsive, hypocritical orators who give assurances and assurances. Everyone whose life does not bring relative catastrophe has never even once turned as a single individual to God; it is just as impossible as it is to touch a generator without getting a shock.

This is the way all Christendom distintegrates into rubbish—in a sense it is to be expected. Just as policemen everywhere when they see one of their professional thieves in a crowd promptly say: If he is here, very likely something has been stolen—so one can say: Wherever "man" is, there is foolish talk.

But in one sense, or seen from another side, how infinitely beautiful that it is not the heavenly majesty who has drawn back, has been unwilling to be involved with men. No, he (O infinite love!) stands unchanged by his word, sits and waits in love——and then it still does not happen, but it is man himself who prevents it, it is man who, instead of acting in earnest, changes the whole thing into mutual chattering, sociable chattering, or into playing that one is doing it in earnest—how typical!

It is in truth a terribly hazardous venture to turn as a single individual to God, or even approximately as a single individual or as a single individual to turn approximately to God. What a hazardous venture it is for a single individual literally to do this is shown by the life of the God-man. This life became sheer wretchedness and distress even to the point —which is part of it—of being forsaken by God, who, still unchanged, is love and suffers together in love.

This I have never denied. But why, then, has Christendom not truly reversed itself long ago and made the admission [*Tilstaaelsen*]: We just won't do as Christians. This is the point I am constantly aiming at. In Christendom one *either* goes along rascally shamming as if nothing were the matter, putting on a bold front, undauntedly carrying on as a Christian, although the. *:* is nothing in his existing [*Existeren*] that even slightly resembles what the New Testament calls being Christian but is rather the opposite—*or* he rascally gives the explanation that he is too humble to aspire to anything as lofty as being a disciple, an apostle (words used synonymously by Christ himself), which is a lie, because humility is not in the way but is the very way to becoming an apostle.

The guilt and crime of Christendom is and continues to be placing dishonesty between God and itself so that God has been unable to be involved with men.

XI^2 A 135   *n.d.*, 1854

« 2082 *Human Existence* {Tilværelsen}

There are two poles in being human: the qualification of animality and the qualification of spirit.

The qualification of animality is connected with propagating the species—and in this direction we are all quite willing to be human.

The consequence of this (and this is the tragedy of existence) is that numbers increase in utter disproportion to the number of single individuals [*Enkeltes*] who actually relate themselves to spirit.

However, this still does not accurately indicate the tragedy. No, the disproportion between numbers and the few single individuals who ought to be the counterbalance is so great that an entire middle category, a medium, interposes itself between these few single individuals and the mass of men—the clergy, the teachers of the populace, etc., who make a living by being yes-men, by changing the true into the false.

If those few single individuals who really relate themselves to spirit could only come to have an influence upon the common man, much would be won. But the misfortune of human existence is just this middle category. And the shocking lie is that this middle category gives the appearance of helping men to come closer and closer to the truth. No, the middle category is and continues to be a half-measure and helps the mass of men into half-measures.

XI² A 149   n.d., 1854

« 2083 *Providentia Specialissima*

To be a Christian means to believe in a special providence, not *in abstracto* but *in concreto*. Only the person who has this faith *in concreto* is an individuality [*Individualitet*]; every one else essentially reduces himself to a copy or specimen [*Exemplar*] of his kind, does not have the courage and the humility, is not tormented and helped enough to be an individuality.

XI² A 259   n.d., 1854

« 2084 *One Person*

In the realm of "spirit" one person is more than 10, 10 more than 100, and so on. Numbers subtract; one person is the highest power. This shows how stupid is all this nonsense which in matters of the spirit supposes that increasing the number strengthens; whereas it weakens and only apparently strengthens. But maybe this is what we really want, and in any case we want to avoid the strenuousness of becoming one, and then again we want to hide this by giving our banding together the apparent purpose of strengthening ourselves spiritually.

At all times one person is enough. But the situation is such that centuries may pass before such a one-person appears.

And then when he is dead only one person again is needed to maintain the cause where he left off. But this does not happen. Therefore what has been advanced must be drilled in. And then begins all the nonsense with assistant professors who make a living by delineating, instructing, presenting, and so on. And so the centuries go on in that nonsense—and the constant need is for only one person.

XI² A 275   n.d., 1854

« 2085 *Natural Cunning, Not to Mention Hypocrisy*

There is always talk about the great tasks, also in the domain of Christianity, which confront our time and that we must work together with united effort, etc.

But you, good God, and Christianity need only one human being, if only he is really willing to stand everything.

Aha, but people do not like that—and in order to conceal it, they let on as if it would be even immodest to want to be alone but modest to want to be united—whereby strenuousness is greatly diminished for each individual, yes, and even becomes profitable.

XI^2 A 360   *n.d.*, 1854

« 2086

Is it the infinite which unites men? No, it is the infinite which makes them into individuals [*Enkelte*]. But the finite (earthly concerns, earthly aspirations, etc.) unites them. But this they will not admit, and this is why they always make it appear as if it were love, enthusiasm for the idea, etc. which unites them, while all the time it is self-love and enthusiasm for the finite—the idea, the cause, etc. are just blinds.

XI^2 A 361   *n.d.*, 1854

INFINITE

« 2087

Philosophers usually give with one hand and take away with the other. So it is with Kant, who indeed taught us something about the approximation of the categories to the genuinely true (νοούμενα), but by making it *infinite* he thereby took it all back. Generally this use of the word *infinite* plays a great role in philosophy.——

II A 47   n.d., 1837

« 2088

Just as there is a future (*ins blaue hinein*), an infinite, continued development, which demolishes all more profound speculation—so the contrasting figure is a "prius," a "prae" in regressive infinity, such as the Alexandrian's *pre*-existence[615] of the λόγος, [616] *pre*-existence of matter, *pre*-existence of the soul, *pre*-existence of evil—and just as misleading for all more profound thought.

II A 448   May 29, 1839

« 2089 *To Be Nothing*

The infinite in the guise of being nothing, purely and simply "man" (somewhat like the lily and the bird, which indeed are not something), is in the world the point outside of the world which can move all existence. If the infinite is something, it can move only relatively.

On the other hand, everything which wants primarily to be something in this world is not a moving power but becomes the untrue established order of things, a kind of secular dovetailing, which the established order is, which stretches itself out complacently in earthly security.

X³ A 430   n.d., 1850

INSTRUMENT

« 2090

The heart of the matter is this: what our age needs is upbringing. And to this end the following has happened: God picked out one who also needed upbringing and brought him up *privatissime* in order that he might be able to teach others.

VIII¹ A 43   *n.d.*, 1847

« 2091

What Luther says (somewhere in his sermons)[617] is true—when the courageous and the strong are afraid, then God has to use the weak.

VIII¹ A 676   *n.d.*, 1848

« 2092

It is a special kind of difficulty. To prove properly that a man is God's chosen instrument we attribute to him visions, revelations, dreams, etc.

I do not speak of the apostles, for whom I always keep a separate account.

But the difficulty is that such a man is then presented as a prototype [*Forbillede*]; although he is uniquely situated, he is supposed to be the prototype for those to whom such things do not happen.

But the problem is: did this happen to him because of his advanced piety, or did the fact that it happened give him the courage, the faith, the intrepidity by means of which his piety advanced so greatly? In the first case the revelations and the like are direct superlatives in a striving undertaken directly; in the other case the paradigm is unique and imitation [*Efterfølgelsen*] is not possible.

We have not been alert to the fact that here in the religious realm a differentiation can arise such as that between the genius, the talented— and ordinary men. This easily happens when religion does not have a vigorous ethic.

X² A 578   *n.d.*, 1850

« 2093 *God's Chosen Instruments*

How does God go about getting an instrument for himself among men?

Simply this way—he isolates such a person in such a way that even if he very much wanted to, it would be impossible for him to make himself understandable to others. As soon as there is an understanding with others, then comes the haggling, the knocking off, etc.—but in this frightful isolation the instrument must persevere, continually alone with God— then the price of being a religious man is sure to be set high enough.

God may isolate "the instrument" with sufferings—sufferings in which he cannot make himself understandable to others, sufferings approaching madness. On the other hand "the instrument" may be isolated by extraordinary events, for example, by visions, revelations, and the like. But is he then isolated? Have we not by the millions lived luxuriously on the fact that Paul was called by a revelation? Undeniably! At a distance (especially at the distance of 1,800 years), a revelation is an extremely comfortable thing—but to be personally in the situation of contemporaneity, to be the one among his contemporaries who has had the revelation—this is basically the most absolute isolation. Such a person continually seesaws between the highest—and madness; he cannot really be understood by a third person, understood as having had a revelation.

x^2 A 602   *n.d.*, 1850

« 2094 *The "Highly Trusted"*

One almost always finds that God's highly trusted ones, God's real instruments, in the beginning have vacillated in one way or another, have spoiled, betrayed, ruined the very cause they were supposed to serve. It is as if God were sure of them, and it also helped them not to be tempted easily by meritoriousness. For no matter how humble a person is, even when he merits nothing with respect to the matter entrusted to him by God, how dangerous, how easy it is for a little notion of his own meritoriousness to slip in. Let us suppose that such an individual personally had a lot to reproach himself for, and then he served the cause all the more zealously—it is still dangerous. There is something fortifying in the fact that it is the very cause he damaged in the beginning.

Peter, after all, had damaged the cause of Christianity by denying Christ—and it was Christ he was supposed to serve. The same with Paul, etc.

x^3 A 764   *n.d.*, 1851

« 2095 *Collision*

A man may be very richly and mightily endowed—infinitely grateful to God for this, asking nothing more.

But see, it may seem to him that actually even more has been committed to him, as if he should go higher—perhaps approach the extraordinary [*Overordentlige*]. And he understands that the moment this happens he will plunge to his downfall, humanly speaking—for the extraordinary, yes, it is forever certain that the extraordinary can only get the worst of it in this world.

This is what I call a collision.

Imagine, now, that he is the extraordinary; consequently he will plunge to his downfall, humanly speaking—and simultaneously this becomes the steady power of agonizing spiritual trial [*Anfægtelse*], the thought that now he has wasted everything—and so it will seem to him at every weak moment.

For the extraordinary can have only the pure relationship of spirit out there, hovering in the witness of pure spirit, which negatively means that all direct signs are dialectical or inverted. For the minor proposition of being the extraordinary is this: to get the worst of it in this world. Human directness wants the God-relationship to be recognizable by prosperity, success in all one does, or if one does not succeed, still to hope for the next time. But for the extraordinary there is no such hope, for him there is only this certainty—his downfall. If he does not, humanly speaking, get the worst of it, then he was not in truth the extraordinary

No wonder, then—as is always the case with the extraordinaries, God's instruments—that God has to constrain them to be the extraordinaries—for no one, to be sure, gets involved in such an affair if he can help it.

But just as everything is taken in vain in Christendom, so also the concept of "the extraordinary."

x³ A 766   n.d., 1851

« 2096 *Instruments of God*

Just because it is God's passion, if I dare say it this way, properly to show men their nothingness, for that very reason he always chooses his instruments accordingly, but it is also for this reason very strenuous for the poor (in a certain sense) human being who is to be the instrument.

To put an end to a world culture culminating in extreme refinement, a simple man of the people is used. If I dare say it this way, it satisfies God's passion to use a grain of sand to overturn a world. The divine passion is present right here in the most decisive hatred of everything which even in the remotest manner resembles human probability and calculation. O, but for that very reason it is so terribly strenuous to be the instrument.

God's passion lies within the absurd;[618] where this sign is seen, there God is present. It is as if one heard God's voice there, more terrible in a sense than in the thunder, for the distance of the absurd is greater. It is as if there one heard his voice to men: Look here, you vipers—see, I am present—see, the absurd! A simple man of the people who has learned nothing, absolutely nothing—to overturn world culture! Do you not detect, you vipers, that I am present, I, the Almighty; do you not see the absurd! A frail, tiny, sickly, insignificant man, physically almost as slight as a child, a figure which every animal-man would almost find ridiculous *qua* human being—this one is used for exertions under which giants would collapse—do you not detect, you vipers, that I am present, I, the Almighty, do you not see the absurd! A single individual being—my God, what is a single individual human being—a mere single individual human being, is used to blow the mass, the millions, apart—do you not see, you vipers, that I am present, I, the Almighty; do you not see the absurd!

This is why it is frightfully strenuous for the poor (in a certain sense) man who is to be the instrument.

XI[1] A 268   n.d., 1854

« 2097 *"God's Instruments"*

The excruciating sufferings of these instruments have certain implications.

When God wants to use a person in earnest as his instrument, he promptly raises obstructions before him in such a way that other men are unable to understand him, and they consider what is actually humility and anguish to be pride and arrogance. If, however, they were able to understand it as in truth it is, how in all the world would it then occur to them to mistreat him—no, then they would sympathize with him and admire him—and then God would not get what he needs. He would not get him out far enough, out into the suffering which is double suffering, and where the essentially Christian is.

But this double suffering comes about because what God forces the person to and demands of him requires such utter strenuousness that others, who do not see that it is God who jabs from behind and harasses him so he does not dare do otherwise—the others think that this terribly strenuous effort is arrogance—*ergo*, they cudgel him.

And then when he is dead, then along come—the professors—and they interpret and interpret and live off his sufferings. Woe unto them,[619] woe unto you for digging the graves of the prophets.

XI[1] A 321   *n.d.*, 1854

« 2098   *The Apostle*[620]

To be an apostle must, after all, be such a terrifying, inhuman, suprahuman torture and horror that I really do not blame us human beings for not daring to be one and wishing to be exempted from it—but, as I have often said, I do blame Christendom for the fraudulent turn that has been given to the matter—namely, that we are too humble to aspire to be apostles. This is the lie which has made God turn away from Christendom, which has been God-forsaken for a long time now. If God condescends to involve himself with us to the extent that he did in Christianity, then we at least ought to be straightforward with him. But here as everywhere the swindling nature in man has probably thought something shrewd along these lines: By being straightforward in this way it will no doubt end with our being unable to avoid becoming apostles, and God will get the better of us and refashion us into his own. Therefore we must shut the door tight on this and secure ourselves so that it even becomes a virtue on our part that we do not aspire to become apostles— then we will damned well know that God cannot possibly get hold of us. O, men, you need not be afraid; God scorns you!

But on the whole it is certain that to be an apostle must be torture and horror, total torture and horror.

Constantly in danger, need, difficulty, and suffering—and constantly denied even the slightest in the calculus of probability. But for man the probable is what water is for the fish and air for the birds. To be denied all probability in this way is to be brought to the limit. Well, then, give him at least the right to sink down, tired and exhausted—no, in the very last moment he is roused up——with the aid of a miracle, great God, a miracle! Well, fine, but to be exercised and drilled in this way is a worse torture than to be broken on the wheel or to be stretched on the rack and split open.

So far from being an aid, humanly speaking, the miracle is more a torture—and in such a way that the world around him either treats him as insane or ridicules him, and when he is in the most elementary need, they say: Ah, we don't need to help him; after all, he can do miracles; and yet his life is such that he quite literally may be in the most elementary need and then perhaps, or perhaps not, perhaps a miracle: frightful torture.

This, you see, is the torture! When a man is actually to be God's instrument, an instrument for this infinite will which is God, then God must first of all take his will from him. A fearful operation. Naturally, no one knows better how to give one the third degree than someone who knows everything and has all the power. No doubt physicians, too, are usually present at tortures to estimate how long the one being tortured can hold out short of death; yet there can be an error in judgment and the tortured one may die right then and there—such a thing never happens to one who is omniscient. No doubt there also are means at hand to bolster up the tortured one so that he can take more torturing; nevertheless his strength is weakened every time and death draws nearer—only one who is almighty can give unconditionally new and totally tenacious powers at any moment.

And it is also a torture that despite all the indescribably great sufferings of being God's instrument, the apostle continually has the additional strain of having to thank, thank, thank for this infinite benefaction.

Yet one thing is reserved for the apostle—to be able to love God in truth. Alas, what is this about the rest of us loving God!

We talk about being obliged to love God by virtue of being created by God—and the only one who truly loves God is the apostle, he who in order to become an instrument is absolutely unconditionally shattered by God.

To love God because he has created you is to love yourself. No, if you want to love God in truth, you must show it by gladly, adoringly letting yourself be totally shattered by God in order that he can unconditionally advance his will.

XI^1 A 400   *n.d.,* 1854

« 2099 *All—Nothing*

God creates everything out of nothing—and all God is to use he first turns to nothing.

XI^1 A 491   *n.d.,* 1854

INTENSITY

« 2100 *The Extensive—the Intensive*

When the Talmudic writers describe the millennium and its perfection, they say that one grape will be so large that it will hold God knows how many thousand barrels of juice (I read this somewhere in Corrodi, *Geschichte des Chiliasmus*,[621] pt. 2, I believe). It would appeal to me more to use the form of intensity: even though the grape is no larger than usual the juice would be so refreshing that one grape would be sufficient for a long time.

On the whole there are no doubt grounds for classifying men into those who are characterized by a sense for extensity and those who are characterized by a sense for intensity.

x^4 A 219   *n.d.*, 1851

« 2101 *The Divine Conception of Christianity*
and the Purely Human Conception

These two conceptions are related inversely to one another. The divine conception is oriented to intensity, Christianity intensively condensed in a single human being who, humanly speaking, makes himself and all unhappy for the sake of Christianity. This he calls loving God and men (and this is the divine); it is out of sheer love that he does all this.

The purely human conception centers in this: Let us love one another, yield to one another, accommodate to one another, each one knock off a little—that is, good-night, idea! By means of this conception Christianity *spreads* itself—the extensive.

The ultimate consequence of the divine conception of Christianity will be: Christianity intensively present in a single human being who is slain for his Christianity, ostracized by the entire human race. Christianity was present in Christ this way when he hung on the cross. In that moment Christianity, according to the divine conception, was unconditionally true as it will never be again. —The ultimate consequences of the purely human conception are: all men have become Christians—and Christianity does not exist at all![622]

x^4 A 392   *n.d.*, 1851

« 2102 *The Intensive—the Extensive*

Movement in the direction of intensive deepening of the intensive is truth.

The extensive movement is sophistry. We want to spare ourselves the mounting rigor which is bound up with having to continue existing intensively, and so we choose to influence by extension, and we do this—as they say—out of love for man. Hypocrisy!

I also have observed this; I was once on the point of swinging away from the direction of the intensive in order to grasp the extensive. This much is sure, however—I did not try to pretty up this deviation to look like love of men. No, I intended to make an admission before God that it was because continuing intensively was too rigorous for me. Yet even this is not right. Intensivity is the truth.

x^5 A 26   *n.d.*, 1852

« 2103 *The Point—the Mass*
    The Intensive—the Extensive

A metaphor. The center is a point, the target is a large body; yet the target is to be hit only in the center; to hit the target elsewhere is not to hit the target. Only the intensive actually lives this way. Extensive being is being which essentially is no being. The extensive is inauthentic being; its being consists only in consuming the intensive. Only the intensive has being in itself; the extensive lives upon or by eating or sucking the blood from the intensive(as the shades in the underworld do to the living).

Just as writing in sand or water leaves no trace, so all that existence which does not become spirit disappears without a trace.

XI^1 A 500   October 11, 1854

« 2104 *The Intensive—the Extensive*

Instead of persevering personally to the uttermost in the direction of intensively becoming a Christian (and becoming a Christian stands in relationship to the intensive; what God wants is the intensive), a person gets busy, as they say, influencing others.[623] And this is called love, although, as it often proves to be, it is self-love, a way of sparing oneself. And this is called Christian earnestness, although it is—distraction, a distraction in which he seeks to forget that he himself deserted intensiveness, a distraction by which he seeks to get God to forget that he deserted intensiveness, a substitute whereby he helps himself and seeks to dazzle and deceive God.

XI^2 A 64   *n.d.*, 1854

INTERESTING

« 2105 *An Esthetic Observation*

There is a certain class of men, in part authors (novelists and the like), whose whole life is preoccupied with the relationship to the opposite sex. They consider themselves to be intellectuals and that the real category is the interesting; the time when it was important to be beautiful etc. is past, and yet it is apparent that they are extremely careful about their external appearance, about looking smart, etc. This means that they have a smattering of intellectuality but no faith in it. Although they protest that mind is still the really important thing, they would despair of achieving anything if they were, for example, malformed or were not dressed in the latest fashion. They are dabblers and dilettantes. Saint-Aubain[624] is a good example of the type. It would be of psychological interest to portray the duplicity of this type, and few would understand it. Such characters are to the erotic world what "assistant professors" are in relation to "scientific scholarship;" they imagine that they have "mind," and yet they would be anxious and afraid if they actually came in contact with mind, or they would find it a ridiculous exaggeration.

x^5 A 162   *n.d.*, 1849

« 2106 *Religion Transformed into the Interesting*

An example of this is the interest with which novels, stories, etc. presenting the old-orthodox Jewish home life are read these days—in Germany, for example, *Erzählungen aus Ghetto* (I have read some of them in *Athenæum*;[625] the author, if I am not mistaken is Kompart, and there is a new collection, *Bohemian* or *Polish Jews*, or something like that),[626] and in Denmark, *A Jew*.[627]

It is so deceptive, as if it grew out of religious interest, as if this motivated the author to produce such things. On the contrary, to produce such a work (the author himself is a Jew) is just the opposite of this and must be regarded as utter blasphemy by the orthodox Jew. But the author is interesting. And we read such stories with a certain sadness, just as when we read of our childhood etc. We find a kind of piety in it—but we are no longer children.

458

Soon we will have similar novels dealing with even essentially Christian matters. They will present the quiet piety which perhaps is still to be found here and there in family life. And then we read it and become sad—but we have grown away from such things.

As far as religion is concerned, the law is: This kind of production implies that its time is past; it has become a curiosity.

x⁴ A 220   *n.d.*, 1851

« 2107 *False Interest*

If one takes almost all of our current literature which could be called Jewish stories or novels, in which the old orthodox Jewish life is portrayed, I wonder if anyone would assert that the authors of these books have any religious interest. Or is it not much more a decisive proof that they are concerned least of all with Judaism as religion, since they are able to sit and occupy themselves with it esthetically—yes, the orthodox Jew may very well regard this sort of production as actual impiety. And yet many others would surely look on it differently—that to portray a particular religion certainly means to be occupied with a religion, but if one is occupied with a religion he certainly has a religious interest.

Incidentally, we shall very likely experience the same thing with Christianity. Before we are aware of it, the novelists and poets will be tumbling all over early Christianity, portraying, sketching, all esthetically —the best proof that for them and their readers Christianity no longer exists as religion. And the oafish preachers we have—they, too, will even praise it as a sign of awakening Christian interest.

XI¹ A 160   *n.d.*, 1854

« 2108 *The Interesting—Earnestness*

Nothing is as interesting to the immature person, there is nothing he is as inquisitive about as sufferings, the secret of sufferings—"described," that is. Earnestness means to suffer in person.

XI¹ A 322   *n.d.*, 1854

« 2109

In margin of 2108 (XI¹ A 322):
Sufferings and accounts of sufferings are for adults what ghost stories are for children—something they like to hear about but of which they are afraid.

XI¹ A 323   *n.d.*

INWARDNESS

« 2110 *He Learned from What He Suffered*

This was said of Christ himself—and yet if anyone should be exempted from this, it certainly should be he who knew all things.

This method is the method of *inwardness*.

III C 25   *n.d.*, 1840-41

« 2111

This is how we save religion in our day. We acknowledge with humor the world of actuality (for presumably finitude is sin, but not something to grieve over), and thus we keep it [religion] healthy. We do not enter the monastery but become fools in the world. One is reminded of Christ's words:[628] When you fast (which means nothing else but "When you grieve," for fasting, after all, was simply the external sign of grieving), anoint your head and wash your face so that your fasting may not be seen by men. With these words all this chittering and chattering about community and living for the idea of community[629] is abolished. The first thing the religious man does is to lock his door and talk in secret.

As a rule inwardness is far more incommensurable with externality, and no man, not even the most candid and outspoken, is able to say everything and to justify all the contradictory expressions.

IV A 86   *n.d.*, 1843

« 2112

Inwardness is earnestness. —the remarkable words of Macbeth.

When inwardness is missing, the spirit is finitized—inwardness is the eternal.

V B 65   *n.d.*, 1844

« 2113

(a) Outline

(b) What is inwardness
    1. Earnestness

460

2. The eternal
   –the various conceptions of the eternal in our age
   a. Avoidance of the eternal
   b. Conceived imaginatively
   c. Conceived comically
                        metaphysically

(c) The more concrete the religious is (consequently the good),
     the greater the range of nuances
          Positive religion
          The historical

(d) It is treated as an appendix to the system. Therefore Poul Møller
     was right, that immortality must be present throughout and
     not brought in as an appendix to the system—to drink of
     Lethe is true to a certain degree.

                                             v b 66   *n.d.*, 1844

« 2114

Inwardness is the eternal, and desire is the temporal, but the
temporal cannot hold out with the eternal. Desire glows less and less
fervently, and at last its time is over, but the time of inwardness is never
over. Inwardness, the need of inwardness for God, has then conquered,
and the supplicant does not seek God in the external world, does not
create him in his desires, but finds him in his inwardness, and finally believes that he himself never did desire so vehemently, never was so confused, and believes that such as he now has become he was from the
beginning. But he does not therefore pray less than before, for that which
made him pray was inwardness, and it has now conquered.[630]

                                             v b 227:5   *n.d.*, 1844

« 2115

Inwardness. If anyone were to give an account of Hegel and say that
he represents thinking, we would have the right to answer: Well, that
says nothing at all; I must have a better idea of which thoughts he represents. So also with inwardness. To say he represents it is to make a
fool of oneself and the one under review, for *loquere ut videam*[631] applies
here, and I have to have an idea of *how* he represents it.[632]

                                             vi b 53:16   *n.d.*, 1845

« 2116

Yet the humorist has an inwardness which is undialectical and only approximates the dialectical inwardness of religiousness. The spheres are ordered in relation to the dialectical development of inward deepening, and to the degree an individual [*Individ*] keeps himself on the outside, fortifies himself against it [inwardness] or even partially fortifies himself, to the same degree his religiousness is less. The inwardness of the immediate person is externality; he has his dialectic outside himself. The man of irony is already turned inward in the exercise of the consciousness of contradiction. The ethical man is turned inward, but the development of inwardness is self-affirmation against himself; he strives with himself but does not remain dialectical to the end because he has fortified himself in a possibility by which he conquers himself. Humor is turned inward in the exercise of the absolute contradiction, is not without the inwardness of suffering, but still has so much of an undialectical self left that in the shifting it sticks its head up like a nisse and raises laughter; the inwardness of religiousness is a crushing of the self before God.

VI B 98:77   *n.d.,* 1845

« 2117

In the Gospel[633] about the unforgiving servant who would not forgive his fellow servant, we read: "As he went *out*." Consequently what took place between the master and him happened *within*. Alas, so it is with all of us—*within* us something takes place between God and us, but then when we come *out!*

VIII¹ A 76   *n.d.,* 1847

« 2118

In previous ages, when they had a properly Christian distrust of these human assurances about one's inner life, etc., they thought it necessary to take seriously actually giving away one's money—in order actually to become poor(as Christ counselled that rich young man), actually to lay down one's secular eminence. But in these honest times such outward precautionary measures are not necessary. In those times when they had a little more distrust of these human protestations about the inner life etc., they also believed that if a man loved, as he said, only one person, this was to be expressed by the fact that his life expressed that he loved only this one; but in our age, the age of tricks, one's outward life expresses the opposite, but one gives assurances, etc.—and we all believe it,* except that we mutually manage more and more to make fools of one another. I wonder, in the final analysis, if that age which required outward expression was not actually more faithful in respect to assurances than our age, which for its mutual comfort has found out that assurances are sufficient.[634]

* *In margin:* It is certainly cozy, and therefore almost every house has this kind of coziness.

VIII² B 91:13   *n.d.,* 1847-48

« 2119

For one who is willing to obey in action what he understands in thought,[635] the dialectical difficulty in being a real Christian is to find the point of rest between rest and unrest.

If a man engaged to a girl were to say: I love her so much that for her sake I would risk my life—and then with a noble distrust of himself (which might be quite in order nowadays) were to add: But this is perhaps just idle talk; therefore I must make good what I have said—he would then bring the greatest unhappiness upon himself and upon her—this happy love or love's happiness ordained of God for him and for her would then become their unhappiness.

So it is with essential Christianity. Yet it must be remembered that the difficulty in erotic love is quite different, because erotic love belongs to this temporal existence [*Tilværelse*] and thus, as far as erotic love is concerned, the worst thing he could do would be to make it impossible for himself in this world.

Now Christianity. Here again the collision is between inwardness and expression.[636] If I transform my Christianity into merely hidden inwardness and outwardly conform completely to the world, if I give absolutely no indication that in my inmost being I acknowledge a completely different criterion (the God-relationship) but am an upright man just like most people etc., then it is obviously a betrayal. The relationship is not entirely the same as in erotic love. There is supposedly no danger involved in confessing my love to others—it is simply lack of tact. But Christianity is not on friendly terms with the world; so I may become unpopular by confessing it. If I refrain from doing it, this is not good taste (as in erotic love) but is betrayal.

Christianity requires of me the inwardness of my being willing to give up everything for its sake. But if I keep Christianity as inwardness within me, in a certain sense I never do really give up anything. How close to troubled mistrust this is. It is obviously a false teaching if one wants to make people think that really to give up the external is to tempt God, that I should wait for God to take it away, for Christianity continually uses the phrase *give up*. On the other hand, if I want to evade and use all my wits to that end, it does not become impossible for God to take it from me (since for God all is possible), but it is made difficult.

What is to be done! I know nothing but this. I believe it is still always preferable to risk a little less, and to make the admission that one does not have courage for more, than to risk too much. The latter can be presumption toward God, which the former cannot be.

This is indescribably difficult when one has the whole day free as I do and has a capacity for thinking as I have. Most men do not give this a thought. Their time is occupied by things completely different; they have neither the time nor the personal development for becoming self-transparent in such a way that they really become self-concerned.

But the relationship to God is eternally inexhaustible, for whether in human terms I risk much or little, both are equally nothing to God; it is to grace that both must go. Here again it is so true: blessed is he who is not offended. That the person who, humanly speaking, honestly and genuinely risks most is the very one who for that very reason is persecuted and mocked, although he nevertheless does not get a bit farther before God than one who cowardly flees all danger—this itself is occasion for offense.

VIII[1] A 511   *n.d.*, 1848

« 2120

A man must be very perfectible in the sense of absence of spirit in order to be loved and cherished. Such a person falls in love, for example, but does it at approximately the same time as his peers. We think this is fine. He is married. Good! His wife dies, and we send condolences. A year later we naturally have forgotten the sorrow—and, sure enough, he too has forgotten it. We think this is all right, because even though he hid his feelings ever so deeply, if we suspected that he secretly sorrowed, we would feel embarrassed, for there would be something almost absolute about his feelings. And then he gets married—we congratulate him.

What a lovable man! Foolish and frivolous like everybody else— and that is exactly why he is lovable.

But inwardness[637]—no matter how hidden it is kept, its presence may still be suspected, and this may well happen if certain outward details are lacking—is distasteful to men. For them it is a thorn in the flesh which would make life strenuous. What men love is a momentary upsurge, then action, spineless nonsense. We are supposed to playact unmitigated grief— it is so becoming to the deeply sorrowing one. He is supposed to say: It is the death of me; I shall never love again—and the year after he is married. Thus he has done what we demand—contributed to life's diversions. But the quiet uniformity of inwardness—this makes men shudder.

IX A 402   n.d., 1848

« 2121

Ne quid nimis[638]—if this is true, then Christianity is a lie, every line in Holy Scripture madness and confusion.

But the unfortunate thing is that in paganism this *ne quid nimis* was openly acknowledged as the supreme maxim of life—but in established Christendom, from generation to generation, those thousands of public officials are rewarded, those men who demoralize themselves and the congregation by assuring and by getting the congregation into the habit of assuring that in their secret hearts they are willing to venture everything, if it is required.

I have never seen a man whose life went beyond *ne quid nemis* with particular audacity—and every single Sunday there is preaching about the highest, about seeking the kingdom of God first. Have you, my friend, ever seen a man who in any way fits this—seek first the kingdom of God —any pastor, for example, who asks first of all whether it is a good parish in a good area?

However, there has to be a little bit of truth—we must make an admission to [*Tilstaaelse*] to ourselves that this lying assuring has to go.

X¹ A 564   n.d., 1849

« 2122

As far as being sure I am going in the right direction is concerned, there is something consoling to me in the fact that of all people, if anyone in my age can be said to be made for inwardness, it is I who after all make a claim for a little bit of externality. In this there supposedly is a guarantee that it does not go off in the direction of work-righteousness. But the fact is that all this about hidden inwardness has become a kind of humbug, and it was necessary for a cunning person to come and attack from the rear.

X² A 46   n.d., 1849

« 2123 *Spirituality—and Spirituality*

We accuse the Middle Ages of overstrained spirituality, that it was in earnest about giving up the world—perhaps.

But is it not far greater spirituality to take possession of it, to spend a great deal of time acquiring and preserving it, and then feel very spiritual because in our deep inwardness we are infinitely elevated above all this.

The Middle Ages were anxious and said: I do not dare trust myself; therefore I will not have honors and position. Nowadays we are more spiritual; we aspire to them, order our whole life toward them—but in our deep inwardness we are so spiritual that we are elevated above all this sort of thing, above mere childish tricks—whether we go around dressed in rags or in velvet with stars and ribbons, it is all quite the same, but yet we do prefer going about in velvet with stars and ribbons.

But this starred and beribboned person declares: I can assure you that in my heart of hearts etc., and if it is required of me—and he gets to be 70 years old in a world he himself claims to be wretched and corrupt—but he found no challenge, nothing was required of him. Yes, in truth nothing was required of him, for no one came to coerce him when he used all his cunning to avoid every danger, used all his cunning to accommodate to that which momentarily was on top—but if it is required etc. This amounts to making a fool of God; it is like a child playing a game of hide-and-seek so that no one shall find him. One says aloud—if it is required, etc.—and then says very softly—look, not even Satan himself will be able to get hold of me—so cleverly shall I hide.

x^3 A 156   *n.d.*, 1850

« 2124 *Introspection*

We are warned against introspection; the warning might just as well be against Christianity.

Using grace, they try to block the path that goes inward and to direct us away from it out into the worldly.

The fact of the matter is—they dread the genuine, strenuous life of the spirit which comes only with introspection; whereas they now live in a secularized mentality and chatter about the highest.

x^3 A 251   *n.d.*, 1850

« 2125 *A Mutually Haphazard Arrangement between Christendom and the World*

With the gradual decrease of concern for being an authentic Christian and of enthusiasm through actually being that, and since on the other hand people did not wish to break completely with Christianity, hidden inwardness arose. Hidden inwardness excuses one from actual renunciation, excuses one from all the inconvenience of suffering for the cause of Christianity. This was agreed to and on this condition men continued to be Christian—it was convenient.

From the other side it was convenient for "the world" as well. If Christianity does not become anything more than such an extraordinary, extraordinary hidden inwardness, which is about *so viel wie nichts*, then the world pledges itself to tolerate Christianity. That was a nice world! It saw, of course, with half an eye that with the aid of hidden inwardness it had conquered Christianity. That enormous power, Christianity, which declared its friendship to be hatred of the world—well, the world really could not take this lying down, nor was it permitted to. But a Christendom which in an utterly, utterly, utterly hidden inwardness hated the world but in other respects was a boon companion of the world in its every expression, completely conformed to the world—yes, go right ahead, the world said and thought—we grant you this kind of hate with pleasure—a perfectly harmless thing—and furthermore, thought the world, this business of hate residing in the hidden inwardness could also be a lie, since one hears it talked about only in preacher prattle, which again is not the preacher's conviction but something he declaims about in an official capacity and in order to make a living as a worthy member of the most recently instituted religious order: The Bread and Butter Brothers.

That a man could be a Christian in such deep inwardness that Satan himself would not be able to spot it came to be glorified and admired as good breeding. It was good breeding—ah, yes, instead of good breeding we sometimes use another expression—to possess the world.

Thus, for example, if Mynster says: Yes, but by being a teacher in the Church I am certainly confessing Christ, I answer: This is a shady trick; for salaried job and office cover over what is essentially characteristic of confession.

Incidentally, I admit that both as an ironist and as a melancholy man I have loved hidden inwardness, and it is equally true that I have had an inwardness and have expended great effort to conceal it. There is also something true in the shyness which conceals its inwardness. But as far as I am concerned, I have on the other hand tried to order my actions in a striving for the essentially Christian. I have not protested that I was a Christian in hidden inwardness and then energetically organized my life secularly. On the contrary, I have worn a disguise over my inwardness and have appeared as egotistical, frivolous, etc.—and yet have acted in such a way that I have experienced the Christian collisions.

In the meantime it is and continues to be an awkward matter—how far may one go in this, since the essentially Christian has the quality of immediately involving me in ridicule, persecution, etc. if I rightly confess it. True enough, by acting according to the Christian standard I incur similar treatment, but it is nevertheless a question whether the exasperation would not become even greater if it became known that this was in order to confess Christ. For if worst comes to worst, the world would rather tolerate the eccentricity of genius or be more lenient toward it than to put up with Christianity.

Then, too, as far as I am concerned, it must be remembered that by my past performance I have already marked my relationship to the essentially Christian by quite another standard than that of the career man and job holder, but the question is whether to do more, and yet I must always keep in mind that I have understood my task to be that of operating as a spy. If I had not had this singular thought, I would have acted differently from the very beginning. But then what has been achieved would not have been achieved: the indirect evidence against Christendom among us—that we imagine ourselves to be Christian and yet cannot recognize Christian action or what conforms to it, but scream that it is eccentricity, exaggeration, etc. This would never have been achieved by direct attack, such as declaring oneself to be a Christian and judging others not to be, for then they would briskly appeal to their hidden inwardness. And the hidden inwardness was the very thing which should be prodded, and this can be done only indirectly.

x^3 A 334   *n.d.*, 1850

« 2126

Every other concern finds its expression in human life. The concern for earning money finds its expression and occupies a long, long time—likewise the concern for honor and glory, and on down to even the most insignificant concern. Only the concern for eternal salvation finds no expression whatsoever—after all, we all have it, we are all Christians.

x^3 A 356   *n.d.*, 1850

« 2127 *How Strange*

In the world, in the world of commerce and trade, the only thing automatically presupposed as a matter of course is—a criterion of the best or the highest. Suppose someone is seeking the lowest kind of a job—his qualifications are by no means presupposed as a matter of course; he is investigated first of all. But it is presupposed as a matter of course that a person is a Christian.

A man seeks a pastoral appointment. The investigation that takes place is unbelievable, and nothing is simply presupposed regarding income, the parsonage, etc.—but that he is a Christian, this, of course, is simply taken for granted; that he loves God above all in hidden inwardness and is prepared to renounce everything the moment it is demanded—this is presupposed as a matter of course.

x^3 A 357   *n.d.*, 1850

« 2128 *The One and Only Thing Which Is Always Assumed in Life*

is: the most important, the absolute, the only thing needful. That a future pastor should know even the most minute trifle in respect to the appointment is not assumed as a matter of course, but that he is a true Christian, in his innermost being (in hidden inwardness) is willing to sacrifice everything for Christianity—this is naturally assumed—O, naturally!

x^3 A 469   *n.d.*, 1850

« 2129 *My Battle against Illusions*

It has never occurred to me to want to get rid of illusions by external means. No, no, no!

For example, Christendom is an illusion.

Do I want to get rid of it? No, I only want the single individual [*den Enkelte*] not to be deceived by it. [*In margin:* I do not have one single moment for doing anything to get rid of it by external means, partly because of inwardness and partly because it is the wrong way to go at it, since the direction is outwards, toward externality.]

Therefore I even want it to remain standing, because just this is the best proof of how victorious one's inwardness is—that one can keep it— and deliberately let the illusion remain, but it does not discompose one, does not deceive one.

x^4 A 21   *n.d.*, 1851

« 2130 *Change of Quality with Respect to the Inward Direction or Outward Direction in Christianity*

If the direction is to be outward, it must be because the established is expressly ungodly (or completely pagan as the world once was). Then it is a matter of conscience.

If this is not the case, then to want to dabble in or be essentially occupied with change in externals is so far from being meritorious that the quality itself changes, and Christianity becomes inwardness.

But not hidden inwardness. No, the ethical aspect of essential Christianity will still provide sufficient collisions with the environment, perhaps occasional martyrs. On the other hand, it is Christian to be neutral toward the projection of changes in the external forms of the Church, for that becomes mere politics or a general inclination for change, which simply is not Christianity.

x^4 A 26   *n.d.*, 1851

« 2131 *Distance*

At one time everything was internal struggle and spiritual trial; whether it was God's will—that was the question, and everything was preparation to that end—a man withdrew into solitude, fasted, prayed, etc.

Now everything is outward: intrigues flourish, the real thing to do is to form a group, etc.

Put two such individuals together and they simply would not understand each other; the one would not understand at all what the other is doing.

x^4 A 151   *n.d.*, 1851

« 2132 *"The Quiet Hours"*

Imagine that a child—after having been taught and admonished by the parents about how they wanted him to behave, what he should and should not do—is put among an enormous swarm of children with whom he must now live entirely on his own without any teacher or superior.

The child can see with half an eye that things here are not as the parents prescribed. Whether the other children never learned anything from their parents previously or had entirely forgotten it, the child quickly sees that things are different here—and that if he is not to make a complete mess of things he must manage to fall in with the ways and customs around him.

This the child does—and finds that everything goes well for him, that he is well regarded by his peers etc.

Perhaps in a quiet hour the child remembers the parents but gets it into his head that his parents are really too far up in the clouds to bother about him and how things are in the children's quarters, that what the parents said, although true, is too exalted.

So it is with the quiet hours in Christendom. We live in entirely different categories, howl with the wolves around us, see with half an eye that it would be plumb crazy for a person to want to apply Christianity to his life.

Finally we delude ourselves into thinking that Christianity is too exalted, that God is too exalted to be concerned about how things are going with us human beings here in Copenhagen, for example, etc.

So we have Christianity-at-a-distance, which is really poetry or mythology.

A person who worships only in quiet hours, thinks of God only in quiet hours—puts Christianity at a distance, sneaks out of the very thing God wants, that religion is to be introduced right in the middle of actual life, everyday, weekdays (the most strenuous of all) and not be satisfied with the Jewish way of doing things—Sabbath worship or an hour or a half-hour each day.

Christianity is nothing else but religion right in the middle of actual life and weekdays—and we have reduced it to quiet hours, thereby indirectly admitting that we are not really being Christians.

That we should have quiet hours to think about God—this seems so elevated and beautiful, so solemn—and it is so hypocritical, because in this way we exempt daily life from "imitation" [*Efterfølgelsen*] and from the authentic active worship of God.

X⁵ A 51   n.d., 1852

« 2133

In margin of 2132 (x⁵ A 51):

The quiet hours and *nichts weiter* are divine worship about as much as worshipping God is binding the Bible in velvet and building marble temples embellished in gold.

x⁵ A 52   n.d.

« 2134 *How Courteous, How Cultured, How Sincere!*

We associate with each other in such a way that we have a mutual expectation that there is never to be any personal conversation about eternity, the matter of salvation, etc.—and we respect this reticence as courtesy, culture, and sincerity. We presuppose, the one of the other, that he—naturally!—in deepest inwardness is most earnestly concerned with the matter.

How tricky! Ordinarily it is not regarded as courtesy, culture, and sincerity to refrain from calling a person's attention to some danger or other to which he is exposed—but in this case it is so courteous, cultured, and sincere—and why? Because all of us prefer to be rid of these thoughts. This also accounts for a good deal of that polite and cultured way of speaking euphemistically of the deceased: "He rests in peace," "He sleeps," "Now he is better off," etc. All of us want to get rid of the thought of death, the sooner the better.

XI¹ A 21   n.d., 1854

« 2135 *The Incognito*

An incognito under which one's God-relationship is concealed is desirable nevertheless.

Alas, among religious people one's God-relationship has long since become a triviality. They smell and sniff at one another to find out whether someone might be in a special relationship to God, and they are preoccupied with this just as people at the castle are preoccupied with someone's having special royal favor.

XI¹ A 255   n.d., 1854

« 2136 *To Believe—Nicodemus*

If believing were a hidden inwardness, Christ must certainly have approved of Nicodemus—an obvious instance of hidden inwardness.

XI¹ A 488   n.d., 1854

JEST

« 2137

Faith is our victory over the world[639]—"Yes, we more than conquer,"[640] as the apostle says. To be specific, when the struggle in which one strives has its full validity in the sphere of actuality so that he actually struggles in it, he cannot more than conquer—no matter how brilliant his victory. But when the struggle does not have its full validity in the sphere of actuality so that this struggle is the ultimate for him, then he can more than conquer—that is, to him the struggle's *discrimen* is secondary, a jest in relation to a far higher struggle. And so it is with the earnestness of faith, its actual struggle, to struggle with God—but the struggle with the world, its joys and sorrows, is like a jest.[641] This is why faith is the victory which conquers the world, yes, more than conquers—that is, it scales that whole struggle down to something secondary. The man of the world does not know anything higher than struggle in the world, and therefore such a person can never more than conquer. If I look upon my adversary as my *ebenbürdige* enemy, I cannot more than conquer, but if he is such a trifle to me that the struggle really has no danger for me, then I can more than conquer.

VII¹ A 207   *n.d.*, 1846

« 2138

O, there is an indescribable bliss in really and truly feeling oneself as nothing before God, less than a sparrow, less than a grain of sand. Let us imagine that God became tired of a man and said to him: I do not wish to have anything more to do with you, and gave him such a kick that he fell forty million miles. Ah, if he really and truly felt himself to be nothing before God—the moment he came to himself, he would say: O, God, just one more thing. Take my gratitude, my indescribable gratitude for every year, every day, every hour, every second I have rested in your confidence; I am still taken care of, for I shall not do anything else than continue to express my gratitude, my indescribable gratitude for every year, every day, every hour, every second I have been aware of the blessedness of your confidence, the blessedness of being with you.

473

But the person who imagines himself to be something would no doubt shout: God is a deceiver. If it is really true that I am literally nothing, then it is an indescribable grace and kindness on his part to let me taste for one single second the blessedness of being with him.

In the relationship to God a person must be willing to strive to the uttermost and must strive to the uttermost. But even if he persevered ever so long, he would guard against bringing into the God-relationship the purely human earnestness which so easily becomes self-important, as if it were something; he must be instantaneously willing to pray for himself like a child and say: It was only a jest. The religious man must speak like this: Humanly speaking, these seventy years have been full of frightful exertion and sacrifice—but when you, O God, look at them, I say "*Bitte, bitte,* it is only a jest; forgive me, forgive me for attempting to express, for so eagerly wanting to demonstrate, my love. If a child sat and worked a whole year on a birthday present, if it had denied itself every pleasure (which, after all, humanly speaking, is a lot for a child) for a whole year, simply to get the work finished and in order not to be delayed by this work from the real work—what a stupid and tiresome child it would be who would come and present his gift in self-important seriousness. No, the child comes lovingly with his gift but is willing instantaneously to change the whole thing to a jest and say: It was only a joke; forgive me for venturing to express my gratitude."

x^2 A 76   *n.d.,* 1849

« 2139

Just as in relation to providence and governance or, more accurately, in relation to what it does, what I do is almost always only a jest (whether I am an emperor or a matchmaker, etc.)—so is it in relation to the Atonement. Christ's Atonement, his suffering and death, is everything and transforms the little I do almost into a jest; whether I reform the whole world or as a hired man take care of my job, it is one and the same, for Christ's Atonement is infinitely everything.

x^2 A 203   *n.d.,* 1849

« 2140 *Faith—Works*

In his sermon on the Epistle for New Year's Day, Luther[642] says that a man is saved by faith—works are only "training exercises."

This is what I have often put this way: Grace is earnestness—my works are only a jest—and so get going, the more animatedly the better, but all the same it is a jest to me and must not mean anything else to me.

And this is Christianity. Lucky is the one who has only heard this doctrine and never got to see on what a horrible scale it is taken in vain, who consequently has not been made anxious by that tragic knowledge as to whether he himself has taken grace in vain and in his anxiety became something of a self-tormentor.

Here again we see how infinitely important it is in respect to the essentially Christian to take the proclaimer along. For they took Luther's doctrine about faith—but Luther's life, that they forgot.

x^3 A 672   *n.d.*, 1850

JOURNALISM

« 2141

Those pen-pushers belong to the gossip carriers; they belong to a species of plants which bear a name very appropriate to them—rubbish mushrooms (see Nielsen's cookbook).[643]

II A 762   n.d., 1838[644]

« 2142 No. 9[645]

Very few realize what an onerous profession journalism is, so onerous that only the consciousness of what one is achieving in the service of truth to the ennobling of mankind can provide the strength to persevere. Imagine a young man in his best years—already looking almost old, almost gray, if not completely bald—to such an extent has everything he has gone through, or everything that has gone through him, left its marks. He is sitting at his desk; we can scarcely see him, he is so surrounded by or buried in papers, books, journals, newspapers, articles, letters, works of art. He sits at his desk, bowed under the enormous strain of bearing the weight which lies upon his shoulders—the fact that nothing, nothing at all, neither the most insignificant nor the most significant event, nothing in the city, in the country, or in all of Europe happens without going through the journalist. —Now the bell rings; it is an author with his newest work. The journalist must be in on everything. Without having once looked into the book, he must immediately be able to say what is wrong with it and suggest what direction the author should now take, what the age demands in politics, philolosophy, theology, philanthropy, art, history, ethics, esthetics, pedagogy, archaeology, tactics, didactics, horoscopes, and metascopes. There is a knock at the door; it is a recently arrived artist. The journalist must be on in everything. Without ever having heard him or heard about him, he must immediately be able to make a judgment, show him what is right, give him the counsel which reveals the art connoisseur—and then read the pile of foreign newspapers the artist carries with him, in which the artist is mentioned and which the journalist must have "lying before him." Now there is a knock at the secret door; it is one of the editor-in-chief's highly trusted men. We see by his face that some-

476

thing terrible has happened—but the journalist must diplomatically control himself, remain calm, or seem calm, must ask him to wait, and he continues his conversation with the artist. There is another knock. It is a note from a person in high authority who feels himself insulted and is threatening. The bell rings; it is an injured party. The journalist must be in on everything, must immediately, without having heard the least thing about the affair, understand it, know the law and the constitutional rights of the land better than all the lawyers. There is another knock; it is the printshop messenger who is to pick up copy.

We almost shudder when we read this; we cannot understand how a man's head can endure this. And yet the journalist has to have ever so much more in his head. Amidst all this he must readily and every moment of the day be able to calculate mentally which of all the thousands of opinions is the public opinion, the cultivated public's opinion. Day in and day out, in this tremendous interchange of the most varied and contradictory opinions, day in and day out, in this shouting and complaining and clapping and clamoring and whispering confusion, in which everyone wants to have his opinion, of course without being obliged to keep it for a half hour but with the unconditional right to change it every second— the journalist has to be able to calculate *stante pede*, in his head, which opinion is the public's, the cultured public's! How should one head be able to endure all this without a consciousness of and faith in the significance of his calling [*Kalds*]. We could well imagine that a person might lose his mind over this, just over the imponderable of how the journalist after all gets the answer out of the public!

And so it goes all day long. When evening comes, there are new demands on the journalist's life. He must be able to cast aside this enormous weight, completely clear his mind, so that when he gets to the party at taverner Mathiesen's he may be young, lively, witty, charming, the ingratiating society man, the ladies'

(to be continued)

VII² B 290   *n.d.*, 1845-47

« 2143

When it comes to literature and criticism (this is not true of its main task—politics) the *Berlingske Tidende*[646] can best be likened to sandwich paper—one reads it while eating. Indeed, I have even seen a man wipe himself with the newspaper for want of a napkin. Yet, as in everything, the setting has great significance. Therefore, without becoming so lofty that it cannot be understood very well by everyone, what is needed is something to make a reader a little more earnest, if possible. Reading should not be done in this manner. This is why I did not want to have anything of mine printed in the *B.T.* Rather than the wide circulation my writing could get by being printed in the *B.T.*, I much preferred only one solitary reader.

VII[1] A 24   n.d., 1846

« 2144

In margin of 2143 (VII[1] A 24):
This lack of self-affirmation is and will be the disaster. Everything revolves about money. If it would pay, I am sure we would get someone to publish a daily designed to be read only in latrines.

VII[1] A 25   n.d.

« 2145

Evaluation by newspapers will gradually be extended to cover subjects never dreamed of. The other day one of the provincial newspapers reported that a man had been executed by executioner John Doe, who performed the job with fine precision; executioner David Roe, present to whip someone publicly, also performed satisfactorily.

VII[1] A 37   n.d., 1846

« 2146

The tyranny of the daily press is the most wretched, the most contemptible of all tyrannies; it is the *begging* tyranny—in the same way that a beggar to whom we say "No" eventually extorts something from us by running up and down the street after us. If we were to imagine an eminent polemical author, the likes of whom has never existed, and set him into controversy with a publication, he will lose out unless he himself publishes a paper, and in that case he has also lost insofar as he has sunk from being an author to becoming a journalist (which is like changing from a philosopher to a sophist). And so the battle begins. The eminent controversialist strikes a blow, and the journalist himself is not unaware that the blow is deadly and decisive. The journalist's puny answer shows the abysmal distance of infinitude between them. Meanwhile the journalist is quite secure. He reasons this way: "An author cannot in all decency continually return to the same theme, and consequently he stops—then I begin. I will keep it up, every evening, or one evening a week; it will certainly take hold. The longer it continues the more muddled the whole affair becomes, and gradually the public has completely forgotten the author's article, and thus I have won the game. The author cannot in all decency suddenly come out with a new article about the same thing, and thus I have him in my power." And all those bunglers, those retired color guards and yes-men and half-baked students rally to this. After all, the joke of it is that each journalist always speaks with enormous importance in his own paper; but if they mutually disagree they do not grant each other two cent's worth of glory and competence—and why? Naturally, because the journalists themselves mutually know best of all what capacities hide behind the "broad rump" of public opinion.[647]

VII[1] A 122   n.d., 1846

« 2147

The government cannot prohibit the natural powers which a man possesses, but it can forbid the possession of dangerous weapons, because they are too powerful and go beyond the human. Accordingly, the government cannot prohibit oral communication, which is a gift of God, but it could very well prohibit the daily press, because it is a much too gigantic means of communication. The printing of notices could be allowed, but on no reasonable basis in the daily press.

VIII[1] A 136   n.d., 1847

« 2148

The daily press is and remains the evil principle in the modern world. In its sophistry it has no limits, since it can sink to ever lower and lower levels of readers. Consequently it stirs up so much foulness and meanness that no state can cope with it. There will always be only a few who truly see the untruth in the existence of the daily press, but of these few, again, there will be very few with the courage to express it, because it is outright martyrdom to break with the majority and the large audience who will immediately persecute the one who does.

VIII[1] A 137   n.d., 1847

« 2149

The relation between the daily press and authors is as follows. An author writes a coherent and consistently clear presentation of some idea —perhaps even the fruit of many years of labor. No one reads it. But a journalist, in reviewing the book, takes the occasion to slap together some rubbish which he presents as representing the author's book—this everyone reads. We see the author's significance in existence—he exists [er til] so that a journalist can have the occasion to write some rubbish which everyone reads. If the author had not lived, the journalist would not have had this occasion—*ergo*, it is important that there be authors.

VIII¹ A 140   *n.d.*, 1847

« 2150

God really intended that a person should speak individually with his neighbor and at most with several neighbors. Man is not greater than that. In each generation there are a few who are so gifted and so mature that they may justifiably use such a tremendous means of communication as the press. But that almost everyone and especially all the bunglers should use such means of communication—with nothing to communicate but nonsense—what a disproportion!

VIII¹ A 146   *n.d.*, 1847

« 2151

How fortunate the modern age, a time when the few authors are the only ones who understand nothing or the only ones of whom it is doubtful that they understand anything. The authors write books. The journalists *evaluate* these books and consequently must understand something, and then they submit the matter to the judgment of the honorable cultured public, who *consequently* must understand something. *Ergo*, the authors are the only ones who do not understand *anything*, or the only ones of whom it is doubtful that they understand anything.

VIII¹ A 399   *n.d.*, 1847

« 2152

The coiled spring in the whole enormous apparatus of *existence* [*Til-værelsens*] and the spring by which every little link (like a ring in a chain) is joined to the whole is personality: all is personality (in the world of nature); each one is personality (in the world of spirit). And now personality has been abolished. God has become impersonal; all communication is impersonal—and here in particular are the two most dreadful calamities which really are the principal powers of impersonality—the press and anonymity.

The highest triumph of all errors is to acquire an impersonal means of communication and then anonymity. It is rubbish to say that the press itself heals the wounds it inflicts. Because all true communication is personal (for personality is truth), it will always have greater difficulty in using the press. But error is always impersonal.

Without the daily press and without anonymity, there is still always the consolation that there will be a definite, flesh-and-blood individual person who voices the error, expresses the impudence, etc. Then there is hope that the mass will shrink from being this particular individual, and in any case his identity will be known. But it is frightful that someone who is no one (consequently has no responsibility) can set any error into circulation with no thought of responsibility and with the aid of this dreadful disproportioned means of communication. And then this irresponsible error is taken up by the public, which again is no one! There is no one anywhere, and for that very reason there is widespread error.

Ultimately truth disappears from the world (for truth is personality), and the only ones who will be heard will be the ventriloquists of this generation.

And so they are unable to understand my teaching about the single individual [den Enkelte]. Well, the fact is that they can understand it all right, but they shrink from it as from madness—that it could occur to any man to want to impose such a task upon himself. But I have not imposed this task upon myself; it has been imposed on me and decided for me. There is a word which for me is a magic formula: Obedience is more precious to God than the fat of rams.[648] If my meager effectiveness, a nothing compared to the task, disappears, humanly speaking, I shall still keep on: Obedience is more precious to God than the fat of rams.

VIII^1 A 540   *n.d.*, 1848

« 2153

It is really impossible to do battle with a journalist. He keeps himself hidden; one cannot get hold of him; and then in the twinkling of an eye he incites those thousands of people against one person, who is actually no concern of theirs, who ridiculously and tragically is both guilty and innocent.

IX A 200   *n.d.*, 1848

« 2154 *Inscription on a Grave*

The daily press is the state's disaster, the crowd the world's evil.

["*hiin Enkelte*"]
"that single individual"
IX A 282   *n.d.*, 1848

« 2155

I have long been convinced that the daily press is a form of evil. But what prospects! And now, on the other hand, now we are brought to the point where the revolutionary governments themselves forbid the press. You can see why a person gets an urge to be an author; he can even glimpse the time when what he has to say about the daily press will be understood.

IX A 320   *n.d.*, 1848

« 2156

Quite true, it will be impossible to prevent gossip, slander, small talk, and all that, even if the press is not used as a vehicle for it; but it nevertheless must be noted that the press's use of it absolutely intensifies a qualitative demoralization. As far as oral communication is concerned, an individual may continually say: I heard "someone" say. But when he cannot personally produce this "someone," a share of responsibility still remains with him and through dexterous handling he could easily be made the more important of the two, and he can be daunted. But the objective tranquillity and, on the other hand, the cocksureness and boldness with which the individual says: Yes, I read it in the newspaper—no, this cannot be daunted.

Furthermore, as far as merely oral communication is concerned, gossip is partitioned, every social class has its own gossip, so to speak; but with the help of the press everything is united, and the most dissimilar people join in chattering about one and the same person.

And what ranges of circulation now prevail!

IX A 357   *n.d.*, 1848

« 2157

Inevitably the time will come when a complete change in the view or conception of the press will take place, but as yet this invention (the press) still intimidates people far too much. People must become even more accustomed to see the misuse of the press so that they can quietly begin to form an estimate of the relationship between the good and the harm this invention has brought to mankind. Everything considered, it has already almost come to a point in the higher classes of society that the press is far more baneful than beneficial. I am speaking only of the daily press.

The change in viewpoint regarding the daily press will be that the legal distinction between the permissible and the impermissible is abandoned, as if the daily press could do no harm by printing and circulating something which by no means can be called untrue or prohibited. Attention must be directed to the disproportion in the medium of communication itself. For example, by telling in print of a young girl (giving the full name—and this telling is, of course, the truth) that she has bought a new dress (and this is assumed to be true), and by repeating this a few times, the girl can be made miserable for her whole life. And one single person can bring this about in five minutes, and why? Because the press (the daily press) is a disproportionate medium of communication. Suppose someone invented an instrument, a convenient little talking tube which could be heard over the whole land—I wonder if the police would not forbid it, fearing that the whole country would become mentally deranged if it were used. In the same way, to be sure, guns are prohibited.

Books are tolerable, but preferably large books; because of their very size they have no connection with the momentary. On the whole the evil in the daily press consists in its being calculated to make, if possible, the moment a thousand or ten thousand times more inflated and important than it already is. But all moral upbringing consists first and foremost in being weaned away from the momentary.

No doubt I shall not live to see this, but nevertheless I am convinced that it will come to pass. As China has come to a standstill at a stage of development, so Europe will come to a standstill at the press and remain at a standstill as a reminder that the human race had invented something which eventually overpowered it.

IX A 378   *n.d.*, 1848

« 2158

That it is the press which has demoralized the states can also be seen in the following way: Only a person of wide culture can read the newspapers and remain unscathed, and there are not many of these in any generation—and the few there are scarcely read newspapers any more. But the mass read the newspapers, the mass for whom this unwholesome diet is in and for itself most pernicious.

The same thing can be seen in another way. The press wants to influence by means of coverage, but coverage is simply the power of the lie, a sensate power, like the power of fists. One is reminded of Goethe's words: We have abolished the devil and gotten devils.

IX A 468   *n.d.*, 1848

« 2159

What a dreadful disproportion! Scripture says that a man shall render account to God for every careless word he has spoken—and yet there is the final consolation that at least in eternity we shall be free of newspapers. Just think of the accounting!

IX A 478   *n.d.*, 1848

« 2160

Strike-anywhere matches are prohibited—on the grounds of *abuse* (as in Russia today); but it occurs to no one to prohibit the press on the grounds of *abuse*. Should we not soon learn that the daily press is a good, the abuse of which far outweighs the benefits.

X¹ A 128   *n.d.*, 1849

« 2161

In ancient times it was the judges and the prophets who guarded a country's morality [*Sædeligheden*].Later it was still customary for the clergy to do this.

Then the Church despaired over the secular mentality—and then the "papers" and the public became the authorities on morality! Finally, the lowest block of the daily press, under the name of satire, kept a watch over morality—which is something like sending a young girl to a brothel —to safeguard her innocence.

X¹ A 341   *n.d.*, 1849

« 2162

The corrupting and demoralizing aspect of journalistic communication is not so much in its communicating something false as in the depraved guarantee it furnishes that there probably are a goodly number who say the same thing and make the same value judgments; just being printed in a paper is, of course, sufficient guarantee for that. What men fear, unfortunately, is not that they may say something true or untrue but that they come to stand alone with an opinion. Such a guarantee is therefore a demoralizing leash which makes men more and more mediocre and base, and this tragedy is far greater than journalistic communication of untruth. The daily press, like all journalism, is more or less impersonal communication and is designed to furnish the guarantee that there are many who think the same way. This does not have to be said explicitly in the paper, for the fact that the communication is in a paper is the guarantee.

X¹ A 409   *n.d.*, 1849

« 2163

Even if my life had no other significance, well, I am satisfied with having really discovered the absolutely demoralizing existence of the daily press.

Actually, it is the press, more specifically, the daily newspaper, and the whole modern way of life corresponding to it, which make Christianity impossible. Think of Christ. The idea that he would use a newspaper to proclaim his teaching is nonsense and blasphemy on seventeen grounds, and this is one of them: the imprint of the personality of the *I* who is speaking must fall upon every word he says—but communication by means of journalism is an abstraction, which supposedly is superior to the individual personality—and with Christ the very opposite is the case.

There are some few who begin to understand me; but at most they admire me—and shrink away; having nothing to risk themselves, they would not recognize themselves again if they dared venture in this way.

x^2 A 17   *n.d.*, 1849

« 2164

Some day people will regard being a journalist the way we now with loathing and abhorrence regard being a Jesuit and the like (because the name Jesuit makes us think immediately of the loathsome degeneration).

Many fine men are to be found among butchers, but a certain brutality is inseparable from being a butcher; it goes with the profession. It is worse to be a journalist. A certain degree of dishonesty is inseparable from even the most honest journalist.

The race's deepest separation from God is epitomized by "the journalist." It is a wicked attempt to make an abstraction into an absolute power, and anonymity is the consummation of the triumph of the lie.

If I were a father and had a daughter who was seduced, I would not despair of her. I would hope for salvation. But if I had a son who became a journalist and remained one for five years, him I should give up. It is possible that I might have made a mistake in the particular case, that the daughter was the one who was lost and the son the one who was recovered, but, ideally, my observation is right: to serve politics by means of the daily press is too much for a man. Who would dare deny having sometimes, perhaps many times, used a little lie; but to use the little lie every day, and in print, so that one addresses himself to thousands and thousands— this is dreadful. We shudder at the brutality of the way a butcher uses the knife: ah, but this is nothing at all compared to the most dreadful recklessness and callousness with which a journalist, addressing himself to the whole country, if possible, uses untruth.

x^2 A 314   *n.d.*, 1849

« 2165 *The Christian Proclamation—the Daily Press*

The proclamation of Christianity customary today is nonsense.

But if Christianity is really to be proclaimed, it will become apparent that it is the daily press which will, if possible, make it impossible.

There has never been a power so diametrically opposed to Christianity as the daily press.

Day in and day out the daily press does nothing but delude men with the supreme axiom of this lie—that numbers are decisive.

And Christianity builds on the thought that the truth is the single individual.

x^3 A 231   *n.d.*, 1850

« 2166 *The Daily Press*

That which has brought about this dreadful evil is, among other things, as follows.

What rules the world is not exactly the fear of God but the fear of man. Therefore this fear of being a single individual [*Enkelt*] and this proneness to hide under one abstraction or another—therefore the anonymity, therefore the editorial "we," and so on.

On the other hand, what envy directs itself entirely against and is opposed to is the single individual [*den Enkelte*]. Envy will not tolerate that a single individual should mean anything, to say nothing of being eminent. Therefore envy fosters pure abstractions: the editorial staff, anonymity, etc. It is to envy's interest to support this—that even the most eminent individual is insignificant before an abstraction, even if this notorious abstraction comes to pass through a particular man's calling himself "the editorial staff." Envy cannot bear to see superiority; therefore it patronizes abstractions, since these are invisible.

Ultimately an abstraction is related to man's fantasy, and fantasy is an enormous power. Even the most remarkable individual is still only one actuality—but "the editorial staff"—well, no one, no one knows what enormous capacity hides behind that!

Summa summarum: the human race ceased to fear God. Then came the punishment, the human race became afraid of itself, fosters the fantastic, and then itself trembles before it.

The discussion about law and the press in France[649] interests me; one is finally brought to the extremity that he speaks out.

There is nothing comparable to hearing the journalists howl that without anonymity the daily press is an impossibility. Truly, a splendid admission of what trash they are; and on the other hand, if everything depends on anonymity in this way, then it is all the more important that this if possible be made impossible.

But the press still defends itself by saying it is impractical, it cannot be done—and the journalists jubilate. Just imagine that the underworld discovered a way of stealing which made it impossible to discover the perpetrator—what joy among the thieves! And what joy among the journalists that it presumably is an impossibility. The journalist is not at all concerned whether it is true that anonymity is one of the greatest moral evils; he merely says: Thank God, it is impossible to root out anonymity. O, of all the abominable corruptions of the human race, you journalists take the cake. Of all the loathesomest tyrants, you are the worst—you who tyrannize through the cowardly fear of man.

In the meantime, however, if the journalists were wrong, it does not matter. The situation is that so far people do not dare come out and say anything. Many people still live in the stupid bliss that the daily press is the greatest and most invaluable good. Others, to be sure, understand that this is not so, but they tremble before the power of the journalists. Even quite recently the person who dared to doubt that the daily press is a priceless good, the pride of the human race, came to be regarded as a dunce who could not lift himself up to such lofty thoughts.

As far as previous attempts are concerned, it cannot be decided whether it would be possible to prevent anonymity by law. Imagine a state in which thieves are regarded as the greatest invention of the human race, an invaluable good, etc. (a self-contradiction, to be sure, but we can certainly imagine it)—well, under these conditions legislation covering thievery would surely be impossible. But when citizens have the sense of order and justice to regard stealing as a crime and the development of sharper and sharper stipulations is regarded as beneficial—then there will be good and proper legislation covering thievery.

This is what should be done with anonymity. Take away its glitter, let the opinion develop that anonymity is vile—not only will very much be gained, but there will also come to be legal provisions against it. It is one thing to have to write laws under the condition that to write them means martyrdom; it is another thing to dare apply one's acumen to working out laws in peace and quiet and then be rewarded with thanks, as for a good deed.

x³ A 275   *n.d.*, 1850

« 2167 *The Daily Press*

It is not my view that laws against it, laws which could regulate it in orderly fashion, are an impossibility. But my real view is that the salvation of mankind from this evil (Satan's personal and proud triumph: "Finally I have invented a depravity so foolproof that every precautionary measure against it is unworkable in practice") is something entirely different: true Christianity.

A little band of true Christians, scattered as individuals, will be able to take up the cause. By true Christians is meant such individuals who believe and whose lives express that this life is dedicated to suffering for the truth, never vacillating in action as if they half hoped that one could serve the truth and at the same time be successful in this world.

These people, you see, have died to the world; only they are able to carry the cause through.

The continual outcry that it would not be possible to gain power over the daily press merely expresses what a puny concept our contemporaries have of what it means to be willing to suffer for the truth, to concentrate a whole life on this; it merely expresses how soft a life men have at present. And I do not deny that the kind of people living now would probably find it impossible to take on the press—these people who have no eternity to hope for and no life to sacrifice.

x³ A 279   *n.d.*, 1850

« 2168 *Jesuits—and the Daily Press*

The Jesuits in their degeneracy were the most disgraceful attempt to seize control of consciences. The daily press is the most infamous attempt to constitute the lack of conscience as a principle of the state and of humanity.

x³ A 280   *n.d.*, 1850

« 2169 *The Daily Press*

This is actually what it signifies—the changing of the public into a kind of person—and then consorting with the public.

x³ A 665   *n.d.*, 1850

« 2170 *The Opposite Direction*

The trend is continually in the direction of perfecting the means of communication so that the communication of nonsense can spread farther and farther. No one seems to think, in view of the nonsense and all that which is killing the states, that the task ought rather be to invent *smoke-consuming* machines.

x^3 A 723   *n.d.*, 1851

« 2171 *The Daily Press*

The demoralizing character of the daily press can also be seen in the following way.

In each generation there are hardly ten who, Socratically, most of all fear to think wrong, but there are thousands and millions who are all too afraid of standing alone with an opinion, be it ever so right.

But when something is printed in the newspaper, this is *eo ipso* sure proof that there is a goodly number who want to have or express the same opinion—*ergo*, you may well venture to have the same opinion.

In fact, if the daily press, like some other occupational groups, had a coat-of-arms, the inscription ought to be: Here men are demoralized in the shortest possible time, on the largest possible scale, at the cheapest possible price.

x^5 A 138   *n.d.*, 1853

« 2172 *The Daily Press*

is well calculated to make personality impossible, for it operates as a huge abstraction, the generation, which has infinite dominance over the single individual.

This is a means which was unknown in the past. In former times the conflict between a personality and the abstract was still not so enormously disproportionate as in our times when someone (impersonally, unscrupulously) can use this enormous weapon against the single individual [*den Enkelte*].

xi^1 A 25   *n.d.*, 1854

« 2173 *"A Public Personality"*

Elsewhere in these journals I have pointed out that the generally accepted view of the "daily press" up to the present time by no means grasps the point. To be specific, we picture it something like this: major premise, the daily press is a good thing; minor premise, sometimes it does harm when it is misused for lies, malice, etc. But what I am driving at is this: the daily press, especially in minor affairs, is evil simply and solely through its power of circulation; in minor affairs it is a disproportionate means of communication and thus a kind of insanity which tends to make society into a madhouse, just as crisscrossing a square mile area with trains would be crazy and, far from benefiting, would confuse everything. No, in and by itself circulation is an evil. I have used [i.e., IX A 378] the example that if the daily press mentioned a young girl by name and said that she had gotten a new light-blue dress (all of which was true), this would amount to an attempted assassination of the young girl which could be the death of her or drive her out of her mind. Only a few people are able to bear the enormous publicity occasioned by the kind of circulation at the disposal of the press, least of all when the press is used in this way to publicize [minor affairs]. Publicity would kill the young girl. And even the most hardened of men needs almost colossal powers to endure for a long time the use of the press in this way in minor matters. Consequently circulation in and for itself is the evil.

I will now point out something similar in relation to "a public personality."

A public [*En off.*] (strangely enough, when abbreviated this way it could also mean an offering or a sacrificed [*en offret*] personality—and they are synonymous, as I will demonstrate) personality must unconditionally be burned a little. Here again one cannot rightly reason as follows: major premise, a public personality; minor premise, if he is proud, arrogant, or if he wants something that is wrong, or if that which he wants is not understood by his contemporaries, etc., he gets burned a little.

No, the point lies elsewhere: publicity, the fact that everybody knows him makes them become sick and tired of him in a way; he gets their goat, etc. Men are guilty here of a curious self-contradiction, for the public figure would no doubt count himself most fortunate to be permitted to go unnoticed. But no, everyone feels duty-bound to notice him and to make those around him, if any, aware of him. Thus he and everything he does are watched day in and day out; the most insignificant thing is evaluated, judged, and related to his character. He becomes more and more widely known—and it is precisely this public acquaintance which irks them. They are unable to endure knowing him in this way; actually, they can stand him only at the distance of imagination. But then they themselves could quit contributing to his mounting public acquaintance. Alas, but this they cannot ever do.

It is the same with any decidedly public personality, regardless of his cause and the kind of sacrifice he is (for if it is truth he serves, it follows as a matter of course that he has to be sacrificed in this world).

The more I look at existence [*Tilværelsen*], the more clear it becomes to me that not only in the world of nature but also in the world of spirit existence becomes unhinged through, if you please, gluttony, except that the law in the world of spirit is the opposite of the law in the world of nature. In the gluttony of the natural world the higher animals eat the lower ones—to eat is superior, to be eaten is inferior. In the world of spirit to be eaten is superior.

To be eaten! Being spirit in the world of nature cannot be otherwise.

To be eaten in this way, or to be sacrificed, is a process of short or long duration. And the significance of this process? Well, once I was inclined to believe that it meant that those who eat him, or those for whom he is sacrificed, thereby come in contact with spirit and are influenced in the direction of spirit. But this is hardly true, and one cannot come to spirit in a brutish manner, anyway. No, the brutish merely become more and more brutish. On the other hand, the significance of the process is that the one in whom there is spirit is more and more purified and transformed into spirit; it is a filtering process.

XI^1 A 232   *n.d.*, 1854

« 2174 *Journalists*

These people call themselves after "the day" (*Journalister*).[650] It seems to me they could better be named after *the night*. Therefore, since journalist is a foreign word anyway, I propose they be called "night-carriers," "night-garbage-carriers." I do not think the word nearly as well fits the sanitation department workers for whom it is used. But journalists are really night-garbage-carriers. They do not carry the trash *away* at night, which is both a noble task and a good work; no, they carry the trash *in* during the day, or to describe it more accurately they spread night, darkness, confusion over men—in short, they are night-carriers.

XI^1 A 342   *n.d.*, 1854

JOY

These are significant words with respect to an inappropriate joy over power and authority in the spiritual sense: "Nevertheless do not rejoice in this, that the spirits are subject to you, but rejoice that your names are written in heaven." Saint Anthony (according to information on Athanasius gathered from Möhler) used these words to warn the ascetics not to forget the one thing needful along with their power to drive out demons.

II A 304   December 6, 1838

« 2176

. . . . . not the laughter which is the playmate of pain—that I do not want, for that I have—nor the *wohlfeile*, the syrup-sweet smile—this I decline—but the smile which is the first fruit of blessedness.

II A 506   *n.d.*, 1839

« 2177 *What It Is to Sanctify One's Joy*

If a man, downcast and troubled, came to you and said, "There is a sorrow which gnaws at my soul, embitters my joy, and makes all the rest of my afflictions still more burdensome,"[651] and it stood in your power to supply the remedy and alleviate *that* sorrow, would you not be right to expect him to find a strength within himself to bear all his other troubles, so that every time he was dispirited he would say to himself: However burdensome it may be, there was one sorrow which lay far more heavily upon my mind, and *it* was taken away, and *therefore* I will be *happy*.

Of course we know that there are in the world many adversities with which one person can greatly help another. But now if a man's sorrow concerned heavenly things, if what he strove after was reconciliation and peace with God, and if he were now to say to God: "There is one sorrow which robs me of all joy, which makes my life a burden; there is one longing in my soul which devours me if it is not satisfied," and then God, because this man sought relationship with the community which witnesses to a forgiveness of sins, gave him the Spirit's witness also to the forgiveness of *his* sins—must not a new life stream through him, must not joy take up residence within him, so that in all his sorrow he still must say: I have nevertheless known a suffering which is more painful than everything which is now happening to me; I nevertheless possess a joy which is as high above all sorrows as heaven is above the earth, and even if earth opened to swallow me, I should still see heaven open to receive me.[652]

This is *Christian joy*, not the world's joy; it is *sanctified*; it is not relished in the fleeting moment, anxious lest it suddenly vanish; it is not behind us, as earthly joy always is, but before us, but yet *not so far ahead* of us that we must say: Who will climb up to heaven to fetch it down— no, it is within us . . . . .[653] Rejoice always! Rejoice, and again I say, rejoice *in Christ!*

But how many there are to whom the earthly joy beckoned and who took it in vain and did not sanctify it; they enjoyed it and it vanished, and their minds were not opened and prepared for heavenly things. Job was an old man, and he prayed that his children might not forget God in their times of happiness.

II A 580   *n.d.*, 1839-40

« 2178

And let us not delude ourselves into thinking that sorrow is more meritorious than joy, self-torture etc.——.

III A 33   *n.d.*, 1840

« 2179

It takes moral courage to grieve; it takes religious courage to rejoice.

III A 213   *n.d.*, 1840

« 2180

. . . . . What was the good of closing your eyes so the world's gloss no longer delighted you, what was the good of closing your ears so the vanity of the world did not force its way in, what was the good of having a calm and cold heart so the traffic of the world no longer affected it, what was the good of it all if your eyes are not again opened to the heavenly glory, your ears are not attentive to the unspeakable words which come from above, if your heart is not moved and filled with heavenly courage?

III C 18   *n.d.*, 1840-41

« 2181

. . . . . and when the pagan poet[654] says that grief rides behind, the

Christian says that joy sits up front, and what is behind we forget.[655]

III A 141   n.d., 1841

« 2182

Paul[656] writes in the letter to the Philippians: *Rejoice*, you people. With that I imagine he pauses for a moment. Listen now—the loud lamentation of all those who believe they cannot be happy, the humble sorrowful, the proud sorrowful, those who are ashamed of sorrowing and those who glory in it—and now he continues—and again I say: Rejoice, you people.

III A 192   n.d., 1841

« 2183

. . . . . Nevertheless, you can always accomplish something by giving witness to joy. Perhaps you say: How can this be; no one knows what I suffer or what I have suffered; the pathway of my sorrow is solitary and remote, rarely trodden by a traveler. To that I would answer: Is it so very important to you that others get to know exactly what you are suffering? Or do you believe that your significance is that you have suffered every possible suffering so that when you yourself have found rest in the world everything is then resolved? Can you not be satisfied with the common lot of humanity? Could not this still keep the way open? Or do you believe this to be impossible and that no one is able to understand you if he does not know your sufferings? Ah, the ear[657] of the sufferer is peculiarly formed. Like the lover's ear, which is trained to hear only the voice of the beloved although it hears everything else in the world, so also the ear of the sufferer picks up every voice of consolation and recognizes it at once if it is the voice of true consolation. Just as Scripture[658] says that faith and hope without love are only sounding brass and a tinkling cymbal, so also the joy proclaimed without mentioning the pain is only sounding brass and a tinkling cymbal; unheeded, it whistles past the ear of the suffering one; it sounds on the ear but does not resound in the heart; it agitates the ear but is not treasured within. But this voice which quivers with pain and still proclaims joy—yes, this forces its way in through his ear and descends into his heart and is treasured there.

III A 194   n.d., 1841-42

« 2184

Therefore my voice will shout for joy at the top of my lungs, louder than the voice of a woman who has given birth, louder than the angels' glad shout over a sinner who is converted, more joyful than the morning song of the birds, for what I have sought I have found, and if men robbed me of everything, if they cast me out of their society, I would still retain this joy; if everything were taken from me, I would still continue to have the best—the blessed wonder over God's infinite love, over the wisdom of his decisions.[659]

III A 232   n.d., 1842

« 2185

Even if you are conscious of having suffered greatly and the human supposition arises in your soul that it will eventually come to an end and better times will be coming, what good is it for you if you merely stare at the past and suck new grief out of it instead of rejoicing that the hour of liberation will perhaps strike soon. You may become so enervated that you will not be able to hear the sound when it does strike.

IV A 146   n.d., 1843

« 2186

If this is properly interpreted, every man who truly wants to relate himself to God and be intimate with him really has only one task—to rejoice always.[660] Even the finest of men, one we would dare rely on with complete confidence, can still require counselling and reminding on various matters; I can actually be wiser than he is, really be right, etc. But none of this is required in the relationship to God, and to begin with such things is nothing but blasphemous busyness, or at least a kind of childishness.

VIII¹ A 12   n.d., 1847

« 2187

It is presented often enough: young people and a delinquent upbringing—but since this nevertheless in so many ways leads to Christianity it is not, at least not here, the major problem. But a wrong Christian upbringing, to be repelled from Christianity by Christianity itself—ah, this they do not think about. And yet here is where the difficulties first arise. At most one thinks of a form of hypocrisy—of being brought up by a hypocrite. But this—to have received from one's upbringing the impression that Christianity never gives joy to the one who sincerely and wholeheartedly adheres to it every melancholy day and night—this is a collision.

VIII¹ A 90   n.d., 1847

« 2188

It is true that our earthly existence [*Tilvær*] is painful, but the possibility of joy slumbers there. —The child cries when it is born but smiles in its sleep (this observation is from Cardanus).[661]

VIII[1] A 97   *n.d.,* 1847

« 2189

The Gospel of Suffering*
No. 2

1. The joy——that we suffer only once
                   but are victorious eternally.[662]
                                      See journal NB 206 [i.e., VIII[1] A 31-32]
2. The joy——that affliction does not take away
                   but recruits hope.[663]
                                      See this book, p. 238 [i.e., VIII[1] A 360-361]
3. The joy——that the poorer one becomes himself
                   the richer he is able to make others.† [664]

VIII[1] A 180 *n.d.,* 1847

« 2190

In margin of 2189 (VIII[1] A 180):
4. The joy——that the weaker I become myself
                   the stronger God becomes in me.[665]
5. The joy——that what I lose temporally
                   I gain eternally.[666]
6. The joy——that it is not the believer who holds the anchor
                   but the author of faith who holds the believer.[667]
                   [*Corrected to:* that if the believer does not
                   succeed in holding on to the anchor in spiritual
                   trial and tribulation, the anchor of faith
                   succeeds in holding on to the believer.]

VIII[1] A 181   *n.d.*

« 2191

In margin of 2189 (VIII[1] A 180):
* Rather: Reassuring and Joyful Thoughts
                   Christian Discourses
                            by
                          S. K.

VIII[1] A 182   *n.d.*

« 2192

Addition to 2189 and 2190 (vɪɪɪ¹ A 180 and 181):

> See pp. 190 and 191 in this book
> [i.e., vɪɪɪ¹ A 300-302, 322-323]
> vɪɪɪ¹ A 183   *n.d.*, 1847

« 2193

Addition to 2189 (vɪɪɪ¹ A 180):

† for all worldly possessions (wealth, honor, power, etc.) diminish the possessions of others to the same degree as mine increase.

The poverty of the spirit.

> the more learned I become,
> the fewer I am able to make
> understand me.[668]
> vɪɪɪ¹ A 184   *nd.*, 1847

« 2194

> See p. 73 in this volume and p. 210
> [i.e., vɪɪɪ¹ A 180-183 and 322-323]

The Gospel of Suffering, No. 2

VII. The joy because it is "for joy" that one does not dare believe the most blessed of all.[669]

> You do not believe it—but take courage, for the reason is really only that it is too joyous; take courage, for it is joy which hinders—is this not joyous?

It is told of the disciples that they did not dare believe for joy. Luke 24:41.

> vɪɪɪ¹ A 300   *n.d.*, 1847

« 2195

In margin of 2194 (vɪɪɪ¹ A 300):

. . . . . that whenever you wish you can close your door and speak with God without a middleman, without the tax and burden of superior condescension—is this not blessed—but you do not believe it? Why do you not believe it? Perhaps it is too joyous—but is it nevertheless not joyous? The forgiveness of sins, etc.

> vɪɪɪ¹ A 302   *n.d.*

« 2196

The joy——that the more the world goes against us, the less we are de-
    layed on our way to heaven.
or
The joy——that, Christianly understood, adversity is prosperity.

Everything that helps us along the way we are to go is prosperity;
but this is exactly what adversity does; *ergo*, it is prosperity.[670]

See pp. 73, 190, and 191 in this book [i.e., VIII¹ A 180-183, 300-302]

VIII¹ A 322   *n.d.*, 1847

« 2197

In margin of 2196 (VIII¹ A 322):

When a fisherman wants to make a good catch he has to go where
the fish are—but the fish swim against the current—consequently he has
to go to that side.

VIII¹ A 323   *n.d.*

« 2198

The Correlation of a Few Joyful Thoughts
4 Discourses
No. 1
Tribulation gives steadfastness.
No. 2
Steadfastness gives competence.
No. 3
Competence gives hope.
No. 4
Hope does not shame.[671]

VIII¹ A 360   *n.d.*, 1847

« 2199

In margin of 2198 (VIII¹ A 360):

or: The coming into existence of hope. Perhaps better to
use in one of the discourses in the "Gospel of Suffering."

See this book, p. 73, no. 2 [i.e., VIII¹ A 180]

VIII¹ A 361   *n.d.*

« 2200 NB

Only 7 themes were used for "Joyful Notes in the Strife of Suffering."[672] Here are three which were set aside.

No. 1. The joy——that if the believer does not succeed in holding on to the anchor in spiritual trial and tribulation, the anchor succeeds in hanging on to the believer.

See journal NB², p. 73 [i.e., VIII¹ A 180]

No. 2. The joyful correlation——that tribulation gives steadfastness, steadfastness competence, competence hope.*

No. 3. The joy——that it is for joy that one does not dare believe what is most blessed.

See journal NB², p. 238 [i.e., VIII¹ A 360]

Thus in Acts 12:14 the girl, Rhoda, who was to open the gate for Peter: when she recognized Peter's voice "in her joy she did not open the gate"—in her joy she let him stand outside.

* *In margin:* They say that misfortunes seldom come singly—the same with joy, it does not come singly.

VIII¹ A 500   *n.d.*, 1847-48

« 2201

No Foreword was written for "Joyful Notes in the Strife of Suffering." If it were to be written, it would be of the following nature. That most valiant of nations in antiquity (the Lacedæmonians) prepared for battle with music—in the same way these are notes [*Stemninger*] of triumphant joy, which tune one [*stemme*] for the struggle, and instead of discouraging a person in the struggle will rather keep him in perfect tune.

VIII¹ A 503   *n.d.*, 1848

« 2202 *The Conclusion*

If you know in truth [feel that God is present] or if it is the truth within you that you have felt that God is present and that you yourself are before him or, more correctly, if you are in the practice of coming here quite often, and every time it is true for you that you feel that here you are before God—then it ought to be detected in you. One ought to be able to detect in a man's bearing that he has fallen in love. One ought to be able to detect in a man's bearing that he has been seized by a great idea. Why, then, should it not be detectible in a man's bearing that he is before God. You should become still and silent, as a person always is when he is before God; warm and ardent, as a person always is when he is before God; strong and courageous, as a person always is when by being before God he is with God; patient, forbearing, yielding, slow to anger, quick to reconcile, as a person always is when by being before God he has God over him; you should be full of hope, rich in comfort, nothing but joy—you should become a benediction to the people among whom you live, since, indeed, God, by the very fact that you are before him, steadily pronounces his benediction over you.

x^5 A 156   *n.d.*, 1849

« 2203 *Joy in Affliction*

It is said that only the secularized mentality wants to have affliction removed in order to be joyful again, that the religious mentality is to be joyful in affliction, although the affliction and the suffering continue.

Let us not exaggerate, however, no matter how true this is, for a human being is still a human being, and if joy in affliction could be or should be the very same as joy without affliction, eternity would be almost superfluous.

x^4 A 183   *n.d.*, 1851

« 2204 *Christian Affection*

A lot of harm has been done by our always having to do it up big right away and proclaiming Christianity as joy, joy—and God knows how joyous we are, after all.

The result is *either* that we transform Christianity radically and leave out whatever is not in accord with purely human notions of joy, *or* that it becomes sentimental drivel and partly hypocritical.

The elemental thing to be said is that Christianity is the unconditioned, that I must accept it, that it then promises me that at some time it will become sheer joy—without implying that it will necessarily be sheer joy in this life or that I am so advanced in Christianity that I already am able to find sheer joy in it.

Besides, I suspect that a slyness lurks underneath all this. The world has gradually completely badgered Christianity into a mouse hole, even though we are all Christians. So we hit on the idea that Christianity is sheer joy—simply in order to make it conceivable that one would want to be a Christian. That's just fine. We would be embarrassed to admit that we do not dare ignore Christianity, that we do understand the suffering—but that we must be Christians. See, here again is that paltriness which really betrays Christianity.

x^4 A 384   *n.d.*, 1851

« 2205 *Believing in God*

That believing in God is impossible without letting go of one's understanding is easy to see, because understanding involves the dialectic of finitude. If I can understand that something is good for one, I think it is easy for me to have faith—yes, but now for the point.

No, to believe in God means essentially always to rejoice impartially in and over God, essentially to be impartially joyous. For the joy of faith is that God is love, which then—if I only let go of my understanding—is just as much love whatever joy or sorrow, according to my notions, comes my way. All, all, all is love.

XI² A 114   *n.d.,* 1854

JUDAISM

« 2206

People often say that someone is a Don Juan or a Faust but rarely say that someone is the Wandering Jew. Should there not also be individuals of this kind who have embodied in themselves too much of the essence of the Wandering Jew? —Is it right for Sibbern[673] in Gabrielis' *Efterladte Breve* to have the hero say that he would like very much to roam around as the Wandering Jew? To what extent is it proper in and for itself—that is, to what extent is it to be preferred to the life his hero leads—and to what extent is it proper in the character of this hero, or does it involve a contradiction?

I C 66   March 28, 1835

« 2207

Now it is certainly true that Paul, for example, in his letter to the Galatians (4:3) calls it [Judaism] στοιχεῖα τοῦ κόσμου,[674] and at that particular point it is by and large placed on the same level as paganism. But this does not help us greatly, for it only leads us to a contradiction, since it is clearly taught in other passages in the New Testament that Mosaism and Judaism were a divine revelation.

I A 48   May 2, 1835

« 2208

For the Christian who now looks at Judaism it is apparent that Judaism was merely a point of transition; but who vouches for its not being the same with Christianity. For it is all very well that the law was given in order to prevent transgressions and consequently was a teacher (Galatians 3:21-23), but how do we account for its actually promising men salvation if they fulfill it.[675] I can well understand that it could mean punishment for transgressions, but the divine (likewise now the Christian) certainly must have perceived that it would be impossible to fulfill it, and how then could it promise salvation on the basis of a condition which it recognized to be impossible.

I A 49   May 2, 1835

« 2209

By the time Christianity appeared, Judaism had developed into its own parody: the Pharisees in the Law and the concept of an earthly Messiah in the Prophets.

I A 287 *n.d.*, 1836

« 2210

How beautifully the preparatory relationship of the Jews to Christianity is intimated in the legend of the Wandering Jew (see *Ein Volksbuchlein*,[676] p. 27), which relates how in the latter part of his life he continually guides those who come from afar to visit the holy land.

I A 299 December 4, 1836

2211 $\sim = \$ = \sim$ [677]

Carl Rosenkranz[678] (Bauer, *Zeitschrift für spekulative Theologie*, II, p. 1), declares as a historical-religious judgment: *Gott ist Gott*, by which, of course, he means Judaism, whose abstract monotheism did not permit anything but tautological predications of God. It seems to me that this is also expressed indirectly by the fact that the Jews never dared utter their עֲרוּנִי.[679] Just as the statement "*Gott ist Gott*"[680] exemplifies the parallelism so characteristic of the Jews, in its wider application their parallelism must lead inversely also to the statement "*Gott ist Gott.*"

II A 71 May 29, 1837

« 2212

This historical interpretation is one side of all knowledge of God. Therefore it is very characteristic of Judaism that it is able to see only the back of Jehovah; because history indeed enters when Jehovah leaves the given in order to go further, since the historical interpretation never becomes identical with the event itself. See Exodus 33:20-23. Verse 22: "*Wenn den nun meine Herrlichkeit* vorüber gehet, *will ich dich in der Felsenkluft lassen stehen, und meine Hand soll ob dir halten, bis ich* vorüber gehe."[681]

II A 354 February 6, 1839

« 2213

In margin of 2212 (II A 354):
On the whole the Jews were a historical nation in a much more profound sense than any other and a nation which emphasized the historical,

as is illustrated in the third person as the root form, which suggests the historical more than either the abstract infinitive or the subjective first person does.[682]

II A 355   n.d.

« 2214

It is like reading a motto on all Judaism: God made a *firmament* to separate heaven and the waters of the earth. It was not merely a separation (this was already characteristic of their monotheism), but it was fortified, a firmament which could never be assaulted.

II A 564   September 11, 1839

« 2215

In what sense the Jews can be called the chosen people is a big question. They were not the happiest of people; they were rather a sacrifice which all humanity required. They had to suffer the pains of the law and of sin as no other people. They were the chosen people in the same sense as the poets and the like often are—that is, the most unhappy of all.[683]

III A 193   n.d., 1841-42

« 2216

When they preach about Job, how speedily they always get to the end where Job got everything back again in double measure. To me it seems strange to preach about this. Is it not true that as soon as this happens, you can see your way clear to going along with it. This is why I prefer to preach about the preceding period.

IX A 191   n.d., 1848

« 2217

Here we see the striking contrast between Judaism and Christianity. Jewish piety always clings firmly to the world and construes essentially according to the ratio: the more pious one is, the better it goes for him on earth, the longer he lives, etc. A proverbial metaphor of how Jewish piety describes impiety is found in the saying: He shoots up like a mighty tree —but in a flash it is all over.

And so I ask: humanly understand (if we do not lie on the basis of subsequent knowledge), is this not a description of Christ's life—a man who in three years shoots up so high that they want to proclaim him king, and then he is crucified as a thief.

Judaism postulates a unity of the divine and this life—Christianity postulates a cleft. The life of the true Christian, therefore, is to be fashioned according to the paradigm which for the Jews is the very paradigm of the ungodly man.

IX A 424   n.d., 1848

« 2218 *Jewish Piety—Christian Piety*

Of all religions, the Jewish religion is closest to humanism. Its formula is: Stay close to God, and things will go well with you in the world.

Christian piety is far, far too high for us.

Thus Christianity has quite properly proclaimed grace as essential; but this, again, has been taken completely in vain.

x³ A 139   n.d., 1850

« 2219 *Judaism—Christianity*

It really makes an infinite difference whether I assume that the mark of my being a pious man whom God loves is that I succeed in everything, possess all the earthly benefits, etc. (this is Judaism), or that the mark is simply that I am the suffering one, always having opposition, adversity (God's fatherly solicitude to keep me awake) and finally suffering the opposition of the world because I adhere to God and confess Christ (this is Christianity).

x³ A 157   n.d., 1850

« 2220 *The Jews*

It is also noteworthy, as Helvig observes in his introduction to the translation of the Book of Ezra (in Kalkar's Bible),[684] that whereas other peoples moved farther and farther away from the faith of their fathers the older they got, until it almost became a joke to them, with the Jews it has been just the reverse. Whereas they ran after false gods in their early period, the religion which they rejected in their younger days became the comfort of their old age. But then, again, they became so prejudiced and set in the old that Christianity had to become an obstacle to them just for that reason. The old culminates in such a way that it has to cut off its own development.

x³ A 230   n.d., 1850

« 2221 *Christianity—Judaism*

One can see how heterogeneous they are simply by observing that

Judaism establishes family life as a form of godliness. Christianity explodes all this by the absoluteness of the God-relationship, which can lead to hating father and mother.[685]

Judaism is godliness which is at home in this world; Christianity is alienation from this world.

In Judaism the reward of godliness is blessing in this world; Christianity is hate toward this world.

The collisions of piety which Christianity itself announces it will bring about must be regarded by the Jews as impiety, consequently as far as possible from being the expression of godliness.

x³ A 293   n.d., 1850

« 2222 *Christianity—Judaism*

Abraham draws the knife—then he gets Isaac again; it was not carried out in earnest; the highest earnestness was "the test" [*Prøvelsen*],[686] but then once again it became the enjoyment of this life.

It is different in the N.T. The sword did not hang by a horsehair over the Virgin Mary's head in order to "test" her to see if she would keep the obedience of faith in the [crucial] moment—no, it actually did penetrate her heart, stabbed her heart—but then she got a claim upon eternity, which Abraham did not get. The Apostle [Paul] was not brought to the extremity where it was revealed to him that he would come to suffer all things in order to "test" whether he personally would keep the obedience of faith— no, he actually did suffer everything, he actually did come to weep and cry out while the world rejoiced, he actually was crucified—but then he got a claim upon eternity, which Abraham did not get.

The Old Testament "test" is a child's category; God tests the believer to see if he will do it and when he sees that he will, the test is over. Actually to die to the world is not carried out in earnest—but eternity is not manifested either. It is different with Christianity.

Thus in one sense Christianity is infinitely more rigorous than Judaism; letting go, giving up, and losing the things of this earth, sheer suffering, and dying to the world are literally in earnest. In another sense Christianity is infinitely more gentle, for it manifests eternity. But to be molded and transformed so that one is consoled solely by eternity means to become spirit, but to become spirit is the most agonizing of all the sufferings, even more agonizing than "the test" in the O.T., and yet it must be remembered that where there is no hope of eternity, every year of life is precious, one does not have many years before it is all over, and this is why every year in the test is so extremely painful—furthermore, if no eternity is expected, the loss of things of the earth is felt all the more. To endure the loss of the things of the earth with the help of the eternal—well, that is not too hard—*aber*, here it comes again, to be able to be helped by the eternal one must have endured the loss of the things of this earth—the eternal does not come without this pain.

Christianity is a matter of being a man, Judaism of being a child. In dealing with a child, we do not place his whole childhood at his disposal and tell him that in 7 or 8 years he will be checked to see how he has used them. No, no, every day, every week, every month we supervise the child. Judaism displays this childishness in the relationship to God. "The test" lasts for a time and then is all over—but, please note, within this earthly life. In Christianity God identifies himself as "spirit"; he pulls himself way back, so to speak, and says: Here is a whole life for you; the examination does not come until eternity. And the task is to become "spirit"; it is not a "test" in time—no, you must actually die to the world.

This preacher-prattle about how easy it is to bear the loss of the things of this earth when one has the eternal is deceptive; the preacher (who, of course, does not get involved personally in such things; otherwise he could not talk so preposterously) does not perceive that this is not the way it goes, for in order to receive the consolation of eternity I must lose, surrender the things of this earth. I do not begin by having the consolation of eternity and then lose and give up the things of the earth—no, I begin by being obliged to give up the things of this earth, and it is in this suffering that eternity comes into being for me. As soon as eternity consoles me, I have surrendered the things of this earth.

Thus in a sense God has become more rigorous in Christianity. Has not the father become more strict if he has heard his son's lessons every evening throughout childhood, but when the lad turns fifteen he no longer involves himself in this but says: At the end of the year comes the reckoning. The child can be deceived momentarily into thinking that he is rid of his father's daily supervision, that this is a mitigation—but it is rigorousness. It is the same with Judaism and Christianity. In Judaism God intervenes in this life, jumps right in, etc. We are released from this in Christianity; God has pulled back, as it were, and lets us men play it up as much as we want to. What a mitigation! Well, think again, for it is rigorousness on his part to deny you the childish supervision and to assign only eternity for judgment. When, accommodating himself to the child, he intervened in the world of time, you were perhaps able to turn back quickly from the wrong way if you were on it. Now, however, your whole life is all up to you—and then judgment comes in eternity.

x⁴ A 572   n.d., 1852

« 2223 *New "Fear and Trembling"*⁶⁸⁷

In margin: This is related to something in one of the journals [i.e. x⁴ A 338, 357, 458] from the time I lived on Østerbro.⁶⁸⁸

. . . . . And Abraham climbed Mount Moriah with Isaac. He resolved to speak to Isaac—and he succeeded in inspiring Isaac—since it is God's will, Isaac is willing to become the sacrifice.

And he cut the wood and he bound Isaac and he lighted the fire— he kissed Isaac once again; now they are not related to each other as father and son, no, as friend to friend, both like obedient children before Jehovah.

— —And he drew his knife— —and he thrust it into Isaac.

At that moment Jehovah in visible form stood beside Abraham and said: Old man, old man, what have you done? Did you not hear what I said; did you not hear me cry out: Abraham, Abraham, stop!

But Abraham replied in a voice half subservient, half confused: No, Lord, I did not hear it. Great was my grief—you know that best, for you know how to give the best and you know how to claim the best—yet my grief is tempered by Isaac's having understood me, and in my joy over being in accord with him I did not hear your voice at all, but obediently, as I thought, I thrust the knife into the obedient sacrifice.

Then Jehovah brought Isaac back to life. But in quiet sorrow Abraham thought to himself: But it is not the same Isaac; and in a certain sense it was not, for by having understood what he had understood on Mount Moriah, that he had been selected by God for the sacrifice, he had in a sense become an old man, just as old as Abraham. It was not the same Isaac, and they were properly suited to each other only for eternity. The Lord God Jehovah foresaw this and he had mercy upon Abraham and as always restored everything, infinitely better than if the mistake had not occurred. There is, he said to Abraham, an eternity; soon you will be united eternally with Isaac, and you will be in harmony for eternity. Had you heard my voice and had stopped short—you would have gotten Isaac back for this life, but that which concerns eternity would not have become clear to you. You went too far, you ruined everything—yet I am making it even better than if you had not gone too far—there is an eternity.⁶⁸⁹

This is the relationship between Judaism and Christianity. In the Christian view Isaac actually is sacrificed—but then eternity. In Judaism it is only a test [*Prøvelse*] and Abraham keeps Isaac, but then the whole episode still remains essentially within this life.

X⁵ A 132   n.d., 1853

« 2224 *Christianity—Judaism*

Actually, of all the religions, Judaism is explicit optimism; even Greek paganism with all its enjoyment of life was nevertheless ambiguous and sad and above all lacked divine authority. But Judaism is divinely sanctioned optimism, sheer promise for this life.

And simply because Christianity is renunciation, Judaism is its presupposition: *Opposita juxta se posita.*[690] Renunciation can never be as radical as when it has divinely authorized optimism in the foreground.

But instead of perceiving this, Christianity in its whole history has had a constant tendency to promote Judaism as the equal of Christianity instead of using it as a point of departure or that which is to be abandoned when renunciation, unconditional renunciation, is proclaimed.

XI¹ A 139   n.d., 1854

« 2225 *Judaism—Christianity*

It cannot be made clear enough or be repeated often enough that Christianity certainly is related to Judaism, but in such a way, please note, that Judaism serves Christianity by helping it become negatively recognizable, is the repulsion of offense, yet they belong together for the very reason that this repulsion is an essential part, for otherwise Christianity would lose its dialectical elevation.*

Take this example. Christianity means renunciation—therefore it is brought to bear upon Judaism, for Judaism is characterized particularly by promises of all kinds for this life, with everything concentrated in this life. Precisely in order to deepen the renunciation, it is brought to bear at the very point where the opposite is manifest, consequently to make the renunciation all the deeper. No one feels more deeply and more painfully what he has to give up than one who had been summoned to receive it.

Further, Judaism is marriage and again marriage: Multiply and be fruitful, blessings on the race, etc.—therefore Christianity is brought to bear on this very point, Christianity, which means virginity, but it must have the repulsion of offense, and it most surely gets it right here.

Further. In Judaism everything is promise for this life, to live long upon the earth, and from this the conception of a theocracy here on earth—therefore Christianity is brought to bear at this point, because Christianity means: My kingdom is not of this world.[691] This is the repulsion of offense, which Christianity must have for its beginning. This is the repulsion of offense, more intense, if possible, when it portrays itself—it is almost ironical—as being the fulfillment of prophecies and expectations.

So it is at every point.

This cannot be emphasized enough, because in Christendom one finds that almost all of the more pious errors are connected with elevating the Old Testament to the level of equality with the New Testament, instead of the New Testament always presupposing the Old Testament in order to make itself negatively recognizable. In this sense the New Testament cannot be properly understood without the Old, for the repulsion of offense is its dialectical sign and the mark of its spiritual elevation.

But men would rather be Jews—sensately holding fast to this life and with divine sanction to boot—than be Christians, that is, be spirit.

XI¹ A 151   n.d., 1854

« 2226

In margin of 2225 (XI¹ A 151):

* In fact, "spirit" can never be represented directly; there must always be a negation first, and the more "spirit," the more care is taken that the negation is the negation of the very opposite.

XI¹ A 152   n.d.

« 2227 *Christianity—Judaism*

It cannot be made clear often enough that Judaism is linked to Christianity in order to make Christianity negatively recognizable—negatively, that is, by the repulsion.

With the divine keen-sightedness of providence everything is arranged to manifest the possibility of offense, and Christianity could not have had any other religion as a foreground, because none negatively manifests Christianity as definitely, as decisively, as Judaism does.

That Jesus is born of a virgin—this would not decisively scandalize pagans, but to Judaism this must be really offensive. Judaism culminates in the deifying of marriage; indeed, God himself has established it. Judaism culminates in the conception of the continuation of the race as a kind of divine worship—and then to be born of a virgin! Fundamentally this negates the whole Old Testament or deprives it of its power.

Besides, the traditional conception has conceded so much in this case that the contemporary age cannot escape the phenomenon by being able to document that this Messiah is not the Messiah. For example, if Christ were not of the lineage of David, this fact would be decisive. But he is of David's line and nevertheless is not, for he is born of a virgin and consequently he is still outside the lineage. As mentioned, in the Jews' high conception of family and lineal descent, to be born of a virgin can never come to mean something higher but only something lower.

XI¹ A 184   *n.d.*, 1854

JUDAS

« 2228

In the situation of contemporaneity Judas would not have been judged very unfavorably. The matter of the thirty pieces of silver would not have been stressed to a great extent. It would have been said: How much or how little does not change the matter. The stress would have been laid rather on Christ's having deceived Judas generally, disappointed his expectations—therefore it was quite consistent for him to take revenge, and this being the case he could just as well have not accepted the thirty pieces of silver, which the high priests might have pressed on him primarily in order not to have him as their confidant and ally.

IX A 431   *n.d.*, 1848

« 2229

One will get a deep insight into the state of Christianity in each age by seeing how it interprets Judas. Abraham of St. Clara[692] is naïvely convinced that he was the most villainous of all scoundrels, about whom one is to say only every conceivable evil—but does not have to explain him. Daub[693] becomes too profoundly metaphysical.

IX A 470   *n.d.*, 1848

« 2230

Until the very end Judas showed that he was astute about money— by getting 30 pieces of silver for someone as scorned as Christ was at the time—or he might also have met the high priests when they were feeling generous.

X^1 A 164   *n.d.*, 1849

« 2231 *Jesus and Judas*

If I dare speak for a moment in a purely human way about Jesus and Judas, I would say that Christ had the benefit of Judas' being quite simply and notoriously a traitor and he thereby got an opportunity to show nobility toward him.

But as the world becomes more and more clever, it also becomes

512

more and more villainous and its villainy more and more cunning. In the modern version the traitor would be so ingenious that ultimately Christ himself would be the only one to see that he was a traitor and the others, the apostles, would think that Judas was his true friend!

In this way the person of nobility is put in the difficult position of having to denounce him—and perhaps not even be understood or believed. Thus the impact of the noble person is also weakened.

XI^1 A 132   *n.d.*, 1854

« 2232 *Judas Iscariot*

Christ himself spoke the terrible words about him: It would have been better for that man if he had never been born.[694]

Although everything has been set in motion in Christendom to make Judas out to be the blackest of characters, I must say nevertheless that I could conceive of him a whole shade worse.

My conception of Judas Iscariot would not be of a desperate man (which he probably was actually) who in a moment of rage sells his master for thirty miserable shekels (how mitigating the paltriness of the sum is in itself and in a certain sense also his frightful end).

No, Judas is constituted quite differently; he is a quiet man with an entirely different understanding of life—what profits. Therefore he goes to the high priests and says to them: I am willing to betray him, but listen to my conditions. I do not care so much about getting a large lump sum which I could go through in a few years. No, I want a certain amount each year. I am a young man, strong and healthy, and in all human probability I have a long life ahead of me, and I would like to lead a pleasant, enjoyable life, marry and have a family. This is my price.

According to my mind this is a whole shade more abominable—I really do believe that such an abomination could not occur in ancient times: it is reserved for our sensible age.

It is easy to detect that I have conceived Judas somewhat *à la* the professor, who safely and quietly leads a tasteful, enjoyable life—aided by the fact that Christ sweat blood in Gethsemane and cried on the cross: My God, my God, why have you forsaken me?

It is this quiet living on in perfect accommodation that makes assistant professors so odious.

O, but in vain do you hope to influence assistant professors. When I am dead, all that is mine will also be exploited by assistant professors.

And these assistant professors will continually bask in the public eye. Just as in the grades the one who was most esteemed by his comrades was the boy who knew how to fool the teacher most cleverly, so the world always admires one thing only—a dishonesty more clever than the previous one.

A Berlin police official (Thiele[695] in his work on the Jewish *Gauner*) tells of a Samuel Joel who was so highly regarded among the thieves that if one of them was asked, "Do you know S. Joel?" he would glow with a smile of admiration. And so the world smiles admiringly every time mention is made of an assistant professor who cleverly deceived the truth.

The point toward which the world is moving before history runs out is that the highly praised honesty prevailing today will turn out to be a swindle.

XI¹ A 374   *n.d.,* 1854

KANT

« 2233

Kant despairs of finding the pure or absolute in the world; therefore he shifts to another position—the newer philosophy abandons this *relative-absolute*.[696]

I A 192   n.d., 1836

« 2234

Isodorus Hisp.[697] refers to a transcendence [*Transcendents*] quite different from that which Kant counsels against—*isti* (namely, *seculo huic renunciantes*) *præcepta generalia perfectius vivendo transcendunt*,[698] although Kant would probably say that it is the same, except in the domain of action, and equally dangerous, since it stands in opposition to the concept of the universally valid.

II A 486   July 20, 1839

« 2235

The Kantian discussion of an *an sich*[699] which thought cannot get hold of is a misunderstanding occasioned by bringing actuality as actuality into relationship with thought. But to conquer this misunderstanding with the help of pure thought is a chimeric victory. In the relation between Kant and Hegel it is already apparent how inadequate immanence is.

VI B 54:16   n.d., 1845

« 2236

. . . . . Let us rather say it straightforwardly with honest Kant,[700] who declares the relationship to God to be a kind of mental weakness, a hallucination. To be involved with something unseen is this, too. Steffens[701] quite properly quotes this somewhere in his philosophy of religion.

VIII¹ A 358   n.d., 1847

« 2237 *Distance*

In a little essay by Kant,[702] "An Answer to the Question: What is Enlightenment," Kant proposes to extend the *public* use of *reason* as much as possible and to limit the *private* use. By *private* he understands, for example, that an official *qua* official should not reason but do what is required. The same person, however, *qua* author, addressing the public, can be granted use of his reason publicly as freely as possible, in order to illuminate quite common irregularities. A pastor *qua* pastor should proclaim what is commanded—*qua* author he can present his doubts about the faith.

I shall not touch on the irregularity (which Kant himself parries somewhat) of an official's thereby becoming a dual being, which especially in the religious realm is lunacy (closely approached now, by the way).

No, what I want to keep is an outburst by Kant. After having placed all his hope in "the public, served by authors," he exclaims: "That the guardians of the people in spiritual things (not the *private* officials but the authors, and the people are the public) themselves should be without authority is an absurdity which eventuates in the perpetuation of absurdities."

Undeniably! But it is simply a prophecy which has been fulfilled, but has it expired? Alas, no—"it eventuates in the perpetuation of absurdities."

x^2 A 517   *n.d.*, 1850

« 2238

What an entanglement in Kant,[703] where he writes that a king ought to say: Reason as much as you wish—but obey. I do not know *whether* I should marvel more over this indirect contempt for reason by a philosopher, that it is to a degree emaciated, *or* the lack of acquaintance with human life. A bit earlier in the same work Kant[704] says that there is only one master in the world who can say: Reason as much as you wish—but obey. I suppose that Kant here means God, and I find it a splendid thought, that God the Almighty could do this—because he can compel. Note, however, whether God does this!

Now transfer this to an earthly king and proceed as if reasoning and obeying did not have the most dangerous close relationship imaginable, as if reasoning and obeying were separated in such a way that they have the least possible to do with each other!

x^2 A 519   *n.d.*, 1850

« 2239

From his standpoint it is jaunty of Kant[705] to say (in one of his small dissertations): It is all right with me for philosophy to be called the handmaid of theology—it must be that she walks behind in order to carry the train—or walks ahead and carries the torch.

X^2 A 539   *n.d.*, 1850

KNOWLEDGE

« 2240

In order to see one light determinately we always need another light. For if we imagined ourselves in total darkness and then a single spot of light appeared, we would be unable to determine what it is, since we cannot determine spatial proportions in darkness. Only when there is another light is it possible to determine the position of the first in relation to the other.

                                                            I A 1   April 15, 1834

« 2241

An example of how something from one angle can contribute considerably to strengthening an illusion and from another angle to unsettling it is found in "The Quaker and the Dancer"[706] in the lord's words: "It is a faked emotion." This can lead us either to think that everything else we see is actuality [*Virkelighed*] or remind us that the whole thing is a comedy.

                                                            I A 23   October 5, 1834

« 2242

Addition to 2241 (I A 23):
Just as in the *Aprilsnarrene*[707] scene: "It is an old man named Rosenkilde who copies [*copierer*] you."

                                                            I A 24   November 6, 1834

« 2243

Is everything, then, daydreaming and disappointment—is the inspiration of the natural philosophers and the ecstacy of a Novalis the vapor of opium—do I grasp there a crude substance where I thought to encounter the ideal in its most beautiful and purest colors?[708]

                                                            I A 91   October 11, 1835

« 2244

What is the significance of different lighting for paintings?

                                                            I A 110   *n.d.*, 1835

« 2245

Actually, the important thing in reasoning is the ability to see the part within the whole. Most people never actually enjoy a tragedy; it falls into separate pieces for them—nothing but monologues—and an opera into arias etc. The same sort of thing happens in the physical world when, for example, I walk along a road parallel to two other roads with interspersed strips of ground; most people would only see the road, the strip of ground, and then the road but would be unable to see the whole as being like a piece of striped cloth.[709]

I A 111   January 7, 1836

« 2246

The same difficulty which arises in the sphere of knowledge with respect to encompassing the mass of empirical data arises also in the sphere of emotions. For example, suppose a person on the occasion of a death were to recall that in Europe 100,000 people die every day—his grief would appear ludicrous to him. From this one sees the necessity of maintaining national distinctiveness in knowledge.[710]

I A 112   January 15, 1836

« 2247

But if even actual cognition is recognized as deficient, how then can the abstract be perfect?

I A 160   n.d., 1836

« 2248

Someone who goes mad by being conscious every single moment that the earth is revolving—

I A 191   n.d., 1836

« 2249

To see[711] is like looking at the sun; we can look at the sun only indirectly; if one wants to stare at it directly, he will see nothing but black spots before his eyes.

II A 663   September 6, 1837

« 2250

Erdmann, *Vorlesungen über Glauben und Wissen* (Berlin: 1837)

The first part of this book seems to me to stand up far better than the second (*Wissen*). It begins, at least according to what I make of it now, with letting the person (the *I*) disappear completely and in its place substituting a subject-object (reason–thought) which the previous development does not warrant. Even if it is so that the subject must stand in an essential relationship to the object (the deeper basis of which might later be shown to consist in the eternal concentricity of both), by being consistent one nevertheless can arrive provisionally only at a rational *I*, which itself becomes conscious of a family relationship with the object. In this case, it is correct for reason to be brought up to think reasonably, for this means, then, the rational *I*, which through a genesis merges in the true subject-object which has amplitude adequate to contain all finite subject-objects. Therefore it is probably true that reason is universal self-consciousness, but one is still not for that reason justified in saying (p. 141) that the question of what constitutes the universality in self-consciousness has the same significance as the question of how self-conscious man distinguishes himself from all other creatures, because reason as such lies above and beyond man.

A similar disingenuousness appears also from another side, which has become very common in more recent times and which has its roots in the ignoring of the historical aspect of Christianity. Although it is true in the development of pagan self-consciousness that the hypothesis first finds support in a universal, an experience (or since the experiment, undertaken by means of the hypothesis, is itself an experience, only the experience confirmed by experience is truth), and that the concept of tradition thereby first appears at a later stage, in the Christian development it has already come earlier, for the paradigm of the hypothesis declined in the experiment is indeed faith (or in this portion the confession) and consequently an experience (by others). In this case, the error is always a going above and beyond a certain traditional linguistic relativity, a going above and beyond which frequently pretends to be speculative. Christianity has really developed the concept of tradition, but now later the corresponding pagan analogy has been discovered,* and what previously was a main section has now become a subsection—a universally human communication based on man's historical aspect (race), a relief for their ideas, given at every moment (naturally, since it is historical) and raised above and beyond every man—then as a subsection comes this universal tradition and the so-called tradition in the strict sense.

Another observation this book prompts me to make is this: what is really the relationship between the deduction of the position and the position itself established historically? At many points it seems to me to be

merely a caricature, which as such naturally bears the marks of acciden-
tality, bears within itself the expression of the will, whereby it terminates
and crystallizes by itself in spite of the necessity of thought. The more the
deduction is concerned with this, the greater is the danger of its becoming
the best possible ordering of the accidental concretions of life and not the
necessary incarnation of the idea. In general the plunging chasm between
abstract deduction and the historical actuality is this: even though it can
be shown that the necessity of thought lays down a certain element of
thought, it still does not at all show its historical actuality—*cur deus
homo?*[712] I shall elucidate by means of an example, which I take from
Lecture 19.

When it is said on page 171 that reason first receives from experiment the confirmation necessary to its being regarded as true, the conclusion, that the "*Beglaubigende, weil das Beglaubigte von ihm abhängt
gegen dieses das Wesentlichere ist,*"[713] by no means follows, partly because if it does not hold true of the particular instance, in which case it
would not be adequate, the expedient is still available, which he did speak
about earlier, that the experiment is a failure, and consequently it can be
said that when one speaks of the particular instance, it does not hold true
of something else. But it is indeed true, if taken in its abstract form, that
reason generally must find its support in experiment; yet it is just as true
that the particular instance must find its support in reason (see page 166:
"*Wenn also nur die* bestätigte *Theorie die Wahreit ist, so andrerseits
auch nur der durch die Theorie erklärte Fall*).[714] If deduction stops here,
it is the accidental empiricism which moves too slowly. This is from one
side. But if we look more closely, then things are not like this in actuality,
for even though this viewpoint accents the historical and thus does not
distinguish between *articuli fundamentales*[715] and *non fundamentales*[716]
and consequently does not make the truth of the content the object of
its consideration but, indifferent to that, merely asks what the Church
Fathers teach, etc., then the same question arises again albeit in another
way, for if I then must ask what the Church necessarily must do, which
Church Fathers teach it, that is, how significant etc., in short, what is their
relationship to the truth,† for the Church still does not vote *per satura-
tum*[717] on the truth—then after closer scrutiny this viewpoint is certainly
not indifferent for the truth, and although there is an attempt to forget
one's viewpoint, oneself, one's interest during the process of inquiring
into what the Church and Scripture teach, it nevertheless arises again later
and is latently present‡ in every instance. Thus deduction as well as the
historical viewpoint appears to be corrupted. He halts the deduction in

order to present a caricature, and he does not use true deduction but
rather a *caricatured* compromise.

* *In margin:*
Although Erdmann heroically maintains faith (see the first lectures)
in its purely historical aspect as not being outside Christianity, he does
not, however, do this with tradition.

† *In margin:*
I find this observation corroborated by Erdmann's own recapitulation
in Lecture 20, p. 187: "*So sucht sie endlich aus den gegebenen Objekten
das heraus was von Andern als wahr bezeugt worden ist.*"[718]

‡ *In margin:*
"*Wie liesest Du? so dass die Lesart Criterium der Wahrheit wird.*"[719]
P. 178.

II C 44   November 21, 1837

« 2251

Lecture No. 21[720]
But here is a new difficulty, for if it must be conceded to Erdmann
that experience is not as passive as we are generally inclined to believe,
and therefore the merit of Erdmann's presentation must be acknowledged
(for example, the observation that we speak of *making* an experiment),[721]
yet one cannot deny that when he employs this kind of thinking particularly in the realm of Christianity he is on most dangerous ground. If all
experience generally has a stimulating effect, a position generally maintained with good justification, then Christian experience has a fructifying
effect, and here the border conflict takes place, because the question then
arises, to what extent can I subsume Christianity, like every other fact,
under my *a priori* judgment. This is the final point which is never clearly
developed, since he says (p. 189): "*So wird also die Vernuft sich damit
beruhigen können, dass irgend ein religiöser Inhalt durch die innere Erfah-
rung sich als wahr zeigt.*"[722]
All this appears also in a characteristic way, employed here and elsewhere, of making a transition to a particularized application, after having
developed a new point of view, with these words: "*Machen wir die Anwen-
dung auf dasjenige Gebiet, mit dem wir es zu thun haben.*"[723] But it may
be that in this way the relationships between the two areas are not investigated with thoroughgoing accuracy.

In spite of the way in which Erdmann limits (p. 196) the aforementioned position, he nevertheless continually uses the expression *reason*, although on the basis of page 196 he must use a sharper expression if he is to be consistent. So much on one side. But when he characterizes naturalism in this way, as he properly does, the whole position seems to take on an eccentricity whereby it lies beyond the scope designated by faith and knowledge, if faith is to be understood in the purely historical, Christian way. I am supported by the fact that all the portions which deal with experience and observation really do not belong within faith properly defined as Christian faith as done here; instead the primary position is that Christian experience rather than reason seeks its corroboration in other experience.

II C 46 *n.d.*, 1837

« 2252

In the presentation (p. 218)[724] of supernaturalism there is a difficulty, for what Kant has pointed out is probably true, that if there is no theoretical knowledge, then this obviously means that the entire sphere of the *an sich* is excluded from human consciousness and therefore never comes to man through consciousness either, and I therefore readily concede to Goschel that nonknowledge consistently ends in nonfaith—but therefore the supernaturalist maintains also that there must be a complete change in consciousness, that a development must begin from the very beginning and [be] just as eternal in idea as the first. It is therefore probably a mistake for the supernaturalist to link his faith to the nonknowledge of Kant, because as stated, from the nonknowledge of Kant must come nonfaith, and the supernaturalist's faith is precisely a new consciousness. The error appears more clearly in rationalism, which remains within the very same limits of consciousness, yet without discovering that if nonknowledge is admitted in the Kantian sense, he can never get faith in his sense within the same consciousness, and that the only means of attaining faith in this way is a more profound investigation of the nature of consciousness.

II C 48 December 4, 1837

« 2253

Upon hearing that some person stimulates his mind with drink, one feels, even though he produces the most magnificent things, a discomposure, an intimation of the forbidden and illicit which lies in this approach to the tree of knowledge—it is what the Middle Ages calls mortgaging his soul to the devil.

II A 698   February 4, 1838

« 2254

Empirical knowledge is a perpetually self-repeating false sorites, both in the progressive and the regressive sense.

II A 247   August 17, 1838

« 2255

In his appropriation of the impression of actuality, the authentic genius is often like someone who is sleeping and hears the fire alarm and conveys everything into his dreaming world, but the factual does not appear to him as such at all. There is something very significant about the relationship between the poetic and the factual (the latter can eminently be the former), as when one says: I do not know whether I have seen it or whether I have dreamed it.

II A 264   September 19, 1838

« 2256

Casuistry is phariseeism in the domain of knowledge.

II A 271   October 8, 1838

« 2257

The development of *a priori* basic concepts is like a prayer in the Christian sphere, for one would think that here a person is related to God in the freest, most subjective way, and yet we are told that it is the Holy Spirit that effects prayer, so that the only prayer remaining would be to be able to pray, although upon closer inspection even this has been effected in us—so also there is no deductive development of concepts or what one could call that which has some constitutive power—man can only concentrate upon it, and to will this, if this will is not an empty, unproductive gift, corresponds to this single prayer and like this is effected, so to speak, in us.

II A 301   December 2, 1838

« 2258

In margin of 2257 (II A 301):
One can therefore also say that all knowing is like breathing [*Aandedrag,* literally the drawing of breath], a *re-spiratio.*

II A 302   December 3, 1838

« 2259

There is a certain *reservatio mentalis* which is absolutely necessary for making a sound judgment.

II A 747   *n.d.*, 1838

« 2260

Just as Socrates had to stand still in order to come to himself[725] (the individual [*Individet*]), just so the Middle Ages had to go to the fairy tale in order to come to itself concerning the world.

II A 748   *n.d.*, 1838

« 2261

There is an incomparable feeling when one has succeeded in breathing the idea into the body of a concept, when one has thereby given it its boundaries—not a rail fence or a Chinese wall over which it *cannot go*, but a shape of beauty within which the *idea swells*, not convulsively but *virginally*. It may well be that for the time being, because of the earthly finitude of our cognition, we are obliged to place it in a *maidenly bower* until we have found a worthy bridegroom—but, after all, a maidenly bower is still no nunnery.

II A 348   February 2, 1839

« 2262

· The image which the mind requires for a period in order to fix its object—this and the externality conditioned by it—vanishes when true knowledge appears, just as the two disciples who journeyed to Emmaus observed, so to speak, that Christ was with them, but not until they in truth identified him did he become invisible.[726]

II A 390   April 3, 1839

« 2263

Especially along toward spring when nature awakens a little from its long sleep but then dozes off again (just as this moment is also the most pleasant in human sleep), there are certain days when nature seems so dreamy,* so pensive that we really feel what it means that the Northmen formed the clouds from Ymir's brains; heaven conceals itself wonderfully in a transparent cloak, as a beautiful girl mantles lovely forms in the luminous dusk of imagination. —And are not all our thoughts clouds which interfuse in relation to the different air currents—nothing but clouds, whether they seem to stand still above us for an hour as if wanting to remain with us or whether they hurriedly displace each other, driven by the storms of passion. You, my reader, whose horizon has still not been darkened by such clouds, this cloud also will drift by you unobserved and forgotten like many other things you have seen but which made no impression on you because they found no response in you.

II A 404   April 28, 1839

* *In margin:* thus *in pausa* we also feel the joy-vowel[727] lengthened.

« 2264

To the same extent that science and scholarship, in the prosaic manner it has now adopted, undertakes to lay out every problem the future has in store, to the same extent the genuine scientific pursuit will lose all its delight, all its adventure, just as hunting has lost it in our day when every head of wild game is known, and several years in advance it is already specified that this animal and that one are supposed to be shot— and in what year—this one in 1840, etc.

II A 441   n.d., 1839

« 2265

It is obvious that there is a cognitive unity of two elements, one of which is not coordinate with the other but subordinate, as when the girl gives up her *name* in marriage (*nomen dare alicui,*[728] precisely in order to take his name).

II A 461   June 26, 1839

« 2266

The philosophers think that all knowledge, yes, even the existence [*Tilværelse*] of the deity, is something man himself produces and that revelation can be referred to only in a figurative sense in somewhat the same sense as one may say the rain falls down from heaven, since the rain is nothing but an earth-produced mist; but they forget, to keep the metaphor, that in the beginning God separated the waters of the heaven and of the earth[729] and that there is something higher than the *atmosphere.**

II A 523   July 30, 1839

« 2267

*In margin of 2266 (*II A 523*):*
The contrast to this I have expressed in one of my other journals [i.e., II A 302] by the statement that all knowledge is *re-spiratio.*

II A 524   n.d.

« 2268

* *In margin of 2266* (II A 523):
Knowledge of this higher something is, of course, fragmentary.*

* See John 16:16: A little while, and you will see me no more; again a little while, and you will see me."

II A 525   n.d.

« 2269

But human knowledge* still has objective reality [*Realitæt*], and anthropomorphism (in the widest sense, not merely as an expression about God but about all existence) involves no transcendence [*Transcendents*],[730] such as we see in Genesis 2:19, which tells that God led all the animals to Adam to see what he would call† them, and the particular name he gave was the name the animal *kept*.

II A 526   August 1, 1839

« 2270

Addition to 2269 (II A 526):
* However circumscribed (limited) it may be as long as we live in the *status constructus*[731] of earthly existence [*Existents*].[732]

II A 527 n.d.

« 2271

In margin of 2269 (II A 526):
† This calling is, of course, essentially different from the divine calling, which is identical with creation: God called light *to be day*, לְאוֹר[733] (note ?), which was not a determination by naming but a substantial, real [*real*] determination.

II A 528   n.d.

« 2272

This is the union of the subjective and objective aspects of observation, as it is always stated in the Hebrew—וַיַּרְדְּהָ אֶת,[734] *he saw* and *see*.

II A 541   August 26, 1839

« 2273

Mark 7:31-37 is a description of human knowledge as it was before Christianity—"He could not hear," for heaven was not opened to him and God's word had not resounded (for everything was indeed created by God, but there still was not the resounding, the resonance in creation), "and he could speak only with difficulty," for since what he had to say was something he himself had found out, it was not worth writing home about. And so great was the error in the world that it was not enough, as it once was, to say: Let there be light;[735] but Christ sighed and said *ephata*, and such is Christian eloquence that it has to praise God even when it is forbidden. ("And Christ charged them to tell no one.")

II A 550   August 30, 1839

« 2274

It is a thought just as beautiful as profound and sound which Plato[736] expresses when he says that all knowledge is recollection, for how sad it would be if that which should bring peace to a human being, that in which he can really find rest, were external to him and would always be external to him, and if the only means of consolation were, through the busy, clamorous noise of that external science (*sit venia verbo*),[737] to drown out the inward need, which would never be satisfied. This point of view reminds one of that which in modern philosophy[738] has found expression in the observation that all philosophizing is a self-reflection of what already is given in consciousness, only that this view is more speculative and Plato's view more pious and therefore even a little mystical, inasmuch as it gives rise to a polemic against the world with the object of subjugating knowledge of the external world in order to bring about the stillness* in which these recollections become audible. But we ought not therefore remain stationary. On the contrary, here in the world of knowledge there rests upon man a curse (blessing) which bids him eat his bread in the sweat of his brow, but just as it does not mean that in the physical realm he must give the earth germinating power etc. but that he is to do everything in order that it can express itself, so it is with knowledge, and we can therefore say that the finite spirit is as it is, the unity of necessity and freedom (it is not to determine through an infinite development what it is to become, but it is to become through development that which it is), and thus it is also the unity of consequence [*Resultat*] and striving (that is, it is not to produce through development a new thing but it is to acquire through development what it has).

See EE, p. 37, DD, p. 59 [i.e., II A 301, 302].

* Not the infinite stillness σιγή[739] which is so characteristically the abstract.

III A 5   July 10, 1840

« 2275

All this big talk about having experience[740] in contrast to *a priori* knowledge is all very well. Nevertheless we cannot deny that it was commendable discretion which influenced that conscientious judge who wanted to try every penalty in order to be the more just in applying them —it was very commendable of him not to include the death penalty.

III A 9   *n.d.*, 1840

« 2276

A walk on the heath. (The wooded area near Hald. The woman and the little boy who hid in the thicket when I came along, and although unwilling to look at me, answered my question.) I lost my way; in the distance loomed a dark mass which restlessly undulated to and fro. I thought it was a woods. I was utterly amazed, since I knew there was no woods in the vicinity except the one I had just left. Alone on the burning heath, surrounded on all sides by sheer sameness except for the undulating sea straight ahead of me. I became positively seasick and desperate over not being able to get closer to the woods in spite of all my vigorous walking. I never reached it, either, for when I came out on the main road to Viborg it was still visible; but now that I had the white road as a starting point, I saw that it was the heathered hills on the other side of Viborg Lake. Simply because a person has such a wide vista out on the heath he has nothing at all to measure with; he walks and walks, objects do not change since there actually is no *ob*-ject [*G j e n-stand*] (an object always requires the *other* by virtue of which it becomes an *ob*-ject [*G j e n -stand*].[741] But this [other] is not the eye; the eye is the associating factor).

III A 68   *n.d.*, 1840

« 2277 *Everything Is New in Christ*[742]

This will be my position for a speculative Christian epistemology.

(New not merely insofar as it is different but also as the relationship of the renewed, the rejuvenated, to the obsolescent, the obsolete.)

This position will be simultaneously polemical and ironical. It will also show that Christianity is not a constriction around a particular object, around a particular normal disposition.

Not like a new patch on an old garment,[743] but like a fountain of youth.

The comparable position in which Christianity has hitherto been placed with respect to the past is this:

There is nothing new under the sun.[744]

This latter position is related negatively to the phenomenon, slays life by the abstract monotony which it teaches; the other position, however, is fructifying.

Even the idea of mediation, the watchword of modern philosophy, is in direct contrast to the Christian position, for which previous existence [*Existents*] is not so readily digestible but lies heavily within it and upon it, just as existence for the single individual prior to faith is by no means mediated without sorrow but is reconciled with profound sorrow; on the the whole the two terms are equally necessary—namely, that Christianity is something which did not arise in any man's thought[745] and yet since it is given to man is natural to him because here also God is creating.

———

When I say that everything is new in Christ, this applies particularly to all the anthropological positions; for the genuine knowledge of God (divine metaphysics, the Trinity) was unheard of before and consequently is new in Christ in another sense; here one sees the superior worth of the concept of revelation over against the purely human position.

The two statements must be distinguished: everything is new as an esthetic view—everything is new in Christ as a dogmatic, world-historical, speculative view.

III A 211   *n.d.*, 1840

« 2278

Addition to 2277 (III A 211):

Fortes fortuna is the pagan position; God is mighty in the weak is the Christian position. We see at once that the former is an immediate qualification, since happiness here is merely the reflex of the given immediate temperament of the individual, is the immediate *harmonia præstabilita*; the latter is a reflected qualification, occurs through the crushing of the individual [the double movement of infinity].

III A 212   *n.d.*

« 2279

If the rights of knowledge are to be given their due, we must venture out into life, out upon the ocean, and scream in hopes that God will hear

—we must not stand on the shore and watch the others struggle and battle—only then does knowledge acquire its true *official* registration.[746] To stand on one foot and prove the existence of God is altogether different from falling on one's knees and thanking him. The former is a delicate silk ladder which one throws up like a romantic knight of cognition and somehow uses in a curious manner to get aloft, simultaneously securing the ladder while standing upon it (unlike firemen who enter each floor to secure the shinning rope)—the latter is a solid stairway, and even if one advances more slowly, he is on the way and all the more securely. —

III A 145   n.d., 1841

« 2280

Notation in a copy of thesis, The Concept of Irony (*S.V.XIII, p.* 153, *line* 30):[747]

It is a shame I did not know at that time the skepticism which Sextus Empiricus maintains with respect to teaching. See Tenneman, V, p. 294.[748]

IV A 198   n.d., 1842-43

« 2281

The definition of science which Aristotle[749] gives in 6,3 is very important. The objects of science are things which can be only in a single way. What is scientifically knowable is therefore the necessary, the eternal; for everything that is absolutely necessary is also absolutely everlasting. —

IV C 23   n.d., 1842-43

« 2282

What is positive? What is negative?[750]

Positive knowledge is infinite knowledge; negative knowledge is finite knowledge. Insofar as positive knowledge is negative, negative knowledge is positive. If I know that I not know, if I know that I am always wrong, this is a negative knowledge, and yet it is positive; if I know that there have been 7,000 emperors in China or I know from experience that this has happened so and so many times, this is a positive knowledge and yet it is negative.

IV C 74   n.d., 1842-43

« 2283 *Interested Knowing and Its Forms*[751]

What knowing is without interest?

> It has its interest in a third (for example, beauty, truth, etc.) which is not myself, therefore has no continuity.

Interested knowing enters with Christianity.

The question of authority.
     of historical continuity
     of doubt
     of faith.
Is knowledge higher than faith? By no means.

IV C 99   n.d., 1842-43

« 2284

Consciousness presupposes itself, and to ask about its origin is an idle question, just as captious as that old one: Which came first, the tree or the acorn? If there was no acorn, where did the first tree come from? If there was no tree, where did the first acorn come from?

IV A 49   n.d., 1843

« 2285

Heraclitus retired from business, wrote his famous work, placed it in Diana's temple as a treasure which was to be accessible only to the knowledgeable.[752]

IV A 58   n.d., 1843

« 2286

Yes, even wanting to regard interest in astronomy[753] as curiosity, silly dilettantism, or even intellectual swindling, which in order to advance and advance does not penetrate into anything but merely makes variations of the sciences and intellectual disciplines—this, also, would be regarded as ethical narrow-mindedness. Socrates,[754] it seems, was also narrow-minded in this way: "He gave up the study of astronomy because he perceived that the heavenly things do not concern us." But at that time Professor Heiberg[755] had not proved that astronomy was what the times required. Now he has proved it, and so it certainly is. Earlier Claudius Rosenhoff[756] expressed something similar, and at Tivoli[757] an observatory has been erected where we can entertain ourselves astronomically for two shillings while poor folk occupy themselves with astronomy free at the Round Tower. And thus it has also been proved that world history is what the age demands.

Yet joking is one thing and earnestness another. Praise be to science and learning. Praise be to daring to begin and despondently abandoning because human limitations frighten a person back.* An objection which merely dreads [frygter] the insurmountable work or merely dreads that it is insurmountable without having anything higher to put in its place is not worthy of attention. Therefore the objection is not formulated in that way. The objection comes from the ethical. It says . . . . .

 * *In margin*: Learned science does not want to see the ethical in the historical, still less to extract from all this what the ethical is; scholarly research is solely in the interest of knowledge.

VI B 40:5   *n.d.*, 1845

« 2287

In relation to the absurd, objective approximation is nonsense; for objective knowledge, in grasping the absurd, has literally gone bankrupt down to its last shilling.

In this case the way of approximation would be to interrogate witnesses who have seen the God [*Guden*][758] and have either believed the absurd themselves or have not believed it, and in the one case I gain nothing, and in the other I lose nothing—to interrogate witnesses who have seen the God perform a miracle, which for one thing cannot be seen, and if they have believed it, well, it is one further consequence of the absurd. —But I do not need to develop this further here; I have done that in the *Fragments*. Here we have the same problem Socrates had—to prevent oneself from foundering in objective approximation. It is simply a matter of setting aside introductory observations, and the old reliables, and proofs based on effects, and pawnbrokers, and all such in order not to be prevented from clarifying the absurd—so that a person can believe if he will.

If a speculator would like to give a guest performance here and say: From an eternal and divine point of view there is no paradox here—this is quite right; but whether or not the speculator is the eternal who sees the eternal—this is something else again. If he then continues his talking, which does have the eternal in the sense that like the song[759] it lasts for an eternity, he must be referred to Socrates, for he has not even comprehended Socrates and even less found time to comprehend, according to his own position, something which goes beyond Socrates.[760]

VI B 42   *n.d.*, 1845

« 2288

The quiet inspiration in driving in the early twilight and seeing one star, until the darkness deepens and one sees more and more (for they were visible, of course, but the light was in the way), until the whole company becomes visible—thus to count the stars.

VII[1] A 230   *n.d.*, 1845-47

« 2289

When a rich man goes driving in the dark night with lights on his carriage, he sees a small area better than the poor man who drives in the dark—but he does not see the stars; the lights prevent that.[761] It is the same with all secularized understanding. It sees well close at hand but takes away the infinite outlook.

VII^1 A 234   n.d., 1845-47

« 2290

But let us never forget that not everyone who has not lost his reason thereby proves incontestably that he has it.

VII^1 A 236   n.d., 1845-47

« 2291

Spinoza[762] rejects the teleological concept of existence [*Tilværelsen*] and declares (at the end of the first book of *Ethics*) that the teleological view can be maintained only by seeking refuge in *asylum ignorantiæ*[763]— ignorant of *causa efficiens*[764] one then creates the teleology. —In the second part of his *Ethics*[765] he justifies his emphasis on immanence by saying that it is universal, except that we do not know what the *causa efficiens* is in every case. But here Spinoza resorts to *asylum ignorantiæ*. The defender of teleology concludes: We do not know it, *ergo* it is not there. Spinoza concludes: We are ignorant of it; *ergo* it is there.

What does this mean? It means that ignorance is the invisible point of unity for the two roads. For it is possible to reach ignorance, and then, as it says in the *Concluding Postscript*,[766] the road swings off. (See *Concluding Postscript*, part II, chapter II, "Subjectivity is Truth.")

VII^1 A 31   n.d., 1846

« 2292

Instead of all this bombast concerning the beginnings of science and scholarship one must, as in olden days, humanly begin with the question, should I beome a scientist.

We begin, then, with a purely ethical consideration, which preferably ought to be framed in a Platonic dialogue in order to get everything as simple as possible.

Just as with the ancient Greeks, it is *wonder* which prompts a beginning. Along with this note on wonder, Descartes' observation[767] about emotions could be used to advantage—namely, that wonder has no opposite—and also what Spinoza says about *admiratio**[768] in the third book of the *Ethics*,[769] that he does not include it among the three emotions (*cupiditas, lætitia, tristitia*)†[770] from which he deduces everything. It could be helpful here to take into consideration beginning with doubt.

That which prompts a beginning is *wonder*. That by which a beginning is made is a resolution.

* *In margin:* See p. 369.

† Note. Obviously he uses the Greek concept κίνησις[771] to mean *in transitio*[772] as he does in saying of *lætitia* and *tristitia* that it is *transitio in perfectionem*, not *perfectio* itself.[773] P. 368.

VII¹ A 34   n.d., 1846

« 2293

Probably the time is coming when people will find it just as *abgeschmakt* [insipid] to communicate results (something the present age demands and makes a big fuss about) as it once was to write a *Nutzanwendung* [instruction for use] at the end of moralistic stories. The person who does not find the result himself with the help of the path does not get it anyway; he merely imagines it.

VII¹ A 75   n.d., 1846

« 2294

Sense impressions are the most mediocre of all categories. Imagine, if you will, a devout woman singing a hymn with inward reverence, enunciating clearly every word, yet without raising her voice at all but rather with a humble, tremulous muffling and muting almost like the resignation of death—so that one has to be completely still to hear it. But sense impressions are like a bellowing watchman drowning out all the others without the slightest inwardness. Having a beautiful voice or not having a beautiful voice neither adds nor subtracts as far as inwardness is concerned.

VII¹ A 76   n.d., 1846

« 2295

If a servant girl asked an astronomer what time it is, he would answer: 12 o'clock. If a business man asked him, he would say: Yesterday, just when I raised the flag, I set my watch, so I know that it is precisely 12 o'clock. But if an astronomer making an observation were to ask him, he would say: It is one minute, 37 seconds, and a few hundredths after twelve. In all three cases he would be stating the truth. What he said to the servant girl was in no way untrue. Such is the relation between the scholarly and the simple.[774] To state it simply: should he who placed the ear not hear[775]—this is exactly the same as a conclusive reconstruction of the idea of God based on a teleological view of the world and the aim and the purpose of the world.

VII[1] A 185   n.d., 1846

« 2296

A conviction [Overbeviisning] is called a conviction because it is over and above proof [Beviisning]. Proof is given for a mathematical proposition in such a way that no disproof is conceivable. For that reason there can be no conviction with respect to mathematics. But as far as every existential [existentiel] proposition is concerned, for every proof there is some disproof, there are a pro and a contra. The man of conviction is not ignorant of this; he knows well enough what doubt is able to say: a contra; but nevertheless, or more correctly, for that very reason he is a man of conviction, because he has made a resolution and voluntarily raises himself higher than the dialectics of proofs and is convinced [overbeviist].[776]

VII[1] A 215   n.d., 1846

« 2297

Knowledge is the infinitely indifferent (in the sense of rank). Knowledge is like an auctioneer who puts existence [Tilværelsen] on the block. The auctioneer then says: Ten dollars (the value of the property)—but it means nothing; only when someone says "I bid," only then is the bid ten dollars.

VIII[1] A 186   n.d., 1847

« 2298

This, you see, is why nothing is learned from history. The great men of bygone days stand in glory; even persecution and the like look attractive; a more specific conception is not communicated. And so a young person rushes ahead and misunderstands, until he himself gets into it in earnest. Yet this is how it must be, otherwise the youth would not learn good and evil in an original or primitive way.[777]

VIII[1] A 479   n.d., 1847

« 2299

Christ says: I will manifest myself to him who loves me.[778] But it is generally true that something manifests itself to the one who loves it; truth manifests itself to the one who loves truth, etc. We usually think that the recipient is inactive and that the object manifesting itself communicates itself to the recipient, but the relationship is this: the recipient is the lover, and then the beloved becomes manifest to him, for he himself is transformed in the likeness of the beloved; the only fundamental basis for understanding is that one himself becomes what he understands and one understands only in proportion to becoming himself that which he understands.

Furthermore, we see here that to love and to know (יָדַע) are essentially synonymous, and just as to love signifies that the other becomes manifest, so it naturally means also that one becomes manifest himself. The relationship is so inward (a "to be" or "not to be") that all protestations and the like about love and loving are neither here nor there.

IX A 438   n.d., 1848

« 2300

In Acts 3:17 Peter declares that the people as well as the rulers acted in ignorance when they killed Jesus. If this is to be taken quite literally, it is impossible to get a definite idea of the necessity of Christ's having to suffer simply because he was love and the world is evil. It is almost as if it were a strategem on God's part. He wants to save men, but men can be saved only by the death of Christ; but how can that happen, how can he be put to death if men see his love—so it happened in ignorance. Insofar as this was the case, there is nothing at all in Christ's life to illuminate the common lot of the Christian in the world.

There is a host of difficulties and problems here. Strange as it may seem, one is reminded here of the Socratic view that sin is ignorance, just as Paul[779] says somewhere that he was forgiven because he had acted in ignorance.

X¹ A 577   n.d., 1849

« 2301 *Knowledge of the Truth*

All this positive talk about wanting so very much to know the truth, etc. is gibberish, illusion, and hypocrisy.

Every person always understands the truth a good deal farther out than he expresses it existentially [*existentielt*]. Why does he not go farther out, then?

Ah, there's the rub! I feel too weak (ethically too weak) to go out as far as my knowledge extends.

That "the truth" existentially introduced into the world means certain downfall is eternally certain, and it is also Christianity.

On a smaller scale everyone experiences something similar. He perceives some greater truth—but he does not dare venture so far out existentially.

In this way everyone becomes guilty before God—and must make this admission.

This is something quite different, you see, from that talk about wanting so much to know the truth, along with the notion that if one only understood the truth he would certainly act accordingly, along with the conceit that if only one were the truth he, of course, would be victorious. O dear one, I am almost tempted to say: Thank God that you are not the truth, because then your downfall in this world would be assured.

This I have understood, and therefore I call myself merely a poet, and therefore it is explicable to me that I may even come through unscathed and perhaps even win out, which would be impossible if I were more than a poet.

x⁴ A 247   n.d., 1851

« 2302   *Blessed Is He Who Does Not See—
and Yet Believes,*[780]

but if one *sees,* then he does not *believe*—therefore why this "yet"?

It must be remembered, however, that Thomas certainly did see, but what did he see? Yes, he saw that which goes against understanding, that a dead person had come to life. In this case seeing does not really help him to believe.

When it is a matter of the kind of certainty related to seeing directly, seeing and believing mutually exclude each other. But what Thomas sees is a phenomenon of a completely different order, containing a contradiction, which makes immediate sense experience (seeing it) an impossibility.

To that extent this "yet" could be interpreted as friendly irony toward Thomas, in that he himself thinks he sees but nevertheless really believes: You see—yet you believe; you think that you see, but such a thing cannot be seen directly, and therefore what you are doing is believing. In connection with such phenomena (contradictory), seeing can be just as much a hindrance as not seeing, because one who merely sees (sensory seeing) nevertheless does not see it, since it cannot be seen.

x⁴ A 310   n.d., 1851

« 2303 *Christian Knowledge*

In Christendom they talk about, boast about, and work to have Christian knowledge in the land.

I will not now discuss having my doubts about this, that the kind of knowledge we have about Christianity is really not about Christianity but about something men themselves have invented; therefore to boast about the existence of Christian knowledge is just as dubious as if a city were to boast about a very remarkable water supply, which actually did supply the city with water, all right, but bilge water .

But this I shall not discuss, but rather that knowledge about Christianity, from a Christian point of view, is of dubious significance. Suppose there really were considerable and true knowledge about Christianity throughout the country—if life does not correspond to it better than it does now, the fact that it is Christian knowledge makes it more blameworthy.

But this talk about Christian knowledge again shows that men still really treat Christianity as a problem of knowledge so that Christian knowledge in and for itself has value in the same sense as, for example, mathematics, history, and so on, intellectual disciplines which are not related to what kind of life a man lives, his character; whereas Christian knowledge, if it does not change life, makes matters worse in proportion to the increase in knowledge; consequently it subtracts and does not qualify as something one can at least cite as documentary proof—no, the very opposite, Christian knowledge gives one so much the less to cite or to use as an excuse.

XI² A 191   n.d., 1854

Bibliography
Collation of Entries
Notes

Bibliography

KIERKEGAARD'S WORKS IN ENGLISH

Editions referred to in the notes .
Listed according to the original order of publication or the time of writing.

The Concept of Irony, tr. Lee Capel. New York: Harper and Row, 1966.
Either/Or, I, tr. David F. Swenson and Lillian Marvin Swenson, II, tr. Walter Lowrie, 2 ed., rev., Howard A. Johnson. New York: Doubleday, 1959.
Johannes Climacus, or De Omnibus Dubitandum Est, tr. T. H. Croxall. London: Adam and Charles Black, 1958.
Edifying Discourses, I-IV, tr. David F. Swenson and Lillian Marvin Swenson. Minneapolis: Augsburg Publishing House, 1943-46.
Fear and Trembling (with *The Sickness unto Death*), tr. Walter Lowrie. New York: Doubleday, 1954.
Repetition, tr. Walter Lowrie. Princeton: Princeton University Press, 1941.
Philosophical Fragments, tr. David Swenson, 2 ed. rev. Howard Hong. Princeton: Princeton University Press, 1962.
The Concept of Anxiety [*Dread*], tr. Walter Lowrie, 2 ed. Princeton: Princeton University Press, 1957.
Thoughts on Crucial Situations in Human Life, tr. David F. Swenson and Lillian Marvin Swenson. Minneapolis: Augsburg Publishing House, 1941.
Stages on Life's Way, tr. Walter Lowrie. Princeton: Princeton University Press, 1940.
Concluding Unscientific Postscript, tr. David F. Swenson and Walter Lowrie. Princeton: Princeton University Press, 1944.
The Present Age and *Two Treatises* by H. H., tr. Walter Lowrie. London and New York: Oxford University Press, 1940 .
On Authority and Revelation, The Book on Adler, tr. Walter Lowrie. Princeton: Princeton University Press, 1955.
Purity of Heart, tr. Douglas Steere, 2 ed. New York: Harper, 1948.
The Gospel of Suffering and *The Lilies of the Field*, tr. David F. Swenson and Lillian Marvin Swenson. Minneapolis: Augsburg Publishing House, 1948.
Works of Love, tr. Howard and Edna Hong. New York: Harper and Row, 1962.

Christian Discourses, including *The Lilies of the Field and the Birds of the Air* and *Three Discourses at the Communion on Fridays,* tr. Walter Lowrie. London and New York: Oxford University Press, 1940.

[The] Crisis [and a Crisis] in the Life of an Actress, tr. Stephen Crites. New York: Harper and Row, 1966.

Armed Neutrality and *An Open Letter,* tr. Howard V. Hong and Edna H. Hong. Bloomington and London: Indiana University Press, 1968.

The Point of View, including *Two Notes about "the Individual"* and *On My Work as an Author,* tr. Walter Lowrie. London and New York: Oxford University Press, 1939.

The Sickness unto Death (with *Fear and Trembling*), tr. Walter Lowrie. New York: Doubleday, 1954.

Training in Christianity, tr. Walter Lowrie. London and New York: Oxford University Press, 1941.

For Self-Examination, tr. Edna and Howard Hong. Minneapolis: Augsburg Publishing House, 1940.

Judge for Yourselves! including *For Self-Examination, Two Discourses at the Communion on Fridays,* and *The Unchangeableness of God* (tr. David Swenson), tr. Walter Lowrie. Princeton: Princeton University Press, 1944.

Attack upon Christendom, tr. Walter Lowrie. Princeton: Princeton University Press, 1946.

The Journals of Søren Kierkegaard, tr. Alexander Dru. London and New York: Oxford University Press, 1938.

The Last Years, tr. Ronald G. Smith. New York: Harper and Row, 1965.

Søren Kierkegaard's Journals and Papers, tr. Howard V. Hong and Edna H. Hong. Bloomington and London: Indiana University Press, I, 1967, II, 1970. Volumes III-V, in preparation.

General works on Kierkegaard are listed in the Bibliography, *Søren Kierkegaard's Journals and Papers,* I, pp. 482-88. Studies of a more limited and specific nature are listed in the appropriate section of topical notes in each volume of *Søren Kierkegaard's Journals and Papers.*

Collation of Entries in this Volume
With the Danish Edition of the *Papirer*

Numbers in the left-hand column are the standard international references to the *Papirer*. Numbers in parentheses are the serially ordered numbers in the present edition.

Volume I A	Volume I A	Volume I A	Volume II A
1 (2240)	160 (2247)	287 (2209)	71 (2211)
2 (1302)	170 (1563)	292 (1181)	73 (1306)
5 (1230)	177 (1964)	299 (2210)	74 (1233)
7 (1231)	178 (1965)	302 (1189)	75 (1681)
21 (1303)	190 (1673)	317 (1567)	78 (1682)
23 (2241)	191 (2248)	337 (1967)	79 (1683)
24 (2242)	192 (2233)	340 (1541)	80 (1684)
29 (1304)	196 (1770)	**Volume I C**	81 (1685)
30 (1305)	205 (1232)	50 (1186)	84 (1686)
36 (1094)	207 (1674)	58 (1179)	85 (1687)
37 (1463)	208 (1626)	66 (2206)	101 (1689)
44 (1095)	211 (1564)	73 (1455)	102 (1690)
48 (2207)	224 (1456)	**Volume II A**	103 (1691)
49 (2208)	225 (1565)	2 (1542)	104 (1692)
82 (1464)	227 (1180)	14 (1630)	105 (1693)
83 (1287)	229 (1566)	22 (1279)	106 (1694)
88 (1177)	231 (1187)	23 (1280)	107 (1695)
91 (2243)	233 (1457)	26 (1288)	108 (1696)
100 (1539)	237 (1540)	29 (1182)	112 (1697)
104 (1178)	238 (1675)	31 (1190)	114 (1698)
110 (2244)	239 (1676)	37 (1679)	134 (1521)
111 (2245)	242 (1627)	38 (1680)	136 (1699)
112 (2246)	247 (1628)	47 (2087)	138 (1700)
125 (1669)	248 (1966)	48 (1568)	139 (1701)
145 (1670)	252 (1188)	49 (1569)	140 (1702)
148 (1625)	256 (1677)	50 (1183)	141 (1703)
151 (1944)	264 (1629)	52 (1570)	142 (1622)
154 (1671)	265 (1678)	53 (1968)	143 (1623)
158 (1672)	273 (1096)	56 (1184)	146 (1704)

Volume II A	Volume II A	Volume II A	Volume II C
147 (1705)	394 (1314)	608 (1711)	41 (1972)
148 (1771)	400 (1979)	621 (1826)	44 (2250)
168 (1969)	401 (1980)	622 (1307)	46 (2251)
172 (1970)	402 (1315)	623 (1543)	48 (2252)
175 (1281)	404 (2263)	626 (1712)	Volume III A
179 (1706)	407 (1316)	627 (1688)	1 (1587)
183 (1631)	408 (1317)	639 (1945)	5 (2274)
187 (1971)	410 (1318)	643 (1973)	6 (1588)
190 (1097)	418 (1319)	650 (1632)	9 (2275)
192 (1707)	424 (1947)	652 (1974)	29 (1321)
194 (1098)	441 (2264)	656 (1465)	30 (1322)
195 (1708)	442 (1546)	657 (1308)	33 (2178)
211 (1975)	448 (2088)	658 (1713)	34 (1589)
214 (1544)	454 (1578)	659 (1714)	36 (1099)
215 (1545)	456 (1238)	660 (1715)	37 (1590)
223 (1976)	457 (1239)	663 (2249)	38 (1983)
237 (1309)	461 (2265)	667 (1505)	39 (1100)
247 (2254)	472 (1320)	672 (1716)	45 (1323)
260 (1573)	474 (1981)	678 (1571)	46 (1721)
264 (2255)	486 (2234)	682 (1717)	48 (1240)
267 (1977)	487 (1579)	689 (1718)	49 (1722)
271 (2256)	488 (1580)	694 (1719)	68 (2276)
278 (1289)	506 (2176)	695 (1772)	98 (1736)
280 (1234)	507 (1466)	697 (1572)	101 (1324)
281 (1235)	516 (1982)	698 (2253)	102 (1325)
298 (1522)	523 (2266)	716 (1523)	104 (1326)
301 (2257)	524 (2267)	729 (1624)	109 (1203)
302 (2258)	525 (2268)	731 (1651)	119 (1282)
304 (2175)	526 (2269)	744 (1524)	127 (1102)
324 (1833)	527 (2270)	746 (1236)	128 (1103)
326 (1200)	528 (2271)	747 (2259)	129 (1665)
330 (1311)	535 (1290)	748 (2260)	130 (1666)
335 (1575)	541 (2272)	752 (1237)	131 (1327)
348 (2261)	550 (2273)	758 (1310)	132 (1834)
354 (2212)	555 (1525)	762 (2141)	136 (1984)
355 (2213)	562 (1720)	766 (1574)	140 (1506)
371 (1576)	564 (2214)	808 (1581)	141 (2181)
381 (1577)	566 (1663)	809 (1582)	143 (1507)
385 (1978)	580 (2177)	810 (1583)	145 (2279)
387 (1946)	591 (1709)	811 (1584)	182 (1104)
390 (2262)	592 (1191)	812 (1585)	186 (1591)
391 (1312)	596 (1710)	813 (1586)	192 (2182)
392 (1313)	605 (1185)		193 (2215)

Volume III A	Volume IV A	Volume IV C	Volume V B
194 (2183)	49 (2284)	81 (1603)	237 (1835)
205 (1737)	58 (2285)	82 (1106)	**Volume V C**
211 (2277)	66 (1204)	99 (2283)	13:4 (1114)
212 (2278)	86 (2111)	108 (1738)	**Volume VI A**
213 (2179)	102 (1328)	**Volume V A**	3 (1743)
215 (1201)	104 (1329)	1 (1111)	5 (1556)
216 (1101)	106 (1330)	4 (1158)	6 (1557)
217 (1664)	109 (1107)	7 (1334)	20 (1989)
232 (2184)	115 (1739)	8 (1335)	21 (1291)
236 (1985)	117 (1108)	24 (1827)	22 (1744)
240 (1508)	121 (1526)	29 (1552)	24 (1161)
242 (1773)	125 (1331)	32 (1112)	38 (1745)
Volume III B	146 (2185)	38 (1636)	49 (1527)
4 (1723)	157 (1332)	40 (1113)	93 (1292)
5 (1724)	185 (1604)	42 (1336)	106 (1990)
6 (1725)	190 (1333)	50 (1337)	107 (1115)
7 (1726)	191 (1110)	53 (1986)	120 (1991)
9 (1727)	198 (2280)	55 (1667)	121 (1342)
10 (1728)	**Volume IV B**	57 (1458)	127 (1343)
11 (1729)	76 (1109)	60 (1987)	148 (1116)
14 (1633)	96:1a,1b,1c	65 (1338)	154 (1467)
15 (1634)	(1550)	66 (1159)	**Volume VI B**
16 (1730)	96:4 (1551)	73 (1605)	35:25 (1638)
17 (1547)	96:13 (1740)	75 (1941)	40:3 (1607)
19 (1731)	118:1 (1246)	83 (1160)	40:5 (2286)
20 (1548)	**Volume IV C**	85 (1741)	42 (2287)
21 (1732)	23 (2281)	86 (1742)	53:13 (1668)
22 (1733)	35 (1635)	89 (1339)	53:16 (2115)
23 (1734)	39 (1241)	90 (1247)	54:12 (1608)
24 (1735)	55 (1242)	**Volume V B**	54:16 (2235)
41:20 (1157)	56 (1243)	5:8 (1340)	54:30 (1609)
Volume III C	59 (1594)	41 (1606)	70:13,14,15
7 (1155)	60 (1244)	43 (1553)	(1746)
16 (1202)	62 (1245)	44 (1554)	98:45 (1610)
17 (1156)	63 (1595)	45 (1555)	98:77 (2116)
18 (2180)	64 (1596)	55:26 (1248)	98:81 (1344)
25 (2110)	65 (1597)	56:2 (1249)	163 (1341)
31 (1592)	66 (1598)	64 (1637)	**Volume VII¹ A**
33 (1593)	67 (1599)	65 (2112)	8 (1459)
Volume IV A	68 (1600)	66 (2113)	19 (1747)
21 (1774)	73 (1601)	148:16 (1561)	24 (2143)
24 (1105)	74 (2282)	227:5 (2114)	25 (2144)
39 (1549)	79 (1602)	235 (1988)	31 (2291)

Volume VII¹ A	Volume VIII¹ A	Volume VIII¹ A	Volume VIII¹ A
34 (2292)	14 (1612)	302 (2195)	587 (1844)
37 (2145)	19 (1121)	303 (1837)	616 (1169)
58 (1162)	24 (1350)	305 (1639)	619 (1122)
61 (1117)	25 (1163)	322 (2196)	643 (1942)
62 (1345)	30 (1351)	323 (2197)	646 (1213)
64 (1748)	41 (1164)	327 (1358)	647 (1214)
71 (1250)	43 (2090)	333 (1510)	649 (1123)
75 (2293)	54 (1775)	335 (1838)	661 (1124)
76 (2294)	57 (1352)	349 (1839)	663 (1215)
81 (1346)	58 (1165)	350 (1840)	670 (1365)
87 (1528)	63 (1353)	356 (1359)	672 (1125)
122 (2146)	76 (2117)	358 (2236)	675 (1216)
139 (1347)	77 (1354)	360 (2198)	676 (2091)
141 (1205)	80 (1283)	361 (2199)	678 (1511)
143 (1348)	90 (2187)	379 (1360)	Volume VIII² B
149 (1994)	94 (1355)	395 (1294)	91:13 (2118)
153 (1611)	97 (2188)	399 (2151)	Volume IX A
167 (1206)	111 (1356)	432 (1841)	3 (1295)
177 (1118)	114 (1207)	438 (2299)	7 (1845)
181 (1251)	115 (1208)	449 (1842)	34 (1366)
185 (2295)	125 (1998)	459 (1210)	49 (1846)
187 (1192)	126 (1999)	462 (2003)	75 (1367)
201 (1349)	136 (2147)	475 (1211)	77 (1368)
203 (1119)	137 (2148)	476 (1212)	78 (1369)
205 (1995)	140 (2149)	478 (1750)	82 (1847)
207 (2137)	146 (2150)	479 (2298)	89 (1460)
208 (1836)	148 (1357)	482 (2004)	91 (2006)
210 (1252)	169 (1749)	499 (1166)	101 (1848)
215 (2296)	178 (1253)	500 (2200)	107 (1752)
228 (1120)	180 (2189)	503 (2201)	109 (1256)
230 (2288)	181 (2190)	511 (2119)	112 (1640)
234 (2289)	182 (2191)	516 (1361)	113 (1370)
236 (2290)	183 (2192)	517 (1751)	116 (1371)
244 (1948)	184 (2193)	522 (1254)	118 (1170)
Volume VII² B	186 (2297)	524 (1362)	151 (1753)
121:6 (1992)	210 (2000)	525 (1255)	157 (1296)
158:3 (1996)	230 (1209)	536 (1843)	160 (1641)
199 (1993)	251 (1558)	537 (1167)	177 (1217)
261:8 (1293)	253 (1509)	540 (2152)	182 (1372)
290 (2142)	262 (2001)	568 (2005)	191 (2216)
Volume VIII¹ A	283 (1613)	569 (1363)	196 (1642)
9 (1997)	286 (2002)	573 (1364)	200 (2153)
12 (2186)	300 (2194)	586 (1168)	202 (1776)

Volume IX A	Volume IX A	Volume X¹ A	Volume X² A
221 (1957)	478 (2159)	555 (1133)	304 (1763)
242 (1373)	482 (1218)	564 (2121)	314 (2164)
247 (1374)	491 (1219)	577 (2300)	317 (1859)
254 (1375)	496 (2012)	590 (1298)	326 (1860)
260 (1958)	**Volume IX B**	605 (1391)	347 (1861)
275 (1297)	45:4 (1643)	629 (1392)	353 (1653)
279 (1754)	63:8 (2013)	631 (1854)	361 (1862)
280 (1755)	66 (2014)	639 (1513)	371 (1136)
282 (2154)	**Volume X¹ A**	646 (1781)	426 (1614)
286 (2007)	12 (1220)	673 (1855)	428 (1261)
305 (1376)	20 (1382)	**Volume X² A**	431 (1615)
311 (1126)	26 (1257)	14 (1172)	438 (1262)
315 (1377)	59 (1383)	17 (2163)	443 (1400)
316 (2008)	60 (1384)	32 (1762)	451 (1654)
318 (2009)	62 (1128)	36 (1856)	452 (1655)
319 (1127)	64 (1385)	46 (2122)	454 (1173)
320 (2155)	128 (2160)	47 (1857)	457 (2022)
323 (1849)	148 (1761)	54 (1134)	465 (1461)
337 (1652)	164 (2230)	72 (1393)	474 (1782)
347 (1378)	179 (1851)	76 (2138)	480 (2023)
356 (2010)	194 (1284)	125 (1394)	481 (1530)
357 (2156)	196 (1386)	140 (1529)	489 (2924)
374 (1379)	203 (1387)	159 (1258)	493 (1401)
378 (2157)	214 (1468)	160 (1259)	494 (1402)
391 (1949)	218 (2015)	169 (1395)	500 (1531)
396 (1850)	246 (1852)	179 (2018)	510 (1783)
398 (1756)	286 (2016)	186 (1396)	516 (1221)
399 (1757)	332 (1388)	188 (1470)	517 (2237)
400 (1758)	341 (2161)	189 (1471)	518 (1263)
402 (2120)	367 (1129)	198 (1472)	519 (2238)
420 (1759)	368 (1130)	203 (2139)	539 (2239)
423 (1777)	372 (1950)	206 (1514)	563 (1299)
424 (2217)	395 (1131)	207 (1135)	564 (1193)
431 (2228)	408 (1389)	219 (1473)	565 (1194)
434 (1779)	409 (2162)	223 (1474)	569 (1403)
435 (1780)	415 (1644)	225 (1559)	578 (2092)
437 (1760)	455 (1853)	226 (1397)	584 (1951)
441 (1380)	463 (2017)	232 (1398)	591 (1404)
450 (2011)	468 (1171)	239 (1475)	602 (2093)
459 (1778)	479 (1390)	241 (1399)	629 (2025)
468 (2158)	504 (1512)	243 (1260)	644 (1405)
470 (2229)	507 (1469)	255 (1858)	**Volume X³ A**
476 (1381)	554 (1132)	265 (2019)	51 (1560)

Volume X³ A	Volume X³ A	Volume X³ A	Volume X⁴ A
72 (1476)	338 (1874)	638 (1533)	77 (1227)
75 (1406)	339 (2028)	658 (1415)	80 (1796)
106 (1477)	347 (1787)	659 (1960)	81 (1228)
116 (2026)	349 (2029)	660 (2031)	82 (1229)
139 (2218)	353 (1480)	665 (2169)	89 (2037)
156 (2123)	356 (2126)	666 (1885)	91 (1961)
157 (2219)	357 (2127)	667 (1886)	99 (1267)
171 (1864)	359 (1409)	668 (1887)	104 (2038)
184 (1137)	360 (1657)	670 (1793)	114 (1142)
200 (1285)	365 (1658)	672 (2140)	123 (1143)
207 (1865)	373 (1410)	687 (2032)	127 (1195)
228 (1764)	374 (1411)	689 (1794)	131 (1894)
230 (2220)	378 (1875)	694 (1416)	132 (1422)
231 (2165)	395 (1788)	712 (1888)	134 (1483)
238 (1784)	400 (1876)	713 (1889)	145 (1196)
247 (1407)	409 (1877)	719 (1534)	146 (1797)
251 (2124)	410 (1481)	721 (1890)	148 (1895)
263 (1286)	411 (1878)	723 (2170)	151 (2131)
264 (1408)	413 (1959)	743 (1417)	170 (1197)
268 (1785)	421 (1412)	747 (1418)	171 (1198)
269 (1478)	430 (2089)	750 (1891)	172 (1199)
270 (1479)	447 (1879)	763 (2034)	175 (1268)
272 (1866)	454 (1880)	764 (2094)	177 (1269)
275 (2166)	455 (1881)	766 (2095)	183 (2203)
276 (1867)	469 (2128)	767 (1892)	188 (2039)
277 (1868)	476 (2030)	772 (1419)	208 (1645)
279 (2167)	499 (1300)	775 (1535)	211 (1423)
280 (2168)	506 (1174)	776 (1893)	219 (2100)
283 (1869)	509 (1789)	778 (2035)	220 (2106)
284 (1532)	524 (1790)	781 (1420)	230 (1484)
293 (2221)	525 (1791)	784 (1482)	245 (1270)
294 (1870)	536 (1141)	786 (1616)	247 (2301)
295 (1871)	552 (1882)	787 (1659)	252 (1424)
297 (1656)	573 (1223)	790 (1421)	253 (1425)
298 (1138)	576 (1792)	792 (1175)	254 (1426)
312 (1786)	581 (1413)	Volume X⁴ A	257 (1271)
314 (1872)	585 (1414)	13 (1266)	269 (1516)
319 (1222)	602 (1883)	21 (2129)	273 (1896)
322 (1139)	615 (1884)	26 (2130)	274 (1897)
323 (1140)	616 (1828)	29 (2036)	275 (1898)
324 (2027)	618 (1264)	39 (1795)	278 (1517)
331 (1873)	619 (1265)	67 (1225)	282 (1798)
334 (2125)	627 (1515)	73 (1226)	293 (1899)

Volume X⁴ A	Volume X⁴ A	Volume X⁵ B	Volume XI¹ A
304 (1427)	572 (2222)	117 (2033)	192 (1149)
310 (2302)	582 (1462)	244 (2021)	194 (1803)
311 (1428)	588 (1661)	Volume X⁶ B	197 (1804)
321 (1900)	618 (1486)	52:1 (2020)	232 (2173)
329 (1660)	619 (1487)	241 (1863)	255 (2135)
340 (1901)	626 (1915)	Volume XI¹ A	260 (2058)
344 (1799)	634 (1147)	4 (1924)	268 (2096)
349 (1902)	635 (1148)	5 (1436)	272 (2059)
352 (1903)	640 (1431)	14 (1619)	288 (1832)
354 (1904)	650 (1916)	21 (2134)	306 (1930)
366 (1905)	656 (1272)	22 (1925)	310 (2060)
369 (1906)	Volume X⁵ A	23 (1274)	319 (2061)
370 (2040)	7 (1488)	24 (1275)	320 (2062)
384 (2204)	8 (1489)	25 (2172)	321 (2097)
385 (1617)	9 (1917)	27 (1926)	322 (2108)
392 (2101)	13 (1273)	35 (1437)	323 (2109)
396 (1536)	23 (1432)	36 (2047)	335 (1963)
401 (2041)	26 (2102)	41 (1927)	336 (1805)
410 (1907)	27 (1918)	42 (2048)	337 (1806)
415 (2042)	39 (1433)	43 (1801)	338 (1931)
419 (1485)	44 (1919)	60 (2049)	342 (2174)
422 (1144)	45 (1920)	81 (2050)	343 (1765)
427 (2043)	49 (1662)	82 (2051)	359 (1439)
429 (1618)	51 (2132)	96 (2052)	368 (2063)
440 (1952)	52 (2133)	104 (1928)	369 (2064)
441 (2044)	54 (1490)	120 (1301)	370 (2065)
455 (1145)	55 (1434)	130 (1802)	374 (2232)
459 (1908)	56 (1491)	132 (2231)	381 (1440)
471 (1943)	64 (1492)	139 (2224)	384 (2066)
478 (1829)	87 (1921)	148 (2053)	388 (1647)
479 (1830)	88 (1922)	151 (2225)	391 (1932)
485 (1429)	97 (2045)	152 (2226)	396 (1933)
489 (1146)	101 (1493)	158 (1929)	400 (2098)
491 (1909)	103 (1494)	160 (2107)	402 (1807)
492 (1910)	108 (1495)	168 (2054)	403 (1808)
499 (1911)	109 (1496)	175 (2055)	415 (2067)
500 (1912)	116 (1435)	176 (1518)	421 (2068)
505 (1646)	121 (2046)	180 (1620)	429 (1809)
521 (1913)	132 (2223)	183 (1621)	432 (1810)
533 (1831)	138 (2171)	184 (2227)	441 (2069)
553 (1962)	139 (1923)	188 (1438)	446 (1648)
556 (1914)	156 (2202)	189 (2056)	447 (1811)
567 (1430)	162 (2105)	190 (2057)	455 (2070)

Volume XI¹ A	Volume XI¹ A	Volume XI² A	Volume XI² A
463 (1953)	588 (1937)	135 (2081)	261 (1277)
464 (1441)	591 (1443)	149 (2082)	264 (1819)
476 (1812)	Volume XI² A	170 (1450)	267 (1820)
485 (2071)	3 (1224)	171 (1451)	271 (1821)
488 (2136)	4 (1537)	175 (1452)	272 (1822)
490 (2072)	5 (1538)	179 (1453)	275 (2084)
491 (2099)	18 (1150)	180 (1454)	284 (1497)
492 (1934)	53 (1444)	182 (1501)	285 (1498)
500 (2103)	64 (2104)	183 (1766)	286 (1499)
501 (1562)	69 (2078)	189 (1767)	294 (1800)
506 (2073)	77 (1816)	190 (1768)	313 (1823)
515 (1813)	84 (1151)	191 (2303)	336 (1153)
518 (2074)	98 (1445)	195 (1817)	342 (1503)
522 (1176)	99 (1446)	197 (1938)	344 (1824)
533 (2075)	100 (1500)	201 (1818)	358 (1939)
539 (1814)	114 (2205)	224 (1519)	360 (2085)
540 (1815)	115 (1152)	226 (1502)	361 (2086)
547 (1954)	119 (1276)	234 (1649)	367 (1504)
550 (1935)	124 (2079)	235 (1650)	380 (1154)
553 (1442)	125 (2080)	237 (1956)	424 (1278)
573 (1936)	130 (1447)	245 (1520)	434 (1940)
576 (2076)	131 (1448)	255 (1769)	Volume XI³ B
577 (1955)	133 (1449)	259 (2083)	199 (1825)
587 (2077)			

Notes, Commentary, and Topical Bibliography

The summary presentation of basic concepts is by Gregor Malantschuk and the notes and bibliography are by the editors.

The following abbreviations have been used throughout the notes:

S.V.   *Samlede Værker* by Søren Kierkegaard, I-XIV (Copenhagen: Gyldendal, 1901-1906).

Pap.   *Papirer* by Søren Kierkegaard, edited by P. A. Heiberg, V. Kuhr, and E. Torsting, I-XI³ (20 vols.) (Copenhagen: Gyldendal, 1909-48). References to the *Papirer* will usually be in the form I A 1, etc.

Titles of studies pertinent to a particular theme are given under the appropriate heading. The editions of Kierkegaard's works referred to in the notes are listed in the Bibliography.

FAITH

According to Kierkegaard's conception, faith expresses a person's existential relation to the eternal. But inasmuch as the eternal can manifest itself to a person in various forms, there are also various forms of faith. Kierkegaard's structuring of the relation of these various forms to one another may be indicated in the following sketch: in the human sphere we find faith in the form represented by Socrates. Men believe that they can actualize in their lives the eternal claim of the ethical. A higher expression of faith is found in Abraham, who in obedience is related to the transcendent God who places his claim upon him. With the revelation of God in Christ, faith receives an entirely new content. The highest and essential form of faith is faith in Christ as the Incarnation of God.

Kierkegaard has tried to distinguish very precisely between these various forms of faith. He has also carried through a rigorous demarcation between the sphere of knowledge and that of faith and has also shown how faith stands in relation to the historical.

Thus in Kierkegaard faith becomes deepened and broadened, and it is this relation he has in mind when he says of his own work on the elucidation of "the whole question of faith": ". . . I venture to declare that in my writings there have been advanced precise dialectical qualifications on particular points which hitherto have not been known" (X^2 A 597).

553

Beck, Maximillian. "Existentialism, Rationalism, and Christian Faith." *Journal of Religion*, no. 4, 1946.

Collins, James. "Faith and Reflection in Kierkegaard." *Journal of Religion*, January 1957. In *A Kierkegaard Critique*, ed. Howard Johnson and Niels Thulstrup. New York: Harper and Row, 1962.

Demant, V. A. *Søren Kierkegaard, Knight of Faith. Nineteenth Century*, January 1940.

Fabro, Cornelio. "Faith and Reason in Kierkegaard's Dialectic." In *A Kierkegaard Critique*, ed. Howard Johnson and Niels Thulstrup. New York: Harper and Row, 1962.

Hick, John, ed. *Faith and the Philosophers*. New York: St. Martin's Press, 1964.

Klemke, E. D. "Logicality versus Alogicality in the Christian Faith." *Journal of Religion*, April 1958.

Letswaart, Willem L. "Kierkegaard's Concept of Faith." Ph.D. dissertation, Princeton Theological Seminary, 1952.

Martin, H. V. *The Wings of Faith*. New York: Philosophical Library, 1951.

Michalson, Carl. "Kierkegaard's Theology of Faith." *Religion in Life*, Spring 1963.

Murphy, J. L. "Faith and Reason in the Teaching of Kierkegaard." *American Ecclesiastical Review*, CXLV, 1961.

Niebuhr, Reinhold. "Coherence, Incoherence, and Christian Faith." *Journal of Religion*, no. 3, 1951.

Paul, W. W. "Faith and Reason in Kierkegaard and Modern Existentialism." *Review of Religion*, March 1956.

Roberts, D. E. "Faith and Freedom in Existentialism." *Theology Today*, no. 8, 1951-52.

Roberts, David. *Existentialism and Religious Belief*. London and New York: Oxford, 1957.

Wilburn, Ralph G. "The Philosophy of Existence and the Faith-Relation." *Religion in Life*, XXX, 1961.

For references in the works to faith, see, for example, *Either/Or*, II, pp. 204, 290; *Fear and Trembling*, pp. 46 ff., 56 ff., 65, 79 ff., 109 f.; *Edifying Discourses*, II, pp. 42-43; IV, 137; *Fragments*, pp. 101 ff., 108 ff., 120 ff., 126 ff.; *The Concept of Anxiety* [*Dread*], pp. 104, 128, 139 ff.; *Stages*, pp. 400 ff.; *Postscript*, pp. 15, 30 f., 33, 53, 118, 174, 182 f., 188, 193, 201, 203, 259, 285 f., 288 ff., 310, 374, 527, 540; *Purity of Heart*, pp. 110 ff., 149 f.; *The Gospel of Suffering*, pp. 27 ff., 73, 112 ff., 128 f., 138 ff., 155 ff.; *Works of Love*, pp. 42 ff., 150 ff., 216 ff., 273 ff., 349 ff.; *Christian Discourses*, pp. 76 ff., 87 ff., 150 ff., 182 f., 239 ff.; *The Sickness unto Death*, pp. 147, 171 f., 213, 262; *Training*, pp. 9, 27 ff., 33, 99 ff., 133 ff., 140 ff.; *For Self-Examination*, pp. 12 ff., 79 ff., 96 ff.; *Judge for Yourselves!* pp. 202 ff.; *Attack*, pp. 5, 277.

1. Friedrich Schleiermacher, *Der christliche Glaube*, 2 ed. (Berlin: 1830), I, pp. 40 ff. This is the edition Kierkegaard owned.

2. For example, Phillip Marheineke, *Die Grundlehren der christlichen Dogmatik als Wissenschaft*, 2 ed. (Berlin: 1827), pp. 6 ff.

3. Romans 8:38.

4. I believe in order that I may understand. See note 18.

5. There is nothing in the intellect that has not previously been in the senses.

6. See *Philosophical Fragments*, pp. 16 ff.

7. See ibid., pp. 137 *et passim*.

8. For a discussion of the term *Mellemværende* and a word coined by Kierkegaard, *Mellemhverandre* (between each other), see Lee Capel's note, *The Concept of Irony*, pp. 361-62.

9. See *The Lilies of the Field and the Birds of the Air*, in *Christian Discourses*, pp. 352 ff.

10. Ibid.

11. Ludwig Holberg's well-known comedy masterpiece, printed in 1731 and first staged in 1747.

12. See *Edifying Discourses*, I, p. 44.

13. See *Fear and Trembling*, p. 37.

14. Acts 27.

15. See *Fear and Trembling*, p. 129.

16. Ibid., p. 132.

17. See II Timothy 1:12.

18. A formulation associated particularly with Augustine and Anselm. F. Schleiermacher used it as the motto of *Der christliche Glaube* (Berlin: 1830). See note 4.

19. Kierkegaard understands spontaneity or immediacy to be what Schleiermacher called "religion" and the Hegelians "faith," the atmosphere in which we breathe in an intellectual-spiritual sense and therefore not properly designated by faith and religion. See I A 273, I A 328 (*Pap.*, p. 142).

20. See *Johannes Climacus or, De Omnibus Dubitandum Est*, p. 116, for the young Kierkegaard's treatment of three assertions concerning doubt as the beginning of knowledge.

21. *Friedrich Heinrich Jacobi's Werke*, I-VI (Leipzig: 1812-25).

22. See *The Concept of Anxiety* [Dread], p. 102; *Postscript*, p. 527, *Philosophical Fragments*, p. 104.

23. Kierkegaard makes effective use of this same kind of analogical paradox of tension and elasticity, weight and lightness, in characterizing the work of an actress. See [*The*] *Crisis* [*and a Crisis*] *in the Life of an Actress*, p. 77.

24. See Matthew 8:5-13.

25. See *Works of Love*, pp. 349 ff.

26. Luke 16:31.

27. See *The Sickness unto Death*, p. 204 n.

28. See *Fear and Trembling*, pp. 57 ff.

29. See *Works of Love*, p. 332; *Stages on Life's Way*, p. 364.

30. Martin Luther, *En christelig Postille*, I-II, tr. Jørgen Thisted (Copenhagen: 1828), I, pp. 165 ff.

31. John 4:48.

32. Martin Luther, *En christelig Postille*, II, pp. 165 ff.

33. "70,000 fathoms deep" is one of Kierkegaard's most characteristic metaphors. See *The Concept of Irony*, p. 137 (70,000 years); *Stages on Life's Way*, pp. 402, 425, 430; *Postscript*, pp. 126, 182, 208, 256; *Works of Love*, p. 334; *Attack upon Christendom*, pp. 43, 111 (70,000 fathoms down). See also X² A 494.

34. Matthew 7:7.

35. Matthew 21:21.

36. See *For Self-Examination*, pp. 63 ff.

37. See Plato, *Gorgias* 454 c ff.

38. Matthew 28:20.

39. Mark 16:17.

FAMILY

In the early period of his life when Kierkegaard still held to the possibility of his "realizing the universal" (to marry), he made numerous important observations on family life. Later, when he concentrated on the category of the single individual, he became more deeply appreciative particularly of the educational significance of the family for the individual. Thereafter family life was evaluated according to its hindering or promoting the mental-spiritual growth of the individual. His later criticisms of family life must be understood as an expression of his conclusion that it does not come up to the requirements Christianity places upon it.

For references in the works to family, see, for example, *The Concept of Irony*, pp. 210, 212, 303 ff.; *Either/Or*, I, pp. 23, 143, 147 f., 152 ff., 157 f., 292 ff.; II, pp. 5-157; *Fear and Trembling*, pp. 98 fn., 121; *Thoughts on Crucial Situations in Human Life*, pp. 43-74; *Stages*, pp. 341, 375; *Postscript*, pp. 130, 155, 212 ff.; *The Present Age*, pp. 18 f.; *Works of Love*, pp. 145, 203; *Christian Discourses*, p. 265; *Training*, pp. 172 ff.; *Attack*, pp. 223 ff.

40. Matthew 6:3.

41. See *For Self-Examination*, pp. 55 ff.

42. See *Either/Or*, II, p. 94.

43. See *Stages on Life's Way*, p. 137.

44. See ibid., pp. 137-38.

45. See Genesis 25:22 and 30:22; *Stages on Life's Way*, p. 205.

46. See Isaiah 3:4; Ecclesiastes 10:16 ff.; *The Point of View*, p. 55.

47. Most likely an expression of Kierkegaard's gratitude to his father for his own upbringing. See *Either/Or*, II, pp. 271-72; *The Point of View*, pp. 76-77; *Works of Love*, pp. 352-53.

48. See *On Authority and Revelation*, pp. 178 ff.; *Attack on Christendom*, pp. 205.

49. See *Postscript*, pp. 305, 314.

FAUST

The Faust figure for Kierkegaard is the symbol of doubt—a doubt that still lies on the intellectual level and is concerned with the possibility of knowing eternal truths. This doubt becomes despair when a person is confronted by the ethical claim, which he cannot fulfill. As a representative of this development, Kierkegaard advances the figure of the Wandering Jew, saying that Faust, as an idea, "must fulfill itself in a new idea (the Wandering Jew)" (II A 56).

Williams, Forrest. "Problem in Values: the Faustian motivation in Kierkegaard and Goethe." *Ethics*, July 1953.

See Lee Capel's compact presentation of Kierkegaard's interest in the Faust theme, *The Concept of Irony*, pp. 20 ff.

For references in the works to Faust and to *Faust*, see *The Concept of Irony*, p. 226; *Either/Or*, I, pp. 25, 55, 86 ff., 90 f., 98, 103 f., 142, 203-13, 346, 436; II, p. 230; *Fear and Trembling*, pp. 116 ff.; *The Concept of Anxiety* [*Dread*], pp. 117 ff; *Stages*, pp. 174 ff.; *Postscript*, p. 164; *The Sickness unto Death*, p. 240.

50. Fit for doing, fit for action or business, active, energetic. (Cognate: practical.)

51. See Kierkegaard's "Gilleleje letter," I A 75.

52. *Ueber Lenau's Faust*. Von Johannes M . . . . . n. (Stuttgart: 1836). Kierkegaard's reference is to *Perseus*, ed. J. L. Heiberg, no. I (June, 1837), pp. 162 ff., which has a version of the earlier work under the title *Betragtninger over Ideen af Faust, med Hensyn paa Lenaus Faust*. See H. L. Martensen, *Af mit Levnet*, I, pp. 183 ff. Martensen used the name Johannes and later the initials H. L.

FICHTE, Johann Gottlieb (1762-1814, the elder Fichte).

Kierkegaard had previously studied Fichte's writings; from the beginning he was critical, because Fichte moved in the realm of abstraction without attachment to concrete actuality. Kierkegaard wrote, "In despair Fichte threw the empirical ballast overboard and foundered" (I A 302). In Kierkegaard's later writings the pseudonymous Climacus in particular ironizes over Fichte's abstract thought in the expressions "the pure I-am-I," "the fantastic I-am-I" (*Concluding Unscientific Postscript*, pp. 169 ff.) which refer also to Fichte's well-known methodological formulation: "*Ich und Nicht Ich*" (see *The Concept of Irony*, pp. 289 ff.). It should be noted that Kierkegaard, as did Hegel, attributes to Fichte's philosophy a primary role in the founding of the German romantic movement (Friedrich von Schlegel et al.).

FICHTE, Immanuel Herman (1797-1879, the younger Fichte).

Kierkegaard's relation to the younger Fichte was more positive. Common to both was their interest in the concrete human person. Significantly, in writing a certain journal entry (II A 31, March 19, 1837), Kierkegaard notes that he had arrived at the ideas before his reading of Fichte's *Die Idee der Persönlichkeit und der individuellen Fortdauer* (Elberfeld: 1834). In a number of his journal entries Kierkegaard notes points of concurrence between him and the younger Fichte. One of them is their critical view of the attempt to create justice and brotherhood through political means, as in the French Revolution (X⁴ A 83).

For references in the works to J. G. Fichte and his son, I. H., see *The Concept of Irony*, pp. 235 (I.H.); 260, 282, 285, 289 ff., 291 (I.H.), 292, 326; *The Concept of Anxiety* [Dread], pp. 105, 123; *Stages*, p. 429; *The Sickness unto Death*, p. 164.

53. F. M. von Klinger, *Der Faust der Morgenländer oder Wanderungen Ben Hafis. Erzählers der Reisen von der Sündfluth* (Bagdad: 1797).

54. J. G. Fichte, *Die Bestimmungen des Menschen* (Berlin: 1800).

55. See *Either/Or*, I, p. 24. For an extended discussion of Fichte see chapter "Irony after Fichte," *The Concept of Irony*, pp. 289 ff.

56. See *Af en endnu Levendes Papirer* (Kierkegaard's first published work, a critical piece on Hans Christian Andersen), S.V., XIII, p. 54.

57. See *The Concept of Irony*, p. 289.

58. See *Philosophical Fragments*, p. 12 and notes on pp. 175-76.

59. Immanuel Herman Fichte (1797-1879), son of Johan Gottlieb Fichte (1762-1814).

60. I. H. Fichte, *Die Idee der Persönlichkeit und der individuellen Fortdauer* (Elberfeld: 1834).

61. F. Baader, *Vorlesungen über speculative Dogmatik* (Stuttgart, Tübingen: 1828) I, pp. 105 ff.

62. Anton Gunther, *Süd- und Nordlichter am Horizonte spekulativer Theologie* (Vienna: 1832), pp. 114 ff.

63. Apparently "the following entry" was not transcribed.

64. I. H. Fichte, *Über Gegensatz, Wendepunkt und Ziel heutiger Philosophie* (Heidelberg: 1832), pp. 165 ff. Pp. xxxi-xxxii: "I. *Die objektive Richtung*: a) *die construirende und dialektische. —Schelling's Lehre . . . Hegel. . . . b) Die mystische . . . Bader, Fr. Schlegel . . . Gunther. II. Die subjektive Richtung: (die reflektirende Philosophie) . . . Kant . . . Jacobi . . . Fries . . . Eschenmayer.*"

65. Ibid., p. 26: *Zu Kürzerer Bezeichnung beider Hauptrichtungen sei es uns erlaubt, jene die "objective" Richtung, oder die "Seinslehre," diese die "subjective," oder die "Erkenntnisztheori" zu nennen.*

66. Ibid., pp. 24 ff.

67. I. H. Fichte, *Grundzüge zum Systeme der Philosophie*, pt. 3, *Die speculative Theologie oder allgemeine Religionslehre* (Heidelberg: 1846).

FORCE

On the basis of a rigorous Christian position Kierkegaard maintains that injustice cannot be removed by force, since one who uses coercion eventually functions on the same level as one who perpetrates wrong. Only suffering love can defeat injustice. Kierkegaard's view of this entire question is most clearly expressed in his important utterance: "Unrighteousness also has its rights, and considering that unrighteousness is unrighteousness, to want to do wrong against it is indeed unchristian. Christianity means: suffering, to allow unrighteousness to have its rights to the uttermost—and in this way to be victorious, to conquer it (X^4 A 135).

McFadden, R. "Nuclear Dilemma. With a Nod to Kierkegaard." *Theology Today*, January 1961.

For references in the works to force (*magt* and other expressions of external compulsion), see, for example, *Stages*, pp. 83, 288, 292; *Postscript*, pp. 147, 308, 528, 530 f.; *Purity of Heart*, pp. 60 f., 101, 201 f.; *The Gospel of Suffering*, pp. 33-43, 156 f.; *Works of Love*, pp. 121 f.; *Christian Discourses*, pp. 54 f.; *An Open Letter*, together with *Armed Neutrality*, pp. 54 f.; *The Point of View*, pp. 28, 121, 134; *Attack*, pp. 39 f., 63, 219.

68. A. Neander, *Denkwürdigkeiten aus der Geschichte des Christentums und des christlichen Lebens*, I-II (Berlin: 1823), II, pp. 227 ff.

69. Matthew 5:39.

70. John 18:23.

71. See *The Gospel of Suffering*, pp. 40-41.

72. Not military service but vice prevents right action.

73. See Luke 4:14-15.

74. See *The Gospel of Suffering*, ch. VII, pp. 138 ff.

75. Friedrich Böhringer, *Die Kirche Christi und ihre Zeugen oder die Kirchengeschichte in Biographien*, I-VII (Zürich: 1842-49).

FORGIVENESS

Kierkegaard battled all his life to win faith in the forgiveness of sins. He had difficulty in gaining confident courage to believe in the forgiveness of sins because of his own experience of the power of sin over man and man's persistent frailty. Such experiences arise as one discovers both the negative consequences of inheritance in human life and one's own powerlessness in seeking to actualize the good. Only Christianity defines man thoroughly as a sinner and offers the forgiveness of sins, but even here these negative experiences are important, for without them a person would be tempted continually by the thought that he achieves something good of himself, and sin and the forgiveness of sins would thereby not encompass the whole man.

Another question in regard to the forgiveness of sins is to what extent a person is freed by the forgiveness of sins from the consequences of sin in his life. Kierkegaard answers this question by saying that through the forgiveness of sins one gains the confident courage to bear the consequences of sin. He says: "It is a crass misunderstanding [to think] that Atonement should exempt one from punishment. No, the spirituality in the forgiveness of sins is that the sinner gains the confident courage to dare to believe that God is gracious toward him, although he still suffers the punishment, but this is a genuine transubstantiation with regard to the punishment" (X^1 A 462).

On the theme of forgiveness in the works, see, for example, *Either/Or*, II, p. 242; *Edifying Discourses*, I, pp. 64 f.; *Thoughts on Crucial Situations in Human Life*, pp. 5 ff.; *Stages*, pp. 216, 230, 304, 322, 348 ff., 428 ff., 433 ff.; *Postscript*, pp. 201 ff., 243, 467, 479, 548; *The Gospel of Suffering*, pp. 41 ff.; *Works of Love*, pp. 79, 114, 191 f., 245, 268 ff., 273 ff., 291, 310, 314, 316, 351 f.; *Christian Discourses*, pp. 55, 102, 111 f., 271 ff., 277, 292, 297 f., 302 f.; *The Sickness unto Death*, pp. 244-55; "The Woman That Was a Sinner," together with *Christian Discourses*, pp. 384 f.; *Training*, pp. 64, 103; "The Woman That Was a Sinner," together with *Training*, pp. 262 ff.; *Two Discourses at the Communion on Fridays*, together with *Judge For Yourselves!*, pp. 9-16, 20 ff.; *Attack*, p. 54.

76. See *Repetition*, pp. 4-5.

77. Confidence and pride of hope.

78. Restitution to original condition. See *Repetition*, p. 26.

79. II Corinthians 5:18 ff.

80. See *Edifying Discourses*, II, p. 49.

81. See *Works of Love*, pp. 349 ff. and also pp. 254 and 295.

82. Ibid., p. 351.

83. Ibid., pp. 352 ff.

84. Ibid., pp. 309-10.

85. Matthew 5:24.

86. *Augustini Aurelii Opera*, I-XVIII (Venice: 1797-1807), Sermon XL.

87. Acts 7:60.

88. Matthew 9:2-6.

89. *Augsburg Confession*, Article XXV.

90. Martin Luther, *En christelig Postille*, I, pp. 551 ff.

91. Matthew 18:23 ff.

92. J. G. Hamann, *Schriften*, I-VIII, ed. F. Roth (Berlin: 1821-43). "As it is said of the three men in the Scriptures, that God forgave them and punished their deed. Psalm 99 [:8]."

93. Mark 2:1 ff.; Luke 7:37 ff.; John 8:1 ff.

FRANKLIN

94. *Benj. Franklin's Leben und Schriften*, ed. A. Binzer, I-IV (Kiel: 1829).

95. ". . . . . and although reformation is the concern of every man (what I mean is that every one should improve others), still in this case it is only too true that everyone's business is at bottom no one's business—and the business is carried on accordingly. After mature consideration I think it well to make 'no one's business' my business" etc.

FREEDOM

As a counterweight to the one-sided emphasis of his age upon the category of necessity in philosophy (Hegel) as well as in the sphere of the natural sciences, Kierkegaard shows the prime significance of freedom for everything that takes place (existence [*Tilværelsen*]). Necessity is only one of the two constituents of actuality. Thus man, as actuality, is a synthesis of freedom and necessity; both of these constituents are simultaneously present.

In his thorough analysis of the relation between freedom and necessity, Kierkegaard points out that necessity is dominant on the lower levels of existence, for example, external nature, whereas freedom is dominant on the higher levels; but the two constituents always go together. Necessity expresses *what* a thing is; freedom *that* a thing is and *how* it comes into existence [*bliver til*].

With his strong emphasis upon freedom, Kierkegaard could not accept the idea of predestination, because in that case the category of necessity would be given too much importance for man. The doctrine of predestination, according to Kierkegaard, finds fertile soil when freedom is not emphasized and when "existential movement is minimized." Therefore he calls predestination the "dogma of sedentary piety" (X^4 A 180).

Grene, Marjorie. *Dreadful Freedom*. Chicago: University of Chicago Press, 1948. Later (1959) published under title, *Introduction to Existentialism*.

Killinger, John. "Existentialism and Human Freedom." *The English Journal*, May 1961.

Malantschuk, Gregor. *Kierkegaard's Way to the Truth*. Minneapolis: Augsburg Publishing House, 1963.

Nagley, W. E. "Kierkegaard on Liberation." *Ethics*, October 1959.

Perkins, Robert. "The Plight of Freedom." *Murray State Alumnus*, no. 1, 1961.

Prenter, Regin. "Sartre's Concept of Freedom considered in the Light of Kierkegaard's Thought." In *Kierkegaard Critique*, ed. Howard Johnson and Niels Thulstrup. New York: Harper, 1962.

Roberts, D. E. "Faith and Freedom in Existentialism." *Theology Today*, no. 8, 1951-52.

Schrag, Calvin O. *Existence and Freedom: Towards an Ontology of Human Finitude*. Evanston: Northwestern University Press, 1961.

Wahl, Jean-Andre. "Freedom and Existence in Some Recent Philosophies." *Philosophy and Phenomenological Research*, June 1947-48.

For references in the works to freedom, see, for example, *The Concept of Irony*, pp. 190, 233 ff., 240, 246 f., 249 ff., 270, 279 ff., 294, 296, 298, 316, 320 f.; *Either/Or*, I, pp. 293, 322, 356, 363, 406 f., 420, 429, 435; II, pp. 44 ff., 68, 99, 116, 129, 148, 156, 177 ff., 181 ff., 217 ff., 226 ff., 235 f., 244 ff., 251, 255 f., 265, 275, 337, 351; *Repetition*, pp. 24, 44, 125 ff.; *Edifying Discourses*, I, p. 67; *Fragments*, pp. 19 ff., 93 f., 96, 102 ff.; *The Concept of Anxiety*, pp. 17, 19, 36, 38 ff., 45, 55, 57, 62, 66 ff., 74 ff., 81 f., 86 ff., 96 ff., 99 ff., 103 ff., 106 ff., 109 f., 113 ff., 118, 120 ff., 127, 139 f.; *Edifying Discourses*, IV, p. 139; *Thoughts on Crucial Situations in Human Life*, pp. 15 f., 44, 49, 62 f.; *Stages*, pp. 107 f., 115, 119, 136, 158, 238, 252 f., 286 f., 295, 313, 323, 335 f., 376, 383, 433; *Postscript*, pp. 5, 111, 121, 124, 131 f., 279-89, 306 f., 321 f., 475, 548; S.V. VIII, p. 62; *Purity of Heart*, pp. 88, 171 ff.; *The Lilies of the Field*, together with *The Gospel of Suffering*, pp. 227 ff.; ibid., pp. 35ff.; *Works of Love*, pp. 52, 119, 147 ff., 324 f., 334; *Christian Discourses*, pp. 64, 186 f., 194; "Does a Man Have the Right To Let Himself Be Put to Death for the Truth?" together with *The Present Age*, pp. 105 ff.; *The Sickness Unto Death*, pp. 146, 162, 210; *Training*, pp. 159 ff.; *On My Work as an Author*, together with *The Point of View . . .* , p. 163; ibid., pp. 78 f.; *Attack*, pp. 159, 184.

96. The term *system* refers almost always to the philosophy of Hegel and more particularly to the presentation and development of it by Danish Hegelians. This is one of Kierkegaard's earliest references to Hegel. See I A 170 (June 12, 1836).

97. C. Daub, "*Die Form der christlichen Dogmen- und Kirchen-Historie,*" in *Zeitschrift für spekulative Theologie*, ed. Bruno Bauer, II, pt. 1. (Volume I contains two parts.)

98. "In what is gone that which has been perceivable is the immortal; in those things which have been the natural is the incorruptible (therefore not that which the apostle teaches 'is sown in corruption and is resurrected in incorruption,' but since it is itself essentially incorruptible it has the appearance of the corruptible only until its re-visualization.)"

99. Three times a week, beginning June 20, 1838, Grundtvig had been giving a series of historical lectures in Borch's Kollegium.

100. See *Either/Or*, I, p. 19.

101. "Wretched man that I am! Who will deliver me from the body of death?"

102. See Ludwig Tieck, "*Sehr wunderbare Historie von der Melusina,*" *Sämmtliche Werke* (Paris: 1837), II, pp. 417 ff.

103. Free will or, more accurately, arbitrary and unconditioned freedom. See *Either/Or*, II, p. 178; *The Concept of Anxiety* [Dread], pp. 45, 100.

104. G. W. Leibniz, *Theodicee*, 5 ed. (Hannover, Leipzig: 1763), para. 311, p. 511, and also para. 319, p. 519, on *liberum arbitrium* as "a nothing." See *The Concept of Anxiety* [Dread], p. 100.

105. W. B. Tennemann, *Geschichte der Philosophie*, I-XI (Leipzig: 1798-1819).

106. See *Either/Or*, II, p. 356, where the verb is *ønske* (to wish) rather than *ville* as in this entry. See IV A 234 for amplification.

107. See *Philosophical Fragments*, title page and p. 89.

108. See ibid., pp. 91-92.

109. See Boethius, *De consolatione philosophiæ* (Agriae: 1758), V, pp. 126-27; *Philosophical Fragments*, p. 99.

110. See G. W. Leibniz, *Theodicee*, para. 406, p. 594.

111. See *Postscript*, pp. 273 ff.

112. See *Stages on Life's Way*, pp. 401 ff.; *Postscript*, pp. 74 ff.

113. See *Stages on Life's Way*, pp. 370, 409-411; *Postscript*, pp. 105-106.

114. See L. Holberg, *Mester Gert Westphaler*, III, 1.

115. *The Concept of Anxiety* [*Dread*], ch. III, pp. 92 ff. Note, however, on page 97 that "the possibility of freedom" (*Frihedens Mulighed*) should read "freedom's possibility" in the sense that freedom *is* possibility.

116. See ibid., pp. 45, 100. See notes 103 and 104.

117. See ibid., pp. 99-100 n.

118. Substance.

119. J. P. Mynster, *Prædikener paa alle Søn- og Hellig-dage i Aaret*, I-II, 3 ed. (Copenhagen: 1837), I.

120. See *Christian Discourses*, pp. 186 ff.

121. Julius Müller, *Die christliche Lehre von der Sünde*, I-II, 3 ed. (Breslau: 1849), II, pp. 61 ff., 70, 76 f., 80 ff.

122. See *Postscript*, p. 55, for the sawing metaphor.

123. Julius Müller, *Die christliche Lehre*, II, pp. 229, 232.

124. See Plato, *Republic*, 379 c ff.; Julius Müller, *Die christliche Lehre*, I, pp. 296-98 n., 337 n.

125. Ibid., p. 571.

126. Friedrich Böhringer, *Die Kirche Christi*. . . .

127. Roskilde-Konvents Psalmekomite, *Psalmebog* (Copenhagen: 1850), p. 374.

128. *For Self-Examination*, pp. 63 ff.

129. Matthew 7:13.

130. John 8:32.

FRIENDSHIP

According to Kierkegaard, friendship presupposes a common interest in a third, consequently an ideal or a life-view. A friendship without a striving for a common ideal does not deserve the name of friendship, and Kierkegaard often pokes fun at such a form of friendship. In Emil Boesen Kierkegaard himself had a real friend, although Kierkegaard's isolation as the single individual with his special task did not promote associations of friendship. But higher than friendship is the relation to the neighbor, since neighbor-love does not make distinctions between "friend" or "enemy" but calls for equal love to all men. (See *Works of Love* throughout.)

On the theme of friend and friendship in the works, see, for example, *Either/Or*, I, pp. 33, 291 ff.; II, pp. 321 ff., 337, 341; *Fear and Trembling*, p. 89; *Repetition*, pp. 124, 127 f.; *Edifying Discourses*, I, pp. 114; III, pp. 10 f., 95, 110; *Fragments*, p. 71; *The Concept of Anxiety* [*Dread*], p. 15; *Stages*, pp. 231, 238, 310 f., 380; *Postscript*, pp. 80, 222, 395, 444, 487; *Purity of Heart*, p. 188 f.; *The Gospel of Suffering*, p. 20; *Works of Love*, pp. 29, 36 ff., 45, 58, 62 ff., 68, 74, 90, 113, 117 f., 122, 125, 129 f., 142 f., 148 f., 155, 162, 164, 168, 238, 249 ff., 254, 282, 290 f., 335, 342; *Christian Discourses*, pp. 191, 292; "The High Priest," together with *Christian Discourses*, pp. 367 f.; *Training*, pp. 119, 138, 180, 237; *Two Discourses at Communion on Fridays*, together with *Judge for Yourselves!* p. 5; ibid., 182 f.; *The Concept of Irony*, pp. 61, 119, 145, 189, 319; *The Point of View*, pp. 65, 70.

131. *Du* is the intimate or informal form of address in Danish and is used properly only with members of one's family and with others who have formally acknowledged this relationship by a toast and pledge.

132. See *Works of Love*, pp. 124-26.

133. "Excuse me, in what school has Professor Sibbern [one of Kierkegaard's esteemed professors of philosophy] learned Danish style?" by C. F. Reiffenstein, editor and former pastrycook, in *Raketten med Stjerner*, ed. C. F. Reiffenstein, no. 141, Dec. 10, 1836, pp. 169 ff. J. K. Blox Tøxen (1776-1848), linguist and writer; Frederik Lange (1798-1862), teacher.

134. See *Stages on Life's Way*, p. 260.

135. Brothers Grimm, *Irische Elfenmärchen* (Leipzig: 1826), p. xiix.

136. See *Either/Or*, I, p. 291.

137. See *Works of Love*, p. 125.

138. See Job 2:10; 3:1 ff.

GENIUS

Kierkegaard writes that "Genius, as the word (*ingenium*) says, means the innate or congenital" (VII² B 261:8). Therefore a genius creates something new on the basis of his inherited qualities, and therefore the activity of genius lies "within immanence."

But Kierkegaard points also to another aspect of genius. Usually in "the lives of the most eminent world-historical figures" (VIII¹ A 161) there is a hidden secret suffering. With regard to this latter aspect Kierkegaard could say of himself: "I could almost say that my genius has really been my suffering" (X¹ A 670).

Since it is a matter of "the innate or congenital," genius belongs to the esthetic stage, but it has the possibility of becoming "religious genius," as it is called by Vigilius Haufniensis (*The Concept of Anxiety* [*Dread*], pp. 90,

92, 102). Kierkegaard himself made such a transition to a religious genius. The genius who is religious, however, always stands on a qualitatively lower level than an apostle (see APOSTLE), because the latter receives his authority from a transcendental source; whereas the religious genius merely uses his eminent innate capacities in the service of the good.

For references in the works to genius, see, for example, *From the Papers of One Still Living*, S.V., XIII, pp. 53, 58 f., 65, 72, 78, 82, 86, 88 f.; *The Concept of Irony*, pp. 24, 308, 337; *Either/Or*, I, pp. 27, 34, 48, 55, 62 f., 70, 73 f., 84, 86 ff., 99, 142, 151, 247 f., 283, 286, 296; II, pp. 21, 113, 143; *Fear and Trembling*, pp. 30, 51, 86, 116; *Repetition*, pp. 58 ff.; *Fragments*, 88 ff., 93 f., 96 ff., 102; *Prefaces*, S.V., V, p. 14; *Stages*, pp. 66, 70, 72, 108 f., 146, 226, 383, 435; *Postscript*, pp. 39, 44, 67, 125, 165, 216 f., 221, 224, 231, 242, 244, 422, 439, 502, 526 f., 543; *A Literary Review*, S.V., VIII, p. 21; *Christian Discourses*, p. 83; *Crisis in the Life of an Actress*, pp. 74, 85, 88; "Of the Difference Between a Genius and an Apostle," together with *The Present Age*, pp. 137-63; *The Sickness unto Death*, pp. 217, 246 f.; *Training*, pp. 52, 88; *For Self-Examination*, p. 45; *On My Work as an Author*, together with *The Point of View*, pp. 146 f.; ibid., pp. 69, 73, 98, 100; *Attack*, pp. 159, 182, 217, 224.

139. See *Attack on Christendom*, p. 182. Kierkegaard criticized (in *Af en endnu Levendes Papirer*, not yet translated into English) Hans Christian Andersen's characterization of a genius (in *Only a Fiddler*) as one who needs to be treated tenderly and carefully.

140. See J. G. Hamann, *Schriften*, ed. F. Roth, I-VIII (Berlin: 1842-43), I, p. x.

141. See "Of the Difference between a Genius and an Apostle," by H. H., together with *The Present Age*, pp. 139-63.

142. The reference is to the story of King Zaher and the genie in "my big edition" (VII¹ A 60), *Tausend und eine Nacht. Arabische Erzählungen. Zum ersten male aus dem Urtext treu übersetzt von Gustav Weil*, I-IV (Pforzheim: 1841), IV, pp. 511 ff.

143. See note 139.

144. The Socratic teaching method involving irony, pedagogical ignorance, and the teacher as a vanishing occasion.

145. No great genius has ever existed without [being possessed] of some madness. See Seneca, *Moral Essays* (*De tranquillitate*), 17, 10.

GOD

In his discourse centered on the theme "What it means to seek God," given on the occasion of a confessional service (*Thoughts on Crucial Situations in Human Life, Three Discourses on Imagined Occasions*, pp. 1 ff.), Kierkegaard sketches the most important steps in man's knowledge of God—all the way from the mythological forms, through trust in fate and in the creator, up to the encounter with the God before whom a person stands as sinner. Kierkegaard shows how a man's conception of God proceeds in gaining greater clarity. This discourse, however, omits God's coming to man in Christ.

According to Kierkegaard man by himself in his seeking after God can arrive at an abstract idea of God and cannot, by way of some proofs, attain to God as genuine reality, inasmuch as all demonstrations lie within the realm of possibility. Only through a person's venturing the leap of faith does God become a reality for him; before this leap, God does not actually exist [er ikke til] for man, that is, God is only an abstract possibility for him. Kierkegaard expresses this quite precisely: "Immanentally (in the imaginative medium of abstraction) God does not exist or is not present [er ikke til]; he is [er]—only for the existing person [Existerinde] is God present, i.e., he can be present [være til] in faith." Therefore "If an existing person does not have faith, then [for him] God neither is nor is God present, although understood eternally God nevertheless eternally is" (VII¹ A 139).

Mourant, John. "The Place of God in the Philosophy of Kierkegaard." Giornale Metafisica, no. 8, 1953.

Ramsey, P. " 'Existenz' and the Existence of God." Journal of Religion, no. 28, 1948.

Thomas, J. H. "Kierkegaard on the Existence of God." Review of Religion, no. 1-2, 1953.

In The Point of View (p. 64) Kierkegaard writes that the relationship to God was the "happy love" of his life, and in the works from the earliest to the latest there are many hundreds of references to God. To pursue this theme requires that one read the entire authorship. For references to "the God" [Guden], a very special term, see the translator's introduction to Philosophical Fragments (pp. ix ff.). For references to "God-relationship" [Gudsforholdet], see, for example, The Concept of Irony, p. 275; Either/Or, II, p. 250; Edifying Discourses, I, pp. 49 ff.; Repetition, pp. 157 f.; Fear and Trembling, pp. 64 ff., 78 ff.; Fragments, pp. 108, 127 f.; The Concept of Anxiety [Dread], p. 98; Thoughts on Crucial Situations in Human Life, pp. 1-41; Stages, pp. 214, 224 f., 238, 244, 252, 376, 383, 415, 417 f.; Postscript, pp. 52, 62 f., 71 ff., 92, 145, 158 f., 178 f., 195, 218 ff., 232 ff., 318, 342, 369, 399, 405, 410 ff., 419, 422 ff., 434 ff., 439, 443 f., 454 ff., 497; The Present Age, pp. 29 ff., 35, 40 f., 65; The Gospel of Suffering, pp. 145 ff., 156, 212 f.; Works of Love, p. 112 f., 117 ff., 121 ff., 129 ff., 140 ff., 184, 188, 195, 217, 222, 259, 296, 313, 332, 335, 348; Christian Discourses, pp. 218 f.; The Sickness unto Death, pp. 146, 165, 179 f., 184, 247 ff.; Training, pp. 92 f., 182; Judge for Yourselves! pp. 137, 218; The Point of View, pp. 9, 64 ff., 76, 88 ff., Attack, p. 221.

146. See Pap. I C 19, Kierkegaard's notes on H. N. Clausen's lectures in Dogmatics; Friedrich Schleiermacher, Der christliche Glaube, I-II, 2 ed. (Berlin: 1830), II, p. 68.

147. See *Edifying Discourses*, IV, pp. 142-43; "The Unchangeableness of God," in *Attack upon Christendom*, pp. 273 ff.

148. See note 146.

149. See John 4:19.

150. *"Der Pantheismus und die Genesis"*, *Zeitschrift für spekulative Theologie*, ed. Bruno Bauer, 2 ed., 1837, II, p. 188.

151. Kierkegaard's library included F. C. Baur, *Die christliche Gnosis oder die christliche Religionsphilosophie in ihrer geschichtlichen Entwicklung* (Tübingen: 1835).

152. Romans 11:33.

153. Genesis 1:31.

154. Genesis 2:2.

155. I Corinthians 13:12.

156. See Luke 19:42.

157. See I John 4:16.

158. See *The Concept of Anxiety* [Dread], pp. 105 ff.: "Dread of the good."

159. Nothing outside God. Nothing beyond God.

160. See *Either/Or*, I, pp. 288 ff.; *Three Discourses at the Communion on Fridays*, in *Christian Discourses*, pp. 382-83.

161. See *Edifying Discourses*, I, pp. 62-63.

162. See Romans 8:38 ff.

163. See *Postscript*, p. 275.

164. See *Philosophical Fragments*, pp. 30, 196-97 n.; *Postscript*, p. 277.

165. Unmoved: the unmoved mover.

166. See III C 27.

167. See Spinoza, *Tractatus theologico-politicus*, VI; *Philosophical Fragments*, pp. 51n., 215-16.

168. See *Philosophical Fragments*, pp. 49 ff.

169. See *Postscript*, pp. 218 ff., 516 ff.

170. Middle term

171. Surprise

172. Kierkegaard had a German translation of Shelley by Julius Seybt. Percy Bysshe Shelley, *Poetische Werke* (Leipzig: 1844), p. 57.

173. See *Philosophical Fragments*, pp. 55 ff.

174. See ibid., Foreword, pp. x ff., 13, 18n.

175. See *Postscript*, p. 485; *The Concept of Anxiety* [Dread], p. 134n.

176. See *Postscript*, p. 484.

177. See ibid., p. 497.

178. See Matthew 10:30.

179. See *Postscript*, p. 296.

180. See ibid., pp. 267 ff., especially pp. 272 ff.

181. See ibid., p. 277.

182. *Philosophical Fragments,* p. 108.
183. See note 146.
184. A. P. Adler, *Studier* (Copenhagen: 1843), pp. 70 ff. Adler was the occasion for Kierkegaard's *The Book about Adler* (English title, *On Authority and Revelation*) which remained in the *Papirer* and did not appear as one of his published works.
185. See *Postscript,* pp. 178 ff., 498n.
186. See ibid., pp. 195, 369, 514; *The Sickness unto Death,* pp. 230, 258; *The Gospel of Suffering,* pp. 91 ff.
187. See *Works of Love,* pp. 177 ff.
188. Matthew 20:1 ff.
189. See *Philosophical Fragments,* pp. 49 ff.; Acts 17:23.
190. See *Works of Love,* pp. 39, 82, 105, 185 ff.
191. Luke 10:42.
192. See Moriz Carriere, *Die philosophische Weltanschanung der Reformationszeit in ihren Beziehungen zur Gegenwart* (Stuttgart, Tübingen: 1847), p. 467.
193. See *The Sickness unto Death,* p. 234.
194. J. Gerhardt, *Meditationes sacræ,* ed. S. Guenther (Leipzig: 1844), Meditatione XXXI.
195. See *The Sickness unto Death,* p. 165.
196. Luke 7:37 ff.
197. See Luke 14:28.
198. See *Works of Love,* pp. 44 ff., 170, 326 ff.
199. Luther, *En christelig Postille,* I, p. 497.
200. See note 186.
201. See *For Self-Examination,* pp. 22-23.
202. *The Gospel of Suffering,* pp. 91 ff.; note 186.
203. *Auswahl aus Gerhard Tersteegens Schriften,* ed. Georg Rapp (Essen: 1841), p. 290.
204. See note 33.
205. Romans 8:31.
206. See Luther, *En christelig Postille,* II, pp. 94, 101 ff.
207. I John 4:4.
208. See *Works of Love,* p. 65.
209. J. H. Fichte, *Sätze zur Vorschule der Theologie* (Stuttgart, Tübingen: 1826).
210. See note 33.
211. A. Neander, *Denkwürdigkeiten aus der Geschichte des Christentums und des christlichen Lebens,* I-II (Berlin: 1823), II, pp. 254 ff.
212. Johann Arndt, *Fire Bøger om den Sande Christendom* (Christiania: 1829).
213. See Luther, *En christelig Postille,* tr. Jørgen Thisted (Copenhagen: 1828), I, p. 307.

214. See *Either/Or*, II, pp. 343 ff.
215. Friedrich Böhringer, *Die Kirche Christi.* . . .
216. Matthew 10:29.
217. Psalm 139:6.
218. See *Philosophical Fragments*, pp. 46 ff.
219. John 3:30.
220. The Danish term *Exemplarer* refers here to men who are copies, duplicates, specimens or particulars of a type, rather than single individuals (*den Enkelte*), authentic persons.
221. J. L. Heiberg, *Nei* (Copenhagen: 1836), sc. 2 and 5.
222. J. L. Jacobi, *Die Lehre der Irvingiten verglichen mit der heiligen Schrift* (Berlin: 1853).
223. See I John 5:19.
224. See article "Salt," no. XI in *The Fatherland*, March 31, 1855, in *Attack upon Christendom*, p. 36.
225. See Suetonius, *Vespasian*, XXIII. Vespasian had levied a tax on public conveniences. When criticized by his son Titus, he held up a piece of money and asked whether the smell was offensive. Titus said it was not; whereupon Vespasian replied, "But it is from urine." See also *Works of Love*, p. 297.
226. John 18:37.
227. See *Postscript*, pp. 520 ff.
228. See, for example, XI¹ A 2, XI² A 130.
229. See, for example, XI² A 96, 97.
230. See, for example, XI² A 8, 118.

GOETHE

In his concentration during 1836-37 upon the question of Faust, Kierkegaard was concerned most intensively with Goethe's *Faust*; but he had also read other works by Goethe, for example the drama *Egmont* and the novels *Wilhelm Meister* and *Die Wahlverwandschaften*, and had been stimulated in various ways.

But Kierkegaard's attitude toward the life-view presented in Goethe's writings gradually became pronouncedly polemical when Kierkegaard discovered that Goethe as a man lacked an ethical stance. For example, he says of Goethe, "At no point has he grasped the idea, but he talks himself out of everything (girls, the idea of love, Christianity, etc.) he can" (V A 57). He upbraids Goethe, saying that he "tampered with the laws of existence and became a genius on the basis of talent" (XI¹ A 197).

Closs, A. *Medusa's Mirror*. London: Cresset Press, 1957.

Williams, Forrest. "A Problem in Values: the Faustian Motivation in Kierkegaard and Goethe." *Ethics*, July 1953.

For references in the works to Goethe and his writings, see, for example, S.V. XIII, pp. 14, 55, 476; *The Concept of Irony*, pp. 226, 294, 333, 337; *Either/Or*, I, pp. 25, 55, 89, 175, 179, 203-12, 261, 307 f.; II, pp. 103, 170;

Repetition, p. 29; *Fear and Trembling*, pp. 117 ff.; *Fragments*, p. 67; *The Concept of Anxiety* [*Dread*], p. 53; *Stages*, p. 148; *Postscript*, pp. 164, 256, 376; *The Sickness unto Death*, pp. 191, 240; *The Point of View*, pp. 88 f.

231. See, for example, J. G. Fichte, *Die Bestimmung des Menschen* (Berlin: 1800).

232. Prototype.

233. *Gedanken über meinen Lebenslauf*, J. G. Hamann, *Schriften*, ed. F. Roth (Berlin: 1821), I, pp. 149 ff.

234. See Goethe, *Aus meinem Leben Dichtung und Wahrheit*, II, ch. 7, *Werke*, I-LV (Stuttgart, Tübingen: 1828-33), XXV; *Stages On Life's Way*, pp. 148 ff.

235. See *Stages on Life's Way*, p. 152.

236. Ah, when I went astray, I had many comrades.
Now that I know the truth, I am almost alone.

Goethe, "Zueignung." The second line is not given quite accurately: "*Da ich dich kenne, bin ich fast allein.*"

237. See note 234.

GRACE

Kierkegaard always unshakably believed that man is saved by grace alone. Yet he points out that "Grace is not something settled and completed once and for all" (X^2 A 198), but in Christendom it "is usually taken to be a dead, once-and-for-all decision instead of being related to a striving . . ." (X^2 A 223).

Falling short in his continual striving, man must continually be convinced that he needs grace. Kierkegaard is progressively more attentive to the relation between faith and striving. By "striving" he means the attempt to realize the ethical claim and, beyond that, imitation [*Efterfølgelsen*]; he regards it as a misuse of grace if such striving is by-passed.

He succinctly states the proper relation between grace and striving: ". . . infinite humiliation and grace, and then a striving born of gratitude" (X^3 A 734). In later journal entries Kierkegaard uses sharper expressions to characterize the misuse of grace which occurs with the omission of striving.

To assist men toward honesty in this relationship he attempts to distinguish between "grace in the first place" and "grace in the second place" (X^4 A 446, X^5 A 44, X^5 A 103). By "grace in the first place" Kierkegaard understands the acceptance of grace in the case of a person who has departed from or does not dare become involved in the requirements of Christianity but nevertheless admits "his distance" from them. By the admission he comes again into an honest relationship to Christianity. As late as his direct critique of the Church (1854-55) Kierkegaard proposes that such an admission is the only possible "means of defending, Christianly, the Establishment" (*Attack upon Christendom*, p. 54).

"Grace in the second place" means that a man's life already expresses "the strenuousness of spirit in the strict sense" (X⁴ A 446) as do "those noble ones," therefore first and foremost the witnesses and martyrs, and in this way one experiences in an existentially decisive way that he is continually thrown upon grace.

For references in the works to grace and gift see, for example, *The Concept of Irony*, p. 236; *Either/Or*, II, pp. 16, 41, 209, 211, 241 ff., 254, 329; *Edifying Discourses*, I, pp. 6, 14 f., 34-55; *Fear and Trembling*, pp. 32, 37, 60, 62, 102; *Edifying Discourses*, I, pp. 92, 101, 116; II, pp. 13 ff.; III, pp. 8, 53, 96, 115, 118; IV, pp. 11 ff., 69, 118; *Stages*, pp. 147, 168; *The Gospel of Suffering*, p. 58; *Works of Love*, p. 356; *Christian Discourses*, pp. 36, 67 f., 71, 83, 87, 182, 196, 218, 275, 308; *The Lilies and The Birds*, together with *Christian Discourses*, p. 335; *The Sickness unto Death*, pp. 240 ff., 257, 371; *Three Discourses at the Communion on Fridays*, together with *Christian Discourses*, p. 385; *Training*, pp. 7, 69, 70 f.; "The Woman That Was a Sinner," together with *Training*, p. 269; *For Self-Examination*, pp. 8 ff., 22; *Judge for Yourselves!*, pp. 156, 165, 198, 202, 206, 209, 212 [omitted in 1.4], 215; *On My Work as an Author*, together with *The Point of View*, p. 160 f.; *Attack*, pp. 38, 54 f., 164, 243, 286 f.

238. *Tidsskrift for udenlandsk theologisk Litteratur*, II (1834), pp. 107 ff.

239. The sprinkled blood that speaks more graciously than the blood of Abel.

240. See *Edifying Discourses*, I, p. 63.

241. Luke 16:24.

242. End or close the parenthesis. See *Postscript*, p. 29.

243. See I Corinthians 15:10.

244. Luther, *En christelig Postille*, I, p. 533.

245. Ibid., II, pp. 370 ff.

246. Luke 14:18 ff.

247. Diogenes Lærtius, *The Lives and Opinions of Eminent Philosophers*, bk. VIII, para. 19.

248. Friedrich Böhringer, *Die Kirche Christi und ihre Zeugen oder die Kirchengeschichte in Biographien*, I-VII (Zurich: 1842-49).

249. "The Reformation is . . . . . the reaction of Christianity as gospel against Christianity as law!"

250. August Petersen, *Die Idee der christlichen Kirche*, I-III (Leipzig: 1839-46).

251. Luther, *En christelig Postille*, I, pp. 479 ff.

252. Luke 2:35.

253. II Corinthians 12:9.

254. See Friedrich Böhringer, *Die Kirche Christi und ihre Zeugen*, I, pp. 222 ff.

255. See, for example, XI² A 96.

GRATITUDE

It is easy to thank God when everything goes well, but Kierkegaard continually stresses the difficult art of thanking God under all conditions. This he had emphasized, as he himself recalls, as early as his first edifying discourses, in which he uses the text "Every good and perfect gift is from above" (*Edifying Discourses*, I, pp. 35 ff.; II, pp. 27 ff. and pp. 45 ff.). These discourses point out how suffering and the difficulties of life are also to be received out of God's hand and borne with gratitude. Characteristically, Kierkegaard pictures himself in eternity as uninteruptedly having "nothing else to do but to thank God" (*The Point of View*, p. 103).

Minear, Paul S. "Thanksgiving as a Synthesis of the Temporal and the Eternal." In *Kierkegaard Critique*, ed. Howard Johnson and Niels Thulstrup. New York: Harper, 1962.

For references in the works to gratitude, see, for example, *Either/Or*, II, pp. 58 f., 100, 211, 247; *Edifying Discourses*, I, pp. 47 ff.; II, pp. 15 f., 58 ff.; III, p. 100; *Thoughts on Crucial Situations in Human Life*, pp. 69 f.; *Stages*, pp. 119 f.; *Postscript*, pp. 59 ff., 125, 158 ff., 209, 399, 405, 553 f.

256. Philippians 2:6.

257. I Timothy 4:4.

258. See *Philosophical Fragments*, p. 45.

259. See ibid., pp. 32 ff.; *Stages on Life's Way*, p. 144.

260. See *Works of Love*, Introduction, pp. 14-15.

261. See Herodotus, VII, 10.

262. Adam Oehlenschläger, *Poetiske Skrifter*, I-II (Copenhagen: 1805), II, p. 248.

263. Luke 17:11-19.

264. A. G. Rudelbach, *Hieronymous Savonarola und seine Zeit* (Hamburg: 1835).

265. Ibid.

GREEKS

Kierkegaard nourished a deep respect for the Greeks and "the Greek principle" (*Postscript*, p. 315). He frequently mentions the Greeks' longing for harmony and shyness before the unlimited. He also emphasizes the Greek thinkers who knew about existence, in contrast to modern abstract thought. Yet Kierkegaard understood that this characteristic of Greek thought, its being more concrete, was linked in part to the level of historical development within which it occurred. Thus Johannes Climacus says: "In Greece, as in the youth of philosophy generally, it was found difficult to win through to the abstract and to leave existence, which always gives the particular; in modern times, on the other hand, it has become difficult to reach existence" (*Postscript*, p. 295). With Socrates a new principle entered into Greek life and sundered the original harmonious conception of the Greeks.

For references in the works to the Greeks, the Greek Spirit, and Hellenism, see, for example, *The Concept of Irony*, passim; *Either/Or*, I, pp. 31, 56, 61 f., 87, 92, 121, 141 f., 156, 232; II, p. 205; *Fear and Trembling*, p. 23; *Repetition*, pp. 3 f., 33 f., 93 f.; *Edifying Discourses*, III, p. 106; *Fragments*, pp. 47 f.; *The Concept of Anxiety* [*Dread*], pp. 3, 58 f., 78 ff., 93 ff., 137; *Stages*, pp. 73, 83, 299, 414; *Postscript*, pp. 54, 89, 91, 100, 128, 143, 161, 170, 184 f., 191, 196, 204 ff., 228 f., 248, 260, 272 f., 277 ff., 297, 315 f., 408, 530, 535; *Has a Man the Right To Let Himself Be Put to Death for the Truth?* together with *The Present Age*, p. 131; *The Sickness unto Death*, pp. 224 f., 258; *Training*, pp. 134, 154; *For Self-Examination*, p. 40; *Judge for Yourselves!* pp. 134, 209; *Attack*, pp. 142, 283 f.

266. Injured by a god.

267. This note has been deleted.

GUILT

Essentially, there is guilt only in relation to God. The guilt men take upon themselves in relation to civil arrangements or moral law is, according to Kierkegaard, on a lower level, since it involves only relations within the finite. Kierkegaard and the pseudonymous authors rigorously carry through this distinction between guilt within the finite and guilt in relation to the infinite. But guilt on the lower level also receives a new qualification when it is confronted by the eternal (God). In order to characterize the guilt that faces man in the encounter with revealed truth (Christ), Kierkegaard uses the customary expression "sin," which then signifies the ultimate and decisive qualification of man's guilt.

De Young, Quintin R. "A Study of Contemporary Christian Existential Theology (Kierkegaard and Tillich) and Modern Dynamic Psychology (Freud and Sullivan) Concerning Guilt Feelings. Ph.D. dissertation, Southern Baptist Theological Seminary, 1959.

Hamilton, Kenneth. "Man: Anxious or Guilty? A Second Look at Kierkegaard's *The Concept of Dread*." *Christian Scholar*, XLVI, 1963.

Heinecken, Martin J. *The Moment before God*. Philadelphia: Muhlenberg, 1956.

Mitchell, J. E. "Some Aspects of the Problem of Guilt with Special Reference to Kafka, Kierkegaard and Dostoevsky." Ph.D. dissertation, University of Edinburgh, 1958.

For references in the works to guilt (sometimes translated as "fault"), see, for example, *Either/Or*, I, pp. 141 ff., 144 f., 154 ff., 157, 305; II, pp. 94, 213, 222, 239, 242, 330, 334, 336; *Edifying Discourses*, I, pp. 11, 64; *Repetition*, pp. 144 ff.; *Fear and Trembling*, pp. 105 ff., 113, 120; *Fragments*, pp. 19, 23, 34, 38, 42; *The Concept of Anxiety*, pp. 11, 32 ff., 39, 46 f., 54 f., 57, 82, 91-96, 108, 144; *Edifying Discourses*, IV, p. 139; *Thoughts on Crucial Situations in Human Life*, pp. 27 ff., 32 f., 39 f., 107; *Stages*, pp. 174, 179-244, 304, 319, 348, 356, 359, 385, 389, 392 f., 405, 408, 417 f., 425, 429, 432; *Post-*

script, pp. 127, 139, 468-93, 497, 505, 517, 524; *Purity of Heart*, pp. 39 ff., 44 f.; *The Gospel of Suffering*, pp. 43, 58, 65-96, 116; *Works of Love*, pp. 39, 110, 135 f., 159, 270 f., 274, 287; *Christian Discourses*, p. 102 (translated as sin-consciousness), 267, 287 f., 298, 300 ff., 307; *Does a Man Have the Right To Let Himself Be Put to Death for the Truth?* together with *The Present Age*, pp. 97, 106 ff., 127 f.; *The Sickness unto Death*, pp. 211, 255; *Three Discourses at the Communion on Fridays*, together with *Christian Discourses*, pp. 372 f.; *Training*, p. 79; *Two Discourses at the Communion on Fridays*, together with *Judge for Yourselves!* p. 22; ibid., p. 186; *The Point of View*, p. 7; *This Has To Be Said; So Let It Be Said*, together with *The Moment*, etc., in *Attack*, pp. 59 f.

268. See *The Concept of Anxiety* [*Dread*], pp. 60 ff.

269. See *Postscript*, p. 482.

270. See *Works of Love*, p. 353.

271. See *The Concept of Anxiety* [*Dread*], passim.

272. Julius Müller, *Die christliche Lehre von der Sünde*, 3 ed., I-II (Breslau: 1849). Richard Rothe, *Theologische Ethik* (Wittenberg: 1848). Dorner, in J. Müller, op. cit., II, p. 559.

273. Change into another category.

HAMANN, Johann Georg

Early in his writings Kierkegaard designated Hamann as representative of the highest human position, the stage of humor as the confinium or border sphere of the Christian-religious. Yet Kierkegaard did not present the stage of humor with Hamann as the representative, analogous to the presentation of irony with Socrates as the representative in *The Concept of Irony*. The reason for this was that Kierkegaard's writing up to and including *Concluding Unscientific Postscript* was on the whole under the sign of humor (expressed by the use of pseudonyms), because the center of gravity for Kierkegaard himself during this period lay in the humorous, yet with the Christian-religious in reserve. He uses Hamann's witty thoughts (for example, I A 100, I A 237), regarding the relation between the human and the Christian, but gives them a more penetrating existential grounding; in Hamann the whole matter is given only in a disconnected and aphoristic form. Kierkegaard says, for example, about his explication of these ideas: "Hamann rightly declares: Just as 'law' abrogates 'grace,' so 'to comprehend' abrogates 'to have faith.' It is, in fact, my thesis. But in Hamann it is merely an aphorism; whereas I have fought it through or have fought it out of a whole given philosophy and culture and into the thesis: to comprehend that faith cannot be comprehended or (the more ethical and God-fearing side) to comprehend that faith must not be comprehended" (X^2 A 225).

Anderson, Albert. "A Comparative Study of the Religious Philosophies of Johann Georg Hamann and Søren Kierkegaard." Unpublished ms.

"Hamann Renaissance." *Christian Century*, June 29, 1960.

For references in the works to Hamann, see *Either/Or*, I, p. 243; *Repetition*, pp. 34 f.; *Fear and Trembling*, p. 21; *Fragments*, pp. 67, 138 (see note); *The Concept of Anxiety* [Dread], pp. 2, 145; *Stages*, pp. 100, 104, 111, 122, 138, 146, 187, 329; *Postscript*, pp. 223 f., 258, 495.

274. J. G. Hamann, *Schriften*, I-VII, ed. F. Roth (Berlin: 1821-43), I. This is from a letter by Hamann to J. G. Lindner in Riga, July 10, 1759. After quoting Hume on miracles Hamann says, "*Hume mag das mit einer höhnischen oder tiefsinnigen Miene gesagt haben; so ist diesz allemal Orthodoxie, und ein Zeugnis der Wahrheit in dem Munde eines Feindes und Verfolgers derselben—Alle seine zweifel sind Beweise seines Satzes.*"—["Hume may have said that with a mocking expression or with a serious one; at any rate, this is orthodoxy, and a witness of truth in the mouth of an enemy and a persecutor of truth—all his doubts are proofs of his statement."]

275. "No—when God himself speaks with him he is forced to send the word of power in advance and to let it go into fulfillment—: Awake, thou that sleepest."

276. Ibid., I, p. 405.

277. "The last fruit of all wisdom is the observation of human ignorance and weakness" . . . . . "Our reason . . . is therefore just what Paul calls law—and the command of reason is holy, righteous, and good; but is it given to make us wise? Just as little as the law of the Jews justified them, but is to bring us over from the opposite, how unreasonable our reason is, that our faults should increase through it, as sin increased through the law."

278. Isn't it an old inspiration which you have often heard from me: Incredible but true! Lies and stories must be probable, hypotheses and fables, but not the truth and basic doctrines of our faith.

279. Ibid., I, p. x.

280. See Kierkegaard's *Af en endnu levendes Papirer* (not presently in English), S.V., XIII, p. 54.

281. J. G. Hamann, *Schriften*, I, p. 497.

282. Ole J. Cold, Rogaardshus, north of Copenhagen near Fredensborg, one of the beautiful wooded areas Kierkegaard visited quite frequently.

283. It allures and its terrifies.

284. Everything divine and everything human. J. G. Hamann, *Schriften*, I, p. 23.

285. Ibid. (1842).

286. "Demonax" in *Lucians Schriften aus dem Griechischen übersetzt*, I-IV (Zurich: 1769-73), II, pp. 254 ff., especially pp. 260-61). Kierkegaard also had *Luciani Opera*, I-IV (Leipzig: 1829). See *Repetition*, p. 84.

287. See J. G. von Herder, *Sämmtliche Werke. Zur schönen Literatur und Kunst*, I-XX (Stuttgart, Tübingen: 1829), XVI, p. 114.

288. See note 290.

289. In the manuscript of *Fear and Trembling*, these lines from Ha-

mann are crossed out. They follow the title-page motto from Hamann concerning interpreting and understanding (Tarquinius and the poppies).

290. A layman and unbeliever can explain my manner of writing in no other way than as nonsense since I express myself with various tongues and speak the language of sophists, of puns, of Cretans and Arabians, of wise men and Moors and Creoles, and babble a confusion of criticism, mythology, rebus, and axioms, and argue now in a human way [κατ' ἀνθρωπον] and now according to power [κατ' ἐξοχήν]. J. G. Hamann, *Schriften*, I, p. 467. See Romans 3:5 and Galatians 3:15; *Repetition*, pp. 34-35.

291. The virgin-children of speculation.

292. Gentlemen, Socrates was no etc. J. G. Hamann, *Schriften*, II, p. 12.

293. Ibid. See *The Concept of Anxiety* [*Dread*], p.2.

294. J. G. Hamann, *Schriften*, III, pp. x ff.

295. Ibid., III, pp. 74, 392.

296. Ibid., V, p. 25.

297. Ibid., V, p. 277.

298. Ibid., III, p. 10.

HAMLET

The figure of Hamlet attracted Kierkegaard's attention not least because of a certain fellowship of fate. Each one had a tragic relationship to the woman he loved because his life in the service of the idea claimed him completely.

Kierkegaard complains of Hamlet's merely reflective and indecisive mind, and his pseudonym Frater Taciturnus avers that Hamlet was "a case of morbid reflection" (*Stages on Life's Way*, p. 410). It is quite typical that Kierkegaard also charges Hamlet with weakness for wanting the recognition of the world so that he could not remain silent to the end. He writes: "It is harrowing when Hamlet at the moment of death is almost in despair that the hidden life he had led with prodigious exertion in the service of the idea should be understood by no one, yes, that no one would know anything of it; but if Hamlet becomes softened at death, he also could have talked in his lifetime, that is, let the whole thing go" (*Authority and Revelation*, p. 54, based upon *The Book on Adler*, VII² B 235, p. 72, H. tr.).

Brophy, Liam. "Kierkegaard: the Hamlet in Search of Holiness." *Social Justice Review*, no. 9, 1955.

Ferrie, W. S. "Kierkegaard: Hamlet or Jeremiah?" *Evangelical Quarterly*, no. 2, 1936.

Rougemont, Denis de. "Kierkegaard and Hamlet." In *The Anchor Review*. New York: Doubleday, 1955.

Rougemont, Denis de. *Love Declared*, including "Dialectic of the Myths" and "Two Danish Princes: Kierkegaard and Hamlet." New York: Pantheon, 1963.

299. Heinrich T. Rötscher, atuhor of *Die Kunst der dramatischers Darstellung*, I-III (Berlin: 1841-46).

300. Ludwig Börne, *Gesammelte Schriften*, I-II (Hamburg: 1829), II, pp. 172-98, especially p. 197. See *Stages*, pp. 409-11.

301. In the *Papirer* there are not many entries concerning *Hamlet* or Hamlet, but Kierkegaard refers to them frequently in the published works. See, for example, *Either/Or*, I, pp. 153, 209; *Philosophical Fragments*, p. 51; *The Concept of Anxiety* [*Dread*], p. 115; *Forord, S.V.*, V, pp. 17, 23; *Stages*, pp. 370, 409-11; *Postscript*, pp. 105 f., 145, 173; *S.V.*, XIII, p. 480; *The Moment*, No. 7, in *Attack upon Christendom*, p. 203.

HEGEL

Kierkegaard's writings contain from the very beginning a polemic against the Danish Hegelians, but they also constitute a reckoning with Hegel's basic philosophic ideas. In contesting Hegel, Kierkegaard treats him as the chief representative of the trend in the modern world which is undermining the beliefs of Christianity.

Kierkegaard attacks and refutes particularly the following of Hegel's philosophical affirmations— (1) Philosophy is superior to faith, since philosophy in the form of concepts gives the same truth that Christianity gives only in the form of representation. In opposition to this assertion Kierkegaard shows the limits of thought in dealing with Christian truths. Thought encompasses only the immanental; the sphere of faith is the transcendent. Whereas contradiction-free thought dominates immanence, such thought collides with the absurd in the encounter with Christianity. The absurd points to a higher reality than that with which philosophy is occupied. (2) The second point in Hegel opposed vigorously by Kierkegaard is the assertion that "the course of the world's events is an inevitable development" (I A 205). In contrast, Kierkegaard stresses the significance of freedom for all that occurs, and this emphasis characterizes all his writings. (See HISTORY.) If Hegel's assertion of "an inevitable development" were correct, the central Christian categories such as Repentance and Atonement would lose their meaning. (3) A third objection to Hegel is that his philosophy "has no ethics." According to Kierkegaard's view there can be genuine ethics only when man relates himself to the eternal as a transcendent reality, but Hegel has wanted "to make the state the highest court of the ethical" (*Postscript*, p. 450, H. tr.) and thereby has reduced all striving to the finite. Ethics on the level of finitude is not ethics in the genuine sense.

In spite of Kierkegaard's critical attitude toward Hegel, attention must be paid to his own declaration that he owed "Hegel himself very much" (X^6 B 128, p. 171).

Beck, Maxmillian. "Existentialism versus Naturalism and Idealism." *South Atlantic Quarterly*, no. 2, 1948.

Berberelly, John, Jr. "Søren Kierkegaard's Criticism of Hegelian Philosophy." M.A. thesis, Columbia University, 1951.

Collins, James. "Kierkegaard's Critique of Hegel." *Thought*, no. 68, 1943.

Kroner, Richard. "Kierkegaard or Hegel?" *Revue Internationale de Philosophie*, no. 19, 1952.

McLaughlin, Wayman Bernard. "The Relation between Hegel and Kierkegaard." Ph.D. dissertation, Boston University, 1958.

Perkins, Robert. "Kierkegaard and Hegel: The Dialectical Structure of Kierkegaard's Ethical Thought." Ph.D. dissertation, University of Indiana, 1965.

Reinhardt, K. F. "Cleavage of Mind: Kierkegaard and Hegel." *Commonweal*, October 2, 1936.

Start, Lester J. "Kierkegaard and Hegel." Ph.D. dissertation, Syracuse University, 1953.

For references in the works to Hegel, Hegelians, and Hegelianism, see, for example, *From the Papers of One Still Living*, S.V., XIII, pp. 53 f., 56, 65; *The Concept of Irony*, pp. 348 f., 72, 83, 132 f., 162, 165, 181, 189, 199, 209, 216, 218, 223, 241, 243, 256, 260, 271, 278 f., 282 f., 286 f., 292, 295 f., 300 f., 317, 323 f., 328, 330, 335; "Public Confession," S.V., XIII, p. 401; *Either/Or*, I, pp. 48, 51 f., 145, 220; *Fear and Trembling*, pp. 43, 53, 65, 79, 92, 121; *Fragments*, passim, particularly pp. 96 f., 100, 102, 107; *The Concept of Anxiety* [*Dread*], pp. 10, 18, 27 f., 32 f., 53, 73, 120, 140 f.; "Prefaces," S.V., V, pp. 49, 60; *Stages*, pp. 271, 401; "A Fleeting Observation . . . Don Juan," S.V., XIII, pp. 475, 477; *Postscript*, pp. 16, 18, 34, 50-55, 65 f., 74, 96-113, 119-42, 164, 167, 170-73, 176 ff., 184 f., 190-208, 216-17, 223-24, 243 f., 248, 263, 267-85, 291 f., 296, 298 f., 301 f., 306, 309 f., 315, 317, 330 ff., 334-40, 354-60, 363 f., 366, 373-77, 450, 458, 481, 498, 505-7, 549; *Works of Love*, p. 34; *Christian Discourses* p. 207; *The Sickness unto Death*, pp. 169, 176 f.; *Training*, p. 88; *The Point of View*, p. 89.

302. Friedrich Schlegel, *Sämmtliche Werke*, I-II (Vienna: 1822-25).

303. See *Kjøbenhavns flyvende Post*, 1828, no. 4.

304. Most likely the reference here is to H. L. Martensen, who returned in the latter part of 1836 from a study tour. In Munich he visited Baader and Schelling and discussed with Baader the relationship between faith and knowledge.

305. Presumably another reference to H. L. Martensen.

306. This phrase appears in various works in various connections (see, for example, passages on "going beyond" Descartes and earlier philosophy, *Fear and Trembling*, pp. 22-23, going beyond faith, ibid., p. 23 and passim, a pupil going beyond Heraclitus, ibid., p. 132, making an advance upon Socrates, *Philosophical Fragments*, pp. 34 and 139 and passim). In *Postscript* his basic criticisms of Hegel's thought (anthropology, ethics, philosophy of religion) continue and deepen, but his most barbed attack is upon Hegelians who "go beyond" Hegel (*Fear and Trembling*, p. 43) as H. L. Martensen

claimed (*Danske Maanedsskrift*, 1836, no. 16, pp. 515 ff.) and as F. C. Sibbern said (ibid., 1838, no. 10, p. 292) J. L. Heiberg had done. See also I A 328, II A 7 and 697.

307. For a discussion of the Hegelian term *ophæve* (German *aufheben*), used here in a pun, see *Postscript*, pp. 199-200.

308. Johannes Climacus became one of Kierkegaard's pseudonyms:*Philosophical Fragments*, 1844, and *Concluding Unscientific Postscript*, 1846. Anti-Climacus (above Johannes Climacus) was given as the author of *The Sickness unto Death*, 1849, and *Training in Christianity*, 1850. In 1842-43 he began a work entitled *Johannes Climacus* or *De Omnibus Dubitandum Est*. Climacus was a monk in the monastery on Sinai and received his name from his book κλιμαξ του παραδεισου (*The Ladder of Divine Ascent*; New York: Harper, 1959), which gives the steps on Jacob's ladder for growth in the spiritual life. Kierkegaard knew of the work through de Wette, *Lærebog i den Christelige Sædelære og sammes Historie* (Copenhagen: 1835). See *Johannes Climacus, or De Omnibus Dubitandum Est*, pp. 103-104.

309. Endless genealogies.

310. See *Postscript*, pp. 102 ff., 120, 301-302, 375 ff.; G. W. F. Hegel, *Logik*, ed. H. G. Hotho, *Werke*, I-XVIII (Berlin: 1822 ff.), III, pp. 147 ff., 263 ff.

311. See *Postscript*, pp. 270 ff.

312. See *Repetition*, pp. 74-76.

313. See note 310.

314. J. I. Baggesen, *Asenutidens Abracadabra*, in *Danske Værker*, I-XII (Copenhagen: 1827-32), VII, pp. 195 ff. See Kierkegaard's parallel in II B 1-21.

315. Insane asylum near Roskilde, a few miles from Copenhagen.

316. See Kierkegaard's *An Open Letter* (1851), printed in English translation together with *Armed Neutrality*, on the theme of ecclesiastics and political parties.

317. "The most summary of summaries."

318. Minimum or insofar as it is enough or sufficient.

319. See A. P. Adler, *Den isolerede Subjektivitet: dens vigtigste Skikkelser* (Copenhagen: 1840), I, pp. 7 ff., 13 f., 18 ff. This was a *magister* thesis by a Danish Hegelian who is remembered now primarily because of Kierkegaard's *Bogen om Adler* (English title: *Authority and Revelation*), written during 1844-47 but not published.

320. Ibid., p. 19.

321. See Hegel's letter to von Raumer (*Werke*, J. A., III, p. 323).

322. G. W. F. Hegel, *Æsthetik*, ed. H. G. Hotho, *Werke*, I-XVIII (Berlin: 1832 ff.), X, pt. 3. In addition to numerous works on Hegel by Danish and German writers, such as A. P. Adler, F. Baader, H. M. Chalybäus, I. H. Fichte, F. C. Sibbern, F. A. Staudenmayer, A. Trendelenburg, and K. Werder, Kierkegaard had in his library, according to the auction catalog, the fol-

lowing works by Hegel: *Werke. Völlstandige Ausgabe durch einen Verein von Freunden des Verewigten*: Ph. Marheineke, J. Schulze, Ed. Gans, Lp. v. Henning, H. G. Hotho, K. Nichelet, F. Förster, I-XVIII (Berlin: 1832 ff.) (Vol. IX, *Vorlesungen über die Philosophie der Geschichte* is not listed in the catalog, but he cites it as early as 1838 in entry II A 282, and vols. XI and XII, *Vorlesungen über die Philosophie der Religion* are listed as 2 ed., 1840); *Hegels Lehre vom Staat und seine Philosophie der Geschichte in ihren Hauptresultaten* (Berlin: 1837); *Hegels Philosophie in Wörtlichen Auszügen . . .*, ed. C. Frantz and A. Hillert (Berlin: 1843). See *Philosophical Fragments*, Commentary, especially pp. 166 ff. and 177 ff. for additional information on Kierkegaard's reading and understanding of Hegel.

323. "For the main right of these great characters consists in their energy in asserting themselves, since with their individuality they bear at the same time that which is universal; while on the contrary the usual morality consists in disrespect for one's own personality and in putting one's whole energy into this disrespect."

324. G. W. F. Hegel, *Werke*, II, pp. 63-65.

325. "Beginning as one (reason), it does not persevere as one but without being aware of it becomes a plurality, sinking down, as it were, under its own burden."

326. G. O. Marbach, *Geschichte der Griechischen Philosophie . . . und Geschichte der Philosophie des Mittelalters*, I-II (Leipzig: 1838-41).

327. G. W. F. Hegel, *Philosophische Propädeutik*, ed. Karl Rosenkranz, *Werke*, XVIII.

328. Category.

329. See D. W. G. Tenneman, *Geschichte der Philosophie* (Leipzig: 1810), VIII, 1, p. 186 and passim.

330. See *Philosophical Fragments*, pp. 51-52 n.

331. I. Kant, *Kritik der reinen Vornunft*, 4 ed. (Riga: 1794), pp. 71 ff.

332. See *The Concept of Anxiety* [Dread], pp. 10-11.

333. Ibid., pp. 11-12.

334. While in Berlin primarily to hear Schelling in 1841-42, Kierkegaard also heard some lectures by K. Werder. Only two entries from the notes on these lectures are in the Danish edition of the *Papirer*. The remainder, edited by Niels Thulstrup, will be included in the forthcoming supplement to a photo-offset reissue of the *Papirer*. Among the notes on Werder's lectures is this entry: "The point in quality is *ist* [is]; it is *seyn* [being] which is *Bestimtheit* [determinateness] and *Bestimtheit* which is *Seyn*. Quantity is *Bestimbarkeit* [determinability]; therefore *Seyn* is still not abrogated. . . . Quantity is becoming determinateness. Quality *is* determinateness; therefore the transition from finite quality to infinite quality is true, *is*. Quantity is the limit in becoming. . . . Measurement is a quantitative [becoming] determined qualitatively and a qualitative [becoming] determined quantitatively; to that extent

it is just as qualitative as it is quantitative and the reverse. Here *is* determinateness.

335. See *Johannes Climacus*, p. 151.

336. See *Postscript*, pp. 293-94.

337. See *Johannes Climacus*, p. 151.

338. Hegel generally uses the term *Vermittlung*; Kierkegaard usually uses *Mediationen* (for example, *Postscript*, pp. 177-78, 330-31, 334-36, 354-60, 373-77). See, however, the use of "mediation" and "self-mediating" in English translation of Hegel, as in *Science of Logic* (New York: Macmillan, 1951), II, pp. 479, 485, 486.

339. See F. W. J. Schelling, *System des transcendentalen Idealismus* (Tübingen: 1800), p. 475; *Vorlesungen über die Methode des academischen Studium* (Tübingen: 1803), p. 310 f. The latter volume is listed in the auction catalog. Kierkegaard had also purchased Karl Rosenkranz, *Schelling Forlesungen* (Danzig: 1843). See pp. 133 f., 187, 241 f.

340. See *Postscript*, pp. 34 n., 107, 275, 458.

341. See *Philosophical Fragments*, p. 96 and note; *Postscript*, pp. 99-100 n., 134 n., 292, 299, 301-302; G. W. F. Hegel, *Werke*, V, pp. 329 ff. (*Science of Logic*; New York: Macmillan, 1951; I, pp. 466 ff.).

342. Philostratus, *Apollonius af Tyanas Levnet*, I-V (Stuttgart: 1819-32), V, p. 10.

343. For Hegel the concrete means the contextual (*concrescere*, to grow together; therefore Portland cement, water, and aggregate are concrete in the Hegelian sense because of the relational solidarity of the parts, not because of the palpable solidity of the whole); the particular or the individual is an abstraction when out of context. The illustration of the orchestra as concrete (manifold) and the lead instrument as clarification *in abstracto* is Kierkegaardian. To Kierkegaard the concrete is "the particularity of the historical" and "the manifold." The lead instrument is abstract in the sense of the theme or idea "in passionless brevity," uncomplicated by the manifold concrete.

344. See *Postscript*, pp. 131-37.

345. See, for example, ibid., pp. 99 ff.

346. See, for example, ibid., pp. 202 ff.

347. See English translation under the title, *On Authority and Revelation*.

348. Kierkegaard refers here to the earlier Schelling and not the Schelling he himself heard in Berlin. This is the Schelling of the Absolute characterized by Hegel as the night in which all cows are black.

349. Julius Müller, *Die christliche Lehre von Sünde*, I-II (Breslau: 1849), I, pp. 537 ff.

350. Extreme.

351. Kierkegaard presumably refers to *Die Welt als Wille und Vorstellung*, I-II (Leipzig: 1844), which he cites two entries earlier.

352. A. Schopenhauer, *Über die Grundlage der Moral* (Frankfurt am Main: 1841), sec. 6.

353. Ibid., "Periode der Unredlichkeit."

HEINE

For references in the works to Heine, see, for example, *From the Papers of One Still Living*, S.V., XIII, p. 65; *The Concept of Irony*, pp. 265, 319; *Either/Or*, II, p. 91; *Stages*, p. 409; *The Sickness unto Death*, p. 261.

354. Heine's *Buch der Lieder* appeared in 1827. It is not listed in the auction catalog.

HISTORY

In his detailed and profound analysis of the historical, especially in *Philosophical Fragments*, Johannes Climacus sought to establish the position that the historical always stands in relation to freedom, which is clearly expressed in the following lines: "All coming into existence takes place with freedom, not by necessity. Nothing comes into existence by virtue of a logical ground, but only by a cause. Every cause terminates in a freely effecting cause" (*Fragments*, p. 93).

Kierkegaard makes a sharp distinction between the "straightforward" historical and the report of God's revelation at a particular historical time. For the straightforward historical, probability-proofs can be presented; the Incarnation, however, regarded from a critical-historical point of view, always bears the mark of improbability.

Kuhn, Helmut. "Champions of Forgetfulness: The Historicist and the Either/Or Philosopher." In *Freedom Forgotten and Remembered*. Chapel Hill: University of North Carolina Press, 1943.

Löwith, Karl. *Nature, History, and Existentialism*, ed. Arnold Levison. Evanston: Northwestern University Press, 1966.

Rowell, Ethel M. "Interplay of Past and Present." *Hibbert Journal*, no. 41, 1942-43.

Schrag, Calvin D. "Existence and History." *Review of Metaphysics*, September 1959.

Stevens, Eldon Lloyd. "The Kierkegaardian Concept of History: an Analysis of the Thought of Kierkegaard as it is related to the Meaning of History." M.A. thesis, University of Minnesota, 1950.

Whittemore, Robert C. "On History, Time, and Kierkegaard." *Journal of Religious Thought*, no. 2, 1954.

Wolf, Herbert C. "Kierkegaard and the Quest of the Historical Jesus." *The Lutheran Quarterly*, February 1964.

Wolf, Herbert C. *Kierkegaard and Bultmann: The Quest of the Historical Jesus*. Minneapolis: Augsburg, 1965.

For references in the works to history, the historical, and inner history, see, for example, *The Concept of Irony*, pp. 47 ff., 66, 96 ff., 131 ff., 137, 222 ff., 243, 277 ff., 288, 293 ff., 325; *Either/Or*, I, pp. 46, 53 ff.; II, pp. 11, 62, 96 ff., 106, 113, 119 f., 128 ff., 135 ff., 139 f., 143, 178, 220, 254, 279 f.; *Fragments*, pp. 1, 16, 68-88, 93-107, 114-38; *The Concept of Anxiety* [*Dread*], pp. 23-34, 44, 47 f., 56, 59, 65 ff., 74-83; *Stages*, pp. 396-404, 437 f.; *Postscript*, pp. 20, 23, 25-47, 75 f., 86-97, 119-43, 188 ff., 227, 275, 282, 288, 309, 316 f., 354, 505-15; *Works of Love*, p. 149; *Christian Discourses*, pp. 232, 285 f.; *The Sickness unto Death*, p. 168; *Training*, pp. 9, 26-39, 40, 60, 67 f., 182, 203 ff., 217; *Attack*, pp. 195 f.

355. It is an old story, but it is always new, and whenever it happens to someone, it breaks his heart. H. Heine, *Buch der Lieder, Sämmtliche Werke* (Hamburg: 1868), XV, p. 109.

356. L. Achim, V. Arnim, Clements Brentano. *Des Knaben Wunderhorn*. Heidelberg: 1806.

357. See Carl Bernhard, *Noveller*, I-IV (Copenhagen: 1836-38), I, pp. 339 ff.; see *Af en endnu Levendes Papirer*, S.V., XIII, p. 60, for Kierkegaard's characterization of the "so-called Bernhard novels" in his first published work.

358. See Carl Bernard, *Noveller*, II, pp. 135 ff., 363-64; *Af en endnu Levendes Papirer*, S.V., XIII, p. 60.

359. In J. L. Heiberg's *Nei* (Copenhagen: 1836) the same melody was used for "*Taarnet skulde styrte sammen*" as was used in Heiberg's *Aprilsnarrene* (Copenhagen: 1826).

360. *Allgemeines Reportorium für die theologische Literatur und Kirchliche Statistik*, ed. G. F. H. Rheinwald, I-XXIX (Berlin: 1833-37), which Kierkegaard had in his library.

361. In such a supposedly exalted, grand, and profound, but actually frivolous, handling of history the persons still count only as bearers or symbols of certain opinions which are ascribed to them arbitrarily. They lose their individuality and all character, just as the appetite, spoiled and debased on such [a diet], gradually comes to disdain the coarser nourishing taste of the genuine, pithy history which is not interpreted and abstracted at pleasure.

362. *Udvalgte Dialoger af Platon*, tr. C. J. Heise, I-III (Copenhagen: 1830-38).

363. See *The Concept of Irony*, p. 341.

364. See G. W. Leibniz, *Theodicee* (Hannover, Leipzig: 1763), pp. 355 ff. Leibniz mentions *Euthyphro* on p. 357.

365. Ibid., p. 355.

366. Without father or mother or genealogy. See Hebrews 7:3.

367. See *The Concept of Anxiety* [*Dread*], p. 127 n.; entry is from draft.

368. See *Postscript*, pp. 86 ff.

369. Matthew 5:44; Luke 23:34.

370. The reference is to Jesus. See *Training in Christianity*, pp. 43-44.

371. See K. F. Becker, *Verdenshistorie*, I-XII (Copenhagen: 1827), IV, p. 121 n. Kierkegaard owned this set.

HOLY SPIRIT

In writing of the Holy Spirit Kierkegaard uses the common expression "the Comforter." The Holy Spirit comforts (strengthens) and guides the Christian in his weakness and imperfection. Because of this mediating, comforting work, Kierkegaard also calls the Holy Spirit "the dispensator of grace," the grace "which Christ won" (X^2 A 451). The way in which the Holy Spirit guides a person in his existence Kierkegaard has presented in the discourse "Becoming Sober" (*Judge for Yourselves!* pp. 113 ff.). Concerning the Christian life in relation to the Triune God Kierkegaard writes: "*What Does It Mean To Be a Christian?* It means to walk under the eye of the Heavenly Father, therefore under the eye of the truly loving Father, led by Christ's hand, and strengthened by the witness of the Holy Spirit" (X^3 A 394).

For references in the works to Holy Spirit, see, for example, *The Concept of Irony*, p. 66; *Either/Or*, II, p. 224; *Edifying Discourses*, II, p. 44; III, p. 124; *Postscript*, p. 41; *The Gospel of Suffering*, p. 233; *Works of Love*, pp. 19, 154; *Christian Discourses*, pp. 71, 112, 142, 262; *The Sickness unto Death*, pp. 255 ff., 262; *Three Discourses at the Communion on Fridays*, together with *Christian Discourses*, p. 361; *Training*, p. 67; *For Self-Examination*, pp. 4, 84 ff., 94 ff.; *Judge for Yourselves!* p. 113.

372. See *Postscript*, p. 113.

373. Romans 4:25.

374. Adolf Helfferich, *Die christliche Mystik in ihrer Entwicklung und in ihren Denkmalen*, I-II (Gotha: 1842).

375. See *For Self-Examination*, pp. 87 ff.

HOPE

Hope can be understood from two viewpoints: either as a hope for this life or as the hope for the eternal life to come. It is this second hope Kierkegaard points to first and foremost. He depicts the way from the purely human way of hoping to the Christian hope: "But the dialectic of hope goes this way: first the fresh incentive of youth, then the supportive calculation of understanding, and then—then everything comes to a standstill—and now for the first time Christian hope is there as a possibility" (VI B 53:13). Christian hope is hope where "there is no hope" (*For Self-Examination*, p. 97), and grounded beyond life it is life-giving in this life, for it is the life of faith, which is the double movement of infinity (*Fear and Trembling*, pp. 52-64).

Croxall, T. H. "The Christian Doctrine of Hope and the Kierkegaardian Doctrine of the Moment." *Expository Times*, no. 56, 1944-45.

Croxall, T. H. *Kierkegaard Studies*. London: Lutterworth Press, 1948.

For references in the works to hope, see, for example, *The Concept of Irony*, pp. 334 f., 339; *Either/Or*, I, pp. 35, 220 ff., 227 f., 288 f.; II, pp. 24 f., 144 ff., 149, 241; *Edifying Discourses*, I, p. 6; *Fear and Trembling*, pp. 31 ff.; *Repetition*, pp. 4 ff., 79, 133; *Edifying Discourses*, I, pp. 111 f.; III, pp. 21,

25, 29; *Thoughts on Crucial Situations in Human Life*, p. 58; *Stages*, pp. 279, 330, 343, 345, 348, 359, 390, 438; *Postscript*, pp. 17, 40, 213, 374, 384 f., 545; *The Present Age*, p. 15; *Purity of Heart*, pp. 111 f., 149 f., 169; *The Lilies of the Field*, together with *The Gospel of Suffering*, p. 170; ibid., 70 ff., 162; *Works of Love*, pp. 60, 174 f., 209, 213, 231-46, 273 ff., 287, 321; *Christian Discourses*, pp. 111-18, 122, 126, 189; *Crisis in the Life of an Actress*, p. 77; *The Sickness unto Death*, pp. 170, 191 f.; *Training*, pp. 152, 163; *For Self-Examination*, pp. 96 ff.; *Attack*, p. 67.

376, See *Edifying Discourses*, pp. 50 ff.

377. Matthew 25:21-23.

378. See note 385.

[HUME]

Popkin, Richard H. "Hume and Kierkegaard." *Journal of Religion*, no. 4, 1951.

HUMOR, IRONY, THE COMIC

The very extensive sphere of the ethical is marked off from the lower by irony and from the higher by humor.

Irony "neutralizes" (*The Concept of Anxiety* [*Dread*], p. 62) the esthetic sphere with its customs and laws, which apply only to finite relationships, and prepare the way for man's deeper self-knowledge and the discovery of the eternal as the first presupposition of the ethical. Humor, on the other hand, as the basis of ethical action, expresses man's existential experience in actualizing the eternal norms of the ethical. Through this experience a person is taught that he cannot fulfill these requirements and he perceives that this mis-relationship cannot be terminated within the ethical sphere. Only on a qualitatively higher level—namely, within the religious-Christian sphere—is there a solution.

In the movement from irony to humor as the boundary between the ethical and the religious-Christian, the comic plays a definite role, as Climacus points out (*Postscript*, pp. 459 ff.). Since the comic is "painless contradiction," every prior position lived through and conquered can be seen in a comical light, because such a position no longer has existential tension. Thus ethical striving must "see the comic in the form of irony." Likewise a humorist who finally arrives at the ethical sphere may look upon his earlier striving from the viewpoint of the comic. Only in relation to the new which Christianity gives is there no use for the comic, since the preceding efforts provide only grounds for repentance and the resultant sense of earnestness. (See JEST.)

Nissen, Lowell Allen. "Kierkegaard on Humor." M.A. thesis, University of Minnesota, 1958.

Rougemont, Denis de. "Kierkegaard Revealed in his Irony." *Arizona Quarterly*, no. 1, 1945.

For references in the works to humor, irony, the comic, and jest, see, for example, *The Concept of Irony*, passim; *Either/Or*, I, pp. 91, 108, 120, 138 ff., 261, 269, 271, 274 f., 382; II, pp. 19, 29; *Fear and Trembling*, pp. 62, 94, 110, 116 f., 119, 120 f., 126, 128; *Repetition*, pp. 24, 27, 53, 58, 68; *Fragments*, pp. 29, 54, 139; *The Concept of Anxiety* [Dread], pp. 13, 62 f., 79, 84 f., 118 f., 120-33, 137; *Stages*, pp. 48 ff., 61, 130 f., 145, 154 f., 231 f., 234, 243, 293, 335 f., 372, 378 ff., 396 ff., 403 f., 406 f., 418, 422, 426, 438; *Postscript*, pp. 35, 42, 53 ff., 73, 74, 77, 81 ff., 92, 121, 123, 125, 159 f., 235, 241 ff., 250 f., 258 f., 268 ff., 287, 378, 393, 400 ff., 408 f., 412 ff., 421, 431 f., 446-68, 476, 486 f., 489-93, 499, 504, 528, 533, 543; *The Present Age*, pp. 11 f., 21, 31 f.; *Crisis in The Life of an Actress*, p. 75; *Has a Man the Right to Let Himself Be Put to Death for the Truth?* together with *The Present Age*, p. 104; *The Sickness unto Death*, pp. 186 f., 221, 226; *Training*, p. 55; *The Point of View*, pp. 54-63, 102; *'That Individual,'* together with *The Point of View*, pp. 125, 130; *Attack*, pp. 97, 157.

379. Carl Christian Rafn, *Nordiske Kæmpe-Historier* (Copenhagen: 1826).

380. G. Schwab, *Buch der schönsten Geschichten und Sagen*, I-II (Stuttgart: 1836), II, p. 357.

381. See *Either/Or*, I, p. 24.

382. See *Fear and Trembling*, p. 62.

383. *Faust*, I, sc. 2.

384. Hayo Gerdes (Kierkegaard, *Tagebücher*, II, note 322; Dusseldorf, Cologne: Diederich, 1962) considers this a possible allusion to the novels of E. T. A. Hoffman, whose works Kierkegaard had (*Auserwählte Schriften*, I-X; Berlin: 1827-28).

385. There are numerous references to and discussions of humor and the religious, humor and Christianity, in *Concluding Unscientific Postscript*. See especially pp. 241 ff., 447 ff., 489 ff.

386. Hidden in the mystery. See Colossians 1:26.

387. In a mystery.

388. Matthew 11:30.

389. Matthew 11:11.

390. Hamann often used this expression in some form. See note 406.

391. The Danish editors think that this most likely is an inadvertent inversion, but as it stands it is consistent with the context of the humorous view. See *Fear and Trembling*, p. 48.

392. See *Postscript*, p. 528.

393. Carl Daub, *Vorlesungen über die philosophische Anthropologie*, volume I of *Philosophische und Theologische Vorlesungen*, I-VII (Berlin: 1838-44).

394. See Psalms 9:13; 107:18; Matthew 16:18.

395. Luke 19:13.

396. Matthew 6:28 f.

397. Matthew 11:25; Luke 10:21.

398. Luke 10:41.

399. Luke 15:7.

400. Mark 10:25.

401. John 8:7.

402. E. T. A. Hoffman, *Auserwählte Schriften*, I-X (Berlin: 1827-28), IX, pp. 127 ff.

403. Adam Oehlenschläger, "Morgen-Vandring," *Poetiske Skrifter*, I-II (Copenhagen: 1805), I, p. 364.

404. J. G. Hamann, *Schriften*, ed. F. Roth, I-VIII (Berlin: 1821-43), II, p. 434.

405. II Corinthians 5:17.

406. See J. G. Hamann, *Schriften*, I, p. 497.

407. Genesis 28:10 ff.

408. Matthew 11:12.

409. G. H. Schubert, *Die Symbolik des Traumes* (Bamberg: 1821), p. 155.

410. *Kinder- und Haus-Märchen, gesammelt durch die Brüder Grimm*, I-III (Berlin: 1819-22), I, p. 379.

411. Jean Paul [Richter], *Sämmtliche Werke*, I-LX (Berlin: 1777-99). Kierkegaard owned this immense work and in the journals makes a number of brief observations on the writings.

412. See *Pap.* I A 75, pp. 57 f.; I A 335; *Repetition*, p. 76; *Either/Or*, I, p. 24.

413. *Mythologie der Feen und Elfen vom Ursprunge dieses Glaubens bis auf die neuesten Zeiten, aus dem Englischen übersetzt*, O. L. B. Wolf, I-II (Weimar: 1828), I, pp. 131 ff.

414. E. T. A. Hoffman, *Auserwählte Schriften*, I-X (Berlin: 1827-28), I.

415. See J. G. Hamann, *Schriften*, I-VIII (Berlin: 1821-43), I, p. 423. Hamann died in 1788. His collected writings, most of them thitherto unpublished, were edited and published by Friedrich Roth over a generation later. Roth writes that Hamann's activity as an author was as hidden and modest as was his life (I, p. viii).

416. See the editor's preface, ibid., p. x.

417. See S. S. Blicher, "Fjorten Dage i Jylland," *Samlede Noveller*, I-V (Copenhagen: 1836), V, p. 212.

418. See *Joannis Calvini in Novum Testamentum commentarii . . .* , I-VII (Berolini: 1833-39), V, p. 601. Kierkegaard had this edition of Calvin's works.

419. We are weak in him. To be weak in Christ means partaking in the weakness of Christ. He makes his weakness glorious since in it he is conformed to Christ, and he no longer dreads disgrace because he shares it with the son of God, but says, meanwhile, that by the example of Christ he will triumph over them.

420. Reference here is to the dogmatic problem of *kenosis*—the self-emptying of Christ. See Philippians 2:6-11.

421. In the form of emptying or in the form of concealment.

422. Though we may seem to have failed.

423. One not standing the test.

424. See *Either/Or*, I, p. 19.

425. Adam Oehlenschläger, "Morgen-Vandring," *Poetiske Skrifter*, I-II (Copenhagen: 1805), I, p. 364.

426. See note 415.

427. The Danish, like German, has a familiar form, *du*, and a formal, polite form, *De*. The familiar form, used between friends and family members, is also used in prayer. Strangely enough, the familiar form in English, *thou*, has become formal and unfamiliar, a linguistic mark of distinction and distance.

428. *Caroline*, from *Caramboline*, a kind of billiard game, also the ball which is placed in the center of the table.

429. See *Either/Or*, I, p. 24.

430. See J. G. Hamann, *Schriften*, I-VIII (Berlin: 1821-43), I, p. 497.

431. See *The Concept of Irony*, pp. 117 ff.

432. *Either/Or*, I, p. 21; *Stages on Life's Way*, pp. 191 f.

433. Soundness of mind, temperance, moderation.

434. See *The Concept of Irony*, p. 49 and note, pp. 364-65.

435. See note 385.

436. See H. Heine, *Buch der Lieder*, "Die Heimkehr," no. 66; *The Sickness unto Death*, p. 261.

437. See *The Concept of Irony*, pp. 341-42.

438. I believe because it is absurd (Tertullian); ibid., p. 341.

439. See *Postscript*, p. 459.

440. See G. W. F. Hegel, *Vorlesungen über die Aesthetik*, *Werke*, I-XVIII (Berlin: 1832 ff.), X, pt. 3, p. 534. On Hegel's consideration of irony see *The Concept of Irony*, p. 406, note 7, for Hirsch's list.

441. The reference presumably is to a review of J. L. Heiberg, *En Sjælen efter Døden*, by H. L. Martensen, *Fædrelandet*, Jan. 10, 1841, no. 398. See *Stages on Life's way*, pp. 374 f.

442. Matthew 21:28 ff.

443. Matthew 21:29.

444. See *Postscript*, p. 459 ff.

445. See ibid., p. 460 n.

446. Ibid., pp. 449 ff.

447. Compare all three paragraphs (VI B 70: 13, 14, and 15) with the footnote in *Postscript*, pp. 459 ff., especially p. 462.

448. Comic power or capacity for the comic.

449. Ludwig Holberg, *Erasmus Montanus*, III, sc. 2 and 5, IV, sc. 2 and 4, V, sc. 5.

450. Danish version of *La camaraderie* by Scribe, presented first November 14, 1839 and many times during the winter season of 1848-49.

451. In his library Kierkegaard had Miguel de Cervantes Saavedra, *Don Quixote von La Mancha*, tr. Heinrich Heine, I-II (Stuttgart: 1837-39), and *Don Quixote af Manchas Levnet og Bedrifter*, tr. C. D. Biehl, I-IV (Copenhagen: 1776-77).

452. A reference to a character in Holberg's *Barselstuen*.

IDEA, IDEALS, IDEALITY

The idea expresses the abstract, eternal content as contrasted to particular, transient, yet genuine things. In human intellectual-spiritual development, the world of ideas, embracing the idea of the beautiful, of the true, and of the good, was first approached in Greek philosophy in the thought of Socrates. Like Socrates, Kierkegaard was concerned primarily with the idea of the good, which is the root of ethical striving. But usually Kierkegaard uses the word *idea* in regard to a good cause: "service of the idea" (X^3 A 689). On the other hand, Kierkegaard designates the ethical requirements which the idea of the good poses to man by the terms *ideals* and *ideality*. Kierkegaard extends the two latter expressions to include Christian striving. In *Training in Christianity* he uses the expression *ideality* even in regard to imitation [*Efterfølgelsen*]—for example: "The requirement for being a Christian is strained . . . to the highest pitch of ideality" (p. 7).

For references in the works to the idea, the ideal, and ideality, see, for example, *The Concept of Irony*, pp. 52, 55, 132 ff., 137, 156 ff., 236, 251, 255, 288, 307, 319 ff.; *Either/Or*, I, pp. 27, 45, 47-56, 62-69, 90 f., 105 f., 109 f., 220, 296, 386 f., 410; II, pp. 26, 61, 96 ff., 122, 138, 214, 230, 256 f.; *Fear and Trembling*, pp. 101, 109; *Repetition*, p. 83; *Fragments*, p. 52, *The Concept of Anxiety* [*Dread*], pp. 4, 15 ff., 85, 141; *Stages*, pp. 28 f., 31, 61, 70 f., 75, 111-19, 152, 158, 163, 166, 238, 290, 330, 384, 386, 395, 396 ff., 412, 416; *Postscript*, pp. 112, 169, 238, 277, 282-307, 312, 315, 347, 369, 374, 389, 486 ff., 553; *A Literary Review*, S.V., VIII, pp. 14, 49, 59 f.; *The Present Age*, 50 f., *Crisis in the Life of an Actress*, pp. 76, 86 ff., 89 f.; *The Sickness unto Death*, pp. 206, 224 f.; *Training*, pp. 7, 71, 91, 185 ff., 190 f., 248; *For Self-Examination*, p. 18; *Judge for Yourselves!* pp. 138, 169, 207 f., 219; *Armed Neutrality*, pp. 33-44; *An Open Letter*, together with *Armed Neutrality*, p. 51; *On My Work as an Author*, together with *The Point of View*, p. 159; ibid., pp. 47 f.; *'That Individual,'* together with *The Point of View*, p. 139; *Attack*, pp. 31 f., 65, 81, 91, 97, 108, 117 f., 181, 262.

453. According to Greek legend, a people living beyond the north wind in a blessed land inaccessible by land or sea.

454. Kierkegaard owned *Herodoti historiarum*, I-II (Leipzig: 1825), and *Die Geschichten des Herodotus*, tr. F. Lange, I-II (Berlin: 1811).

455. Johannes von Müller (1752-1809), German historian, author of *Reisen der Päpste* (Aachen: 2 ed. 1831), *Schweizergeschichte*, I-V (Leipzig:

1786-1808), and others. We have not been able to find the source of the statement attributed to Müller. None of Müller's books is listed in the auction catalog.

456. Martin Luther, *En christelig Postille*, I, p. 460.

457. Wise men. See *Armed Neutrality*, p. 42.

458. Lovers of wisdom. Ibid.

459. Kierkegaard says in many places in the works that the writer is "without authority," is only a poet. See, for example, *Fear and Trembling*, pp. 42 ff.; *Philosophical Fragments*, pp. 43-45; *The Sickness unto Death*, pp. 208-209. See also *Armed Neutrality* throughout, "A First and Last Declaration" at the end of *Postscript*, pp. 551-54, and *Attack upon Christendom*, pp. 201-202.

460. H–t [R. P. K. Varberg], *Striden mellem Ørsted og Mynster eller Videnskaben og den officielle Theologi* (Copenhagen: 1851), pp. 28 ff.

461. "Subordination" here means lesser fulfillment or under-achievement. See X³ A 347, "The Christian Order of Precedence."

462. The indispensable condition.

463. See *Attack upon Christendom*, p. 156.

464. See *Fear and Trembling*, pp. 92 ff.

465. Concluding or final parenthesis. See *Postscript*, p. 29.

466. See J. L. Heiberg, *En Sjæl efter Døden* (Copenhagen: 1841); *Intelligensblade*, June 1, 1842, no. 6; *Nøddeknækkerne* (Copenhagen: 1845).

467. In *Intelligensblade*, February 1, 1844, J. L. Heiberg called his *Urania* (Copenhagen: 1844) "a New Year's gift designed for the esthetically cultured public." See also *The Concept of Anxiety* [Dread], pp. 5, 17.

IMAGINATION

Imagination [*Fantasi*] or fantasy is a capacity for knowing, or better expressed, the creative capacity of providing the elements of all thinking. Therefore Kierkegaard fully agrees with the elder Fichte in regarding imagination as the highest mental capacity (*The Sickness unto Death*, p. 163). Kierkegaard calls it the "capacity *instar omnium*" ("the capacity of all capacities").

Man is distinguished by the creative capacity of imagination from the animals, since through imagination man constructs the specifically human existence (the productions of mind and spirit, culture, etc.). Imagination, however, must be tempered by logical thought and by the ethical consciousness in order to avoid degenerating into the fantastical.

For references in the works to imagination, see, for example, *The Concept of Irony*, pp. 132 ff., 137, 320; *Either/Or*, I, p. 386, II, p. 59; *Fear and Trembling*, pp. 44; *Repetition*, pp. 42-50, 89, 99; *The Concept of Anxiety* [Dread], pp. 23, 135; *Stages*, pp. 39, 42, 64, 242, 356, 381, 390, 423 f., 442 f.; *Postscript*, pp. 61, 90 f., 106 f., 112, 226, 307, 310 f., 313, 345, 347, 349, 356, 374, 376, 397 f., 409, 447, 514, 524, 530 f.; *A Literary Review*, S.V., VIII, pp. 14, 18; *Works of Love*, p. 238; *The Sickness unto Death*, pp. 163

ff., 168 ff., 174, 192, 208; *Training*, pp. 185 ff.; *The Point of View*, pp. 80 ff.; *Attack*, pp. 30, 117, 201.

468. Matthew 25:29.

469. See C. M. Wieland, *Geschichte des Agathon, Sämmtliche Werke*, I-LIII (Leipzig: 1818-28), I, pp. 95 ff., 115-16, 149.

470. See note 455.

IMITATION

According to Kierkegaard, Protestantism rightly maintains that Christianity and the Christian life are most appropriately defined by grace, but grace has meaning only against the background of the unfulfilled requirements. Kierkegaard points out that if, therefore, a person does not find continually that he falls short again and again in his ethical striving, grace will come to seem abstract and be taken in vain. This gives Kierkegaard occasion to emphasize and reemphasize the importance of imitation [*Efterfølgelsen*] as an essential element in the Christian's life and one which impels to grace, because imitation brings him to experience his weakness in a wholly concrete way.

Of the timeliness of emphasizing imitation Kierkegaard says: "It is entirely clear that it is Christ as the prototype [*Forbilledet*] which must now be stressed dialectically, for the very reason that the dialectical (Christ as gift), which Luther stressed, has been taken completely in vain . . ." (X^2 A 361).

Kierkegaard thereafter stresses very frequently that imitation must be "a glad fruit of gratitude" (X^3 A 767). He sees the relation between imitation and grace this way: "(1) imitation is the direction of decisive action whereby the situation for becoming a Christian comes into existence; (2) Christ as gift—faith; (3) imitation as the fruit of faith" (X^4 A 459). (See GRACE: "Faith in second place.")

In his later years Kierkegaard expressed himself more and more incisively on the misuse of faith, which he considered to be particularly prevalent in Protestantism.

Eller, Vernard. *Kierkegaard and Radical Discipleship*. Princeton: Princeton University Press, 1968.

Hansen, Olaf. "Kierkegaard's Understanding of 'following Christ' (*Efterfølgelse*) and its Basis in the Concept of Atonement." M.A. thesis, University of Chicago, 1946.

Holmer, Paul. Review of W. Lindstrom, *Efterfølgelsens Teologi hos S. Kierkegaard. Lutheran Quarterly*, no. 1, 1959.

Thulstrup, Marie M. "Kierkegaard's Dialectic of Imitation." In *A Kierkegaard Critique*, ed. Howard Johnson and Niels Thulstrup. New York: Harper, 1962.

Malantschuk, Gregor. *Kierkegaard's Way to the Truth*. Minneapolis: Augsburg, 1963.

For references in the works to imitation, see, for example, *The Gospel of*

Suffering, pp. 5-20 (tr. "following"), 34 (tr. "disciple"); *Christian Discourses*, p. 286 (tr. "follower"); *Training*, pp. 231-50 (tr. "follower"); *For Self-Examination*, pp. 79 ff.; *Judge for Yourselves!* pp. 151 ff., 161-220; *Attack*, pp. 27, 130, 147, 161, 264, 268 f., 280, 287.

471. John 1:29.

472. See *Gospel of Suffering*, pp. 7-9.

473. See *Christian Discourses*, p. 286.

474. J. Gerhardi, *Meditationes sacræ*, ed. S. Guenthner (Leipzig: 1842), p. xxx.

475. To rejoice in Christ . . . , to imitate Christ.

476. See *Attack on Christendom*, pp. 5 ff.

477. II Timothy 3:12.

478. Matthew 13:21.

479. Johann Tauler, *Nachfolgung des armen Lebens Jesu Christi*, ed. N. Casseder (Frankfurt am Main: 1821), which Kierkegaard had in his library, as well as Thomas a Kempis, *Imitation of Christ*, in French (1702) and Danish (3 ed., 1848) translations.

480. A. G. Rudelbach, *Christelig Biographie* (Copenhagen: 1848). This is a direct quotation from Rudelbach and stops short of the reference to Matthew 5:10. "No. 7" refers to number seven and the last of a series which Rudelbach attributes to Luther. Jesper Swedberg (1653-1735) was professor of theology at Uppsala and Bishop of Skara in Sweden.

481. I think therefore I am [Descartes' formulation] . . . I am therefore I think.

482. See *Training in Christianity*, pp. 231 ff.

483. Alpha intensive.

484. Alpha privative, like a-social etc.

485. See *Three Discourses at the Communion on Fridays* in *Christian Discourses*, pp. 357 ff.

486. See *En christelig Postille*, I, pp. 59 f.

487. Romans 13:11-14.

488. Matthew 22:1-14.

489. Matthew 27:43.

490. See *Judge for Yourselves!* pp. 201-203.

491. John 7:68.

492. See *Training in Christianity*, p. 232.

493. Matthew 27:51-52.

494. See *Judge for Yourselves!* p. 197.

495. This is an expression from an old game (still sold in Denmark) called *Gnavspillet*. See *Philosophical Fragments*, pp. 27, 194; note 549.

496. See *Postscript*, p. 171.

497. See *Judge for Yourselves!* pp. 201-203.

498. This entry is one of the many indications that Kierkegaard's conception of "situation" is remote from the so-called "situational ethics" of the

1960's. Kierkegaard's emphasis is upon "situating" the doctrine, the belief, upon belief-ful action, not upon construing norms of action out of the situation. See *Postscript*, pp. 302-303.

499. See John 7:17.

500. See *Either/Or*, I, p. 22.

501. See, for example, *Fear and Trembling*, p. 109; *Philosophical Fragments*, pp. 12 ff.; S.V., V, pp. 44-45; especially *Postscript*, pp. 180-85, 496-97.

502. See *Postscript*, pp. 523 ff.

503. See Matthew 28:19 ff.

504. Mark 16:16.

505. We have not been able to locate the source of this quotation.

506. Slotskirken, November 24, 1850; Matthew 11:24 ff.

507. As such.

508. See *Training in Christianity*, pp. 204 ff., 231 ff.; also *Judge for Yourselves!* pp. 197 ff.

509. J. A. W. Neander, *Der heilige Johannes Chrysostomus und die Kirche besonders des Orientes, in dessen Zeitalter*, I-II (Berlin: 1821-22), I, p. 745; . . . seeks the support of immorality rather than the prototypes of morality.

510. See *Training in Christianity*, pp. 202 ff., 231 ff. and passim.

511. Friedrich Böhringer, *Die Kirche Christi und ihre Zeugen oder die Kirchengeschichte in Biographien*, I-VII (Zürich: 1842-49).

512. See *Training in Christianity*, pp. 231 ff., *Christian Discourses*, pp. 135 ff., *Judge for Yourselves!* p. 207, *For Self-Examination* (on Socrates), p. 3.

513. See *For Self-Examination*, pp. 10 ff.

514. Ibid., pp. 78 ff.

515. John 7:17.

516. See X^4 A 237 (Luther).

517. J. L. Heiberg, Danish author and Hegelian; *Clara Raphæl, Tolv Breve* (Copenhagen: 1851).

518. See *Judge for Yourselves!* pp. 197 ff.

519. See *For Self-Examination*, p. 10.

520. A legal term meaning a trust.

521. Matthew 6:24. See *Judge for Yourselves!* pt. II, pp. 161 ff.

522. Ibid., p. 215.

523. H.H. [Søren Kierkegaard], *Two Minor Ethical-Religious Treatises:* "Has a Man the Right to Let Himself Be Put to Death for the Truth?" and "Of the Difference Between a Genius and an Apostle" (Copenhagen: 1848), in English together with *The Present Age*, pp. 71-163.

524. J. P. Mynster, leading bishop in Denmark, friend of Kierkegaard's father and in a paternal way also of Kierkegaard. See Walter Lowrie, *Kierkegaard* (Oxford: 1938), for a discussion of Mynster and the Kierkegaards' re-

lation to him. See note 528. See also volume V of *Søren Kierkegaard's Journals and Papers*.

    525. See Friedrich Böhringer, *Die Kirche Christi . . .* , I, p. 424.

    526. Matthew 11:6.

    527. See *Attack upon Christendom*, pp. 268 ff.

    528. Ibid., pp. 31, 32, 55, 84, 117, 122, 147-48, 150-51, 183-84, 231, 252-54, 279-80.

    529. See ibid. pp. 5 ff.

    530. Ibid., p. 121.

    531. See ibid., p. 144; Ludwig Holberg, *Ulysses von Ithacia*, II, sc. 1.

    532. Psalm 22:6.

    533. The expression "Behold the man" is closer to the Danish "*See hvilket Menneske*" than the newer English translation, "Here is the man" (John 19:5).

    534. See note 531.

    535. See *Attack upon Christendom*, pp. 287-88.

    536. See ibid., pp. 268 ff.

IMMEDIACY

    According to Kierkegaard there are two kinds of immediacy, the first and the second; the first refers to man's natural condition and powers, the second to the reality of spirit.

    Every man begins life in the first immediacy; as a natural being he is related spontaneously or immediately to the surrounding world without the intervention of reflection. A further development occurs when immediacy acquires an admixture of "quantitative reflection" (*The Sickness unto Death*, p. 184). Aided by this reflection, one seeks to manage his life within the world of finitude (the quantitative world). Only through infinite reflection or reflection upon the infinite is he led in the direction of a new actuality, the actuality of spirit, which is a contrast to the natural condition. But he cannot achieve the new actuality through reflection, for reflection always renders actuality in the form of possibility. Kierkegaard calls the new actuality the second immediacy or second spontaneity, and the transition to it occurs through the leap of faith. Therefore he can say that "faith is immediacy or spontaneity after reflection" (VIII¹ A 649-50); the first immediacy lies prior to reflection. In a genuine sense it is only the leap of faith into the Christian life that yields the second immediacy, since the actuality of spirit is fully present only there. (See *Stages on Life's Way*, pp. 435-36, including footnote.)

    [This is another of the themes that are of great importance in Kierkegaard's works but are represented directly in the *Papirer* by only a few entries. In the works the theme is treated in some way in every one of the fourteen volumes, from the multifarious embodiment of immediacy in volume I of *Either/Or* and analysis of it in volume II, to numerous characterizations and contrasts in *Fear and Trembling*, *Stages on Life's Way*, and *Concluding Un-*

scientific Postscript, to telling allusions and analogies in the various *Discourses* and in *The Moment* at the end of his career.]

For references in the works to immediacy or spontaneity, see, for example, *The Concept of Irony*, pp. 51 ff., 225, 248; *Either/Or*, I, pp. 43-134, 69, 80, 204 f., 209; II, pp. 20, 30 f., 46 ff., 57 f., 96, 185 ff., 193 ff., 261; *Fear and Trembling*, pp. 79, 108; *Fragments*, pp. 78, 83 ff., 100 ff., 254 ff.; *The Concept of Anxiety [Dread]*, pp. 10, 33 f., 88; *Edifying Discourses*, IV, p. 35; *Thoughts on Crucial Situations in Human Life*, p. 13; *Stages*, pp. 74 f., 107 ff., 126, 157 ff., 162 ff., 375 ff., 430-36, 437 ff.; *Postscript*, pp. 37, 101 ff., 160, 217, 250 f., 258, 261, 310, 353, 367 f., 386 ff., 397, 406, 412 ff., 446, 450 f., 463 ff., 468, 507, 526; *A Literary Review*, S.V., VIII, p. 61; *Purity of Heart*, p. 113; *Works of Love*, pp. 41 ff., 49 ff., 144, 342; *Crisis in the Life of an Actress*, pp. 75 f., 88 ff.; *The Sickness unto Death*, pp. 158, 184-94, 197 f.; *Training*, p. 124; *Attack*, pp. 221 f.

537. F. A. Trendelenburg, *Erläuterungen zu den Elementen der aristotelischen Logik* (Berlin: 1842), which Kierkegaard purchased February 13, 1843. He also had Trendelenburg's *Elementa Logices aristelicæ* (Berlin: 1842), *Platonis de ideis et numeris doctrina ex Aristotele illustrata* (Leipzig: 1826), and four other works, as well as forty-two volumes of Aristotle or secondary works. See *Philosophical Fragments*, Kierkegaard's note, p. 103; *Either/Or*, I, pp. 140-41.

538. See F. A. Trendelenburg, *Erläuterungen . . .*, I, pp. 24 ff.

539. See *The Lilies of the Field and the Birds of the Air*, in *Christian Discourses*, pp. 311-56.

540. See *Either/Or*, I, p. 19.

IMMORTALITY

Every human being has in him the possibility of the eternal. That is, he is designed for immortality. But only Christianity gives reality to this possibility, for Christianity promises an eternal life. Kierkegaard explains: "On the whole, immortality first appeared with Christianity, and why? Because it requires that a person shall die to the world. In order to be able and willing to die to the world the eternal and immortality must remain fixed. Immortality and dying-away correspond to each other" ($\dot{X}^4$ A 440).

Just as there are no proofs of God, so also there are no proofs for immortality—there can only be a conviction of faith in it.

Kierkegaard does not set immortality and resurrection in opposition to one another; he often makes parallel use of the two expressions (see *Christian Discourses*, p. 210). The distinction between these two expressions for man's eternal qualification (existence) is that immortality as the possibility of the eternal is linked to God's creative thought (that every human being is created for eternity), whereas faith in Christ and resurrection give it reality.

For references in the works to immortality, see, for example, "Yet another Defence of Woman's eminent Talents," S.V., XIII, p. 6; *The Concept* of Irony, pp. 99-113, 118 f., 139 f.; Either/Or, I, pp. 34, 401; II, pp. 172 f., 211, 218 ff., 245, 257, 269, 274 f., 284; Fear and Trembling, pp. 109, 115 f., 126; Repetition, p. 43; Edifying Discourses, p. 48; Fragments, pp. 11, 42; The Concept of Anxiety [Dread], pp. 92, 124 f., 136 f.; Prefaces, S.V., V, p. 44; Stages, pp. 28, 71 f., 163, 426; Postscript, pp. 137, 152-58, 160, 180, 268, 384 f., 496; Purity of Heart, pp. 34 ff., 101; Works of Love, pp. 73, 289, 308; Christian Discourses, p. 108, 210-20, 231; "Of the Difference Between a Genius and an Apostle," together with The Present Age, pp. 155 ff.; The Sickness unto Death, pp. 153, 190; "The Activity of a Travelling Esthetician," S.V., XIII, p. 431; "The Dialectical Result of a Literary Police Business," S.V., XIII, p. 432 f.; The Point of View, pp. 56 f.

541. See Mark 12:18; Acts 23:6 ff.; Christian Discourses, p. 211.

542. Joh. Arndt's Vier Bücher vom wahren Christentum . . . (Schiffbeck bey Hamburg: 1721).

543. For God will judge you as he finds you.

544. See Christian Discourses, pp. 210-20.

545. See Postscript, pp. 153 ff.; Christian Discourses, pp. 211 ff.; The Concept of Anxiety [Dread], p. 124.

546. J. L. Heiberg, Julespøg og Nytaarsløier (Copenhagen: 1817), Act II, p. 189.

547. The Danish here is Gavtyve and in parentheses the German version. See Ludvig Holberg, Pernilles korte Frøkenstand, II, sc. 7.

548. Pardon the word or expression.

INDIRECT COMMUNICATION

All communication of knowledge is direct communication (VIII² B 83, "Second Distinction, B"). Knowledge is occupied with thought objects; they can be transmitted directly from the communicator to the receiver who obtains them through the medium of imagination. A genuine engagement, however, can never be transmitted directly from the communicator to the receiver. For that, indirect communication must be used. The receiver is thereby confronted by a choice between two possibilities; by choosing one of them he becomes genuinely engaged. Kierkegaard's works are an example of how the indirect method can be employed. He epitomizes the central idea of using the indirect method in these words: "This art consists in reducing oneself, the communicator, to nobody, something purely objective, and then incessantly composing qualitative opposites into unity" (Training in Christianity, p. 132). See COMMUNICATION.

Anderson, Raymond E. "Kierkegaard's Theory of Communication." Ph.D. dissertation, University of Minnesota, 1959.

Anderson, Raymond E. "Kierkegaard's Theory of Communication." Speech Monographs, no. 1, 1963.

Broudy, H. S. "Kierkegaard on Indirect Communication." Journal of Philosophy, April 27, 1961.

Cumming, Robert. "Existence and Communication." *Ethics*, no. 2, 1954-55.

Holmer, Paul L. "Kierkegaard and Kinds of Discourse." *Meddelelser fra S. K. Selskabet*, no. 4, 1953.

Holmer, Paul L. "Kierkegaard and Religious Propositions." *Journal of Religion*, July 1955.

' Lee, R. F. "Emerson through Kierkegaard: toward a Definition of Emerson's Theory of Communication." *Journal of English Literary History*, September 1957.

Malantschuk, Gregor. *Kierkegaard's Way to the Truth*. Minneapolis: Augsburg Publishing House, 1963.

On the themes of indirect communication and indirect method in the works, see, for example, *Either/Or*, I, p. 418; *Repetition*, pp. 21-27; *Fragments*, pp. 11-22, 28-43, 68, 88, 111-38; *Stages*, pp. 234, 278 ff., 389; *Postscript*, pp. 65-74, 111, 197, 216 ff., 222 f., 225-66, 275, 279, 289, 312-22, 332, 339, 342 f., 375, 416, 450 f., 456, 472, 490 f., 499-508, 535, 542, 551 ff.; *Christian Discourses*, pp. 115, 121 ff.; *Training*, pp. 96 f., 124-44; *Judge for Yourselves!* pp. 188 f.; *On My Work as an Author*, together with *The Point of View*, pp. 146-51, 162; ibid., pp. 5 f., 24 f., 38-41, 58, 92, 96; *Attack*, p. 14.

549. *Gnavspil*. A game played with small pieces with various pictures, including a cat (from which the game gets its name as a borrowing from Italian *gnau* or *gnao*) and a fool. See note 495. See *Philosophical Fragments*, pp. 14, 183.

550. Johannes Climacus, *Postscript*, p. 545.

INDIVIDUAL

Kierkegaard uses various designations for the individual human being, by which he indicates the various levels in a man's mental-spiritual development. His lowest designation is *specimen* or *copy* [*Exemplar*]. He notes ironically that "to be a specimen is the easiest kind of life, a life shielded against direct relationship to the idea, which would be as fatal as sunstroke (XI^1 A 42). His next and frequently employed expression, which means the same as the word *person*, is *individual* [*Individ*]. As an individual one stands in a relationship of thoroughgoing dependence upon the race and environment. Vigilius Haufniensis characterizes this relationship of dependence thus: "The individual is himself and the race" (*The Concept of Anxiety* [*Dread*], p. 26). The individual must work his way out of his dependence in order to win self-dependence, and Haufniensis extensively describes the freeing process, which consists in the individual's assuming the guilt of the race as his own.

On a higher level than *individual* stands *individuality* [*Individualitet*], which corresponds approximately to the expression *personality*. In individuality particular prominent individual qualities and acts manifest themselves as belonging consciously to one selfhood. Highest of all is *the single individual* [*den Enkelte*]. One first becomes the single individual through an existential

God-relationship. For Kierkegaard the category of the single individual is central. He often points out that he was the first to propound this category as central and predicts that it will become very significant in the future. He wished that his grave would bear the inscription, "that single individual" [*hiin Enkelte*] (*That Individual,* together with *The Point of View,* p. 131; VIII¹ A 482).

In brief, according to Kierkegaard, human existence lies between "two poles": "the qualification of animality," represented by specimen or copy, and "the qualification of spirit," which appears in "the single individual" as characterized by Kierkegaard (XI² A 149).

Berdyaev, Nicholas. *Solitude and Society.* New York: Scribner, 1939.

Cherbonnier, Phyllis. "The Preservation of the Individual in the Thoughts of Nietzsche and Kierkegaard." M.A. thesis, Columbia University, 1950.

Croxall, T. H. *Kierkegaard Commentary.* New York: Harper, 1956.

Harper, Ralph, *The Seventh Solitude: Man's Isolation in Kierkegaard, Dostoevsky, and Nietzsche.* Baltimore: Johns Hopkins, 1965.

Miller, Libuse. *In Search of the Self.* Philadelphia: Muhlenberg, 1952.

Ruitenbeck, Hendrik M. *The Individual and the Crowd.* New York: Nelson, 1965.

Schwandt, Jack. "Alienation and Reconciliation in the Works of Søren Kierkegaard." M.A. thesis, University of Minnesota, 1959.

Smith, Constance J. "The Single One and the Other." *Hibbert Journal,* no. 4, 1947-48.

Wade, D. V. "The Concept of Individuality in Søren Kierkegaard." Ph.D. dissertation, University of Toronto, 1944.

Wolf, William. "Alienation and Reconciliation in the Writings of Søren Kierkegaard." Ph.D. dissertation, Union Theological Seminary, 1945.

For references in the works to individual (*Individ*), individuality (*Individualitet*), the single individual (*den Enkelte*), and that single individual (*hiin Enkelte*), see, for example, *From the Papers of One Still Living,* S.V., XIII, pp. 78 f.; *The Concept of Irony,* pp. 206, 209 f., 221, 234 f., 241 f., 245 ff., 296 ff., 314; *Either/Or,* I, pp. 123, 140 ff., 157 f., 220 ff.; II, pp. 70 f., 85 f., 94 f., 184, 244 f., 256 ff., 260 ff., 333 ff.; *Fear and Trembling,* pp. 64 ff., 72 ff., 77, 80 ff., 85-91, 102 f., 106 ff., 120, 122-29; *Repetition,* pp. 42 ff.; *Edifying Discourses,* I, p. 59; II, p. 5; III, pp. 69, 71 f., 79; *Fragments,* pp. 14, 48; *The Concept of Anxiety* [*Dread*], pp. 14, 18, 26-32, 34, 42 f., 45, 47 ff., 51 ff., 54 ff., 64 f., 69 ff., 88, 99 f., 110 ff., 123 f., 133, 140 ff.; *Edifying Discourses,* IV, p. 5; *Thoughts on Crucial Situations in Human Life,* pp. vii, 38, 104 ff.; *Stages,* pp. 218-19, 292, 315; *Postscript,* pp. 18 f., 47, 50-55, 67, 93, 109, 113, 116, 123, 127, 131, 133, 142, 270, 272, 305, 308 f., 313, 317, 337, 342, 347, 352, 357 f., 364 ff., 375 ff., 416, 436 f., 452, 484 ff., 506 ff., 510, 517 f.; *A Literary Review,* S.V., VIII, p. 20; *The Present Age,* pp. 16 ff., 21 ff., 27 ff., 61-65; *Purity of Heart,* pp. 99 ff., 184-97, 206, 211 ff., 217; *The Gospel of*

Suffering, pp. 144 ff.; *Works of Love*, pp. 17, 31, 43, 61, 80-98, 104, 120 ff., 139, 142 ff., 217, 282 f.; *Christian Discourses*, pp. 40, 43, 121, 220, 244 ff., 276 f., 278 f.; *The Lilies of the Field and The Birds of the Air*, together with *Christian Discourses*, p. 313; "Has a Man the Right to Let Himself Be Put to Death for the Truth?" together with *The Present Age*, pp. 115 f., 132; *The Sickness unto Death*, pp. 159 f., 250 ff.; *Three Discourses at The Communion on Fridays*, together with *Christian Discourses*, pp. 359, 374; *Training*, pp. 52, 57, 71 f., 83, 86-95, 205, 217 f., 223 f.; *Two Discourses at the Communion on Fridays*, together with *Judge For Yourselves!* pp. 5, 7 f.; ibid., p. 109; *An Open Letter*, together with *Armed Neutrality*, pp. 48, 51, 52; *On My Work as an Author*, together with *The Point of View*, pp. 151 ff., 160 ff., ibid., pp. 21, 61, 89, 94, 102; '*That Individual*,' together with *The Point of View*, pp. 106-40; *Attack*, pp. 109, 166 f., 186, 221 f., 262 f., 285, 287.

551. See *The Concept of Anxiety* [Dread], p. 26.

552. See Clemens Brentano, *Die Mehreren Wehmüller und ungarischen Nationalgesichter* (Berlin: 1833). See *Either/Or*, I, p. 258.

553. A navel contemplator.

554. See *Works of Love*, pp. 251 ff.

555. J. E. Erdmann, *Vorlesungen über Glauben und Wissen* (Berlin: 1837).

556. See *Postscript*, p. 402.

557. See *The Sickness unto Death*, p. 207.

558. "No. 250," "available at P. W. Tribler, Holmensgade 114."

559. See *Either/Or*, I, p. 21.

560. The editors of the large Danish dictionary, *Ordbog over det danske Sprog*, do not know the origin of this expression, either, but the editors of the German equivalent, Grimm, *Deutsches Wörterbuch*, claim a clue to the German cognate *mutterallein*: absolutely alone as in the mother's womb.

561. Hard necessity. Horace, *Odes*, III, 24, 6. See *Either/Or*, II, p. 293.

562. See *Postscript*, p. 235; *Works of Love*, pp. 140, 353-54.

563. See *Either/Or*, II, pp. 259-60, 309, 334 ff.; *Repetition*, pp. 151 ff.; *Fear and Trembling*, pp. 78 ff.

564. See *Postscript*, pp. 118-19.

565. See *Edifying Discourses*, IV, p. 107.

566. A tale concerning yourself. Horace, *Satires*, I, 1, 69 f.

567. Wallowers in pleasure. Cicero, *Lælius on Friendship*, XV, 52.

568. See *Postscript*, pp. 484-85.

569. See *The Present Age*, pp. 27 ff.

570. See ibid., pp. 36-37.

571. See ibid., pp. 34-35.

572. See *Works of Love*, pp. 29-30.

573. See, for example, Kierkegaard's Foreword to *Works of Love*, p. 17, and pp. 80-81, 217.

574. Dr. Rasmus Møller, *Veiledning til en andægtig og forstandig Læsning af det Nye Testamente, især for ulærde Læsere* (Copenhagen: 2 ed. 1824). Bishop Møller was the father of Poul Martin Møller, professor of philosophy, University of Copenhagen.

575. See *'That Individual,' Two 'Notes' concerning My Work as an Author*, together with *The Point of View*, pp. 105 ff. This work and the two "Notes" were published in 1859 after Kierkegaard's death.

576. See *Stages*, p. 61.

577. Abraham of St. Clara, *Sämmtliche Werke*, I-XXII (Lindau: 1845), XV-XVI, p. 387. Kierkegaard owned this set.

578. See *'That Individual,' Two 'Notes' concerning My Work as an Author*, no. 2, "A Word about the Relation of My Literary Activity to 'the Individual,'" together with *The Point of View*, pp. 130 ff.

579. See *Works of Love*, pp. 251 ff.

580. Genesis 4:1, 24:16; I Kings 1:4.

581. See note 578.

582. The term *historical* was added in the margin. In the final copy it reads *ethical*.

583. See "A Word about the Relation of My Literary Activity to 'the Individual,'" no. 2 of *That Individual*, together with *The Point of View*, pp. 130-32.

584. Pantheism refers to Hegelian thought and its implications. See *Postscript*, pp. 111, 203, especially pp. 317-18.

585. See *The Present Age*, pp. 136-38.

586. See *Works of Love*, pp. 58-98.

587. Matthew 10:29.

588. Kierkegaard, contrary to Sartre in *Existentialism Is a Humanism*, does not maintain that existence precedes essence in the sense that man has no nature. Kierkegaard is closer to Augustine when he says in *Confessions*, "Thou hast made us for thyself and our hearts are restless until they find their rest in thee." See *The Sickness unto Death*, pp. 166, 176, 232; *Works of Love*, p. 199. See ANTHROPOLOGY.

589. The background of this generalized reference is a play *Kammeraterne* (*The Boon Companions*) by Scribe, presented in the Royal theater for the first time in Danish translation by C. Borgaard on November 14, 1839, and many times thereafter.

590. See *That Individual, Two "Notes" concerning my Work as an Author*, no. 2, in *The Point of View*, p. 134.

591. *Om Christi Efterfølgelse*, tr. J. A. L. Holm, 3 ed. (Copenhagen: 1848), p. 26.

592. Matthew 4:1; Luke 4:1.

593. See "Regarding the 'Two Notes' A Postscript" together with *The Point of View*, pp. 139-40.

594. See note 578

595. Julius Müller, *Die christliche Lehre von der Sünde*, I-II, 3 ed. (Breslau: 1849), I, pp. 48 ff., 536 ff.

596. Ibid.

597. This discourse (English translation together with *Training in Christianity*), dedicated to his father, was published, without the Preface, in 1850, and *The Accounting* (in *The Point of View*) and the *Two Discourses at the Communion on Fridays* (together in English translation with *For Self-Examination* and *Judge for Yourselves!*) were published in 1851.

598. See *Attack upon Christendom*, pp. 32-33 and 127, 166 f., 182.

599. For a Christian believes in the species' fall into sin and the restoration of the individual.

600. A Vinet, *Der Sozialismus in seinem Princip betrachtet* (Berlin: 1849).

601. We grant this pardon, and in turn we seek a favor. Horace, *Epistles*, II, 3, 11.

602. I. H. von Wessenberg, *Die grossen Kirchenversammlungen*, I-IV (1840), I.

603. I Corinthians 9:24.

604. A work by the title *For Self-Examination* was published later (Copenhagen, 1851) and is addressed to the single individual (see, for example, Foreword, the letter analogy, pp. 25-34, Nathan, pp. 39-45, a version of the Good Samaritan, pp. 45-51, etc.). The "first discourse" is part I of *For Self-Examination*.

605. See *Postscript*, pp. 317-18.

606. A Danish gossip-satire journal, edited by A. M. Goldschmidt, which Kierkegaard attacked by asking why he (under a pseudonym) alone should be commended in *The Corsair* and by which he was lampooned (1846). Kierkegaard himself had nothing to gain, and he felt abandoned by those high and low whom he sought to serve by his opposition to *The Corsair*. Much of the lampooning was foul and in any case exacerbating to one as sensitive as Kierkegaard.

607. Roskilde-Konvents Psalmekomite, *Psalmebog* (Copenhagen: 1850), p. 175.

608 See note 598.

609. Matthew 24:41.

610 See *Postscript*, p. 272.

611. See, for example, *The Point of View*, p. 41; *For Self-Examination*, pp. 1-3; *Philosophical Fragments*, pp. 28 ff.

612. See *Works of Love*, p. 219; *The Sickness unto Death*, p. 176; *Attack upon Christendom*, pp. 188 ff.; Plato, *Apology*, 29b.

613. H.H. [Søren Kierkegaard], *Two Minor Ethical-religious Treatises*, together with *The Present Age*, pp. 71 ff.

614. F. Böhringer, *Die Kirche Christi oder die Kirchengeschichte in Biographien*, I-VII (Zürich, 1842), I, p. 83 f.

INFINITE

The infinite [*det Uendelige*] is used by Kierkegaard in the sense of the eternal. Both of these expressions are used in the definition of man as a synthesis, in which the infinite (the eternal) is one of the two components that comprise the synthesis. The very use of the concept *the infinite* in characterizing man in existence frequently prompts Kierkegaard to point out that the infinite must not be understood abstractly but as a concrete qualification of man's essence. The existential movement whereby man reaches the eternal Kierkegaard calls the "movement of infinity" (*Fear and Trembling*, pp. 48, 79).

For reference in the works to infinity and the infinite, see, for example, *The Concept of Irony*, pp. 59, 63, 65, 82 f., 155, 162 f., 221, 231, 238, 243, 250, 252, 278, 290 ff., 297, 313, 324 ff.; *Either/Or*, I, pp. 36, 386 f.; II, pp. 62, 85, 96, 113, 225 ff., 234 ff., 270, 352 ff.; *Fear and Trembling*, pp. 46-64, 79, 109; *The Concept of Anxiety* [*Dread*], pp. 77, 100, 139 ff.; *Stages*, pp. 85, 167 f., 373, 425, 430, 438; *Postscript*, pp. 19, 23 f., 25 f., 36, 42, 53 f., 75 f., 79 f., 82 ff., 102 f., 105, 127, 134, 137, 156, 162, 174, 179 f., 209, 282, 288 ff., 301 f., 375 f., 436; *A Literary Review*, S.V., VIII, p. 100; *Works of Love*, pp. 78, 107, 111, 136 ff., 149, 173 f., 176 ff., 217 f., 223; *Christian Discourses*, pp. 66, 103, 109; *The Sickness unto Death*, pp. 146 f., 162 ff., 201 ff., 210 ff., 230, 238, 248, 258; *Training*, pp. 72, 129; *Judge for Yourselves!* p. 130; "The Activities of a Travelling Esthetician," S.V., XIII, p. 429; *Attack*, p. 275.

615. See *Philosophical Fragments*, p. 12, fn. 1.

616. Word, reason.

INSTRUMENT

"God's instruments" are what Kierkegaard calls those men who are especially chosen to carry through a particular task. God isolates such an instrument by "sufferings" or by "visions, revelations, and the like" (X² A 602), which also bring suffering. One who is taken "under arrest" (*The Point of View*, p. 69) by God finds that it is "impossible for him to make himself understandable to others" (X² A 602). Through isolation and suffering God takes the instrument totally into his service. Kierkegaard felt that he was such an instrument in God's hand, and in the following entry he imagines how God would speak if he were to try to open men's eyes to the thankless situation of an instrument: "A frail, tiny, sickly, insignificant man, physically almost as slight as a child, a figure which every animal-man would almost find ridiculous *qua* human being—this one is used for exertions under which giants would collapse—do you not see the absurd!" (XI¹ A 268).

For references in the works to instrument, see, for example, *The Concept of Irony*, p. 280; *Edifying Discourses*, IV, p. 52; *Works of Love*, pp. 94, 333 f., 336; *Judge for Yourselves!* pp. 120, 130.

617. See M. Luther, *En christelig Postille*, I, p. 559.

618. See section on ABSURD, Vol. I of this edition.

619. Matthew 23:29.

620 See "Of the Difference between a Genuis and an Apostle," English translation printed together with *The Present Age*.

INTENSITY

For Kierkegaard the extensive means the development or diffusion of a content or an idea in the external world. Intensity, on the other hand, means the individual's concentration and deepening in a spiritual content. Consistent with his entire spiritual attitude, Kierkegaard could only emphasize intensity over extensity.

For references in the works to intensity and extensity, see, for example, *Either/Or*, I, pp. 287 f., 294; II, pp. 24, 135 f., 141, 203, 270 f.; *Fragments*, p. 115; *Stages*, p. 141; *Postscript*, p. 345; *The Present Age*, p. 48; *A Literary Review*, S.V., VIII, p. 103; *Crisis in the Life of an Actress*, pp. 70, 90; *The Sickness unto Death*, pp. 169, 179, 182, 196, 231, 240, 245; *An Open Letter*, together with *Armed Neutrality*, p. 54; *Attack*, p. 34.

621. (Frankfurt, Leipzig: 1781), II, pp. 496 f.

622. See note 598.

623. See *For Self-Examination*, opening prayer.

INTERESTING

The words *The interesting* and *interest* have various meanings in Kierkegaard. The pseudonym Johannes de Silentio calls *the interesting* a "border category, a confinium between the esthetic and the ethical" (*Fear and Trembling*, p. 92). Socrates is cited as an example of the interesting; others are aware of him as an interesting personality. This aspect still lies within the esthetic. Preoccupation with it often remains there, but one can be led from this aspect to the Socrates who represents the ethical claim on man.

An analogous use is made of the word *interest* by Kierkegaard's pseudonyms when the word signifies that a person's awareness is focused on the next higher existential stage, for example, the transition from the abstraction of metaphysics to a concrete faith in God. (See *Repetition*, pp. 22-23, *Postscript*, p. 173, and *The Concept of Anxiety* [Dread], pp. 16-17, footnote.)

For references in the works of interest and the interesting, see, for example, *Either/Or*, I, pp. 9, 98, 108, 300, 305, 335, 341, 347 f., 364, 368; II, pp. 87, 238; *Fear and Trembling*, p. 92; *Repetition*, pp. 30, 33; *The Concept of Anxiety* [Dread], p. 16; *Stages*, pp. 317, 403, 413; *Postscript*, pp. 19, 23, 28, 51, 67, 125 f., 127 f., 129 f., 143, 155, 173, 184, 234, 278 ff., 282 ff., 302 ff., 345-85, 511 f., 540 ff., 551 f.; *The Present Age*, p. 61; *Crisis in the Life of an Actress*, p. 70; *The Sickness unto Death*, p. 202; *The Point of View*, pp. 93, 96 f.; *Attack*, pp. 230 f.

624. Andreas Nicolai de Saint-Aubain (1798-1865), Danish novelist who wrote under the name of Carl Bernhard. See notes 357-58.

625. *Athenæum, Wochenschrift für Litteratur, Wissenschaft, und Kunst* (London: 1827-).

626. Leopold Kompert, *Geschichten aus den Ghetto* (Leipzig: 1848); *Bömische Juden. Geschichten* (Vienna: 1851).

627. Adolph Meyer, *En Jøde*, ed. M. Goldschmidt (editor of *The Corsair*) (Copenhagen: 1845).

INWARDNESS

By *inwardness* Kierkegaard wants to say that man is no longer defined by externality (the external situation and law) but by the eternal. Through inwardness the eternal receives a foothold in man; therefore, "Inwardness is the eternal" (V B 65). Growth in inwardness is determined on the one hand by the form of the eternal to which a person relates himself (the eternal in man, God, Christ), and on the other hand by whether he still believes in the possibility of his own actualizing the eternal or has already perceived his limitations and guilt, which gives inwardness a greater depth.

Flottorp, Haakon. "Kierkegaard and Norway. A Study in 'Inwardness' in History with Illustrative Examples from Religion, Literature, and Philosophy." Ph.D. dissertation, Columbia University, 1955.

Nelson, C. A. "The Dimension of Inwardness in Christianity." *Augustana Quarterly*, no. 2, 1941.

For references in the works to inwardness, hidden inwardness, inward deepening, inner/outer, etc., see, for example, *From the Papers of One Still Living*, S.V., XIII, p. 84; *The Concept of Irony*, pp. 88 ff.; *Either/Or*, I, pp. 3, 6, 176; II, pp. 99 f., 126, 137 ff., 155, 251, 268, 91-129; *Edifying Discourses*, I, pp. 67 f., 92-119; II, pp. 67-87; *The Concept of Anxiety [Dread]*, pp. 110 ff., 119, 123 ff.; *Edifying Discourses*, IV, 124 f., 132 f.; *Thoughts on Crucial Situations in Human Life*, p. 78; *Stages*, pp. 196, 335, 387 ff., 399 ff., 410, 422 f., 430; *Postscript*, pp. 37, 44, 51, 52, 67 f., 78, 83 f., 123, 125, 154 f., 169-224, 225-66, 267-322, 341, 346, 362 ff., 366 ff., 387 ff., 445-68, 479, 482, 486, 489, 494 ff., 497, 535-44; *The Present Age*, pp. 17 f.; *Purity of Heart*, pp. 39 ff., 185-97, 215 f.; *The Gospel of Suffering*, pp. 138 f.; *Works of Love*, pp. 132 ff., 137 f., 140, 144, 146, 304 f., 354; *Christian Discourses*, 102, 113; *The Sickness unto Death*, pp. 147, 182-94; *Training*, pp. 87 ff., 90 f., 136, 138, 209 ff., 214, 223; *For Self-Examination*, passim; *An Open Letter*, together with *Armed Neutrality*, pp. 41, 49 ff.

628. See Matthew 6:17 ff.

629. Presumably a reference to the adherents of N. F. S. Grundtvig's conception of the Church. See *Fear an' Trembling*, p. 121; *Postscript*, pp. 35 ff.

630. See *Edifying Discourses*, IV, pp. 132-33.

631. You speak so that I may see.

632. See *Postscript*, p. 266.

633. Matthew 18:23 ff.

634. This entry in the *Papirer* may be considered a footnote to the discussion of words and acts in *Christian Discourses*, page 57.

635. See *Postscript*, pp. 302-305.

636. See *Works of Love*, pp. 23 ff.

637. See ibid., pp. 132-33 on the inwardness of the love-relationship and pp. 137-39 on the inwardness of personal transformation; also pp. 281 ff.

638. Nothing in excess.

JEST

The term *jest* is used by Kierkegaard primarily to characterize a relationship in existence. He wants to emphasize that all human efforts must be regarded as a jest in relation to the infinite ethical requirement which confronts man; man is saved by grace alone (see X² A 203). But although all human striving appears as a jest in relation to the high requirement, man is in no sense released from striving.

Secondly, Kierkegaard employs the term *jest* instrumentally in his dialectic of communication, which always contrasts one concept to another. Jest stands in contrast to earnestness, and the recipient must discern, without the aid of the communicator, whether what is said is in jest or in earnest. An example of the use of *jest* in indirect communication is, Kierkegaard says, "so to compose jest and earnest that the composition is a dialectical knot—and with this to be nobody" (*Training in Christianity*, p. 133).

For references in the works to jest, see, for example, *The Concept of Irony*, pp. 265, 275, 317; *Repetition*, pp. 154 f.; *Edifying Discourses*, III, p. 96; *The Concept of Anxiety [Dread]*, pp. 67, 85, 133 f.; *Thoughts on Crucial Situations in Human Life*, p. 78; *Stages*, pp. 121, 148, 163, 234, 317, 335, 377, 381, 399, 402, 403, 421; *Postscript*, pp. 60, 65, 73, 81, 92, 94, 121, 123 ff., 226, 235, 251, 257 f., 301, 304 f., 311, 366, 392 f., 400, 408, 412 f., 421, 451, 473, 491; *Judge for Yourselves!* pp. 195 f.; *The Point of View*, p. 92; *The Unchangeableness of God*, together with *Judge for Yourselves!* p. 230.

639. I John 5:4.

640. Romans 8:37. See *Works of Love*, pp. 48, 307.

641. Although there are few entries on the *jest* in the *Papirer* and also relatively few direct references in the various works, they are strategically placed and qualitatively significant.

642. *En christelig Postille*, II, p. 91.

JOURNALISM

Kierkegaard's attitude toward the daily press was extremely sharp. Of the main reason for his attitude, he writes: "On the whole, the evil in the daily press consists in its being calculated to make, if possible, the moment a thousand or ten thousand times more inflated and important than it already is. But all moral upbringing consists first and foremost in being weaned away from the momentary" (IX A 378).

By making important the incidents which in Kierkegaard's view are usually trivial and very transient, the daily press falsifies the true picture of actuality. With a certain irony Kierkegaard says of the dissemination of untruth by the press: "Who would dare deny having sometimes, perhaps many times, used a little lie: but to use the little lie every day, and in print, so that one addresses himself to thousands and thousands—this is dreadful" (X² A 314).

Swenson, David F. "A Danish Thinker's Estimate of Journalism." *Ethics*, no. 1, 1927-28.

————. *Something about Kierkegaard*. Minneapolis: Augsburg Publishing House, 1951.

For references in the works to journalists and the press, see, for example, *Either/Or*, I, p. 282; II, p. 210; *Prefaces*, S.V., pp. 22, 26; *Stages*, pp. 29, 229, 317, 440; *Postscript*, pp. 113, 325, 420 f., 472, 484; *Purity of Heart*, p. 139; *Works of Love*, p. 292; *Training*, p. 63; *The Point of View*, pp. 44 f., 49, 55 f., 118 f., 127, 130; *Attack*, pp. 18, 49 f., 53 f.

643. Margrethe Sophie Nielsen, *Vejledning i Kogekunsten for Huusmødre og Huusholdersker* (Copenhagen: 1829), p. 120. This reference to a cookbook is another, and admittedly somewhat unexpected, indication that Kierkegaard's reading far outran his own books as listed in the auction catalog covering the books sold publicly after his death.

644. It is of some importance to note that Kierkegaard's reflections upon and criticism of journalism and the press did not begin *after* the controversy with *The Corsair* in 1846. On November 18, 1835 (at the age of 22), he presented a paper, "Our Periodical Literature," to the Student Union (*Papirer* I B 2). The *Samlede Værker*, XIII, contains, among other things, pieces relevant to this subject published from 1836 on. See also Ulf Kjær-Hanson, *Søren Kierkegaards Pressepolemik* (Copenhagen: 1955).

645. This entry is part 9 of a projected piece entitled *Handwriting Specimens*, by A.B.C.D.E.F. Rosenblad, a takeoff on Johan Ludwig Heiberg's *Urania*, yearbook for 1844. *Urania* was printed on heavy paper and each page had a printed border. In *Prefaces* [*Forord, Samlede Værker*, V, pp. 27 ff., not translated into English] the pseudonymous Nicolaus Notabene writes about this luxurious publication and Herr Rosenblad prescribes that *Handwriting Specimens* should be provided with all possible elegance, with "a border around every page (as in *Urania*), every section with its own type face" etc. (*Pap.* VII² B 274:2).

646. Denmark's oldest newspaper and one of the oldest and most highly regarded newspapers in the world. The name comes from the founder and has nothing to do with Berlin.

647. This entry presumably reflects Kierkegaard's controversy with *The*

Corsair [*Corsaren*]. More extensive and explicit entries about the controversy are assigned to the final volume in this edition.

648. I Samuel 15:22.

649. *Berlingske Tidende*, June 26, July 4, July 9, July 11, July 13, 1850 (nos. 146, 153, 157, 159, 161).

650. *Jour*, French for day.

JOY

A person's first joys are spontaneous and immediate. They are dependent upon external circumstances and for this very reason are transient and accidental. Although Kierkegaard describes these shifting emotional-mental states, nevertheless his concern is centered on enduring joy, the joy won only in relation to the eternal. Christianity in particular is able to give man imperishable joy.

Comparing Christian joy to the joy occasioned by evanescent external conditions, he says: ". . . it is *sanctified*; it is not relished in the fleeting moment, anxious lest it suddenly vanish; it is not behind us, as earthly joy always is, but before us . . . (II A 580). The latter joy always continues, even though everything is taken from us. But in this life genuine joy always has the background of renunciation and suffering. Of the way the two opposites, pain and joy, are found in the individual's life (but with joy preponderant), Kierkegaard writes extensively in *The Gospel of Suffering* (pp. 118 ff.) and in *Christian Discourses* (pp. 101 ff.). Only in eternity is there joy without pain (X^4 A 184).

For references in the works to joy or gladness (sometimes *Glæde* is translated "happiness" or "pleasure"), see, for example, *From the Papers of One Still Living*, S.V., XIII, p. 57; *The Concept of Irony*, pp. 103, 296, 301; *Either/Or*, I, pp. 20, 25, 39, 74, 76, 144, 165, 167 f.; II, pp. 24, 48, 88, 108, 209, 213, 238 ff., 258, 281 f., 309, 316, 329; *Edifying Discourses*, I, pp. 13, 38; *Fear and Trembling*, pp. 28, 45, 47, 119; *Edifying Discourses*, I, p. 92; II, p. 36; III, pp. 43 f., 58 f.; *Fragments*, p. 37; *Thoughts on Crucial Situations in Human Life*, pp. 35, 38, 43, 49, 58; *Stages*, pp. 137, 140, 156, 171, 341, 424, 439, 443; *Postscript*, pp. 116, 140, 198, 254 f., 277, 294, 321, 368, 404 f., 497; *The Gospel of Suffering*, passim, particularly pp. 27 f., 79, 116, 161 ff.; *Works of Love*, pp. 75 f., 221, 260, 271; *Christian Discourses*, pp. 35 f., 72, 78, 97-163, 228 f., 245, 269, 280; *The Lilies of the Field and the Birds of the Air*, together with *Christian Discourses*, pp. 315, 347-56; *The Sickness unto Death*, pp. 159, 258; *Training*, pp. 71, 151, 253; *For Self-Examination*, p. 8; *Judge for Yourselves!* p. 177; *The Point of View*, pp. 68, 76, 91.

651. See *Either/Or*, II, p. 239.

652. See ibid., p. 353.

653. See *The Concept of Irony*, p. 320.

654. See Horace, *Odes*, III, 1, 40; *Edifying Discourses*, I, p. 85.

655. See Philippians 3:13-14.

656. Philippians 4:4.

657. The text reads *eye*, which from the context, is apparently an error in transcription.

658. I Corinthians 13:1.

659. See *The Lilies of the Field and the Birds of the Air*, together with *Christian Discourses*, p. 355.

660. I Thessalonians 5:16.

661. Hieronymus Cardanus (Cardano), *De rerum varietate* (Basel: 1557), XVII, p. 707.

662. In 1847 Kierkegaard published a work entitled *Opbyggelige Taler i forskjellig Aand*. The first part has been published in English translation as *Purity of Heart*, the second part as *The Gospel of Suffering*, and the third part, "What We Learn from the Lillies of the Field and the Birds of the Air," together with *The Gospel of Suffering*. This outline is directly related to "Joyful Notes in the Strife of Suffering," which is Part II of *Christian Discourses*, pp. 97-163. For section one see *Christian Discourses*, pp. 101 ff.

663. See ibid., pp. 111 ff.

664. See ibid., pp. 119 ff.

665. See ibid., pp. 129 ff.

666. See ibid., pp. 139 ff.

667. See ibid., pp. 149 ff.

668. See ibid., pp. 120 ff.

669. See ibid., pp. 154 ff. and VIII^1 A 322.

670. See ibid., pp. 154 ff. and VIII^1 A 300.

671. See ibid., pp. 111 ff.

672. See ibid., p. 99.

JUDAISM

In the earliest entries on Judaism Kierkegaard takes particular note of the Jews' special place among other peoples. He cites the following characteristics:

(1) The Jewish people had become oriented, through promises, toward the future; they had thereby gained a sense of history, inasmuch as the future goal implied a consciousness of the future; other peoples, immersed in the present, did not possess such a sense of history or historical outlook.

(2) The Jewish people also have a special place because of being chosen from among other peoples. It is very characteristic of Kierkegaard to stress in this connection that to be chosen means to be unhappy, and he says of the Jews: "They were not the happiest of people; they were rather a sacrifice which all humanity required. They had to suffer the pains of the law and of sin as no other people (III A 193)."

(3) Judaism was supposed to be a preparation for Christianity. The Jewish people had received the law from God and were to enact it in life, but

in time they learned that they could not fulfill the law. Through the resulting scepticism about its own capacity Judaism prepared the way for the new which was to come in Christianity (*The Concept of Irony*, pp. 279-80). Through the pseudonymous writers Kierkegaard also points to the main emphasis in Jewish piety as expressed by Job and Abraham, who continue to be paradigms for other persons in crucial life-situations.

Kierkegaard's later writings tend to stress the distinctions between Judaism and Christianity. This is consistent with Kierkegaard's oft-expressed view that trends in Christendom toward conformity with the world are a retrogression to Judaism.

The difference between Judaism and Christianity is stated in this way: Judaism is wholly oriented to present life; it is optimistic in relation to the world; this optimism, in contrast also to pagan optimism, is "divinely sanctioned optimism, sheer promise for this life." Christianity, on the other hand, is first of all pessimistic, because its aspiration is directed toward the eternal. So viewed, Judaism and Christianity may be said to stand in contrast to each other, "*Opposita justa se posita*" (XI¹ A 139).

Fox, Marvin. "Kierkegaard and Rabbinic Judaism." *Judaism*, no. 2, 1953.

Gumbiner, Joseph Henry. "Existentialism and Father Abraham." *Commentary*, no. 2, 1948.

Halevi, Jacob L. "Kierkegaard and the Midrash." *Judaism*, no. 1, 1955.

Harrellson, Walter J. "Kierkegaard and Abraham." Andover Newton Bulletin, no. 3, 1955. (Kierkegaard centennial issue.)

Hems, John M. "Abraham and Brand." *Philosophy*, no. 148, 1964.

For references in the works to Judaism and the Jewish people, see, for example, *The Concept of Irony*, pp. 52, 235, 279 f.; *Either/Or*, I, pp. 27, 148, 232; II, pp. 29, 41, 45, 218, 222, 260; *Edifying Discourses*, I, pp. 63, 94; III, pp. 42, 53, 106; *Fragments*, p. 37; *The Concept of Anxiety [Dread]*, pp. 65, 81, 92; *Prefaces*, S.V., V, p. 17; *Edifying Discourses*, IV, pp. 27 ff., 67; *Stages*, pp. 46, 103, 125, 129, 222, 354, 426; *Postscript*, pp. 43, 82, 89, 188, 191, 193, 196, 260, 296, 340 f., 360, 385, 408, 433, 480, 530, 532, 535; *The Gospel of Suffering*, pp. 25, 75, 94 f.; *Works of Love*, pp. 40, 354; *Christian Discourses*, pp. 186, 195, 224, 234, 268, 305; *"Has a Man the Right To Let Himself Be Put to Death for the Truth?"* together with *The Present Age*, pp. 81, 87 ff., 97; *The Sickness unto Death*, pp. 230, 231 f., 247, 262; *Training*, pp. 44, 85, 134, 154, 169 f., 175, 199; *For Self-Examination*, pp. 103, 196, 209, 214; *An Open Letter*, together with *Armed Neutrality*, p. 50; *The Point of View*, p. 55; *Attack*, pp. 35, 104, 142, 190, 206, 222.

673. *Efterladte Breve af Gabrielis*, ed. F. C. Sibbern (Copenhagen: 1826), p. 32.

674. Elemental spirits of the universe or, as some scholars translate the phrase, elemental religious forms.

675. Deuteronomy 4:40.

676. *Ein Volksbüchlein. Enthaltend: Die Geschichte des ewigen Juden* . . . (Munich: 2 ed. 1835).

677. The unusual heading appears only once in the *Papers*, as far as we know. Its meaning is unclear, except that the sign used first and last indicates infinity and the whole heading indicates tautology. Another possibility is that it symbolizes the Trinity (see text in work cited).

678. Karl Rosenkranz, "*Eine Parallele zur Religions Philosophie*," in *Zeitschrift* . . . , ed. Bruno Bauer, 1837.

679. Adonai (Lord).

680. God is God.

681. And while my glory *passes by* I will put you in a cleft of the rock, and I will cover you with my hand until I *have passed by*.

682. In Hebrew grammar the third person singular is the basic form in conjugation.

683. See *Either/Or*, I, p. 19.

684. *Bibelen . . . ledsaget med Indledninger og oplysende Anmærkninger* . . . , tr. C. H. Kalkar, I-III (Copenhagen: 1847), I, p. li.

685. Luke 14:26.

686. See *Fear and Trembling*, passim.

687. Ibid., pp. 27 ff.

688. Østerbro 108A. The corner of Østerbrogade and Willemoesgade, at the end of the artificial lakes. The building has been replaced since then and the numbering changed. This was the next to the last apartment Kierkegaard had (April, 1851–April or October, 1852).

689. See *Fear and Trembling*, pp. 27-29.

690. Opposites placed next to each other in close proximity.

691. John 18:36.

JUDAS

The fate of Judas was one of Kierkegaard's continuing preoccupations; he believed that one "will get a deep insight into the state of Christianity in each age by seeing how it interprets Judas" (IX A 47). Reference may be made to Kierkegaard's reading of Carl Daub's book, *Judas Ischariot*, I-II (Heidelberg: 1816). Kierkegaard concluded that Judas's position is more common than supposed. In *The Sickness unto Death* (p. 218) he writes, for example, ". . . he who first invented the notion of defending Christianity in Christendom is *de facto* Judas No. 2. . . ." His point is that all apologetics are of negative value. In *Training in Christianity* (pp. 239, 247-48) he equates the Judas figure and those who simply admire Christ but do not imitate him.

For references in the works to Judas, see, for example, *Fear and Trembling*, p. 74; *The Concept of Anxiety* [Dread], pp. 123, 139; *Postscript*, p. 122; *Purity of Heart*, p. 102; *The Gospel of Suffering*, p. 53; *Christian Discourses*, pp. 259, 286 f.; *The Sickness unto Death*, p. 218; *Training*, pp. 239,

248; *An Edifying Discourse*, together with *Training*, p. 267; *For Self-Examination*, p. 72; *Judge for Yourselves!* p. 186; *Attack*, pp. 36, 242.

692. Kierkegaard's library included Abraham of St. Clara, *Sämmtliche Werke*, I-XXII (Passau, Lindau: 1835-54).

693. Carl Daub, mentioned frequently in the *Papirer*, is represented in the auction catalog by *Philosophische und Theologische Vorlesungen*, ed. Marheineke and Dittbrenner, I-VII (Berlin: 1838-44).

694. Matthew 26:24.

695. A. F. Thiele, *Die jüdischen Gauner in Deutschland*, 2 ed. (Berlin: 1843), p. 234. The reference is to a Marcus Joel.

KANT

Kierkegaard's attitude toward Kant (1724-1804) is marked by his appreciation of the philosopher's sobriety of mind—he calls him "honest Kant" (VIII[1] A 358). Kant's definition of the beautiful (the esthetic) as "disinterested satisfaction" (IV C 114) is the particular point of congruence with Kierkegaard's own view.

Nevertheless, from the outset Kierkegaard had to make critical observations on Kant's thought at three points. The first concerned Kant's position that thought must stop with *"das Ding an sich"* as something with which it cannot cope (*The Concept of Irony*, pp. 138-39). Johannes Climacus calls this position a "misleading reflection" (*Concluding Unscientific Postscript*, p. 292), because Kant, for whom there is an ethical actuality which is above thought, did not need to halt at *"das Ding an sich"* as the boundary of thought. According to Climacus (ibid., pp. 292-93), Hegel wanted to transcend this Kantian position by way of his eternal idea in which "thought and being are one" but did not achieve ethical actuality (neither did he attribute "actuality to the ethical").

Secondly, Kierkegaard criticizes Kant's concept of "radical evil." Where Kant thinks thought must stop, at *"das Ding an sich,"* according to Kierkegaard the new actuality begins, which has its ground in a transcendent relationship and which ultimately has the characteristic mark of the absurd.

Kierkegaard also takes a critical view of Kant's confidence in man's ability to penetrate his empirical actuality with the categorical imperative. The division of personality into two principles, of which the higher is to penetrate the lower, Kierkegaard calls self-redoubling. But in the form of self-redoubling found in Kant the ideal cannot be realized. According to Kierkegaard realization can occur only with the aid of a constraining third, that is, a transcendent power: "Real re-doubling [*Selvfordoblelse*] without a constraining third factor outside of oneself is an impossibility and makes any such existing [*Existeren*] into an illusion or an experiment" (X[2] A 396).

On all three points Kierkegaard charges Kant with a lack of reference to the transcendent reality. The first traces of this critique appear as far back as 1839 (II A 486).

For references in the works to Kant, see, for example, "Yet another De-fence of Woman's eminent Talents," S.V., XIII, p. 8; *The Concept of Irony*, pp. 138 f., 173, 260, 289 f., 293; *Either/Or*, II, p. 327; *The Concept of Anxiety [Dread]*, pp. 10, 16; *Stages*, p. 150; *Postscript*, pp. 292, 491.

696. See *Postscript*, p. 292; *The Concept of Anxiety [Dread]*, pp. 10-11; *The Concept of Irony*, p. 260.

697. See W. M. L. de Wette, *Lærebog i den christelige Sædelære og sammes Historie* (Copenhagen: 1835), p. 141.

698. Those (renouncing this age) *transcend* general precepts by living more perfectly.

699. See *The Concept of Irony*, pp. 138-39, 289-90; *Postscript*, pp. 292-93.

700. See *Stages on Life's Way*, p. 150.

701. Henrich Steffens, *Christliche Religionsphilosophie*, I-II (Breslau: 1839), I, pp. 212-13.

702. I. Kant, *Vermischte Schriften*, I-III (Halle: 1799), II, pp. 689 ff., especially pp. 692 ff. The auction catalog lists this set and also *Critik der Urtheilskraft*, 2 ed. (Berlin: 1793) and *Critik der reinen Vernunft*, 4 ed. (Riga: 1794).

703. *Vermischte Schriften*, II, p. 700.

704. Ibid., III, p. 692.

705. Ibid., p. 491.

KNOWLEDGE

In thinking through the problem of knowledge and its various aspects, Kierkegaard reached his own characteristic solutions, of which the most im-portant are the following.

Knowledge is closely linked to existence: "If the rights of knowledge are to be given their due, we must venture out into life, out upon the ocean, and scream in hopes that God will hear—we must not stand on the shore and watch others struggle and battle . . ." (III A 145).

To the question of the relation of knowledge to the eternal in man, he answers that the eternal presupposes itself because it is always in force. It can be reached through self-awareness, and in this connection he refers to Plato's doctrine of recollection (III A 5, IV A 49).

Kierkegaard distinguishes between positive and negative knowledge. Knowledge of finite things is negative knowledge, whereas knowledge of the eternal is positive knowledge (IV C 74). Kierkegaard deepens this distinc-tion and later uses it to distinguish the spheres of knowledge and of faith from one another.

He also considers the problem of whether it is possible to overcome scepticism in the medium of thought and declares that scepticism can be overcome only through a resolution of the will.

Finally, just as Kierkegaard in his doctrine of the stages has sketched the existential stages of human development, he has also described the stages of knowledge which must be gone through in order for thought to reach its highest level. He adduces the following stages: (1) mythological thought, (2) imagistic or metaphysical thought, (3) conceptual (abstract) thought, (4) scientific and scholarly thought, and (5) thought about the absurd.

The earliest human thought is mythological thought, and in later periods everyone goes through this form of thought during childhood, even though in foreshortened perspective. Kierkegaard maintains that this kind of thinking corresponds to the idea "in a condition of estrangement," its externality, i.e., its immediate temporality and spatiality as such" (*The Concept of Irony*, p. 132).

The next stage signifies the awakening of the individual. Men discover that they are not in possession of the idea but have only an image of the idea or "a reflection of the idea" (ibid., p. 134). In this way arises the question of the correspondence between image and idea.

In the third stage man reaches abstractions as the basis of a conceptual world. The pseudonymous writer Johannes Climacus says that Greek thought in particular strove to achieve this level (*Concluding Unscientific Postscript*, p. 295). According to Kierkegaard's view Plato did not go beyond the stages of metaphorical and abstract thought (*The Concept of Irony*, p. 134).

The fourth stage is an expression of the attempt, by way of logically consistent thought, to find the connectedness between phenomenon and concept. By means of concepts and regularities the attempt is made to encompass the entire range of given actuality.

In the fifth stage clear scientific-scholarly thought is placed in relation to the ethical and to the actuality which from the scientific-scholarly point of view must be characterized as absurd, that is, in relation to Christianity. In order to reach this level, the highest level in Kierkegaard's view, and to maintain it throughout thought upon the essence of Christianity, scientific-scholarly thought is an inescapable presupposition. Concerning thought upon the absurd, Kierkegaard says, "The absurd is a category, and the most developed thought is required to define the Christian absurd accurately and with conceptual correctness" (X^6 B 79).

Brown, James. *Subject and Object in modern Theology*. New York: Macmillan, 1956.

Carnell, Edward J. "The problem of Verification in Søren Kierkegaard." Ph.D. dissertation, Boston University, 1949.

Holmer, Paul L. "Kierkegaard and the Truth." Ph.D. dissertation, Yale University, 1946.

For references in the works to knowledge, see, for example, *The Concept of Irony*, pp. 47 ff., 55, 57 f., 63, 67 f., 74, 77, 82 f., 96 ff., 104 f., 112, 124, 128 ff., 145, 156 f., 195 ff., 202 f., 209, 211 f., 249, 259 f., 325; *Either/Or*, I, p. 35; II, pp. 257, 262 f., 268 ff., 351, 356; *Repetition*, pp. 3 f., 33 f.; *Edifying Discourses*, II, pp. 27 ff., 83 ff.; III, p. 49; *Fragments*, passim; *The*

Concept of Anxiety [*Dread*], pp. 9-21, 99, 123 f.; *Prefaces, S.V.,* V, pp. 65 f.; *Edifying Discourses,* IV, pp. 91 f.; *Postscript,* pp. 15 f., 18, 25 ff., 34, 37 f., 41 f., 74 f., 85-113, 126 f., 134 f., 155, 162, 169 ff., 176 ff., 181 ff., 185, 208 f., 270 ff., 274 ff., 278, 280 ff., 293 f., 299, 310, 314 ff., 504; *Purity of Heart,* pp. 113 ff.; *Works of Love,* pp. 32 f., 111, 214 ff., 220 f.; *The Sickness unto Death,* pp. 142, 162, 175-80, 181, 220 ff., 224; *Training,* p. 202; *Judge for Yourselves!* pp. 122 f., 130 ff.

706. A comedy, *Qvækeren og Danserinden,* by Scribe and Dupport, tr. J. L. Heiberg (Copenhagen: 1832), sc. 12.

707. J. L. Heiberg, *Aprilsnarrene* (Copenhagen: 1826), sc. 23.

708. The handwritten text is not clear. The word could be *form.*

709. See *Either/Or,* I, p. 121, footnote.

710. The object of this irony is unclear, but it could be Grundtvig's cultural nationalism (See VIII¹ A 245). Grundtvig is mentioned directly in other connections in *Either/Or* (1843) and presumably, according to E. Hirsch, earlier (1841) in *The Concept of Irony,* p. 82.

711. Presumably the word *God* has been omitted.

712. Why [did] God [become] man? Title of Anselm's book on the Atonement.

713. "The certification, in contrast to this [that which is certified], is more fundamental, because the certified depends upon it."

714. "If then only the confirmed [or established] theory is the truth, then on the other hand also only the instance explained by the theory [is the truth]."

715. Fundamental articles.

716. Not basic.

717. As if infallible.

718. "So she seeks out finally from the given objects that which has been certified as being true."

719. "How do you read? So that the manner of reading becomes the criterion of truth."

720. See heading of II C 44.

721. The Danish is *gøre Erfaring.* We lose the active character of this expression in the English *have experienced* or *experienced,* which is present in *making an experiment.* A more literal translation would be *making experience.* See Rollo May, et al., *Existence* (New York: Basic Books, 1958), p. 9, on a Continental Leibnizean view of mind and a more Lockean Anglo-American philosophy of mind.

722. Thus reason will be able to console itself that any religious content proves itself true through inner experience.

723. Let us make the application in that area with which we have to do.

724. See II C 44.

725. See *The Concept of Irony,* p. 49 and note.

726. Luke 24:31.

727. See *Philosophical Fragments*, p. 100; J. C. Lindberg, *Hebraisk Grammatik* (Copenhagen: 2 ed., 1828), p. 13.

728. To give a name to some one.

729. Genesis 1:7.

730. Presumably Kierkegaard has in mind Kant's epistemology with its affirmation of the *transcendental* or formative capacity of the human mind and its denial of a *transcendent* capacity to apprehend reality in itself (*das Ding an sich*). The Danish terms are the same as in English. In this entry Kierkegaard uses a third term (*Transcendents*). The meaning of the paragraph seems to be an affirmation of the mind-relative capacity of man in knowing and also of the object-relative character of that knowing—both of them necessary yet relative.

731. See J. C. Lindberg, *Hebraisk Grammatik*, 2 ed. (Copenhagen: 1828), p. 205; *Philosophical Fragments*, p. 125. The change which a noun undergoes when it is related to another noun which qualifies it, as in the genitive case.

732. Contextual relationship of earthly existence.

733. Day to be.

734. See Genesis 1:31, 40:6; Ezekiel 8:10. Vulgate: *vidi, et ecce*.

735. Genesis 1:3.

736. Plato, *Phædo*, 72 c, *Meno*, 81 d. See *Philosophical Fragments*, pp. 11 ff.

737. Pardon the word or expression.

738. See J. L. Heiberg, *On Philosophiens Betydning for den nuværende Tid* (Copenhagen: 1833), pp. 49 ff.

739. Silence, stillness.

740. See note 721.

741. Here Kierkegaard is drawing epistemological significance from the Danish word for object, *Gjenstand*, which is a modified loanword from German (*Gegenstand*), that which stands over against the observer, which, like the English word *object*, is based upon the Latin *objectum*, that which is thrown before or presented to the mind or thought. Here the distinction is not between object and subject but between two objects which require each other.

742. II Corinthians 5:17.

743. Mark 2:21.

744. Ecclesiastes 1:9.

745. I Corinthians 2:9.

746. *Tinglæsning*, literally, registration in the official record.

747. English translation of *The Concept of Irony*, p. 96.

748. See note 752 for edition.

749. *Nicomachean Ethics*, 1140 a, 1 ff.

750. See *Postscript*, pp. 74-75.

751. See *Johannes Climacus or, De Omnibus Dubitandum Est*, pp. 151-53; *Postscript*, p. 279.

752. See W. G. Tennemann, *Geschichte der philosophie*, I-XI (Leipzig: 1798-1819), I, p. 210; *Fear and Trembling*, p. 132.

753. See, for example, *Postscript*, pp. 146, 162, 255, 300, 445. See VI B 40:5.

754. See *The Concept of Irony*, p. 161; *Postscript*, pp. 76-77, 144, 419.

755. *Urania* (Copenhagen: 1844), p. 122.

756. "Stjernehimlen," in *Den Frisindede*, October 4, 1842, no. 117.

757. See *Postscript*, pp. 254-55; *Tivoli Avisen*, May 18, 1845, no. 1.

758. For an explanation of the expression *the God* [*Guden*], see *Philosophical Fragments*, Foreword, pp. ix-xii.

759. See J. L. Heiberg, *Kong Salomon og Jørgen Hattemager*, sc. 23.

760. See *Concluding Unscientific Postscript*, pp. 181 ff., especially pp. 188 ff.

761. See *The Gospel of Suffering*, p. 123.

762. Kierkegaard had Benedict de Spinoza, *Opera philosophica omnia*, ed. A. Gfroer (Stuttgart: 1830).

763. Refuge of ignorance.

764. Efficient causes or secondary causes as distinguished from the first cause.

765. Proposition 45.

766. *Postscript*, pp. 169 ff. The word order of the chapter title in *Postscript*, published in 1846, is "Truth is subjectivity."

767. Renati Cartesius, *Opera philosophica* (Amsterdam: 1678), *De passionibus animæ*, Pars II, artic. LIII.

768. Wonder.

769. Benedict de Spinoza, *Opera philosophica omnia* (Stuttgart: 1830), *Ethices*, pars III, defin. IV.

770. Passion, pleasure, melancholy.

771. Change, becoming.

772. In passage, in process of passing over, in transition.

773. Transition or change in perfection, not perfection itself.

774. See, for example, *Postscript*, pp. 143-44, 161-62, 445.

775. See *Purity of Heart*, p. 111.

776. See *Works of Love*, pp. 214 ff. and note.

777. See *Training in Christianity*, pp. 185 ff.

778. John 14:21.

779. I Timothy 1:13.

780. John 20:29.